Praise for *The Harbour*

'Sydney Harbour. I know what it looks like.
I know what it feels like. Now with this wonderful book,
I know its story. This book is a joy to read. And essential for
anyone who loves Sydney Harbour . . . and who doesn't?'
Ken Done

'The finest harbour deserves the finest book . . .
A colourful, fascinating and enduring account of
the greatest waterway in the hemisphere.'
Simon Winchester

'A remarkable piece of work'
The Spectator

'Novel, ambitious, and inspiring . . . a beautiful mosaic of
space through time, covering art, architecture, biography
and history, with a sprinkling of memoir'
The Age

'History, adventure and meticulous research,
delivered with a punch'
The Courier Mail

About the author

Scott Bevan is a writer, journalist, broadcaster and
playwright based in Sydney and Port Macquarie.
He is the author of four critically acclaimed books:

The Hunter
Battle Lines: Australian Artists at War
Water from the Moon: A Biography of John Fawcett
Bill: The Life of William Dobell

His documentary work includes:

Oll: The Life and Art of Margaret Olley
Arthur Phillip: Governor, Sailor, Spy

THE HARBOUR

A city's heart, a country's soul

SCOTT BEVAN

**SIMON &
SCHUSTER**

London · New York · Sydney · Toronto · New Delhi

A CBS COMPANY

THE HARBOUR
First published in Australia in 2017 by
Simon & Schuster (Australia) Pty Limited
Suite 19A, Level 1, Building C,
450 Miller Street, Cammeray, NSW 2062
This edition published in 2018

10 9 8 7 6 5 4 3 2 1

A CBS Company
Sydney New York London Toronto New Delhi
Visit our website at www.simonandschuster.com.au

© Scott Bevan 2017

 A catalogue record for this book is available from the National Library of Australia

Cover image: Ken Done *Sydney Harbour, June 2018*
Cover design: Christabella Designs
Typeset by Midland Typesetters, Australia
Printed and bound in Australia by Griffin Press
Internal photographs by Scott Bevan

Not fare well,
But fare forward, voyagers
T.S. Eliot, 'The Dry Salvages',
Four Quartets

For William, Tom and Jo – my harbour

CONTENTS

LIST OF ILLUSTRATIONS

Section 1

1 The journey's beginning and end. The memorial to champion sculler Henry Searle, rising out of Parramatta River.
2 A shipwreck in Homebush Bay carries a cargo of mangroves.
3 Shells along the shoreline at Cabarita, Parramatta River.
4 An arc of concrete: Gladesville Bridge.
5 Spanning the water and touching the sky: Sydney Harbour Bridge and Blues Point Tower.
6 The tourist photo essentials: the Bridge, the Opera House and Luna Park, as seen from Lavender Bay.
7 The other side of an icon: Sydney Harbour Bridge, from below.
8 Securing a slice of waterfront real estate for New Year's Eve: McMahons Point.

Section 2

1 HMAS *Sydney* Memorial at Bradleys Head, and in the distance North and South heads guard the harbour entrance.
2 Reflections of another time: an old explosives store, Bantry Bay, Middle Harbour.
3 A city of sails at sunset: twilight racing on the harbour.
4 Harbour life and death: the former Quarantine Station's Third Cemetery on North Head.
5 Escape from high-density living: stacks of kayaks below apartment blocks at Elizabeth Bay.
6 Famous face of the harbour: Sydney Opera House.
7 Layers of history, as seen from Nawi Cove, Barangaroo.
8 Early-morning harbour view from *Pulbah Raider*.

INTRODUCTION
FARE FORWARD, PADDLER

EVERYONE KNOWS Sydney Harbour. At least, we think we do.

So much of the globe is covered in water, about 71 per cent. What is cupped beneath the 5000 hectares of Sydney Harbour's surface is some of the most famous water in the world.

Everyone can see the harbour, whether we have ever been to Sydney or not. With just a word or two, the harbour floats into our mind's eye. The Bridge. The Opera House. Fireworks on New Year's Eve. Flotillas on Australia Day. When we conjure up those mental images, we feel a sense of belonging, if we live in Sydney, and longing and desire, if we don't. No matter who we are or where we're from, we picture the harbour, and we feel good.

The harbour also makes us feel safe. It has held the promise of shelter since James Cook sighted the harbour's entrance in 1770. Not that he entered it. Cook had just sailed out of Botany

Bay, which he considered 'safe and commodious', so he was not about to steer HM Bark *Endeavour* left again. However, as he sailed past the great sandstone headlands that marked the entrance, he did note that *Endeavour* was 'about 2 or 3 Miles from the land and abreast of a Bay or Harbour wherein there apperd to be safe anchorage which I call'd *Port Jackson*'.

Eighteen years later, Captain Arthur Phillip used that reference and passed between the Heads seeking more than safe anchorage; he wanted to find somewhere to build a penal settlement. He had led the First Fleet to the new land, and for its cargo of convicts, the harbour was meant to be about banishment and confinement half a world and an eight-month voyage away from Britain. Yet the harbour quickly came to be seen as holding the potential for escape – physically for a few, and metaphorically from their past for many. Rather than isolate them from their origins, the harbour connected these convicts with possibilities and potential. For the officers on board those eleven ships, the harbour offered natural protection like no other waterway they had sailed into. They were rhapsodic in their descriptions, beginning the unbroken tradition of visitors lavishing praise on Sydney Harbour.

'Port Jackson, I believe to be, without exception, the finest and most extensive harbour in the universe, and at the same time the most secure, being safe from all the winds that blow,' the expedition's chief surgeon, John White, noted. White's fellow officer and surgeon George Worgan thought the harbour was unequalled in its 'Spaciousness and Safety' and, what's more, 'exhibits a Variety of Romantic Views, all thrown together into sweet Confusion by the careless hand of Nature'. The man entrusted with starting a colony predominantly populated by criminals and cast-offs on the furthest edge of the Empire was less prosaic but no less impressed in his description of the harbour. From his flimsy base by the water, Arthur Phillip penned some of the earliest letters from Sydney. He sent a dispatch to the man after whom he had named the cove that cradled the colony, Lord Sydney. He told the Home Secretary back in London of the 'satisfaction of finding the finest harbour in the world'. Phillip also wrote to the Marquis of Lansdowne about five months after arriving. That letter is held in the archives of the Mitchell Library, less than a kilometre from where Phillip dropped anchor to begin this extraordinary social experiment. Louise Anemaat, a senior curator at the library, showed me the letter. In a florid font, Phillip explained why he had decided to found the colony on the shore of Sydney Cove.

'Botany bay, offerd no Security for large Ships,' he wrote. 'Here a Thousand Sail of the Line may ride in the most perfect Security.' Reading those words on the fragile paper, I could have run my finger across the reason why Sydney came to be where it is. I could have touched the words of the founding Governor who had so much belief in what the colony could become. What some considered a dumping ground for Britain's unwanted, he saw as a most valuable acquisition for the Empire, and he envisaged a great city by the water. In no small way, the harbour carried Phillip's hopes and ambitions.

The harbour continued to play that role from the 18th century through the 19th and well into the 20th century, carrying ships filled with the hopeful, the ambitious, the weak and the war-weary from the Old World and ruined empires to the wharves of a fresh beginning. Sydney may not have a Statue of Liberty at the mouth of its harbour, or any great proclamations of 'Give me your tired, your poor/Your huddled masses yearning to breathe free/The wretched refuse of your teeming shore', but the topography articulates that kind of welcome as clearly and as profoundly. Once an immigrant or a refugee passed between the sentinel sandstone bluffs at the harbour's entrance, they would have had their first inkling of having at last found shelter. In the process, the harbour helped create a new country. It carried to the shores the raw materials for building a nation.

Yet there have also been fears about who, and what, else would come through the Heads into the harbour. Threats, real and imagined, have always been in the water. Concerns about foreign powers attacking from the sea have shaped – and helped preserve – the harbour's headlands, while the fear of being eaten by sharks has led to stretches of the shoreline being trussed and stitched in netting.

The harbour also encourages us to imagine possibilities. Just as it has carried ships into the city's heart, the harbour has coaxed vessels out into the world. Those departing ships have been loaded with exports manufactured and nurtured in Australia, from sheep and wheat to brilliant and creative minds seeking further education or simply a great adventure. The quest for adventure is inscribed on the harbour just about every day, whether it is the helter skelter of skiffs inhaling the north-easterlies on summer afternoons, the sleek yachts of the Sydney to Hobart fleet dashing towards the sea each Boxing Day, or the floating hotels in the shape of cruise ships.

The harbour has not just carried the fortunes of a continent in and out of the Heads, it has also supplied vast wealth to many. Entrepreneurs have seen financial opportunity in the harbour. They always have. The harbour was considered an extraordinary asset, to transport products to the wharves, to cradle industries on its shores, or to swallow all the waste that could be dumped and discharged into it. And it wasn't just the industrialists sullying the water; everyone was. For many years, it was treated as one big sewage outlet. The city was poisoning the very thing it was suckled by. Sydney continued to exploit the harbour, as if believing that anything that went into the water would be washed away. As a result, Sydney Harbour was, for a time, one of the world's most polluted ports. Changes in regulations and public attitudes to protecting the harbour have stopped a lot of the worst practices. What's more, it is no longer the 'working harbour' it once was. Most cargo ships now berth in other ports along the coast, and the factories have been largely removed from the shoreline, making way for yet more residential and office developments. But that doesn't mean Sydney Harbour is now as clean and healthy as its beautiful face would have you believe. Pollution continues to make its way into the water, and the harbour remains scarred by decades of abuse, even if we can't see it, or choose not to.

To Sydneysiders, the harbour is beyond compare. Visitors have also deemed it incomparable. As an American preacher and writer floridly declared in 1894, 'He only belittles and be-dwarfs and demeans Sydney Harbor who compares it to the Bay of Naples or the entrance to Rio Janiero [sic]'. Even so, Sydney Harbour is used as a comparison. Sydharb is an unofficial measurement, based on how much water the harbour holds, which is about 500 gigalitres. Although at high tide, it can hold up to 562 gigalitres of water. Not that anyone really cares about the actual volume; it is the comparison to Sydney Harbour that counts. No matter how big a waterway is in Australia, and there are quite a few larger than Sydney Harbour, spruiking that capacity alone is not impressive enough. Authorities somehow have to state how many Sydney Harbours it can hold.

Yet it is the immeasurable that makes the harbour so special. For something whose body literally slips through our fingers, Sydney Harbour has a tight grip on the heart and soul of the city, and of the nation. We imagine it flowing through our lives, defining not just where we live but who we are. The novelist Robert Louis Stevenson reckoned if an Englishman wished to have a patriotic feeling, it had to be about the sea. For a Sydneysider to experience a similar emotion, it would have to be about the harbour. It fills Sydney people with confidence and pride, and rarely in a quiet way. They love showing off the harbour to visitors. To do that, in many Sydneysiders' eyes, is to reveal the most attractive feature of themselves. But how Sydneysiders see themselves can be seen as smugness and arrogance by other Australians.

When Melburnians sometimes argue they have superior cafés and a greater commitment to the finer cultural things in life, Sydneysiders can be relied on to dismissively reply, 'Yes, but we have the harbour'. Which is kind of like saying, 'So what if you're smarter? I'm more beautiful'. It is as though having a stunning harbour means a Sydneysider doesn't have to try in any other way. As Tim Freedman, leader of rock band The Whitlams and charmingly cheeky chronicler of Sydney life, sings, 'You gotta love this city for its body and not its brain'.

The most seductive bit of the body is, of course, the harbour. It is the part people lust over. They become obsessed with just being close to it. For that pleasure, you must pay dearly. A harbour view, no matter how thinly sliced, can cost the purchaser millions of dollars. The harbour is the Lorelei of Sydney. Its song is so intoxicating that many people sail closer and closer to the wind just to have a glimpse of its beauty, until, finally, some are smashed onto the rocks of financial ruin. Still, a few get to buy the rocks and build a mansion on top of them. Many Sydneysiders value not just their home but the worth of themselves by their proximity to, and view of, the harbour. And quite a few sell chunks of their own soul to buy into the dream and move as close as they can to the holy grail of Sydney property ownership: water frontage. Even when more and more people are crammed into phenomenally expensive housing and commercial developments on waterfront land reimagined and reclaimed, shrinking the shoreline, somehow the harbour responds by seeming not smaller and besmirched but serenely beautiful and filled with endless possibility. No matter what we do to its foreshores, or to the water quality, the harbour itself delivers on the ridiculous promises of real estate marketing slogans of living a dream. Which means yet more want to be near the harbour, to gaze at the water and into what is almost like a magic mirror. If the harbour is a reflection of how Sydneysiders imagine themselves to look, then in our desire to be close to the water, to stare into it, perhaps we really are – as some Melburnians would have it – a pack of shallow narcissists.

If they can't stare into the water, Sydneysiders can always laugh at a refracted version of themselves presented by playwright David Williamson. He is originally from Melbourne, but the popularity of his wry observations and one-liners about Australian life helped Williamson shift to Sydney into a harbourside house. A few years after moving, Williamson wrote a play about Sydney, titled *Emerald City*. Its main character is Colin, a scriptwriter who moves from Melbourne to Sydney and, like just about every other character in *Emerald City*, covets a home with a harbour view. Elaine, the scriptwriter's agent, tells Colin, 'No one in Sydney ever wastes time debating the meaning of life – it's getting yourself a water frontage. People devote a lifetime to the quest. You've come to a city that knows what it's about, so be warned.' Colin is warned but hardly deterred. How could he be after he has seen the harbour view from her office?

However, the problem with just looking at the harbour, especially when you're staring at undeniable beauty, is that you miss what is going on beneath the surface. You can miss the personality, the soul and the brain contained in the body. You can miss the complexity. After all, what we refer to as 'the harbour' is actually a series of waterways: Parramatta and Lane Cove rivers, which feed into the main harbour; the inner harbour, which extends to just east of the Bridge; the outer harbour, which presses through to the Heads, and, before reaching the sea, there is a deviation to the left, into North Harbour and Middle Harbour. Each section contains more than just water but its own character, its own challenges and idiosyncrasies. Yet as each body flows into the next, it is easy to miss all that. Especially if you are engrossed in your view of the harbour, whatever it may be. You can become blind to the fact there are so many other ways to look at the harbour. After a while, when you're caught in a routine, you barely notice what you are looking at.

And then it hits you. You see the harbour through the prism, and the prison, of your view and realise, 'I hardly know you'.

THIS BOOK was born in an old cemetery.

Each day, on the way to and from work, I would walk through St Thomas' Rest Park, on the fringe of Crows Nest, on Sydney's lower North Shore. More than strolling through history, in this park you're treading on the dead.

Before it was handed over to the community in the 1960s, this urban sanctuary was a cemetery. From the time its ground was consecrated in 1846 to the last burial more than a century later, St Thomas' Cemetery accommodated about 4000 souls. As part of its conversion from a resting place for the dead to a refuge for the living, many of the headstones were re-sited or removed altogether. About 450 headstones, and some grand monuments, remain. As well as providing excellent obstacles for kids and dogs to run around, they tell the story of a harbour city.

A number of the headstones are etched with the names of Sydney pioneers and settlers whose memory is retained beyond the rest park, on street signs and maps, such as the Milsons. There are the names of fortune seekers and finders, such as Bernhardt Holtermann, who helped unearth the world's biggest lump of gold quartz in 1872. With his dug-up wealth, he built a mansion with a tower, from which panoramic photos of the harbour were taken. There are the builders, the law-creators and the decision-makers of a colony clawing its way towards nationhood. And seeping out of the stone, through the inscriptions, there is the harbour. The headstones remind you of the connection many of those buried here had with the water. They were born by it, worked on it, and, in quite a few cases, it led to their grave.

As I walked through the park, the first headstone I would see each morning was that of Jacob Hooper A.B., who died in 1879. The insignia of a rope-furled anchor and Union Jack is engraved in the headstone, erected by the officers and crew of HMS *Emerald* 'in memory of their shipmate'. There is no indication of how Hooper died, but the 29-year-old's headstone is etched with a verse. Its first line reads, 'SAFE HOME. SAFE HOME IN PORT'.

A few steps further on is the headstone of Thomas Langford Snr, 'native of Sydney, yacht & boat builder'. Like navigational beacons, more headstones mark the tidal zone of the harbour's history, guiding you through the shoals and perils of another time. There are the names of ships' captains, and the resting place of a coxswain, Robert Chambers, who 'was drowned when diving in Farm Cove' in 1880. There are the headstones of those who notated the shape and form of the harbour, such as the renowned colonial artist Conrad Martens, who had been a topographer on board HMS *Beagle* alongside a young naturalist named Charles Darwin, before he was beguiled by Sydney and stayed to sketch and paint it. There is the memorial for a Royal Engineer who reshaped the harbour, George Barney, who blew the top off the harbour island known as Pinchgut to build Fort Denison. Near Barney's memorial is a plaque commemorating the descendants of William 'Billy' Blue, a convict who became a notorious ferryman and raconteur, rowing passengers from the North Shore to the town – that is, when he wasn't cajoling the passengers to row him. For his efforts and wit, he had a headland named after him, Blues Point.

The most prominent monument in the park is a neoclassical stone pyramid, built by Alexander Berry. He had arrived in the colony as a ship's surgeon. Berry and his business partner, Edward Wollstonecraft, made much of their fortune from the harbour, particularly in shipping. Berry married Wollstonecraft's sister, Elizabeth, who wrote regularly to her cousin back in England, the author of *Frankenstein*, Mary Shelley. When his wife died in 1845, Berry gave this land for a cemetery and built the monument. Beneath the pyramid is a vault containing the remains of his wife and his brother-in-law, as well as his own. In keeping with the grandeur and faintly Gothic air of the monument, an instruction is etched along the pyramid's base, indicating the 'ENTRANCE to the VAULT 4 feet below this face', along with an arrow pointing down. The symbol is reminiscent of the broad arrow that was imprinted on convicts' clothes, which marked both the fabric and its wearer as property of the British government.

The rest park is stubbled with the memory of explorers who voyaged out of the harbour, into the Pacific, into the unknown, and, finally, into the earth. Captain Owen Stanley, who was surveying the New Guinea coast when he died of malaria in 1850, is commemorated here. Buried underneath a shared monument to the early colonial judge Ellis Bent and his good friend, the explorer Major John Ovens, is the skull of Lieutenant Bower. The Royal Navy officer was killed in the Solomon Islands in 1880. His skull and a necklace fashioned from his teeth were handed over by locals to the crew of a visiting British warship the following year and brought to Sydney.

The largest and perhaps most poignant memorial for lost mariners is the gravesite of Commodore James Goodenough, who was in charge of the Royal Navy's presence in the Pacific, the Australian Station. He died on board HMS *Pearl* in 1875, after being pierced with arrows on the island of Santa Cruz, which, his memorial says, he was 'visiting for the purpose of establishing friendly relations with the natives'. On each side of Goodenough's memorial is the grave of a sailor killed in the same incident, and neighbouring these are headstones commemorating other seamen from *Pearl*, who died on duty between 1873 and 1876.

This cluster of memorials is fenced off with chains and symbols of crossed anchors. The site is a few kilometres from the harbour, too far for the scent of salt to lace the air, but for many years, sailors would traipse up the hill to pay their respects. Almost a century and a half on from the enormous funeral ceremony for Goodenough that brought the city to a halt, I would often deviate from the path to stand in front of the crossed anchors and the cold stone commemorating the officer and his men. I would read the inscriptions, and those words that were so redolent with adventure and drama and tragedy would feel so removed from this somnolent suburban park, and from me. The earth united all these souls now, but I wanted to write about what had connected them in life, the harbour. However, I didn't have time. Having disrupted my routine for a few minutes, I would return to the path and walk to the train.

On the rail journey along the lower North Shore, I would catch glimpses of the harbour squeezed between the buildings or cradled in the yacht-speckled coves. As we trundled across the northern approach to the Harbour Bridge, I would peer down at Milsons Point, where Commodore Goodenough's body was brought ashore before a crowd of thousands in 1875, and where, for many years before the Bridge was opened in 1932, commuters would pile on and off ferries for the journey to the opposite shore. I would look at the famous clown's face entrance to Luna Park. Its manic grin reminded me of occasional childhood visits to the amusement park, my stomach flitting with excitement on the ferry ride over, and churning with fried food mushed by the Big Dipper roller coaster on the way back.

Crossing the Bridge, I would look to the right, watching the harbour wriggle in and out of coves and inlets, and pirouetting around Goat and Cockatoo islands. I would look down at the press of terrace houses and hotels in Millers Point, for so long the rowdy domain of sailors and wharf workers. I could see Gladesville Bridge arcing through the sky in the distance, as the harbour squiggled on towards Parramatta.

Then I would look to the left, towards the surreal sails of the Opera House, down to the calligraphy of ferries' wakes, as the craft cut in and out of Circular Quay, and at the office towers rising from ground that was once swamps and mudflats. I would see Lieutenant Colonel Barney's Fort Denison, with its stone Martello tower, like a fairytale fabricated in the middle of the harbour, and the grey warships docked around Garden Island. My gaze would bounce across the headlands, each packed with billions of dollars in real estate, until it reached South Head, crowned with the historic Macquarie Lighthouse. When it was lit by the morning sun, the lighthouse gleamed like a white exclamation mark, punctuating land's end and the beginning of the blue immensity of the Pacific. Then the harbour would sink and disappear, as the train slipped into a tunnel.

Seeing the harbour, and the life on it, never failed to bring me pleasure as I headed to work. It was a necessary part of my routine. And it often made me think of those I had walked around and over half an hour before, the dead mariners. Perhaps it was because I was thinking of them, and how the harbour enriched life and took it away. But I do remember it was while I was travelling over the Bridge that I was slapped with the realisation, 'I hardly know anything about this harbour'.

It wasn't as though I had been estranged from the harbour. I thought I had engaged with it, and often. I had criss-crossed it on ferries. I had sliced through it in cruise ships, tall ships, and warships. I had dined and jogged along its shores and waded into its shallows at quite a few of its many beaches. Yet the closest I had felt to the harbour was when I kayaked on it.

I usually kayaked on my own, paddling the same nine-kilometre return route along the length of Middle Harbour. I would also regularly paddle on the inner harbour and the lower reaches of Parramatta and Lane Cove rivers with two friends, Bruce Beresford and George Ellis. Commuting over the Bridge, I could see the stretches of the harbour where the three of us would paddle, and the patch where we would meet. Bruce and George would kayak from the south, from Birchgrove, and I would paddle from the north, out of the bushy crescent of shore-line behind Berry Island, having agreed to 'see you in the middle of the harbour'. Our meeting area was usually off Manns Point, which is considered a marker of the border between Parramatta River and the inner harbour. From there, the three of us would set off and, punctuated by the paddle strokes, we would talk, learning what each of us had been up to. Our friendship has been grouted with water. It is more solid because of water. Being together on the harbour would encourage us to talk, to confide and to laugh. And being on the harbour would encourage us to not talk, to simply immerse ourselves in the joy of being there.

Water is a conductor. It gives you energy, and it makes you feel connected. At least, that's how I feel when paddling. When you just look at the harbour, it is often as a diversion, an escape, from life. It breaks the rhythm of whatever you're doing. When you are on the harbour, you become part of its life. You sink into its rhythm. And you feel more alive. The sensation reminds me of a famous speech by US President John F. Kennedy. Addressing a dinner for America's Cup crews in 1962, President Kennedy said it was an interesting biological fact that we had the same percentage of salt in our blood as what there was in the sea. And so, he argued, when we headed to the sea, we were, in a sense, going back to where we came from.

That moment on the Bridge when I realised I knew so little about the harbour arrived not long after I had decided to resign from my job as a television presenter. I needed a break from wearing a suit and tie and reading an autocue. When I quit, I knew it was not so much about disconnecting from a job but reconnecting with who I am. I resolved to play more music and to kayak on the harbour as much as I could. I would get to know the harbour better, and me. I resolved to get back to the water.

NO ONE has observed Sydney Harbour more closely than Kenneth Slessor. He did the closest thing to capturing lightning in a jar. He spun the rhythm of water into the metre of words. Slessor was the harbour's poet laureate. His stipend was a fathomless sea of ideas. He was rewarded handsomely.

My favourite Slessor poem is 'Captain Dobbin'. When I read the poem as a young man, I wanted to be like Captain Dobbin and have great adventures in life. When I read the poem after quitting my presenting job, I wanted to be sure I didn't end up like Captain Dobbin. In the poem, the retired South Seas captain 'Now sails the street in a brick villa, "Laburnum Villa",/ In whose blank windows the harbour hangs/Like a fog against the glass/Golden and smoky, or stoned with a white glitter'. Slessor has Captain Dobbin riding the ebb tide of his memory, surrounded by his artefacts and mementos of 'mummified waves', reading of the places and cultures he once voyaged into. I wanted to be Captain Dobbin in reverse. I wanted to get out on the harbour and journey upon it. Leaving behind the water and merely reading about it is a kind of death for Captain Dobbin, as he sits in his room, 'In his little cemetery of sweet essences'. For me there was renewal, even rebirth, in stepping away from news reading, no longer feeling tethered by tightly constructed sentences, and heading out onto the water for a while. I would find what Captain Dobbin was grieving for.

I decided to take my time exploring the 316 kilometres or so of the harbour's shorelines, to delve into its dozens of bays and inlets, and to circumnavigate each of its islands. I would get to know this waterway that was 'many lobed', as D.H. Lawrence described it in his novel *Kangaroo*. And that description suggested to me, contrary to Tim Freedman's lyrical observation, that Sydney did have a brain. I wanted to get inside that brain, and learn about its soul.

The vessel for my voyage of discovery – and re-discovery – was to be my long-time paddling companion, my kayak, *Pulbah Raider*. I didn't give the kayak its name; its maker in the Hunter Valley did. The *Pulbah* part I love, as it is a word from the Awabakal people of Lake Macquarie, 90 minutes north of Sydney, and it means 'island'. However, the *Raider* part of the vessel's name makes me a little uncomfortable, for the implied aggression in that word is diametrically opposed to the gentle passage you experience in a kayak. That gentleness takes you a lot further than aggression ever could; the kayak allows you to nudge into other places and lives, causing barely a ripple.

When I bought *Pulbah Raider* in 2004, I chose a colour for her deck that could have been seen from space. It was a radioactive green, creating the impression that the kayak had been paddled around Fukushima. Over the years, the colour has softened, until now it is like the milky turquoise of a tropical lagoon, or of the waters off a sandy harbour beach. *Pulbah Raider* has aged into a vessel that looks like it belongs on Sydney Harbour. Actually, it is suited to Sydney Harbour, because it was designed for lakes and rivers. So *Pulbah Raider* can usually handle estuarine conditions, where the rivers and the sea meet, mixing the different characters of their water to become one. And as marine scientists keep telling me, Sydney Harbour is an estuary. Although the name 'Sydney Estuary' somehow makes the harbour sound less beautiful, more pungent, and kind of swampy. Even if it had been known as Sydney Estuary, some tourism marketing wizard would have decided long ago that it had to be grander and more inviting. It *had* to be Sydney Harbour. Just as Norma Jeane Baker had to be Marilyn Monroe. After all, icons of beauty can't have plain names.

Pulbah Raider, I knew, would take me where I wanted to go, and where I needed to be. From its cockpit, I could see the harbour from a different perspective. While out on the water, I would imagine what all those sailors and paddlers before me – from the original inhabitants in their canoes, or nawi, to the captains of ships – had experienced as they interacted with the harbour.

But even from the water, you can't learn just by looking. So I planned to pull up on the shore and talk with people who lived by the harbour, worked and played on it, dived into its depths, and drew inspiration from it to create art. I wanted to meet those who fought to preserve the harbour, who worked to repair and regenerate it, and those who were determined to reshape and redefine parts of it. I would drift into the lives of those who had travelled great distances to be on the harbour, and those who had delved into its character and past, before bobbing up with insights into our character. I would try to understand how this body of water has divided us and made us different, and how it has united us and made us who we are. I would get to experience this beautiful, complex, wilful harbour through the beautiful, complex, wilful souls who are bound to it. I would find more than shelter in this harbour; I would find knowledge.

Water can create the intoxicating illusion that you are the first to scratch its surface, by quickly rubbing out the wakes of all the boats that have been before you. However, any library will quickly smack down any notion that you're treading – or paddling – into uncharted territory when writing a book about Sydney Harbour.

'So much has been said and written about Sydney Harbour that he must be a bold man or a specially well-informed man, or otherwise well-equipped above the average, who will undertake at this time of day to add to the literature on the subject.' That is what the *Sydney Morning Herald* published more than a century ago, in 1903, in a review of a book on the harbour by a Mr E.J. Brady.

I am not a bold man, nor a specially well-informed man. And clearly I'm not a man to take the hint that a subject has been already covered. But I'm a curious man. And there is no better way to satisfy my curiosity than to accept I can look only as far as the eye can see, slip into *Pulbah Raider* and paddle around the next headland to find what is there.

1

FOLLOWING HENRY: UP PARRAMATTA RIVER

THE OBVIOUS place to set off on a harbour journey is under the Bridge or in the shadow of the Opera House. But the appropriate place for me to begin paddling is beside a broken stone column holding the sky off the water in Parramatta River.

For the column is a symbol of just how far a paddle can take you.

About a kilometre upstream from Gladesville Bridge, and just off the northern bank in water that has the character of cloudy tea, the column appears to rise out of the river. But it is actually sitting on one of a trio of rocks known as the Brothers, which only show themselves at low tide. The column is out of the way of boating traffic and all but out of sight of those sitting on the fast catamaran ferries rumbling upriver and down between Circular Quay and Parramatta. The RiverCats' wake washes past the column like time itself.

The column is a memorial to a young man who rowed this reach of the river, and into immortality. His name was Henry Searle, and, as a plaque facing the river reads, he was 'Champion Sculler of the World 1888-89'.

Henry Searle was born to row. He had to. Searle grew up on an island in Clarence River on the New South Wales north coast. He would row himself and his siblings more than ten kilometres to and from school. Having dominated local regattas, Searle headed to Sydney, where a talented oarsman could make both a name for himself and a good deal of money.

In the later part of the 19th century, sculling was a very popular sport in Australia, and Parramatta River was the main course. And like just about anything else involving competition in Australia, the river provided a platform on which to gamble. Professional scullers heaved and pulled 3 miles and 330 yards (just over 5.1 kilometres) from near the present-day Ryde Bridge downriver to the Brothers rocks. Where this column – and the memory of Henry Searle – rests was the finish line. This was the point where history was made, and so was money, as the betting on the races was huge.

Australians' interest in professional sculling had surged in 1876, when Edward Trickett travelled to England to take on the Mother Country's champion for the world crown. Trickett had lived by, and trained on, Parramatta River. He won the race, becoming the first Australian to be a professional world title holder.

From then on, those around the globe would learn what many Australians already knew. The colonials were a powerful force on the water. Never mind rule Britannia; Australians ruled the sculling world title for twenty-two of the following thirty-one years. Parramatta River became a stage for intense competition, with forty-five world professional sculling championships held on its waters between 1876 and 1914. When the champions took to the water, so did the crowds. Fleets of launches and ferries, packed with spectators, moored in the river. People lined the shores, filled the wharves, and pushed onto pub verandas along the course.

Searle, in particular, was lionised. He looked like a champion. The illustrations and photos of him show a handsome young man, with a groomed moustache and eyebrows arching over sharp eyes. He was criticised for having a crude rowing action. Even so, Searle literally left other champions in his wake. He became known as the Clarence Comet. What made Searle extraordinary was not just how quickly he rowed, but how it took him such little time to row to greatness.

Having arrived in Sydney in April 1888, Searle was on Parramatta River just six months later to compete against the world champion Peter Kemp. Searle had raced on the river just three times before, and he had won each race, pocketing £200. This time he was racing for £1000, and the world championship. An estimated 30,000 spectators had crammed onto and along the river.

On that October Saturday, Searle carved through the water and the record books. He reached the Brothers in 22 minutes 44.5 seconds. Those statistics, in clinical digits and across the distance of time, may barely register. But often, while paddling along Parramatta River, I think of Henry Searle and those statistics. To row more than 5.1 kilometres in less than twenty-three minutes; I can only imagine the acidic burning in the muscles, the heart hammering against the chest, and the desperate gulping for breath. Actually, I can more than imagine. I only have to paddle a little harder, feeling the river take on the viscosity of molasses and my muscles melt to the density of water, to be in awe of what Searle achieved.

While ordinary paddlers draw breath and rest, Henry Searle rowed on to more milestones. After defeating every other Australian sculler of note within a year, he travelled to Britain. The journey in itself would have been a challenge for Searle. This man who could crush all on the water was, in his own words, gripped with 'fear travelling by sea' and suffered motion sickness.

In September 1889, Searle took on the Canadian champion William O'Connor on a 4¾-mile course along the River Thames. Searle won easily and as soon as the telegraph message reached Sydney, celebrations erupted.

Henry Searle was run down on the voyage back to Australia by typhoid, which he presumably contracted in Europe. By the time he arrived on home soil, he was very ill. When the ship docked at Melbourne, he was taken to hospital. Henry Searle died of peritonitis on 10 December 1889. He was aged 23.

A country that had been readying to welcome home a hero was now preparing for a funeral. The *Sydney Morning Herald* reported Searle's death was met with 'expressions of unfeigned sorrow and regret that the life of so promising a young man should have terminated in such a lamentable manner'. The newspaper's editorial mourned the loss of a young man who personified what was good about Australia, declaring, 'he did us honour, for he was of us, and had the strength of our soil, of our atmosphere, of ourselves to some degree, within him'.

On the same page the *Herald* reported on Henry Searle, it printed an item about Sydney Harbour cradling hopes for a growing export trade: 'At daylight today the largest cargo of wool ever loaded into one vessel at this port, it is believed, leaves for Europe'. The shipment of 10,428 bales 'includes some of the best samples of wool ever exported from this colony'.

Henry Searle's body had not even been returned to Sydney when calls for a monument began. In a letter to the editor, one suggested 'a monument be erected on the Brothers rocks . . . Surely no more appropriate spot could be found . . . The winning post was the beacon light that beckoned him to victory . . . Then in future struggles on the historic course, the goal to be reached by the victor will be the monument to Australia's greatest aquatic champion, typical of honourable perseverance, courage and integrity. Henry Searle may justly, in disposition, action, and character be held up as an example of perfect manhood to the rising generation.'

The funeral for Henry Searle was, according to the *Sydney Morning Herald*, 'one of the most imposing and remarkable events ever witnessed in New South Wales or, indeed, Australia'. An estimated 170,000 mourners lined the route to Circular Quay. The procession following the coffin was more than a kilometre long. The coffin was loaded onto the steamer *Australian,* with the sculling champion's colours fluttering from the foremast. Henry Searle's remains were to be sailed out the Heads and back to Clarence River. Even this service at the quay, at a time when the country was not yet a nation, was seen as a uniting force: 'The coffin lying upon the deck of the steamer covered by wreaths from every one of the Australian colonies spoke that we were now an Australian nation, and federated as one people.' That belief was not quite unanimous. An editorial in the Melbourne *Age* expressed concern the enormous outpouring of grief sent the wrong message to Australian youth that 'the development of biceps, not brains, is most desirable . . . All that can be fairly claimed for him is that he was a good-natured but illiterate young man with a magnificent muscular development, who had proved that he could pull a wager-boat faster through the water than any other man in the world.'

Still, the eulogies and paeans to what those muscles achieved were created, including this verse, written by 'O.S.W.' and published in *The Sydney Mail*.

> *Past are his glories on harbour and river,*
> *Never again will a people acclaim*
> *With wild cries of triumph his prowess, who never*
> *Will uphold again fair Australia's fame.*

The broken column, a symbol of a life cut short, was unveiled on the second anniversary of Searle's death.

As I paddle around the memorial, I read the plaques eulogising the birth and death of Henry Searle. Yet it is the panel above the plaque proclaiming Searle as 'Champion Sculler of the World 1888-89' that speaks so much. It is a pair of oars crossed and bound with a ribbon.

A north-easterly gust skitters across the water, and the strengthening tidal flow is pushing me upriver, away from the monument. It is as though time and tide, or perhaps the memory of Henry Searle, are willing me to put the blades in the water and get paddling.

HENRY WOULD be disappointed. I paddle only fifty or so metres before I guide *Pulbah Raider* onto a beach strung along the Henley shoreline.

Above the sandy bank, looking over Searle's monument, is a row of large homes. One, in particular, stands out. The historic pile has Gothic windows that look as though they have been plucked from a cathedral in Europe, and a tower on its eastern side. The tower looks fortress-like, giving the impression it was built as much to protect those within as it was to provide a platform from which to look out. The Victorian-era mansion has a slightly spooky look about it, like an imperious old spinster peering disdainfully at the deserted shoreline.

Below the house is a pontoon, listing on the sand and holding a rusting crane. I trudge along the beach and onto Henley Point for another look at Searle's monument. A man in his sixties walks his Jack Russell dog onto the gently sloping point. While the dog, Spot, follows his nose through the grass, I yarn with his owner, Henry Hart. I wonder if this point used to be an approach for a car ferry or punt. No, Henry replies, there used to be a ferry wharf here; he remembers it from when he was a kid.

'There used to be the little boats going down to the Quay and back,' says Henry.

Henry points to the old mansion and says he lived there as a child and young adult. It was the family home. He calls it 'The Castle'. The house's name is Burnham, but it is commonly known as Burnham Castle. As a teenager, Henry set up his bedroom in the tower.

'You could see the [Harbour] Bridge from there,' recalls Henry, 'and you could actually see the tower from the top of the Gladesville Bridge.'

The Castle, he says, was built in the 1880s and had been home to diplomats, and a sea captain whose ships ploughed up and down the river, carrying coal from Hexham on Hunter River to fuel the gasworks at Mortlake. Henry remembers seeing the colliers gliding past until the late 1960s.

'There were many more industries along here, when I was a kid,' he says as he scans the opposite shore at Chiswick and Abbotsford, with its cluster of new apartments. The Nestlé factory was over there, he says, pointing. A little further downriver was the Lysaght wire works.

'There used to be a low frequency hum, but it didn't worry me,' Henry recalls.

A RiverCat whizzes by, rolling a set of small waves to the bank. Henry says the RiverCats' wake has pushed the sand up the bank over the years, all but burying a low stone wall on The Castle's property line. Henry's son used to body surf the RiverCats' waves, which can curl up to more than half a metre at low tide. But it was surfing dictated by the ferries' timetable.

'There was a long wait between waves,' he chuckles.

Henry comments how much cleaner the water is compared with when he was a boy. He used to swim at nearby tidal baths, long since gone.

'You'd come out with black stuff sticking to your hair and skin from all the rubbish in the river,' he says. 'I'd swim in there now. But I don't.'

PADDLING AROUND the point at Henley and into a bay, I slalom through a motley fleet of moored cruisers and yachts, some glistening and expensive, a few having seen better days. I notice an older man with a grizzled beard sitting in a rowboat that is tethered to a restored former navy fast auxiliary boat. Not having my map handy, I ask the man the name of the bay.

'Bedlam Bay, so you have to be a bit mad to be here,' he says, in a deadpan tone, before grinning.

Ahead the bay slaps into a sandstone wall and small wharf. Beyond the seawall, the land sweeps up to a collection of buildings that had been part of the Gladesville Hospital for psychiatric patients.

The man in the boat introduces himself as Lloyd and says he is the secretary and caretaker for the Bedlam Bay Boat Club. I ask him where the clubhouse is. 'Burnt down', he says glumly.

In August 2015, fire tore through the 19th century boathouse at the wharf. Lloyd says the flames consumed more than a piece of history by the bay; most of his possessions had been stored in the boathouse. With what he has left, Lloyd sometimes stays on a yacht in the bay. He's been living around Bedlam Bay since 1994.

'It hasn't changed much in that time,' mutters Lloyd. 'It's very quiet here.'

So this bay, it seems, is a rarity in Sydney. It is a backwater.

These waters also cradle big dreams and high hopes in the shape of small boats. Lloyd's mate and fellow Bedlam Bay Boat Club member, Colin Campbell, is restoring a cruiser, *Elenka*. One look at the cruiser tied up at the hospital jetty tells me Colin is either an optimist or very patient – or both.

'I'm stupid!' he declares. 'These projects come up, and I can't say no.'

The waters of Bedlam Bay have flowed through more than half a century of Colin's life. He worked at Gladesville Hospital for almost twenty years, starting as a nurse in 1963. He would sail sabots across the bay. The little sailboats were built by a colleague in the old boathouse, with the aid of patients.

Back then, Colin recalls, it was possible to sail freely on the bay, for there were very few boats moored in it. He used to swim in the bay, but he wouldn't now. Too many bull sharks around, he explains. Not that he's seen any, but he's heard plenty of stories of recent sightings in the waters around here. He eyes my kayak then looks at me with a mild expression of warning.

'A kayak got bitten four, five years ago in Morrisons Bay [a couple of bays upriver].'

It's more than twenty years since Colin worked at Gladesville Hospital. But his boat restoration passion (and he has bought another cruiser to do up, once *Elenka* is finished) keeps him anchored to the bay, and to his past.

'I've never left this place, because of the bay,' he says, looking up the hill to where he used to work. He smiles and pats *Elenka*. 'And I've still got my office here!'

FROM BEDLAM Bay, the grounds of the former Gladesville Hospital are a picture of restfulness. Old buildings, in burnished brick and sandstone, huddle along the ridge line behind clumps of trees. The land forms an amphitheatre as it tumbles down to the water. Before it reaches the bay, it flattens onto a cricket oval. The terrain bending around the oval, the trees, the buildings, they combine to create a good feeling. And that would please Doctor Frederick Manning.

In 1868, Frederick Manning was appointed Medical Superintendent of what was then known as the Tarban Creek Lunatic Asylum.

The institution had been on the site for thirty years. Until it was built, the growing issue of mental illness in the colony was being literally moved around and hidden away, wherever patients could be put. What facilities did exist were overcrowded.

The colony's Governor, Richard Bourke, wanted a solution. A slice of land between Parramatta River and a tributary, Tarban Creek, was surveyed in 1835. The site for the asylum was chosen, in part, because of the river. It provided access to the facility from both Sydney and Parramatta. What's more, it helped provide a serene environment. As Manning's predecessor, Francis Campbell, noted, the patients would 'derive eternal benefit' from the views. Not that patients were given the full opportunity to respond to that environment; many were languishing in cells, passing through dark, tunnel-like passages, and behind high walls.

When Dr Manning took up his appointment, he didn't like the asylum's gloomy prison-like atmosphere. Further, he felt the site was isolated, making it difficult and costly to supply the asylum. Frederick Manning set about turning isolation into self-sufficiency, in the process improving the facility and the lives of those placed there. New buildings, many of them fine sandstone structures, were erected. Extensive gardens were planted, additional land was bought, and agriculture practised, with patients helping out. A vineyard was planted on the slope leading to the bay. Dr Manning advocated the medicinal benefits of wine, and at one stage recommended the drop as part of a diet to combat scurvy at the facility. The vines flourished, and, as seen in photos from the late 19th century, helped give the asylum the look of a successful farming estate by the river.

Manning was credited with making improvements not just in bricks and mortar and to the land, but also to flesh and blood, adopting a more humane approach in the treatment of those here, even at the most elemental level. He replaced the term 'lunatic' with 'patient', and the facility was to become known as a hospital.

'Frederick Manning should be a household name,' says Peter Colthorpe, the co-ordinator of the Friends of Gladesville Hospital community group. 'He brought a dignity into the system, his approach changed the way New South Wales thought about mental health. That approach lived on, and it still does.'

Peter is showing me around the site. The hospital's long history, from colonial times and through most of the 20th century, can be seen in the different architectural styles. As a hospital, Gladesville was decommissioned in the mid-1990s. However, the site continues to house a range of health facilities, both public and private. The grounds themselves are an ongoing source of well-being, with the public welcome to walk around them.

Peter, along with his Labrador, Chloe, meets me outside the thick perimeter stone walls. Heading through the open gate, we have glimpses of the river through the bush.

'The water was the easiest way to transport people here,' Peter explains. 'The first patients came by river.'

Those thirty-nine who stepped ashore here in 1838 were the first of many patients who arrived via the water. We follow roughly in their footsteps, along a straggly stone path up the hill. Along the way, Peter points out remnants of the gardens Manning had planted. The walk takes us past a fine two-storey home built for the Medical Superintendent. The path slides between two rows of casuarinas, which soften the fact that beyond the trees are stone walls leading to the asylum designed by the Colonial Architect, Mortimer Lewis. The walk is appealing, but the destination, a stern pile of stone dating back to the late 1830s, is imposing. As we inspect the building, Peter indicates the timelines set in bricks and stone, from the ground floor extensions in the mid-19th century to the first floor additions done in the early 1900s. Behind the original building are others constructed in the late 1800s and the early 20th century. In 1940, Peter says, there were up to 1700 patients here.

We trace the lip of the hill towards the north-east. Not even the thick perimeter walls can keep out the ceaseless noise of road traffic. Near the entrance off Victoria Road are more buildings, including a hospital built in the late 1800s, and a string of brick buildings used as wards in the early 20th century. Peter says the collection of buildings close to the road reflected the shift in emphasis away from the river as the main link to the hospital. Yet the river played a role beyond being a highway.

As part of their therapy, patients would immerse themselves in its waters, with baths built in the river. But whether it was hygienic is questionable, for the river had also long been a dumping ground for the hospital. When he was heading the facility, Francis Campbell praised the infrastructure built to sluice the waste to the water, calling it 'a splendid piece of perfect drainage in itself; it is the finest in the colony'.

The river was repeatedly encroached upon as demand for more land grew. A map from 1931 shows how part of Bedlam Bay had already been reclaimed, its original incision into the valley filled in to become more of a curve. According to Peter, ash from the power stations around the harbour was used for more reclamation, and, by 1950, where there was once water was the oval.

As we stand at the top of the hill, looking down the slope that had been cloaked in grape vines and market gardens more than a century ago, we can see a cricket match being played on the oval. The bay is just beyond the boundary, with masts poking above the seawall. As the batsman sweeps the ball towards that boundary, a ferry glides by in the background.

As for the future of the Gladesville Hospital site, Peter Colthorpe is hopeful. It may sit on a prime waterfront position, and, in the past, parcels of the land have been sheared off and sold for development. However, the land along the shore is part of Parramatta River Regional Park, and Peter believes the remainder of the site will be protected by growing community awareness of what is here.

'I'd like to see it continue as a functioning part of the Health Department. The tradition is there.

'And I think it should remain an open parkland, somewhere you can walk your dog,' Peter says, looking down at a panting Chloe.

'But the river links it all.'

LEAVING THE bay cradling the former hospital grounds, I stop at Bedlam Point for a drink of water. But I'm hardly the first to pull in along here for a break.

'We stoped [sic] at a Neck of land to Breakfast,' wrote Lieutenant William Bradley in his journal, on 15 February 1788. Bradley was among the crew in boats journeying up this river with the colony's founding governor, Arthur Phillip.

It had been less than three weeks since Phillip had stepped ashore at Sydney Cove with almost 1500 other souls to found the penal colony. In that time, the Governor had barely scratched the surface in establishing a transplanted community. But scratching the surface of the soil around the cove was enough to convince Phillip he had to find more suitable land for farming.

The exploration party's breakfast spot by the river had been a place of nourishment for thousands of years for the Wallumedegal people, who lived on the river's northern side. The men speared fish from the bank, and the women guided bark canoes across the river and used hooks and lines to catch a feed.

The original inhabitants and the explorers met on the headland just across from Bedlam Point. Those two headlands marked the entrance to a bay off the river. Bradley recorded their meeting with a 'Native arm'd'. He noted how the Wallumedegal man was very curious and carefully examined the boats and their contents.

'The Governor gave this Man a hatchet & a looking glass,' Bradley wrote, 'which, when he looked into, he looked immediately behind the Glass to see if any person was there, & then pointed to the Glass and the shadows which he saw in the water, signifying they were similar.'

As a result of that meeting, both the cove and the western neck of land at its entrance received new names: Looking Glass Bay and Looking Glass Point. As for the other knoll at the bay's entrance, it would become known as Bedlam Point. This point was part of a vital link across the Parramatta River, and in the development of the colony. As settlers pushed further north, the Hunter Valley was opened up. That heightened the need for a land route between Sydney and the Hunter; relying on shipping was not enough. From 1826, gangs of convicts hacked and picked through the bush to form the Great North Road. In spite of toiling in terrain as tough and indifferent to suffering as many of their overseers, the gangs managed to bend the will of Mother Nature and built a road. But in places along the 264-kilometre route, nature was not about to be bowed by the lash of human endeavour. Parramatta River brought the road to a halt. Planners plotted a way across the river, so that travellers didn't have to journey upriver to present-day Ryde, or as far as Parramatta, to cross. The colony's Surveyor-General Thomas Mitchell searched for the best place to operate a punt and determined the narrowest part of the river along this reach was from Bedlam Point to Abbotsford, a distance of 220 yards (201 metres). Yet even when so short a distance is involved, it can still take a long time to turn a recommendation into reality. It took more than three years and many complaints from farmers beyond the northern bank of Parramatta River before the punt was operating.

But it was rarely a relaxed crossing. The puntman had to haul the vessel across by pulling on chains or rope tethered to the banks. The work was so heavy that passengers usually had to help. Occasionally the punt was left stranded in the stream. W.S. Campbell, the son of the Medical Superintendent at the nearby asylum, recalled how passing steamers or large sailing boats would sometimes snag and snap the punt's haulage rope, 'causing great delays and much strong language and worry, until the ends could be fished up and spliced'.

Protruding from the point into the river is a low wall of old sandstone blocks. They are the remains of a wharf built in the 1830s. The blocks wear the marks of their makers, for the stone would have been cut and the wharf built by convicts. Walking up the track from the bank, I'm roughly following the route taken by travellers almost two centuries earlier. Over the rise is a stone cottage, restored and resplendent above Looking Glass Bay. The cottage is called Rockend. The building looks sturdy; its origins are shaky. Just when Rockend was built, and why, is debated. It may have been an inn at one stage, trying to lure travellers on the Great North Road. It could have been built in the 1840s, perhaps the 1850s. What is certain is that Rockend was a boyhood home of one of Australia's best-known poets, Andrew Barton 'Banjo' Paterson.

Paterson's maternal grandmother, Emily Mary Barton, owned the property. She gave the house its name, and she developed her grandson's love of literature and told him stories about the wider world. Rockend became a gathering place and home for her children and grandchildren, including Andrew. He was a country kid, growing up on Illalong Station, near Yass in southern New South Wales, and he had attended bush schools. From the age of twelve, Andrew was sent to Sydney for schooling and lived with his grandmother. Andrew would catch the ferry at the bottom of the hill to Sydney Grammar. He was keen on sports that allowed him to be on or by Parramatta River – boating and fishing – for, in a way, it connected him to the country life he missed. As he would later write in one of his poems, 'the man who's born a bushman, he gets mighty sick of town'. Paterson returned to the farm on holidays. But the city was where he lived for many years, working as a solicitor after completing his education. However, Paterson's imagination would go wandering in verse. Andrew, in print, became 'The Banjo', taking his nom de plume from the name of a horse back on the farm. Inevitably he would be drawn to the rhythm, imagery and stories of the bush, creating not just characters in verse but sketching what his readers perceived to be the very character of Australia in poems such as 'The Man from Snowy River' and 'Clancy of the Overflow'. And Banjo helped turn the tale of a sheep-stealing swagman who kills himself into a rallying cry that metamorphosed into an unofficial anthem in 'Waltzing Matilda'.

While his words roamed the Australian countryside and were recited far and wide, the writer himself had been exposed to a broader education at Rockend. It helped lead him out into the world, as a journalist and Boer War correspondent. So no matter where he went and what he wrote, it's interesting to try to read between the lines the lessons learnt in his grandmother's house. And perhaps what also helped open Paterson's ears to the cadences of life was the environment below the cottage. Or, to use the poet's own words:

> The song of the river
> That sings as it passes
> For ever and ever.

While Banjo's ballads were assured of immortality, the cottage where Australia's best-known poet had lived and had developed some of his ideas seemed doomed.

The view from the back of the cottage had been radically changed in 1923, when a linseed oil producer, Harold Meggitt, bought Rockend and established a factory along the eastern shore of Looking Glass Bay. It was one of the few factories built on Parramatta River's northern bank. The historic cottage was used as the company office. A 30-metre high silo, emblazoned with the company's logo, was built on the waterfront. Land was reclaimed and a wharf built. The factory operated until 1974.

The plan was for the 2.5 hectare site to be cleared for an apartment complex and marina. The cottage was to be demolished. But residents and the local council fought the proposal and eventually won. In 1979, the State Government agreed to buy the property, and it was to be parkland. At a time when battles to save historic properties from developers were raging on many fronts, this was seen as a watershed in public and official attitudes towards conservation. Physically saving the cottage was a longer battle still. Rockend had become, according to the committee which had joined the fight to save it, a burnt and ragged wreck. The cottage's interior had been stripped and vandalised, and its grounds overgrown.

As Rockend was restored, the cottage's future use was uncertain. In the end, it became a restaurant, but the building is also a museum of sorts. And in its very name, it is a monument to its famous former resident: Banjo Paterson Cottage Restaurant. Ross Pitts, who secured the restaurant sublease in 1986 and has been running the business ever since, is passionate about history and Banjo's writing.

I meet Ross at the cottage door, in the shade of the veranda. He wears a jovial expression, but Ross' face is not the only one that grabs my attention. In the front garden, a bust of Banjo peers at passers-by. The sculpture is of an older Paterson, with a pipe in his mouth and a roadmap of life experiences in the wrinkles and creases etched across his face. He is looking at the sky, lost in his thoughts, as he contentedly draws on his pipe. Ross commissioned the sculpture of the 'Singer of the Bush' to acknowledge not just the poet, but also how Paterson used his writing to help make Australians 'who they are, what they are'.

In the foyer hangs Paterson memorabilia, including a photo of Banjo at the front gate of Rockend in the early 1900s.

'He used to come back to stay with his grandmother,' explains Ross.

We walk through the cottage, tracking thick sandstone walls that keep at bay the heat of the day and the noises of the 21st century. Ross guides me to an enclosed veranda offering a terrific view of Looking Glass Bay, the river and life along the opposite banks. From here, for more than thirty years, Ross has watched the elements of the past disappear and the character of the area change. He shows me a photo he took in 1986. There are large storage tanks in the background, at Mortlake. The tanks have long gone. In the photo, in the bay below, there are only a few moored boats; there are more now, and the spaces between the buildings on the opposite shore have been largely filled in with yet more structures or larger houses. The promise of open space on the old Harold Meggitt factory site has been realised. It is Banjo Paterson Park. When he arrived at Rockend, Ross recalls, the foreshore looked neglected, saying 'it was pretty rough'.

We wander out into the cottage's garden, past the bust of Banjo, to another sculpture. It is of Governor Phillip, holding the 'looking glass' or telescope, and the Wallumedegal man. Both are peering out over the bay named after the looking glass, taking in the landscape that has been so dramatically altered in the years since.

Ross commissioned the sculpture because the event it commemorates 'puts this part of the harbour into the very early history of the first settlement'. Ross mentions that just behind the statue are strewn more reminders of the river's history: stones that were used as ballast in ships, along with lumps of coal and coke.

Paddling away from Bedlam Point and looking back into Looking Glass Bay, I note what remains of the past, what has returned, and what has gone. Rockend is a gracious presence from the mid-19th century on the slope of the hill. The building looks so solid, and so embedded in the landscape, it is hard to believe it was ever under threat. Below the cottage is the band of green honouring Rockend's famous former resident. Little evidence of the linseed oil factory remains, other than a commemorative plaque under the trees. Yet for all the changes, through what has been and what will be, the song of the river flows on.

AS I KAYAK up Parramatta River, I'm pushing against both the tide and the direction that generations of competitive rowers took on this waterway. Amateur rowing regattas had been held along this part of the river since the mid-19th century, and for more than four decades from the 1890s, these waters were the venue for competitions between the Greater Public Schools. The schools' crews raced for up to 2.5 kilometres down the river, in front of thousands of spectators, and finished around here, where the water blooms to the south into what's called Hen and Chicken Bay. The GPS Regatta was moved to Nepean River, near Penrith, in 1936. The traffic on Parramatta River had forced the rowers to look for another waterway on which to compete. The regatta, known as the Head of the River, has remained in Penrith but is now held at the Sydney International Regatta Centre.

Parramatta River remains a training ground and nursery for champion rowers. Nestling along the banks and bays around this part of the river are many of the schools' boatsheds. Although they are hardly sheds; they are testament to how prized rowing remains in the private schools system – and how much money is committed to the sport – for they are beautifully appointed buildings.

The most distinctive and elegant boatshed along this reach of the river belongs to Scots College. Built into a steep slope on the northern bank at Gladesville, the building, from the water, has the look of a country club. On the ground level is the boats storage area, and, on the storey above, the building's face is dominated by large windows. From the outside looking in, I can make out an honour board flanked by photos, and displayed in the centre window are two crossed oars. The building's weatherboard exterior is painted a blue-grey, the colour the sky can turn when a squall is approaching. I'm told later it's called garter blue. The front wall also wears the college insignia, along with the declaration that the boat club was established in 1914. The clubhouse is one of those places that by its very appearance speaks of tradition and arouses a desire to gain access, to stand in front of that honour board and look out of those windows. Yet I figure that's wishful thinking for someone who isn't an old boy, doesn't have sons at the school – and paddles a kayak. *Pulbah Raider* simply wouldn't fit in here; its milky turquoise colour would clash with the garter blue.

However, wishful thinking – and perhaps being a paddler – can open doors. Steven Adams, the college's Director of Property and Works, kindly arranges to guide me through the boatshed. I've made it into the club, at least for an hour or so.

The Chinese general Sun Tzu, in his *Art of War*, advised that if you are far from the enemy, make him believe you are near. The members of the Scots College Boat Club don't have to make believe they are near. All they need do is stand before their front windows and they can see a few of the other schools' boatsheds and watch their crews training on the river.

Not that Steven Adams views the competitors as the enemy; they are all part of the rowing community, and the river unites them. That, and the pain.

'It's so devastatingly debilitating,' says Steven, of competitive rowing. And he should know; he rowed on the river as a schoolboy in the early 1970s.

'It takes so much out of you. I think it's the ultimate team sport. You need to work completely in sync with the rest of the crew. An error by one can affect everyone.'

Steven explains the Scots College boathouse was built in 1936. Beyond the champions developed in this club and celebrated in the memorabilia on the walls, Steven views the walls themselves as a trophy. For this building that shelters the future generation of champion rowers is also upholding the past.

'The timber shed has largely disappeared from the harbour,' says Steven. 'The texture of the waterfront has changed from wood and steel to residential developments. And if you look at the texture of the waterfront, these sheds add interest.'

Steven looks up and down the river, at the neighbouring houses sprouting extensions and architectural 'features', and at the residential developments on the opposite bank. As he sees it, the loss of texture means a diminution of interest, and of character, along Sydney's waterfront. Steven doesn't really like what he sees.

'The whole morphology now smacks of maximisation. You can't get a pizza box between them [the buildings].

'I like dishevelled waterfronts.'

The character of the waterfront was not only about what you saw but also what you smelled. Rowing in the 1970s, Steven could navigate by his nose. When he had a whiff of chocolate, for instance, he knew he was passing the Nestlé factory at Abbotsford. There was the scent of linseed oil, the gas odour near Mortlake; each peninsula emitted a clue as to where the rowers were.

'But you can't navigate by smells these days,' he says almost ruefully.

Perhaps it is because rowers face backwards, looking at where they have been. Perhaps it is because Steven used to be the Collection Manager at the Australian National Maritime Museum. Whatever the reason, for Steven, the beauty of rowing on Parramatta River is shaped by history.

'You are retracing the steps of those who have raced before you. Essentially the river hasn't changed since Henry Searle rowed here.'

Little wonder, then, Steven Adams loves the Scots College Boat Club house. It may not have a dishevelled look, but touch the walls and you can feel the texture, and the tradition. Beyond retaining the building, Steven and his colleagues battled to protect the colour scheme. Some bureaucrats wanted the building painted in 'recessive colours', so it blended into the landscape. Steven insisted it be garter blue, so that it told all who saw it that this building belonged by the water and was deeply connected to it.

Of course, the shed is more than a blue trophy; it is a training centre and home to dozens of young rowers. Steven introduces me to the shed manager, Garry Elliott.

When the river is glass and its surface is cut by few other boats, when there is barely a light on in the neighbouring homes, Garry is at his busiest. Each morning of the rowing season, from September to March, Garry ensures the rowers are on the water. Up to twenty of the students have stayed overnight in the shed.

In the pre-dawn, the rowers shuffle down to the shed's lower level, where about forty boats are stored. On the racks is a stack of money pressed into carbon fibre and moulded into racing shells. A boat for a crew of eight can cost up to $75,000. Once the shed's doors are open and the morning chill claws its way in, urging the boys to get paddling, it's just a few metres down the ramps, onto the pontoons and into the river.

By 4.45am, the crews are cocooned in their shells, heaving and huffing as one, all the while watched over by coaches in tinnies following them. Garry says the training sessions tend to be finished by 7am, because after then, 'it gets pretty busy on the river'. The rowers then head off to school and return in the afternoon for more training, before turning in early, preparing to beat the sun, other boats, and their own racing times.

Competing against other boats in regattas is what they train for. But the young rowers are finding training on Parramatta River increasingly difficult because of other boats, especially the RiverCats.

Steven argues that with the ferries ploughing through the water at twenty-two knots an hour, they push out pressure waves that create a swell, and a challenge, for the crews. As he says bluntly, 'you can't easily row now'. The ferries' waves are pushing the rowers off the river; the crews of Scots College, and those of other schools, head for the relatively calmer waters in the coves, such as Hen and Chicken Bay, to train and to stage smaller competitions.

Steven says crews are also dealing with the 'in-fill' of waterways with developments, especially marinas. And with the marinas come more pleasure boats, and some of those with engines, he argues, are plainly aggressive towards those who rely on paddles for power.

A tradition is literally at risk of being swamped on Parramatta River.

As residential development continues along the banks, many feel even bleaker about the future of rowing on the river. With more residents comes the need for more ferries and more wharves, and the New South Wales Government has committed millions of dollars to building infrastructure along, and on, the river. Rowers have resisted the encroachment into their sport. In early 2016, a representative body, Rowing NSW, voiced its concerns about a new ferry wharf and interchange planned for about half way up the river at Rhodes, where industrial plants have been replaced by clusters of apartments. The organisation warned it would make rowing more dangerous on this stretch of the river, and it called for the government to give rowers a stronger voice in deciding how the waterway was used. However, as Steven Adams well knows, you need a very strong voice to be heard over the din of construction and the ringing in politicians' ears of what sounds like progress.

'We'd like to think it will keep going as long as it can,' Steven says of the future of rowing on Parramatta River. 'But we're up against it, and there's not enough support from the government to protect the heritage.'

Inscribed above the crossed oars in the Scots College Boat Club's centre window is a phrase in Gaelic. Steven and Garry tell me it roughly translates as, 'Go Together in Brave Hearts'. That motto ripples downstairs and into the river. Competitive rowing, on even the calmest of waters, takes more than toned muscles; it requires resilient souls, determined minds, and brave hearts together. As for rowers remaining on this river, it may well take all those qualities and more to pull against the inexorable flow of political and commercial demands. For the very same waters that can help build character for the future can also wash away all that stand in the way of those who seek money, power and, that most amorphous and 21st century of words, lifestyle.

GLADESVILLE. THE very name sounds green. Say 'Glades' and you picture trees. But the suburb along a stretch of Parramatta River's northern bank was named not because of some environmental inspiration but after John Glade, one of the earliest British settlers in the area. Glade bought additional land, which folded around a bay, from John Doody, a former convict who had the ability to draw glades; he was a botanical artist. In time, Glade's name was attached to not just the land but the water as well. Doodys Bay became Glades Bay.

As I kayak into the bay, it is possible to see a semblance of a glade on the shore. The mangroves thicken, and the muddy bank slurps at the water. Having flowed out of the river, the water becomes sluggish, as though it is taking on the consistency of its colour: chocolate. Just as the water slows, so does the sense of time, as I look at the bushy eastern shore. I figure this is a view of how the banks used to be in these little coves, before the arrival of Glade and Doody, but a walking track beside the bay teaches me otherwise.

The Wulaba Track takes you through a corridor of bush following a creek to the bay, and back to the time when the Wallumedegal people lived around here. Back then, there were few mangroves; instead, the banks were sandy and the rocky outcrops encrusted with oysters. But with the Europeans came land-clearing, and this led to silt and nutrients being washed down the creek into the bay, allowing the mangroves to thrive. Still, the sight of growth is taken as a healthy sign by those who remember when the shore was degraded.

'Oh, it's good to see them sprouting,' says a man walking along the boardwalk, who has stopped to look at the green buds of mangroves bursting out of the mud.

His name is Sen. He has lived in the area for more than twenty years and enjoys wandering along the Wulaba Track to the water.

In the 1990s, Sen would watch the fishing trawlers still working in the river. The trawlers disappeared, as the authorities declared fish caught around here might not be fit to eat due to contaminants in the river bed and water. That didn't dissuade Sen.

'I used to fish around here, and I wasn't afraid to eat the fish,' he says. 'And nothing's happened to me – yet!'

Sen points to the rocks next to a public ramp, where I've landed *Pulbah Raider*.

'I used to eat oysters from here in the mid-90s,' he says.

The rocks still wear a girdle of oyster shells, but I presume they are empty, long eaten out or dead from pollution.

'No, there are oysters here,' counters Sen. 'I'd be still game to eat one or two. It wouldn't do anything drastic to you.'

After meeting Sen, I think of him whenever I see a trawler moored in bays along the river. Not that I see many. They may be outnumbered by pleasure boats, but the trawlers stand out as a reminder that this river was once more of a workplace than a playground. Paddling the river, I see few commercial vessels operating, only the occasional barge carrying equipment.

Just off the peninsula at Putney, I see an apparition slowly moving on the water. It is a vehicular ferry, providing a link not only across the few hundred metres of the river from Putney to Mortlake but also to a service that has disappeared from the rest of the harbour. Launched in 1928, the Mortlake ferry – or the Putney punt, depending on which side of the river you are on – is grasping the past as tenaciously as it holds the cables that guide it across the water. The ferry's operation exudes a gentle rhythm. It waits on one bank as up to eighteen vehicles drive up the ramp and park on its deck. The gates come down, and the punt sets off. For the next five minutes, the vehicles' occupants are compelled to go with the flow of another time and soak in the experience of slow travel. Other vessels, even the RiverCats, have to wait while the punt trundles across the river like a dignified old lady. Then the punt nudges up the bank on the other side, the gate is lifted, and the vehicles fire up and prepare to accelerate back to the tempo of the 21st Century.

As the punt marks time travelling across the river, the RiverCats scurry up and down the waterway. They weave a jagged pattern from terminal to terminal along the banks. Between Circular Quay and Parramatta, there are eighteen ferry terminals and about 22 kilometres of river. They may be running to a schedule, but the ferries are also carried along by history. Commercial passenger craft have been on this river since 1789. The first boat built to carry goods and passengers along the river was named *Rose Hill Packet*, but this reputedly ugly assemblage of wood was better known as 'The Lump'. Relying on sails and oars, which the passengers had to grasp as well, 'The Lump' could take up to a week to finish the return voyage. The RiverCats cover the journey from Circular Quay to Parramatta in just under an hour. Then again, ferries in the 1890s were taking only roughly an hour and a quarter.

'The Lump' was followed onto the river by a mangy fleet of small passage boats. The first regular service on the river was in 1793, with passengers being charged the substantial fare of one shilling. From March 1831, the oars and sails of those little vessels were shrouded by steam. The future puffed onto the river with *Sophia Jane* and, shortly after, the first locally built steamship, *Surprise*.

On Parramatta River, fortunes rose and fell like the tide, as different ferry designs and companies came and went. One vessel that could carry about 100 passengers relied literally on horsepower. *Experiment* had four horses running on a treadmill. Occasionally, the horses would stop and *Experiment* would float backwards, as did the business, until she was fitted with an engine.

As land transportation improved, the pressure on river ferries increased. Passenger services were shut down a number of times, as demand dwindled. But the ferry has ploughed back into relevance on the river. These days more than three million journeys are taken each year on Parramatta River catamaran services.

THE RIVERCATS do as boats have done for more than two centuries on Parramatta River; they stop at Kissing Point. And with an evocative name like that, Kissing Point is almost a siren call to all on the water. Indeed, many have pulled up on the bank to rest on the grassy verge, including the colony's early governors. One report has it that the point earnt its name when the second governor, John Hunter, was rewarded with a kiss for helping a woman step onto dry land. What lures me ashore, however, is not any air of romance around the rocky outcrop's name but my bladder.

Aside from environmental considerations, there is nothing practical about urinating from a kayak. What's more, it could be lethal. Just off Kissing Point in the early days of the colony, a sailor was 'easing himself' at the edge of his boat, when he fell overboard and drowned.

So I paddle onto the bank just below the Concord and Ryde Sailing Club, its weatherboard and corrugated iron home perched over the water on piers and reminding passers-by that sails can still be seen on this river, especially on summer weekends. The shore is studded with shells, so when the kayak's hull is rubbed by the bank, *Pulbah Raider* sounds as though it is sighing with relief. Perhaps that's just me anticipating the sound I'm about to make.

Once comfort is restored and I have time to look around, I notice the Wallumai wind sculpture on the bank. As well as honouring the Aboriginal people who have drawn sustenance from the river, the sculpture gives shape to what so many seek along this reach – it features three fish suspended on poles, their polished steel scales gleaming in the noonday sun. Wallumai is an Aboriginal word for 'snapper'. Sitting under the fish sculpture is an older couple. I wonder if they have been moved to visit Kissing Point because of the name. But no, Donald and Beryl Chivas, married for more than sixty years, are here for a picnic lunch and a little reminiscing.

When I mention how the point's name may give visitors ideas, Donald sets me straight on its origins.

'Oh, there are rumours about why it's called Kissing Point,' he says, 'but how it got its name was back in the early days of the colony, when the boats were coming up here. If they came too close to the point and weren't careful, the hulls touched the bottom of the river. They "kissed" it. A nice way of putting it, isn't it?'

Donald and Beryl have lived near here for as long as they've been married. For forty years, Donald worked for the Australian Gas Light company, which had the large works just across the river at Mortlake. His job took him all over Sydney, but when he was in the area, one of Donald's unofficial tasks was to collect green weed from the shallows around Kissing Point, for the boss to use as bait on his weekend fishing trips. Apparently the weed was terrific for catching luderick. He doubts he could collect as much green weed these days, with the river cleaner than he remembers it.

Donald pauses and gazes across the river to the peninsula where the massive gasworks he knew so well once stood. Then his eyes drift back to this side of the river, to the present. He looks at Beryl and gently murmurs, 'There are a lot of memories triggered by different points of this river.'

MEMORIES ARE under the surface as well. Buried in the bed of Kissing Point Bay is the keel of HMAS *Stuart*. The Royal Australian Navy ship served in operations in the Mediterranean then around New Guinea during the Second World War, only to have her battle honours recognised after the war by being decommissioned, placed on the disposal list and sold for scrap. From cruising the world's seas, she ended her days in pieces by Parramatta River.

Other remnants of Australia's maritime history are along the bank. A few hundred metres upriver from Kissing Point was one of the country's most successful boatyards. This was where the Halvorsen family built hundreds of vessels for almost four decades and, in the process, helped shape Australians' idea of a luxury boat. Some very beautiful and very well-known craft slid into the water here.

In late 1924, Norwegian-born Lars Halvorsen arrived in Sydney, bringing boatbuilding skills learnt from his father and in shipyards in the United States and South Africa. He also brought a dream of establishing a family company. Even before his wife and seven children had reached Sydney, he had his first commission, building a yacht in a rented boatshed at Drummoyne, further down Parramatta River.

As orders flowed in and word of his craftsmanship spread, Lars Halvorsen kept upgrading his boatsheds, ending up in a large yard in Neutral Bay, on the harbour's North Shore. Lars Halvorsen also bought and sold boats, including a yacht called *Sirocco*. He sold that to a Professor Flynn, from Tasmania, who was buying it for his son, Errol. Young Errol arrived to pick up the yacht and sail it on to New Guinea. He invited Lars' son Carl to join him, but that was vetoed. The yacht was wrecked in New Guinea, but once he was in Hollywood and became a movie star, Errol Flynn had another *Sirocco* built.

Lars Halvorsen died in 1936. His sons carried on the business. They bought a couple of hectares of land on Parramatta River to build a new yard just near Kissing Point, at Ryde. When the main shed, a massive building that could have sheltered a football field, was erected, the family was concerned about attracting enough work to pay for it. However, world events took care of that.

During the Second World War, Lars Halvorsen Sons Pty Ltd built about 250 vessels for the Australian, US and Dutch armed forces. At the peak of production, the company had a workforce of 350. Author and Lars' granddaughter Randi Svensen says the Halvorsen brothers pioneered the concept of mass production for Australia's defence department and were able to build two 38-foot air-sea rescue boats a week at their Ryde yard.

In addition to the boats they built for the war effort, others that the Halvorsens had constructed for pleasure were seconded from their owners. When the navy commandeered those boats, they became known as 'the Hollywood Fleet'.

After the war, the boats that gave the 'Hollywood Fleet' its lustre attracted Hollywood when the stars visited. The Halvorsens produced a fleet of motor cruisers at its Ryde boatshed, and they were hired out for glamorous holidays on the Hawkesbury River, or to entertain the famous. Among those who went cruising on a Halvorsen boat were Bob Hope, Humphrey Bogart and Alfred Hitchcock.

More than highly polished boats of beauty took shape in the big shed. On the Parramatta River bank, the firm also built yachts that raced in the Sydney to Hobart competition, and its workers created Australia's first America's Cup challenger for the 1962 bid. Randi Svensen recalls the yacht was shrouded in tarpaulin in the shed, but she took a peek and saw the stars of the Southern Cross painted on the bow. Randi was convinced the yacht would be called *Southern Cross*, and she was shocked when the boat's owner, Sir Frank Packer, named her in honour of his late wife, Gretel.

Randi holds childhood memories of visiting that 'cavernous space' at Ryde, which 'was basic but functional and highly organised'.

'It was always a thrill to see the boats, either under construction or being repaired or maintained,' Randi recalls.

The Halvorsens sold the Ryde yard to the Royal Australian Navy in 1980, but it has since become a commercial boat repair operation. The big shed remains on the bank, although the sum of the years has knocked it about. The wharves and jetties have also been battered by time; in places, the timber is warping, bowing and soughing towards the river. I've seen a diverse fleet tied up around the yard, including jetboats that give tourists a thrill on the main harbour by turning their stomachs to swill. I reckon Lars Halvorsen and his sons would approve of those boats. To make ends meet during the Depression, they charged a shilling for joy rides on the harbour in the family's speedboat, *Kangaroo*.

To Randi Svensen, the Ryde yard was pivotal not just to the family business but to the development of boatbuilding in Australia. In that massive shed, new ideas and designs were tested and formed. As Randi says of the Halvorsens' venture by the river, 'Ryde was ahead of its time when built and continued to keep up with the times, until the times caught up with wooden boatbuilding.'

LONG BEFORE there were boats being produced on this site along the river, there was beer. Shakespeare once had a character declare, 'I will make it felony to drink small beer', but it was a felon who was Australia's first big brewer.

James Squire was convicted of highway robbery in England and transported to New South Wales with the First Fleet. In 1795, having received a conditional pardon, Squire was granted a 30-acre (12.1 hectares) plot near Kissing Point. Within a few years, he had established an inn, the Malting Shovel, on the banks of the river. Being roughly halfway between Sydney

Cove and Parramatta, the public house became a beacon that couldn't be passed by boatmen and their passengers. His beer, simply called Squire's Brew, may have attracted drinkers from upriver and down, but the tavern was merely value adding for James Squire.

In his land at Kissing Point, Squire sowed hops and harvested opportunity. Governor Philip Gidley King was encouraging colonists to drink beer rather than what he saw as the more debilitating rum. So Squire was satisfying official tastes, and his land holdings grew. He also built a large brewery. Randi Svensen says the foundations of the brewery, along with Squire's wharf, were still visible when the Halvorsen family had their yard on the site.

By the time he died in 1822, James Squire was one of the wealthiest men in the colony. His efforts were preserved not just in bottles of beer but works of art. One watercolour image of Squire's riverside property in the early 19th century shows the buildings and a jetty, with a sailing boat tied up to it. A man is rolling a barrel along the jetty, and also standing in the foreground near the boat are two Aboriginal men. As in that piece of art, the life of James Squire was closely connected to the original inhabitants, in particular one of the most significant and influential men in the early colony, Woollarawarre Bennelong.

Bennelong had grown up on the southern bank of the Parramatta River as a member of the Wangal people, whose territory stretched to what would become Darling Harbour. In 1789, Bennelong would meet the leader of the new arrivals, Governor Arthur Phillip. Keen to learn more about the Aboriginal people, Phillip's noble intentions fell apart in the practice; he had Bennelong and another man snatched and brought to him.

In spite of that brutal beginning, Bennelong and Phillip became friends, to the extent that the Wangal man sailed with the Englishman when he returned home in 1792. Bennelong and another young Aboriginal man, Yemmerrawannie, who travelled with Phillip were, as the renowned human rights lawyer Geoffrey Robertson is fond of proclaiming, Australia's first expatriates in Britain. The pair dressed in fashionable clothes, met with high society, perhaps even the King, and attended the theatre. Yemmerrawannie died in Britain and was buried in a churchyard in the village of Eltham, now on the outskirts of London. Homesick, Bennelong returned to Sydney in 1795. As he wrote to a friend in Britain, 'Not me go to England no more. I am at home now.' But it wasn't an entirely peaceful homecoming; he struggled with alcohol use. In the final years of his life, Bennelong lived around Kissing Point and came to know James Squire. Bennelong died in 1813 where his life had begun, by the Parramatta River, only on the opposite bank. Bennelong was buried on Squire's property, but exactly where became vague with time, until an investigation and announcement in 2011. Bennelong's grave was on a suburban street corner, which was once Squire's orchard.

Even the oranges grown around Kissing Point were reputed to be historically significant. Australia's first Anglican minister, the Reverend Richard Johnson, had saved seeds from oranges he had bought in Rio de Janeiro on the voyage out on the First Fleet. In Sydney, he planted those seeds, which grew into trees. Reverend Johnson's fruit trees also made their way to Kissing Point, perhaps by the hand of the clergyman himself, since he used to be rowed to Parramatta to hold church services.

In what seems like symmetry, the Kissing Point oranges became so popular they would be transported by water down to Sydney, where shipmasters would buy them for long sea voyages. As the orchards spread across the paddocks of Kissing Point, at least an early 20th century poet, David McKee Wright, remembered what was first planted here:

> Some common fruits are grown out here
> Where once were fields of waving beer!

RUMBLING AND grumbling over my head is an incessant line of traffic crawling to somewhere. I'm paddling under the Ryde road bridges. As I look up, I'm grateful I'm down here on the water, taking it slowly. For a river teaches you it really is about the journey, not the destination. The reason that lesson has been lost in the rush looms above me.

The first Ryde road bridge was opened in 1935, effectively replacing a punt service that had been operating for about 135 years. Finally, motorists could just cross the river, with barely a glance at the water. That sturdy construction of steel and concrete is still in heavy use but shares the load of traffic with a newer bridge, built in 1986, just downriver. At least the older structure is a reminder of how relevant the river once was for transportation and commerce. It had an opening span that lifted to allow through ships heading to industries upriver.

The original road bridge is also a headstone on the grave of the sailing ship trade that once extended as far as the Kissing Point and Ryde stretch of the river. Ships unloaded goods at wharves and jetties along the bank, and took on produce from the area's farms. Beyond here, the river became too shallow for most vessels, and they risked doing more than 'kissing' the bottom.

A few hundred metres on from where the traffic crosses the river are the rail bridges. Trains have been trundling over the river since the 1880s. In between the road and railway bridges, the land is being recolonised and reshaped. The suburb on the river's northern bank may have a bucolic name – Meadowbank – but there is no meadow to be seen. Instead, on that wedge of land, there is block upon block of apartments, progressively shoving off the warehouses and factories.

Before there were apartments, before the industries, there were actually meadows around here. The land was originally granted to a naval surgeon whose name was given to another harbourside suburb, William Balmain. By the end of the 1820s, that stretch of land supported not just a farm but also affairs of the sea. The property owner William Bennett was a ship's captain who sailed in the Pacific. When his vessel needed an overhaul, he would bring it ashore at Meadowbank, and his crews, including men from the Pacific islands, would camp on the bank.

Beyond the railway bridges, the bank is gradually being covered by mangroves. Apart from a smattering of litter, the bank looks untouched by humans. The light amid the mangroves is dim, the mud smells ancient, and there is an incessant deep thrum. Only that sound is not prehistoric; it is industrial. Paddling further way from the bank and looking over the shaggy heads of the mangroves, I can see the roofs of light industry and storage sheds, and high tension power-lines stitch the sky over Ermington Bay.

Paddling around a gentle bend, a view of the future further dilutes the primeval effect of the mangroves. A couple of kilometres upriver is the Silverwater Road Bridge, beyond that are a few industrial stacks and in the distance, reaching ever higher, are the commercial and residential towers of Parramatta.

If only Arthur Phillip could see this view. Just as I'm doing, the Governor would have traced the thick, forbidding bank up the river. He was looking for possibilities, and he was confident that the river would lead him to them. Phillip had discovered his own potential on the banks of another river, the Thames. In *Heart of Darkness*, that extraordinary novel about a river journey deep into a country and the soul of man, author Joseph Conrad had his narrator observe of the Thames, 'What greatness had not floated on the ebb of that river the mystery of an unknown earth! . . . The dreams of men, the seed of commonwealths, the germs of empires'. Arthur Phillip had floated down that river many times. He had been educated by the Thames, at Greenwich, for a life at sea. And here he was in 1788, up a river marked on no map, deep in the mystery of an unknown earth, at least unknown to the British. In accepting the job of leading the First Fleet and founding the colony in New South Wales, Arthur may have planted the seeds of a commonwealth nation, but first, he had to find somewhere to sow the seeds of grain to help ensure the infant settlement didn't wither and die on the shores of Sydney Cove.

The river evidently held promise for Arthur Phillip, or stoked his determination to find out where it led. During his first exploratory journey in mid-February, he reached a junction. He followed what he thought was the main river for about six kilometres before it was blocked by fallen timber. Phillip returned to the junction in April and on foot roughly followed the other watercourse. After a couple of days, the exploration party reached a spot where, as Surgeon John White detailed, 'the tide ceased to flow; and all further progress for boats was stopped by a flat space of large broad stones, over which a fresh-water stream ran'. Phillip and his party had found a tidal limit of the harbour. In the countryside around here, they found what they had been looking for.

To the Aboriginal people, this was the place of eels, or Burramatta, so it was a rich source of food. Such was the importance of this place, the local people were known as the Burramattagal. Initially named Rose Hill by the British, Burramatta would become known as Parramatta and a source of food for the new arrivals as well. As Phillip wrote to Lord Sydney, the Home Secretary and his great supporter back in London, he now knew there was good country near the harbour settlement, that he intended to cultivate in the spring. True to his word, in November 1788, Phillip sent a man with substantial farming experience, Henry Dodd, upriver with a detachment of marines and a hundred convicts to plant grains. After a couple of precarious years and, at times, reduced rations for everyone, including the Governor, the farm overseen by Dodd helped ensure the colony could survive. Some of the seeds of a common-wealth had taken hold in Parramatta. The dreams of men would be realised.

JUST BEFORE the Silverwater Road Bridge, the mangroves peter out and a new residential development has been taking shape. The site was once a navy stores depot, and it stretches along more than 700 metres of the river's northern bank. The development is called Royal Shores, and those behind it assert the architecture celebrates the Ermington area's naval history.

Although the development is about thirty kilometres by kayak from the sea, the marketing proclaims the landscaping will tantalise the senses with ocean scents. That would be somewhat different to the scents that wafted over from the plant producing gas, solvents and tar, which used to be on the other side of the river.

I paddle up to the Silverwater Road Bridge, only to be confronted by a sign that warns beyond here, 'Access to RiverCats and Authorised Vessels Only'. A bloke in a tinny putters up behind me, reads the sign and, in a disappointed tone, mutters, 'I was hoping to go to Parramatta.' He looks at my kayak and adds, 'You probably can though.'

Actually, I can't. Kayaks are classified as vessels in New South Wales, so I can't go to Parramatta by water.

But I figure I can paddle just a couple of hundred metres further to see the junction of Parramatta and Duck rivers. This was where Arthur Phillip mistook Duck River for the main waterway in February 1788, and it was where he and his party left their boats a couple of months later when they trekked over the countryside and came across Burramatta.

Duck River, as John White indicated in his journal, was filled with birds, which the party wanted to hunt but couldn't get close enough to shoot. In the years since, someone or something got to the birds. I see no ducks on Duck River, just a couple of industrial-looking bridges straddling the water, when I paddle to its mouth on the southern side of Parramatta River. While it may not have led Arthur Phillip to what he sought, Duck River has nurtured huge wealth. On the land bordered by the two rivers, the colony learnt to ride on the sheep's back. On one side of Duck River, Captain Henry Waterhouse established a merino stud with a small flock he had brought out from South Africa in 1797. On the other side of the river, army-officer-turned-entrepreneur and thorn in the side of a succession of governors, John Macarthur, along with his wife Elizabeth, built a fortune on fleece, expanding his landholdings and spearheading the export of wool to England in the early 1800s. A century or so later, on that same land along Duck River, a large oil refinery was established. The water was integral to the refinery; barges carried the crude oil upriver from a terminal at Gore Cove in the main harbour, and millions of litres of water were pumped out of the river each day to cool the facility.

Through the years, the demands and expectations heaped on the land and water by the sum of development and competition took its toll. Signs at the Silverwater boat ramp near the river junction warn those fishing to not eat what they catch. One sign prohibits fishing of any sort in Duck River because of the high levels of industrial pollutants found in the marine life. Before heavy industry arrived, the rivers were already suffering, with farming along the banks. Parramatta River progressively silted until, by the end of the 19th century, the ferry service had to be moved downstream. A terminal was built near the confluence of the rivers, with a connecting tramway to Parramatta. These days, the ferries can once more reach Parramatta. The river was dredged, and the RiverCats have a shallow draught. At low tide, however, the service has to terminate one stop downriver from Parramatta, at Rydalmere. But for me, just as it once was for the ferries, my Parramatta River journey has to end just beyond the junction of Parramatta and Duck rivers. Even if the law didn't forbid me from going further, the reality of sharing a narrow, shallow waterway with a RiverCat soon stops me anyway.

I am sitting out of the channel, just near a sign that points out this is as far as unauthorised vessels can go. I study the river's languid course towards Parramatta, less than five kilometres upstream. The waterway is progressively constricting, as the banks press ever closer. Just then, a RiverCat rumbles around the bend towards me. I'm confident I'm well out of its way, and it is cruising slowly, less than seven knots. However, just before it reaches me, the RiverCat accelerates and it pushes out a larger wake, which balloons into a set of waves up to half a metre high. I glance at the advancing waves, then peer into the river underneath the kayak. I realise I'm in shallow water. It also dawns on me that I'm in deep trouble. I paddle frantically towards the waves, to try and ride over them before they break. For *Pulbah Raider* is not designed to surf RiverCat-generated waves. I ride over the first of the waves, just as it breaks, timing it perfectly to have the second one pour into the cockpit.

Pulbah Raider is swamped and I'm saturated. I head to the bank, empty the kayak, and continue my journey – downriver.

2

DOWN PARRAMATTA RIVER

IN A country settled by the British to serve as both a human dumping ground and the land of a second chance, perhaps no patch of dirt is more representative of Australia's origins than Sydney Olympic Park.

For this stretch along the southern bank of Parramatta River was for decades a dumping ground for all manner of waste, as well as hosting industries, before the area was given a new life as parklands, homes, and fields of dreams for the world's best athletes.

Yet it took years and hundreds of millions of dollars to remediate the site. And the clean-up is not finished. Before remediation began, the land was so polluted in places, it oozed toxins, while what had been poured and leached into the river created a poisonous brew that killed marine life, along with any desire to engage with the water. You could well have been paddling the River Styx.

But here I am paddling down Parramatta River, trying to picture how the bank on my right was once a wasteland. To the eyes, at least, the pall over a dead shoreline has been lifted and the land has been resuscitated with trees, shrubs and a walking track. Clumps of mangroves are sprouting on the water's edge. As for the water itself, it is an olive-brown colour, but there are no psychedelic swirls from oil or chemicals visible on the surface.

Virtually since the British arrived, this land had endured enormous demands being heaped upon it, and so much being extracted from it.

In the early 1800s, it was part of the large Newington Estate of John Blaxland. The entrepreneur and politician created an array of industries on his property. He set up saltpans near the river, shipping about eight tonnes of salt to Sydney each week. He bred cattle and created a bone-crushing mill. He felled trees for logs, he built a lime kiln, to help feed the colony's appetite for building materials, and he dug for coal. A census in 1828 indicated Blaxland's property was the largest 'household' in the district, with ninety-seven people.

In the 1880s, an eastern portion of Newington was bought by the Colonial Government to set up a storage depot for armaments and gunpowder. The site was chosen not just because it was well away from the heart of the city but also because it could be accessed by the river. A large wharf was built for the delicate loading and unloading of products that could obliterate the area, if something went horribly wrong. Not that anything did. According to maritime historian Graeme Andrews, in 150 years of munitions being transported around the harbour to here and other sites, there was never an explosion. The land later came under the control of the navy. As the demands and requirements of the navy increased in the course of two world wars, so did the land set aside for the armaments depot. The site ate up about 250 hectares, the armaments hidden away in magazines hunkering behind earthen mounds and blast walls.

Much of the land that was strictly out of bounds and run by military rules is now open to the public to walk and cycle at leisure. A few tracts of Newington Armory are still no-go areas, but that is due not so much to the military's obsession with keeping secrets but to give the wildlife somewhere to call their own in a city where housing is a growing issue for all creatures. Those restricted areas are marked as nature reserves.

Paddling towards the armoury, I see the old wharf valiantly holding the weight of two large cranes standing guard by the river. I clamber onto a bird poo-spattered pontoon and head to a wharfside café, which looks a little like a bunker, only one that is aesthetically pleasing. The terrace wears a veil of retro military chic; it's covered with camouflage nets. The sun filters through the camo, creating shadows that flutter like butterflies on the ground etched with old rail lines; trains used to carry the munitions to and from the wharf.

Back in the kayak and tracing the bank, I can see regeneration and reinvention flourishing across the flats. A gleaming symbol of that regeneration juts into the water near Wentworth Point. It is the Sydney Olympic Park ferry wharf, looking vaguely futuristic. Near the terminal are residential complexes seemingly growing by the day, increasingly obscuring the view to what signalled the transformation of this area, the arenas and stadiums built for the Olympic Games in 2000.

The possibility of the Homebush Bay area becoming a major sports hub was considered as early as the 1970s. In the

1980s a regional environmental plan was made for the site to be remediated and sports and recreation facilities built. Within a few years, that was realised, to an extent, with the opening of the State Sports Centre and the Bicentennial Park. But once the International Olympic Committee president Juan Antonio Samaranch announced in 1993 that the city to host the 2000 Games was Sydney, plans and hopes for Homebush Bay accelerated and turned into a massive works project.

One of the Sydney bid's key points was that this would be a 'green Olympics', with the latest ideas on ecological sustainability applied to the site's development. While the venues were designed to include initiatives such as solar energy and recycled water, the biggest obstacles to a clean, green Olympics still lay under everyone's feet. The site had to be remediated. It was estimated that by 1988, there were nine million cubic metres of waste and contaminated earth on the site. A strategy for cleaning up the Homebush Bay area had been put in place even before Sydney lodged its bid. Waste had to be removed, leachate controlled and collected, and contaminants contained and capped. The mountainous clean-up task is symbolised by a series of artificial hills that serve as lookouts around the site. What visitors stand on as they gaze over the transformed landscape is a great mound of waste materials.

Just as Arthur Phillip had ventured up Parramatta River in search of land richer than he could find around the main harbour, the politicians and planners wanted to lead the world up the river to Homebush, to show everyone that the city was about more than a bridge and an opera house. It would be where Sydneysiders would also learn a lot more about their own city.

Debbie Watson still recalls her reaction when she heard where the heart of the Sydney Olympics would be.

'I'm from Manly. Who goes to Parramatta, to Homebush? That's a long way!' she tells me.

Debbie is one of Australia's greatest ever water polo players. In the same year Sydney was announced as the host city for the 2000 Olympics, Debbie was voted the best in the world at her sport. She was the captain of the national team. She had helped win World Cup and World Championship crowns. Yet the dream of competing at an Olympic Games, especially in her home city, seemed more than just distant. Women's water polo was not part of the Olympic program.

Yet a couple of years later, women's water polo was slated for the Sydney Olympics. Debbie was selected for the national team. She would be an Olympian, competing in her hometown – even if it was on the other side of town.

The Australians tussled towards the finals, graduating from the aquatic centre's water polo pool to the 'big pool' for the gold medal match against the United States on 23 September 2000. The home team knew that pool so well – 'it felt like ourselves' – but what the Australians had never experienced was the reception that awaited them.

'It was super special,' recalls Debbie. 'It was unbelievable walking out to the pool. There were 17,000 people in there, and over the years I've met 18,000 of them.'

This match was an 'I was there!' moment from the Sydney Olympics. It was a frenetic, water- and gut-churning experience for the competitors and spectators, with the Australians winning with just a second to spare.

'It was like a dream,' Debbie says. 'We were just looking at each other. "We've actually won!".'

In the pristine waters of a pool set into earth that for so long had been sullied and shunned, the Australians had made Olympic history, becoming the first gold medallists in women's water polo. They had turned water into gold. And Homebush would always be a place that held great significance to Debbie Watson.

These days, Debbie is a mother and a teacher. But she gladly travels from Sydney's Northern Beaches to attend events at Homebush, or to visit the aquatic centre – 'it's my son's favourite pool'.

'What I loved about it, and still love, when driving from home, was coming up over the hill at Ryde and looking down at the Olympic site and being able to see the venues. That was really beautiful. That's now almost been lost with all the other buildings, which brings a tinge of sadness, but for me, it's still, "There it is!".'

'I think it's exceeded everyone's expectations,' Debbie says of the Olympic park. 'It's turned something that was ugly into something very vibrant. And the sporting facilities are great.

'I love it. And for me, it's still very special.'

OLYMPIC GAMES leave their mark on lives and places, but the events themselves are ephemeral. The Olympics, and the grand circus of humanity attached to them, move on. An Olympic site has to become something else. Homebush was no longer a waste-land, but no one wanted to see it turn into a white elephant.

In addition to the permanent sports venues, the Olympic Village was transformed into a residential suburb. As the firms behind building that precinct boasted, the opportunity of creating a new suburb on ninety hectares of land close to Sydney was a developer's dream. What had been accommodation for 15,000 athletes and officials for a few weeks was to become home for about 5000 residents. In deference to a portion of the land's history, the suburb was named Newington.

Along with John Blaxland's estate, another prominent name in the early colony, D'Arcy Wentworth, held extensive property on what would become part of Sydney Olympic Park.

Wentworth was a doctor with a strong entrepreneurial streak. He was part of a rum deal struck with Governor Lachlan Macquarie in 1810. Wentworth and his partners would build a hospital with convict labour in return for a monopoly to import spirits. The building project was allegedly dragged out, so the developers could import more spirits. The arrangement didn't provide the healthy returns they had been hoping for, but it was beneficial to Sydney. 'The Rum Hospital' has been a distinguished part of Macquarie Street for more than 200 years.

While he was busy in town, Wentworth also developed his land along Parramatta River. He called his estate Home Bush. The origin of the property name has been debated. In his memoir, *Homebush Boy*, author Tom Keneally told of his form-ative years in what was then a western Sydney suburb. Keneally thought Homebush had received its name because it had been a tangle of scrub in the early days of the colony. If that was the case, D'Arcy Wentworth set out to change that. Land was cleared to such an extent that a later resident on the property, the author and artist Louisa Anne Meredith, noted not a native tree, not even a stump, was visible.

Wentworth was turning his bush home into a horse stud. He imported an Arab stallion from India that provided enormous service to Australian equestrian heritage. That stallion was behind the basic strain for many of the country's racehorses, as well as for the animals that became a renowned breed known as the Walers, ridden by Australian Light Horse soldiers in Palestine during the First World War. Having bred the horses, Wentworth built a racecourse at Homebush. The Australian Jockey Club held its first meetings at the course from its foundation in 1842 until it moved to Randwick in 1860. Many punters travelled by ferry to the Homebush race meetings.

For much of the 20th century, the land where horses had been bred became a vast killing ground of beasts. It was the site of the State Abattoirs. The slaughter of thousands of animals each day fed more than humans; sharks feasted on the abattoir's effluent dumped into Homebush Bay. Another part of the former Home Bush estate was gouged when the State Brickworks was established in 1911. The brickworks closed in 1988, but the scars of an industry that produced about three billion bricks remain. A deep pit, where machines dug through the layers of Sydney's geological life to obtain clay, has been remodelled. Visitors can circumnavigate the pit on an elevated walkway and peer into the great big hole that is now a reservoir as part of the park's water recycling program, and a home to the endangered green and golden bell frogs. It seems appropriate these frogs have taken up residence, since green and gold are the colours predominantly worn by Australia's athletes in the nearby stadiums.

More than provide materials for homebuilders to construct the great Australian dreams, the brickworks helped create the perfect nightmare of a post-apocalyptic world. One of its pits was a location in the 1985 film, *Mad Max Beyond Thunderdome*. The pit was transformed into the film's trading community, Bartertown, which has a motto over its gates: Helping Build a Better Tomorrow. What was disturbingly ironic in *Mad Max Beyond Thunderdome* was strangely prescient for the Homebush location. Indeed, most of the Homebush Bay area seems to be living out a line uttered by one of the film's main characters, Aunty Entity: So much for history.

Paddling out of the flow of the river and into Homebush Bay, I can see the past rusting into the water, and the future rising along the shores. Much of the bay's edge was reclaimed from the water for industries; now much of that land is being reclaimed for homes. Warehouses and storage sheds are being nudged aside by the new apartment developments.

Sitting in the bay, like a conscience, are a few old wrecks. In the 1960s, the Maritime Services Board granted permission to a number of companies to use the bay's shore as a ship-breaking yard. While the shoreline now cradles infant communities, the waters are a cemetery for ships.

Just ten metres from the shore, with a cluster of apartments dead ahead off its bow, sits the wreck of SS *Ayrfield*. She was built in Britain in 1911 and was launched as SS *Corrimal*. The following year, *Corrimal* was in Sydney's waters. During the Second World War, she saw service in the Pacific, transporting supplies to American troops. After the war, she was renamed *Ayrfield* and was a collier for more than 20 years, operating between Newcastle and Blackwattle Bay in the harbour. In the early 1970s, her time was up. The 79-metre-long ship was sent to Homebush Bay to be broken up. She has lost much, *Ayrfield*. Her steel skin is rusting and is afflicted with barnacles, and in places the hull has withered away, exposing her old bones. Indeed, you can see straight through her, like a ghost, to the apartments on the shore. On part of the deck, there are still bollards that look naked without rope swaddling them. And yet she still serves a purpose. These days, *Ayrfield* carries a cargo of mangroves, which sprout out of her hull like hair out of an old man's ears.

About 50 metres away, sitting alone, is a chunk of SS *Mortlake Bank*. She was also a steam collier, built near Newcastle upon Tyne in 1924 and then, on the other side of the globe, spent much of her life transporting coal from Hexham, in the Hunter Valley, to the gasworks at Mortlake, just a few kilometres from where her corpse lies. *Mortlake Bank* has been here since 1972, meeting the same ignominious end as *Ayrfield*. Yet, in a way, time has whittled beauty out of the wreck. Plates at the stern have been rusted and sculpted into delicate filigrees of steel that filter the afternoon sun. And while she was brought here to be broken up, the former collier has been reincarnated as a play-ground for seagulls.

Just across the way, on the other side of the mouth to Haslam Creek, are two wooden wrecks piled onto a nodule of land. Near the shambles of wood there is a clue as to what this place used to be. Along the shore is a tideline of old bricks. This small penin-sula was created in the 1950s to load bricks from the nearby works onto barges. Hiding in the mangroves is the wreck of a barge.

Around the point are two more wrecks lying side by side. The one on the left is listing onto its port side, leaning towards its water grave, but its funnel remains defiantly in the air. The wreck is that of the tug SS *Heroic*, which was built in the UK in 1909 for the Sydney tugboat operators Thomas Fenwick. It wasn't long before the steam tug was dragged into military service. During the First World War, she was commandeered by the British Admiralty and was involved in rescue work. During the Second World War, *Heroic* was again involved in the military effort, including rescuing a freighter that had been torpedoed by a Japanese submarine off Sydney. *Heroic* continued to work as a tug up to the 1970s, before ending up in the bay. From the bow, with rope through one of the portholes, it looks like a sad, tethered elephant. Yet near a rusted, arthritic winch at the bow, a mangrove has sprouted. It looks like a figurehead, symbolising growth and life, while around it is decay and neglect.

To the starboard of *Heroic* is the wreck of HMAS *Karangi*. She is sitting upright and still looking sturdy, while the elements are gradually taking shreds off her. *Karangi* was a boom defence vessel, to protect harbour entrances from enemy ships entering. *Karangi* was built downriver at Cockatoo Island and launched just a few months before Australia was at war against Japan in 1941. She helped defend Darwin Harbour from attack during the war. *Karangi* ended up in Homebush Bay in 1970. Over its steel hull, *Karangi* still wears a skin of wood in many places, and when you look through the barnacle-lidded portholes, it is like peering into a dragon's eye.

Only a few metres away from the wrecks, behind the mangroves along the shore are parklands and a waterbird refuge, with a viewing tower's crown poking above the mangroves. No matter what humans did to Homebush Bay, the birds still came. A 1978 study noted that one of the remarkable aspects of the bay, even in its degraded state, was its diverse birdlife. The local environment has been much improved, and the birds have a more attractive home or place to visit, with some migrating from as far away as Russia. Birds with evocative names such as the Bar-tailed Godwit, the Chestnut Teal and the Red-necked Avocet can be seen gliding across the water or wading in the shallows around the refuge. And because those birds can be seen, the wetlands also attract birdwatchers.

Standing still on the refuge's shore, with his binoculars tracking a pair of black swans, is Simon Dobrée. Originally from Great Britain, Simon considers birdwatching an indicator of an advanced country. 'There aren't many birders in Australia,' he says, with the hint of a smile.

Simon tends to watch alone. But around here, birding is rarely a solitary pursuit. He usually has to share the surrounds with cyclists tearing along the pathways and children revelling in the outdoors. Still, Simon regularly travels from his home in the city's north to Sydney Olympic Park.

'There are places to hide,' he says, both from the crowds, and to remain out of sight of the birds. Indeed, there is a bird hide perched on the refuge's northern shore.

Simon tends to make a day of it, arriving mid-morning and staying until dusk. He works his way around the park's 500 or so hectares of public areas, all the while noting the species he sees, from the teardrop-shaped ponds in the Narawang wetlands – 'you can see a Buff-banded Rail there' – to the stretch along the river near the Newington Armory – 'I saw a Mangrove Heron there once'.

'I've never been around everywhere in the one day, so you have to be selective,' explains Simon.

He usually spots forty to fifty species in a day, and in his notes recording all his visits to Sydney Olympic Park, he can count more than ninety species. Simon has many more to see. According to the authority overseeing the site, more than 200 native bird species have been recorded throughout Sydney Olympic Park.

'I've certainly found it a cornucopia for birds,' Simon tells me.

'My favourite one of all is the Pink-eared Duck. Even if it was pure luck when I saw it. It was sitting near Pacific Black Ducks.

'It's not just the numbers but the quality of what you see in a day.'

Before us are a couple of birds wading and picking in the shallows. I ask Simon what they are.

'Black-winged Stilts,' he says without hesitation. 'Pretty birds.'

Mindful that Simon tries to see up to fifty birds each visit, and the shadows are lengthening on the fringes of the refuge, I wonder what his tally is so far.

'Hmmm. Thirty-five.'

I take my leave, to allow Simon to focus and scan the waters, which are beginning to take on the sheen of pewter in the afternoon sun and – to my eyes at least – making the birds harder to identify. But in his quiet way, Simon seems to relish the challenge. As he tells me, there is something deeply satisfying in being out in the open and observing nature. And, as he reasoned, this is an act of nation-advancing. It is surely a sign of a nation learning from its errors when it restores a part of the environment it all but destroyed, so that birds – and birdwatchers – have somewhere to find themselves.

'I think for all round bird numbers and variety,' concludes Simon, 'this is the best place in Sydney.

'It is good to see an area that has been so improved, especially for birds. It provides a local antidote to the problems that Sydney faces, with population growth and the rise in traffic and development, and the pressures on birds due to the loss of wetlands and other suitable habitat.'

ACROSS THE bay from where the wrecks of historically significant ships rot in the water, barely noticed and all but forgotten, large residential and retail developments have sprouted at Rhodes.

Thousands of people are living in the hundreds of units built on a peninsula that was once congested with, and polluted by, heavy industries. A large flour mill that perched on the Rhodes peninsula was converted into a stock feed factory. Its neighbours were chemical factories, including the Timbrol plant, which produced a range of chemicals, from timber preservatives to pesticides. In 1957, the plant was taken over by the industrial giant Union Carbide. The factory continued to produce pesticides and herbicides, including ingredients for Agent Orange, which was used by American forces as a defoliant during the Vietnam War.

What was produced in Sydney would have a huge impact on not just the jungles of Vietnam. The chemicals contributed to the reshaping of Rhodes and the poisoning of a bay, and beyond. The production process resulted in dioxins, which are carcinogenic. Dioxins have been linked to cancer and birth defects. Dioxins are also long-lasting in the environment.

For decades, when the factories needed to expand and more land was required, the shore was extended into the bay. Contaminated soil and waste were used as fill. Dioxins were discharged into the bay and dumped into the wetlands along the shore. When regulations finally tightened in the 1970s, chemical waste was stored in drums. By the time Union Carbide shut down the plant in 1986, the legacy was a bay considered among the world's most contaminated with dioxins. The New South Wales Government told the company to clean up the mess on the land. Ultimately, the remediation of the site to a level that made it acceptable to build and live on was largely done with public money.

But what had happened in the water and to the bed of the bay could not be contained as easily. The dioxins don't remain at the bottom of the harbour. They enter the marine food chain, as fish eat organisms in the contaminated sediment. As a result, in 1989, the government prohibited fishing in Homebush Bay and its tributaries, and that ban has remained. Perhaps that explains why I've seen so many fish jumping and plopping back into the water around me as I've paddled in Homebush Bay. These are the ones that got away; at least, from the fishing hook.

The dioxin problem seeped from the bay into other parts of the harbour, and from the past into the present. Data collected by a state government department in 2008 indicated that dioxins were detected more than 10 kilometres upriver and down from Homebush Bay. Those findings affirmed what was already known. Due to the elevated levels of dioxins, commercial fishing in the harbour was banned in 2006. While recreational fishing is still allowed in most parts of the harbour, signs in popular places to cast a line deliver unpalatable dietary advice. Any fish or other crustaceans caught west of Sydney Harbour Bridge should not be eaten. And if you eat what you catch east of the Bridge, then you should restrict your intake to 150 grams a month.

For years, Gavin Birch has been delving into the polluted soul of Sydney Harbour. As an adjunct associate professor from the

School of Geosciences at the University of Sydney, Gavin has studied and written about the pollutants in the harbour.

He mentions the huge effort put into cleaning up the Homebush Bay area. The developers around Rhodes peninsula scraped back the earth to the bedrock, and the New South Wales Government remediated the eastern margin of Homebush Bay, using suction dredges to clean up to a metre through the bottom, then covered it with clean material. But Gavin says studies have indicated that with the movement under the water, dioxin-affected sediment from outside the cleaned area covers the remediated strip. While the problem has been lessened, it hasn't been removed. He doesn't know what the future is for cleaning up dioxins, because 'the dioxins have been remobilised so comprehensively, including outside Homebush Bay'. As it is, he says, there's no way he would eat fish from here, or from Parramatta River.

Gavin and his teams have taken sediment cores throughout the harbour. In regard to heavy metals, those cores show the more recent deposits are much cleaner than in the lower, older layers.

'For some areas, there will be natural remediation or relaxation, in other words, the concentration is declining, but I can't say that for dioxins,' Gavin says, although he points out that testing for dioxins has been limited because the research budget stretches only so far.

The declining levels of heavy metals are 'all very good news, which is attributable to the Clean Waters Act of 1978, and the removal of heavy industry from the foreshores of the estuary', which is what Gavin calls the harbour.

He considers the change along the banks of Parramatta River 'a remarkable transition'.

'It's transformed from having high-polluting industries to high-rise, high-value communities,' he says. 'In one way, that's good, but you're coming to a situation where the sewerage systems are being overtaxed. While the high-rise developments create more sewage discharges, they're much better than the factories that were there.'

But the major problem for the harbour now comes not so much from along the shoreline, but from much further up, out of the webs of creeks bringing down contaminants from the catchment areas, and from stormwater drains.

He cites the example of organochlorines, mostly no longer in use, but they were used for years to clear land and protect new homes from insects. They continue to leach from the soil and eventually end up in the harbour. Gavin points out that unless there's an improvement in the catchment, 'the potential for improvement at the bottom of the harbour is very small'.

What comes out of the stormwater drains is also drugging the harbour. His teams' testing has found surprisingly significant levels of pharmaceuticals in the water. The drugs dulling headaches and treating depression among the city's residents are potentially creating a different kind of pain for water quality. He reckons it is an indication that the increasingly burdened sewerage system is leaking. And there is the issue of stormwater overflow.

'A key to cleaning up the harbour is to clean up the stormwater going into the harbour,' Gavin argues, which also means more money has to be poured into upgrading Sydney's sewerage system. Because for too long, he cautions, what has poured into that system is the waste from multi-storey residential developments in areas that were designed for mostly single-family houses. And if you keep putting pressure on it, the system eventually craps itself. When that happens, the harbour is the toilet.

DOWNRIVER FROM the Ryde road bridges, there is a distinct change of view on the water and along the southern bank. The homes have grown in size and luxury, and the waterway they preside over, Brays Bay, has its mouth filled with boats.

The flotilla devoted to pleasure is also a job creator. Fluttering on a smaller boat is the code flag alpha, indicating there are divers below. The boat is tied to a cruiser. I notice a line snaking from the smaller boat, across the surface to the cruiser. It is attached to two divers, feeding them air. They are underwater boat maintenance workers, and they are cleaning the cruiser's hull. One, in a black wetsuit, looks like a seal lolling under the boat, before he dives to check something, while his buddy breaks the surface. His mask-framed eyes widen at the sight of a bloke in a kayak watching them. I introduce myself, he pulls out his regulator and introduces himself as Marshall. Having seen his diving buddy doing a fine seal impression just a few moments earlier, I ask Marshall what's been in my mind since.

'Do you ever see sharks?'

In the couple of years he's been doing this work, Marshall replies, he's seen only two sharks. They were bull sharks. I ask him did he see those sharks around here. No, Marshall says, they were down in the main harbour. He then smiles as he bobs around in the murky water.

'You wouldn't see *anything* up this far.'

Marshall Michael's dive buddy is Paul Nind. He owns the business, called Boat Buddies. When Paul dives under the harbour's surface, he's not just doing a job, he's following his passion.

'We see a very different harbour to what most people see,' Paul says.

Paul hasn't always worn a wetsuit for a living. He used to wear a suit and tie, working for an international logistics company. Paul's hobby was scuba diving, a skill that came in handy in 2006 when he was crew on a boat in the Sydney to Hobart yacht race. He was the yacht's clearance diver. After that race, he was asked more and more to do underwater maintenance on yachts. Gradually, while under the surface, Paul saw the possibilities of a business and the makings of his future.

These days, Paul and his team do maintenance work on between ten to twenty boats daily – 'the record is thirty in a day' – in all sorts of conditions. The working week is average, about forty hours, but the work environment is anything but. He has swum with dolphins, penguins, a blue marlin and fur seals, and he's seen about half a dozen sharks.

Through the depths, when the water is clear, he has seen sunken boats squatting like phantoms on the harbour bottom. And when the water is murky, such as in the upper reaches of Parramatta River, he works not by sight but feel.

'And there are all sorts of things at the bottom there,' he explains. 'Bits of metal, concrete, cars.'

Still, he believes the harbour is cleaner and healthier than it used to be.

'When I was a kid,' Paul says, 'you wouldn't swim in the harbour. It was disgusting. But now, in many places, you can see to the bottom.'

Having changed careers in his early 30s, Paul intends to stay in the water for the rest of his working life.

'When it's great, it's unbeatable,' he says of the harbour. 'But even on the worst days, it's still good – even if it's miserable and disgusting.

'The harbour will remain my workplace in one shape or form. I love it.'

THE CURVE of the shoreline explains why the waterway I'm paddling into was once called Horseshoe Bay. But deference to the family who settled this land, and whose progeny included the first Mayor of the local Concord Council, meant its name was changed to Brays Bay.

The western side of the horseshoe was once studded with industries, and, during the Second World War, there was a ship-building yard tucked into the toe of the bay on reclaimed land. These days, the yard is commemorated with a bitumen- and concrete-covered public reserve. The spare-looking memorial includes the remnants of the slip, with the names of some of the ships that slid down it embedded in the concrete. It may not be a classically pretty reserve, but it is a clear reminder of how stretches of Parramatta River's banks once looked.

Just beyond the skeleton of the shipyard and slicing through the riparian bush is a path that leads walkers back to another chapter of the Second World War. It is the Kokoda Track Memorial Walkway. The route is punctuated with information markers for key battles and sites from that critical campaign in 1942, when the survival of Australia seemingly lay in the jungles of New Guinea, and in the hands of young soldiers who were poorly equipped and up against two enemies: the Japanese and Mother Nature herself. The landscape was ruthless to all who stepped into it, irrespective of their uniform.

What those men endured is hard to imagine, especially while standing on the shores of Sydney Harbour three-quarters of a century on. The well-formed path skirting Brays Bay is far removed from the treacherous muddy tracks, river crossings and ravines the soldiers contended with. Yet the path is but a conduit to the most evocative element of the memorial: the stories of men who were there.

On most days, Reg Chard heads to the walkway and returns to his youth. He guides groups and educates anyone who listens.

Born in 1923, Reg was a teenager when he fought on the Kokoda Track. As he tells visitors to the walkway, he was one of the more than 4000 Australians who became a casualty due to sickness during the campaign.

'I collapsed with scrub typhus and malaria,' says Reg.

Sickness eventually ended the war for Reg. But all these years on, his service continues.

With a purposeful walk and a mind full of facts and anecdotes that he readily summons from under his thatch of silver hair, Reg seems younger than he is, as he takes visitors along the path to a memorial, etched with iconic images from the Kokoda campaign. Reg lost a lot of mates in that campaign. That's why Reg comes to Brays Bay most days; to honour 'all the ones who didn't come home'.

Within sight of the Kokoda Track Memorial Walkway is the place where Reg Chard ended his war service: Concord Hospital. The collection of buildings presides over a sliver of land on the other side of the bay. The area was once known as

Levy's Folly, because one of the early landowners apparently built his house using mortar mixed with salt water from the bay. His house collapsed. Levy repeated the process, with the same result. The hospital, commissioned in 1940 as war crept ever closer to Australia, was evidently built to last. From the water, the main building's conglomeration of glass and bricks looks like a Mondrian painting, as though a modernist idea has climbed out of the mud and mangroves at its feet.

At the height of the Second World War, the 113th Australian General Hospital, as it was known, was one of the largest medical facilities in the southern hemisphere. It had more than 2000 beds, treating troops brought in from across the Pacific theatre. Private Reg Chard was one of them.

Reg spent three months in the hospital in 1943, before returning to his unit. When scrub typhus and malaria ravaged him again the following year, Reg was sent back to Concord. This time his stay was for 14 months. The war ended, and Reg was still a patient when he received special leave to be married in October 1945.

'I was known as the Malaria King of Concord,' Reg chuckles.

After the war, the facility became known as the Concord Repatriation General Hospital, or simply, the 'Concord Repat'. The hospital's services may have broadened, but it is still called that by many locals.

'I sometimes still get a funny feeling looking at the hospital,' Reg says.

Concord Hospital is one of a string of health facilities in historic buildings along this reach of the river. Entwined around those facilities in one way or another is the Walker family.

Thomas Walker was a highly successful businessman, politician and philanthropist in the middle and late 19th century. His only daughter, Eadith, inherited not just the family fortune but his generosity. As a result, paddling along this shore, I'm treated to a tour of how a pile of money can be converted into beautiful architecture and community service.

Kayaking out of Brays Bay and around Rocky Point, I see a Dutch tower squatting on the river bank. The vision is fantastic, as though someone has picked up the building out of a fairytale and plonked it by Parramatta River. Yet this was the gatehouse to the large, stately brick and sandstone building on the hill behind, which was no place of fairytales. It was the Thomas Walker Convalescent Hospital.

Walker had written in his will that he wanted some of his fortune to be used to fund a convalescent hospital, to be built on part of his estate, Yaralla. When Walker died in 1886, twelve hectares of land and £100,000, a fortune in those days, went to the hospital project. The building constructed with the endowment was designed by the renowned architect John Sulman and was dressed in fine features, including marble fireplaces and ornate woodwork. Indeed, it was so fine, the family had to contribute another £50,000 to its construction. The hospital opened in 1893. The following year, a children's convalescent hospital, named in memory of Walker's sister, opened nearby.

Most patients arrived by water, disembarking at a jetty at the gatehouse, which was praised at the time as being 'a veritable Paradise'. The air of paradise continued up the hill. The hospitals and their staff quickly garnered a reputation for being gentle and refined, and there was no charge for patients. The hospital, and Thomas Walker, was praised as being 'the most magnificent charity created by the benevolence of one man in all the colonies'. Among those who sought refuge at the Thomas

Walker Convalescent Hospital was the poet Henry Lawson, who spent a lot of time in the facility's library. More than a century on, the Thomas Walker Convalescent Hospital remains a place of healing; it is a mental health facility for young people.

Drifting past the little tower where patients once entered the facility, I can see through its arch and up the immaculately tended lawn to the main building. The ethereal look of the gate-house, especially in the late afternoon, when the water soaks up the colours of the sky, fits in with the surroundings. For the grounds are now called Rivendell, the name of the elves' haven in J.R.R. Tolkien's epic novels, *The Hobbit* and *The Lord of the Rings*.

I paddle into a sense of the ancient earth around the shoreline into Yaralla Bay. A thick curtain of mangroves skirts the bay. With a soundtrack of cicadas and birds, the trees help create the impression I've paddled into somewhere primordial. Yet the mangroves are like a magician's trick; the sense of isolation is a mere illusion. I peer through the curtain and can see snippets of Concord Hospital. The illusion is further shattered when I look to my left; a small fleet of industrial barges is resting in the bay. The primacy of nature sharply returns. A mosquito has been having afternoon tea on my arm. It is the first mosquito I've been aware of while paddling Parramatta River, which is a relief compared with the amassed squadrons that used to patrol here. In her book written in the 1840s, Louisa Anne Meredith bemoaned how mosquitoes would rise in clouds from the banks, forcing her to retreat indoors.

The Walkers had a majestic place in which to retreat from mosquitoes and just about any other annoyance. Thomas Walker had engaged the former Colonial Architect Edmund

Blacket to design a 'cottage at Concord' in the 1850s. Beyond the mangroves on a nodule of land pressing into the bay, that 'cottage' still stands.

Having climbed out of *Pulbah Raider* onto a greasy rock shelf at the shoreline, I know I'm at the right place. An old set of stone stairs and a wonky path are remnants of the grandeur that once greeted visitors. The Walkers had a private wharf here, and they would often have a band playing on a pontoon to welcome guests. I follow the stone path through a grove of groaning bamboo, and gradually Yaralla is revealed. It is a two-storey mansion with wide verandas and an Italianate tower.

Eadith Walker had built on her father's vision with Yaralla. After Thomas Walker died, his daughter commissioned John Sulman to design extensions to the house, which became the scene of lavish parties and balls. Eadith Walker hosted royalty and stars at Yaralla. Yet she would also host events for returned and wounded troops, including setting up a camp in the grounds for soldiers with tuberculosis during the First World War. To Walker, Yaralla was more than a house; it was a self-contained estate. It even had its own power station, the first private electricity plant in Sydney. As it was, she had water on three sides of her home, but Eadith Walker had created an island of luxury, with a buffer zone of meticulously tended gardens. The Walkers had brought the world to Yaralla, with an Indian Room, a 'Norwegian House' in the gardens, and a stone terrace constructed by Italian masons. Yet it was a world unto itself. For all their contributions to the community, the Walkers lived like few others in the country.

After Eadith Walker's death, the Yaralla mansion and the land surrounding it were given to the State Government. The family home became the Dame Eadith Walker Convalescent Hospital.

It retains the look of a grand residence. There is an extensive rose garden and a lawn adorned with urns and fountains leading down to Majors Bay.

I leave behind the beautifully ordered world within the world created by the Walkers, walking back down the stone path to the shoreline of mud and mangroves and gouged sandstone. There is a public walking track around the shore, and no sooner have I set off than two Labradors leap off the rock shelf, sending arcs of water – and excited yelps – towards the kayak. Two women appear and laugh at their pets playing with abandon.

'It's great for the dogs here, except for the bull sharks,' says one of the women.

I ask has she seen any here.

'No, but they've been sighted over there,' the woman replies, pointing towards Meadowbank, a distant smudge well out of the bay and on the other side of the river. It seems the sharks are always somewhere else in the harbour.

As the dogs lope in the water, the women talk about Yaralla. They say locals love walking around here, the Walker legacy still providing convalescence from the pressures of daily life.

'Don't tell anyone about here,' says one of the women. 'Keep it secret!'

Yet it's not a kayaker who the women fear will spoil their secret. They, and other locals, are concerned the State Government will one day sell Yaralla, and this haven will be recrafted into just another peninsula on Parramatta River packed with apartments and marketing slogans about perfect living.

As I paddle away before a dog jumps onto the kayak, one of the women reiterates, 'Keep it secret!' I know I won't, yet I trust this is a secret that should be shared in order to keep it.

As I kayak around the point into Majors Bay, I trace the ongoing outline of Yaralla. Filtered through the bush along the shore are the mansion and the grounds. They look like something lifted out of an English pastoral scene. It is an extraordinary juxtaposition. It is, in microcosm, the story of the British settling on the shores of Sydney Harbour. It looks faintly ridiculous, but somehow it works.

On the other side of the bay, a few hundred metres away, is Mortlake. What those two women don't want for Yaralla has already taken hold over there. The tip of Mortlake is a hive of residential developments. And more are on the way, with foundations being gouged into the earth.

Long before a rash of new housing broke out over its skin, Mortlake was the site of the Australian Gas Light Company's works. The complex was vast, with enormous storage tanks that could be seen for kilometres around. The AGL Company bought the land on the peninsula in 1884 and within a couple of years, the works were operating. As the city expanded, so did the Mortlake facility. Around the gasworks themselves, a community grew, with housing and businesses.

The river was crucial to the works' operation. The gasworks, and the surrounding community, was garlanded with coal smoke. Coal was the key material for producing the gas for many years, so shiploads of coal were delivered in colliers tracking back and forth from the Hunter River to Mortlake. The gasworks' wharf accommodated the river, with landing stages for both high and low tides. The ships hauling the coal were known as 'sixty milers', the approximate distance by sea from Newcastle, at the mouth of the Hunter, to Sydney. The vessels wore the names of the places involved in producing the gas, including *Mortlake Bank*, whose bones I saw in Homebush Bay. When the Mortlake to Putney punt began operating in the 1920s, one of the main reasons was to transport workers from the other side of the river.

The business that helped fuel a city also fed thousands of families, including that of Donald Chivas, whom I had met on the other side of the river, at Kissing Point. Donald was with the company through the change from coal gas to natural gas. He retired from AGL before the gasworks closed in 1990, and Mortlake's transition began. Donald mentioned he didn't feel the need to visit the site for old times' sake.

'Gasworks aren't the prettiest of places,' Donald said. 'But it's only a skeleton of what it was.'

Those skeletons of the industrial past have been largely buried under the houses and apartments along the riverfront, which wears a name retrieved from the earliest days of the colony: Breakfast Point. The first journey of a British boat along this river was in February 1788, just a couple of weeks after the ships of the First Fleet dropped anchor in Sydney Cove. Captain John Hunter, later to be the second Governor of New South Wales, and his shipmate Lieutenant William Bradley were undertaking the exploration. In his journal, Bradley noted that on February 5 they stopped at a point to cook breakfast. The party made signs to a group of Aboriginal people on the northern bank to come over, and seven of them did, in two canoes. According to Bradley, the meeting was friendly, with the Aboriginal men leaving their spears in the canoe, and the British tying beads around the locals' necks. The visitors offered to share their breakfast, but the Aboriginal group declined, instead waiting for the British to leave so they could use the fire to cook mussels. Hunter named the place Breakfast Point.

Neighbouring where the punt hauls itself onto the Mortlake bank with a screech and grunt, there is an old slip and a marine business, River Quays. The business was started in the mid-1980s by an architect and keen sailor, especially of wooden boats, John Wood.

John had lived by the harbour at Birchgrove and used to watch imported Oregon logs being unloaded from ships into the water near his home, herded into a raft and towed to timber yards up Parramatta River. After the mills had gone and the voyage of the logs had ended, John made the same journey, to Mortlake. He was looking for somewhere to lift his beloved historic wooden sailboat, *Kelpie*, out of the water for a major service. He found a boatyard between the punt and the gasworks, where he could work on his 30-foot yacht.

'In the process, the more time I spent at Mortlake, the more I was convinced this was a brilliant site,' John recalls.

'I had seen around Sydney Harbour there were lots of little boatyards on prime waterfront land that was far in excess of the value of the yards themselves. I could see the writing on the wall for these little yards. You could make an income as long as the land and development costs weren't prohibitive, so it was logical Mortlake was a good place for a marine business. And because it was industrial, you didn't have the residential issues.'

More than restore his boat, John bought the Mortlake yard and expanded it. Some of the fastest and best-known racing yachts of the 1980s made their way up the river to be serviced at the yard, much to the surprise of many who didn't think elite sailing craft would venture west of Sydney Harbour Bridge.

'John had a bit of foresight, because anything west of the Bridge then was considered a non-boating area; it was just for fishermen,' says Ian Smith, who worked at River Quays.

Ian is a shipwright and sailor, with a great respect for maritime history and an even greater passion for crafting wood into beautiful boats. He began the Sydney Wooden Boat School at River Quays in the late 1980s. As well as teaching traditional methods of boatbuilding and restoration, Ian, along with John, celebrated the results. They organised Sydney's inaugural wooden boat festival, returning a flotilla of traditionally built vessels to the waters that once cradled many timber hulls.

'We were basically trying to generate interest in that part of the river,' Ian says.

Wooden boat owners embraced the idea. On a weekend in October 1990, about fifty vessels were moored on the marina, and another twenty-five were displayed on trailers. While some queried, 'Why Mortlake?' John was confident the crowds would come. His faith was rewarded.

'Word about the festival spread, so by the Sunday afternoon, there were about eighty craft moored out in the river; all these people had turned up by boat,' says John. 'We were flat out running a tender, and the ferries were having to slow down and weave in and out of the moored boats. It was absolutely incredible.'

A second wooden boat festival was held at Mortlake before it was moved downriver to Balmain.

John Wood misses the six years he spent by the river at Mortlake. What he doesn't hold fond memories of is the water quality.

'It was unbelievably polluted, it was toxic, horrendous,' he says.

'On the bottom, there was this crust, but underneath that was this oily, oozy mass, and that black ooze contained dioxins, oils, all the industrial pollution that had settled into the sediments.

'So the river quality is pristine compared to what it was like then.'

THE HOMES in the Breakfast Point development are a mix of detached buildings, townhouses and apartment blocks. Many are clothed in the colours that seem to be spreading across the peninsulas up and down the river and around the harbour: soft greys and browns, creams, yellows, apricot and salmon, pale terracotta. Paddling past, Breakfast Point looks like a bricks-and-mortar salad. A cluster of new homes are being built close to the point itself, and on many, the 'sold' signs are already up.

In marketing real estate, some things haven't changed. Back in 1840, when land that would become part of Yaralla was being sold, the agents rhapsodised about the 'enchanting' scenery and the steamers, 'as they glide through the romantic waters of the Parramatta River'. The marketing also assured the climate was 'free from any humidity injurious to the constitution'.

Almost two centuries later, a sign on the Cabarita shore across from Breakfast Point on Kendall Bay indicates there are other elements under the water that could be injurious to the constitution. The sign has a map and a warning that the marked zone is a contaminated land remediation site. It recommends the public not enter that area until investigation of the sediment in the bay is completed. The marked zone is along the Breakfast Point shoreline, which I've just paddled. Still, I reason, my blades are hardly going to stir up the sediment. I barely finish my thought when a RiverCat pulls into the Cabarita Park ferry terminal, its powerful engines swizzling the water into a fury. According to the map, the wharf is just outside the 'sediment investigation area'. Still, the flow of contaminants probably doesn't strictly adhere to a map.

Cabarita Park has a long beach, which wears an apron of shells. There are thousands of them along the bank. It looks like a conchologist's dream. For *Pulbah Raider*, it's a nightmare. The kayak protests loudly, as its hull is scratched and picked at mercilessly as we land. From the beach, I walk up onto a grassy headland, where there is a memorial to William Beach.

As the plaque on the stone obelisk proclaims, William Beach was an undefeated champion sculler of the world. Beach seized the world championship from Canadian Edward Hanlan on Parramatta River in 1884, before a crowd estimated to be 100,000. As the renowned bookseller and publisher James R. Tyrrell recalled in his memoir, 'A sculling match, in those halcyon days, was not merely a sporting encounter; it was the big event of the moment.' When Beach raced against Hanlan again the following year, Tyrrell joined the 'swarms' making 'the pilgrimage' to the river. When he defeated Hanlan a third time, after beating a string of other challengers, Beach retired. But his feats were not forgotten. Three years after he died in 1935, his 'friends and admirers' erected this monument. Long after his own marks on the water have fizzed into nothingness, long after the crowds who cheered for him have dispersed into history, William Beach still has a place by the river.

Cabarita is an Aboriginal word, and it's believed to mean 'by the water'. The people of the Wangal clan collected oysters and mussels along the shores and caught crayfish in nets of woven bark. They headed onto the river and bays in canoes shaped from bark and sealed with the gum of Xanthorrhoea.

The traditions and identity of the Wangal were disrupted and dislocated when the settlers and speculators moved in. Cabarita Point was identified relatively early, in the 1850s, as ideal for recreation. In 1880, almost ten hectares of the point was set aside as a public park. An entrepreneur, Thomas Correy, established a pleasure ground and dance hall next to the park. Until it shut just after World War One, Correy's Gardens were among the most popular resorts in Sydney, attracting ferries filled with picnickers.

The area remains a pleasure ground by the water, and on it. At Cabarita Point there is a large marina, poking its fingers deep into the mouth of Hen and Chicken Bay and providing berths for dozens of vessels, including some large private and commercial craft. The name of one cruiser I paddle past echoes across the river to Banjo Paterson Park. It is called *Waltzing Matilda*.

I kayak around the marina, into the bay. My view is filled with the scrimmage of hulls and masts around the marina, so I miss the sandstone outcrop at the point that is believed to be the reason behind the bay's name. On their voyage up the river in February 1788, Hunter and Bradley noticed the formation and apparently thought a large rock was like a hen, and a group of smaller ones like chickens. Others have surmised the explorers may have seen an emu and her chicks on the shore around the point.

While the definitive reason for its name may have drifted off, there is no missing the bay, as the shoreline balloons. The bay is almost three kilometres long. Little wonder it has been a long-time drawcard not just for rowers but also boaties – and those hardy souls who enjoy being towed behind powerboats. The shallow waters of Hen and Chicken Bay were apparently the first in Australia to be slashed and cut by water skis. In 1934, 20-year-old Ted Parker was pulled across the bay, and into history, wearing skis his neighbour had made based on a magazine photograph.

Hen and Chicken Bay has a series of inlets along its western shore that contain the names and legacies of faraway places.

There is France Bay. When it comes to access to the water, there doesn't seem to be much 'Liberté, égalité, fraternité' going on. The water's edge has been largely sliced up and cut off by private residences. In the bay, boats are moored, and the seagulls who have taken up residence on the vessels screech at me as I pass, seemingly giving voice to what the fences on shore indicate: 'Go away!'

I paddle around the peninsula festooned with fancy homes, where there once stood a number of industries, including a sheep dip manufacturing plant and the Wunderlich factory, famous for its pressed metal ceilings, and I arrive in Exile Bay. In the bay's south-west corner, next to a golf course, is a towering reminder of what used to inhabit much of this area – a factory. With its stack looking like a defiant finger, it seems as though the plant is sending a message to the Johnny-come-lately residents, golfers and boaties surrounding it. However, the factory is also a monument to one of Sydney's abiding obsessions. Coffee is roasted in there. So the building must still have a place.

On the southern tip of Exile Bay is Bayview Park. Just metres away from the shore in the park, there is a small stone monument that explains the name of the bay, along with those of nearby France and Canada bays.

In 1837, rebellions broke out in British-ruled areas of Canada. British forces crushed the uprising. One hundred and forty-nine of the captured rebels received sentences of transportation for life to the Australian colonies. Those of British descent were transported to Van Diemen's Land, and fifty-eight French-Canadian rebels were sent to Sydney. When the French-speaking prisoners arrived in this far-flung British colony in 1840, they 'gazed with horror' from the ship's deck. Their first impression, as recorded by one of the exiles, Leon Ducharme, was that they had sailed into one big prison. The exiles saw 'miserable wretches' harnessed to carts and dragging blocks, while others were breaking up stones.

Their opinion of the place would not have improved when they were taken up Parramatta River, to a stockade in a marshy area near the shores of Hen and Chicken Bay, known as Longbottom. Being about half way between Sydney and Parramatta, Longbottom had begun life as an overnight holding area for convicts being marched along the rough road between the two centres. The stockade later housed prisoners, whose work included the dispiriting task of wading into Hen and Chicken Bay and collecting oyster shells to burn and create lime for the colony's building projects.

By the time the French-Canadians arrived at Longbottom, the stockade had shrunk in use and importance. Petitions for the exiles' release were being sent across the globe. The group had the backing of the local Catholic clergy, along with the Governor himself, who said their behaviour had been exemplary. In November 1842, the French-Canadian prisoners were released on tickets of leave, and, by February 1844, they had received pardons. The Canadian exiles were finally free to leave.

All but three returned to Canada; two had died, and one stayed, marrying a local woman.

The Canadians' saga would have a huge effect on lives across the British Empire. As a result of the rebellion, the British granted its territory in Canada 'responsible self-government'. The same principle was applied to the Australian colonies. Consequently, long after the Canadian exiles had left the shores of Hen and Chicken Bay, their memory remains in ways far more profound than a small stone monument.

AROUND PAST Bayview Park and into Canada Bay, there is another residential development, Phillips Landing. He may have spent less than five years in the colony but, based on the number of places that has his name attached, you'd think Phillip landed just about everywhere around Sydney Harbour. However, Phillip would probably bristle at what the path skirting this residential estate is called: Frenchman's Walk.

Prior to being the founding Governor of New South Wales, Phillip, in his long naval career, had fought against and spied on the French. In 1788, when the French expedition, led by Jean-François de Galaup, comte de La Pérouse, sailed into Botany Bay less than a week after the ships of the First Fleet had, it shocked the British, who hastily hoisted the Union Jack on the shores of the much better harbour just to the north. Phillip assiduously avoided meeting La Pérouse and worked at keeping the two French ships away from Port Jackson. Instead, Lieutenant Philip Gidley King did most of the talking with the French, sailing for several hours in a cutter to Botany Bay to pass on Phillip's greetings and offer of assistance, before reporting back to the

Governor. The French not only received King and his crew 'with the greatest politeness & attention', but La Pérouse offered additional stores for the fledgling British colony, since his two ships had plenty to share. The French commander also sent back a message to the Governor that a few escaped convicts had begged to be taken on board, 'but he had dismissed them with threats and gave them a day's provisions to carry them back to ye settlement'. After six weeks in Botany Bay, the crews of *La Boussole* and *L'Astrolabe* sailed away, never to be seen again.

A gardener is trimming the edges along Frenchman's Walk, as I paddle along Canada Bay. He sees me and points to something in the water. I offer to grab it for him. I attempt to pull it up out of the water, but it's so heavy.

'It's a tent,' I call out. He then utters what I'm thinking: 'I hope there's no body in it'. The tent contains nothing but water, so I drag and prod it to a large wharf, with a ramp, below Frenchman's Walk.

The gardener introduces himself as Mark and says he's pleased to see me pull up at the wharf, because few ever use it. He jokes he keeps the shoreline clean for the 'water lookers' living in the homes along the shore.

Mark advises I'm seeing Canada Bay at its best. At high tide, he says, it is 'lovely and peaceful'. But when it is low tide, and the water drops about a metre, this part of the bay can be 'muddy and horrible'. Mark sometimes heads onto the water, fishing for bream and flathead, in a shallow-draught boat. He points over to two small clumps of mangroves on the opposite shore and says there are good spots around them. But he releases what he catches; Mark wouldn't eat the fish from here, because he's concerned about what remains in the mud. You only have to dig a little, he explains, and it emits an odour. On this day, there is no stink, just the faint scent of coffee wafting from the factory.

Paddling out of Hen and Chicken Bay, the view is expansive. Little wonder when Governor Lachlan Macquarie toured this area soon after his arrival in the colony in 1810, he noted how it was located on 'the southern side of the arm of the sea or river between Parramatta and Sydney'. It would be too generous to view Parramatta River as a sea, but from Abbotsford Point, it does look impressively wide.

On Abbotsford Point, sail and oars co-exist and have done so for decades, with the bases of the Abbotsford 12-Flying Squadron and the Sydney Rowing Club. The rowing club has had a base at Abbotsford since 1874, when it bought an inn that was a popular watering hole for those taking the punt across the river from Bedlam Point. The new facility was launched by a festive flotilla rowing up the river to Abbotsford from the club's base in the main harbour at Woolloomooloo.

The boatshed perched on the point these days was dismantled and transported from Woolloomooloo in 1946. The old clubhouse at Abbotsford had been ravaged by fire a dozen years earlier. Like many of the private schools' rowing bases dotting the banks along this reach of the river, this is no shed. It is a distinguished building, with a steep-pitched roof, observation areas facing upriver, and a storage area packed with expensive racing shells.

I want to stop and have a drink at the rowing club. The ramp outside the boathouse is designed for ease in getting in and out of the water. Perhaps it is the sight of all those fancy craft in the club's belly that compels me to paddle a little further and look for another, more humble, spot to hop out of *Pulbah Raider*.

I find an older ramp below the restaurant, but its slimy skin ensures all I can do is keep sliding helplessly back into the river. I paddle on, defeated and sober, slime-coated and wet.

Between the rowing and sailing clubs is a shed brimming with character, and a pontoon that allows a kayaker to alight with a degree of dignity. No sooner do I clamber onto the pontoon in front of the Abbotsford Point Boatshed than I'm surrounded by the past. An old Maritime Services Board launch berthed out the front is in the throes of restoration, and a rambling collection of artefacts are on the deck and leaning on the boathouse, including a life-ring from a tug that was renowned on the harbour, *Monterey*. But the most compelling artefact is the boathouse itself.

Although a sign on the boatshed indicates the business was established in 1851, it's believed this two-storey weatherboard building has been here since the 1890s. The Abbotsford Point Boatshed is one of the oldest surviving commercial operations on the harbour.

In all its years, the boatshed has been in the hands of only three families. The present owner, Roger Kyle, has been at the boatshed since 1983, taking over from his father. Bruce Kyle was well known not just for his business by the river, but he was also a world champion in boomerang throwing. He would practise throwing the boomerang from the front of the boathouse. For a time the business was called Bruce's Boats and Boomerangs.

When Roger inherited the business, he reverted to the boatshed's old name, and he retained the reminders that this building has been here a long time. Walking into the shed is like entering Davy Jones' Locker, only without any sailors' bodies, just the spirits of another age. Posters, photos and memorabilia hang on the walls and from the ceiling, and just about every square centimetre of the time- and tide-seasoned wooden floors carry the weight of history, from old ropes to bits and pieces of boats. Roger's father used to call these items 'nautical niceties'. Although not everything attached to the boatshed is old or deeply significant. I ask him about a model of a reindeer perched like a figurehead on the roofline.

'That's just a Christmas decoration I haven't taken down,' shrugs Roger, who is in his mid-50s and looks like he is prepared for a voyage out to sea, wearing a beanie and a fleece jacket.

'Maybe I should make up a better story about the reindeer. You'd be amazed by the number of people passing on ferries who photograph it.'

Roger shows me a photo from the late 1800s of a rowing race. The competitors heave their way past the boatshed, whose façade is daubed with the words, 'Boats for Hire'. The shed's appearance hasn't changed much in more than a century. All around it has. The surrounding bush has turned into buildings. In the photo, a rowboat in the foreground is filled with spectators, decked out in their finest clothes.

'Abbotsford used to be like Bondi,' Roger says, adding there were river baths that also attracted many visitors.

The boatshed remained a leisure destination well into the 20th century, as commemorated by one of Bruce's boomerangs hanging on the wall. Roger tells how during the Vietnam War, US servicemen on leave would hire boats to go water skiing, and they would also buy boomerangs and receive a quick lesson from Bruce. Before the boomerangs were thrown, Bruce would explain if any dropped into the river, the visitor would still have to buy it. Sure enough, a boomerang would often plonk into the water. After the soldiers had left, having paid for their lost souvenir, Bruce's dog would retrieve the boomerangs from the river.

From where he sits in the shed, Roger has a perfectly framed picture of change; he need only look out the doors at the river, observing what passes, and no longer passes.

Growing up in Abbotsford, he saw the final days of the colliers, as *Hexham Bank* huffed towards the gasworks at Mortlake, and he and his mates would jump on the rafts of logs being towed to the timber yards upriver. Roger also remembers the fishing trawlers working the river. Sometimes his father would rig up an old gramophone in the boatshed and play *O Sole Mio* at full volume. The Italian fishermen would float closer to listen, and their singing voices would ripple across the water.

Just as he's talking about how the workboats have all but disappeared off the river, a trawler chugs by.

'It *used* to be a trawler,' says Roger. 'It now services moorings.'

Then one of the biggest symbols of change rumbles into view just off the boatshed: a RiverCat. The Abbotsford ferry terminal is next door. The RiverCat's engines churn up the water, and the old launch moored at the pontoon rocks restlessly.

Yet Roger looks beyond the RiverCat, beyond the churn and changes.

'It's like a postcard, looking out,' Roger smiles.

AS PART of their business, the Abbotsford Point Boatshed's original owners ferried workers along Parramatta River. One of the popular destinations was more or less around the corner. The Nestlé factory snuggled into Abbotsford Bay for the best part of seventy years. The factory was in the grounds of Abbotsford

House, a mansion built in the 1870s by a prominent doctor and parliamentarian, Sir Arthur Renwick. The property was later owned by department store tycoons, the Grace family, before Nestlé bought it in 1917. The company built the largest chocolate factory in Australia around the mansion, which it used for offices. The factory buildings have gone, but Abbotsford House remains. Only the mansion now has to share its grounds at the head of the bay with townhouses and apartments, in a development called Abbotsford Cove.

Nestlé had its own jetty, and the shoreline was used in filming part of the convict epic *For the Term of His Natural Life* in 1927. The shore is hardly cinematic these days, as I land on a slice of sand below the stone seawall. However, if you take a long, tight shot straight ahead, the picture would be impressive. The two-storey mansion, with its wide verandas, looks majestic.

Around the mansion exists a community. Paul Roman is playing with his grandson on the large common lawn that sweeps from the mansion to the waterfront. The dips and terraces are ideal for the grandson's billy-cart to rip down.

Paul has lived here since 2000. When he moved in, the lawn was still a construction site, and he could see heavily armed troops in inflatable boats on the river, on security patrol for the Sydney Olympics. He and his family had moved from a house in suburban Strathfield. He gladly traded a big yard for a harbour view.

'From our place, you can look straight down the river to Gladesville Bridge,' he enthuses.

As Sydneysiders do when they're standing near the harbour, we talk property prices. He points to a townhouse that had recently sold for more than two million dollars, and he gestures across the lawn to another place that went for three million. In this city, to ensure capital gain, just add water.

Paul is unwilling to do more than dip his feet in the water, because of the ongoing pollution problems upriver.

'Apart from that, the river is wonderful,' Paul says.

'People pay good money to go overseas and stay in a resort. I've got one here!'

PADDLING OUT of the bay, I think about how many place names along Parramatta River carry echoes of the Thames. Chiswick, Henley, Mortlake, Putney. Ahead of me, downriver, are the suburbs of Woolwich and Greenwich. These are all names that can be found by the river threading its way through the heart and soul of London.

I think about how those who named these places along a river in the colony were probably driven not by what they saw but how they felt. After all, the land along this river could not have been further removed in distance or appearance from that great, sprawling, dirty city many of them had sailed away from. These transplanted place names were likely an expression of homesickness, or, at least, of longing for something familiar in the midst of everything that was so alien.

The bank approaching Blackwall Point is unmistakably, beautifully of this land. The sandstone face is etched with marks and squiggles. They tell an epic story stretching back more than 200 million years, when vast amounts of sand were deposited across the area by floods. As layer fell upon layer and the sand was compressed, it eventually became stone. The mass of ages held in that stone was exposed merely thousands of years ago, when the last Ice Age ended, and the water flowed in to form the harbour and the river valleys. The stone became a parchment on which time, with the help of water, could continue to tell its tale. And with each rise and fall of the tide, with each boat that passes, with each moment, the story on that sandstone face continues to be written.

Squatting right on top of that sandstone wall is a block of brick apartments, about forty years old. The contrast between the naturally sublime and the architecturally ridiculous is glaring. But in so many places around the harbour, the ridiculous is perched on the sublime, which somehow only highlights the beauty of one and the ugliness of the other.

Rounding Blackwall Point into Five Dock Bay, I see a tidal pool, enclosed in netting. It is the first pool in the river I've seen. On the eastern side of the bay's opening is the reason the waterway was given its name. The sandstone headland was once indented with five small coves that looked like docks. Two of the coves remain. In one are the remnants of steps cut into the stone, and above them is a gnarled flowering gum reaching out to the water.

Moulded in and around the 'five docks' is a wall of sandstone blocks, plunging into the water. As I bob around at its oyster-encrusted feet and look up, the sandstone wall has the formidable air of an old fortress. It is actually an abutment of the first Gladesville Bridge, which opened in 1881. The wrought iron, lattice-truss structure was a vital link from north to south. It was the first bridge across the river east of Parramatta, and an answer to the entreaties and demands of those living on the north side. They had been calling for a bridge for at least three decades. Gladesville Bridge had an opening swing span to allow ships through. Yet in the years ahead, what allowed for the flow of river traffic became an ever growing cause of frustration for motorists, as the numbers of cars increased. Paddling across the river to trace the northern bank, I recall chatting with Donald Chivas, whom I had met at Kissing Point, about the old Gladesville Bridge. Donald told me how he spent many an hour sitting at the end of the bridge. With only two road lanes and a tramway, traffic could be congested at the best of times. But when the bridge opened for a ship, the wait – and the lines of vehicles – stretched interminably. The colliers heading for the Mortlake gasworks would barely squeeze through the opening, with only centimetres to spare on each side. In summer, Donald remembered, when the heat made the steel expand, the bridge's components would occasionally not close properly. The fire brigade was called in to hose down the bridge, so that everything could align once more.

Sydney had outgrown the bridge. The solution to that growing pain arcs through the sky a few hundred metres ahead.

3

GLADESVILLE BRIDGE TO WOOLWICH (VIA COCKATOO ISLAND)

FROM A distance, the arch of Gladesville Bridge looks like a concrete rainbow. When it opened in 1964, this was the longest concrete arch bridge in the world. And in replacing the old Gladesville Bridge, it offered something better than a pot of gold to commuters on both banks of Parramatta River: time saved.

Every hour, thousands of vehicles ride the 305-metre span across the river. From the crest of the bridge, you feel as though you are not so much driving as flying. Sneak a glance to the left and you can take in the bridge that gets all the attention, along with the Opera House and the city centre. Look to the right, and you have Parramatta River unravelling through the suburbs, and the mountains in the distance. For a few brief moments, soaring through the sky, you can appreciate the beauty and the scale of the harbour city.

But to appreciate the beauty and the scale of Gladesville Bridge itself, you have to be under it. Sitting in the kayak just off the northern bank, I crane my neck and track the flow of concrete above me. The perspective gives the impression of the concrete narrowing as it pours onto the Drummoyne shore. The underside of the arch is ribbed and, accompanied by the guttural roar of trucks on the bridge, I could be peering into the belly of a monster. It is a humbling view. From here on the water, you can appreciate the engineering and all the labour involved in creating this great curve of concrete.

Ossie Cruse is one of Australia's most revered Indigenous leaders. He has devoted much of his life to helping Australians understand the importance of Aboriginal culture, and to share his passion for preserving it. Ossie Cruse is, in a most important sense, a bridge builder. But when he was in his mid-20s, Ossie helped build a different kind of bridge.

'We knew it was going to be massive,' Ossie says of the Gladesville structure.

He began work on the bridge soon after construction began in 1959. Ossie's initial job was digging the bridge's foundations, cutting deep into the river bottom. The waters were held back by a cofferdam, as Ossie and his co-workers drilled and jack-hammered through solid sandstone, cutting almost 20 metres into the rock.

'It took us a fair few months to get down through the rock,' Ossie recalls. 'It was a big chasm by the time we'd finished.'

As Gladesville Bridge took shape, Ossie's roles expanded. He operated the cranes, became a rigger and 'dogman', often riding the load of building materials high above the water. He wasn't bothered by heights, he assures. He just enjoyed the views when he was hanging more than forty metres above the river.

Ossie was hardly alone in expanding his skills on Gladesville Bridge. Ideas and techniques were being pioneered on its design and construction, particularly with the use of concrete as a dominant bridge-building material. Hundreds of pre-cast boxes to form the bridge's arch were barged up the river and then lifted and pushed into place. According to Ossie, each box weighed about 50 tonnes, and they were secured with cabling and more concrete. After each block had been manoeuvred into place, Ossie would put his faith in the sum of everyone's labour.

'I used to lie on my back and inspect the concrete,' he explains. 'It was just above my face, and I'd make sure there were no cracks.' When I ask him if he was a little worried having all that concrete looming over him, he simply replies. 'We took it in our stride. We were told even without the grout, the blocks would stay there, with the weight on them.'

Ossie adds that no workers were killed during the bridge's construction, even though safety standards were less stringent then and, as far as he remembers, he was the only one who wore a hard hat, which was an old miner's helmet.

Ossie Cruse was a young Aboriginal man at a time when racism continued to trample its way through the attitudes and policies of Australia. While he was helping build a symbol of the nation's future, Ossie had no official say in what that future might look like. Aboriginal people around the country were not given the same voting rights as other Australians until 1965. And it was only in 1967 that Australians voted in favour of Aboriginal people being counted in census figures. Yet on the construction site, Ossie says, there was a sense of community, 'a really good spirit, we were good mates'. I ask Ossie had he been mindful he was building a link from the land of the Wallumedegal people on the north side over to the traditional area of the Wangal people on the south bank. No, Ossie replies, people didn't think like that back then.

In the years ahead, Ossie Cruse would be instrumental in advancing social justice and recognition for Aboriginal Australians. He was a member of key delegations to the United Nations and Commonwealth Heads of Government meetings. He was a member of the World Council of Indigenous People. He has chaired boards and councils in Australia and has been the prime mover of education and cultural programs. He is also a Christian pastor, and he founded the Aboriginal Evangelical Fellowship. In a remarkable life that has made a difference to not just other lives but that of this nation, Ossie Cruse ranks his work on Gladesville Bridge right near the top.

'It was a great experience, I just got so much out of it myself,' he explains. 'And I was leaving something beautiful behind.'

'Sydney got an icon. It also got a freeway, after the bottle-neck of the little old bridge. I reckon it's equal to the Harbour Bridge really.'

The city never did get the north-west expressway that was planned to improve traffic flow, but at least it got the bridge that was intended to be its gateway. And if it weren't for that other bridge about six kilometres downstream, this construction would perhaps feature more prominently as a symbol of the city. It might even have been accorded that most Australian of honours, a nickname, just like 'the coat hanger'. Gladesville Bridge did inspire the poet Les Murray. He crafted into verse his impressions of the view of the 'flooded valley, that is now the ship-chained Harbour', the surrounding suburbs and 'the new city standing on its haze above the city', and he marvelled at the construction, all the while sitting in a car that had run out of petrol,

> *on the summit that exhilarates cars, the concrete vault on*
> *its thousands*
> *of tonnes of height, far above the tidal turnaround.*

More than half a century after Gladesville Bridge was completed, Ossie Cruse still experiences joy when he drives over it. Only where most of us look around, he thinks about what went into building the bridge.

'It's what's on the inside, it's not just what's on the outside, that's the strength of it,' Ossie concludes.

'I remember when we took out all the stuff from underneath the bridge, it was awesome to look at it from below. And it still is an awesome sight, a beautiful sight.'

AS I paddle downriver past a line of homes, the compensation for living in the shadow of a bridge is revealed. The thrum of traffic above subsides, and the harbour view rises. The skyscrapers of the CBD appear over the headlands, while further around to the west is the top of Anzac Bridge. The bridge's pylons, threaded with supporting cables, look like a pair of Bedouin tents being erected above the Balmain peninsula.

Straight ahead is the suburb of Hunters Hill. It was once known as a 'garden suburb'. But as successive booms and busts rolled over the ridgeline, some gardens were ripped out and the grand properties they belonged to were subdivided. The later arrivals, especially close to the waterline, grab the attention.

Actually, many demand attention, with their large display windows. But if you look carefully up the slope, you can make out the more subtle symphony of sandstone, slate and cast iron in the older colonial homes. What bonds all that architecture – the historic and the modern, the dignified and the ostentatious – is the grout of green. While the number of grand gardens has shrunk, from out on the water, Hunters Hill still looks like a finely treed suburb.

Before I paddle over to Hunters Hill, there's another diversion (that's another pleasure of kayaking; there are always diversions). Tarban Creek flows in from my left through a canyon of mansions. A couple of hundred metres up the creek is the mini-me of Gladesville Bridge. Tarban Creek Bridge was built around the same time, opening in 1965. The design isn't quite the same as Gladesville Bridge, but it does have a large arch that spans the creek, giving the impression this stretch of water is more significant than being just another barely-noticed tributary feeding the insatiable hunger of the main harbour. Tarban Creek Bridge is apparently more than a vital piece of transport infrastructure. It is also an arts incentive program, a blank surface on which philosophers and painters can make their mark with graffiti.

Just as the work of the subversive bridge painters is all but out of sight, so was life along Tarban Creek in the early colonial days. Perhaps it was made to feel all the more so by the presence of the asylum, which took its name from the creek. There were few homes neighbouring the Tarban Creek Lunatic Asylum, according to W.S. Campbell, the son of one of the facility's superintendents. Walter Campbell wrote about one Tarban Creek couple who put their marriage vow of 'for better, for worse' into action. Whenever the husband made the journey by water to Sydney, he apparently drank up to the point he couldn't walk by the time he returned. His wife would be waiting at the wharf with a wheelbarrow. Then, when she travelled to Sydney, he did the same for her.

In 1847, the creek meandering out of the bush became a path of spiritual guidance. When two Catholic priests voyaged from France to establish the Order of the Marist Fathers in Sydney, their quest led them up Tarban Creek. The order bought a property just near where the creek tasted the first lick of salt water. The priests extended the sandstone farmhouse and named it Villa Maria. This was to be their base for missionary work in the Pacific. The Tarban Creek property held the promise of home comforts to fortify the Fathers in preparation for long voyages and arduous work in the Pacific. One of the founding priests, Father Rocher, wrote to his superiors in France how the orchard and garden were magnificent, and that the 'vines are coming along very well, already it seems that there will be sufficient to provide everyone in the procure with wine for one year'. When the Marists later sold the property, it received a more ecclesiastic name, The Priory, before it was bought by the New South Wales Government to become part of the asylum.

By then, the Marist Order had firmly settled on higher ground on the other side of the creek. The Fathers had built a new home and the Villa Maria Church, with its stunning bell tower that continues to thrust its way into prominence on the local skyline. In 1872, the teaching brothers of the Order arrived in Sydney, and they bought a plot of land near the church to build a boys' boarding school. St Joseph's College opened in 1881. What began as wooden huts in a clearing created by the Brothers' own hands grew into the multi-storey sandstone solidity of the college's main building. Just as the college grew, so did its population, until it was the largest boarding school in Australia.

From the creek, there's no sign of the college buildings, but the influence of Joeys has flowed down the hill. Skimming across the creek's surface, powered by the staccato orders of a megaphoned voice and their own youthful ambitions, are the school's rowers. Their base is a two-storey brick and weatherboard affair on the creek's northern bank. From the rowing club's pontoon, there is a beguiling view of an arch within an arch, with the top of Sydney Harbour Bridge framed by Tarban Creek Bridge. But only a kayaker with no one barking orders at him and no hope of paddling a competitive time can relax and enjoy that view. As the creek upstream constricts and is clotted by the bush on the northern bank, I turn around and paddle into the view.

TRACING THE Parramatta River shore of Hunters Hill, where the air is almost fragrant with money and gentility, it is hard to believe that it was once described as the place where 'the very worst characters find an undisturbed place of abode'. The 'very worst characters' may have gone, but from the water Hunters Hill still looks and feels like an undisturbed place of abode – if you can afford it. Many of the homes around here have private slipways, private wharves, even private beaches. The only thing not private is the display of wealth.

While much of the harbourfront land along this reach is off-limits to all but those who hold the title deeds and their friends, there are still slivers where anyone can access the water. One of those spots is at the end of Ferry Street. However, the ferries no longer stop here. What has been the passengers' loss is the fishing enthusiasts' gain. On the weekends, there can be a row of anglers standing above the seawall. But on this weekday early afternoon, there are only two older women fishing. Vicky and Hayat are friends and neighbours from up the river at Parramatta. Hayat has been fishing for five years. She was taught by Vicky, who has been fishing for more than twenty years.

The friends travel to Ferry Street about once a week to fish. They like it here, especially when it is quiet and there are few lines in the water, but Hayat reckons some of the locals would prefer they stay away.

'Sometimes they're not happy with us,' she says.

'Why not?'

'Don't know. Maybe they have too much money!'

As Vicky threads a pilchard onto the hook, she explains they normally catch up to five fish each session.

'Bream, flathead and trevally mostly,' she says, as she flicks the rod, sending the pilchard-weighted line curving through the air.

'Sometimes here, you put the line out and the fish catch themselves.'

Vicky and Hayat say they eat the fish they catch. Nearby, on a power pole, is one of the signs issued by the government and erected at popular fishing spots around the harbour, particularly west of the Harbour Bridge. It provides 'dietary advice' for fish caught locally. Basically the advice for this part of the harbour is, don't eat the fish. The women have their backs to the sign.

I ask Vicky does she worry about eating the fish she catches here.

'No, no problem,' she replies. 'I don't know about the future. But for now, all right.'

As for this day, Vicky and Hayat have nothing to worry about.

'We're safe, because we haven't caught anything. Terrible!'

Even so, it's relaxing, adds Hayat.

'It's better than being at home. At home, you have to work.'

AS WAS often the case, the British didn't see things clearly when they named Hunters Hill. The original Australians were more descriptive of the landscape in their name for it; Moocooboola or Mukubula, which means 'meeting of the waters'. For Hunters Hill is a peninsula, with the land in pincers between Parramatta and Lane Cove rivers.

By virtue of having rivers on either side of it, Hunters Hill feels self-contained. It could well be another island in the harbour. All of which makes it very desirable to those wanting to be close to Sydney's centre but feel removed from it, and for those seeking something that can be often hard to find in a city: a sense of community.

'You come here, and you don't need to go anywhere,' enthuses David Ward. And David should know. He came here in the 1970s to sell real estate, and four decades on, he isn't interested in going anywhere else. David loves historic homes, which is what brought him to Hunters Hill, since there are so many here. Over the years, he has sold dozens of the landmark properties along the peninsula.

The day I meet David, he and his son Matthew are holding an 'open for inspection' at a gracious two-storey mansion, Woodbank, which was built in 1879. Just before Woodbank was built, its land was valued at £100. David and Matthew expect to sell the house, on a much smaller allotment now than in the 1870s, for about $6 million.

Resplendent in a blue blazer and a tie adorned with a flotilla of colourful yachts, David shows me the pocked sandstone blocks of the original building and explains that over the years the house has been extended. The older homes, he explains, were built up high for the views and the cooling breezes, and their land stretched down to the water.

David reckons buyers' interest in historic homes is diminishing. People love the views but they also want direct water access and preferably somewhere to put their boat. Wealthy Chinese are a growing part of the local market, David says, and buyers often come from Sydney's Eastern Suburbs.

'Although the young ones sometimes feel it's too much like the country here; too quiet.'

But the quiet and sense of distance are what attract many to Hunters Hill.

Woodbank neighbours Bulwarra, another sandstone mansion and the former home of the actor Cate Blanchett and her director-writer husband Andrew Upton. 'She was part of the community; their kids went to the local school,' David says, as he guides me outside.

What is viewed by many now as glorious – and highly marketable – isolation was once seen as a drawback to Hunters Hill.

'The water was both a blessing and a curse for the development of Hunters Hill,' explains Graham Percival. Graham has lived on the peninsula since 1963 and is a member of the Hunters Hill Historical Society. 'It's beautiful, but it also meant a lot of people didn't want to settle in the area, because it was reachable only by boat from the main part of Sydney.'

The area remained largely untamed and unknowable to Sydneysiders until two brothers originally from France recognised the potential in Hunters Hill.

Didier Numa Joubert was a wine and spirit merchant from Bordeaux. He arrived in Sydney in 1837. His younger brother, Jules François de Sales Joubert, arrived in Sydney a couple of years later. Like many before him and since, Jules was smitten with what he saw as he came through the Heads into Port Jackson. After visiting some of the great ports of the world, Joubert declared after his first glimpse of Sydney that 'all other harbours dwindled down to almost insignificance'.

In 1847, Didier Joubert bought a property on the north side of Hunters Hill from the convict-turned-businesswoman, Mary Reibey. She had been among the first to invest in Hunters Hill. But her farm on Lane Cove River was not productive enough to supply her business in town.

'She used to come up on a Sunday to visit the farm, but it was a waste of time for what she brought back by boat,' Graham Percival says. 'People knew what Hunters Hill was like as a farming area – a dead loss.'

Yet Joubert didn't see the peninsula's future in farming. When his brother joined him in Hunters Hill in 1855, they became, according to Graham, 'a formidable force' in developing the area. They began slicing up the peninsula into housing allotments. When Italian stonemasons arrived in the colony, the Jouberts arranged for them to build a string of cottages and villas, using locally quarried sandstone. The Jouberts established a ferry service. They argued it was necessary, for the service provided by the passing Parramatta River ferries was so haphazard, some locals resorted to rowing all the way to Sydney. Both brothers also served as Mayor at various times after Hunters Hill was proclaimed a municipality in 1861.

Hunters Hill was named after a British officer and gentleman, John Hunter, the First Fleet naval officer who surveyed the harbour and was the second Governor of New South Wales. But under the influence of the Jouberts and other arrivals from France, including the Marist Fathers, the area came to be known as 'the French village'. Even France's official representative in Sydney took up residence in Hunters Hill. According to Graham Percival, the Consul, Louis Francois Sentis, visited the Jouberts, who convinced him this was an ideal area for the French to make their presence felt in the midst of a British colony. The brothers arranged for the purchase of a parcel of land that stretched all the way from the top of the hill to Lane Cove River, and a fine two-storey stone house was built for the Consul. The mansion was named Passy, after the precinct in Paris, and when the tricolour flew from the roof of the house, it could be seen from both Parramatta and Lane Cove rivers. In recent years, the historic landmark has been seen far and wide in the media, for Passy has been the home of the notorious former politician Eddie Obeid.

The Jouberts were not the only ones threading the look and feel of Europe through the sandstone and gums on Hunters Hill in the mid-19th century. A young Swiss immigrant, Leonard Etienne Bordier, imported a handful of prefabricated wooden houses, along with German workers to assemble them, in 1854. One of these buildings, called The Chalet, has survived on the southern side of Hunters Hill. For almost half a century, from 1954, it was the home of artist Nora Heysen. I visited Nora at The Chalet in 2003. That Nora Heysen lived in a house that was both pioneering and unique was in keeping with her character. With her talent and resolve, Nora had worked her way out of the public shadow of her famous landscape artist father, Hans, and, with those steely eyes of hers, she had stared discrimination and adversity straight in the face. She was the first female winner of the Archibald Prize for portraiture, she was the first woman to be appointed an Australian official war artist, and, throughout her career, she steadfastly pursued her vision, painting what she wanted, no matter what trends and 'isms' in art swirled and eddied around her. Nora Heysen wasn't fashionable. She was a classic. Little wonder I was nervous at the prospect of meeting her in her pre-fab chalet by the harbour. Yet neither the artist nor her home was anything like what I had imagined. Nora was a warm and generous soul, especially with her memories and her whisky. And her house was not some austere Baltic log cabin out of joint by the harbour, but a beautiful resonant space with broad verandas and potential Nora Heysen still life painting subjects wherever you looked, both in the house and out in the garden. Like its owner, the house was comfortable in its own skin, and it belonged. Nora died in late 2003, but her art lives on, as does The Chalet.

Hundreds of old buildings peppered along the peninsula are not just reminders of another age. They're also testament to the residents who fought to conserve them. By 1960, many were concerned their quiet and historic garden suburb was about to be concreted over with high-density housing. As the Town Clerk of Hunters Hill prophesied at the time, 'it seems likely the face of the district will change considerably in the next decade'. To residents, that would be an intolerably ugly face. As progress pushed its way towards the peninsula, some older homes in Hunters Hill were demolished, and others seemed doomed. The residents pushed back, forming the Hunters Hill Trust. Their efforts helped save many of the suburb's buildings. Hunters Hill has more than 220 places listed on the Register of the National Estate.

As a result, Hunters Hill is a wonderful place for wandering. The historic commercial buildings and houses, with their stone fences draped in leaves along tree-lined streets, make for an enriching yet disorienting experience. The sandstone from which many of the buildings have been constructed is quintessentially of this land, as it glows from the light of the eucalypt-filtered sun, and yet it has been sculpted and assembled in accordance with the memories and influences of distant lands. The suburb of two rivers provides two experiences at once.

While it resisted a lot of development, Hunters Hill has been recycled in parts. Paddling east, I reach Pulpit Point, named after a rock formation that was shorn and shaved long ago to make room for the religion of money-making. For a time in the 1800s, there were pleasure gardens on the shores of Fern Bay, but then the site was sold and turned into a large oil depot. For ninety years, ships cruised along the inner harbour to the depot, berthing at the long jetty that reached out into Fern Bay. Pulpit Point was a cluster of storage tanks and sheds. But after the depot closed in the 1980s, Pulpit Rock was converted from an industrial site into a luxurious housing development. The estate has the look of a resort, and its residents could be anywhere that includes palm trees. The only thing really anchoring them to the idea they are in Sydney is the uninterrupted view out of Fern Bay to the Harbour Bridge. The exclusivity of this place is explicit in the signs attached to its marina. They warn a passing kayaker that the marina is private and for residents only, so KEEP OFF.

From this pocket of tightly held privacy, it is little more than a stone's throw to the scene of a historic victory for the preservation of bushland and the public's right to access the water.

Kelly's Bush is a thick patch of green covering almost five hectares of the peninsula. In the midst of the reserve, you can catch thin slices of harbour views between the tree trunks, which rise from a bed of sandstone and ferns. In the heart of Kelly's Bush, nature is at its most tenacious and defiant. Which are the very qualities its saviours displayed.

For many years, a tin smelter operated by the Kelly family was on the foreshore. The harbour was an important component of the Sydney Smelting Company. Supplies of ore were shipped to the works, and the slag created during the smelting process was carted away by barges and used as fill across the water at Drummoyne and Birkenhead Point. Eventually, no one would take the slag, so it was dumped around the site. The patch of bushland above and beside the smelter had been preserved by the company as a buffer between it and the residents, to offer at least some distance from the slag heaps and the emissions the industry created. Yet the land was also a playground for local kids, a shortcut for locals heading to and from the ferry, and it was the largest remaining parcel of native bush along Parramatta River.

In the 1950s, the council had bought 2.8 hectares at the top of the parcel for a park. But when the smelter closed in 1967, the real estate developer A.V. Jennings, took out an option for the rest of the land, to build apartments and townhouses on it. With the developer having the backing of the state government, it seemed another part of the harbour foreshore was about to be built on and locked up. But what no one counted on was the Battlers for Kelly's Bush.

Thirteen local women formed the residents' action group in 1970 to oppose the development. One of the 'Battlers' is Doctor Joan Croll.

'We were the original greenies!' exclaims Joan, when I meet her in her Drummoyne unit, with views across the harbour – all the way to the peninsula she helped conserve.

Joan is a feisty, energetic character. She gives the impression that she is still a 'Battler', not in the interpretation most Australians apply to the word, but that she would be up for a fight, if necessary. Indeed, as Joan remembers it, she joined the campaign to save Kelly's Bush not just because of what she was fighting for, but who she was fighting against.

'Nobody likes developers,' she declares. 'To save the waterfront from a developer, that was important.'

When Kelly's Bush came under threat, Joan lived further east along the peninsula than most of the other Battlers.

'I was one of the few who didn't live in Red Square,' she says, applying the term disparagingly used to criticise those in the group who lived in blue-ribbon Hunters Hill yet, as part of the conservation campaign, formed an alliance with the union movement.

The Battlers met in each other's homes, with the aim of raising the money to help the state government buy the land. But when it turned out the state was not interested in that option, they changed tactics: they would enlist the public's help to save the bushland.

I ask Joan whether the activists, who lived in a well-to-do part of Sydney, were being ironic in calling their group, Battlers for Kelly's Bush.

'No, they meant it!' she counters. 'They were used to getting what they wanted.'

'So why were there only women in the group?'

'In those days, women did things, and men did things. We didn't need them!'

The group organised public meetings, they wrote letters to politicians and departments, and they organised essay writing competitions for school children. They held 'Boil the Billy' fundraisers in Kelly's Bush and sold an information leaflet, with a foreword by the writer and Hunters Hill resident Kylie Tennant, who argued this was more than a struggle to save land: 'It is a confrontation of values. Kelly's Bush is a symbol of our lost land. Take away Kelly's Bush and you take away one more assurance that in man is left a possibility for the future. The unborn Australian will ask for his birthright and be handed a piece of concrete.'

Despite that combined pressure, in June 1971, the state's Minister for Local Government signed the documents to rezone the land for residential development. The middle-class women then reached across the water to some working-class men. They sought the assistance of the union movement. The State Secretary of the Builders' Labourers Federation, Jack Mundey, became involved, holding a meeting with a few of the Battlers.

'I nearly had a fit when I heard the BLF was involved,' recalls Joan, who left the group in protest. 'My husband was so disgusted [with her], he told me to go back immediately.'

'Why were you disgusted by the involvement of the BLF?'

'Well, I was a Liberal voter, for God's sake! But I quickly resolved that issue.'

The BLF offered its support, imposing a black ban on the Kelly's Bush site. This became known as a green ban, the first of its type in the world.

The Battlers eventually prevailed. The bush was saved. In 1983, the State Labor Government announced it would buy Kelly's Bush for public open space. It marked the end of the fight, and the dissolution of the Battlers for Kelly's Bush. Their success inspired other campaigns to protect areas around Sydney Harbour, particularly the formation of alliances between action groups and the union movement to save bushland and historic buildings.

'It helped us rethink the harbour,' Joan muses.

Joan Croll has achieved much in her life. She has been a renowned doctor in the area of breast cancer, pushing for the widespread introduction of ultrasound technology and mammography. She has also figured prominently in Australian art, both as a collector and subject. She features in one of John Brack's best known portraits, as she stares directly at the viewer with a determined look. I presume it's a look many a critic of the Kelly's Bush campaign would have received. Yet, despite all she has done, in Joan's opinion, the battle to save Kelly's Bush 'is the most significant thing in my life'.

I point to the distant slash of green that Joan helped save and ask her how often she looks over there. Joan squints and shakes her head.

'It's funny, I don't think to look,' she says. 'Maybe it's because I've got all this greenery here out the front and I can't see the bloody thing!'

THE PENINSULA is divided between Hunters Hill and, further east along the ridgeline, Woolwich. For a time, it was also divided between the residential and the industrial. Hunters

Hill was predominantly fine homes and big gardens; Woolwich was more working class.

Before Woolwich became a hub for industries, it was promoted as an ideal place to live. In 1841, Joseph Simmons, who was an actor, theatre entrepreneur and auctioneer, promoted land at Woolwich, declaring that 'to attempt even an outline of its many advantages would occupy an unlimited space'. But he went on to outline its many advantages, anyway; the proximity to Sydney, 'the finest views of any known spot in the Colony', along with the residents being able to enjoy 'health in the breeze'. Mr Simmons' exhortations didn't attract land buyers to Woolwich at the time.

I inhale that health in the breeze as I paddle along the Woolwich shore towards Clarkes Point. The stretch is devoted to recreation, with a marina, a broad area known as the Horse Paddock, because work horses used to graze here but is now a playground for dogs to run leash-free, and the Hunters Hill Sailing Club. Just beyond the club is a strip that looks like a beach, but it contains faint and rotting reminders of the area's industrial days. Sliding from the foreshore into the harbour are the remains of a slipway. Ferries were built here before the First World War, and a few more were constructed on the shore during the 1920s. During the Second World War, work began on the construction of two large cargo ships. Photos taken at the time show a great iron shell on the shore being tended to by cranes towering over it. That scene of earth stripped bare for shipbuilding is hard to reconcile with the gentle space dotted with trees that I'm looking at.

The parkland curls around Clarkes Point. The view of the harbour from here is what made the actor-auctioneer Mr Simmons so rhapsodic in 1841, and while it may have changed, it still warrants purple prose, or quiet contemplation. It takes in the sandstone headlands, the CBD's clump of towers, and the Harbour Bridge curving across the water, so Clarkes Point is, to quote Mr Simmons, 'delightfully situated'. The shoreline, however, has undergone dramatic shifts through the years. In the 1880s, the Atlas Engineering Company bought a large chunk of land on the waterfront, cleared it and built a series of workshops and imported a floating dock from England for ship repairs. The company itself was taken over by Mort's Dock and Engineering Company, whose base was across the harbour at Balmain, but the shipbuilding yards, docks and workshops remained in operation until 1959. The writer P.R. Stephensen hated what had been done to tip of the peninsula, decrying in the 1960s that the dormant industrial site 'had the appearance, in contrast with its naturally beautiful surroundings, of the Abomination of Desolation – a man-made scar on the landscape, which perhaps time would heal'. Time, and a whole lot of human effort, has helped the scars on the point to fade. Yet there remains one awesome incision deep into the sandstone skin of Moocooboola. Woolwich Dock.

When Mort's Dock and Engineering Company took over the site in 1898, it set out to build a dry dock capable of accepting the largest ships sailing in Australian waters. To build that dock took teams of men hacking and cutting into the stone face for more than three years. The sandstone cut out was carted by horses around the point, to build a seawall and reclaim land. That knobbly yet majestic wall is still largely in place; I had paddled past it and remember thinking how these sandstone seawalls are yet another character marker of Sydney Harbour.

By the time the labourers had finished in 1901, they had carved a dock about 188 metres long and about 27 metres wide. At high tide, it had a draft of 8 metres. When Woolwich Dock officially opened in December, the first ship that sailed into it was *Neotsfield*. She was the first of many ships over more than half a century to enter the dock, have the caisson close behind her, and have the water pumped out beneath her until she rested on keel blocks. During the Second World War, battle-damaged ships limped into the dock for repair. For some of Mort's workforce, which reached a peak of 1500 in 1917, a ship in the dock meant not just employment but a feed. When the water was pumped out, there was usually a large haul of fish flapping on the dock's floor. In tough times, when few ships were in dock and men were laid off, they did as Woolwich families had done before the industries arrived: they fished. During the Great Depression in the early 1930s, to make ends meet, the wives would walk up the ridgeline to the households more resistant to downturns and sell their catch. When a ship was in the dock, it brought not only work but also sailors into the community. Woolwich even had a club for the visiting seamen.

When the dock closed in the late 1950s, 700 men were out of work. A few years later, the dock and surrounding land became a base for army water transport squadrons. The army stayed for more than thirty years, and, once the military had transferred its operations to Townsville, developers wanted the site. Locals who united under the name Foreshore 2000 Woolwich and another action group called Defenders of Sydney Harbour Foreshores fought for the preservation of the dock and the surrounding area, and they won.

As well as retaining the area for public access, a maritime community has mushroomed once more in and around the dock. In the large sawtooth-roofed shed that was built in the 1940s, shipwrights and detailers whittle, grind and polish, and outside, yachts are cradled and manoeuvred by crane into the water. While this hubbub of boating maintenance is reassuring in a harbour that is watching its 'working' title slowly sink, the most impressive part of Woolwich Dock is experienced when you paddle into the incision, in the wake of ships long gone.

With the dock's sandstone walls and above them the carved cliffs, I'm kayaking into a chasm. Near the entrance, on the wall to my right is a series of Roman numerals inscribed in the stone, measuring the depth of the water. Above the wall on the left are a few masts, with yachts being worked on outside the big shed. Berthed in the dock is a row of larger yachts. The legendary Sydney to Hobart race record breaker, *Wild Oats XI*, is often resting her carbon fibre body in the dock. The supermaxi's 44-metre mast towers above the toil of men etched into the cliffs. But not today; she is off scooping more silverware from the deep blue somewhere. However, a couple of head-turning vessels are berthed in here. For those who consider ocean-racing yachts to be the sports cars of the sea, there is compelling evidence in the dock: a sleek beauty called *Maserati*.

At the end of the dock, the rock wall curves like a ship's bow. The rock is dark and weeping groundwater, and it wears a wispy beard of ferns. This ancient striated rock face stares at the state-of-the-art sailing technology behind me. One holds time in its layers; the other is designed to race time. Between the rock and the fancy yachts, lying beside me, is an old barge, which is gradually being broken down by time. Here, at the meeting of the waters, the past meets the future.

Where the peninsula ends is called Onions Point. It is named after Samuel Onions, who bought this patch of land in 1835. Perched on the end of the point and hovering over those meeting waters is an old boatshed. In one sense, the shed is like a border post between the Parramatta and Lane Cove rivers. The shed's entrance is facing away from the main harbour, with a slipway leading from its wooden doors into Lane Cove River. Those doors are open and, inside the shed, Ross Gardner is hunched over a wooden boat, carefully tending to a plank. He is concentrating so hard, initially he doesn't notice a kayaker bobbing outside the front door. And he looks content, with a soft smile across his face.

'For me, this is heaven,' Ross tells me, as he takes a break from the restoration work. 'I don't have to die, I'm already there. Working on the boat gives me such great pleasure.'

The source of his pleasure is also his creation. Ross built the boat, which he named *Ellen Mary*, in honour of his mother. *Ellen Mary* is a 12-foot yawl crafted from Huon pine. Ross took three years to build her, treating it as an after-work project. The creation of *Ellen Mary* was a celebration of traditional skills. He would split the wood, make the planks and shape them, then secure them using copper nails clinched with rooves.

'It used to take me a week to put two planks on,' he grins.

The current restoration of *Ellen Mary* has also seen weeks flow into months, but Ross doesn't mind because when he is in the shed, 'I feel as though I'm out on the boat'.

The shed is also a wonderful ramshackle museum that holds the tools and clues as to where Ross learnt his boatbuilding skills. Crammed into old wooden chests and drawers are old chisels, planes and patterns, each with a story attached, and most handed down from one generation to the next. Ross comes from a family of boatbuilders. On a wall hangs a bronze plaque, which reads, 'E.H. Gardner, Boat Builder'. He was Ross' great uncle.

Ross was born so close to the water, the harbour might just as well have been his cradle. His first years were spent in Balmain, above Johnstons Bay. Ross can still picture the P&O and Union Steamship vessels coming and going. The Gardners ventured onto the harbour, often in boats crafted by their own hands. The first vessel Ross recalls going on was an 18-foot sailing boat his grandfather had built in 1911.

Ross' father was also handy at woodworking, so much so it secured him part-time work at Mort's Dock at Balmain. But he planned for a monumental shift for his family, all the way across the harbour. He bought a plot of land on Onions Point, built the boatshed, with his wife mixing the concrete, and, at the top of the escarpment just outside the shed, a house. In March 1949, the Gardners moved in, and Ross has been there ever since. As Ross declares, he lives 'at the most easterly point of the Western Suburbs'. His favourite room is what he calls 'the wheelhouse'. It used to be a glassed-in veranda but has grown into a walled-in room with a bay window that is filled with views across the harbour.

When Ross was a boy, the big windows reminded him of the wheelhouses of the old *Lady* ferries that graciously glided around the harbour, 'and being a ferry driver was an ambition of mine as a very young bloke'. So, whenever he is in the room, he is realising an ambition.

'It doesn't go anywhere, but a lot goes floating past.'

Ross' parents already knew this part of the harbour when the family moved into the house. Ross gestures for me to look across the wide expanse of the bend in the river to a building on the opposite bank. That's the Greenwich Flying Squadron, he explains, 'and that's where Dad met Mum, at a dance'.

As a boat sails, it is only a few kilometres from Johnstons Bay to Onions Point, but it felt like another world to Ross when he was a boy. There was not as much boating traffic on Lane Cove River, although the ferries ran regularly, and punts would wait for the high tide to transport raw materials to industries upstream. It was quieter over here as well. At night, Ross would sometimes hear the heavy splash of sharks. As a result, he never swam in the river, and he still won't. Ross guides me onto the small deck wrapped around the shed and gestures straight down. Not long ago, he saw a shark, which he thinks was a bronze whaler, lying there in the shallows. He estimates it was 16 feet (about 4.9 metres) long.

Ross then points at a half-cabin launch at a nearby mooring. He helped his father build that boat, named *Bouquet*, in the late 1950s, and the family would head out on her.

But where Ross collected the bulk of his knowledge about building vessels – great and small – can also be seen from his shed. He gestures downriver to a nest of buildings.

'See that grey roof? That's where I worked.'

COCKATOO ISLAND commands a stentorian presence in the middle of the harbour. It sits a few hundred metres off the Woolwich shore. The island's name is embedded in the vernacular and 'Cockatoo' sounds almost playful, but its appearance is far more serious. Whether it is the hard face of sandstone on the eastern side, the austere structures of brick and iron, or that this mass of severity is accentuated because it is surrounded by shimmering, light-polished water, the island looks like a prison. Which it was for many years.

When you arrive by ferry, which regularly stops here, there is a sign attached to a reception building that spells out the dimensions of what is the largest island in Sydney Harbour: 'Length 500m. Width 360m. Area 18 hectares'. But those arbitrary measurements give no clue to the depth and texture of human experience on Cockatoo Island.

It was used as a meeting place for Aboriginal groups, who called it Wareamah. When British settlers turned up, they saw little value in what was a solid lump of sandstone thatched with red gums, in which sat and screeched the cockatoos that the new arrivals named the island after. What's more, the island was apparently snake-infested. What was of little interest to settlers was attractive to Governor George Gipps. The island held the promise of solving two problems: fluctuations in food supply and prices, and housing convicts.

In 1839, Gipps decided to use convict labour to excavate underground grain silos on the higher part of the island. His plan was to store wheat in the good seasons, which would soften price rises in poorer times. The silos hacked out of the rock were shaped like bottles, almost six metres deep, and they could hold up to 140 tonnes of grain. By the end of 1840, about 560 tonnes of wheat were stored in the silos, and the Governor was pleased.

'Being hermetically sealed, grain of any kind may be preserved in them for years,' Gipps wrote.

The British Government was less impressed. It effectively told Gipps to shut the silos and let the market determine grain prices. Still, the colony had a new place to put convicts, which was needed with the closure of Norfolk Island as a penal settlement. The island within an island was well suited to being a prison.

Cockatoo Island earned a reputation for being the dumping ground for some of the toughest and worst-behaved of convicts. The cruellest torment of being locked up here, I imagine as I walk through the prisoners' barracks, was not the cold stone or cramped conditions but viewing the harbour's beautiful northern shoreline through bars. Then again, to a convict, perhaps the opposite shore looked dispiritingly like yet another wall, another obstacle.

Near the barracks was the military guardhouse, which was built in 1841. The ruins are on an exposed patch on the western end of the upper part of the island. It is open to the finest of views and all the moods of Mother Nature. The guardhouse neighboured twelve isolation cells next door, where prisoners would be lowered through a ceiling trap-door. This was a horrible place to do time. Sitting in the darkness, the inmate would have to fight off the rats when his meal was delivered. Even the Hunters Hill developer Jules Joubert, who had acted as a magistrate on the island, referred to the cells as a tomb.

The obsession of many convicts was to escape. Stories of the waters teeming with sharks were not enough to dissuade some. Guards were posted along the shore, and others were in boats rowing around the island, particularly when the harbour was fog-veiled. A few convicts planned to escape by staying on top of the water, as a diary entry by a police sergeant in 1859, indicates: 'mast, paddle and sail discovered . . . an attempted escape'. Others tried their luck in the water. Some didn't get far or were drowned, and a few made it to the mainland shores before being caught. The writer Louis Becke, who as a boy lived at Hunters Hill in the 1860s, recalled how, having heard the tell-tale sounds of a sentry's rifle shot and the clamour of a bell in the night, he went down to the rocks at dawn and saw 'a wretched, exhausted creature clinging with bleeding hands to the oyster-covered rocks beneath our house, too weak to drag himself from his pursuers'. The only known successful escapee was horse thief Frederick Ward. With the help of his wife, who had swum to the island and left tools for him to use to break out, Ward and another prisoner swam towards Birchgrove at night in September 1863. His fellow escapee drowned, but Ward made it. He resumed his career as a criminal, becoming renowned as the 'gentleman' bushranger Captain Thunderbolt, before he was shot by a police officer near the town of Uralla in 1870.

All the prisoners finally escaped the island in 1869, when they were transferred to Darlinghurst Gaol. Two years later, the island was once more a prison. It became an industrial school and reformatory for girls, which was named Biloela, an Aboriginal word meaning 'white cockatoo'. In the same year, *Vernon*, a sailing ship that had been converted into a training vessel for boys, was moored off the north-eastern part of Cockatoo Island. Hundreds of boys lived and learnt trades on the ship, and they grew vegetables on the island.

Inevitably, the residents of Biloela and the company of *Vernon* found each other. The girls' institution moved on in 1887, and the buildings reverted to a prison to relieve overcrowding at Darlinghurst Gaol.

Cockatoo Island closed as a prison in 1908. However, by then, the island had been fulfilling another major role for more than half a century. Indeed, the island had become bifurcated, not in shape but in function. As well as being a prison, it was also the centre of shipbuilding in the colony. The industry was built on a sandstone base and with convicts' sweat, for, like so much development in the colony, before any ship could be docked or built, a lot of rock had to be hacked out.

Construction on a dock began in 1847 on the south-eastern part of the island, with a 91-metre indent cut into the rock. It was designed to be long enough to take a large man-of-war ship. Overseeing the construction was Captain Gother Kerr Mann, a former Royal Engineer. Aside from this gash in the island, Mann is remembered by a headland on the northern shore opposite. It's called Manns Point.

On Cockatoo Island, Mann had to deal with an obstinate convict labour force. As a result, it took about ten years to build the dock, even though the original estimate was less than sixteen months. The dock was named after the 10th Governor of New South Wales, Sir Charles FitzRoy. It finally opened in 1857.

More shipbuilding facilities were grafted onto and carved into the island. In 1870, the government's Harbours and Rivers Department built slipways on the southern shore. Over the next half a century, more than 150 ships, including tugs and barges, were built on this part of the island. These days, next to what's called the Shipwrights' Shed, is one of the old slipways. It is fenced off and its cradle is empty. Where the harbour laps at the slip there is a fringe of rubbish.

In 1880, the New South Wales Government proposed building a second dock on the island, one that was capable of accepting the largest ships in operation. The Sutherland Dock was cut into the south-western part of the island. This time free labour was used. It was completed in 1890 and, at 193 metres long, was the largest dry dock in the world. More than cradle ships, Sutherland Dock was also a training pool for Barney Bede Kieran, a world champion swimmer who worked in the carpenters' shop on the island. Kieran broke a string of swimming records in 1904 and 1905.

The docks were never busier than in wartime. Just before the First World War, the Commonwealth Government took over the island from the New South Wales Government, and it became the first dockyard for the young Royal Australian Navy. Sutherland Dock was extended to accommodate the RAN's battle cruiser, HMAS *Australia*. When war was declared in August 1914, the Australian Naval and Military Expeditionary Force left from Cockatoo Island on board HMAS *Berrima*. The ship had been converted into a military cruiser from a liner in just six days. This was just one of twenty-seven vessels converted to troopships. The island's workforce of more than 4000 maintained, refitted and repaired hundreds of ships during the war.

After the First World War, the island seemed to grow taller, with the construction of the *Titan* floating crane. The massive crane, sitting on a pontoon half a football field long, would be manoeuvred around the harbour by tugs for the next seventy-two years, doing the heavy lifting on some of the city's major projects, including the building of Sydney Harbour Bridge and Gladesville Bridge. As well as being able to stretch its main jib more than 58 metres above the harbour, *Titan* could also be used to reach deep into the water, fossicking sunken tugs and ferries from the floor.

Between the wars, the island was scratching for work. In 1933, as the Depression gnawed deeper into the economy, the Commonwealth Government leased the island to the Cockatoo Docks and Engineering Company. The lease came with a lifeline, as it guaranteed naval ships docking there each year. Still, the company looked for further cost cutting. Some of the gardeners were replaced by sheep, which grazed on the island for many years.

During the Second World War, the island surged back to life, with more than 3000 workers. The island was further reshaped and its sandstone face shaved in places to accommodate new buildings, and additional wharves and another slipway were installed. When the war ended so did the busiest time in the dockyard's history.

The focus for naval vessels moved further east along the harbour. In 1945, a larger dock was opened on the other side of the Harbour Bridge, at Garden Island. At one point after the war, there were plans to join Cockatoo Island to the mainland, as there were concerns about the costs of having a dockyard on an island. After all, everything had to be transported across the water – including the payroll. The risk of that was revealed in April 1945, when almost £12,000 was robbed by machine-gun-wielding robbers at a Drummoyne wharf, as the dockyard payroll was about to be taken by launch to the island. It was one of the biggest payroll robberies since the bushranging days.

Despite the expansion of Garden Island, some work for the navy still flowed further up the harbour. During the 1950s, the RAN destroyers *Voyager* and *Vampire* were built on Cockatoo Island. The *Voyager* was lost, as were the lives of eighty-two of her crew, when she collided with the aircraft carrier HMAS

Melbourne during exercises off Jervis Bay in southern New South Wales on 10 February 1964. She was split in two by the impact and sank. With a badly damaged bow, *Melbourne* limped to Sydney Harbour and into Sutherland Dock for repairs. She would undergo the same operation in the same dock five years later after a collision with an American destroyer during night exercises.

In addition to being a cradle for new ships and extending the lives of vessels, Cockatoo Island was a nursery for skills and ideas. In a cavernous, convict-built sandstone building on the south-eastern side, and from the sum of experience brought onto the island by older workers each shift, apprentices would learn their trade. One of them was Ross Gardner. He left school as a 16-year-old and trained as a fitter and turner on the island that he could see from the family boatshed.

'There were 300 apprentices [on the island] the year I started,' Ross says. His abiding memory of the apprentice training school was that the building measured the seasons by being either boiling hot or freezing cold. He gave little thought to the history in the walls. Instead, he gained a sense of the island's heritage from his co-workers.

'There were people on Cockatoo whose fathers or grand-fathers had been warders in the prison,' Ross says.

'It was a very interesting place to work, because there was a lot of knowledge there.'

Ross worked on harbour ferries, the Mortlake colliers, which often came in for a 'haircut and shave' (painting and anti-fouling), and he helped with the building of the *Empress of Australia* passenger ship, which was the largest vessel of its type constructed in the world at the time. He also worked on naval ships and was on the island both times the damaged *Melbourne* arrived for repairs. He particularly remembers his reaction when the aircraft carrier docked after the *Voyager* disaster.

'Everyone was terribly upset; when the ship came in with bits hanging off the bow, it was very distressing,' he recalls. 'I knew someone on *Voyager*. He survived, but I didn't know if he was alive or dead at that time. It was all very close to home.'

At the end of the 1960s, Ross was moved to the drawing office at the top of the island for three weeks. He stayed there for twenty-seven years. He was involved in purchasing, a role he loved, since he was dealing with every trade on the island. Ross learnt that the building where he was based had been home to an aircraft factory during the late 1920s and early 1930s. The workers had rebuilt Sir Charles Kingsford Smith's *Southern Cross* after it crashed.

At the launch of HMAS *Vampire* on Cockatoo Island in 1956, the Governor-General, Field-Marshall Sir William Slim, told the gathering, 'An island which does not provide itself with ships, and with the means to protect them, gives, as tragic hostages to fortune, its own people'. A quarter of a century on, Cockatoo Island's future as a shipbuilding centre was clouding. The contracts were drying up, the facilities were ageing and in need of an overhaul, and the very element that had made the site attractive in the first place – it was an island – was increasingly seen as a problem. The last navy ship built on the island, HMAS *Success*, was launched in 1984. It was the largest naval ship ever built in Australia. As always, the launch was a celebration, which Ross watched from the roof of the Planning, Estimating and Supply Offices building. At that time the workers didn't know this would be the final naval vessel to be built here.

A major refit program on the navy's Oberon submarines continued, but that was not enough to ensure the dockyard's future. The yard ground to a halt at the end of 1991. Ross' own employment ended early in 1992. He returned as a contractor to help oversee the stripping of the dockyard and the removal of materials off the island. As he describes those six weeks of work, 'it was sort of like getting ready for a funeral'.

Then the final day arrived. Ross vividly remembers the date: 3 January 1993. The island had already gone from being a shipyard to a graveyard. There was next to no one on the island, and the machines were still and silent, the rust and rictus setting in. At the end of the day, with the facility handed back to the Commonwealth, Ross, along with the dockyard's chief executive and the production manager, hopped onto a workboat and left the island.

'And that was it,' Ross shrugs. 'It was the most anti-climactic end to 150 years. We didn't even stop to say good-bye. I now know why we didn't. It was upsetting for everyone.

'To me, we'd lost a huge pool of engineering knowledge. The location was not ideal, but I don't think the decision to close [the dockyard] had anything to do with that. It was political.'

After it had effectively killed off Cockatoo Island as a shipyard in the late 1980s, the Federal Government wanted to sell the island. Developers were keen, but the workers and the broader community pushed back, demanding it be kept in public hands. A hundred workers even staged a fourteen-week sit-in on the island.

The workers lost their place of employment, but the public retained the island. Under the management of the Sydney Harbour Heritage Trust, Cockatoo Island has slipped into a new role in recent years: tourist attraction. Each day, visitors step off ferries and stroll through the old buildings and among the historic machinery. They can even sleep on the island, camping in tents along the northern apron, or staying in historic cottages on its crown. You can also arrive by kayak, sliding into Slipway No. 2, where ships were built for the war effort.

The island has been given World Heritage listing because of its remnants of the convict era, but a reminder of its maritime past bobs in Sutherland Dock and a camber wharf on the southern side. Pleasure boats are berthed where ships were brought to life. Just south of the dock, and lying under the jib of an old crane, more boats are stored in racks on the edge of a wharf.

If the island's name appeals to the birdwatcher in you, then you could be in luck. As long as you love seagulls. At times there are thousands loitering and swirling around parts of the island's sandstone faces. The birds have become a tourist attraction of sorts, particularly around nesting time, when the seagulls do their squawking, screeching, poo squibbing best to deter visitors. Those expecting to find kooky gulls crying, 'Mine! Mine! Mine!', like in *Finding Nemo*, are instead confronted by something closer to the characters out of a certain Hitchcock movie.

Walking on the island, you can see the different layers of human effort. A patina of experience covers the buildings. There is the corrugated iron skin wrapped around some of the build-ings, speaking in a guttural, no-nonsense tone of heavy industry. Inside one of those buildings, the mould loft, are the phantoms of great ships. Its top floor wears the markings of full-scale templates for the components of ships built on the island from the end of the First World War right through to when computers took over.

From the water, the different eras nudge and flow into each other. On a gloomy winter's morning, I paddle into Fitzroy Dock. The stepped stone walls on either side of me are like shackled arms, reminding me of the convicts who built this dock. The walls gradually press closer, following the outline of ships the dock once held, until they touch about 144 metres beyond the entrance. On the right side is a steam-powered crane, which is branded with the name of another harbourside dock, Mort's, and is proudly tattooed, 'Sydney 1891'. Cranes of different ages are dotted along the dock like gibbets, their hooks hanging lifeless on the jibs. On each side are also buildings from various times; a utilitarian brick office on the left, towering corrugated iron workshops and a convict-created sandstone building on the right. Ahead, beyond the dock, is a sandstone cliff, hacked and gouged out of the island's soul. From where I bob deep in the dock, the mix of the penal and the industrial feels Gothic. The air sounds dead, punctuated by the seagulls' shriek and the hiss of the bitter westerly trying to exfoliate the skin of the aged buildings. The cold wind is more effective on my skin. I shiver like crazy, as though a ghost has floated over me. But it's me who is floating over ghosts.

ON COCKATOO Island, where shipbuilding was seen as a symbol of nation building, there is now imagination building.

Since 1998, the island has been a venue for the Biennale of Sydney. The catchphrase for the 20th Biennale, held in 2016, was 'The Future is Already Here – It's Just Not Evenly Distributed'. But for the twenty-one artists exhibiting on Cockatoo Island, 'The Future is Already Here' was staged amid the hulking pieces of the past. Among heavy industrial machinery imported from Glasgow and Bath and Leeds were the creations of artists from South Korea to France, from Germany to China.

In the shed where Ross Gardner, and thousands of other apprentices trained, there was an installation titled, 'Nowhere and Everywhere at the Same Time, no. 2'. Hundreds of plumb bobs, similar to those used for setting a vertical reference in boatbuilding, were hanging from strings and swinging like pendulums. You were encouraged to negotiate your way through the ranks of plumb bobs, assuming you weren't first lost and tangled in the artist's statement. I still don't know what 'unconscious choreographic competence' is, but I think it means 'don't bump into the plumb bobs'.

The convict precinct on the upper island also provided exhibition spaces. The hard stone walls that once spoke of confinement were used as screens to project images of people talking freely on mobile phones in open fields.

The sum of roles the island has played through its life means it has the kind of character that attracts not just visual artists but movie-makers. It has been used as a set for Hollywood movies, and it has hosted a film festival. And the island's buildings have provided stages for a range of live performances, including what is possibly the most theatrical and beautiful statement of 'I love you' ever created in this town.

When the acclaimed sculptor and performer Ken Unsworth was seeking a space large enough to stage a tribute to his late wife Elisabeth in 2009, the answer was before his eyes. From their home on the harbour's edge at Birchgrove, Ken could see Cockatoo Island. But it was only when a friend suggested the island as the venue for what he was quietly planning did Ken visit.

'Once I went to the island, things fell into place,' Ken smiles, as we talk in his home. His lithe frame is clothed in black. Behind him, trickling in between the trees and through his lounge room windows, is the harbour, which on this day has the appearance of tin. It is as though the water has been pressed in one of the old machines on the island and then rolled out in a sheet to Ken's windows.

To stage his production, *A Ringing Glass (Rilke)*, Ken hired the old turbine hall and set about turning the cavernous and industrial into something intimate and magical. On one winter's night, about 170 invited guests in dinner suits and ball gowns were transported across the harbour, and deep into Ken's imagination.

As they approached the island, guests could see the water tower shimmering in an ethereal blue light. After the formally attired crowd disembarked, they walked through an old tunnel, accompanied in the low light by a soundtrack of noises before they emerged into another fantastic world. They were guided through a marquee then through four galleries Ken and his team had created in the turbine hall. Inside the galleries were installations, from a large skeleton, which moved with the slow deliberation of a Tai Chi master, to suspended toy pianos and the pieces of a dismembered piano, casting long shadows, and with two automated sticks tapping out a mournful beat on the lid. The art was honouring a life; Elisabeth had been a superb pianist.

Yet the most extraordinary experiences occurred in a ball-room plotted out among the machinery. Recordings of Elisabeth playing reverberated through the hall, as a piano descended from the ceiling. The audience became performers, dancing to an orchestra. They were choreographed through a dream. Then, for these Sydney Cinderellas, the Cockatoo Island dream was over. The performance ended and they were ferried off the island. But for those who were there, it is still talked about as an amazing night.

While he staged another production and installation on Cockatoo Island a couple of years later, Ken says he couldn't afford to do it again. The barging costs alone have risen dramatically, he explains.

For all the expense and effort, what remains of Ken's Cockatoo Island creations are little more than memories. Still, Ken feels he added another layer to the archaeology of human experience on the island. What's more, there's an overlap of experiences between the industrial workers of the past and the creative conjurers of more recent times. For a few years until the mid-1920s, the Cockatoo Island workers had a choir, which practised on the ferry as it transported them to Circular Quay.

'Well, they would have approved, wouldn't they?' Ken says, smiling.

Ken has not returned to the island since he dismantled his last project there. Although he can look at the island from his home whenever he wants. But when he does, he doesn't think about what he created there, and how he let imaginations soar.

'I never look back,' he says shaking his head, swishing his gleaming white hair. 'I'm not one of those people who look back.

'The island can't remain a mute museum of the past, it has to change to mean something to present society.

'I just see it as an island that has not really found its future, and in many ways that's sad.'

*

THE PAST repels Ross Gardner from returning to Cockatoo Island.

From his boatshed on Onions Point, he could easily sail or row his own beautiful creation, *Ellen Mary*, across to the island. But he has no desire to. Ross has visited Cockatoo Island only a couple of times since he left on that summer's day in 1993 but he was uncomfortable, because 'there are too many ghosts'.

'I think it's gone,' Ross replies when asked is there any hope of reviving industry on Cockatoo Island. 'But there's to be some consideration for somewhere to repair things or build things, and, with a boat, that's got to be near the water.

'If industries such as Cockatoo Island are continually shut down, you'll end up with a desert, because there'll be no reason for people to be here. If there aren't jobs, who is going to pay the rent for all those apartments?'

Yet to Ross Gardner what cut deepest with the dockyard closure was not the loss of jobs or even an industry.

'It wasn't the physical rock on which it was built, it was the people,' he says. 'It was a community, and that's what was destroyed when they closed Cockatoo Island.'

But not all has been lost. The skills Ross learnt on the island are being carefully, even lovingly, applied to *Ellen Mary*. While his past, and an entire tradition, can be seen through his shed window, Ross concentrates on what is before him, in restoring his wooden boat and sliding her back out the front doors and down into the river, where both she and he belong.

'We don't live on the harbour here; we live on Lane Cove River,' Ross says as he looks at the water, the skin around his eyes crinkling, perhaps from the glare, more likely with delight.

'We're sort of river rats, I suppose.'

4

LANE COVE RIVER

IN OUR search for something that symbolises the flow of time from the cradle to the grave and beyond, we often rely on rivers. At least, a torrent of poets and philosophers, musicians and writers through the ages has relied on the idea that a river is like life itself. Which makes sense. After all, a river has a beginning and an end, it twists and turns, it occasionally runs dry or breaks its banks, and its waters can carry hopes or drown them. On a river, as in life, you can float or go under. You can push against the current and feel your defiance stretching and grinding the moments into a seeming eternity, or you can go with the flow and embrace time.

Yet for a symbol of life and time, rivers can give the impression of being timeless. Their waters carry history and the future, and their course changes through circumstance. And yet, when you're on a river, it can seem unchanged, as its waters forever stream through the present. A river seems to transcend time; it is simply there.

But that's not how I feel when I paddle on Lane Cove River.

As soon as I enter the river's mouth, the past flows back. I think of each time I've kayaked up here with my friends, Bruce Beresford and George Ellis. Actually, I don't even need the river as a symbol to remind me time is whooshing by. I have George and Bruce to do that for me, mercilessly.

The three of us have been kayaking different parts of the harbour for years. We have watched each other age, if not mature, on the water. We help each other age. No matter what George and Bruce say, I've aged the least.

We call ourselves the Gentleman Kayakers' Club. It is a very exclusive, if woefully misnamed, club. Although we *are* kayakers. We describe ourselves as a 'B-grade conductor', 'an old film director', and 'a burnt-out hack'. Of course, we don't refer to each other in these terms. We say far worse.

Bruce began paddling in the mid-1990s.

'Kayaking's one of those things that help you,' he muses. 'You have various problems on films, trying to work out how to solve them, and you go out paddling, you relax, and the problems seem to solve themselves. You come back and go, "I know what I can do". It's exhilarating out there.'

More than provide a slate on which Bruce can solve problems, the harbour has starred in his latest movie. Sydney Harbour helps set the scenes, and the golden light mood, for his comedy-drama, *Ladies in Black*.

George has been paddling since early 2009. A wonderful conductor and arranger who possesses the hair and on-stage energy of a rock star, George had been cast by Bruce to be in his film *Mao's Last Dancer*. He was to play a conductor. George reckons it wasn't his conducting skills but his late 1970s–early

1980s 'outdated hair', which fitted the setting of the film, that gained him the role. But, more importantly, his hair was an entrée to the glamorous world of kayaking and its beautiful people. In other words, Bruce and I.

Water, with all its cadences and rhythms, has the sound and feel of music. In his novel *The Refuge*, Kenneth Mackenzie wrote how the harbour on an early winter's morning conjured up the opening of Brahms' Fourth Symphony in E minor.

'It is a beautiful opening line in that symphony,' agrees George. I ask him what music he hears while paddling.

'Mine is much less romantic,' he replies. 'What I hear is my huffing and puffing, trying to keep up with you blokes. That's about as rhythmic as it gets for me.'

One of Bruce's acclaimed movies is *Black Robe*. It is a beautiful, at times harrowing, film set in North America in the 1630s. A Catholic missionary and his young offsider undertake a perilous journey by canoe deep into the wilderness. As one of the characters mutters before the party sets off, '1500 miles by canoe in that country, at the beginning of the winter, death is almost certain'.

It is as though Bruce were directing a film based on our harbour kayaking adventures. Only when we paddle, we almost die laughing.

The beauty of kayaking alone is you revel in sounds other than your own voice, and you learn to observe more carefully. The beauty of kayaking with George and Bruce is revelling in the sounds of their voices and their wry observations of us, the world and life. We talk – and laugh – so much, we often forget to dunk our blades in the water, until we're going at a pace that makes the stately car in Bruce's *Driving Miss Daisy* seem like an F1 racer.

But the main purpose of our paddling is not about getting somewhere. It's just to be out there. The harbour is our men's shed. In the harbour, there are secrets; on the harbour, we share ours. Indeed, in the Gentleman Kayakers' Club, we don't drown our sorrows with a bottle. Instead, we paddle our sorrows out into the harbour or up the river, slice their throat with some sharp comments, tie some heavy sarcasm around their feet, and we laugh in their face as we toss them overboard and watch them drown. As a result, by the time I return to shore after paddling with Bruce and George, my kayak feels lighter, and I feel more buoyant.

So whenever I kayak into Lane Cove River – actually, around most parts of the harbour west of the Bridge – I think of my gentleman kayaking mates and smile at the knowledge of all the drowned sorrows lying beneath my hull.

We could choose deeper water than Lane Cove River to be rid of our worries. The water beneath our kayaks had been plumbed and measured soon after the First Fleet arrived. As part of his survey of Port Jackson in 1788, John Hunter and his party had rowed into the river. The plan indicates Hunter explored the lower reaches of the river and noted the depths were mostly less than 4 metres. Among Hunter's party was Lieutenant William Bradley. He was the first to refer to 'Lane Cove', but no one is exactly sure why the river was named that. Bradley and his party may have been officially surveying the river, but he saw this waterway was already well used. Ahead of him, Aboriginal people in canoes were paddling away.

The peninsula that holds Hunters Hill and Woolwich is not just defined by two rivers; it seems to possess two faces and characters. It is like Sydney Harbour's Janus. That sense of difference, of transiting from the company of one character to another, greets me whenever I paddle out of one river into the other. No sooner am I in Lane Cove River than I'm struck by what I see or hear very little of: boating traffic. On the other side of the peninsula, vessels are constantly trundling and tearing past; on this side, the occasional pleasure craft putters by.

The shoreline looks different as well. This seems like the gentler side of the peninsula, and the more genteel. There are fewer new mansions on the water's edge; instead, many of the homes keep their distance up the hill. The historic houses of sandstone and brick are swaddled in trees and landscaped gardens, while on the riverfront are tennis courts and boatsheds. These homes don't scream, 'Hey, I'm rich!' Rather, they murmur in mellifluous tones, 'Well, yes, we're comfortable'.

The more meditative mood along the Lane Cove River side is underlined by one building in particular that I notice while kayaking towards Newcombe Point. High on the hill is a sandstone church, with large stained-glass windows facing the river. It is a Catholic church, St Peter Chanel, and it was built in the late 19th century. Like the harbour itself, the church has a link with the Pacific Ocean. It was named in honour of Peter Chanel, a French missionary who was killed on the island of Futuna, near New Caledonia, in 1841.

From the water, the church has a quiet dignity; up close, St Peter Chanel maintains that air. In the grounds is a sundial, and on its face is inscribed the words, 'Some Tell of Storms and Showers/I Tell of Sunny Hours'. On this day, a shadow creeps across the dial. The sun is shining, and the air is still. Although it could well be blowy on the peninsula's other face.

As I consider the peninsula's split personality, I recall my conversation with Graham Percival, from the Hunters Hill

Historical Society. Before he moved further up the peninsula, Graham had Lane Cove River at the bottom of his property. He liked the peninsula's northern face because it wasn't whipped by the southerlies that would skip across the water and harass the homes on the other side.

'But I know people on the Parramatta River side who say they wouldn't live anywhere else because they'd miss all the activity on the water,' Graham mused. 'There's always something happening on that side.'

On this side as well, there's always something happening in small, subtle ways. I pull ashore at a relatively untamed strip known as the Ferdinand Street Reserve. As I look through the screen of trees and over the muddy banks, a solitary tinny grumbles by. It all feels very distant from one of the world's greatest harbours, rather than being an arm of it.

A stairway, hewn from stone, climbs the hill beside a rambling Port Jackson fig. As I climb the steps, there's a distinct change in atmosphere, from the Australian shoreline to something remotely European, with the slush of autumn leaves underfoot and stately sandstone homes on either side of the path. The historic houses on top of the hill are identified not so much by number but name, such as Cleverton (1876) and Maruna (1856), whose original owner gave his address as 'Lane Cove River'.

Yet along this reach, the house that is synonymous with the river, because it is virtually in it, is Figtree House. The building sits under Fig Tree Bridge, which carries thousands of vehicles across the river every hour, and yet somehow the house seems removed from all that rushing and roaring above its head. From the road and on the water, Figtree House, especially its wooden tower, grabs attention. While it looks like it is from another place, perhaps New England, Figtree House is from another time. Its origins stretch to 1836, when the Sydney business-woman Mary Reibey established her farm on this land. She built two stone cottages and named the property Figtree Farm, after a Port Jackson fig on her land. The massive tree not only survived through the years, it stamped its presence on the main house as it took shape. It grew through the bathroom, and the residents would hang their towels on nails in the trunk.

In 1838, Reibey leased the property to Joseph Fowles, who was an artist and later author of *Sydney in 1848*. Fowles intended to farm the land and ship the produce downriver to Sydney. As Reibey had already discovered, the soil did not easily yield a living. But the river always offered a feed. As Fowles recorded in his journal, 'we have plenty of sea fish and the rocks are covered with oysters'.

Didier Joubert, one of the developers of Hunters Hill, bought the property in 1847, and he set about converting the two stone cottages into the heart of one house. His son, Numa, added the tower in about 1890, and it was built by a shipwright. Didier had constructed another home on the property, St Malo, which was a single-storey sandstone home with a deep veranda. The home wore the trimmings of affluence, with marble mantel-pieces imported from Italy.

Didier and his brother, Jules, began a ferry service on Lane Cove River in the 1860s. The first of the Joubert fleet was a paddle-wheeler, *Kirribilli*, which would churn its way along the river, stopping at wharves owned or leased by the Jouberts. Their fleet expanded to about a dozen vessels, and a few of the ferries were built on the property at Figtree Farm. The ferries not only transported residents to and from the city but also brought day-trippers upriver. The Jouberts developed a recreation area near the wharves at Figtree in the 1880s. Hundreds of passengers dressed in their finery would pour off the ferries to visit The Avenue Pleasure Grounds, with its luncheon pavilion and dance hall. In the 1930s, the old dance hall was converted into a film studio, then it was a storage depot for the Royal Australian Air Force during the Second World War, and when Hunters Hill High School opened on the site in 1958, it became a gymnasium.

Although the Jouberts made money from ferries, they pushed for bridges to be built, to further develop the peninsula. In 1885, the first Fig Tree Bridge was completed. Yet as the Jouberts would have known, progress comes at a price. Almost eighty years after the first Fig Tree Bridge opened, it was replaced with a concrete girder structure. The approaches to the new bridge cut through what had been Joubert land, and some of the most important houses they had built were demolished, including St Malo in 1961. The loss of the developer's home ironically galvanised the push for the preservation of Hunters Hill's most significant buildings.

From the river, Figtree House looks like a wonderful conglomeration of structures that rambles through different architectural styles and eras. And there is still a fig tree between the house and the bridge, its presence helping ensure Hunters Hill's most historic home stays true to its name.

Under the bridge, a sandbank emerges from the river at low tide. Bruce, George and I have run our craft up onto the island and claimed it for the Gentleman Kayakers. Actually, we've had no such thoughts of triumphalism when we've landed on the sandbank. We've just been grateful to find somewhere to stop and stretch our legs. Which is why we've been disappointed when the tide has been high or, worse, against us. With our cherished territory, The Island of Caught Breath, submerged, we've been reduced to being three cranky old buggers pushing against nature itself.

AS SOON as I kayak under Fig Tree Bridge, I notice a change of environment. Along the left bank, in the outside bend of the river, the houses have retreated and the bank is lined with mangroves. Paddle in close, and the river's edge looks primordial. It seems as though time itself is trapped in there, stuck in the mud and dank air. A large pile of oyster shells rests on the mud, like a cairn marking where the original Australians sourced food for thousands of years, and where some of the early colonists eked out a living. The Aboriginal people sought the oysters; the new arrivals wanted the shells.

Alexander Harris, who wrote a series of books based on his experiences as an 'emigrant mechanic' in New South Wales in the early 19th century, described how men journeyed up the river to collect oyster shells. They would shovel the shells into their boats then transport them downriver, where they would be sold and burnt to create lime, for building houses. While the money was good, Harris said this was filthy, hard and perilous work, especially if a boat 'loaded down to the very gunnel' was hit by bad weather. It could easily sink on the journey across the harbour, taking a living and lives to the bottom. Harris wrote about his brief time as a shell-getter, and a tense episode when his heavily laden boat was caught in a storm.

'Before we got through the rough water we could hardly work the long oars to make any headway, so deep did we lie between the short, broken swells,' Harris recounted.

The water close to the muddy banks is murkier and more furtive. When the water takes on this character, it is easier to imagine there are sharks about. Old newspaper reports don't help quell that uneasy feeling. Along this reach there was a string of attacks in the early 1900s. One report breathlessly recounted how a young man was bitten while collecting oysters in shallow water. One of the victim's companions grabbed him by the arm, 'and for a moment it was a tug-of-war as to whether he or the shark should have him'. The man was saved but not before the shark tore a chunk of flesh from his thigh. Others weren't so fortunate. In one fatal attack in 1912, a man was taken as his girlfriend watched from the bank. Only moments before he was attacked, the 21-year-old victim had reassured another swimmer there was no need to fear sharks in this part of the river, because 'it's too far up'. Two bystand-ers risked their own lives to bring the man ashore, but he died from a 'frightful' wound, which 'bore eloquent testimony to the power of the monster's jaws', as the *Sydney Morning Herald* reported.

Sharks are still in Lane Cove River. They are all over the harbour. Scientists have shown that through programs following tagged bull sharks. These creatures have a reputation for being vicious, and they tolerate lower salinity. Tracking of their move-ments has also indicated bull sharks tend to be in the harbour during the warmer months, when they are breeding.

Professor Bill Gladstone, a marine biologist and Head of the School of Life Sciences at the University of Technology Sydney, points out that improving our understanding of sharks is a way of managing what is already a minimal risk: being attacked.

'If we know there are certain times of the year when sharks are around, and also under what conditions you're more likely to be attacked or encounter a shark, then you can manage a risk with that understanding.

'The risk [of attack] is very, very small, but still it's a primal fear that people have and respond to in very emotional ways. And sometimes it's difficult, or impossible, to rationalise a fear with what the reality of the risk is.'

What's more, we need sharks in the harbour for ecological balance.

'If we take sharks out of there, the ecosystem would look very different,' Bill argues. 'You could predict that if you took out a big predator, that would then influence the numbers of other animals that are normally preyed on. If the next level down is a slightly smaller predator and it goes up because there's no bull sharks, and its food is bream and whiting, then the numbers of those species would go down.'

Along this reach, the river is still a couple of hundred metres wide, but the curtain of mangroves, along with the ceaseless soundtrack of cicadas, gives the feeling the waterway is closing in. Slithering out of the mangroves along this reach are spindly watercourses. Waterbirds are pecking and drilling into the mud and sandbanks close to shore. Perhaps I'm too preoccupied watching the birds because I run onto a sandbank. It is only then I notice the navigational markers for boaties to remain in the channel and avoid the shallows. I take heart that I'm not the first to miss the signs or misread the river. Picnic parties used to transfer at Figtree from ferries into smaller boats. Even so, the little craft would frequently be grounded, and the operators would have to pole the vessels off the mud, or if they were really stuck, lead the passengers in 'sing-songs' until the tide rose. I don't have to sing, just grunt and curse, as I heave and push the kayak out of the clutches of the sandbank.

The buoys and signs along the river, with one advising what I had already learnt – 'Navigation Past This Point May Be Hazardous' – indicates pleasure boats still make their way upstream. The river traffic used to be heavier. One of the newspaper stories on the fatal shark attack in 1912 reported a witness saying the water was muddy because it was stirred up by launches 'that were going up and down all the time'. It wasn't just recreation that brought boats up and down the river. So did industry.

These days, you can see warehouses and offices set back from the river, raising their heads above the riparian zone and clumped together in business parks, but few occupy the banks. Just downstream from Epping Road Bridge is an industrial plant, and while it is tucked away on the inside bend, it is conspicuous because it is so close to the water. I paddle right past it, while listening to the groaning of machines and sniffing at the suddenly malty air. The scent is a reminder that around here there has been a mill since 1894, when the Chicago Cornflour and Starch Mills opened. The river brought materials and people to the mill, transported in small lighters.

The mill was far from a lone presence. Along these banks and beside the creeks feeding into the river there has been a string of industries, and not all of them welcomed. In the 1880s, when a wool-washing business was proposed on Wilson's Creek, just downstream from the modern-day Epping Road Bridge, there was uproar. Local councillors and residents protested, arguing the waste water would destroy the oysters and poison the fish, bathers would contract diseases, and, one declared, it 'would be the means of carrying death and destruction along the banks of the river'. Another conceded while this sort of business was necessary, Lane Cove was not the place for it: 'Lane Cove was a favourite pleasure ground for boating parties, and the establishment of a factory such as this would go very far to destroy it for recreation purposes.'

Industry won out; the wool wash went ahead. About twenty-five years later, when a paper mill was established in the same area, it received a warmer welcome, at least in the press. The Cumberland Paper Board mill, the *Sun* newspaper declared, would 'materially improve the Lane Cove River, and add another beauty spot to that already charming waterway'. In particular, the building of a dam across Wilson's Creek to supply water to the mill was applauded as a wonderful improvement, 'converting what was an unattractive rocky creek into a pretty and expansive sheet of water'.

As more industries were built upstream, those further down the river were not impressed with the outfall. One resident, who had lived by the river for many years, complained in 1920 about the shocking state of the water, which was often soapy, and that 'dirty masses of black slime are now to be seen floating about'. The resident lamented that the authorities had been unsuccessful in getting the river cleaned up, and 'it would be impossible to prevent the factories from emptying their waste'.

It was a complaint that flowed through much of the 20th century. The river and its tributaries were badly degraded, and there were reports of fish kills. In recent years, the river has been cleaned up, through tighter laws and the efforts of environmental groups and volunteers. And there are fish to be caught. That's evident not just from the occasional angler on the banks. I paddle past a bird wrestling with a mullet in its beak. For human fishers, there are restrictions, including catch-and-release rules, for sections of Lane Cove River. But this bird pays no heed to rules. While the mullet puts up a fight, flapping and floundering, the bird ensures this is not the one that got away.

BEYOND EPPING Road Bridge, the river narrows and the world hushes. The sound of vehicles subsides and is replaced by the call of bellbirds. I can finally hear the river murmuring in its soft voice. The water's complexion also changes. It is less flushed by sunlight and takes on colours seen along the banks; olive and khaki, and browns. There has been a change along the banks as well. The mangroves have been largely left on the other side of the bridge, and now the bush pushes between sandstone boulders to the water's edge. The entanglement of tall trees and thick undergrowth is what enticed some of the colonists up the river in the first place.

Convict gangs were sent in boats to cut grass for hay to feed livestock, and the timber was keenly sought. Teams worked their way along the river and up the gullies and valleys, felling the ancient blue gums, stringybark, turpentine and blackbutt trees. During Lachlan Macquarie's time as Governor from 1810 to 1821, his vision for more impressive buildings resulted in the axes being swung with greater conviction. While the trees were disappearing from the landscape, they made their way onto the map; the waterways were named in recognition of what was once there, with titles such as Blue Gum Creek.

If the trunks of those trees were tough, those hacking into them could be even tougher. Many went into the bush to not just exploit it, but to escape what or who they once were. Alexander Harris, who wrote of his experiences in the book, *Settlers and Convicts; or Recollections of Sixteen Years' Labour in the Australian Backwoods*, went up the river and into the bush in the 1820s. He quickly became aware that 'the whole bush in this part of the country was then thronged, as indeed it was almost all round Sydney, with men who get their living by various kinds of bush work'. To get the timber to town, Harris explained, they relied on the river. The author himself travelled in one of the 'snug little 2½ or 3 ton boats that the Lane Cove settlers manage to stow with top-heavy loads of wood, and yet bring safely down the stream to Sydney'. The craft had a sail, but sometimes the boatmen used blankets, and Harris saw one even using his jacket to try to scoop up more wind.

Other boatmen relied on their own muscles rather than the fickleness of the wind. In another book, Harris recounted meeting a nuggety bushman who pulled 'long heavy oars with three tons of wood in the boat' from his camp at the head of the river to Market Wharf in Darling Harbour, 'a journey of eleven or twelve miles'. On top of that, he chopped, loaded and unloaded the wood.

Apparently some didn't ply the river in such a strenuous way. A journalist in the early 1900s wrote about a fleet of 'Lane Cove Varnishers', which, despite their name, were not varnished but were 'commodious craft'.

'It was no unusual thing for the "skipper" to be accompanied on his journeys up and down the stream by the members of his family, who occupied quarters aboard, much in the same way as the Thames barges provide for a home afloat,' the journalist wrote. At the time of the article being written, the Varnishers had long disappeared off the river. As the land was cleared, the river silted up and the boats could no longer navigate their way as easily to the timber camps and sawpits.

In those camps, life was far from commodious. Alexander Harris noted there were few women in the world among the trees. He visited a homestead serving as a de facto public house. One of the patrons was an old boatman who 'had never slept in anything other than his day clothes for years', and often bedded down under the overhanging rocks along the river.

Those working in the bush may have helped build Sydney into a more substantial town, but they had a poor reputation among those enjoying the finer life downriver. Before the developer Jules Joubert had even arrived at his future home in Hunters Hill, he had heard about the area's dubious characters, such as old convicts and runaway sailors, who made a living by stealing timber and transporting it by boat to Sydney. After being confined in prison or in the bowels of a ship, life by a river, and on it, may well have felt like freedom. After all, in the words of a famous river adventurer, Huckleberry Finn, 'other places do seem so cramped up and smothery'.

Just as Huck Finn revels in 'the lonesomeness of the river', I always appreciate being alone on this reach. Even when I've been paddling here with my fellow Gentleman Kayakers, I let them plough ahead, so that I can listen to the river and let my eyes wander along the banks. At the end of one stretch, a sand-stone escarpment scooped out by floods and time gathers up the water's whisper and amplifies it, so that by the time it ripples back to me, the river sounds like it is chuckling. I smell the scent of the bush sprinkled over the water and marvel at how nature has regenerated through here. It hides the scars of all those years of timber-getting. There is the occasional reminder that humans have had their way in here. A solitary palm tree pokes its head above the canopy of eucalypts. The bush also largely disguises the fact that just beyond its fringe there are vast tracts of suburbia, which, with a dash of indifference mixed with run-off down the drains and gutters, can easily flush modern-day environmental threats down to the water. Yet the further I paddle along this reach, and the more the bush presses in on the banks and the river narrows, the further away in distance and time the city and suburbs feel. That's a gift of a river. Its waters can carry you to where you least expect.

Yet this reach of the river also holds a mystery. Along the right bank downstream from Fullers Bridge, two bodies were discovered on New Year's Day, 1963. Only hours earlier, Dr Gilbert Bogle and Margaret Chandler had been at a party at nearby Chatswood. Margaret had arrived with her husband, but when he headed off to another party and Dr Bogle had offered to drive her home, the pair ended up together by Lane Cove River at a place renowned as a lovers' lane. Sometime in the early hours of the brand new year, they had died. Their bodies were found in the morning by a couple of boys.

The deaths had a city talking and speculating. The theories about what or who killed them ranged from murder by a jealous lover to an accidental overdose of LSD, and even assassination, because Bogle, as a scientist, had been working on secret projects tied in with the Cold War. When the massive police investigation and the coroner couldn't provide a definitive answer, the theorising about the pair's deaths continued through the years.

One hypothesis was the river had killed Bogle and Chandler. A 2006 documentary explored the possibility that the pair had died from accidental poisoning due to hydrogen sulphide gas. The residents had been complaining for years about an odour like rotten eggs rising from the river. In the 1940s, the government commissioned a major study, and the tests discovered that the muddy bottom was saturated with the gas, believed to have largely come from a factory that had pumped waste into the river. The worst affected section was where Bogle and Chandler had been found. The speculation was the couple had been lying in a hollow beside the water, and that a lethal amount of the gas, which had erupted from the river, had accumulated in that area. Without knowing it, they breathed in the hydrogen sulphide, and their systems shut down.

After more than half a century, so many questions about what happened to Bogle and Chandler still linger. Time, and perhaps the river, has kept the secret. As I sit in the kayak, near where the mystery began, the river looks serene, even innocent. And yet the knowledge that two people died on the bank sullies the atmosphere.

THE CONTEMPORARY world dashes out of the bush and across the river at Fullers Bridge. The vehicles are relying on a crossing that has been here in one form or another since 1918. Locals had been pushing for a bridge for many years before then, so they could be better connected with the rest of the world. But when the bridge was finally constructed, it was so people could also be better connected to the after-world. They could reach the Field of Mars with greater ease. The Field of Mars sounds like it has sprouted from ancient mythology, but it was the name given by Governor Phillip to an area on the western side of the river, where land was granted to a couple of marines who had served in the colony. A century on, the ranks of the dead were assembling in the area, with the opening of the Field of Mars Cemetery. The bridge was initially intended to enable trams to cross the river to take mourners to the cemetery.

The bridge's name also connects to the area's past. The Fullers were one of the pioneering families who established orchards near the river, and they would transport their fruit in boats to the Sydney markets. The original farmer in this part of the valley, William Henry, even planted a vineyard in the early 1800s. If only Henry's vines had survived to provide something medicinal to those who have paddled as far as they can up the river.

A few hundred metres beyond Fullers Bridge, a weir straddles the river. Of course, it would be possible to porter a kayak around the weir and keep paddling deeper into the bush, which is part of Lane Cove National Park. The spillway looks benign and the incline gentle enough to carry a kayak up. But the fine algal coating ensures the slipway is true to its name, and so I slide without a shred of dignity into the water.

Long before the weir was built in the 1930s, residents had been pushing for this sort of infrastructure along the river, not to ward off kayakers but to shore up the local economy. As early as 1900, the New South Wales Government had considered a weir or lock near Fig Tree Bridge, so that the river was navigable at all times for its 15 kilometres upstream. The pleas kept coming, with a letter writer to the *Sydney Morning Herald* calling for the locking of the river, 'in the interest of the orchardists and settlers, to enable them to start irrigation and thereby earn a living. The river flats would produce any fruit or vegetables with the assistance of water.'

The orchards and market gardens withered and were turned into parks, residential plots, and playgrounds. In the early 1900s, a little downstream from here, the Fairyland Pleasure Grounds flourished where vegetables once had. For a couple of generations, Fairyland was an enormously popular destination. Old photos show a flotilla of small ferries and launches lined up across the river. Such was the attraction of a river journey to the pleasure grounds that it wound its way into Christina Stead's novel set in the 1920s, *Seven Poor Men of Sydney*. The characters 'made tea and ate fish just caught in the river', then 'going back in the launch they sang sentimental songs'. The pleasure grounds exist now only on paper and in memories; the site is part of Lane Cove National Park.

Sydneysiders still head up the river in pursuit of relaxation. The national park, which was opened in 1938 in response to community demands for some bushland to be retained along the river, is an escape from urban existence, if not from other people. While I gingerly crab my way up the slipway with the kayak, on the other side of the weir families in hired paddleboats gently churn the water. Cyclists plough across the top of the weir, their wheels tossing out fans of water, and walkers head for tracks threaded through the national park, or for the picnic area by the river. We're all interacting with the river in myriad ways, but no one is actually in it. A sign just beside the weir cautions against swimming in Lane Cove River, due to the potential of submerged logs and pollution, especially after heavy rain. The setting may look idyllic, but even in this national park, there can be no real escape from the city and all the pressures and problems that we who live in it bring upon ourselves and the environment.

Yet a couple of hundred volunteers and a group called the Friends of Lane Cove National Park help to reverse the damage of the past and present. Margaret Reidy is both a Friend and active supporter of the river and the national park.

'When I retired, I was looking for something significant to do,' explains Margaret. 'And I'm a bushwalker, a birdwatcher.'

Margaret found what she was looking for in the park. Since 1992, she has been a volunteer worker, helping improve the bushland, and the river and creeks that meander through the national park. In that time, Margaret has seen, and been part of, some 'noticeably huge improvements' to the environment. Sites along the river have been cleaned up, with weeds removed and native vegetation planted. What happens along the banks has an impact on life in the water. The native bass living in the upper reaches, for example, have a better habitat and a greater chance to breed.

Yet while Margaret and her fellow volunteers work along the river, new challenges are frequently washed down. The river is integral to the beauty and health of Lane Cove National Park, but it is also the carrier of outside threats to that very integrity.

'What happens above and comes down, the health of the river will always be dictated by that. Urban run-off is always our problem,' Margaret says. She is confident that more Sydneysiders are becoming aware of the impact their actions may have downstream.

'The significance of having a national park so close to Sydney is enormous,' Margaret muses.

'We have to fight to maintain it.'

*

IT MAY be the same stretch of water, but a river can markedly change in look and feel, depending on whether you're paddling upstream or down. And what felt easy on the way up can be painful on the paddle down. Kayaking out as the tide is coming in, Lane Cove River feels loath to let me go. The narrowness of the river heightens that impression. Yet gradually the banks loosen their embrace, the river broadens, and, back at Fig Tree Bridge, its course turns and unravels towards the east, towards the sea. Downstream from the bridge, the land along the northern bank keeps grasping at the river; locals refer to the handful of peninsulas along this reach as the five fingers of Lane Cove.

Between the fingers of Linley Point and Riverview is Burns Bay. Where factories and tanneries presided there are now houses and blocks of apartments jostling for a water view. The water looks turbid, probably due to run-off down a creek that has been effectively transformed into a stormwater drain, with concrete walls and a small weir. However, there are fish in the bay. A mullet leaps beside the kayak, almost landing in the cockpit with me.

The bay's eastern shore is largely untamed, and its chipped and flaky sandstone face looks ready to stare down any developer. Close to the waterline around the point are a couple of caves, which would make ideal hiding holes for those who have occupied the top of this landform since 1880. For up there is the Catholic school for boys, St Ignatius' College, better known as Riverview.

'You can see why it was out of bounds to the boys. The things you could get up to down here,' says David Mort, grinning. Despite that mischievous look, David is no schoolboy; he's an old boy.

David attended the school from 1962 to 1968. The river would carry him to Riverview. He lived a few hundred metres across the water at Hunters Hill. As we stand on the northern bank, David guides me through his school days. He points out a historic mansion, called 'The Haven', one of the grand residences of Hunters Hill. It was built in the 1850s and through the years was home to a couple of the suburb's mayors. The grounds of 'The Haven' stretched down to the river. No, he didn't live in 'The Haven', David adds, but behind it. He was allowed to keep his dinghy beside the stone boathouse at the bottom of the estate's garden, so that he could row to school.

'It'd take only five minutes – as long as the wind wasn't against me. And if it was raining, well, I just got wet.'

Occasionally, when the tide was very low, David would have to drag his dinghy over mudflats in the middle of the river.

'Hard to believe you had to drag your boat over part of what is the harbour, isn't it?'

Some students still arrive by water, with a daily ferry service to and from the city, and a few boys even travel across the river in their tinnies. But these days, the obvious point of entry to the college is by road, and the drive into the grounds takes you past sporting fields and impressive buildings. But the river remains the more interesting, if more demanding, approach to Riverview.

From the water's edge, it is a chest-heaving climb to the college, past a sleek modern building and up a stairway cut through rocks and picking its way through bush. They are called Whitfield's Stairs, named after George Whitfield, who in the mid-19th century owned part of the land on which Riverview stands. Jesuit Father Joseph Dalton bought a parcel of the Riverview Estate in 1878 on behalf of the Society of Jesus to build a school. In less than two years, classes were under way in a cottage on the old farm, with just a couple of pupils. The college has grown to be one of the largest in the country and has about 1500 students.

Near the top of the hill is a rose garden, which is on the site of the original Riverview Cottage. The garden is adorned with a small octagonal pavilion called the Teahouse. It was constructed by a Brother Thomas Forster, who had been a builder. Gradually revealing itself through the foliage is the college's main building. This edifice in sandstone presides on the rise. It was gradually built between 1885 and 1930 and was to be just one side of a huge square. However, only this part of the main building, facing south, was built. The building's gaze is firmly fixed on what has defined this college and helped bring it into being: the river.

As we stand at the top of the hill, David Mort's gaze extends beyond the river to the main harbour, and to the history of his own family. For Sydney Harbour shaped his family. In turn, the Morts shaped life around the harbour. David is the great-great grandson of Thomas Sutcliffe Mort, a commercial giant of the colony, whose broad business interests ranged from dock-building to wool and mining. Mort's Dock was downriver and across the harbour from where we stand, at Balmain. When that dry dock opened in 1855, it played a huge role in developing Sydney as a port and trading hub. He also built some magnificent buildings around the harbour, especially a beautiful multi-storey wool store near Circular Quay. His memory remains on the map: Mort Bay.

David and I turn away from the view and head into the life of the college. We step on the shadows of the colonnades as we walk along the main building's arcades, out of the sun and sheltered by history. The sense of the past grows stronger as we head into the basement. The corridor is lined with photos of rowing champions past, and with oars, their blades wearing the names of triumphant crews. The school has had a rowing club since 1882, barely two years after the college was founded. One of the first buildings constructed on the campus was a boatshed.

We step out of the corridor and into a series of rooms holding the college archives. Catherine Hobbs, the college's archivist, explains that this was the air-raid shelter during the Second World War. These days it's a bunker from the 21st century, which can be spied in slivers through the narrow windows set into the stone walls that are almost a metre thick. Catherine has set up the rooms like a museum. Among the memorabilia are references to the river and rowing, with one of the key exhibits the Riverview Challenge Cup, a golden trophy splendidly isolated in its own glass case. The first Riverview Regatta was held in 1885, and crews have been competing for this cup since 1893. Catherine points to another trophy and explains there's a competition for girls as well.

The archives not only chart the changing nature of the landscape around the college, but also highlight the character and achievements of those who have studied here.

The poet Christopher Brennan, born in Harbour Street in the city, was a Riverview student in the 1880s. In one of his best known poems, 'The Wanderer', the character reflects,

> So I sit and muse in this wayside harbour and wait
> till I hear the gathering cry of the ancient winds and
>   again
> I must up and out . . .

Through lessons he received here in the Classics and literature, Brennan heard those ancient winds whistling through the college's colonnades and out across the surrounding bushland, calling him far away to Europe. He returned to Australia, crafting beauty and drama in verse and life. He died poor in 1932. But Brennan's memory has been returned to his first muse; Riverview's library is named after him.

Another alumnus who used words to help make his way beyond Riverview was the author and art critic Robert Hughes. His way of seeing the world, and writing about it, was nurtured by his schooling at Riverview, and by the harbour itself. Hughes grew up in an old home overlooking Rose Bay on the harbour's south-east shore. As a little boy, he watched with wonder the flying boats taking off and landing on the bay. Hughes learnt to swim in a harbour pool, and its waters fed his lifelong passion for fishing. He would fish from the Rose Bay pier, waiting to catch the elusive. In the process, he also developed the skills to be a writer, particularly one that can be as difficult to hook as a fish: how to embrace solitude.

In 1951, the teenage Hughes was sent to a distant shore, following the trail of other males in his family, to become a boarder at Riverview. His harbour view had changed. 'You never had the feeling that Riverview was part of the great city of Sydney,' Hughes wrote. 'Riverview straddled its hill in isolation, a self-contained and monosexual world of boarders and priests against whose limit the bungalows of Lane Cove pressed in a suburban tide.' Yet while cloistered in that isolation, Hughes was educated in how to make his mark in the world. A few key Jesuits encouraged him to broaden his reading, to look more deeply at art, and to speak up in public. Those lessons remained with him.

Having seen the trophies and photos in the archives, David and I head back down to the river, where the college's boatshed is located. It is a fine building sprawled across the point between the river and the western shore of Tambourine Bay. On the lower floor are dozens of racing shells. The name of one craft honours the roots of the college – *Spirit of Ignatius* – and another acknowledges the people on whose traditional land the college stands – *Cammeraygal*. On the upper floor is a gym with large windows that allow views of the river and of the distant high-rises in the CBD to wash in. On the back wall are more old photos of past champions and glories. In one 1970s photo of a victorious Second Eight crew, third from the back, is A. Abbott. The former Prime Minister Tony Abbott is a Riverview old boy.

The boatshed and pontoon provide direct access to the scene of the Riverview Regatta; the finish line is just around the point. David can virtually see the invisible line in the water; he explains he used to roughly follow it when he rowed to school. For the rest of us, there are indicators on the bank as to where the races are held. Just above the water is a small but ornate octagonal building. It is another Brother Thomas creation. The pavilion was the bandstand for the musicians playing at regattas. On a higher point overlooking the river is what's called the Vice Regal Pavilion, built in 1892, for very important guests to sit and watch the rowing. Yet irrespective of importance, thousands would pack along the banks, and on the water, for these events.

'The attendance of visitors, always strong at these regattas, appeared to be more numerous than on former occasions, and the fleet of steamers, yachts and smaller boats gave the river quite an animated appearance,' wrote 'The Referee' in his report of the 1890 annual regatta.

That much has not changed. The regattas still attract large crowds, and the competitors still strain and train in the hope of holding the golden trophy and having their names etched into history in the college archives.

Yet the environment in which they train has dramatically changed. As we stand on the boatshed's pontoon, David looks into Tambourine Bay, which is knotted with moored boats. Yet he notes what has gone. Next to the boatshed, he says, there used to be tidal baths where he and his mates would swim. Now there is just the ghost of the baths, with the remains of a stone wall and a few blocks in the water. On the shore, the ruins of an old shelter are being gradually reclaimed by the bush. Soon the shelter will be bush rocks once more.

TAMBOURINE BAY may have received its name because a woman who sang and played a tambourine in Sydney streets lived in a cave along this shore. At the head of the bay, where mangroves cluster around a creek mouth, there is no sight of a cave, let alone the din of tambourines; rather, there's the more subtle sound of ticking and clicking rising from the mud, which looks as though it is trembling. Thousands of soldier crabs are scrambling across the squelchy shore. The mouth of Tambourine Creek seems to be a busy place for nature. Wader birds are picking around in the mud. Only the fish seem to be taking it easy. Rather than darting away when I approach, the fish sluggishly sway and swish to move just a little.

Paddling into the next cove, Woodford Bay, I'm in the midst of a boating playground. There are hundreds of vessels moored in the bay. When you paddle into a waterway where you could virtually walk across the water from one deck to the next, and you realise this is replicated in one bay to the next, the dry statistics of almost 5000 private moorings and about 17,000 recreational vessels on Sydney Harbour form into a staggering reality. If the surface looks cluttered, the harbour bottom looks increasingly scarred. The moorings' chains and blocks are cutting a swathe through seagrass beds. Scientists have been surveying the harbour floor and the impact of moorings on marine life, and it's estimated about half of Sydney's seagrass beds have disappeared in the past sixty years. This is worrying for the harbour, for seagrass plays a vital role in maintaining its health. Seagrass slows down water passing over it, so that not only decreases erosion on the shore-line, it also means fine sediment drops to the floor. That makes the water clearer. Seagrass also provides vital nurseries for fish, and it has an algal coating that absorbs nutrients, so it is like an underwater filter. For environmental and economic reasons, scientists argue, seagrass has to be maintained.

But it is possible for boating and the seagrass to co-exist. Marine biologist Professor Bill Gladstone has told me about work his team has been doing on environmentally friendly moorings. Instead of using a block and chain, a screw is inserted into the floor, with an arm that sits above the seagrass. The line is attached to the arm and taken up to the surface, so it doesn't come into contact with the bed and doesn't cut through the seagrass. Better still, research indicates that seagrass beds can recover.

'So you can still have a high level of boating, and a healthy seagrass bed,' Bill says.

That is encouraging, in the face of increasing demand for moorings in the harbour. The waiting lists can be long, for, just like with real estate, Sydneysiders hold on tenaciously to their little piece of the harbour. Even if some hardly ever untie their boat from its mooring.

I talk with a bloke who is launching a tinny from the shore to row out to his sailboat in Woodford Bay. He's travelled from the western suburb of Seven Hills, and he regularly makes the journey to go sailing. He is surprised not so much by the number of boats moored in the bay, but how many remain unused.

'I think some have forgotten they even have boats in here,' he remarks. 'They don't move.'

For half an hour or so, there is one less vessel in Woodford Bay. I pull *Pulbah Raider* out of the water, so I can get into the water. Jutting out from the bay's south-west shores are Lucretia Baths. The harbour pool is between an old slipway and a boatshed, with a wooden canoe sticking like a highly varnished insect to one of the walls. On the shore is scattered a marooned armada of dinghies, kayaks and tinnies. A couple of boats are tied to the baths' protective timber bars, so it is doubling as a marina.

Although it is a hot day, I have the baths to myself. Tip-toeing across the burning sand, the sting on my soles makes me nostalgic for childhood days at the beach. The baths are about a century old and are considered historically significant, because of their timber paling construction, designed to keep out unwanted flotsam and jetsam – especially those with fins. In the unmown grass on the shore is a plaque explaining these are actually the 'Jean Mitchell Lucretia Baths', in honour of her 'many years of service' to the baths. They could do with having Jean back, by the look of it. The setting is charmingly unkempt.

The bottom of the baths is tiled with muddy sand and studded with shells, including the occasional oyster shell. The clammy feeling under foot is only further inducement to start swimming.

Nancy Phelan, who wrote of her childhood further east on the shores of Middle Harbour in her book *A Kingdom by the Sea*, recalled swimming in a similar pool in Tarban Creek.

'After our crystalline beach and rock pools these baths were rather frightening, dark and sinister, undisturbed by tides,' Phelan wrote. 'There was the sense of something dangerous and slimy in the obscure depths; you dived in with panic and got out as fast as possible, yet with far more excitement than on our wholesome beach.'

Once I'm floating, any discomfort washes away. At the pool's end, I can see to the other side of the bay and distant high-rise buildings on the lower North Shore. To the east, I can view the top of that stunning steel arch marking the heart of the harbour. This is the wonderfully democratic element of these harbour pools. You may not exactly swim with the rich – after all, they have their own pools in their harbourside properties – but you're swimming among the rich.

Occasionally, that's not all you're swimming among. Under the New South Wales Government's Beachwatch monitoring program, the water quality of a couple of dozen harbour pools and beaches is regularly tested. In one table of results I looked at on the program's website before heading out, the water in these baths in Woodford Bay was listed as 'Fair', which means it is generally suitable for swimming when it is dry. But after rain, the run-off rises, and so do the levels of microbial contamination. I've revisited the website after it has rained and have read the warning that pollution was likely and to avoid swimming in the baths. Still, on this day, there's been no rain, and it's so hot, the harbour water feels like a blessing.

Pollution, and the sheer cost and effort of maintenance, has seen a few public pools in the harbour disappear. Paddling along the shores, I've also seen the rusting and rotted legacies of private harbour pools that have fallen into disrepair and been abandoned.

Even so, harbour baths have an enduring allure. When you dive into them, you may be advised to not swallow the water, but most have heightened levels of something you'll rarely find in a backyard pool: heritage. One harbour pool considered historically significant is just across the river. Woolwich Baths took shape in the first decade of the 1900s. For the local working men and their families, the timber palings and pylons pressed into the harbour bottom defined fun. But it didn't come for free. The entrance fees helped pay for a caretaker, who lived in a tent besides the baths during the summer. For their money, the swimmers received more than a protective fence; there was a diving tower. Apparently one local, Vincent 'Ned' Kelly, developed diving skills at the baths that may have saved his life. While working on Sydney Harbour Bridge during its construction, he fell into the water and survived.

More than a century on, Woolwich Baths still attract swimmers from near and far. One late summer afternoon, as I paddle past, the waters are bursting with humanity. Children are jumping from the deck, squealing with delight before they shatter the surface. Parents cradle their babies and toddlers in the shallows, and, in the deeper water, a few older swimmers are meditatively doing laps. One of those is Warwick Richardson, from West Ryde, about twenty minutes drive away. Whenever he is in the area, he fits a dip at the baths into his schedule. At least, he does from October to about April.

'I'm a summer swimmer,' Warwick smiles.

In the decade or so he has been swimming here, Warwick reckons the water quality is much the same, becoming more turbid after rain but overall fairly clean. What's more, he feels safe swimming here. The nets keep out sharks and large jelly-fish, he says. Not that Warwick thinks about all of that when he's performing the adagio of laps in the historic harbour pool.

'It's nice to be in salt water from time to time.'

IF ONLY the convicts who camped along Woodford Bay, nursing their aching bodies after long days of felling trees or cutting grass for hay, could be brought back from a couple of centuries ago and see these shores now.

The forbidding bush in which those poor souls toiled has been replaced with some prohibitively expensive homes. Even the boatsheds are impressive. One double-storey shed squatting over the water looks bigger than many terrace houses in the inner city. But the bush has not been totally dominated. As I sit in the kayak, I look at the houses that have sprouted on the slopes around this bay over to the next 'finger' of land, Northwood. In spite of all that brick, concrete and steel grafted onto the landscape, this stretch still looks bushy. The eucalypts are hanging on tenaciously amid the big homes, just as they grip the sandstone ledges hanging over the water's edge. The composition of tree trunks and sandstone sculpted by Mother Nature, the sheds on the shore, the boats in the bay, all washed with water and light, has the beauty and intensity of a piece of art.

Indeed, this setting inspired one of Australia's great landscape artists, Lloyd Rees. For more than half a century, Northwood was Rees' home, and the bays and bush surrounding it were often the subjects of his art.

Rees learnt from, and was inspired by, the works of the European masters. You can see that in his highly detailed drawings and rich paintings. But he was besotted by Sydney. You can feel that in just about every image of his adopted hometown. As a 20-year-old from Brisbane, he sailed through the Heads in 1916 and was 'confronted by the golden sandstone portals of Sydney Harbour'. Lloyd Rees would travel far and wide in his long life, but his vision kept returning to the harbour.

For a time, Rees lived a few bays to the east at McMahons Point. From the top of his apartment block, he would depict the harbour to Balmain, along with the headlands, and he would wander those peninsulas and along the shore, searching for subjects. He didn't have to search far; it was all before him. Rees' sketches of the rocks and trunks of Port Jackson figs are like academic studies of muscular torsos.

In 1934, Rees moved to Northwood, which, back then, felt isolated to the artist. He wondered why there was no corner shop. It may have lacked convenience, but the area nurtured his art.

On a small knoll of weathered rock above Woodford Bay's eastern shore is a bronze plaque honouring Rees and etched with a quote of his, 'If you look for light you find it'.

On this very spot, Lloyd Rees found light and so much more. This was one of his favourite views, and I can see why. I gaze across the bay, through the yachts' masts and up the river until the water and landscape are smudged, as though Rees himself has scumbled the view with a paintbrush, just to make it even prettier. Sitting here, I'm looking at more than a beautiful view, thanks to Lloyd Rees' art. What he created in works such as *Three Boats, Lane Cove River* is what I see.

The viewing spot is part of Lloyd Rees Park. I reckon he would like the look of this park. It is not gently undulating with carefully laid paths. Rather, there is no clearly defined path, and it is on a steep slope, peppered with rocks, making it difficult to negotiate. This park seems like a metaphor for pursuing a career in art in Australia. Yet, like a Rees painting, when you look for beauty, you find it. There is a nest of ferns in a gully, dinghies along the shore, and the boats can be seen through the stands of gums and casuarinas. The only thing missing are Rees' beloved Port Jackson figs.

At the end of the point, just below where Lloyd Rees sat and sketched, there is a small sandstone shelter and a ferry wharf. Rees said Northwood community life once revolved around the ferries and, until the end of the Second World War, there was a half-hour service until midnight. The artist was saddened by the diminishing role of ferries in his time. He would be thoroughly disheartened now. The Northwood wharf is little more than a fishing platform. While ferries do occasionally stop here, the wharf has no timetable on its noticeboard. But at least along the shoreline are weathered lumps of sandstone. They look like a Lloyd Rees drawing. Or a portrait of Sydney.

Rees delighted in hopping on a ferry at the Northwood wharf, taking an outside seat at the stern and watching the view slowly unfold. Yet the harbour provided him with more than a source of inspiration for his art. Once, while riding on the ferry, he was struck by where he was and what it meant to him. 'I looked out upon it all and suddenly I thought: I don't want to go to Heaven because it can't be as beautiful as this.'

In perhaps the cruellest of deprivations for an artist, Lloyd Rees gradually lost his sight. And yet he kept finding the light. The details disappeared from his paintings, and shapes softened and liquefied. But there was still the light, especially the way it sparkled on the harbour. He didn't need to see to express how he felt, and, in doing so with his paintings, he bestowed on Sydney Harbour, or pulled from its depths, a beauty for the rest of us to view. So whenever I'm paddling on the harbour, and the sun ignites the water until I can see nothing but light and quicksilver, I think of Lloyd Rees.

FERRIES MAY be rarely spotted on Lane Cove River these days, but you can see an aircraft. Occasionally, as I've been paddling in the river, I've heard an engine clear its throat and roar to life, and then have watched a seaplane slowly slalom its way through the moored boats, preparing to take off on the harbour. When not turning heads near the mouth of the river, the plane is on a slipway at the foot of a house near Greenwich Point. On either side of it, there are some fine looking boats moored at jetties jutting out from some lovely houses in lush gardens. But as an eye-catching water feature, nothing outdoes a seaplane.

Along the left bank tracing Greenwich Point are deep shaded glades, and the rocks are coated with oysters. In the midst of multi-million-dollar homes, incredibly expensive boats and a seaplane is a symbol of simple pleasures: a rope hanging from a tree, just waiting for some kids to latch on, swing out, let go and shriek with delight as they plunge into the water. Leaving me with those impressions, Lane Cove River pushes me out of its mouth.

5

GREENWICH TO LAVENDER BAY

GREENWICH ON the River Thames may be associated with measuring time and distance around the globe, but its namesake in Sydney is packed with markers of the past.

Serried up Greenwich Point are historic homes. One of the more prominent properties is Greenwich House. The sandstone mansion was built on the land of boatbuilder George Green, who subdivided his property, Greenwich Estate, in 1840. His marketing for the subdivision was apparently the first time 'Greenwich' had been used.

Tucked into the cove just beyond the Greenwich Point ferry terminal are the local baths. For more than a century, generations of kids have learnt to swim in this little patch of the harbour, pegged out with protective iron rods. The baths and the raggedy shoreline around Greenwich were more than places to swim; they were cradles of friendships. In the late 1920s and early 1930s, two boys living locally, Paul and Peter, mucked around in the water. The good mates almost drowned once, when the leaky canoe they were in was sinking and they had to be rescued. The world would have never known what it had lost if the harbour had taken those two boys. For in time, both of them would be internationally renowned for playing with words – Paul Brickhill as the author of the bestselling books *The Dambusters*, *Reach for the Sky* and *The Great Escape*, and Peter Finch as an Oscar-winning actor.

Even Greenwich Point, with a crown made shaggy from all the trees growing on it, is an indicator of how times have changed – and changed again. I've seen old photos of the point on the Lane Cove River side, and the slope is bald but for grass. The stripped slope was probably seen as scenic, providing unimpeded views of the water. But the denuded landscape was a deep wound, gashed into the landscape ever since the first gangs of convicts had been sent up the harbour and the river to cut down trees. When the author and 'emigrant mechanic' Alexander Harris trudged along the harbour's northern shore from a timber camp on Lane Cove River, he observed, 'I could not but take notice of the immense numbers of tree stumps. Each one of these had supplied its barrel to the splitter or sawyer or squarer: and alto-gether the number seemed countless.' So on Greenwich Point, at least, parts of the past have been healed over, if not cured.

As I paddle east along the peninsula, gliding by the baths bubbling with excited kids, time flows not just past the kayak but underneath it.

About 250 million years ago, the land around what would be Sydney was a basin, which held a huge lake system. Over millions of years, the sandstone that would be Sydney's bed and give character to its face was formed. Sediment was carried in and dropped by ancient rivers, and then, layer upon layer, it would be compressed. About ninety million years ago, Sydney's bed was dramatically ruffled, as the earth heaved. The land around Sydney rose, and all the ructions and rifts in the earth cut into the sandstone a rough template for where and how the harbour and the surrounding landscape would take shape.

Water flowing from higher ground followed the template, slicing through the sandstone. Integral to the harbour's formation was Parramatta River. The river that is holding me helped carve the Greenwich headland I'm paddling by, and the trench to cradle the harbour.

Water flowing from the east largely filled the harbour. Seawater poured in and then dropped away a number of times. During the last Great Ice Age, about 15,000 years ago, the ocean was about 140 metres lower than it is now, and today's Eastern Suburbs would have been outer Western Suburbs; it is estimated the sea was about 30 kilometres east of the Heads. Thousands of years ago, as the last major glaciation ended and the seas rose, the harbour and valleys leading into it filled. So in kayaking Parramatta and Lane Cove rivers, I've been paddling in partially drowned valleys.

The river is about to release me.

One of the most powerful men in the early colony was William Charles Wentworth. Not content to be a lawyer, politician, landowner and media baron, he was also a writer. In 1823, Wentworth penned a paean to the land of his wealth and influence, 'Australasia'. In his poem, Wentworth rhapsodised how the harbour, on its way to the sea, 'Fled loath from Parramatta's am'rous touch'. This must be the first and last time Sydney Harbour has been portrayed as some chaste maiden. I think about Wentworth's hopelessly romantic verse as I approach Manns Point, and I dunk a hand over the side. The water is warm to the touch, but I'm not feeling any of that amorous quality. Which is just as well, because I'm about to love and leave the river.

Not that there is any clear line to cross. There is no obvious photo opportunity to have the kayak's stern in the river and the bow in the harbour. Water knows no such boundaries and respects no borders. However, the stretch of a few hundred metres from Manns Point across to the western shore at Long Nose Point, or Yurulbin Point, at Birchgrove is considered the dividing line between Parramatta River and the harbour. Not that it makes any difference; it flows all into one.

Along the shore near Manns Point, I spot embedded in a retaining wall a couple of large sandstone blocks that must have once adorned a building. They are etched with fine geometric patterns, and intricate floral designs bloom on the stone. This is the aspect of Sydney Harbour that the tourist advertisements don't highlight. It is also a graveyard for massacred heritage. To me, those sandstone blocks are a monument to the generations of commercial greed and political bastardry that have shaped so much of the harbour's shores.

Time to keep paddling. On the map, the very outline of Manns Point seems to be telling me where to go. It looks like a finger pointing down the harbour. Instead, I trace around the finger into Gore Cove. Not that I can paddle directly into the cove. Just off the finger is a mooring dolphin with a sign attached to it that encourages me to take a wider arc: DANGER. MOORING LINE SNAPBACK AREA. But it's the ship attached to those mooring lines that is the great persuader.

The cove is home to a large oil terminal, and it has been for more than a century.

'The present peaceful suburb of Greenwich promises to become a hive of industry in the near future,' the press excitedly reported in 1900. 'A large firm, with headquarters in London and with branches in all parts of the world except Australasia, has obtained the permission of the Lane Cove Council to establish large petroleum works on a site which it has purchased and which has a frontage to the river.' That firm was Shell. The company initially imported kerosene, and for many years it shipped in crude oil. The oil was transported from the terminal up Parramatta River to its Clyde refinery by barges until a pipeline was installed.

Just before the terminal opened in 1901, a newspaper reported, 'The company guarantees that the industry is not of a noxious or offensive character and that the waters of the river will not be polluted.' Through the years, the terminal has received complaints from residents, ranging from environmental concerns to worry at having something extremely flammable for a neighbour.

Paddling along the south-western shore, past the twenty or so large tanks sprouting like metallic mushrooms in the curve of the cove, I'm reminded this is how much of the shoreline used to look, hosting industry, but also this is what the harbour used to be: a bustling workplace. This cove is one of the few parts of the harbour where you can still see ships filled with a cargo other than holidaymakers. Often, while paddling around the tip of Berry Island, I've been confronted by a great wall of steel, as a tanker slides in or out of the cove. It is an awesome sight to be so close to a ship, as its bow gently nudges aside the harbour, while at its stern the propellers churn the water into a boiling pot of energy. What's more, as the names on the ships indicate, the furthest reaches of the world, from Hong Kong to Majuro, have floated into this wedge of water.

On early mornings, I have seen ships disappear like a spell as they slip their lines at the terminal, head down the harbour and sink into the fog. In those moments, I feel as though I'm watching one of those wonderful photos by David Moore of the working harbour in the post-World War Two years lift off the paper and emerge out of the past and the skeins of mist. Moore was a master photographer who had grown up near the harbour, and, throughout his career, he used cameras to capture the movements of ships, and of time, on the water. In many of his black-and-white photos, the harbour looked dirtier, but undeniably busier, with smoke chuffing from the funnels of vessels of all sizes, as well as from factory stacks on the shore. Even the light seemed to become tangled in the thick air levitating over the water. But that's gone now. By the time the fog lifts, the ship will be out to sea, and the light can settle unimpeded by funnel smoke on a harbour cut mostly by pleasure cruisers.

This cove once cradled ships to be scrapped. Among those sent here to die and be dismembered was the sailing ship *Sobraon*. After many years carrying passengers and cargo between Australia and Britain, the three-masted *Sobraon* was moored off Cockatoo Island and became a training ship for disadvantaged boys in 1891. Twenty years later, she was given a new life and new name, HMAS *Tingira*, serving as a naval training ship. After 1927, *Tingira*, which is an indigenous word meaning 'open sea', was paid off and the ship mouldered in nearby Berrys Bay before making its way to its grave in Gore Cove, where she was broken up in the 1940s. Yet *Sobraon* was reincarnated to sail again. Or, at least, parts of her were recycled. When the renowned boatbuilders, the Halvorsen brothers, were constructing their yacht *Peer Gynt*, they used teak decking from the wreck of *Tingira*.

As I trace the shoreline, the tanks and pipelines surrender to bush and sandstone outcrops. Unlike most inlets and bays around the harbour, the head of Gore Cove has not been lopped off, filled in and turned into a park. I paddle through a thick band of mangroves, picking my way towards the sound of trickling water. I reach the end of the cove, where a creek trips through a bush-arched gully into the harbour. Some things in here have changed, however. This waterway has grown, in name at least, from 'cove' to 'bay'. These days it is often referred to as Gore Bay. The shoreline to my left, as I paddle out of the mangroves and back down the cove – sorry, bay – still wears a name that is no longer true: Berry Island.

The island was part of the estate owned by an entrepreneur who came to be one of the wealthiest men in the colony, Alexander Berry. The Scottish-born Berry was a ship's surgeon for a time, but he moved into the mercantile world. After an initial venture in 1808 when he arrived in Sydney with thousands of litres of grog, Berry returned a decade later and put down roots. He had gone into business with another merchant, Edward Wollstonecraft. The pair set up an operation in the north-west corner of Sydney Cove, just above the mudflats. Berry and Wollstonecraft sought more land by water; they headed south, and in 1822 they applied for, and received, thousands of hectares of land around Shoalhaven River. What they felled or grazed on their estates they could transport in their ships and sell in Sydney.

More than business partners, Wollstonecraft and Berry became neighbours in Sydney. In the early 1820s, Wollstonecraft was granted land on the harbour's northern shores, 212 hectares ('exclusive of rocks and sand') that he called Crow's Nest Farm, because of its views of the harbour and surrounding country-side. More than offering views, Wollstonecraft's grant stretched to the water. Berry obtained a grant of 28 hectares next to Wollstonecraft's, and his land also tumbled down the gullies to the harbour. His grant included a small island that reconnected itself to the northern shore by a sandy isthmus at low tide. The pair also became brothers-in-law. In 1827, Berry married Wollstonecraft's sister Elizabeth.

Edward Wollstonecraft died in 1832, and his property was given to Berry. On the estate's fringe, Berry built a stone wharf and four-storey warehouse, and in his fleet of small ships was one named *Edward*. He and Elizabeth lived in Crow's Nest Cottage, originally built for Wollstonecraft, 'on the brow of a ridge overlooking the Harbour, Town, & Botany Bay to the South'. When they built a larger home in the early 1840s, they also called it Crow's Nest.

Berry's wealth afforded him great influence in politics and business, and it fuelled significant enemies. He was attacked in the newspapers and the parliament by another powerful figure, the Reverend John Dunmore Lang, for being greedy and an oppressor of the poor: 'even Mr Berry should have said, "I have got enough land, now let other people get a little also".' Yet a lot of land was never enough for the 'Laird o' Crow's Nest'. By the time he died in 1873, Alexander Berry was the owner of the largest freehold estate in the colony, and he was worth more than £1.2 million, an eye-popping figure for the 19th century, and a phenomenal inheritance for his brother David.

Beyond place names, the legacies of Alexander Berry are sprinkled around the lower North Shore, notably the pyramid-shaped monument above his remains, and those of his wife and brother-in-law, in St Thomas' Rest Park. People picnic and play in the shadow of Berry's memory.

For those who prefer not to picnic with the dead, there is Berry Island. After all, Berry used to picnic here. He joined his small island to the rest of his holding by building a stone causeway on the sandy isthmus. In 1906, the island was transferred to the State Government, as part of an exchange for the building of a hospital in the Shoalhaven town of Berry, in accordance with the will of David Berry. The mud flats on either side of the causeway were gradually filled in to create the lawns that people now relax and party on. Occasionally, the reserve is an unofficial camping spot. One morning, while lifting my kayak out of the water, I chatted to three young German backpackers, two women and a man, who had pitched a tent in the fringe of bush by the water. 'Yes, we stayed there,' said one of the women. 'We don't know if it's legal, but it's beautiful!' In Sydney, if it has a view and there's room for a tent or, better still, a beaten-up campervan, you will almost certainly find backpackers. And no number of council signs or censorious looks from locals will dissuade them. Yet it is one of the mysteries of nature how backpackers can find their way to the remotest of harbour spots that most Sydneysiders don't know of, let alone have ever visited. Then again, maybe it's not such a mystery. 'Google maps,' shrugged the young German man.

On the eastern side of the 'island' is Balls Head Bay, which includes a couple of smaller coves. Long before backpackers pitched their tents, others camped around here. In the early 20th century, artists from *The Bulletin* magazine had a campsite, giving them somewhere far but near to sketch and paint in the landscape. And before all of them, the Cammeraygal people lived along these shores. The oysters that helped feed many generations also provided the name of the cove here. The shores hold the Wondakiah residential development, but amid the hives of apartments are a few concessions to the site's past, with a chimney and old brick buildings. Oyster Cove was home to a succession of industries, including a sugar refinery, a kerosene plant, and, from the early 1900s, a large gasworks.

The wharf that was once integral to industry in Oyster Cove is now a promenade. With people strolling above, I paddle under the wharf, among the concrete piers. A few birds are flittering about, and the sound of the water swells and bounces off the concrete. I turn and look out at the light-washed harbour. All that has happened above – the industries, the apartments – doesn't matter; for right now, sitting in here, it is just me and the water. Not even a backpacker is in sight.

Neighbouring Wondakiah is the HMAS *Waterhen* naval base. *Waterhen* is fairly unassuming, tucked into the cove and flanked by two bushy headlands. Minehunters can be seen ploughing the harbour as they head in and out of the bay. When the grey shapes glide by, they can look menacing. But that sense quickly fizzles when, as happened one morning while I sat in the kayak waiting for HMAS *Gascoyne* to pass, an officer on the bridge gives you a wave. The base's long finger wharves reach back to a cluster of buildings hunkering under a cliff. What was sliced from the landscape here was used to shape another naval base. When the graving dock was being built at Garden Island, rock was quarried on this site and transported down the harbour. The *Waterhen* site was used during the Second World War by both the Australian and United States navies. These days the base is the main home for the RAN's mine warfare facilities.

As if the presence of navy ships doesn't hold the promise of a secure place to berth, the landscape curling around the bay offers protection. Even if the wind is ruffling the harbour, it can be fairly still in here. What's more, while the CBD's crown can be seen over Balls Head to the east, it can feel wonderfully distant in the bay. As a result, Balls Head Bay draws in yachties.

On a stunning day, under a sky freshly rinsed and blue, I paddle past a catamaran in the bay. From its mast an Australian flag flutters, but at the stern, the Stars and Stripes are riding the gentle breeze. I see a woman on the aft deck, we chat, and she introduces herself as Pam. Her husband, Eric, appears. I'm guessing they're in their 60s, but they have a vitality that makes them seem much younger. They invite me on board.

'Sorry about the washing,' Pam says. A string of clothes along the deck and a couple of waterproof jackets hanging at the bow are waltzing in the light breeze. I ask if there's a washing machine on board. 'There it is.' She points to a five-gallon bucket. 'It's actually good exercise.'

This 38-foot catamaran, *Pied a Mer III*, is Eric and Pam Sellix's world. And it's taken them half way around the world. They are from a small town, Clatskanie, in Oregon.

'It's a river town,' they explain, as we sit in the catamaran's saloon. Clatskanie is a sea-going community of sorts; Alaskan fishermen live in the town in the off-season. Not that Pam and Eric had thoughts of heading to sea. Pam had trained as a teacher and Eric, a Vietnam veteran, as an electrical engineer. They ran restaurants together. They liked their life in Clatskanie.

'I was never going to move out of my home,' says Pam, 'let alone cross the ocean. It wasn't my dream.'

'It wasn't even mine,' adds Eric, who had done some sailing.

'I couldn't see the point,' says Pam.

After the global financial crisis in 2008, Eric and Pam decided to downsize. They sold up most of their possessions and had a catamaran built on the other side of the world – in Wollongong, south of Sydney. They took delivery of their catamaran in 2010, and a couple of years later, they declared, 'we're going sailing'. They've been sailing ever since.

They cruised off Mexico, sailed up to Canada and, in March 2015, they set off across the Pacific, island hopping, until they finally reached Australia, making landfall in Newcastle, before sailing down to Sydney.

'When we came through the Heads, I was just glad to be here,' exclaims Pam. 'I didn't think we'd ever get here. Sailing through the Heads made it real, but not as real as seeing the Opera House and the Bridge!'

Sailing in, Eric was particularly surprised by the numbers of moored boats.

'Obviously, even if you've never been on the harbour, a lot of Sydney residents think they're going to be, judging by all the boats here!'

The couple had moored in a few coves around the harbour before dropping anchor in Balls Head Bay, which, Eric reckons, is 'one of the nicest, cleanest places we've been'. In the few months they've been in the harbour, Eric and Pam have been absorbing Sydney experiences on the water. They've watched the start of the Sydney to Hobart race. They observed the curious episode of a pleasure boat running ashore at a nudist beach, and the bathers wading out to help the stricken boaties. They've sat on their boat with Australian friends they'd met on their voyages and stared at the night sky blossoming on New Year's Eve. And Pam has been riding the ferries. They make for a leisurely change after the catamaran.

'Oh, I like to use the ferries,' she enthuses. 'I don't have to work then when I'm on the water!'

Eric and Pam intend to keep sailing, back across the Pacific, and then over to the Atlantic, to Europe, to wherever their catamaran takes them.

'I think we very well might sail for as many years as we can,' says Eric.

And they will sail 'home' to Oregon, adds Pam, before she hesitates and looks around the well-ordered world within the catamaran. She smiles, perhaps thinking about the sum of their adventures, before she murmurs with satisfaction, 'This is home.'

JUST ACROSS the water, at the foot of Balls Head, two chapters of Australian maritime history remain afloat and are being gradually restored by supporters. *Cape Don* is a former tender that was built in Newcastle, commissioned in 1963, and spent a quarter of a century on the seas, helping service manned lighthouses, mostly off the Western Australian coast. Now *Cape Don* sits, docile, at an old wharf. Her white paint is spattered and mottled with rust, and a loading crane's jib bows to the deck.

Berthed at the stern of *Cape Don* is one of the beautiful old workhorses of the harbour, *Baragoola*. The ferry was built only a couple of kilometres away at Mort's Dock. *Baragoola* was launched in 1922, and for sixty years, she carried passengers on the legendary run between Circular Quay and Manly. Through those six decades, she rode over all manner of obstacles that both the ocean and developing technology tossed at her. She survived the conversion from steam to diesel, massive waves and high winds tearing through the Heads, collisions with other boats, and even banging into a whale in the harbour. But time itself eventually stopped *Baragoola*, and she ended up in Balls Head Bay. Paddling close to her and looking up at the curling wave of iron, *Baragoola* still looks powerful and majestic. She is tethered, but she is rarely still. The old ferry rocks slightly whenever a set of small waves is pushed through by a passing vessel. She makes a low rubbing sound, as though the harbour is scratching her belly, when she rises a little, then there's the sound of water trickling off her hull.

The ships are in better shape than the old timber wharf in front of them. A rusting steel barrier girdles the wharf's base, and there are signs warning people not to go underneath it. Not that you need any signs. It looks forbidding enough; with so many planks missing from the deck, sunlight is peppered through the wharf on to the water. The structure was built about 1917 as part of a coal storage and loading facility.

When industry began grinding its way towards Balls Head, there was an outcry. The prospect of this dramatically beautiful landmark being defaced with a coal loader provoked a protest from the most famous poet in the land and sometime resident of nearby Waverton, Henry Lawson. Not only did Lawson write to a local paper, voicing his opposition to what he considered vandalism of the North Shore, he also composed a poem, 'The Sacrifice of Ball's Head':

They're taking it, the shipping push,
As all the rest must go –
The only spot of cliff and bush
That harbour people know.
The spirit of the past is dead,
North Sydney has no soul –
The State is cutting down Ball's Head
To make a wharf for coal.

Lawson predicted the 'grimy trucks' and the 'soulless cranes' dumping their 'grimy loads' would bring an end to the natural beauty and spoil the place where 'boating couples land'.

No more our eyes shall be relieved
In the city's garish day –
A sordid crime has been achieved!
And none has ought to say.

Eloquence and indignation helped protect some of the headland, which was declared a public reserve in the 1920s. But industry had its way on the western face. The coal loader was built and operated for more than seventy years. Bulk carriers offloaded their cargo at the finger wharf, and the coal was stockpiled on a large platform near the top of the hill. Underneath, tunnels had been crafted, and coal-heaped skips rolled on rails through them. The tunnels are still there, and you can now walk through them, deep in the soul of Balls Head, towards the sliver of light on the other side. On top of the hill, there are a few old buildings. In a delicious irony, what were facilities for handling fossil fuel have been converted into a centre for environmental sustainability.

While Henry Lawson feared the spirit of the past would be killed by the coal loader, it wasn't. That spirit has prevailed, and it is etched into Balls Head. On a rock platform near the centre for sustainability is the engraving of a whale. That this open-air work of art has survived is remarkable, because it has defied the ravages of the years and industrial activity. The engraving is more than a symbol of survival. It is a celebration of the animal and the importance it held to the Cammeraygal people, who carved the image. The Cammeraygal, who lived on the lower North Shore and Northern Beaches, occupied this headland for thousands of years. It is awesome to stand near the rock and look down at the engraving, which must be five metres long, tracing the tail and fins of this creature swimming across the sandstone. Inside the whale, near the tail, is the outline of a man.

'No, he's not inside the whale,' corrects Professor Dennis Foley. 'He's on top of it. He's riding the whale.'

Dennis is a lecturer at the University of Newcastle and a Cammeraygal (Gai-maraigal) descendant. This engraving, explains Dennis, is not telling some imagined story. This is what young men did as part of their passage in life.

The water off Balls Head is some of the deepest in the harbour, and whales would gather in that area and calve. Even though large sharks were also lurking, young men would swim out from the headland to the whales. Dennis says the figure on the whale is depicted with his feet wrapped. 'That's seal skin or penguin skin,' he explains, and that gave the young men grip to climb on to the whales.

The engraving, and the ritual it records, explains not only the close relationship the Cammeraygal had with the whales, but also with the harbour itself.

'Sydney was the Venice of Australia,' Dennis says of the number of canoes on the water, as people fished from them and paddled from one location to another. They canoed where their ancestors once walked, before the valleys were flooded. The Cammeraygal continued to carry the knowledge of the terrain at the bottom of the harbour. It is knowledge that has flowed through to the present-day, to Dennis. He can't see it, but Dennis can give directions on how to make your way along the hills and valleys below the water. His heritage is his guide map of the harbour and its foreshores. It is different to the maps I have looked at.

On those maps, the name of Lieutenant Henry Lidgbird Ball is attached to the headland that holds the whale engraving. Ball commanded HMS *Supply* in the First Fleet and was part of the early surveys of the harbour. He was also involved in the abduction of a local man, Arabanoo, from Manly in 1788, as part of Governor Phillip's desire to learn more about the Aboriginal people and their culture. When Ball returned to England in 1791, he took with him a live kangaroo, the first to be exported.

Standing on a rocky lip protruding from the southern face of the headland that holds his name, I don't think of Lieutenant Ball. Rather, I think of the Cammeraygal. For I'm standing on the ground that they did. They called this landmark Yerroulbine. And I'm doing what I imagine they did: absorbing the view. From this rock shelf high above the water, and with no safety fence or warning signs pushing you back, you can look west, south, and east. What I take in along the shoreline and on the harbour is vastly different to what the Cammeraygal would have seen, but what connects us over the millennia is the water itself. To my right, I look at Parramatta River, just as they would have done. Ahead of me, over Goat Island is Darling Harbour, and turning to my left, there's the harbour reaching for the sea. In Sydney, values are often determined by the views. But how can you value this? For it's not what you see – as spectacular as it is – but how you feel when you stand here on Yerroulbine. It's the feeling of not just the spirit of the past, but the spirit of the land, and of the harbour.

Out of respect for the original inhabitants, Dennis Foley believes we should use Aboriginal place names, either in conjunction with, or in place of, the names they were given after the British arrived.

'It's like if you go into someone's house, and you start speaking French or German,' he says. What's more, Dennis argues, using Aboriginal place names would help all of us to better understand the significance of the harbour and the land.

From the harbour itself, Yerroulbine has the look and feel of a resilient character, like an old boxer. Little wonder artists such as Lloyd Rees returned time and again, sketching and painting that beautiful, compelling face, with its pock-marked sandstone skin and scrabbling thatch of angophoras and gums. Rees loved what he called the sculptural quality of the harbour foreshores. In one of his pencil on paper works, titled *Balls Head, Sydney Harbour* (1931), the great gnarled knob of rock and bush dominates the image. Passing the headland is a tiny figure, little more than a squiggle in the shaded graphite water.

It's a rower. At least we who hold a paddle have a place, no matter how small, in the art of Lloyd Rees.

Around the time Rees sketched that image, a lot of the bush had been hacked off Balls Head. The vegetation was battered during the Great Depression, when desperate job-seekers cut down the trees to sell for firewood. In the caves and overhangs, where the Cammeraygal once sheltered, the homeless fashioned shacks. From the 1930s, residents and conservationists worked at regenerating the bush on Balls Head. But when fireworks are involved, people can still find a viewing platform. On New Year's Eve and Australia Day, tarps and tents sprout on the southern and eastern faces of Balls Head, and this motley camp clinging to the rocks provides a fleeting glimpse of how this landmark must have looked during the Depression.

Paddling close to the shoreline around Balls Head, you can see where the harbour has been incessantly scratching away at the sandstone, scooping out a string of caves and shells. The water is sucked into the caverns and swilled around until it echoes. It is a delicious sound.

The water off Balls Head presented me with a chance to bring an end to a torment perpetrated by my fellow Gentleman Kayakers, Bruce Beresford and George Ellis. We three members usually convene our meetings just out of Balls Head Bay. One autumn morning, as I paddled towards the gentlemen, Bruce hollered, 'Did you see the dolphins?!' No, I didn't. Bruce and George then tripped over each other's words, excitedly recounting how one, then two, then, ultimately, five dolphins dipped and gambolled right in front of them! And then they followed the dolphins all the way to here!

'They were so graceful,' George cooed.

With eyes sparkling even brighter than the water, Bruce declared that in all the years he'd been paddling on the harbour, he had never seen dolphins before. He punctuated his sentence by declaring, 'And I can't believe you missed them!'

'And you *just* missed them,' said George, feigning bitter disappointment for me.

After that episode, whenever and wherever we paddled, no matter what the topic of conversation was, George and Bruce would somehow weave into our chats, 'Hey, remember the time we saw the dolphins . . . Oh, that's right! Sorry, Scott, you didn't see them, did you?' I'm not sure what caused me greater distress; that I had never seen a dolphin in Sydney Harbour, or that I was a member of the Gentleman Kayakers' Club.

And so it was, until one late winter morning. The air was still and crisp and the water an unblemished mirror reflecting a flawless sky. Suddenly a beautiful day became even better. Bruce and I were going for a paddle and we had just met at the foot of Balls Head. No sooner had we set off than I thought I saw a fin. Before saying anything, I waited and watched. Just in case I had to yell, 'Shark!' Then the great sheeny curve of a dolphin's body broke out of the mirror before sliding back into it.

'Did you see that?!'

No, Bruce hadn't. I was preparing to rib him about missing the perfect moment, when two dolphins appeared. They were synchronised as they slowly curled out of the water. We paddled towards the pair, as they continued their loping journey towards Parramatta River. Then a speedboat passed too close, and we didn't see the dolphins again. But the curse on me had been broken. The torrent of torment had been dried up. Never again could Bruce and George proclaim, 'You haven't seen a dolphin in the harbour'.

Others have seen even more impressive creatures in this part of the harbour. In 1889, a 'Resident in Elizabeth Street' wrote how he was in a skiff near Blues Point (the next peninsula east of Balls Head) when he saw three whales coming down Parramatta River. The writer recounted how the whales, which he estimated were between 20 feet (6 metres) and 80 feet (24 metres) long, dived under his boat and resurfaced just beyond it. So that I can tease my fellow club members, I live in hope of seeing a whale off Balls Head – as long as it doesn't swim under the kayak. Or over it.

THE ENDURING influence of Alexander Berry hurdles Balls Head, which was part of his estate, and lands in the very name of the waterway on the other side. It is called Berrys Bay.

On the bay's western shores, Berry built a wharf and warehouse for the ships bringing produce from his property further down the coast. Berry's buildings are long gone. But the commercial empire-builder would have been pleased to know that, since his time, a succession of entrepreneurs have sailed into this bay and turned the water into money. Yet it's not all business in Berrys Bay.

The time-sculpted northern shoreline burrows into Balls Head to form a narrow cove, all but tucked out of sight. It would be an ideal site for a getaway, to forget about the rest of the world and its cares. But for three-quarters of a century from 1912, this was a base for those watching out and keeping at bay some of those cares of the world. This was a quarantine depot. From here, Commonwealth Government launches would chug out to meet arriving ships and fumigate their cargo. The depot has shut, but what remains on the site are a collection of old buildings and a well-ordered, almost old-world atmosphere, straight from a Somerset Maugham story. The buildings, including an old coal bunker, sit on manicured lawns and recline under a pine tree and aged palms. The grounds strike a contrast to the unruly bush tumbling off Balls Head to the property's back fence. In recent years, the former depot has been providing quarantine from the everyday for those with money; it has been home to a luxury yacht charter business.

Neighbouring the old depot, but worlds apart in atmosphere, is a sliver of sand, which is given the rather dry title of North Sydney Council Beach. A 2012 study of Berrys Bay for the State Government noted there was no formal maritime facility on the beach. However, there is a wonderfully eccentric informal maritime facility. In other words, a shack. If the neighbour sips on the spirit of Somerset Maugham, then this structure has drifted in from *Robinson Crusoe*. The shack is garlanded in the flotsam and jetsam of harbour life: thick ropes, mooring buoys, a life-ring, and a bizarre collection of caps and thongs. On the shack's door is the image of a pirate. It looks as though a castaway or beachcomber should live here. But the barbecue, a wonky table and a couple of chairs, along with the overturned dinghies lying around the shack, indicate this is actually a retreat for local boaties. For the shack's decor, the designer wouldn't have had to go far. Rubbish is washed up at the shack's door. The tideline is a noose of wood and plastic; toys and bottle tops, bags, even a section of barricading tape that reads 'Danger'. It is an indication of just how much rubbish is funnelled into Berrys Bay, or dropped along its edges.

The shack may look like it is from *Robinson Crusoe*, but local resident Michael Stevens must feel like he *is* Robinson Crusoe when he walks along a small stretch of beach at the head of Berrys Bay, picking up rubbish and trying to get the message out to Sydneysiders to clean up after themselves. Yet each time, the message in a bottle he gets back is that too many people are either careless or lazy. He is left to pick up the bottle, and the plastic, and every other kind of garbage imaginable.

'I got into this by accident,' Michael, who is retired, explains of his passion for cleaning up the shoreline. 'In September 2011, I was walking on Waverton Oval then decided to go down and walk on the sand.'

Michael was disturbed by how much broken glass was along the little beach. So he picked up a piece, then another, and another. He returned the next day and did the same. And still there was more glass and other rubbish. He began noting what he collected. His first recorded entry in his journal, on 6 September 2011, showed he picked up 60 litres of rubbish and dug out a boat cover half buried in the sand.

His pattern was set. He kept returning to that strip of sand, barely 100 metres long, picked up the rubbish in 20-litre buckets and noted what he collected. By the end of that year – just four months – he had collected 2403 litres of rubbish.

By early 2017, Michael's tally had reached 16,517 litres – 'I've calculated that as two garbage trucks full'. He has mostly collected it at that same little strip. Occasionally, he wanders further around the bay's western shore, picking rubbish out of the rocks.

'I get an awful lot of plastic, in all shapes and sizes,' he says. 'Fishermen are big offenders, because the bags they buy their bait in ends up in the water, where it is a danger to the fish they're trying to catch.'

From what he picks up, Michael is convinced a lot of rubbish is blown – or tossed – off boats, or it has come down the storm-water drains on the other side of the harbour and is carried across into Berrys Bay, particularly when the southerly winds are strong.

'I find a lot of City of Sydney parking tickets,' he says. 'Perhaps the strangest thing I've picked up is a packet of sausages.'

Michael is no longer alone picking up rubbish on the local harbour beaches. He began a volunteer group called HarbourCare in 2013 and used his daily collection records to convince North Sydney Council to support it. He's hopeful more councils will join the HarbourCare campaign, for he argues that while there are clean-up events, one day a year is not enough to deal with the ceaseless tides of rubbish; it has to be every day.

Some days Michael finds staggering volumes of junk. On 27 December 2011, his records show, Michael picked up 200 litres of rubbish, including 120 litres in bottles. As a result, that Robinson Crusoe feeling can be overwhelming.

'Sometimes I think, "I should give up, I'm getting nowhere". But I'm getting somewhere. The message gets out that someone is taking care, and that rubs off. We get more people doing it.'

'But there's no future in picking up rubbish; we've got to stop dropping rubbish.'

Yet while ever there is rubbish on the beach, he will continue to walk with his buckets along the little harbour beach in Berrys Bay. He has received awards and recognition for his harbour care work, but that is not what motivates Michael Stevens. In his gentle voice, he simply concludes, 'I'm just someone who likes to leave the place tidy for the next person.'

MOORED ON the bay is a pleasure armada, from yachts and cruisers to former tourist boats. Historic vessels that once helped move a city also rest in these waters, including the steam tug *Lena*, with its name and year of construction – 1898 – carved in wood and attached to the stern, and the beautiful Manly ferry turned floating function centre, *South Steyne*. There's something about old work vessels that suggests they have an A-type, high-achiever personality. Even when they're just gently rocking in the water, they don't seem as though they've been retired; they're just waiting for the next job, the next voyage. They may be going nowhere, but these unreformed workaholics give the impression they're about to set off to – somewhere.

Helping give vessels, and their owners, hope that the journey continues is a shipyard along the bay's north-eastern shore. Actually, the Noakes yard helps give hope that there's life yet in Sydney as a working harbour. In a cradle in one of the yard's sheds, a wooden ferry is being caressed back to good health. A couple of sleek yachts are out of the water, sitting haughtily in the yard and showing off their lines, as they wait for a little cosmetic surgery. Squatting near the yachts are navy landing barges about to be repaired. Out the front in the water are more vessels waiting for their moment with the dozens of tradesmen and engineers working in the boatyard.

The boss is Sean Langman. Not that he is dressed like a boss when we meet. He is wearing safety glasses and a helmet, and he is a high-vis blur as he dashes in. He has just been down in the yard. Sean takes off his helmet and glasses, unharnessing a nest of sandy hair and sun-reddened skin. Now he looks like the sailor he has always been. Only a few days before, he had brought a yacht across Bass Strait and up the coast.

Sean is all energy, like the gusts of wind he captures in sails whenever he can. Yet he also knows how to slow down, by accepting you can't really control the elements; just learn from them. When I tell him I'm paddling around the harbour to slowly see Sydney from the water, he recounts how for months prior to the 2006 Sydney to Hobart race, he would row a 12-foot clinker dinghy from Woolwich to this yard.

'I was at a dinner party, and someone said, "There's this crazy guy who is rowing every day from Woolwich to Berrys Bay", and I had to say that I was that crazy guy,' he says.

But there was method to Sean's craziness. He was preparing not just for the gruelling race but also accruing knowledge of water and an even greater appreciation of the harbour.

'You understand the tidal flow, and the timelessness of the outcrops, the eddies swirling just as they have probably done for thousands of years,' Sean says. 'It was a case of taking my watch off. The rowing made me appreciate what's around us.'

Sean Langman was born for the water – 'I'm a Piscean' – and he was born on the water. Home for the first two years of his life was an old gaff rigged boat moored in Rushcutters Bay, further down the harbour, and his mother would row them to shore for showers. As a teenager, he lived up Parramatta River at Rhodes. Whenever he could, he'd be sailing either model boats or the real thing. He didn't fulfil his ambition to join the navy, but nothing could keep him off the water.

'I don't exist without being around boats, around the water,' he asserts.

Sean has made a living working on boats around the harbour. And he has sailed them out of the Heads and into the wide blue yonder. Sean has competed in twenty-six Sydney to Hobart races so far. He has endured horrendous experiences, such as competing in the 1998 race, when six sailors died. But Sean Langman's motivation for being part of the iconic race hasn't dimmed. He loves the 'have a go' attitude that pervades the race. He points out you can come from nothing, and your fellow crew members may be multi-millionaires, but out in the ocean, none of that matters. As Sean says, 'the sea doesn't discriminate'.

Sean Langman has run his Berrys Bay operation since 1994. He maintains not only boats but a tradition. For the business is literally built on the harbour's past. This was where the Stannard family operated its large yard, building boats from the 1960s. Long before then, all manner of vessels took shape along the bay's eastern shore. *Wallaby*, the first double-ended ferry on Sydney Harbour, was built in 1878 in a yard run by William Dunn. His yard built more than 400 vessels. Neighbouring Dunn's operations, the Ford family built a yard in the 1870s. The Fords built colliers, trading ketches that sailed the Pacific, and luxury motor yachts, including *Lady Hopetoun* in 1902. She was built to transport VIPs for the Sydney Harbour Trust, but through the years, this graceful steam vessel has accomplished other roles with aplomb. She has been everything from a naval command post during defence exercises to a rescue boat when vessels ran into strife on the harbour. And 'The *Lady*' is still chugging around the harbour, as a member of the Sydney Heritage Fleet. She is still trim and lustrous, and the smoke she exhales from her funnel carries the scent of the Edwardian era. Having paddled in her wake, I believe there can be no finer backside to follow in Sydney than that of *Lady Hopetoun*.

The shipbuilding that took place along the shoreline is officially commemorated by a plaque and steel walkway, which is known as Boatbuilders' Walk. At the Noakes yard, Sean Langman and his team of about 50 full-time workers continue making, building and restoring history. In 2008, he bought Rosman Ferries, with its historic wooden boats. The ferries are moored outside the yard, when they're not out on the water. They are popular for chartering, but for Sean the business is as much about the heart as it is the head.

'We've got to hold on to some things we call iconically Australian,' he declares. 'We should keep those things that are at the core of us, and wooden ferry boats are part of that. Some of these boats are more than 100 years old, and that's in a country not even 240 years old. Once they're gone, they're gone.'

To pay for the passion for boats, there has to be profit. The yard has to survive, not just financially but also in the face of public opinion. He has had to contend with those who want their harbour to be little more than an adornment in their windows.

'They like the romantic notion of it being a working harbour, but . . .' Sean says, adding that some locals don't want the sights and sounds that come with a maritime industry.

Debate over how Berrys Bay should be used in the future has been chopping up the waters locally. On the bay's western side is the site of a slipway and marina that operated for almost a century to 2011. The name of the marina – Woodleys Pty Ltd – remains in bold letters across the main shed. The noonday sun tattoos the letters in shadows onto the building's corrugated-iron skin. The wharf out the front of the shed has all but given up and collapsed into the bay. Yet where old infrastructure sinks, developers' dreams float. A plan for a marina capable of holding about eighty vessels, including super yachts, has been opposed by an action group which doesn't want to see the western shore turn into a parking lot for big boats.

Sean is confident about the bay's future. He has seen seals in the bay, and sharks. He was once in the water, helping manoeuvre a racing yacht down a slip, while its crew of visiting European sailors watched from the seawall. One of them yelled out to ask Sean what he did when he saw a shark. Sean replied that he would wrestle the shark and throw it back in the water. 'Well, what about that one?' the European said, pointing to a fin cutting the surface nearby. Sean was out of the water in a flash.

Sean Langman is adamant about one future use for Berrys Bay. It will be his resting place.

In the harbour where Sean was born, works and sails, a place where every cove and bay holds a memory, Berrys Bay is to him the most significant. So when he dies, he wants his remains to be sprinkled into the bay off the *Young Endeavour* replica sailing ship, which he has done a lot of work on. Not that he's thinking that far ahead. Just as he rarely stands on the shore and contemplates all that has happened for him around this bay. He hasn't had time to count how many boats he's worked on during his career – 'thousands' – let alone chart his place in the harbour's history. Sean remains right here, in the moment, a man who is happy when he is on the water.

A LOT of the waterfront around the bay has been opened up for enjoyment. On the western shore is Carradah Park. From the water, it doesn't look like a park, with its faces of cut and sliced sandstone. Generally, faces record a life story, but here, the sculpted cliffs tell only part of the terrain's tale. Alexander Berry's storehouse was built on these western shores. A torpedo and seabed mine base was also here during colonial times. Berry's warehouse was later converted into a distillery used by a local hotel. But from 1922 until 1993, the site was a major oil storage facility. Along the waterfront was a series of wharves. With ships no longer tying up to them, the older timber wharves have deteriorated, and paddling close to the time-silvered piers is like gliding through tree trunks in an ancient forest. When the terminal was operating, lumped around the curve of the bay towards Woodley's slipways were more than a dozen storage tanks, and a few of them doubled as billboards for the oil company.

The prominence of industry on the waterfront annoyed a few influential observers. C.E.W. Bean, the renowned war correspondent and author, complained about the 'disfigurement of the harbour foreshores by oil companies and other industrial concerns'. Bean reportedly told a town planners' meeting in 1931 that, 'One could not blame the oil companies if they chose prominent sites with a view to advertising their products . . . Citizens were to be blamed for taking no steps to prevent them.' One of those attending the meeting had an interesting proposal to tone the industrial structures into the landscape. He suggested they 'could be castellated on top to resemble mediaeval castles'.

As it is, the hill has the look of a fortress. The landscape is scabrous, and there are also the in-grown carbuncles of industry. The storage tanks have been removed, but their footprints remain, and grasping the rock are sections of the thick bund walls that were designed to contain spills and leaks. However, from the top of the hill, just near where tanker trucks used to be filled, there are platforms to soak in the view over the harbour. In some ways, the lookouts return the scene to how it was before the oil terminal was built, when famous artists who lived locally, such as Will Ashton and Roland Wakelin, would sit up here and paint. With their brushes and oils, they were creating art, but they were also recording history. Wakelin's *Down the hills to Berry's Bay*, painted in 1916, shows the boat-sheds along the eastern shore, including one where the Noakes yard is today.

On the ridgeline, a large sign has been erected by the local council. The sign stands next to the skeleton of a gum tree, and it barges into the view, with the declaration, 'WARNING. Trees in this area have been wilfully destroyed by selfish vandals'. Just across the bay is a reminder of when trees were felled in huge numbers not by vandals but to build an economy. Sawmillers Reserve is a crescent of green pressed between the sandstone hill and the harbour. Casuarinas along the shore catch the sun and sprinkle the light onto the grounds. Every couple of years, the reserve becomes an open-air art gallery, when it hosts the 'Sculptures at Sawmillers' exhibition, the brainchild of a local resident. Crowds wander around materials recycled, reshaped and reimagined into story-telling shapes. Where these sculptures are exhibited was once the site of a timber yard. It was started in the late 19th century by a merchant whose name suggests he was born for this business, John Wood Eaton. The forests of the globe, from Baltic pine to oak and kauri, were shipped into the bay and unloaded at the company's wharves. The sawn timber would make its way around the city and even back out of the harbour, being exported as pre-fabricated buildings for the Pacific islands. The disembodied forest grew along the foreshore, as Eaton's yard expanded through the 20th century. Large rafts of timber floated in the water, and wharves stretched for hundreds of metres along the curve of the bay. The company ceased operating at Berrys Bay in the early 1980s. Some of the land was sliced off for home units, the rest becoming Sawmillers Reserve.

The frenetic waterfront activity has been replaced by a lone shipwreck lying in the shallows just off the reserve. I paddle into the wreck and pick my way among its bones. The vessel is gradually shedding its iron-plate skin, exposing its skeleton, while part of the concrete deck and a number of thick wooden planks cling tenaciously to the structure. The wreck is that of a Maritime Services Board barge. While the other vessels that berthed here are but ghosts and memories, this barge has kept its shape, trying to defy the incessant scratching of the water and the years.

This stretch of the harbour could have held a vastly different look. It could have been 'modernised', according to the plans and vision of Australia's best-known architect, Harry Seidler. When he moved to Australia after the Second World War, Austrian-born Seidler carried a head full of modernist ideas and influences in building design. He didn't want to be part of a process that plonked people in dark boxes to live and work, as though they were still in England and stuck in the past. He desired to create buildings that respected the environment, helped build a sense of community, and encouraged its inhabitants to live in the here and now. While many were still grappling with what Australian architecture actually was, Harry Seidler had a clear picture of what Sydney needed in its buildings. On the serrated sandstone peninsula heaving out of the water from Blues Point and McMahons Point, Seidler had found a canvas on which to create on a grand scale.

In the late 1950s, Harry Seidler envisaged a tiered residential development that followed the lie of the land: low buildings close to the water, medium-height buildings staggered up the slope, and high-rise towers along the ridge. Seidler saw this design as a practical way to approach high-density living, giving everyone access to public transport, open space, and a view of the water. He and a group of other architects drew up plans and made a model of how the peninsula would look. To Seidler, the development would be a harbour showpiece, demonstrating what could be done on other peninsulas. However, the proposal was about more than bringing contemporary building design to Sydney; it was also a bulwark against the local council's plans to designate the McMahons Point area an industrial zone. Seidler railed in the media that no country in the modern world would allow such a beautiful harbour foreshore to be defiled by factories. Seidler's vision for the peninsula had the backing of locals opposed to the idea of industry in their suburb.

However, Seidler's plan for the peninsula wasn't realised, and in many areas in the years that followed, the opposite happened, with towers being built on the waterfront, blocking the view for all behind. From Seidler's musings and hopes for the peninsula, only one apartment tower was built, in 1961. Blues Point Tower was then the tallest apartment building in Australia and, according to his biographer Helen O'Neill, larger than anything that was in his plans for McMahons Point.

Blues Point Tower sticks up like a defiant finger at the local authorities who rejected Seidler's ideas. But being a 24-storey building alone at the tip of the peninsula, Blues Point Tower also sticks out. Wherever you are, be it travelling over the Bridge, on a harbour ferry, standing on the shore, or kayaking around the reserve at its feet, you can see the tower. While architects and students rave about the building's design, and Seidler himself said he liked its facades, to its detractors the tower holds all the aesthetic appeal of a public toilet. That concrete and brick finger has been viewed by many as a poke in the eye to all trying to appreciate the harbour's beauty. Arguably more than any other building, Blues Point Tower has copped the blame for changing Sydney's face for the worse.

Still, it all depends on your perspective. For those on the inside looking out, it's a fine building. A friend used to live in Blues Point Tower, and whenever I stood in his lounge room at the small 'french' balcony that faced south-west, I felt the unit's windows were not big enough. But that is the problem with harbour views; they make you greedy to the point you're never satisfied.

Iconic buildings around Sydney that Seidler designed, from Australia Square to the Horizon apartment tower, reach for the sky, but the memorial to him is a small horizontal patch next to his old office at Milsons Point. From Harry's Park, you can peer across to that architectural exclamation mark of his, Blues Point Tower.

Harry Seidler was hardly the originator of big and bold statements around Blues Point. The man behind the headland's name, Billy Blue, was, by all accounts, the master of the big statement. Billy Blue is believed to be originally from Jamaica. Whether it was Jamaica in New York or in the West Indies remains a topic of discussion. He was working on the docks in London when he was charged with possessing a stolen bag of sugar and sentenced in 1796 to transportation to New South Wales. It wasn't until 1801 that he sailed into Sydney. A decade on, the harbour that had been his prison was the making of Billy Blue. As well as being appointed a waterside watchman by Governor Macquarie to prevent smuggling, Blue had a private ferry service, rowing passengers across the harbour to the North Shore. His fleet grew from one rowboat to eleven, apparently prompting the Governor to exclaim that Blue should be called 'Commodore'. After that, Billy Blue was widely known as the Old Commodore. He wore a naval uniform and top hat and insisted on being greeted in a manner in keeping with his rank of Commodore.

Billy Blue was notorious for jesting with, and insulting, any passenger who tried to lord it over him, and for regaling those on board with tales about his long and apparently adventurous life. The Old Commodore was also loath to row. Alexander Harris wrote in his book, *Settlers and Convicts*, about being a paying customer of Billy Blue: 'He told us, with quite a fatherly sort of authority, that he had been across a good many times that day; that we must pull him over to the other side, and he would take the boat back. The "Old Commodore" being considered to possess a sort of universal freedom of speech to everybody, no demur was made. We pulled him across in his own boat, and paid him our fares for pulling himself back again.'

When Billy Blue died, there was much conjecture in Sydney about his age. Some claimed he was 100. What was certain is that he was a celebrity on the water. Around the time of his death, a poster of Billy Blue was printed and sold. The poster featured the words 'True Blue!' and a sketch portrait of him in top hat and uniform, and rattling the stick he was fond of carrying. The poster was also adorned with some of his favourite sayings, including, 'No rows, my child' and 'Go along, you long legg'd brute'.

The Old Commodore's influence flows around Blues Point and McMahons Point into the next bay. It has such a pretty name. Lavender Bay. Yet it is not named after bunches of soft purple herbs but after George Lavender, a Royal Navy man who had worked on a floating convict barracks, *Phoenix*, that sat in the bay. Lavender made his way into local lore, marrying Billy Blue's daughter, Susannah. Eventually, after being a ferryman like his father-in-law, Lavender was the owner of the Old Commodore Hotel up the hill in Blues Point Road.

The bay itself is an intoxicating place, because it possesses more than a pretty name. And its Aboriginal name is even prettier – Quibaree, believed to refer to the fresh water spring that used to be here. No matter what it is called, this is a beautiful alcove, so near yet removed from the hurly-burly of the main harbour as it approaches the Bridge, a few hundred metres away. Even when it is being lashed by a southerly, and its waters are tussled, the bay still feels serene.

These days a few dozen boats are usually moored in the bay. Along its shores there used to be boatsheds and slipways, a ferry wharf and a grand bath house, owned by Fred Cavill. His son Dick, a champion swimmer, trained in the baths and is credited with inventing the stroke known as the Australian crawl.

A wharf remains but hosts only the occasional charter ferry these days. Although it is a fishing platform. I chat with Reece, a young man who has caught the train from Ryde to cast his lines into the bay. He's been fishing here for fifteen years, since he was a boy.

'There are not many wharves left in Sydney where you can fish without it being packed,' he explains. Not that his fishing rods have bent even slightly so far on this day.

'There's usually something around,' he murmurs, peering into the clear green that darkens as the harbour drops away. 'It's pretty clean around this spot.' As the water quality has improved in recent years, so have the stocks of fish, especially bream, in the bay. If he does catch a fish – and he remains confident – Reece will eat it, despite the official warnings about toxic levels.

'I eat fish from here, but I wouldn't from anywhere further up,' Reece says, as he slices a fresh sardine for bait.

If he doesn't catch a fish, Reece can always cook the sardines – or wait until he returns to work. He has a job in a fish shop.

On the steep slopes around the bay are a few historic mansions. But there used to be more; time and a city ever hungrier for land knocked them over. Further up the hill, with perhaps the finest views of the harbour, was a mansion built from gold. Bernhardt Holtermann had been scratching away for years at Hill End with little success. But then in 1872, a syndicate he was part of hit a massive lump of reef gold, the largest ever uncovered at that time. It became known as Holtermann's Nugget. Using some of his fortune, Holtermann built a home on the heights above the harbour, with a 27-metre tower that included a stained-glass window portraying him standing with the nugget. Yet the tower was more than a shrine to himself and the source of his wealth. It was a mount for another of his passions: photography. From the tower, Holtermann and a photographer he had met in Hill End, Charles Bayliss, captured a panorama of Sydney. The pair would carefully carry large and bulky glass plates up the staircase to the camera Bayliss had installed at the top of the tower.

A brief time in the history of the harbour city was preserved on the plates. Holtermann had performed alchemy of sorts, turning gold and light into a series of extraordinary images of Sydney.

The panorama was displayed at major exhibitions in Philadelphia and Paris. Holtermann and Bayliss opened the eyes of the world to a city still straggling out of the scrub, and with buildings shaped out of the sandstone on which they stood. What binds the foreground and background is the great anguine shape of the harbour slithering through the middle of the panorama. In the images, the harbour cradles ships, under sail and steam, from the wharves of Sydney Cove to the distant bays to the east. The viewer's eyes drift from left to right, pushing against the journey of the harbour from the rivers to the sea. And the harbour seems to flow on, beyond the margins of the panorama, from another time into ours. It is an extraordinarily important series of photos, exposing how much a city has developed, and regressed, around the harbour.

In one of the photographs is Lavender Bay, with a couple of sailing ships and a steamer in its embrace. The image also showed the bay had a longer reach than it does now. The cove was shaped like an arrowhead piercing the land, but it softened the blow with a sandy tip that was a popular beach. From 1890, the cove was filled in and the bay's shoreline was sculpted for a rail line to the nearby Milsons Point ferry terminal. It is no longer the main line, but the rails remain, running like an old scar close to the shore.

While the rail line partially cut off the water from those living up the hill, a viaduct it ran over did provide a nest for one harbour tradition. For more than a decade, a renowned wooden boatbuilder, Bob Gordon, had a workshop under the arches. Before then, he built boats out in the open on the bay's shores.

Life jogged by the graffiti-marked brick walls with barely a sideways glance. But if you stopped and peered into the space under the viaduct, it was like following the white rabbit into a wonderland. You were treated to the scent of wood and the sight and sounds of time-seasoned skills being practised, as Bob and his son, Robert, used hand-tools to whittle and plane, saw and shape timber into elegant boats. It felt as though you were observing something you had presumed was extinct.

At the front of his workshop was a slipway. Boats had taken shape there since the late 19th century, and it was once used by the Neptune Engineering and Slipway Company, which pioneered the design and building of marine diesel engines in Australia. When that business closed in the bay in the late 1980s, much of the land had housing piled on top of it, but the slipway remained. Bob Gordon considered it an insult for the historic slip to be left decrepit.

He bemoaned how heritage was allowed to fade away.

'No one is interested until it's too late,' he said.

Bob Gordon launched his last boat in 2005, and he died the following year. The arch was sealed, and so was a window to the past. The world kept jogging past, largely unaware that the city, especially the harbour, had lost yet another character. All that is left as a reminder of the bay's boatbuilding past is the idle slipway. It may have a plaque in front of it, but that doesn't mean the historic landmark is accorded the respect it deserves. Once when I paddled onto the small beach that has formed at the slipway, I noticed a used syringe floating in the shallows.

But regeneration can occur in the unlikeliest of places.

Just up the hill, peeking out from behind the gangly limbs of a massive old Moreton Bay fig, is a white Federation house with a fairytale tower. It is the home of Wendy Whiteley. She is half of a formidably creative couple. Wendy was the wife, muse and painting subject of the acclaimed artist Brett Whiteley.

Wendy and Brett Whiteley, along with their daughter Arkie, moved to Lavender Bay in 1969, after visiting a friend here.

'We'd never been in Lavender Bay before, we didn't even know of its existence, and, of course, we instantly fell in love with the harbour,' recalls Wendy, as we sit in the kitchen of her home.

In those days, the baths and its wooden change sheds were still on the shore, and the Whiteleys would swim in there. Early in the morning, they would wander down to the wharf in their pyjamas and buy fish directly from the trawler of an Italian–Australian fisherman.

When they moved here, the Whiteleys rented a flat in this house. Like many older homes in the area, it had been carved up inside. The Whiteleys' flat was on the floor where we are chatting. It is now a gleaming space, opened up to the view of the harbour and the Bridge, which is perfectly framed by the branches of the Moreton Bay fig. But before the Whiteleys bought the house in 1974 and renovated it, the harbour was effectively locked out.

'All these houses were built to keep the light out, and therefore the view, because they didn't want all that sun coming in and bleaching their red velvet curtains,' Wendy explains, while managing to keep a straight face. 'This had stained glass and everything. Why would you want stained glass between you and the harbour? We got rid of all that crap very fast.'

Brett also arranged for the quirky tower to be built, partly for the view, but it was also functional, encasing a spiral staircase that linked the house's floors. I ask Wendy does she often go to the top of the tower.

'No. There's a perfectly good view out there on the veranda.'

In the mid-1970s, Wendy could see straight over the Moreton Bay fig, but it has doubled in size since then. Not that she has ever sought a clear view; she finds it less interesting. That attitude puts her at odds with many in Sydney.

'I love the tree!' she says. 'I looked after it. A lot of people who have come here have said, "Oh Christ, why didn't you kill that tree!", and I've said, "Why do I need to have a completely open view of some rather mediocre buildings on the other side of the harbour." I love the Bridge, but I can see the Bridge perfectly well, and Luna Park.'

The view from the Whiteleys' windows has become our view of Sydney Harbour. The palm trees, the wharf prodding at the bay, the smears and slashes of boats' wakes, we've seen it all through Whiteley's eyes. For the artist was seduced by the harbour, in all its moods and colours. When the sun was shining, he used his favourite colour, French ultramarine blue, to create a glazed harbour; when it was rainy and subdued, he made the water creamy, like a rock oyster. Just as the harbour's response to the weather could be capricious, so could the artist's be to the harbour; he even painted it orange. What was constant was his love for this slice of the harbour at Lavender Bay.

The way he responded to the curves of the shoreline, the headlands, the water itself, resulted in images that are very sexual, I suggest to Wendy. She pauses, before replying diplomatically, 'Yeah, sensual maybe.'

'Of course, the harbour's sensual, because it's beautiful, so it's sensual – and sexual, in that sense of it being beautiful and interesting, and alive. But you're not going to look at it simply because it's got a curve in it and you see a tit or a bum every time, otherwise you'd go nuts, because that's so clichéd in a way.

'The fact is Brett used that kind of abstraction in his early paintings, and he loved the curve, he didn't like straight lines. He wasn't a straight-line person.'

'So, he didn't look at the harbour and see a tit or a bum?'

'He saw visual ecstasy, as he described it. So is that sensual or sexual, or both?' Wendy asks in a way that sounds like more of a statement.

'Both.'

She smiles, as though she has finally got through to a none-too-bright student.

'There you go,' she says quietly.

Between the visual ecstasy and the house lay an eyesore. The gully filled in for the railway line had become a dump over the years, descending into a tangled mess of weeds and rubbish, impenetrable to all but a few homeless people.

But the wasteland was to be a place of healing for Wendy Whiteley. In an area that had been given up for dead, she nurtured life, and a purpose for living. When Brett died in 1992, Wendy dealt with her grief by wandering into the wasteland and began hacking and clearing. As a little girl, her favourite book was *The Secret Garden*, about an orphan and her cousin transforming a neglected patch of earth – and themselves – into something beautiful and healthy. Just as in the story, Wendy Whiteley did the same with the harbourside railway land. She created a 'secret garden'. Wendy and a gang of helpers became 'guerrilla gardeners'. They recycled materials; old railway sleepers became steps, the sandstone rubble that had been used as landfill was the key material of drystone walls, and discarded objects were turned into little sculptures. And there was a lot of planting. The garden was not formal in design, nor was it officially on the books.

'I'm not a horticulturalist, I wasn't a gardener,' Wendy explains. 'I did it by eye and hard work.'

The garden again became a place to work through grief and loss for Wendy, when Arkie died from cancer in 2001. Through the years, the garden was not just a place for Wendy to find peace. More and more people wandered in, looking for somewhere beautiful to have lunch, to meet with friends, or to gather their thoughts. The secret was out. For Wendy's garden offers not just visual ecstasy but also qualities increasingly hard to find in Sydney, serenity and joy.

You don't walk into Wendy's Secret Garden; rather, it seems to invite you in. More than enchant you, Wendy's garden embraces and envelops you. You observe the sudden change in environment, as you can't see too far ahead down the squiggly paths for the profusion of trees and plants. But that is how the garden changes you. It calms you down and gently encourages you to enjoy the moment. Don't look for the wide view, or gaze too far ahead; just revel in what is right before you. It is a magical garden.

Little wonder this place is now very much on the map, even if there are no physical signs pointing to the garden. Tour groups and wedding parties traipse in, it features on visitors' websites, and it is the subject of a beautiful coffee-table book, *Wendy Whiteley and the Secret Garden*. Even the State Government has had to acknowledge its existence, and priceless community value, with a long-term lease. Wendy's secret garden is now everybody's haven.

'I can't get my knickers in a knot, can I, when I look out there and see people are loving it and enjoying it and writing in the [visitors'] book, because that's what it's for,' she says.

Wendy still loves wandering down into the valley, getting her hands dirty and, in effect, being that little girl in *The Secret Garden*.

'Somebody transforming something,' she murmurs. 'Alchemy.' Which happens to be the title of one of Brett's best-known paintings.

The garden has given Wendy a greater sense of belonging and an even deeper love of Lavender Bay. She calls it her heart and soul place.

'I love the bay. It's just spectacular. It has a very, very special thing about it, Lavender Bay, that I haven't felt in any other bay in Sydney, or anywhere else.

'There's something very protected and heart-warming about this place. People feel it when they come here, and it's not just the garden. They feel it's very peaceful, and it's not dangerous, and it's just got a very good *feng shui*. And that's got nothing to do with me. I've just made it accessible.'

6

MILSONS POINT AND THE BRIDGE

THE ENCHANTMENT of Lavender Bay wends its way out of Wendy's Secret Garden and down to the water. A boardwalk meanders for a few hundred metres towards Luna Park. On the right is the boat-dotted harbour. On the left, playing hide-and-seek in the vegetation, are cute little statues of characters that have shaped many an Australian childhood, including Blinky Bill, Bib and Bub, and Ginger Meggs, along with sculptures of local icons – a ferry and the clown's face entrance to Luna Park.

The procession of characters is mostly from the hands of artist Peter Kingston. From his nickname, 'Kingo', to his love of comic books and his passionate approach to conversations, Peter is like a kid. But that's not why he created what he calls 'The Comic Walk'. Rather, it was out of a sense of atonement, Sydney Harbour style.

Peter Kingston lives just above Lavender Bay, in an old house neighbouring Wendy Whiteley's. From his lounge room and veranda, Peter has a view through coral trees to Luna Park and the Bridge. The trees are bursting with red flowers, which look like a wig plonked on the amusement park. It looks somehow appropriate, given Luna Park's catchphrase is 'Just for Fun'. Yet there was a time when the red wig was too shaggy, and the trees blocked the view. So Peter gave them a trim.

'To sort of compensate for doing that, I put in those sculptures,' Peter explains. 'If you do something, you've got to give something back a bit more.'

Peter Kingston loves preservation. He helps preserve childhood memories with his little sculptures along the boardwalk, which has been officially named Peter Kingston Walkway. And he's helped preserve Luna Park.

When Luna Park opened in 1935, that big mouth at its entrance offered what was missing on so many Sydneysiders' faces. After years of privation during the Great Depression, a North Sydney alderman, James Street Stanton, noted the city needed brightening, and that the park would supply 'a big want in the lives of Sydney and North Sydney'. Alderman Stanton's comment underlined a separation between his side of the harbour and the other, as though something other than the kilometre or so of water was between them. But the city had a common desire for fun, so it seemed Luna Park would achieve what has always been a challenge ever since the British sailed into Port Jackson; pulling people to the opposite shore.

Even before it opened, Luna Park had its critics. Some were worried it would attract undesirables and threaten the morals of the good people of North Sydney, while others believed it would be another eyesore on the foreshore. Yet the criticisms were trampled under the rush to the new face beside the harbour.

Like moths, Sydneysiders were drawn to the lights of Luna Park. During the Second World War, the park was an escape for soldiers on leave, along with the young women they took out on the town. The harbour was incorporated in the fun. There were speedboat rides on Lavender Bay and to the Bridge. For a time after the war, a decommissioned Dutch submarine was moored next to the park, with customers shuffling through its cramped interior. The excitement of Luna Park pressed itself onto the pages of literature, including Dymphna Cusack and Florence James' best-selling novel set in wartime Sydney, *Come In Spinner*, and it crackled through the lives of boys and girls growing up in a world juggling a precarious peace.

'Luna Park was always the place we loved to go to as kids,' Peter Kingston recalls. 'Luna Park's heyday was the 1950s, '60s; that's when it had all the great rides, like the River Caves, and the roller coaster was a *proper* roller coaster, the Big Dipper.'

The harbour also added to the sense of adventure for Peter.

'It was like Luna Park was on an island. You'd get the ferry from Circular Quay, and that's how you'd approach Luna Park. And on beautiful heritage ferries as well. It was so magic.'

The magic threatened to fade. The fun park occupied land where serious money could be made with development. Yet it was saved. In the mid-1970s, artist and Luna Park enthusiast Martin Sharp was commissioned to put colour back into the place. Sharp assembled a team of artists, including Peter Kingston, who had moved into the old house above Lavender Bay, which is now his home. Back then, it was a jumble of flats.

For Peter, the job was not just creating artworks, but restoring what had fed his imagination as a kid. Arthur 'Art' Barton was an artist and Luna Park's chief decorator. He had been there virtually from the outset and helped give the park its irresistibly quirky look. On the walls and around the rides, Barton painted faraway places, fantasy scenes, and wide-eyed characters in a colourful, comic style.

Peter says he was 'besotted' by the paintings, because Barton absorbed ideas from other cultures yet in what he created gave it 'an Aussie twist'. Barton's paintings were among 'the jewels of the city'.

Barton also devised what Peter considers the best of the grinning faces at the entrance. The years and the salt rubbed away the smile, so there had to be facelifts, about nine by Peter's count. In recent years, he urged the park's management to return the face to the Arthur Barton design, 'which is sort of like old King Cole'. Yet it's still not quite right, Peter argues, before pointing to a model he has made of Luna Park's entrance.

'That's the right face,' Peter says, picking up the model. 'That's Arthur Barton's mouth.'

Peter Kingston worked mainly in Coney Island, which was adorned with Barton images and housed simple pleasures, such as slippery dips and the spinning 'Joy Wheel'. Coney Island is still there. Peter points to the building's crown of a silver onion dome. It looks at once exotic, like something plonked onto Coney Island from the steppes of central Russia, and familiar. It has been there by the harbour for eighty years.

On a winter's night in 1979, the fun was replaced with tragedy. A fire tore through the Ghost Train. A man and his two sons, along with four other children, died. Peter Kingston was away, so didn't see the blaze that horrified Sydney.

To honour those who died, Peter, along with cartoonist Michael Leunig, designed a small sculpture atop a plinth with

HENRY ERNEST
SEARLE
CHAMPION SCULLER
OF THE WORLD 1888-9

the seven victims' names etched into it. The memorial is near the other little statues along the waterfront.

After the fire, Luna Park was closed for a couple of years, and for a time its future was threatened. Peter was instrumental in the formation of the Friends of Luna Park. He thought it was vital Luna Park survived. This wild nest of popular culture, with its wide-eyed face at the entrance, stares across the water to the soaring home of high culture, the Opera House. To lose Luna Park, Peter reckons, would have lessened the very look of Sydney Harbour.

'I think it's amazingly important,' argues Peter. 'The relationship between the Opera House, Luna Park and the Bridge – along with the wharves and the ferries – makes Sydney very special. They're all the anchor points, aren't they?

'But there was also a great fear of what would replace it.'

Peter points to the wall of luxury apartment blocks looming over Luna Park. The site could have easily ended up being buried under high-rise buildings. With the support of enthusiasts such as Peter, a listing on the State Heritage Register, and legislation to protect the site passed by the New South Wales Parliament in 1990, Luna Park lives on.

In Peter's eyes, the park isn't quite what it was. However, in his art, Peter Kingston has restored the Luna Park he remembers. In his studio, downstairs from where we're sitting, he has created images that have boisterous life crawling all over them; the rides, the crowds, the sense of abandon, Kingo has them all going off like a party popper across the paper. More than being just for fun, his Luna Park works seem to pay homage to the art of Arthur Barton. Yet the title of one etching indicates that it is not all joie de vivre for Peter: *Au Revoir Old Luna Park*.

'I'm glad it's there,' Peter shrugs, as he peers towards Luna Park. 'I can't imagine that not being there.'

From his studio window, Peter can see the harbour. He doesn't always like what he sees, or what he can no longer see. In the bay is one of the old wooden ferries that transported passengers across the harbour to the Quay for decades. Peter fought for the service to be retained, but it finally ended in 2003. A couple of the little ferries were given another life as charter vessels, but Peter wonders how much longer they will stay on the water.

The working harbour remains in Peter Kingston's images. Tugs skitter across the water, and the ferries plough on, through grey days and into the night, their shapes like phantoms, made barely visible by their lights that dribble onto the dark harbour. Peter adores the old ferries.

'They're well built, well made, they're beautiful, they add to the furniture of the harbour, like the cable cars in San Francisco.'

Unlike his former neighbour Brett Whiteley's sensual depictions of the harbour and life by Lavender Bay, Peter Kingston's images are often pensive, varnished with melancholy. They are an evocative lament for what is disappearing from the harbour.

'It's not really a working harbour anymore. I think it's sad. Its diversity, things to draw and paint . . .'

Still, some aspects of harbour life have changed for the better. In 1973, Peter starred in, and co-produced, a short film inspired by one of his comic book heroes, The Phantom. In *Fanta*, Peter plays a young man who imagines himself as The Phantom. His neighbour, Wendy Whiteley, has a major role, and so does Lavender Bay. Watching Peter Kingston's character sitting on a ferry, I notice three marked differences between then and now.

He is sitting on wooden bench seats, he is smoking, and he throws a match out the window into the water.

'Did I now?' Peter asks, when I mention the littering scene.

'Times have changed, haven't they? You rarely see people chuck something into the harbour these days. It's the rise of consciousness, isn't it?'

The harbour will remain Peter Kingston's muse 'till the end, will always be'. He can't imagine living, or painting, anywhere else.

'I really wouldn't know where to go,' Peter shrugs, as his gaze drifts off through the space between the coral trees to Coney Island and its crazy onion dome.

WHILE I kayak along the shores of Lavender Bay and look up at the wall of apartments on the ridge, the words of Peter Kingston spring to mind.

'Have you ever seen a more miserable group of buildings?'

Yes, I have. But the cool aloofness of many of the apartments seems at odds with the sounds in the air, as shrieks of laughter and fright, and warped phrases of rock music, are flung out from the rides at Luna Park.

The new residents and the old fun fair have been awkward neighbours at times, with complaints about the park. Yet I imagine the annoyance of some apartment dwellers would seem like a model of tolerance compared with the reaction of James Milson, if he could see Luna Park.

Milson was the first permanent British settler in North Sydney. After arriving as a free emigrant in 1806, he secured land on the peninsula now named after him. Milson complained about his land being only rocks and stones but he was advised that was as good as money; they could be sold as ballast to the ships. Milson soon grasped the idea that in this young colony, you made the most of what you had, and soon you would make something of yourself. He sold to ships' crews fruit and vegetables, and, with the establishment of a dairy farm on his land, milk.

The first recorded burials on the North Shore occurred on Milson's land. Three crew members of the visiting ship *Surry* died of smallpox in 1814. In time, the headstones were uprooted and used in the construction of cottages on Milsons Point but were retrieved when the buildings were demolished to make way for the Sydney Harbour Bridge. While he accommodated the dead on his land, Milson was less appreciative of those swimming at the beaches on what he considered his piece of the harbour. If he were still here, how would he cope with hordes of revellers at an amusement park on what had been his land?

Visitors arrive at Luna Park not just for fun, but also to get married, attend concerts and conferences, and even to dine out in an eye-bulging pop-up restaurant. The carriages on the Ferris wheel are converted into mobile private dining rooms. Yet many still turn up for the rides. In school holidays, the crowds queue out of the entrance, putting their money where its mouth is.

Other visitors head for neighbouring North Sydney Olympic Pool, which was built soon after Luna Park opened. Dozens of world records were set in this pool, which hosted the swimming events for the 1938 Empire Games. These days, people go there to slow down time, swimming outdoors, glancing at the harbour right beside them as they stroke out their laps.

Long before it became a relaxation destination, Milsons Point was a hub for ferries. By the late 19th century, the vessels were steaming across the harbour around the clock. There were also large ferries carrying carts and livestock. The passenger ferries servicing Milsons Point and Lavender Bay had their own wharf at Circular Quay and an elaborate terminal on the North Shore. The Milsons Point complex was built in 1886. It featured a stunning leadlight window, welcoming passengers as they headed under the arched roof. The terminal's construction coincided with the introduction of a cable tram service, delivering people from further up the North Shore to it, and those numbers only grew when the rail line was extended to Milsons Point in 1893.

Thousands of commuters poured onto the harbour in the morning and were disgorged onto the North Shore of an evening. The artist Lloyd Rees, who lived nearby, recalled the 'great evening rush' of passengers from the Milsons Point terminal to the trains and trams.

'Young men in their dozens line the sides [of the ferry], poised to jump at the earliest safe moment (sometimes they misjudge and go home wet),' Rees recalled.

You wouldn't want to end up in the water around Milsons Point; it seems to be always cantankerous. No matter if the day is still and the harbour seems calm wherever else you look, the water here forms into little fists and punches the seawall. Worse, it grabs the kayak and contemptuously shoves it around. *Pulbah Raider* is usually content in the harbour. But at Milsons Point, as I deal with the churn, I feel I'd be better off in a sea kayak – or a ferry.

The washing-machine effect is exacerbated by the water being funnelled between Milsons Point and Dawes Point on the southern shore. This is among the narrowest parts of the main harbour. And nearby is some of its deepest water, up to about 45 metres. All sorts of things are down there. In 2015, the Port Authority discovered on the floor near Blues Point a ship's propeller, with each blade about 1.5 metres long. The authority speculated the propeller had been dumped, and the culprit was probably aiming for a hole on the harbour floor but missed.

Despite the churn and wash, when paddling past Milsons Point, I tend to look not down but up. I stare at a sky of steel.

SYDNEY HARBOUR Bridge carries more than vehicles and pedestrians. It carries expensive advertising and marketing campaigns, breathless superlatives from tourists, and the demands of Sydneysiders for it to be simultaneously a piece of gleaming costume jewellery and an unmistakable identity badge for their city. In short, it carries the weight of the world's expectations and emotions. It's a wonder the Bridge doesn't collapse into the harbour.

Yet whenever you lay eyes on the Bridge, it is so transfixing, you not only feel as though you're the first to ever see it, you're overcome with a televangelist's urge to tell everyone else about it. Sydneysiders who can barely remember their phone number are able to rattle off the vital statistics of the Bridge. Which is why the resigned tone of Sydney's great poet, Kenneth Slessor, is so funny. In his otherwise loving essay, 'A Portrait of Sydney', Slessor concedes the Bridge 'elbows itself into any description of Sydney as truculently as it forces its presence on the city'. Slessor then takes a big breath, presses his tongue into his cheek, and spews figures: 'The Bridge is 20 miles high, weighs 736,000

Persian Yakmans (which is roughly equivalent to 24,000,000 Turkish yusdrums), is 142 miles, 17 rods, 23 poles, 5 perches in length, carries everything from rickshaws to electric buggies, and feeds on paint.'

Actually, Sydney Harbour Bridge is 134 metres high, from the water to the top of the arch, its steel weighs 52,800 tonnes, which may well be 736,000 Persian Yakmans, and it is 1149 metres long, including the approaches. As Slessor proclaims, the Bridge has carried everything, perhaps even rickshaws. As an infant, it fed on paint. About 272,000 litres of paint were used in the first three coats applied to the structure. Contrary to Slessor's assertion, the Bridge has never had to truculently force its presence on the city. A bridge has been there, in the imagination of Sydneysiders and visitors, long before there was the Bridge.

Erasmus Darwin was a British man of many skills: naturalist, philosopher, physician and poet. His verse, 'Visit of Hope to Sydney Cove, near Botany Bay', written in 1789, just a year after the arrival of the First Fleet, suggested Darwin may have been a prophet as well. Darwin was inspired to write his poem after a friend and colleague, the master potter Josiah Wedgwood, showed him an engraving of a medallion he proposed to mould from the first clay sent back from the new colony. Wedgwood produced his renowned 'Sydney Cove Medallion', with its image of the figure of Hope being met on the harbour shores by Peace, Art and Labour. At that time, Sydney dirt could barely produce enough to feed the wretched souls sent to live here, but it could nurture art.

In his poem, amid the lyrical description of Sydney Cove's 'lucid bosom' swelling, Darwin foresees a great city rising by, and over, the harbour. He writes of 'embellished villas', 'tall spires, and dome-capped towers', 'piers and quays', and:

There the proud arch, colossus-like, bestride
Yon glittering streams, and bound the chasing
Tide . . .

Darwin imagined this harbour city from afar; he never visited Sydney. But his grandson did. Charles Darwin sailed into Sydney Harbour in January 1836, on board HMS *Beagle*, as part of its round-the-world surveying voyage. Australia, especially its wildlife, apparently had a profound influence on Darwin's thinking towards his world-changing theory of evolution by natural selection. Comparing the strange animals to the fauna of the Northern Hemisphere, he mused they couldn't have all been the work of one creator. The young scientist was also impressed by the evolution of Sydney, writing back to England that his grandfather had prophesied most truly in his poem. However, there was no proud arch bestriding the harbour. The Bridge was still almost a century into the future.

In the early days of the colony there was talk of a harbour bridge. In 1815, Francis Greenway, the man who helped put Sydney on surer footings and spruced up its face with the buildings he designed, proposed a bridge to Governor Macquarie. A decade later, Greenway suggested a bridge from 'Dawes Battery to the North Shore', to encourage development on both sides of the harbour and as a symbol 'that would have reflected credit and glory on the colony and the Mother Country'.

Through the years, all manner of designs were drawn up and presented to the government. Politicians and major landholders on the North Shore, in particular, lobbed proposals over the water. A People's Bridge League was formed, then a Sydney and North Shore Junction League, which suggested building a bridge or a tunnel, or both. And all the while, the ferries kept running, as more and more relied on water transport.

By 1908, thirteen million passengers a year were being carried across the harbour by five major ferry companies. The ferries would line up in Circular Cove, awaiting a berth, as seventy-five vessels docked there each hour. A decade on, it was estimated that in one year, there were about 7,500,000 passenger journeys from the Milsons Point and McMahons Point–Lavender Bay ferry terminals alone. The pressure on the transport system had been the source of commuter complaints and was considered in a royal commission into the improvement of the city and suburbs in 1908 and 1909. Many passengers believed no bridge would be built until there was a ferry disaster and lives were lost.

Yet while people despaired at the increasingly clogged harbour and the yawning gap between the shores, and as politicians kept talking, an engineer was looking at the possibilities. John Job Crew Bradfield had sailed into Sydney Harbour from Queensland in the 1880s to study engineering. As a draftsman and engineer, he tested the various designs for a bridge when the government called for tenders, only for the plans to never leave the paper. By 1912, Bradfield was the Chief Engineer of the Harbour Bridge, along with the city's railway network. He pursued plans for a cantilever bridge. Yet a decade on, after overseas study trips, the shape of his plans was changing; he could see a great arch spanning the harbour from Dawes Point to Milsons Point. In 1922, the sum of Bradfield's investigations and planning helped prod political will to finally pass the Sydney

Harbour Bridge Bill. For Bradfield, this had been the unrequited love of his life, but, as he wrote determinedly in his diary, 'I will see my Romance of the Bridge become a Reality'. Perhaps the romance was buttressed by the reality of being a long-suffering commuter. Bradfield lived on the North Shore.

The following year, tenders were called once more, and work actually began on preparing the approaches to the bridge. On a drenched day in July 1923, thousands gathered in the rain in North Sydney to watch local and state politicians, and Bradfield, preside over the turning of the first sod. That slight irruption of soil was but the start of a swathe of destruction to tear through North Sydney, and a community on the other side of the harbour at Dawes Point.

Life was thickly packed around Milsons Point, with terraces, boarding houses and flats, and small businesses. The clustering of commuters and workers around North Sydney had not impressed one sometime-local, the poet Henry Lawson. He wrote verses about the rush for the ferry in 'The North Shore Business Girl', while in 'Old North Sydney', he lamented that the area's community spirit had been lost to accommodate more 'busy strangers':

> But the Spirit of North Sydney,
> It vanished long ago.

No one listened to the poet. Old North Sydney kept shifting. As work on the Bridge picked up pace, hundreds of the area's residents and shopkeepers received a letter telling them their lives were to be upturned: 'Sir, I hereby, as Agent for the Minister Public Works, your landlord, and on his behalf, give you notice to quit and deliver up possession of the house and premises . . . '. Within a few years, nearly 500 houses had been demolished and businesses shut. Many locals received nothing to compensate them, other than 'removal expenses' for tenants pushed out. A community was being reduced to rubble and ghosts. The commuters lost their ornate terminus. By its very design and architecture, the arcade and ferry building at Milsons Point had always looked less like a place where things came to an end but where something grand began. But for the building, and for many of the ferries which used the terminal, the Bridge spelt the end. The ferry arcade was demolished, disappearing under what would be the Bridge's northern pylon.

The grave of a community demolished is in a park just near the Milsons Point railway station. Sandstone kerbs that once defined a lane and a street cut across the park like scars. The footings of buildings long gone are also visible, and now that they've been inscribed with their street name and number, they look like headstones. Through the trees in the park, you can see what pushed the homes and businesses into the earth; the stone edifice of the Bridge's northern pylon, and part of the arch. The ground in which these remnants lie is named after the man who oversaw the need for these buildings and their inhabitants to go: Bradfield Park.

A few hundred metres away, Christ Church has fared better. The sandstone building has stood on the same ground since the 1870s. The harbour views from here are glorious. You can see the structure that carried so much change into this church and suburb. In the 1920s, the Rector of Christ Church, the Reverend Frank Cash, reflected on the change happening around him. The congregation was fast dwindling, as homes and businesses disappeared. A keen photographer, he captured on film what was being lost. Frank Cash turned his point of proximity into an opportunity to record history. As he later wrote, 'A telephone call, that a fine wall was coming down in five minutes; or a demolisher coming soon after seven o'clock in the morning, with a hurried message, "*come on, we are waiting*," speak plainly of the privileges of living on the ground.'

The Reverend Cash took many photos of chimneys being torn off homes, and the walls of terrace houses standing defiantly, only to be toppled. 'Without fear of correction,' the Reverend Cash opined, 'it is safe to say, that no part of New South Wales has undergone such far reaching change within the last sixty years, as Lavender Bay, and Milson's Point.'

As the demolition continued, the Bridge design's options for a suspension, cantilever, or arched structure were further considered. British firm Dorman, Long & Co's option of an arch with pylons was selected to be Sydney Harbour Bridge. The Bridge and its approaches were expected to cost about £5.5 million. It ended up costing almost double that.

Work on the Bridge itself began in 1925, but it wasn't until a few years later that the great arms of steel began reaching out over the harbour. Much of the steel was shipped from Britain, and some came down the coast from the BHP works in Newcastle. The steel was unloaded at a wharf built on the Milsons Point waterfront, then cut and assembled in large workshops that dominated the foreshore. Completed steel sections were lifted by crane onto barges and floated the short distance to the Bridge construction site.

After the Bridge was completed, the workshop site would become Luna Park. However, in the early days of the project,

Bradfield had a radically different vision for the Lavender Bay foreshore. He wanted it to be adorned with a long gracious building, decorated with hanging gardens, lounging in the curve of the bay. All that remains of the industrial site are some of the piers that supported the wharf. But to see those, you have to be sitting low in the water, as I do in *Pulbah Raider*, so that you can peer into the gloom under the Crystal Palace.

The harbour also played its part in the building of the pylons that rose like ancient temples on each side of the Bridge. Granite was transported in custom-built ships from quarries further down the coast at Moruya.

The Reverend Cash trained his camera lens on the preparatory work and the construction. He became a Bridge convert. As Lawrence Ennis, the Director of Construction for the Bridge Contractors, later noted, the Reverend Cash was their most constant visitor, and the only one, outside of those connected with the project, to have unlimited access to the work. In the pursuit of a shot, the Reverend Cash often put his faith in beams and platforms high above the water, acting like one of the workers to portray what they were creating – 'the greatest pioneering work of its kind ever attempted'.

The Reverend Cash estimated he took more than 10,000 photos up until 1930 alone, when he published a book titled *Parables of the Sydney Harbour Bridge*. In images and words, he expressed his admiration for the workers, and he saw the divine in what was being built.

'The Bridge is truly *sacramental*,' he declared. 'It displays, against our southern sky, day by day, a further and progressive visible expression of a faculty, which can be seen and known, in no other fashion.' By the end of his tome, the Reverend Cash was prophesying, 'The finished Bridge . . . will bestow upon the people of this land the same gift, as the Sacred Word speaks of God conferring upon the whole world.'

The monumental geometry of steel and stone was seen as both a marvel of engineering and a work of art. And a muse for artists. Grace Cossington Smith and Roland Wakelin painted the arms as they crept across the sky, ever closer to touching. Through their dynamic paintings, these artists used the Bridge to help carry a modernist vision onto Australian shores. Other artists chronicled the progress of the Bridge in more conservative styles. A series of etchings by Jessie Traill portrayed the ant-like scale and energy of the construction workers. In 1932, Lloyd Rees sketched 'Sydney Bridge'. In the drawing, a section of the Bridge barges into the picture from the left and works its ways across the top of the image, which is an otherwise bucolic scene. It's like Rees was showing the industrial age creeping into Arcadia. However, like everyone who saw it, Rees was seduced by the Bridge. He wrote how one night he saw the structure, before its arms were joined, by moonlight, and he was awed by 'a colossal work of modern sculpture against a background of eternity'.

Arcadia was changed forever late in the night on 19 August 1930, when the arms met and the arch was formed. The moment was marked with ships blowing their horns. Sydneysiders, who had been observing the Bridge's construction for years, jumped out of bed when they heard the noise and added to the symphony of celebration, according to one local, by standing in the street and banging on saucepans.

Flanking the arch were the stone and concrete pylons. They were symbols of stability. But their role was simply symbolic, in part to reassure people, looking at all that knitting of steel and cables, that the Bridge would be safe and sturdy. The architect and writer Robin Boyd thought the pylons played another role, acting as diversions to make all the ugly steel presentable in the public eye.

'The pylon features thus successfully destroyed the visual reality of the steel bridge, while relieving Sydney of the expense of covering the whole arch with stone veneer,' Boyd offered.

The Bridge arches were held in place by tension, using massive steel cables. The project itself was riven with tension, with arguments over who designed the Bridge. Yet in the public mind, there was no argument. Bradfield was synonymous with the Bridge.

In the vernacular of Sydney, the Bridge was already part of the Australian landscape, and not just in a physical sense; it was honoured with nicknames. It was the 'coathanger' and, perhaps more respectfully, the 'Iron Lung', because at the height of the Great Depression, it had employed up to 1650 workers. For the 300,000 or so residents on the North Shore, this piece of infrastructure may have been connecting them to the 600,000 on the other side of the harbour, but it belonged to them. They called it 'The North Shore Bridge'. For property speculators and real estate agents, the Bridge meant money. In 1931, Arthur Rickard & Co Ltd advertised land on the North Shore, saying 'Up goes the last girder, up go land values' . . . 'Are you going to be one of the fortunate folk to make big profits from North Shore land?'

As well as satisfying the prospect of soaring real estate prices, the Bridge fed another Sydney obsession: something to brag about. The media made a point of comparing the Bridge to other landmarks and icons. With its span measuring 503 metres between the pylons, the Bridge was almost three times as long as HMAS *Australia*. What's more, the Bridge was twice as high as the General Post Office, and most of the city's buildings would have slotted into the space between the deck and the water.

By the time the Bridge was completed, it had rewritten the record books as the largest steel arch in the world, it had reshaped the physical and social landscape of Sydney, and it had become the talk of not just the town but a nation. Even Melbourne lauded Sydney Harbour Bridge. In its editorial, Melbourne's *The Age* pointed out how the Bridge was begun when times were good and was completed in the Depression, but the fact it reached the other side was symbolic of how 'Sydney and the rest of Australia [will] find safe conduct over the Bay of Despond on the Bridge of Faith, whose concrete is the inflexible will of the people and whose steel is reinforced with the national courage'.

Saturday, 19 March 1932, was a clear day, ideal for an official opening. Detractors argued the dire economic climate meant this was not an appropriate time for big celebrations. But the city was in the mood to celebrate. Hundreds of thousands turned up from near and far. Lennie Gwyther, a nine-year-old boy from Victoria, was so keen to attend, he rode his pony 1000 kilometres from his family's farm to Sydney. His four-month ride ignited enormous interest in towns worn down by the Depression, and Lennie was such a celebrity by the time he arrived in Sydney, he and his pony were included in the procession across the Bridge. The pageantry was also played out on the harbour, with a flotilla of ships and boats, powered by steam, sail, muscles, whatever could get them on the water.

Yet it was the theatrics of Captain Francis De Groot at the

opening that raised eyebrows and hackles. A member of the right-wing New Guard, De Groot was determined that Labor Premier Jack Lang would not have the honour of opening the Bridge. The New Guard believed a member of the royal family or one of its representatives should cut the ceremonial ribbon. So De Groot cut it, by galloping up on a borrowed horse and slashing the ribbon with a sword. He was promptly detained and his antics were barely noticed on the day. The ribbon was rejoined, and Lang officially cut it, setting off a 21-gun salute. But the rebellious act was reported around the world and has reverberated through the years. De Groot and his sword stunt are probably what most people associate with the Harbour Bridge's opening.

Ultimately, bridges aren't about openings but closing gaps and providing passage. Once the pomp and ceremony passed, the vehicles drove onto the Bridge and crossed the harbour, but at a price. Drivers and passengers, horse riders, even cyclists had to pay a toll. Pedestrians were also to be charged, but the Lang Government dismissed that proposal. Initially, there were far more pedestrians than vehicles on the Bridge each day. Within a couple of years, the number of vehicles had climbed to 12,000 daily. Eight decades on, about 160,000 vehicles use the Bridge each day.

The Bridge is also often referred to as a dividing line between the inner and outer harbours, as though the water and all that lives in it suddenly change as they pass under the deck. The State Government's Department of Primary Industries, for instance, advises no fish or crustaceans caught west of the Bridge should be eaten, because of contaminants, mainly from the Parramatta River. Gavin Birch, who, as an environmental chemist, has been studying the harbour's health through its sediment for about thirty years, reckons the Bridge is an understandable threshold.

Generally speaking, Gavin, an Adjunct Associate Professor from the University of Sydney's School of Geosciences, points out there are physical differences either side. The harbour on the seaward side of the Bridge broadens. The character of the water and the sediment changes as the harbour approaches the Heads. The impact of the sea, including salinity and wave action, contributes to those changes. Then there's the human impact; testing has indicated the harbour west of the Bridge is generally more contaminated.

'It's not a fence or wall, but the Bridge is a convenient threshold, and that thinking flows through to regulations,' Gavin says. However, dioxins dumped by industry many years ago into Homebush Bay have been carried from the west and been detected east of the Bridge.

'So you mustn't think that all contaminants stop at the Bridge.'

A statement in itself, the Bridge has also been used to convey all manner of messages. Crowds have marched across it in celebration or commemoration, such as the estimated 300,000 who walked on the Bridge in 2000 in support of Aboriginal reconciliation. It has held the pounding feet of runners, including Olympians competing in the Sydney 2000 marathon. Some have leapt from the Bridge. In the first year of the Bridge's operation, thirty-nine people jumped off, prompting the erection of a protective barrier. A few have climbed its frame in protest or to seek attention. Millions more have legitimately clambered to the top of the arch, with guides from commercial operator BridgeClimb.

While you could pay up to a few hundred dollars to climb the arch in a tour group, you can walk along the pedestrian path on the deck, weaving amid the power-walking commuters and joggers, for free. You have to peer through the mesh of the protective barrier, but even so, the view to the east, over the Opera House and the headlands towards the Macquarie Lighthouse near South Head, is stunning. Looking down, ferries scurry like insects across the harbour, and, most afternoons, a cruise liner pulsating with holidaymakers passes underneath, its funnels seemingly close to scratching the Bridge's underside. For a few moments, you can almost see the excitement in the passengers' eyes. No moment is left unrecorded on the Bridge. As the unblinking eye of mounted security cameras watch those on the Bridge, the people being observed snap their own images. Watching tourists perform camera-acrobatics, manoeuvring their devices through the thin gap between the protective barriers, I wonder how often their captured memories end up tumbling through the air into the water more than 50 metres below. When the Bridge was being built, something more noxious was tossed into the water. With no portable toilets, the labourers would use bags. At least once, the toilet bag landed not in the harbour but splatted on the deck of a ferry.

WHILE THE Bridge offers a platform from which to view Sydney, on at least one night of the year the eyes of the world are on the Bridge.

The New Year's Eve fireworks display is to Sydney what bread and circuses were to Imperial Rome. No matter how much money has been wasted by politicians on other things in the previous twelve months, all is forgiven as we pack around the harbour, and on it, to watch millions of dollars more bloom into meadows of psychedelic dandelions in the night sky, before they sputter and trail away.

Yet the greatest display doesn't require a severe craning of the neck; it spurts and spills from the structure of the Bridge. It is known as 'the Bridge effect'. And the effect, basically, is to reduce conversations to 'ooh-ah'. Waterfalls of light cascade from the deck to the water, tufts of colour explode off the summit, and, after weeks of guessing, a symbol for the theme of the New Year's Eve show is revealed in dazzling fashion on the eastern arch.

The most moving symbol, for me, was one word that danced to life across millennia. Perhaps it was the circumstances in which I saw it lit up that gave the symbol such meaning and hope. For New Year's Eve 1999–2000, my wife and I were at the Governor-General's Sydney residence, Admiralty House, on Kirribilli Point. It was perhaps the best location on earth to see in the new year. I was working, but it felt like a 'pinch yourself' privilege. I was there to cover a party being thrown by Admiralty House's then-residents, Governor-General Sir William Deane and Lady Deane. Being the generous souls they are, Sir William and Lady Deane were hosting a 'sleepover' for young organ transplant recipients, along with their families, kids waiting for an organ, medical staff, and the loved ones of donors. The Governor-General and his wife sat on the floor and talked with their little guests. I remember when one of the children thanked the Governor-General for having them over to his house, Sir William smiled – and he has perhaps the gentlest smile you would ever wish to see – and replied this was not his house. It was everybody's house. And so it was, at midnight, we were standing on the lawns of everybody's house, looking at the Bridge, when that one word appeared: Eternity. The word ignited in the handwriting style of Arthur Stace, returned soldier, recovering alcoholic and devout Christian. Stace had tagged the city's footpaths and walls with 'Eternity' every night for years from the 1940s until his death two decades later.

At that moment, as the nocturnal graffito of Stace lit up the face of a brand new year, I felt anything was possible. Sydney Harbour Bridge was illuminated with how I felt. But not even 'Eternity' lasted long. Within a few weeks, the lights were off, and people were already plotting where they would plant themselves for the ephemeral pleasure of watching the 2000–2001 fireworks.

Each year, expert pyrotechnics crews install the fireworks onto barges and into firing points on city landmarks. The process is painstaking and time-consuming. Almost as painstaking and time-consuming as it is for those who claim the prime positions to watch the display. Days out from the fireworks, the keenest of souls move in with tents and supplies. The first rule of life by Sydney Harbour on New Year's Eve is the same as every other day of the year: those closest to the water win. One of the best locations to feel like a winner on New Year's Eve is around McMahons Point.

Mid-morning on 31 December 2015, I paddle under the thrusting finger of Blues Point Tower and around the tip of the peninsula, only to be confronted by a thick crust of humanity – and tents – along the shore. There must be thousands already packed in here.

The crush of people intensifies as I paddle around the curve of Lavender Bay. Some are in such precarious spots, I worry they'll end up in the drink. No one seems concerned. A few are already well and truly into the drink. Many are reading, resting, observing – and happy to wave at a passing kayaker and yell out, 'Happy New Year!'

'Good day for a paddle,' a young man hollers. 'Good day for camping,' I shout back. 'How long have you been here?' 'Since Tuesday!' Today is Thursday. He smiles triumphantly, as though he is about to win a marathon. Which, in a way, he is.

Streaming down the harbour is an ever growing procession of boats, all heading for a favourite spot to moor and wait. In Lavender Bay, I see craft from far and wide, including a yacht flying the Canadian flag. Close by are three blokes on the deck of a sailboat named *Priority II*.

Priority II has ticked off Priority 1: securing a fantastic location. The trio has an uninterrupted view across the water to the Bridge, about half a kilometre away. Charlie Jensen owns the boat, a 30-footer in good nick. He's from Carcoar, about three and half hours drive west of Sydney. He keeps his boat moored on the harbour and comes down about once a month to go sailing. Also on board are his older brother Barry, who is from the city of Orange, and their mate, Les Fordham, from Newcastle. They sailed into the bay this morning. This is the third year they've moored early for the fireworks. Previously, they were on the other side of the Bridge off the southern shore, at Farm Cove. They're surprised more boaties haven't turned up here – yet.

We yarn for about an hour, when Les says, 'Want a beer?' 'No. Yes,' I reply. Charlie looks up. 'The sun's over the yardarm.' And so bobbing in my kayak next to *Priority II*, riding the jelly-rolls of water sent our way by the passing boats, I sip their beer, as we look at the view, and imagine what the night will hold. We think no further ahead.

As I prepare to paddle away, Charlie invites me to return later. So, just after the 9pm 'family' fireworks display, I follow the flow of people down the hill to Lavender Bay. Wendy Whiteley's Secret Garden is even less of a secret tonight. It's packed with revellers, seeking vantage points amid the foliage. At the bottom of the steps is a long queue of people, standing patiently. The line leads to the solitary toilet block on the foreshore. The jetties are barnacled with bodies who have claimed a skerrick of deck space in readiness for the fireworks. I pick my way along a jetty, where Charlie is waiting in his little rubber boat. I step gingerly aboard and feel water seep into my trainers. 'Here,' he says, handing me two glow sticks, one orange, one green. 'Hold the orange one in your left hand, and the green one in your right. Navigational lights. Now we're legal!'

Chicaning amid the motley fleet of skygazers, time counters and pleasure seekers, Charlie guides us to *Priority II*. Once all aboard, we open a bottle of Hunter white and watch the procession of ships in the dark, outlined like ghosts by thousands of LED lights.

On a cruiser neighbouring us, Charlie says, there are eight kids who have spent the day diving into the water and having a great old time. 'You wouldn't want to know what's below you though, would you,' says Barry.

We look expectantly at the Bridge. On the pylons are screens with images projected onto them. We yarn away the minutes until the countdown begins on the pylon, the numbers getting ever closer to zero – and to 2016. At the count of two, the first of the fireworks fizz above the Bridge, and then it's on for the next ten minutes. It is a fantastic display in the sky and, by reflection, on the water. When the curtain of fireworks showers down from the deck of the Bridge, lighting up the water, a silhouette armada appears before us. For the first time, I appreciate just how many boats are in the bay. It's easy to imagine, when you're looking skyward, that the harbour is all yours.

The fireworks end, and Charlie declares this spot is better than Farm Cove. Anywhere on the harbour would provide a fantastic experience, I reckon, for I now realise fireworks are best enjoyed from the water. After one more drink, I step back into the supple but unconvincing embrace of the rubber boat, hold up the glow sticks, and we murmur our way back to the wharf. Crowds are climbing the steps, past Wendy Whiteley's garden, leaving behind another year and a whole lot of rubbish.

A few days after the big celebrations, I paddle into Lavender Bay. Strewn along the sand on the old slipway is a tideline of hedonism. Lying on the little beach are plastic bottles, party poppers, champagne corks, condom wrappers, glittering silver tinsel and spangled baubles. Floating in the shallows is a dead fish, as though it's been asphyxiated by all the flotsam and jetsam of pleasure. For the harbour itself, all these good times come at a cost.

PETER MANN works inside what he calls the castle. He is referring to Sydney Harbour Bridge's south pylons, where the Roads & Maritime Services' maintenance team is based. Peter is the Strategic Infrastructure Manager, which means he is in charge of keeping the Bridge in top shape.

As we walk through the security door at the base of the stone pylons, Peter, a tall slender man with kindly eyes, welcomes me inside the 'dungeon'. It doesn't feel like a dungeon; it is a vast space, several storeys high. And it is also busy. Peter takes me into a workshop where a tradesman is using a large drill that has been here since the Bridge was built. He shows me some of the 132 Art Deco-style lamps to be mounted on each of the Bridge's light arms. The originals were removed in the 1950s, so Peter commissioned the casting of replacements. It may not add up as a 'business case', he reasons, but there's enormous social value in 'putting the jewellery back on the Bridge, out of respect'.

A train rumbles overhead. Since we're in the bowels of the Bridge, it sounds like the icon has bad indigestion.

'You get used to it; it's ambient background noise,' laughs Peter, who adds that, in peak hour, twenty trains in each direction travel across the Bridge.

An engineering graduate, Peter says the motivation for his job is 'to look after an icon'. There are about 100 workers in the Bridge maintenance team, including carpenters, metalworkers, and riggers, whose duties include operating the cranes on the arch and setting up platforms for the painters. Before his career as a comedian and actor took off in the 1970s, Paul Hogan was a rigger on the Bridge. He was apparently chasing the danger money, working at heights. As a primer for standing alone on a stage, telling jokes to an audience, balancing on beams without falling would have been ideal. Just as his former workplace has done since it was erected, Hogan also helped sell Australia as a tourist destination to the world. In one of the 1980s television ads he featured in for the American market, Hogan stood on the arch of the Harbour Bridge – and pretended he was the Statue of Liberty. Ironically, having done so much to attract tourists to Australia, Hogan has said he doesn't know how anyone can work on the Bridge anymore, with so many gawkers going over the arch on tours.

The biggest component of the workforce is the painters. The Bridge has about thirty painters, with fifteen support staff.

'Most parts of the arch still have the original paint system applied in the 1930s,' explains Peter. 'It's just been overlaid with layers of paint.'

Contrary to popular belief, the painters don't begin at one end of the Bridge and work their way across. 'We're leapfrogging all around the Bridge, chasing areas where paint breaks down the quickest.'

The paint is called Bridge Grey, and while it is a light tone when applied, it darkens with age. Peter says that's why there are so many shades of grey on the Bridge. The workers still use brushes to apply paint around the six million or so rivets. To prevent corrosion, the primer has zinc in it. That protection is sorely needed.

The very thing that complements the Bridge's beauty is unceasingly working to tear it apart. The harbour's salt water, along with the sea breezes, rain, and sunlight, conspire to gnaw away at the structure.

'The salt air is a major enemy of anything metallic, especially steel,' explains Peter. 'Steel doesn't exist naturally in this environment, it wants to rust, it wants to go back to dust. The job of the paint is to stop it rusting, as a barrier, like a sunscreen, so the structure can live on.'

Depending on how exposed the paint is, it can last between ten and forty years.

In the quest to maintain the Bridge, the human team has been joined by robots, doing unpleasant, even unsafe, jobs. One robot, called Croc, inspects the structure by delving deep inside small chambers that are awkward 'wombat holes' for humans. Peter likes the idea that the state-of-the-art is being used to maintain what he calls 'the matriarch of the harbour'.

The annual budget for maintaining the Bridge is about $20 million. While no one likes paying a toll each time they drive south across the Bridge, most are content to see their money going towards the upkeep of something that not only helps them get from one place to another, but helps define who they are.

'Because the Bridge is so iconic, they [the public] want it well preserved, they don't want to entertain the prospect that the Bridge has a finite life,' Peter says. 'What we're trying to do is to redefine what was intended in an engineering design sense.'

Bridges, he explains, are generally designed for a 100-year life. Yet with the Harbour Bridge, he and his team are looking much further into the future.

'What we're trying to do is to defy the laws of engineering, to keep a bridge alive that wants to rust back into the soil.'

Although a newspaper published an April Fool's joke article about government plans to build an exact replica beside the original Bridge, Peter says that could not happen. For one thing, there is a heritage curtilage around the Bridge, to protect its integrity, and, from an engineering sense, it would be near impossible to exactly replicate it. If the Bridge were to be pulled down and replaced, Peter reckons the favoured design would be something that is cheaper to maintain.

Yet you could never really replace Sydney Harbour Bridge. While its book value is about $1.3 billion, according to Peter, what price do you attach to an icon? Which is why Peter and his team are working towards the Bridge spanning the harbour for another thousand years. Surprised by that figure, I ask him could the Bridge last that long?

'Yes, certainly,' he replies. 'That's the sort of conversation I have with our senior management and our bridge engineering team. How do we keep this Bridge for another thousand years?'

How to keep the Bridge alive is just one question Peter asks himself as he drives across it each morning and evening. Looking through the steel arcing over him, he asks, just as everyone else does, 'How did they build this thing?' As an engineer, he knows the answer. But even so, the Bridge remains, in his eyes, a wondrous thing.

Paul Hogan may have misgivings about the Bridge being opened up to tour groups, but Peter sees the benefits.

'If we were to be selfish, you could argue they get in our way. But holistically, it's a good outcome for the Bridge.'

'Having that accessibility to the Bridge feeds its popularity.'

Even though he climbs the Bridge regularly for work, Peter is but one of many Sydneysiders who has paid to do a tour, along with his wife.

'There's that curiosity factor for people who live near the Bridge,' he muses. 'To see it from the ground or a car window is different to actually planting your flag at the summit, if you like, to conquer the Bridge or to feel the power of the Bridge by standing on top of it. It's what you'd feel standing on any mountain peak.'

I'VE NEVER felt the need to climb to summits. 'Because it's there' doesn't seem like a good enough reason to clamber to the top.

A mountain looks awesome from its base and majestic from a distance. And so it has been with Sydney Harbour Bridge for me. I didn't want to join a bunch of other overall-suited visitors and climb the arch. The view from the Bridge deck has satisfied me, and the structure itself has looked even more extraordinary from a kayak.

'Oh, no,' counters Peter Mann. 'You've got to go to the summit. You can't be living in Sydney and not have gone to the top of the Bridge.'

Peter invites me to join him on an inspection of Sydney Harbour Bridge. But we don't go directly to the top.

We catch an elevator in the south-west pylon to the sixth level and step out just below the deck. The Bridge occasionally groans in response to all that traffic roaring and rumbling over our heads. The structure is designed to accommodate the contracting and expanding of the steel, and the weight of vehicles on its deck. But just to be sure, attached to the Bridge under the bus lane is a series of structural health monitors – 'just like electrodes attached to the body,' explains Peter.

As traffic using the Bridge has increased through the years, steel cables have been installed in the hanger posts to share the load on the deck. What's more, the pylons are not just pretty faces and play a part. They support the section of the deck above their footprint.

We step out onto a walkway underneath the western edge of the Bridge. Just above us, only a few metres away, trains rush by, their steel wheels pushing down on the wooden sleepers and the rails. And about fifty metres below is the harbour foreshore and the water, its turquoise surface cut by vessels. What looks menacingly large from the cockpit of a kayak looks almost inconsequential when staring down to a boat from this height. Not that I look down very much; I look ahead, watching the walkway narrow into a thin line before it reaches the other side, on the North Shore. A BridgeClimb group appears on the walkway ahead. We shimmy past each other. It seems like an apt symbol for how the relationship between the tourists and the workers has developed. Peter explains that, during the high tourist season, the workers concentrate on the places where the paying customers can't go, such as the Bridge's north side.

The workers also have to negotiate cruise ships' schedules, moving out of the way the painting gantries that hang under the Bridge. We head down onto a gantry on the northern side, which is loaded with tins of Bridge Grey paint. For the painters, this is hard work, combating the elements. If Mother Nature revolts at the painters' presence and the wind is blowing hard, then they have to retreat.

'These are all the painting jobs that people don't see,' says Peter, as we head back up to the walkway and make our way past a recently coated section.

'It's nice to see freshly painted steel.'

But there are always more sections waiting to be cleaned and painted. Along the walkway, there can be seen the bubbles and blemishes of rust, creating new projects for the workers. It is superficial rust, but it creates a deep and constant challenge for those who work on the Bridge. The rust blooms in places that are all but inaccessible, and the workers are rarely presented with a smooth beam or plate of steel to clean and paint. It is usually nubbly with rivets, which, Peter says, have been superb in holding the body together.

'So far we haven't had to replace any rivets,' he says.

'The rivet, once its head is formed into the rivet head shape, it cools down and it's there to stay. With the vibration on the Bridge, and there's a lot of that, the rivets don't come loose. So they're a great part of engineering, a part of our heritage.'

The nuts and bolts now used on the Bridge do come loose, but, as Peter says, they are a lot safer to create and use than rivets. They used to be cooked on the Bridge and then were tossed, glowing, to the riveter, who often caught them in an empty paint tin or bucket. That sort of practice is no longer acceptable. Like so many of the work practices then.

Sixteen men were killed during the building project. Eight fell to their death from the Bridge. Standing on the walkway and looking down, it is hard not to think of those men. And looking at the gantries and platforms, I feel admiration for where today's workers go and what they do to keep the Bridge safe.

When the Bridge was built, there was no safety net. These days there are nets to protect workers, and to catch any objects that fall off the deck. Peter points out a caught plastic bottle and says it was probably thrown from a passing vehicle above: 'That way the bottle doesn't end up in the harbour or hitting someone below.'

Almost an hour since we stepped foot onto the walkway, we reach the other side and head up to the deck through the north-eastern pylon. We emerge through a hatch, leaving behind the Bridge's underworld only to find ourselves in the midst of Sydney's frenzied life. We are on an island between the traffic lanes.

'I reckon we should walk over the arch,' says Peter. We pass through a couple of security gates and climb steel stairs on the arch. They are on a surprisingly gentle gradient, so it feels merciful at first. But that fades. The view steals my breath, anyway. During the climb, I look at the slices of harbour encased between the steel beams. I look down at the deck, at all the cars dashing across the Bridge, driving over the girders' shadows on the roadway. And I look up and follow the track of the arch, a sinuous curve, which is actually composed of straight beams of steel, and all those rivets. Then we reach the top.

I may once have been satisfied with the view from the deck. But no more. The view from up here is incomparable. Which is why, near the summit, the BridgeClimbers are literally queuing and waiting their turn to shuffle to the top and have their photo taken with everything they need to show they have been to Sydney: Bridge, Opera House, and harbour. Then, with the moment recorded, if not fully absorbed, they shuffle down the other arch.

I'm fortunate to be able to stand at the summit longer, to not only be seduced by the harbour but also to look where it's headed. The distant sea is the colour of a sapphire, with a south-westerly ruffling its surface. Directly below, the harbour is serene. Just above me, however, is a gentle rustling, as the wind irons out the Australian and New South Wales flags.

Peter confesses the arch is not where he loves to be the most on the Bridge. He prefers to be on the underside, looking up and within, rather than gazing out. He constantly looks for, and finds, repairs that need doing, but he also feels something more.

'Under there, I feel like I'm a part of the Bridge,' he says.

Sydney Harbour Bridge has a humanity, which it seems to project; or perhaps it is what we project onto it. More than steel and stone, Sydney Harbour Bridge has a heart and soul. And more than provide an identity for Sydneysiders, the Bridge is one of us. As Peter says, 'it represents how we see ourselves'.

Indeed, the man who is in charge of maintaining the Bridge is studying its humanity. Peter is undertaking a PhD on the sociology of Sydney Harbour Bridge. He is trying to get under the steel skin that he and his team work to preserve.

'It's awe-inspiring,' Peter murmurs. 'I've grown to appreciate the Bridge for what it provides to the people. And it's not just a bit of steel that enables you to drive across the harbour, it's an icon. Even to newcomers to Sydney, it has that symbolic representation of being a great place to live.

'Without it, Sydneysiders would feel an emptiness. It's symbolic of being home in Sydney.'

IN A thick band of shadow cast by the Bridge, a piece of Australian naval history modestly pokes its head out from the stone seawall along the northern shore. It is part of the bow of the first HMAS *Sydney*. When the Royal Australian Navy was barely a few years old, *Sydney* was involved in a fierce battle against the German ship SMS *Emden* during the First World War. The German raider had been creating havoc with shipping in the Indian Ocean. After *Emden* raided the Cocos Keeling Islands in November 1914, *Sydney* was sent to the area and confronted the German ship. The battle lasted less than two hours, but when the badly damaged *Emden* ran aground on North Keeling Island, the efforts of *Sydney*'s crew reverberated around the nation and the British Empire. The young Royal Australian Navy had achieved its first victory at sea.

HMAS *Sydney* was paid off and then broken up at Cockatoo Island in 1929. Given the enormity of what she achieved in the First World War, this memorial to *Sydney* seems insufficient.

Dwarfed by the great grey bulk of the Bridge, and ignored by the boating traffic scurrying in front it, the only acknowledgement from the water that this innocuous-looking nodule of steel may hold some significance is a rust-streaked sign that states simply, HMAS *Sydney*. A larger monument to *Sydney* exists further along the harbour at Bradleys Head, so I look forward to passing it and quelling my disappointment at the lack of interest shown in this memorial.

Just off the point, thousands of vehicles are rumbling along the bottom of the harbour. They're travelling in Sydney Harbour Tunnel, through concrete tubes that at their deepest are 25 metres below sea level. The tunnel wears a helmet of rocks to protect it from anything coming from above, such as an anchor or a sinking ship. The project was undertaken to alleviate some of the pressure from an increasingly clogged Harbour Bridge. The idea of a tunnel under the harbour had been around for more than a century. In 1887, the Government noted it was seriously considering a proposal for twin passageways, one for trams and trains, the second for other vehicles. The project would have reshaped more than timetables. It was proposed the excavated material could have been used 'in filling up some of the bays on the northern side of the harbour in which the water stagnates and engenders disease'. Newspaper reports in 1887 estimated the project would have cost £450,000, and there was 'every reason to hope' work would begin that year. Construction began on the Sydney Harbour Tunnel in 1988, and the project cost close to $750 million. It opened in August 1992.

There is a proposal for another, 'Western Harbour', tunnel for vehicles. And preparations for a rail tunnel under the harbour have begun. Barges have been working to the west of the Bridge, drilling into the harbour bed, seeking to identify the best route. At the risk of sounding like those optimists in 1887, the Government expects trains will be travelling through that tunnel by 2024.

While Sydney Harbour Tunnel carries about 90,000 vehicles for 2.3 kilometres from one shore to the other every day, it happens deep under the water. It is out of sight of Sydneysiders, until there is a crash or a major jam in the tunnel; then everyone curses it. And that is why in this city, where a quiet achiever receives, at best, scant praise, the tunnel can never be the Bridge. Cool efficiency somewhere in the mud on the harbour bed is no match for a stunning ballet of steel vaulting through the sky above the water.

7

KIRRIBILLI TO MIDDLE HEAD

AROUND THE harbour, there are richer suburbs than Kirribilli, but none is home to more powerful residents. Kirribilli Point holds the Sydney homes of the Governor-General of Australia and the nation's Prime Minister.

Long before it was the residence of the Governor-General, Admiralty House was the home of the powerful, often the rich *and* powerful, of the colony. The land on which the mansion was built was bought in 1806 by the merchant and builder of the colony's first commercial wharf, Robert Campbell. The house, or the beginning of what it would grow into, was built in 1845 by the Collector of Customs, Lieutenant Colonel John George Nathaniel Gibbes. He called his single-storey stone home Wotonga. Among the influential characters who later moved into Wotonga were a politician, Thomas Cadell, MLC, a successful auctioneer George Lloyd, and, before them, Lieutenant Colonel George Barney, the Royal Engineer who reshaped parts of the harbour with his construction of Fort Denison on the island to the south-east of Kirribilli Point, and Semi-Circular Quay in Sydney Cove. With each owner came some changes to Wotonga.

In 1855, with the Crimean War blazing on the other side of the globe, Governor Sir William Denison was concerned Russian ships might sail through the Heads. So he resumed a portion of Kirribilli Point and had gun emplacements built into the sandstone. Ironically, a few decades earlier, the headland was briefly known as Russian Point, when the crews of Russian ships on a science mission were allowed to camp there. Russian ships never did invade Sydney Harbour, but a succession of British admirals set up a luxurious beachhead on Kirribilli Point.

In 1885, the property's name was changed to Admiralty House. It was the residence of the Admiral of the Royal Navy's Australian Squadron. To give these gentlemen a greater chance to survey all they ruled over, a second storey was added to the home, and it was girdled in the grand colonnaded veranda, which it still wears. In 1913, the final officer to live in Admiralty House suggested he was handing the property to the Commonwealth. That came as a surprise to the Government of New South Wales, which countered it had loaned the house to the British.

Nevertheless, Admiralty House became the Governor-General's Sydney residence in 1913. During the Great Depression, Admiralty House was closed as a belt-tightening gesture, but within a few years, the Governors-General were back in the home and, by 1948, the property's title was in the hands of the Commonwealth.

Admiralty House is at the end of a narrow street filled with apartment blocks, some gracious in their Art Deco finery, others more modern and ostentatious, and all facing the harbour, or craning for a glimpse of the water. Yet the minute you're allowed through the gates and are heading down the drive to Admiralty House, with its sandstone skin glowing in the sun and light flushing through the building's grand windows, you feel gloriously isolated.

The harbourfront lawn is shaded by a giant fig tree. Dotted around the property, and along the front and filtering the views, are native flora, including angophoras and a towering Gymea lily. While the setting may have been inspired by the English, the Australian vegetation can't be denied or pushed out of the harbour picture.

Huddling just below the edge of the lawn and at the foot of a small escarpment are some reminders of when the tip of the point was resumed for defence. The historic marines' barracks is only metres from the water. As I discovered while working during the 2014–2015 New Year's Eve celebrations, it is a great position to not just watch the fireworks, but to be part of the fun. For an outpost of vice-regal pomp and circumstance, Admiralty House feels as though it is in the midst of the public celebrations during big events, especially as the showboats thump past close to shore.

A spectacle has always drawn the crowds to the harbour's edge, but sometimes not for a celebration. On 14 December 1921, thousands watched the wool store of the Pastoral Finance Association on the Kirribilli shoreline burn. The seven-storey warehouse was known around the harbour, because it was crowned with a large advertising sign. When a fire broke out in the building around dawn, the combination of about 30,000 wool bales and the lanolin-soaked floors created what the press called a furnace. At one stage, there were concerns the flames might jump onto Admiralty House. Millions of litres of water were pumped from the harbour, but the wool store burnt to the ground.

Sharing Kirribilli Point with Admiralty House is an east-facing gabled home that is the Prime Minister's Sydney residence. Kirribilli House was built in 1854 by merchant Adolphus Feeze, who had paid for a slice of Wotonga's land. About 1920, when Prime Minister William Hughes heard the land was slated to be subdivided, he had the Commonwealth buy Kirribilli House. In what monarchists might discern as a marvellous symbol, Kirribilli House was used for a while by staff of the Governor-General.

From 1956, Kirribilli House was used as accommodation for visiting guests, and as a Sydney residence for prime ministers. The house's name has worked its way into the lexicon, with the term 'Kirribilli Agreement'. 'Kirribilli' is believed to be derived from an Aboriginal word meaning 'a good fishing spot'. In political speak, 'Kirribilli Agreement' means 'a good spot to do a leadership deal'. In 1988, then-Prime Minister Bob Hawke met his Treasurer and deputy, Paul Keating, in Kirribilli House and agreed to resign during his next term of office, if the Labor Party won again, and hand the reins to Keating. But the deal all came unstuck. Australians were bequeathed not just a political mess but also a new term.

*

THE ENTRANCE to Careening Cove, as you would expect from the name, is clogged with boats. But they are not laid up on their sides having their hulls scrubbed, as they used to be in the earliest days of the colony. Instead, these days, some fabulously expensive boats are moored around the cove's mouth and at the marina of the Royal Sydney Yacht Squadron.

The private yacht club has been in existence for more than a century and a half. Among the club's drivers were members of the Milson family, who were keen to formalise their passion for sailing. James Milson had been competing on the harbour since the first regatta was held in the 1820s, and his son, James junior, was appointed the club's first Vice-Commodore in 1862. Young Milson had already created his mark along the shoreline, establishing an abattoir, which led to the cove bearing the pungent name Slaughterhouse Bay for a time.

I paddle around the Royal Sydney Yacht Squadron's marina into Careening Cove. I'm headed for a smaller clubhouse, where history is launched and skitters across the water each Saturday from October to April. It is the Sydney Flying Squadron, the home of the famous 18-foot skiffs. These are the craft that the bigger club along the bay reputedly rejected from an Anniversary Day race, prompting businessman and sailor Mark Foy to set up his own competitions for smaller open boats.

The races for small craft, especially the 18-footers with their sails that open and bloom like butterflies' wings, soon became spectator favourites on the harbour. And more than a century on, they still are favourites.

The skiffs are rigged on the grounds of Milson Park, which was formed from fill and rubbish at the head of the cove. They may be less than 6 metres long when they are rolled out of the clubhouse on the edge of the park, but the skiffs grow in dimensions and attractiveness. As the hulls lie on the grass beside the water, their varnished wooden bodies sheeny like a sunbather's, the skiffs are fussed over by crews. The sailors mount and rig bowsprits and masts, gaffs and booms, sails and bundles of 'kites', or spinnakers. The skiffs become stunning, and passers-by stop and stare at the craft and listen to the arcane language and terms the crews speak. But no skiff is more beautiful than *Britannia*. I may be biased, for I've been invited to sail on *Britannia* by her skipper and creator, Ian Smith.

Compact in stature, Ian Smith is a giant of the wooden boatbuilding tradition in Australia. Ian grew up near the beach in the industrial city of Wollongong. His love of the water led to him building boats from plans out of magazines when he was a teenager. That hobby grew into a living, and he trained others how to build traditional wooden boats. Ian's skills dovetailed with his interest in history, and he researched what used to be sailed on Sydney Harbour. He resolved to build an 18-foot skiff, and, for his inspiration, he traced a line to the past.

Ian's skiff is a replica of, and homage to, the original *Britannia*. It was built in 1919 by George Robinson, who was a star of the Balmain Tigers rugby league team. 'Wee Georgie' Robinson and his team would play footy in the winter and, being Balmain boys living by the harbour, would go sailing in summer.

'Everyone had a boat or knew someone with a boat, so they'd go out,' Ian explains.

'If you were a fit young man, that's what you did, that's what your mates did, that's what your family did.' There were at least five Robinsons on Georgie's crew.

Nicknames in Australia tend to be ironic, but 'Wee Georgie' was just that; he was only about 1.5 metres tall. Wee Georgie was a local hero in his working-class suburb, and he was a champion on the water. He sailed *Britannia* for more than a quarter of a century, and he won at least thirty championships.

When he decided to base his skiff on Wee Georgie's *Britannia*, Ian wanted to copy it as closely as he could. The original is housed at the Australian National Maritime Museum at Darling Harbour. To Ian's good fortune, *Britannia* had been taken out of display for restoration, so he was able to take lots of photos and pore over it, studying the details from the smallest fittings to measuring the plank widths.

Ian spent 1100 hours crafting his *Britannia* from Oregon and cedar, kauri and spotted gum, copper and bronze, and a deep respect for tradition. On the bench near the transom, Ian attached a plaque that reads: '*Britannia*. Dedicated to "Wee Georgie" Robinson. Builder and skipper of the original boat 1919. Replica by Ian Smith – 2002.'

'I think he'd be pleased to know,' Ian replies, when asked what he reckons Wee Georgie would make of this.

'We use modern sail cloth and ropes. Everything in the hull is the same as the original. If you plonked Wee Georgie down in it, he'd go, "Something's different, but I can't put my finger on it!".'

Ian considers his skiff an 'old friend'. But he also has plenty of flesh-and-blood friends. On racing day, friends become crew. Many have raced with him for years. But Ian also accepts newcomers and no-hopers, which are my two qualifications to be on board.

Rigging *Britannia* is a labour-intensive job that takes the best part of two hours. What's more, just about everything on this boat is heavier than what is on our competitors'. Crew member Wally says *Britannia* weighs about 400 kilograms before being rigged, about double that of the others. Once the rigging begins, the weight really piles on. The Oregon mast takes at least four of us to carry and another few to lift it into place. Wally says other skiffs tend to use lighter-weight masts, sometimes made of aluminium. But Ian counters the extra weight is worth it, to honour the boat's heritage.

'If we're going to find out how it [the boat] was used and to pay respect to the blokes who built and raced this, I thought I must do it this way. Do it right,' says Ian. The mainsail unfurls, revealing the red British Merchant Marine flag emblazoned on it. As I look at the symbol, Ian explains he's a republican.

'I feel it's part of history the way the boats were built,' he muses. 'The racing is important, the history of the people is important, but the history of the boats as artefacts is also important and hasn't received enough attention.'

Just before the race, Ian hands out jumpers to his seven crew members. They're footy jerseys in the original Balmain colours of black and gold stripes, with the flag and 'Historical 18-footer Britannia' embroidered on them. We look like a swarm of bees in our jerseys, and *Britannia* is a hive, as we nudge her down the ramp and into the harbour.

We pile into the skiff and head out of the cove for the start of the race. Once we're crushed in, the 18-footer feels like an 18-incher. Thankfully, just before entering the water, I had asked Michele, one of Ian's long-term crew, is there anything in particular I should remember out on the harbour.

'Yes. You're going to get yelled at, and sworn at. But it's nothing personal.'

On land, Ian is a considered and erudite conversationalist, and a generous and lovely bloke. On the water, he's a fantastic leader, which means he can be as hard as the wood that he works with. When the skipper talks through his neatly trimmed beard, we listen and react. Even a novice is left in no doubt what the skipper wants, and where we have to move to. And we have to move quickly, constantly, and as one. It's shin-knocking, hand-stinging, back-aching work, as we lean out, jump in, duck and weave, pull out the spinnaker poles and attach the sections, then pull them back in. While it's the skipper giving the instructions, Mother Nature is determining what we're ordered to do. Joe, a large man from Nebraska ('cow country') who has learnt to read the air and sea and spends his days working in a boatyard, looks intently ahead.

'There'll be a blow in five, four, three . . .'

The sail blossoms and *Britannia* tilts. And so we all shift yet again, as the boom swings above us. No wonder the footy players enjoyed this sailing. The tacking is like scrummaging, pushing and shoving each other to get on the gunwale. There is nothing pretentious about this sailing; it's bloody hard work. It dunks under the water any stereotype of sailing being elitist.

Ian later says it's an exaggeration that historically the crews were only working class. He mentions a string of professionals who were 18-foot skiff sailors, including a Solicitor-General.

'If you were one of the core crew, you had some kudos,' explains Ian. 'I think their seamanship was respected, but I think there would have been "right of way" clashes.'

Those clashes continue to bounce across the water. At one point, a large charter catamaran tries to barge through.

'FUCK OFF!' hollers Ian. The charter skipper tries to argue, wrongly and in vain, that he's got right of way. He's told, in no uncertain manner, he's wrong. 'Dickhead!' mutters Matt, a calm-natured crew member, at the end of the cross-water debate. The calmness comes through familial experience for Matt; his grandfather was a champion sailor and sailmaker, and his father was a shipwright, whose business was in a shed opposite the Sydney Flying Squadron clubhouse in Careening Cove. 'That's what I love about Australians!' chuckles Mike, a young Irishman who has volunteered to be crew on this most English-sounding of skiffs. 'You know exactly where you stand!'

Sydney Harbour holds many beautiful sights, but there can be none more breath-stealing than sitting in the hull of a skiff, when the wind puffs out the 'kites'. It is as though an old sepia photo of skiffs on the harbour has been breathed to life – in glorious colour. To celebrate and honour Wee Georgie Robinson, Britannia's spinnaker features the logo of the Balmain Tigers rugby league team.

There is no 'rule Britannia' on this day. We come last, clocking in at 1.52.07, more than half an hour behind the winners, and just ahead of the storm that comes skulking in from the west to pummel the harbour. Just before we push Britannia out of the water, Ian takes out a flask filled with rum. We each take a swig. It's a ritual he practises at the end of each sail. Ian explains that Wee Georgie instituted this tradition on the original Britannia.

'He called it the "Block and Tackle". One drink and you'll do your block, two drinks and you'll tackle anyone!'

The rum tastes as warm as the camaraderie on the skiff. Despite my being little more than human ballast, Ian invites me back as crew. The next time we taste not just salt spray but victory. *Britannia* wins, even though we have to round a bulk carrier, and at one point it looks as though a kayaker is playing chicken with us.

'I know you're one of them, but we don't worry about kayakers,' says the skipper, with the hint of a smile, when I point to the paddler just off our bow.

What makes our victory better is that in fairly light conditions, the skiff is packed, with a crew of eleven. The artist James R. Jackson, who was renowned for depicting harbour life, loved sailing on the 18-footers as a young man. He recalled when the boat had to be lightened for the run home, he would be ordered overboard and left to swim back. As tempting as it must have been, Ian orders no one overboard during the race. As a competitor on another boat, *Tangalooma*, quips when he sees the crush of us on board, 'You look like a ferry!' Still, James R. Jackson said in his day there could be up to eighteen on board a skiff, so we still have plenty of room.

The pleasure of the skiffs is not just in the pain while racing, but also yarning with members of the other crews on the shore. Occasionally, sailors wear T-shirts that hint at their life and near-death connection to the water. Members of *Top Weight* sometimes wear shirts that read, 'Careening Cove Swimming Club'. This is an invitation-only club you don't want to be welcomed into; it depends on how many times you capsize.

A T-shirt worn by Marshall Flanagan, a crew member of *Tangalooma*, is not so lightly earned or worn. The message and insignia on the front of Marshall's shirt look like a joke, 'Bite Club', with a drawing of a shark fin. At first, I think he might be wearing it as good-natured psychological warfare, to make competing crews think twice about entering the harbour. Yet the back of the T-shirt reads, 'Shark Attack Survivors Support Group'.

I ask Marshall if the Bite Club is real. He lifts his cargo shorts to reveal the upper part of his left leg. A divot has been dug out of his skin. Marshall was attacked by a great white shark while surfing in South Africa in 1976. He escaped only by repeatedly punching the shark in the snout until it opened its jaws and released him. During the fight for his life, Marshall was bitten on the arm, and had a tendon in his hand torn through.

The shark was estimated to be three to four metres long. That estimate is based on part of a tooth that had been embedded in Marshall's knee. The tooth was removed and given to Marshall. He still has it, which is either a jagged reminder of how he was in the wrong place at the wrong time, or a good luck charm.

'It was tough,' Marshall says of the attack, 'but, hey, at least I got this T-shirt.'

FOR ALL the joy they bring to the harbour, and despite the heritage they carry in their varnished wooden hulls, the 18-foot skiffs are not assured of a future on Sydney Harbour, Ian Smith fears.

'I've got to say I'm not optimistic.'

'There is a bit of an element that wooden [boat] sailors are looked at the way vintage car people are looked at – "It's nice they're doing it, but they're nuts!"'

Many sailors, he reckons, are only interested in replicating their life on land, ripping along at great speeds and in maximum comfort.

'They don't want to be one of these weird people sailing these funny old boats,' Ian shrugs.

'There are a few younger people but not in the numbers to keep the fleet going for too many more decades. I'll keep going for as long as I can physically handle it.

'We have to interest more people in maritime history, and in the sheer joy of sailing.'

ROUNDING THE point from Careening Cove into Neutral Bay in *Pulbah Raider*, I feel momentarily lost. The ferry terminal is marked 'North Sydney'. Lesson learnt – don't navigate by ferry wharf signs. A little further along is an imposing 115-metre-long wharf where submarines once berthed. This is the site of the former HMAS *Platypus* base. *Platypus* was commissioned in 1967, and for more than thirty years the navy's Oberon submarines slid in and out of the bay to this base. The black fenders, which would have softened the nudging of the subs against the wharf, remain. Those who knew this area when it was a navy base can still hear the submarines in their memory. Kayaking with a friend in Neutral Bay, he pointed to where his father had lived, just a few doors from the base. My friend used to listen to the subs' engines rumble to life and see the smoke billowing out of them.

The submarines were hardly the first contributors to pollution along this section of the harbour. In 1876, the farmland that existed on the western shore became the home of a gasworks, tucked into the excavated sandstone cliff. Colliers would unload at the long timber wharf at night, sending out great plumes of coal dust. The works survived until the early 1930s, but their closure spelt only a change of industry for neighbours. During the Second World War, part of the gasworks site was resumed for a torpedo manufacturing and maintenance factory, servicing the Australian, British and US navies. Then, after the war, the submariners came.

The sites' industrial stories are scattered around the site in the surviving buildings, from the gasworks' coal stores to the massive RAN Torpedo Maintenance Establishment factory and the *Platypus* facilities. The Sydney Harbour Federation Trust – the agency formed in the late 1990s to oversee the return of Commonwealth land, particularly former Defence properties, to the public – has been given the task of moulding this rich yet dirty industrial past into something useable for the future. The site is to be a foreshore park, and some of the historic buildings are to be reinvented for public and commercial use. Change is already under way. A few buildings have been demolished or dismantled, and teams have been undertaking stonework and landscaping. There are even plans for a facility that is surprisingly sparse around the main harbour: somewhere to launch a kayak. More than $40 million have been spent on remediating the site, and another $20 million have been earmarked to bring new life to the old base. Whenever waterfront land becomes available, there are many ideas and not enough money to create something everyone will be happy with. But at least a slice of the harbour is being opened to the people, particularly in an area where much of it is in private hands.

AT THE head of Neutral Bay, as with so many of these harbour inlets, there was once a stunning creek and waterfall, which attracted picnickers. And like so many of the bays, its head was trussed behind a seawall, filled in and converted into a park. On 17 July 1934, the park became a runway for the famous aviator Sir Charles Kingsford Smith. His plane, *Lady Southern Cross*, had been shipped from the United States then transferred on a barge to the park. Kingsford Smith had lived near here years before and remembered the park, so he figured it could be used as a runway. Crowds gathered to watch the plane take off. They collectively held their breath as *Lady Southern Cross* hung low over the bay before it climbed above the harbour. The following year, Kingsford Smith, his flying partner J.T. Pethybridge and *Lady Southern Cross* were lost without a trace on a flight from England to Australia.

Near the park on the bay's western shore and staring across the water at the former navy base is a training centre for Australian Customs, or, as it has been rebranded, Border Force. I've paddled past clumps of earnest-looking people, swaddled in Customs overalls, combing over yachts berthed outside the depot. Border Force's presence, and its efforts to control what comes in and out of the harbour, echoes how the bay received its English name.

Governor Arthur Phillip didn't want foreign ships mooring wherever they wanted in the harbour, with all its discreet coves and inlets. So, in 1789, he ordered that all visiting non-British 'neutral' ships were to drop anchor in this bay. In that way, the colonists could keep an eye on them. Yet the expected foreign ships were slow in arriving. Phillip himself was readying to sail out of the Heads and leave Sydney when the first foreign trading ship, an American brig named *Philadelphia*, sailed into the harbour in November 1792.

The Customs complex sits on land that once held the home and business of a man who arrived in the colony in the sort of yacht that its officers could have searched for hours. Ben Boyd was a Scot. He sailed into the harbour in 1842 in a luxurious schooner, *Wanderer*, bringing with him plans to develop the resources of the colony and promises of funding to realise those ambitions, by way of money through the appropriately named Royal Bank of Australia. Boyd had formed the bank back in London, where he had been a stockbroker. In time, the bank would turn out to be little more than his cash cow. But he milked that cow and turned it into sheep. He established sheep stations, built up a steamship business, and, to transport the livestock and wool from his properties to Sydney, he built towns on the New South Wales south coast, modestly called Boyd Town and East Boyd.

On the shores of Neutral Bay, Boyd built a large dam and facilities to wash the wool, and a multi-storey building in which to store the bales, ready for shipping to England. Boyd lived in a large home, Craignathan, by the bay and was renowned for being a generous entertainer. Yet it all came crashing down and, by the late 1840s, he lost just about everything except his yacht, in which he sailed away in search of new fields of gold. Boyd went to California, but when that did not work out he sailed back across the Pacific, possibly with grandiose plans of starting his own Papuan republic, only to disappear, presumed killed, in the Solomon Islands. When Boyd's woolstore was dismantled in the 1870s, some of the great sandstone blocks were recycled and built into the seawall in Neutral Bay.

Just beyond the Neutral Bay ferry wharf, with its lavish Art Deco entrance, and a slice of sand with the urban name of Hayes Street Beach, sits the home of magical bushland creatures. Nutcote is a house built by gumnut babies. For this was where author and illustrator May Gibbs lived for more than forty years. Gibbs had already made her name with *Snugglepot and Cuddlepie* by the time she moved into Nutcote, but the property would inspire more book adventures. She would sit on the balcony of her home, nestled in the curve of the bay, or walk in the cottage's gardens down to the shore, all the while conjuring characters and settings that made their way from the harbour into children's imaginations, such as *Bib and Bub*, and *Scotty in Gumnut Land*.

In the days after the controversial opening of the Sydney Harbour Bridge in 1932, Nutcote housed another almost mythical character. Captain Francis De Groot stayed here after he had been released from detention for defiantly cutting the official ribbon before Premier Jack Lang could. May Gibbs' husband James Ossoli Kelly was a friend of De Groot.

While the design of Nutcote has Mediterranean influences, further along the point a touch of Venice seems to have been plonked right on the shore. Next to the Kurraba Point ferry wharf is a three-storey apartment block with sumptuous curves, like an ocean liner's. Living in there, you would feel as though you were on a boat. On the ground floor, the harbour is just a couple of metres below the windows, so the sound of water would be a constant companion. In 'A Portrait of Sydney', Kenneth Slessor saw his harbour town as a kind of Venice, comparing the coves and inlets to the Italian city's canals, and the ferries to the gondolas.

Around the point is Shell Cove. Along the cove's eastern shore, which is Cremorne Point, the sense of the landscape remaining how it's always been is palpable. On the waterline there are no houses, just oyster-clad rocks and bush, like nature's own green ban. It is part of a 30-metre reserve skirting the point, ensuring the waterfront is kept in public hands. Hiding under the trees are overturned tinnies, waiting to take their owners out to the larger boats clotting the cove. The bush slowly surrenders its territory to housing as I near the tip, but the feeling of another time stays. With its waterfront reserve and behind that a row of predominantly older homes, Cremorne Point, from the water, looks like some seaside resort town from a century earlier. There is even a fantastic swimming pool, hiding behind a curtain of Port Jackson figs, on the water's edge.

The MacCallum Pool may be made of concrete but it is virtually a rock pool. Indeed, it began life as a pool defined by rocks, assembled by an Olympic swimming gold medallist, Fred Lane, in the early 20th century. A local, Hugh MacCallum, took over the pool's maintenance, and, for his efforts, the facility was named after him in the 1930s. The pool is set like a jewel into the sandstone shoreline. As I float in the water, I can hear the waves splashing onto the rocks, just on the other side of the picket fence. I could well be swimming in the harbour. I'm undoubtedly, gloriously, swimming in Sydney. For what makes Sydney magical washes through the spaces in the wooden fence and into the pool. It's the view, not the early-morning water temperature, that takes my breath. I can see down the harbour to the Bridge peering over Kirribilli Point, and on the opposite shore, there's the Opera House, the Botanic Gardens, the warships at Garden Island. Between there and here is Fort Denison. MacCallum Pool is hardly Olympic standard in dimensions. An older man, whose freestyle stroke has the gentle rhythm of Tai Chi, tells me he's paced it out to be thirty metres. Not that it matters. I spend most of my time at the end of the pool, gazing out. This utterly beguiling pool is perhaps the least conducive in the harbour, if not in the world, for swimming laps. Or, as the Tai Chi swimmer proclaims with a sweep of an arm across the harbour, 'Who needs New York, eh?'

Cremorne Point has a beauty that attracted admirers from the early days of the colony. Some wanted to be nurtured by what the point offered, others wanted to be made wealthy by it. The owners of the Cremorne Gardens combined the two motives, when they opened their pleasure ground in 1856. The owners had named their venture after the renowned Cremorne Gardens in London. Steamers brought revellers across the water from Sydney Cove. The commercial pleasure gardens shut after a few years, but, as a picnic destination, Cremorne Point remained popular. However, some wanted the land for a few. James Milson junior sought to subdivide the point – right down to the waterline. He was told the waterfront reserve would remain, but he advertised in 1889, anyway, showing blocks for sale with nothing between them and the harbour. The matter went to court, the developer lost, and the point still wears its green trim. The predominance of green slides around the tip into Mosman Bay, as residents in the Federation homes along the point's lip maintain the foliage between them and the harbour. Stone paths and stairways shyly reveal themselves between the plants and trees on the steep slope. The residents are tending to not just a garden but a tradition. For one section along here has been revered locally for more than half a century. In 1959, a resident, Lex Graham, planted an elephant ear bulb that he had grabbed as it floated past while he was swimming in the bay. From that one act, more than the elephant ear grew. Lex and his wife Ruby cleaned out the garbage – some of it very old, including women's whalebone corsets – that had been thrown over the edge, removed the weeds, and slowly created a wonderland that holds the slope firm and sets your mind free when you wander into it. Birdsong sprinkles from above, and the rhythm of water on the rocks is whispered from below. The secret of Wendy Whiteley's garden in Lavender Bay is well and truly out, but somehow Lex and Ruby Graham's harbourside creation remains barely known – which is probably how those who care for it, and use it, want it to remain.

Cremorne Point's beauty was once threatened from below the surface. A couple of bores were sunk in the late 19th century, in the search for coal. A thick seam was located, and the coal company wanted to push ahead with a mine. The locals pushed back. The debate whether to approve the development raged in the parliament, and the *Illustrated Sydney News* featured a drawing in its 2 December 1893 edition, titled 'A Glimpse of the Future: Cremorne 10 Years Hence'. The illustration is a dystopian vision of a ruined suburb, with a colliery chuffing away, and ships clustered around the point to load the coal. Yet the picture never came to life. The mine was not given the green light.

I paddle on past the Sydney Amateur Sailing Club headquarters and a ferry terminal with the evocative name Old Cremorne. A creek trickles down a steep gully and into the bay through a rainforest bower. The bay itself holds maritime history. The vessel that carried the unprepossessing beginnings of a nation into this harbour, the First Fleet's flagship *Sirius*, was careened in this bay in 1789. Apparently the frigate was to be repaired on the other side of the harbour to remove its crew from the temptations of idleness and bad company in Sydney town. *Sirius* was in the bay for more than four months, and as a result it was named Great Sirius Cove. However, that name seems to have largely drifted off the map. Instead, the bay's name is attached to a prominent early local landholder, the shipowner and whaling industry pioneer Archibald Mosman.

Mosman Bay became a haven for whalers chasing their fortune in the southern seas. The bay had been selected largely because it was beyond smelling distance from the main town. The pungent smell of whale oil filled the air. What was repugnant to many of the good folk of Sydney town was the sweet scent of money to those in the industry. In 1826, the value of whale oil and other products exported from New South Wales was £34,850. A decade later, the whale exports were valued at £140,220. At this stage, the colony was riding more on the whale's back than the sheep's; the poor creature was a huge earner. The mix of oil and water was particularly lucrative for Archibald Mosman. In the early 1830s, he developed a whaling station in the bay. After he sold up in the early 1840s, Mosman left behind infrastructure for an industry that had already peaked, and a name for the bay. For a while, the ships continued to sail into Mosman's Bay, their masters praising the facilities and 'the locality would be very favourable to a ship of war from the absence of the temptations of grog, &c., &c., which she would be exposed to at the Sydney wharves'.

Commercial shipping gradually moved out, but the picnic boats steamed into Mosman Bay. It was advertised as a largely undiscovered wonder, 'a rough, rural and romantic place worth seeing', with 'magnificent scenery; such nice shady nooks for picnic parties'. More than a century and a half later, the bay is far from rough, and at the bottom of the steep slopes curling around its head is a congestion of facilities devoted to water and fun: a marina, dinghy racks and boatsheds, and the Mosman Rowers Club.

From what was Great Sirius Cove, I paddle around to Little Sirius Cove. Somehow the bay has shrunk in name. It was Sirius Cove. However, the 'Little' often drifts off when people talk about it. So I paddle into (Little) Sirius Cove. At its head, dogs scamper in the shallows, while their walkers call in vain from the reserve, and along the eastern shore, just beyond a Sea Scout hall tucked into its own little cove, is a visually intoxicating picture of an oyster-covered sandstone shoreline buttressing thick bush leaning over it. The scene is at once refreshing for the eyes, and familiar. For along this stretch was the bush idyll of a couple of enormously influential late 19th century artists who helped open Australians' eyes to who they were and the beauty of where they lived. Arthur Streeton and Tom Roberts painted and stayed here, in what was called Curlew Camp. Near the head of the bay, I stand roughly where Streeton stood in 1892 to paint his *Near Streeton's camp, Sirius Cove* and pretty much see what he saw. The scene is little changed from what Streeton captured with his paints, although the young lady in a sunhat in his picture has been replaced by two women in bikinis lying in front of the Scout hall, and the steamer off the point has metamorphosed into a navy landing barge undergoing trials.

Streeton loved the boating activity, the way in which the light pulled colour out of the water, and 'the soft, dark breath of the harbour playing through my hair'. He thought the area around Mosman Bay was a land of passionfruit and poetry. It was all intoxicating to his eyes; little wonder he considered Sydney an artist's city. Streeton went on to London, but he was drawn back to the harbour city. He wrote to Roberts in 1907 about Sydney's 'fascinating, warm, grey sky and yellow rock . . . and long, undulating shore lines and luxurious languor of expression'.

Under a Streeton sky of cerulean blue, I kayak around Little Sirius Point and listen for lions and elephants. From Athol Bay, I had been told, you might hear these animals. I hear nothing but water murmuring. On the slopes, however, live thousands of creatures, including lions and elephants, in Taronga Zoo.

The zoo has been by the harbour for more than 100 years. The original site was at Moore Park, on the city's south side, but the animals needed more room. In 1916, they were transferred across the harbour on barges and ferries to Athol Bay. Boats followed the floating cavalcade, so that if any animals jumped overboard, they could be picked up.

Before the zoo was built, this section of the northern shore had already housed creatures from around the globe. In the early years of the 20th century, there was a quarantine station for livestock and imported dogs. The landscape above the bay, as photos of the time show, was fairly sandy, dotted with low scrub and trees. These days, from the water, the slopes around Athol Bay are thick in foliage and with tourists wandering the paths through dozens of replicated habitats for about 4000 animals.

Yet it's no longer enough to merely look at animals in a zoo. You can also sleep with them (but not in the same compound), and wake up to a harbour view, with accommodation offered at Taronga. And in its grounds, you can experience that most beguiling of creatures up close, the rock musician, with a series of outdoor concerts staged over summer. As the sun slid towards the eucalypts on a perfect March evening, I wandered through the zoo's grand entrance and down its paths to attend the concert of Colin Hay, the co-creator of Australia's sardonic unofficial anthem, *Down Under.*

On the journey to the amphitheatre, I passed a tree kangaroo dining on a branch, brush turkeys ambled across the path, and Gung, the male Asian elephant, was moving a few things around with his trunk. From the sloping lawn in front of the stage, I could see vast swathes of the harbour, which looked gauzy in the late afternoon light. Just before the sun set, a sea-bound cruise ship cut across the diamond harbour. The setting was a superb opening act for Colin Hay and his band. Near the end of the show, the band played a cover version of *You Shook Me All Night Long*, but the Sydney night flowed by unruffled.

The shore of Athol Bay is a gem. A couple of beaches are set between the bush-encrusted rocky outcrops like gold between emeralds. During the Second World War, the great *Queen* liners from Britain moored around the bay, as they were transformed from the epitome of floating luxury to troop carriers. In 1940, *Queen Mary* sailed out of the Heads with about 5000 Australian troops on board, bound for the Middle East. *Queen Elizabeth* was also fitted out and loaded with troops in the harbour. Cruise ships still occasionally moor around Athol Bay, if they are so large they can't fit into Circular Quay or under the Bridge, or on special occasions such as Australia Day.

As those troops destined for a distant war sailed out of the bay, on the first headland they passed on their port side, they could have seen a monument to the feats of Australians in another conflict. Standing tall on Bradleys Head since 1934 has been the foremast of HMAS *Sydney*. The tripod crowned with an Australian naval flag looks like some giant survey marker embedded into the point, as if helping ships gain their bearings. When you are sailing east and pass Bradleys Head, you have a sense that the sea and adventure lie before you, as the Heads come into view. Conversely, when you are sailing into the harbour and round the head, you feel the embrace of security and the binding of routine as the CBD appears.

Long before the foremast was planted on Bradleys Head, naval men made their presence felt here. No sooner had the British arrived in 1788 than they began renaming the harbour's landmarks. What had been known as Borogegy for generations was named after the Royal Navy lieutenant involved in the initial survey of the harbour, William Bradley. While that may be the official reason behind Bradleys Head's name, whenever I paddle around the point, I look up at the great swathes of bushland marching up from the water to the ridges and I figure its name is, by default, a tribute to two tenacious local sisters. Eileen and Joan Bradley spent decades gaining an understanding of the bush along the northern shores by walking through it and helping it to regenerate. The sisters would hand-weed where they walked, carefully returning the bush litter as they went, after they noted how the authorities' slashing-and-clearing approach ultimately didn't help. They formulated what became known as the Bradley method of bush regeneration. One of the core principles was to let the bush itself determine the pace of work; when it regenerated, continue. Eileen died in 1976 and Joan in 1982, but the Bradley sisters' memory flourishes in the undergrowth and under the shade of the gums not just along the harbour's edge, but in bush regeneration programs around the country.

If the bush is a memorial of sorts to the Bradley sisters, the HMAS *Sydney* foremast on the headland is a reminder for all members of the Royal Australian Navy of who they are and what they do. The naval men and women acknowledge the foremast every time they sail past it, and a commemorative service is held on the headland each year to honour *Sydney*'s defeat of the German ship SMS *Emden* in the Battle of the Cocos Islands in the early days of the First World War in 1914.

The significance of that battle has reverberated through the years undimmed. On 8 November 2015, underneath the foremast, a service commemorating the 101st anniversary of the battle was held. In the audience were descendants of those who served on *Sydney* I, which is remembered on this site, and *Sydney* II, which was sunk with the loss of all 645 on board during the Second World War. A group of those who served on *Sydney* III and *Sydney* IV were also attending, along with RAN representatives, dressed in their whites that shimmered against the oyster sky, sulking and threatening to rain at any moment. A friend of mine, Commodore Peter Leavy, who was representing the Commander of the RAN Fleet, read 'The Naval Ode'. Pete was ideally suited to do the reading. He is a former commanding officer of HMAS *Sydney* IV. As the ode's solemn words were recited, and *The Naval Hymn* was sung, beseeching that mariners be protected from 'rock and tempest, fire and foe', life on the harbour flowed on in the background. The ferries ploughed determinedly past the headland, yachts leant away as they grasped at the wind, and tourist jet boats created whirlpools of spume and shrieks from their passengers.

The passing of time, and the creating of history, was perhaps most keenly felt by those from *Sydney* IV. Just the day before, their ship had been decommissioned in a ceremony across the harbour at the RAN's Fleet Base East. As they well knew, and the crowd at that ceremony was told, *Sydney* had inherited more battle honours than any other ship in the fleet and had added to that tally through its own actions. This *Sydney* had cruised 959,627 nautical miles or about 1.78 million kilometres, the equivalent of circumnavigating the globe forty-four times, and about 4000 men and women had served on her.

A day on, a few of those members of the now-decommissioned ship's company were gazing wistfully across the harbour. I didn't notice what they were looking at until one of them pointed out *Sydney* IV berthed at Garden Island. There was much speculation about what would happen to the frigate, with one ruefully muttering, 'She'll be turned into scrap.' But on this day, she looked beautiful in the distance, giving shape to the sum of words we had heard during the commemorative ceremony.

Just below the tripod, incongruously rising out of the harbour like some ancient Greek ruin is a single Doric column. It was once part of the General Post Office in the city but when that building was demolished, the column was salvaged and placed here to mark a nautical mile from Fort Denison, so ships could measure their speed. The ships rounding the point sailed into the verse of Henry Lawson, in his paean to the harbour city, 'Sydney-Side', in 1898.

And the sunny water frothing round the liners black
  and red,
And the coastal schooners working by the loom of
  Bradley's Head;

And the whistles and the sirens that re-echo far and wide –
All the life and light and beauty that belong to
   Sydney-Side.

Bradleys Head may be a long-standing landmark for mariners, but that finger of land has occasionally conspired with Mother Nature to catch out shipping. The ferry *Curl Curl* ran aground on the headland in 1936. Despite the small lighthouse just off the point, thick fog had dissolved any distinction between land and water. Off Bradleys Head and sitting on the harbour bed close to the shipping channel is the wreck of SS *Currajong*. The steamer collided with a much larger ship, *Wyreema*, in 1910, and quickly slid under the water.

Tim Smith is a maritime archaeologist and has done so much to bring to the surface knowledge about our nation's past. He has dived on *Currajong*. His first impression of approaching the wreck was watching its shape form through the gloom. Where it sits, on the edge of the shipping channel and in an area where any silt carried down the harbour is likely to rest, is often gloomy and beset with poor visibility. But when she does come into view, Tim says, *Currajong* is a sight to behold.

'It's the biggest intact shipwreck in Sydney Harbour,' Tim explains. 'You feel the bulk and scale of it when you land on the bow and follow it down to the harbour bed. Then you look back up and see the bow towering over you.

'If you follow the port side down, you can come to the damage caused by the collision. You pass across a couple of metres of this big gaping hole.'

While hundreds of ships have sunk in Sydney Harbour, Tim says there is comparatively little on the bottom of the harbour.

Many shipwrecks were salvaged, and, in the past, recreational divers picked the bones clean, because much of the harbour is relatively shallow and accessible. Still, to dive on a wreck in Sydney Harbour, he says, is 'just magic'.

'It's such a spectacular setting, and every time you dive into the water, you're jumping into these pages of history,' he says.

If Bradleys Head signals a change in direction for shipping, it can also mark a change in the harbour's mood for a kayaker. When I've paddled around the headland, past the Doric column and the HMAS *Sydney* sign set into the rock below the mast, I've often been smacked in the face by a north-easterly, along with a few waves that have ridden in through the Heads. The calm of Athol Bay is already a memory. The *Sydney Morning Herald* editor and writer, J.M.D. Pringle, observed, after arriving from Britain in the early 1950s, that Sydney was ruled by three winds, 'which command the city in turn like the chiefs of an invading army': the southerly, the north-easterly and the westerly. He reckoned those winds set the different rhythms of the city's life but also represented the conflicting elements that shaped Sydney's character. The southerly, Pringle reckoned, was the wind of conscience, cooling the city down and reminding its inhabitants to work hard. The westerly was the voice of Australia, hot and dry as it blew in from the heart of the continent. The north-easterly, he wrote, was intent on turning the city into a South Pacific town, with its warm and humid character impelling people to slow down and take it easy. Mr Pringle must never have kayaked around Bradleys Head into a north-easterly. The wind that he reckoned makes Sydneysiders relax can make the going tough for a paddler.

*

NO SOONER had the British ridden those 'invading army' winds into Sydney Harbour than the colonists began worrying about who else would come through the Heads. And that worry never abated, because Britain was usually arguing or fighting with some power or another: France, Spain, Russia, the United States of America. For many years, in response to the concerns, there was more debating and fretting about how to protect the harbour than any actual fortifying. Still, there were some bursts of activity, and the shape of those fears of attack is still particularly evident along the harbour's northern shore. Many of the points jutting into the harbour from Bradleys Head to the sea were reserved for defence. Camouflaged in the bush, gouged into the rock and sticking out from the sandstone are gun emplacements and old buildings, their faces turned eastward, constantly watching what the seas have carried in.

Ultimately, the installations sort of achieved what they were built for. They defended much of Sydney Harbour's northern shores. They saved the headlands on which they were based from being overrun by residential development. At the end of the 20th century, large tracts of Defence land were handed back to the people. So while the old defence facilities are a monument to history, the bushland saved is a testament to a quirk of history.

In the bush just above the HMAS *Sydney* monument are the remains of gun emplacements dating back to the 1870s. The emplacements have a stone inscribed 'VR 1871', and one cannon, steadfastly pointing towards the east. While the 'VR' spells out the ties to Britain and Queen Victoria, the presence of the emplacements represents the colony standing on its own feet, or being forced to. In 1870, the soldiers of the last of the British regiments providing protection to the colony boarded ships in Circular Quay and sailed away, leaving the local authorities to determine how to best defend New South Wales. The Bradleys Head emplacement was part of a broader plan of fortification, recommended by a government commission into the Defences of Sydney Harbour in 1870. And as far as some were concerned, the facilities were grossly overdue, with the *Illustrated Sydney News* at the time being critical of the reliance on a 'few fragile forts' to defend the harbour.

I kayak around Bradleys Head and follow the shaggy and rock-studded shoreline along Taylors Bay, which is the picture of serenity – even if it doesn't sound it. A moored yacht is playing a Jimi Hendrix song at a leaf-curling volume. I head out of the storm of *Purple Haze* and paddle on to the next cove, Chowder Bay. Its name is courtesy of 19th Century American whalers who moored in the bay and collected oysters from the rocks to cook up 'clam' chowder. Those with the patience to rely on the harbour for a meal still head to Chowder Bay. The long jetty pushing into the bay is often prickled with fishing rods.

The area around the bay was also dressed in a resplendent name, Clifton Gardens. In the early years of the 20th century, Clifton Gardens was described as the most extensive playground in Australia, with ferries bringing hordes of visitors to the bay. They would bathe in the large circular swimming pool, dance in the hall, picnic in the grounds, or stay in the three-storey hotel that overlooked the harbour. The hotel and dance hall may be gone, and the great circular pool has been replaced by less imposing netted baths, but the pleasure-seekers still come to Clifton Gardens. When I paddle by early one April morning, part of the baths' netting had collapsed into the water, leaving it open. Just as I'm contemplating whether that would deter swimmers, an older bloke comes along, drops his towel and wades in. He has the look of someone honouring a daily ritual. Just before he finds his rhythm in the water, I ask him how long the net has been open. A month, maybe two, he replies. Then, reading my mind, he says, 'Only small sharks could get in.' He smiles and starts swimming. His strokes are syncopated by a hollow drumming sound bouncing across the water. The harbour is playing a tune on a large mooring buoy in the bay, as the waves slap against the metal and knock out some wonderful polyrhythmic energy.

On the bay's eastern shore are old wooden and stone buildings, which have been converted into cafés, restaurants and offices, and the headquarters of the Sydney Institute of Marine Science, a training and research facility involving scientists from four universities, and government agencies.

One of the institute's major programs laps at its feet. The Sydney Harbour Research Program involves scientists from a range of disciplines, and it aims to improve decision-makers' and the public's understanding of the waterway's natural systems – and the impact we have on it. Much of the research is designed to determine not only the harbour's health now, but to provide direction on how to make it healthier, or at least do less damage to it, in the future.

Some of the research SIMS is engaged in is there for all to see on a wharf at Chowder Bay. Tanks pumped with harbour water are being used to study threats from climate change to the biodiversity on rock shelves. The researchers manipulate the water's temperature and acidity to see what effect that has on mussels. The study could well help ensure there are mussels and oysters in the future, so that those diners sitting on the restaurant verandas above the tanks can continue to enjoy seafood – even 'clam' chowder – by the bay.

'The water around here is clean, so it's perfect for labs,' says Professor Bill Gladstone, a SIMS member, as well as being Head of the School of Life Sciences at the University of Technology Sydney.

As a marine biologist, Bill's workplace is the harbour. It serves as his study and laboratory for his research, including into seagrasses and sharks. But the harbour is also his playground. It has been since he was a kid. He has been scuba diving in the harbour for almost half a century.

'To me it's just as beautiful underwater as it is above water,' he says, as we look out on Chowder Bay.

Having been diving since he was thirteen, Bill need only look through his mask to determine the water is cleaner. What's more, fish numbers are strong, which he says reflects good management.

'The numbers of people [in Sydney] have skyrocketed, and there are lots of people fishing around the harbour, but the fish population appears to be pretty healthy,' he says.

'There are other huge changes, like whales coming back into the harbour, and the seals. We never saw those things ten years ago. So there's been a major shift in what people can experience in a pretty short period of time.'

A key to Bill's enjoyment underwater is not just the numbers of fish but the different species he sees. About 575 fish species have been recorded in the harbour, which is more than twice the number of those around the entire coast of the United Kingdom. Yet he warns the types of fish appearing in Sydney Harbour are also a concern for the future. The rising temperatures and acidification of the water mean the harbour could be increasingly 'tropicalised'. Bill says tropical fish arrive in the harbour in the summer months and die off during winter. If the water temperature doesn't drop, and those species survive, they will become permanent residents. So *Finding Nemo* won't be just a movie; there could be all sorts of tropical fish in the harbour, but that is not necessarily a good thing.

'It changes the ecosystem, it may lead to competition with the existing species,' says Bill.

One fish Bill is not concerned about seeing when he's diving is the shark. Not that he sees that many, he adds. 'The occasional grey nurse, and the Port Jackson shark.'

Although he explains that the shark whose name is taken from the waterway we're looking at is not strictly a Port Jackson shark.

'They're Port Jacksons for only a couple of months of the year, then they're either Eastern Australian, or Bass Strait or Tasmanian sharks,' he says.

For Bill Gladstone, the harbour continues to be a place of research, and of fascination.

'I've dived all around the world, and worked all around the world, but the fact we can still enjoy Sydney Harbour, and the way it is in such a beautiful state is amazing.'

WHERE SCIENCE is now housed, along with the cafés and restaurants, the military once ruled. Some of the buildings around Chowder Bay were the base for the Submarine Mining Corps from the early 1890s to 1922. As part of the defence of the harbour, mines were attached to cables from Chowder Bay to the southern shore. The plan was to detonate the mines if an enemy ship reached this far into the harbour. It was incredibly dangerous work, as the Mining Corps members demonstrated in 1891. They were showing off their skills before a crowd of thousands, when suddenly there was an explosion, killing four servicemen. Changes in technology led to the cables being pulled out of the water, and the Corps was disbanded.

Playing hide-and-seek among the trees all the way up the hill at Georges Head and on the heights that they dominate are more old military installations and buildings, which were integral to the defence of the outer harbour. Many of the buildings were constructed in the 1870s, beautiful structures crafted from sandstone and blending into the setting. Yet what is remarkable is how these defences were furnished with their firepower. In 1870, a road was hacked through the bush from North Sydney, and a band of 250 soldiers rolled the gun barrels on skids to the emplacements on Georges Head and further along on Middle Head. A newspaper reported at the time how the 'military road' was an impressive 66 feet (20.6 metres) wide. That dimension would sound woefully inadequate to anyone who has been trapped in the daily vehicle chokehold of Military Road. If only they had bigger guns in the 1870s. Still, it did take three months to roll the guns to the emplacements, which is only slightly longer than it takes to drive from Mosman to North Sydney in peak times these days.

Georges Head became the command post in the 1890s for all the defences around Sydney Harbour, and it maintained that role until the 1930s. The army stayed much longer, until the early 21st century, when the land was handed over to the public.

In their time at Georges Head, the soldiers didn't just build on it, they burrowed into it. For a tour of the shafts and tunnels worming under the headland, I meet with a Vietnam veteran and former sergeant in the artillery, Ron Ray. He trained around here in the 1960s, staying in the spartan First World War-era barracks. However, the views from Georges Head and Middle Head were a revelation, and even being here was amazing to young Ron, 'because, being a Western Suburbs kid, the harbour, especially the North Shore, was toffy stuff'.

These days Ron is a volunteer guide for the Sydney Harbour Federation Trust, which is based at Georges Heights. The Trust also renovated and leased out the buildings that Ron would have used as a soldier. Ron has a jovial face, a friendly manner, and an authoritative voice that by its very tone commands you to listen. Vocally, at least, he is still a sergeant.

We meet at the lookout at nearby Georges Head, where a battery of large guns was once embedded. A plaque at the lookout makes it clear that long before the army occupied the site, this was an important meeting place for Aboriginal people. What made it so significant to them, and so strategically vital to the military, is what makes it a joy to visit now: the views. Unlike the soldiers and their guns, with their attention largely trained to the east, I can look back to the south-west. A sailing ship leans around Bradleys Head, and that sight makes me wonder what the Borogegal people would have thought the first time they stood here and saw vessels cutting across their space and into their world.

We march down the hill and past the sandstone Gunners' Barracks, built in 1872 and made more gracious in recent years by its restoration and conversion into a restaurant. As we trundle by finely-clothed diners enjoying high tea, Ron mentions that as part of his military training, he used to run down the steep slope to the shore more than 50 metres below then clamber up again, while wearing a full pack – and all before breakfast.

Beyond the barracks, we enter the tunnels. The sun is locked out, the temperature drops, and the air thickens and clings to me, as we walk through the zig-zagging tunnels, designed to prevent any blast from travelling too far. The 19th century underground construction was still used a century later, as Ron explains. He takes us into a larger, concave-ceilinged room that was once a magazine, but in his day was used by the officers for parties. Further on the tour, he tells another story about his former superiors. He points to a pit where the submarine cables to protect the harbour were coiled and stored, but many years later, it had been fashioned into a fishing pond for the officers.

The tunnels lead out to a large gun facing the south-east. Ron says when it fired, the gun had a 4-kilometre reach. The battery was another installation constructed in the frenzy after the British left harbour defence to the colonials, as evidenced by the 'VR 1871' etched into the stone. The rigidity and discipline of the military past on Georges Heights are softened by the harbour views that wash across the grounds. Perhaps the views always did soften this place a little.

'I like the way the government has given the military sites to the public, and made them accessible,' Ron says, smiling.

'I would've hated to see the harbour built out and it being sold off.'

WALKING ALONG the peninsula to Lower Georges Heights, I'm passing through Aboriginal land, not just in the traditional sense that it belonged to the Borogegal clan, but in the British understanding of property. For around here was Bungaree's Farm. Bungaree was a Garigal man, from Broken Bay, about thirty kilometres north of Port Jackson. He was also one of this country's great sea explorers. In 1799, he accompanied the navigator Matthew Flinders on a voyage to Moreton and Hervey bays along what is now the Queensland coast. When Flinders set off the following year to circumnavigate the continent, he included in his crew Bungaree, who often acted as liaison, if not interpreter, as they encountered Indigenous groups on their marathon voyage.

Bungaree journeyed further into the ways of the colonists in 1815, when Governor Lachlan Macquarie granted a plot of land on Georges Heights for a group of Aboriginal families to farm. It was the first time land was allocated by the colonial authorities to Aboriginal people in Australia. Macquarie anointed Bungaree the leader of the group, and the Governor presented him with a breastplate inscribed with his name and the words, 'Chief of the Broken Bay Tribe'. The farming venture failed, despite two attempts. Bungaree returned to the water, joining the expedition of Lieutenant Phillip Parker King in 1817 to chart the coast of north-western Australia. Later in life, as his health declined, he was often seen on the harbour, boarding ships or rowing over to Sydney Cove. As an Irish sailor and actor, James O'Connell, described him, 'King Bungaree' was 'boarding officer, and official welcomer and usher of newcomers'. O'Connell also observed that 'King Bungaree' was 'better entitled to his rank than the English to his land'.

When he died in 1830, Bungaree was buried across the harbour at Rose Bay. While there's no trace of his farm on

Georges Heights, Bungaree's memory was illuminated on the headland in 2015, the 200th anniversary of the land allocation. Mosman Art Gallery held an exhibition in his honour, and it included images projected onto a Second World War fuel tank. Yet there is an unofficial memorial to Bungaree on the peninsula. Stand on a high point, gaze between the Heads, and think of him sailing out to sea, away from his people and into the unknown. For his voyages of exploration alone, Bungaree should be better known.

The practice of former military assets being reinvented and recycled continues further along the peninsula at Lower Georges Heights. Buildings that had been erected in the late 19th century for soldiers in the artillery became part of the 21st Australian Auxiliary Hospital during the First World War, as more and more casualties returned from the Western Front. By mid-1918, this military hospital in the most peaceful of locations was the third largest facility in Australia, treating some of the 152,000 Australian soldiers wounded during the war. Here, men, smashed and shattered, gassed and broken, and 'taken off strength', as their personnel files read, were put back together to resemble, as closely as possible, their peacetime selves.

Where soldiers' bodies and souls were once treated, the muse is now nurtured. The Army buildings have become an artists' precinct. Outside an artillery store, built around 1889, a French-Australian artist plays the piano accordion, while her sensual works of tango dancers mingle inside. In the former administration hut, a corrugated iron structure built during the Second World War, is part of the Julian Ashton Art School. History has presented a kind of symmetry by having the art school here. Ashton, one of Australia's highest profile artists during the late 19th and early 20th centuries, painted and stayed in a camp nearby at Edwards Beach in Balmoral. The artists' camp attracted other creative types. Performers and writers also stayed under the canvas, including the author of *Treasure Island*, Robert Louis Stevenson, for one night. At the camp, Ashton immersed himself in harbour life; he slept in an old boat on the sand.

Just across from the hut housing the Julian Ashton Art School is the studio of painter, sculptor and conservator Stephen Coburn. He is based in a large former workshop, built during the Second World War.

'It used to be where they did up the PT Boats,' Stephen explains.

Moping outside the studio is a boat that looks as though it is in need of doing up. A sailing mate of Stephen gave him a 1920s wooden fishing boat. It's beyond repair, Stephen says, so he's looking at turning it into a work of art, a sculpture perhaps, and 'make it look like a beached whale'.

Stephen has been in this studio since 2005. When he first came here, the transition from military to art was still taking place, with army material stacked and scattered around the building. He recalls one evening walking outside and seeing soldiers, dressed in black and carrying serious weaponry, looking at him. Surprised, Stephen could only utter, 'Are you on our side?'

One of the soldiers replied, 'Yeah, mate, don't worry, we're on your side.'

As the son of a Second World War veteran and one of Australia's great post-war abstractionists, John Coburn, Stephen has been in a lot of studios, but this is his favourite.

'I'm very lucky to have a big messy art studio here in well-to-do Mosman,' he says.

'And if you get sick of working, you can go down to the beach.'

MANY OF the fortifications on the headlands were designed to repel invaders who could have landed on the shore and climbed the slopes. From the water, those defences look unnecessary. Mother Nature had already provided the defences. By the time anyone had clambered up the sandstone cliffs and through the bush, they would have been exhausted.

The intrepid still pick their way down to the waterline to fish. At the bottom of Georges Head are two fishermen. One standing precariously on the rocks tells me his name is Thomas. He's travelled from Epping, a north-western suburb, to fish here for the first time. So far, he has caught one leatherjacket.

He says it's a bit dangerous, with the occasional wave rolling through, but the view is fantastic. As I talk to Thomas from my kayak, which bobs above a kelp garden swaying with the flow, his outline is cast against the distant North Head in a soft, diffused light. He's right; it is a fantastic view.

Along the shore, barely above the waterline are small concrete observation posts and bunkers sprouting from the rocks, or even set behind them. They date from the Second World War. I paddle into Obelisk Bay, and the source of its name is thrusting above the scrub near the shore. The white obelisk has served as a navigational aid for mariners seeking the right course along the harbour. Gripping the escarpment nearby are the remains of one of the harbour's earliest defences. In 1801, a fortification was designed, in the words of the colony's Governor Philip Gidley King, to 'prevent any attack from without'. From the rock on the headland, convicts cut the platform and a curved parapet for a battery. The fortification sat about 15 metres above the harbour, with walls almost a metre thick. Everyone and everything had to be brought in by boat, and the six guns installed at the fort had to be hauled from Obelisk Bay. All the effort and expectation piled onto the battery quickly amounted to nothing but hewn rocks in the bush. The guns fell into disrepair within a few years, and the battery was abandoned. As I stand near the ruins, I look to where the guns pointed, to the Heads and out to sea. Below two men are fishing from the rocks, ignoring the harbour growing ever testier as it tosses broken waves at them.

Leaving the ragged fringes of the harbour to the fishermen, I head back out onto the water. The sea is pushing a lumpier swell through North and South heads, straight into Middle Head. On a map, the tip of Middle Head looks as though it is trying to head north, to slot into the relative safety of Manly Cove, and escape the ceaseless attention of the sea. But it is a relationship that goes on. The sandstone face of the headland bears the scars and marks of that long, at times tempestuous, relationship. It is a face constantly changing as the water caresses and pounds it, shaves and picks at it. As I paddle around the headland, the waves crash into its feet, exploding in starbursts of spume. Yet the headland remains resolute, even if great chunks of it lie shattered at the water's edge. It is an awesome sight looking up at Middle Head. And it is more comforting to gaze up at its solidity than out to sea, beyond the limits of the harbour, into the unknown and unknowable.

But the sea still has its way with me. The waves rebuffed by Middle Head play with the kayak instead. *Pulbah Raider* rises, then its prow kowtows like a vassal towards the opening between the Heads, as if honouring the might of the sea. But the sea blithely ignores any respect it is accorded. I watch a yacht that has sailed in through the Heads disappear into a trough, only for me to drop and lose sight of it once more.

Somewhere beneath me on the harbour bed are two anchors, symbols of how quickly the harbour, when angry, can destroy a ship and the lives of those on board. The anchors are all that remains of *Edward Lombe*, a three-masted barque that was smashed onto the rocks at Middle Head in a gale in 1834. Twelve people were killed. While at least four other ships had been wrecked in the harbour since European settlement, this was the first time there had been loss of life. The tragedy horrified Sydneysiders. They saw passengers and crew desperately clinging to the shattered stern in the storm, they helped rescue survivors, and they grieved for the dead. Newspapers were filled with dramatic accounts of the event, artists sketched and painted the destruction of the ship, and the authorities responded by improving navigational aids in the harbour. That is the legacy of *Edward Lombe*; that, and the anchors.

They may be in shallow water, about ten metres, but the iron anchors hold deep meaning and poignancy for maritime archaeologist Tim Smith, who has dived to them.

'They are like a signature to the event,' Tim says, explaining how the captain most likely dropped the anchors to try and stop his ship being pushed onto the rocks on that dreadful August night in 1834. Tim has sent me a photo of one of the anchors, and it looks both haunting and beautiful. For this symbol of destruction and death is festooned with life, including soft corals.

'It shows just how vibrant the marine life is in Sydney Harbour,' Tim says.

With no desire to tempt the same fate as that of *Edward Lombe*, I paddle further away from the rocks, and from the exhilarating danger of the waves smashing into them, until I can look back and see the fortifications on top of Middle Head. Their days of power have passed. One concrete bunker at the northern end of the headland has been besmirched with graffiti.

Back in 1848, while preparing yet another review of the harbour's defences, Lieutenant Colonel Gordon had identified the headland as a very tempting site for a battery, and he compared Middle Head with Gibraltar. During the 1870s, temptation turned into action. On the northern side, Inner Middle Head fort was built, to cover Middle Harbour. On the southern end, the Outer Middle Head defences took shape to protect the entrance to Port Jackson. Gun pits and trenches were hacked out of the solid sandstone, and about twenty support and residential buildings were constructed in the scrub.

The defences were modified in the First World War and during the Second World War. Searchlights were installed at the Inner Middle Head fort, which was used as an observation station, while the guns remained trained between the Heads at the other installation, a few hundred metres away. After the war, the guns and searchlights were removed, but it remained a training ground for troops during the Vietnam conflict.

The machines and minds dedicated to warfare have left Middle Head, and it is now part of Sydney Harbour National Park. The remaining buildings have been occupied by the National Parks and Wildlife Service, and the views to the north, east and south that made this such an important strategic position are now a highlight for any visitor. Reminders of the military still hold some ground. Old stone tunnels and trenches cut through the bush like earthquake cracks, and teetering on the edge are the shells of gun emplacements and observation posts. Walking around the remains of the Outer Middle Head fort, I get a sense of what an immense facility this was. Five minutes' walk through the bush and I come to what is left of the Inner Middle Head fort and some legacies of the Second World War. The view from an old concrete observation post is revelatory. From there, I've watched the sun rise. When a Manly-bound ferry cut across the harbour, the water looked molten. The vessel hardened into a silhouette and its windows were backlit and filled with ingots of gold. Way below, kayaks were cruising like sharks, and power boats were cutting in and out of the Heads.

Long after the guns have gone, the elevation and the outlook invest this place with enormous power. Yet to stand here looking over the harbour and out to sea, you feel humble. On that morning in the observation post, I felt particularly humble. For this headland also gave me perspective. From up here, I could see where I had already kayaked, where I was not going to paddle – out through the Heads – and, as I gazed to my left towards Middle Harbour, just how far I had to go.

8

MIDDLE HARBOUR

STRICTLY SPEAKING, I have not yet entered Middle Harbour. Going by the map, I will have paddled into Middle Harbour when I pass an imaginary line between Grotto Point on the northern shore and Middle Head. As far as I can tell, that boundary mark is still quite a few strokes ahead of me. But if I go by how I feel, having curled around the north-eastern tip of Middle Head, I'm already there.

Even the swell tells me I'm in a different part of the harbour. The water has relaxed and displays a gentler character. It helps rather than hinders me, as it nudges me towards Balmoral.

I can see Balmoral across the water, with its Art Deco Bathers' Pavilion on the shore, and Awaba Street, rising even more steeply than the heart rates of those who jog up it. From the harbour, the gradient still looks cruel. The road that has become famous for an annual charity run known as the Balmoral Burn sears you even out here on the water.

I paddle past the navy base HMAS *Penguin*, which is holding onto the steep northern side of Middle Head. A navy workboat is moored in Hunters Bay in front of the base, and a few yellow buoys standing sentry warn all those in vessels to 'Stop. Naval Waters'. Just beyond the prohibited area are dozens of moored pleasure boats casually bobbing about. From the water you can observe a lot more of HMAS *Penguin* than you see from the front gates, of course. The different architectural styles and eras form up in ranks down the slope to the water. Those serving on the base would vehemently argue otherwise, and with good reason, but from out in the bay, HMAS *Penguin* has the look of a recreation camp.

Then again, just about everything feels relaxed in this bay. Even the shore curves leisurely, feeding the illusion of Balmoral being a beachside village rather than an expensive harbour-side suburb in a massive city. I paddle onto the beach beside a boatshed protruding on piers out into the bay. On the decking around the shed is a garden of umbrellas shading tables. For these days it's more than a boatshed. It is the Balmoral Boatshed. It is no longer where boats just get fixed; it is where people get their coffee fix. The Boatshed has transmogrified into a Destination.

I sit on a bench near the end of the jetty, drinking a coffee, peering into the water, where thousands of tiny fish form a fibrillating cloud around the piers. As much as I'd like to sit here all day, I have to keep paddling. I pass the harbour baths, with a few swimmers gently stroking the surface, and the long stretches of sand that are Balmoral Beach and Edwards Beach, punctuated by a knoll called, predictably enough, Rocky Point. On this late morning there are only a few walkers and joggers on the beach. But on hot days, the combination of relatively calm water and superb views attracts big crowds. Special events also bring the people down the slopes to Balmoral. Shakespeare plays are staged on the beach in summer, and, on Australia Day 2016, there was a re-enactment of the arrival of the First Fleet. The flotilla consisted of rowboats with flimsy home-made sails. A number of the boats flew Union Jacks at their stern, but one curiously had the French flag, presumably in honour of La Pérouse. The presence of the tricolour and the arrival of the First Fleet at Balmoral were not the only questionable historical points of the re-enactment. The boats were greeted on the beach by a team of lifesavers.

He may not have landed here, but Arthur Phillip would have seen this section of Middle Harbour even before he led the First Fleet through the Heads. A few days earlier, Phillip and a small crew had rowed up from Botany Bay and into Port Jackson, seeking a better place to found a settlement. The party first tracked around the lower part of Middle Harbour before heading to Manly, then over the next couple of days towards Sydney Cove, where Phillip found what he was looking for.

Within months of the First Fleet arriving, Phillip and his men further explored Middle Harbour. Captain John Hunter tracked and surveyed the harbour to its tidal limit by boat (so I'm roughly following in Hunter's long-faded wake), and Phillip led an overland expedition, determined to find arable land close to the shore. The terrain not only refused to offer potential for farming, it made the going tough for the expeditioners. As one of the party, naval surgeon John White, observed, 'The country all around this place was rather high and rocky, and the soil arid, parched and inhospitable.'

First Fleet re-enactments and plays on the beach were hardly the first pieces of outdoor theatre in Balmoral. For more than a year from 1923, a large amphitheatre took shape at the northern end of Edwards Beach. The amphitheatre featured a stage with a white-columned structure, like part of a temple, framing the view across the harbour and between the Heads. Up to 3000 people could sit and stand on the tiered platforms, taking in the view and – if the builders' plans had to come pass – a spiritual experience. The amphitheatre was built by a Theosophist group called the Order of the Star of the East to greet the expected arrival of one of its leaders. That so-called World Teacher from India did visit Balmoral, but only once. The order disbanded, and the amphitheatre was used for a time to stage more conventional theatre, before it was demolished and replaced by what the Order of Sydney Developers would consider a temple: a block of apartments.

The strip of sand gives way to a rocky outcrop at the northern end of Balmoral, where a couple is practising yoga, performing downward dogs and chair poses in their swimwear. Above them, staring out to sea, are the display windows of mansions along Wyargine Point. The rocks pushing out from the bluff into the water have been made sculptural by the years and the elements. Wherever you turn around here looks like a picture – or at least holds the potential of being made into one. And no one knows that better than the couple who live a little further along the shoreline, Australia's best-known painter and a brilliant visual interpreter of Sydney, Ken Done, and his wife Judy, who is a designer.

*

IN THE eyes of many people, Ken's art is synonymous with the Opera House and the Harbour Bridge. When I lived in Tokyo in the early 1990s, friends told me they were introduced to Sydney through Ken Done images, which were widely reproduced in magazines, including on the cover of one Japanese journal, *Hanako*, every month. They saw a Done, then they wanted to see the harbour city.

Like Sydney itself on special occasions, Ken's paintings are ebullient and feel uninhibited. Most of us have forgotten what that feels like. His paintings are as refreshing as an ice block on a summer's day. For a Ken Done image is not only a bold reflection of the city he lives in and loves, they are an extension of the man. To me, he's a fantastic colourist and a good friend.

Yet the man who opens eyes with his art says of himself, 'I have bream eyes'. He makes this declaration just after he has helped me carry the kayak out of the water and across rocks carpeted in frangipani and so beguilingly carved by the harbour that they look as though Rodin had been here. We head through a little wooden gate into the Dones' front yard, which is actually their backyard, but when you live by the harbour, your perspective turns 180 degrees. Despite having a crook shoulder from a recent skiing accident, Ken is the most lithe 70-something-year-old bloke I know. With his tanned face and luxuriant moustache, his preferred wardrobe of board shorts or loose-fitting pants, and his generally relaxed air, Ken perennially looks as though he's about to head to the water or has just returned from it. And it is often the case. It can't always be so, because he's also a prolific and disciplined painter.

We plonk the kayak down on the lawn under a gnarled old tree holding a swing from one of its branches, and we peer over the stone wall marking the boundary between Ken and Judy's property and the harbour, looking at life in the water – 'There's one! See? A bream.' That's when he tells me he has the eyes of a fish. Ken goes on to explain that he often sees bream in the water, when the fishermen on the rocks don't seem to. 'But I never tell the fishermen. I'm happy to see them casting in the wrong place.'

In his art, Ken sometimes applies those bream eyes, painting underwater views, guiding you through gossamer light and veils of colour. He takes you into somewhere most people view only from the surface. He invites you to go deeper. The inspiration for those works comes from distant places, in Pacific undersea gardens or on the Great Barrier Reef, but it is also found on the other side of the stone fence. Ken and Judy often snorkel in the cove outside their home, and they swim along it for a hundred metres or so every morning. Having immersed himself in what he paints, Ken heads to his studio. He usually paints in a space high on the hill, overlooking Chinaman's Beach. Named after those who tended the market gardens that once existed beyond the dunes, Chinaman's Beach is, in my eyes, Done's Beach. The beach is as ingrained in his art as its sand is under his toenails. The ribbon of beach, the swimmers and bathers who become dots and daubs of paint, the gentle surf swizzled and stroked in cool colours, the sails inhaling the wind and then exhaled onto canvas in triangular shapes of colour; Chinaman's Beach may have helped make Ken Done's name, but he has also made Chinaman's Beach his own. Everyone seems to know Ken around here. Even navy divers in training out the front have surfaced and yelled out, 'Nice paintings, Ken!'

Ken Done's other studio on the property is the Cabin. The structure itself seems modest, as it grows like a bush orchid out of the rock face behind it. The Cabin has been here for many years. As a teenager living in nearby Cremorne, Ken would rock-hop past here, looking at the view and coveting the old shack at the bottom of the steep slope, being embraced and smothered by the Port Jackson figs flanking it. Little did he know that many years later, he and Judy would buy the Cabin, restore it, and the two-storey building would serve as more than a studio.

The Cabin has been one of the artist's regular subjects, its bare beauty featuring in many of his paintings, whether it be the veranda on the second floor, the view framed by the kitchen door, or the louvre windows shifting the shapes and perspective on the world through the glass. The Cabin itself is a work of art. Before walking in, you are greeted by a frangipani clothesline, or, as Ken and Judy call it, the 'cossie tree'. Swimming costumes are hung from the frangipani's branches to dry, but the assemblage looks like a Ken and Judy work of art; colourful, colloquial and quintessentially Australian. The Cabin's interior is casually dressed. Downstairs, there are terracotta tiles on the floor and a couple of day beds with fishing rods hanging above them. In the middle of the space, separating the kitchen from the living area, is a large lump of a rock. It is no design feature, Ken explains; the rock would have been the original shelter, long before the Cabin took shape around it.

'Aboriginal people would have slept there for thousands of years, because it was north facing and offered shelter,' he says.

Up a narrow flight of stairs, like something on a ship, and you're in a living space that essentially puts you inside the eyes and soul of Ken Done. It certainly gives you the sense of standing in a Ken Done painting. He has created so many works looking out from this space. As Ken says, everything he needs is here: the

French doors, the frangipani trees, the rocks, and the turquoise blue of the water, perhaps more paradisiacal in colour than any other part of the harbour I've seen. On coffee tables seemingly crafted from driftwood are books about idyllic seaside places around the world. But nothing in those books beats the Cabin. And this is to be my home for the night.

Waiting for the sun to set, Judy, Ken and I have a drink in a stone courtyard guarded by the natural rock face. Massive hibiscus flowers provide bursts of colour with the wash of Middle Harbour just behind. We talk a little about sharks. In all their time living here, more than three decades, the Dones have hardly seen any. Judy mentions she once swam with about a dozen baby sharks just off here. Wasn't she worried Mum might be around? 'No, she would have gone on ahead,' says Judy in that unflappably calm voice of hers. Ken says he was once swimming in the shallows when he felt jaws bite him on the lower leg. He soon realised he had been attacked – by a small dog.

He may inhabit the busiest parts of the harbour with his paints, but Ken and Judy feel a greater connection to the more removed stretches. Judy grew up close to where we are sitting, in North Harbour.

'It was pristine, and everybody had a boat,' she remembers. Growing up in a quieter part of the harbour has shaped Judy's view. The main harbour is almost another world: 'it's the city'. She finds the world a little further up from their home, past The Spit, 'claustrophobic'. So she prefers looking the other way, towards the Heads and the opening to the sea. It is easy to imagine her outlook has also nurtured the way she is. Judy possesses a serene aura, like the harbour itself on the calmest days.

Night arrives and I head into the Cabin. Once the light has gone, I realise that while Ken's studio up the hill allows him to see further, with its sweeping views, the Cabin is a more sensual space. Its proximity to the water makes it so. Sounds are compressed and amplified. I hear the distant clang of a yacht's mast, the throaty moaning of the wind and the splashing of waves on the Rodin rocks. The air is laced with salt and the creamy aroma of night-scented jasmine. There are dribbles of lights on the water, from a street lamp near Chinaman's Beach, and from homes on the opposite shore at Clontarf. A little further to the east along that shore is a block of darkness. The peninsula's tip has been spared from development; it is part of Sydney Harbour National Park. I fall asleep to the calming sounds of the wind and water; silence is never a sleeping companion on Sydney Harbour.

I wake just before dawn. A paddle boarder glides by out the front. By the time I'm sitting on the stone fence, the water around Wyargine Point is the colour of copper. A couple of kayakers and a cruiser etch the surface. The copper turns to gold, as the sun rises above the headlands. Ken and Judy come down from their home above to perform their morning ritual, a return walk along Chinaman's Beach, then a swim. The stroll along the beach is only a few hundred metres, but it is a cleansing one, for the mind, and for the beach.

Ken walks ahead, a solitary figure in colourful boardies, leaving footprints in the sand. I walk with Judy. She sees a small fish flittering on the shoreline. 'Oh, darling!' she says and picks it up and puts it back in the surf. Ken has turned back to see what the issue is. The little fish doesn't look like it's going to make it. It has turned upside down and is at the mercy of the wave movement. 'That's nature,' says Ken gently.

Walking along, Ken and Judy say the harbour is much cleaner. They regularly see dolphins, and a southern right whale was recently here for a few days. The number of moorings off the beach is also slowly reducing. It would be amazing to look out on a slice of Sydney Harbour and see no boats moored. We reach the end of the beach, which we share with only one other, a man jogging. Ken says he's surprised how few use the beach of a morning. He shows me a 'beautiful enclosed rock pool', which he peers into like a little kid. I guess that's the key to being an artist. They always peer like a little kid into things.

As we walk back, Ken and Judy begin the second part of their ritual, picking up rubbish dumped by the waves or beachgoers. By the end of the beach, we've picked up enough to fill a plastic bag, which was also collected. 'That's the amount we normally get each morning,' Ken notes.

The swim is next. To reach the harbour entry point, we have to scramble across rocks and thin strips of lawn on neighbouring properties. Along the way, we stop at a dripping sandstone overhang, and Ken pulls back the foliage to reveal inscriptions in the rock. They are initials, a sketch of a pennant and stick figures in a boat, and the date, '30 December 1885'. Nearby is a more elaborate, and later, carving, the Australian coat of arms. Ken is delighted by these works, not only because he loves mark-making of any kind, but they are reminders in stone of those who have been here before him.

In the space between the mystery rock carvers and Ken Done, other artists and writers have created some evocative pictures of the harbour around Chinaman's Beach. In her beautiful memoir about growing up by Middle Harbour, *A Kingdom by the Sea*, Nancy Phelan recalled how families lived in homes of canvas and sand, dug into the dunes near Chinaman's Beach. Nancy would pick her way down the steep, bushy slopes to remote harbour beaches then escape the clutches of the land and adult rules by swimming out into 'The Open'. She also did something I'm not game enough to do, paddling at night. Young Nancy would steer her canoe towards the Heads, 'where the sleeping ocean gently breathed'. She could just make out shapes in the dark, but mostly she listened and imagined, including visualising being dragged under by a bombora, 'fear heightening the night's enchantment'.

Half a century before Ken moved into the area, James R. Jackson lived and painted above Chinaman's Beach. Jackson was renowned for his harbour paintings, and from the start of the 20th century to the early 1970s, he chronicled on canvas and board the changing waterfront. He was often simply referred to as a painter of Sydney Harbour.

Jackson was apparently quite territorial about the harbour as a subject. He would mark his painting spots, with his trademark being two palette knife swabs of harbour blue on the side of a rock. If he saw another artist's paint marks on a rock, Jackson would get annoyed. James R. Jackson has long gone, relinquishing 'his' territory to Ken Done. Not that Ken views it that way.

As he gazes through the branches of the cossie tree, across the frangipani-coated rocks to the water, Ken muses, 'If you sat here and try to make it the same as that, it's not going to work, because it's so beautiful. You can only use the experience of being here to take you to other things.

'We never take it for granted. I understand how privileged and lucky we are to be here.'

*

NOT POSSESSING bream eyes as Ken Done does, yet wanting an insight into what he sees, I pull on a diving mask and snorkel and plunge under the surface outside their home.

The morning light fractures as it hits the surface before sinking and flapping on the sandy bottom. I feel as though I'm floating over sand dunes. I imagine this is what it would be like to have a bird's, or fish's, eye view of the planet Tatooine from *Star Wars*. Clouds of algae suspended in the water stick to my mask. Judy told me the algae were the legacy of ships coming in from distant waters. I swim out of the *Star Wars* set into deeper water. I float over soft corals and observe the fish gliding around kelp-covered rocky clumps. The plant life sways gently, as if it is conducting a lullaby. I can hear the high-pitched whine of a distant motor churning through the water, so I break the surface and look around – which occurs to me later is probably not the wisest response to hearing a boat engine. I put my head back under and watch a school of garfish pass like a floating cache of swords. My eyes are grabbed by a plant that is a stunning mauve. It strikes me that I've seen that colour before, in a Ken Done painting. For a moment, I feel as though I almost have bream eyes. If only I had an artist's skill.

PADDLING AWAY from the Cabin, I have a mud map drawn by Ken in my lap, and in my memory his descriptions of the little beaches strung like pearls along the shore between his place and The Spit. I'm on a self-guided kayaking tour of Ken Done's Middle Harbour.

'Just beyond Chinaman's Beach, you'll see a little house with a boatshed underneath.' Sure enough, I pass an older two-storey house, gleaming white, soaking up the light reflected off the water. 'It's one of the few houses around here right at the water,' Ken had explained. Before reaching the 'boathouse', as he had called it, I'm to look for a larger rock with a small beach below it. Ken has called that beach 'Tony's Rock'. The name had been daubed on the rock, but 'Tony' has faded through the years – except in Ken's mind: 'I can only assume Tony was a fisherman.'

The next 'secret beach' is a couple of hundred metres further along. Ken calls it the 'Sea Frame', because embedded in the sand is a rectangular concrete frame encrusted with sea life, including barnacles. Within the frame is an ever-changing subject.

'You can never be sure what you'll find in the frame, but it will always be beautiful,' Ken had enthused. 'Sometimes it's seaweed and a few fish, sometimes crabs; whatever, it's always wonderful. It's a picture being made by nature.'

I land on the sand and find the sea frame on Sea Frame. It is marooned on the sand in a low tide, but within the frame, there are still pools of water, which have arranged the sand into a beautiful abstract picture. Glancing up, the view out towards sea is beguiling as well. As Ken had told me, from Sea Frame, 'you can see South America'.

I paddle further, leaving behind nature's art gallery, and follow the strip of sand until it bumps into a long flat rock. This is 'Japanese Tree'. Ken thought the tree that defiantly clung to the rock looked like a bonsai. The tree is now nothing but a dead trunk, but at least it is honoured in Ken's name for the beach.

'Then a little bit further on is a great big round rock, and half the rock has been eaten away. I call this "Big Brain Rock", because it really does look like a big brain,' Ken had explained.

Big Brain Rock hovers over one small beach. I think Ken has been generous calling it a beach. It is a few grains of sand between a few rocks. It looks like a Zen garden at Ryoanji temple in Kyoto. So in my mind, I amend Ken's tour; neighbouring 'Japanese Tree' is 'Kyoto Temple'.

Writer Nancy Phelan had her own name for these slips of beaches that she would sneak down to as a girl. She called them 'Treasure Island' beaches. Nancy had a finely honed skill in seeing somewhere exotic in her local environment she knew so well. She referred to two concrete buildings squatting beside the harbour – one near The Spit, the other directly across the harbour at Clontarf – as Egyptian temples. Paddling past the age-mottled lump of concrete below Parriwi Head, I admire Nancy's powers of imagination. For it was built for a more down-to-earth purpose; as a valve house for the sewerage system carrying the waste to the outfall pipe at North Head. It has served its purpose, but when it is the first main building you see as you approach The Spit from the water, the concrete lump looks not so much like a temple but a severe monument to how bureaucracy can approve the ugliest looking structures so close to such a beautiful waterway.

In the stretch between the 'temple' and The Spit Bridge, the water and shoreline are clogged with boats and services dedicated to them. With yachts and cruisers berthed to the left of me and dozens more tethered to moorings to the right, I feel as though I'm paddling through the eye of a needle.

Kayaking in the boat-flanked channel, I think of Ernest Flint. During the Second World War, Ern was a member of a unit called the US Army Small Ships Section. Ern and his First World War veteran father had signed up to be crew on vessels flying under the American flag, taking supplies to Allied soldiers fighting to Australia's north, then cruising back down the coast with a cargo of the wounded, the broken and the dead. The 'small ships' were actually a motley collection of requisitioned and seized vessels, ranging from old fishing trawlers and ferries to tugs and sailing ships. The US Army Small Ships Section was nicknamed the Ragtag Fleet. With so many vessels requisitioned for the war effort or confiscated, so the Japanese could not use them in the event of an attack, Ern recalled the harbour's edges looked stripped during the war. Which is why, more than sixty years later, when I was cruising with him on the harbour, Ern found it hard to reconcile how many boats there were.

Almost out of sight among the recreation armada, and housed in what was once part of the yacht club, is the Marine Rescue Middle Harbour headquarters. Every year, the unit's volunteers help tow and guide dozens of boats out of sticky, embarrassing or dangerous situations.

According to the Deputy Unit Commander, Lyndie Powell, the service comes to the aid of boaties throughout Middle Harbour, around to the Harbour Bridge, and out to sea for up to thirty nautical miles. The jobs range from using the unit's launch to tow vessels that have broken down to medical emergencies, through to rescuing occupants off sinking or burning boats.

Lyndie, whose father was a Sydney to Hobart race-winning sailor, grew up on boats, and she sees her involvement as 'giving back to the community'. She says most of the eighty or so volunteers at the Middle Harbour unit come from a boating background. Since she sees Sydney boat users at their most vulnerable, Lyndie is generous in her assessment of their behaviour.

'In general, boaties are pretty good,' she says. 'Every now and then, you'll get a young yahoo.

'But boaties know they can call us when they need us.'

THE PLEASURE-on-the-water industry that is embedded along this shore, and on the western side of the point leading to The Spit, is hardly a new arrival. From the late 1800s, there were boatsheds, refreshment rooms and moorings. Yet crossing the water here was not always a pleasure, but a necessity, and frequently a pain. It still can be painful.

In naming the place where Middle Harbour separated the southern shore from the north, the early European settlers concentrated not on the water but the tongue of sand licking it. They called it The Spit. A correspondent in 1908 noted the 'streak of sand . . . stretches like a natural bridge nearly across the channel'. But it was no bridge. From the mid-1800s, a hand-operated punt transported people and goods across the couple of hundred metres of water. No sooner was the punt in service than those who used it were calling for a bridge to be built. Like the punt itself, the bridge was slow in coming. The first Spit bridge, a timber structure, opened in 1924. It also had an opening span, to allow through boating. As more people travelled by car to and from the Northern Beaches, a new bridge was built in 1958. However, it also remained close to the water, with a clearance of little more than 6 metres. So, as a concession to those using the harbour, the bridge has an opening span. The traffic on the deck above has continued to grow; about 70,000 motorists and another 60,000 bus commuters trundle across each day. Even so, up to six times during weekdays and more on the weekend, the bridge's opening span is raised, like an enormous hand indicating 'Stop!' For a few minutes, one of the main routes to the Northern Beaches is cut, and the increasingly frenetic life of a Sydney driver is pushed into 'park'. Those in their vehicles can do little but watch the tops of yachts' masts and very large cruisers glide gracefully through the opening. It is a strange experience to paddle under the bridge when its span is open. The towering block of tilted bridge is an imposing sight. Then the span is lowered, you hear the monstrous grumble of a thousand engines being ignited, and commuter life returns to what passes for normal.

On the western side of The Spit is Pearl Bay, and on its shores is the training shed of the Mosman Rowing Club. Pearl Bay is only a kilometre or so from the main body of Middle Harbour, which is elongated and runs roughly north to south for about 4 kilometres. So it is terrific for rowing. Early in the morning, I have often seen rowers parting the tendrils of mist, as their shells make incisions on the surface. Unlike on Parramatta River, the rowers on Middle Harbour don't have to compete with many other boats. Indeed, on some weekdays, it is only them and me on the water. All you can hear is the sound of blades cutting the surface and the coxswain urging more effort, before the harbour quickly mops up any human-made sounds, wipes over the oar-stirred flurry, and restores the serenity that seems wondrous in a city.

Pearl Bay also cradles a rarity on Sydney Harbour: permanent houseboats. There are believed to be only four permanently and officially moored on the harbour, with leases required from the NSW Government's Roads and Maritime Services. Three of those houseboats are in Pearl Bay; the other is squatting in a bay on the opposite shore, on the other side of The Spit Bridge.

With the three houseboats in Pearl Bay, one looks like a renovator's delight, its neighbour is much larger and fancier, as though some fine home has slid down the slope from Mosman and ended up in the water, and the third is a two-storey Cape Cod design.

Their presence in the bay is charming, even whimsical. They give shape to what many people dream about; living on the water. As an article in the late 1800s posed, 'Wonder has often been expressed by travellers that the houseboat idea has not been adopted in our city of many bays.' These days, the answer to that is simple: regulations. While the government may not be issuing any more leases for permanent houseboats in the harbour, in the past they have served as homes in straitened times, such as during the Great Depression. In the early 20th century, a newspaper reported there was even a boarding houseboat on the harbour, moored at McMahons Point and offering 'all the comforts of a refined house, with the delightful experience thrown in of sleeping on the water, and a further thrill is offered by the fact that variety of scene is splendidly achieved by simply moving the house to a fairer and more charming spot'. In the late 1800s, a group of investors, known as the Sydney Harbour Residential Club Company, was trying to raise the money to buy and fit out a vessel, complete with a harbour pool and concert hall, for about 350 'gentlemen only' to live on board. Like so many ideas involving water and money in this city, the plan doesn't seem to have taken hold.

In Pearl Bay, I paddle in close to the Cape Cod houseboat. A tradesman is working on the floating cottage. I ask who lives on a houseboat these days, and he mentions that a family had been raised on board.

The air of relaxation floats out of Pearl Bay and along the shoreline of Beauty Point. However, before it was called Beauty Point, someone had responded not to the intoxicating mix of water, sandstone and trees but to the gradient of the slope, by naming it Billy Goat Hill. In the end, beauty won out. A little further on is an eye-catching natural sandstone sculpture, whittled and pocked, rising from the tip of the headland. A reverential soul named it Pulpit Point. The remotely religious theme continues in the next cove, with Quakers Hat Bay.

In 2016, on the cusp of his 95th birthday, I went canoeing in Middle Harbour with a mate, one of Australia's artistic elder statesmen and Archibald Prize winner Guy Warren. In both his art and life, Guy seeks adventure, which is why, despite my suggesting we hire a boat, we were paddling. Guy is constantly curious and sharply observant. I figure it has not only made him the artist he is, but it has given him the fuel to live such a long and vital life. I remember as we approached Quaker's Hat Bay, his gaze turned away from the cove, with its mansion-stubbled shore, and he looked up Middle Harbour, taking in the few kilometres of water pushing through the undulating, wriggling landscape of a drowned valley. The headlands still held a lot of bush, and the further you looked, the housing pinned to the steeply sloped peninsulas thinned and disappeared into the trees.

'Incredible,' murmured Guy in his voice that is simultaneously authoritative and gentle. 'That's how the main harbour would have looked before we all arrived.'

Squiggling off Middle Harbour is Willoughby Bay. The head of the bay is bushy and green, but in the late 1800s, the mudflats were covered with a sewage treatment works. By 1930 the plant was closed, and, since then, where there was waste, there has been the fragrantly named Primrose Park. As we paddled around the bay, Guy recalled playing there in cricket matches between Sydney artists and their Melbourne counterparts. Typically, he said, the Melburnians took the game far more seriously.

Willoughby Bay's northern side is defined by Folly Point. It is delightfully scruffy, with casuarinas and gums. When my sons were small, we would wander on the point's scarified and fissured sandstone ledges at low tide and count the periwinkles. Whenever we did that, I would think of the photographer David Moore, who described how growing up near Sydney Harbour provided 'a world of delight, adventure and privilege'.

One brave and entrepreneurial man took adventure to new heights above this part of the harbour. In 1877, a Melbourne circus performer, Henri L'Estrange, announced he would walk on a tight-rope across Willoughby Bay, reportedly up to 100 metres above the water. L'Estrange proved himself to be a master of juggling the media and public hype. By the time the rope had been stretched across the bay on a warm Saturday afternoon in April, an estimated 8000 spectators were clustered in the bay on boats, including on specially chartered steamers, and thousands more were perched on every vantage point in the ravine. Apart from a few who had managed to sneak through the bush, all had paid to watch L'Estrange perform his stunt. With a balancing pole in his hands and a red turban on his head, L'Estrange stepped onto the rope 'with a confidence that was discernible by the spectators below'. Indeed, his every step was being scrutinised and counted to the extent that the *Sydney Morning Herald* journalist could report that L'Estrange 'walked fearlessly at the rate of eighty steps to a minute'. He put on quite a show, and for his efforts, Henri L'Estrange was called the Australian Blondin, a reference to the Frenchman who had walked on a tight-rope across Niagara Falls. He also walked away with an estimated £25,000 in takings, a huge amount at the time.

Rounding Folly Point into Long Bay, the land presses in, with homes and the Cammeray Marina along the left shore, and bushland and the Northbridge Golf Club on the right. Long Bay was once longer, as it reached further into the valley. But the bay's head was progressively filled in and turned into playing fields. Stretching high over the fields, looking like a castle in the sky, is a concrete and sandstone bridge with Tudor-style towers at each end.

When construction of the bridge began in 1889, it was to traverse the bay cradled in a valley, and to bring the ambitions of a real estate developer closer to fruition. The North Sydney Investment and Tramway Company built the suspension bridge to foster land sales at what was called Northbridge. Sandstone blocks were barged along Long Bay and hoisted to construct the castellated towers for housing the suspension cables. When the bridge opened in 1892, many people came to gawk at what was considered a masterpiece of engineering but few crossed to buy land. The company went under, and the builder tried to recoup some of the bridge costs by charging a toll. The government took charge of the bridge in 1912, tram tracks were laid, and the real estate marketing assured this was 'The Bridge to Health and Wealth at Northbridge'. At last, the land buyers came.

Due to concerns about the stability of the bridge, it was shut to all but pedestrians in 1936. Commuters had to walk across the bridge, until the suspension cables were replaced with a reinforced concrete arch. Even so, decades after the cables were taken down, it is still called the Suspension Bridge by most locals. In 2011, even the state's road authority officially accepted the name, after years of listing it as Long Gully Bridge.

Flowing into the bay, under the sporting fields, is Flat Rock Creek. It cuts through the valley, up to where there used to be a renowned waterfall, which was the highest in Sydney. Yet Naremburn Falls were slowly strangled as the flow was impeded by development further upstream. Then they were destroyed. The falls were filled in when the area was turned into a rubbish dump in the early 20th century. Near the ruined waterfall, a local, Edward Hallstrom, had his factory, manufacturing Silent Knight refrigerators. Hallstrom earned a fortune, allowing him to indulge his passions: zoology and ornithology. Hallstrom lived only a few kilometres away at the end of Long Bay, on Fig Tree Point, in a two-storey house. When the house was built in the 1870s by a dentist who rowed to work in the city, it was known as The Hermitage. The owner apparently thought the land on the point was suitable for only goats. But Edward Hallstrom found it suitable for many other animals. After he bought the property in the 1930s, Hallstrom renamed it Fig Tree House and crowded the grounds with creatures great and small, from kangaroos to deer, and aviaries filled with exotic birds. Hallstrom's interest in animals was not contained by the private zoo he created around his home. He was a major contributor to, and trustee of, Taronga Park Zoo. He made Fig Tree House pleasant for the human species as well, building a ballroom on the harbour's edge and installing a swimming pool filled with water pumped from Middle Harbour.

*

THE BOAT ramp at Tunks Park into Long Bay is the escape hatch for thousands of Sydney boaties. On weekends, they queue to slide their boats into the water. And it's from where I usually set off in *Pulbah Raider*. Within a dozen strokes, I feel as though I'm in a different world. The land-fettered life is left on the ramp and I paddle past the sandstone clumps guarding the shoreline, as they have done for thousands of years. After rain, the sandstone darkens and seems denser, and when the sun is blazing, it seems to shed its weight and glows. The sandstone is swept by ferns and fractured by trees. Thank goodness plans in the 1850s for a dockyard to be built in this part of the bay never materialised. But boats and ships have found their way into the bay.

I pick my way through moored yachts, some of them with distant places of origin, from The Netherlands to Nuku'alofa, tattooed on their stern. For a few craft, however, their adventures have ended in this stretch of water. In an indent off the bay is Salt Pan Cove, believed to be the site of an early salt-gathering operation in the colony. The cove has been a graveyard for ships, and the skeletons of a few can still be seen. The remains of a steamship built in Balmain and used for training during the Second World War reveal themselves at low tide. Pointing imperiously towards the shore is the rusting bow of a 19th century British barque, *Itata*. The sailing ship may be buried in Middle Harbour, but it died sixty nautical miles to the north. In 1906, *Itata* was unloading nitrate and taking on coal in Newcastle Harbour, when it caught on fire. As the newspapers reported, 'in ten minutes waves of fire and smoke were rolling out of the vessel with such fury that nothing could save her'. *Itata* was reduced to a 'gaunt and bare hull', which was towed to

Sydney and scuttled in Salt Pan Cove. Looking into the water, you can see fish flitting around the hull, and its bones are fleshed out with sea plants growing from them.

Paddling down Long Bay always brings me joy, but never more so than on the day when I heard a blast of air, like an old man harrumphing, right beside the kayak. Initially, the sound scared me; I wondered if sharks harrumphed. But I couldn't see anything. I had taken barely a couple of strokes when I heard the harrumphing again. I swivelled to see just centimetres away from my blade – indeed, I just about hit it – a seal. Not only did the seal sound like an old man, he looked like one, with his whiskers. And it was big; about half the length of my 3.8-metre kayak. The seal eyed me off, I eyed it off, and it dived without so much as ruffling the surface. I tried to follow the seal down the bay, trying to photograph it, for it kept popping up. However, following seals is like chasing rainbows. But just as it is with rainbows, I felt invigorated by having seen a seal.

When you reach the end of Long Bay and round Fig Tree Point, you see for kilometres up Middle Harbour. The water may be constrained by the steep land on either shore, but I always feel unconstrained when I see that view. When land in these parts was first auctioned, the deep water frontage was emphasised, as the agents pointed out it would be good for shipping. Instead, ship-sized yachts can be seen moored here. The northern nodule along this stretch was saved for recreation in the 1880s. The length of time this has been used as a picnic spot hasn't quite rubbed out initials and a date carved into a rock near the water:

R.M H.M

E.N. B.M.

A.D. B.N. 1905

Time, in concert with the water, has been more successful at dismantling an old harbour pool here. The pool was built at the end of the Second World War from rock and concrete by the Northbridge Volunteer Defence Corps Association. It was one of the smallest tidal rock pools in the Sydney area. Now all that remains are concrete piers and sections of the rock wall.

Near the mouth to Sailors Bay is an old shipwright's shed. At first glance from the water, Northside Shipwrights looks out of place. It is a small green weatherboard shed on piers over the water, with its paint peeling and corrugated roof rusting, the odd one out in this land of meticulous mansions. But then, on second glance, I'm utterly beguiled and think it is the one building that looks just right for the surroundings.

I paddle in beside one of the two small slipways, and I'm greeted, or confronted, by a black dog. Then I meet his owner, Andrew Hay, who introduces me to the dog, named Halvo, after the Halvorsen boats.

Andrew has been the tenant here since 1988. He had just earned his shipwright's ticket, at the age of 20, when he took over the place. The years have been kind to Andrew. Working in an old shed by the water must help keep you looking young. Or perhaps the unhurried air he exudes has helped him age slowly. That unhurried air seems to extend to his workplace. I tell him I love the look and feel of his shed.

He smiles and replies, 'We're in a time warp here.'

Inside the shed, sawdust whorls, conjuring up the scents and ghosts of trees, whenever the breeze skips across the bay and through the door, which is gloriously open to the water. Along the walls are workbenches, including a stack of old hand tools. The shed is full of history, including Andrew's. A tool box under a bench holds the hammers, planes and chisels he's had since he was an apprentice shipwright and boatbuilder at Cockatoo Island. 'You still see hand tools in this trade,' Andrew says proudly.

Hanging from the rafters is a little wooden canoe, wearing the name *Mintie*, because 'it used to be painted green on the inside'. The canoe was built by his father when Andrew was seven. He used to convert it into a sailing boat by holding up a paddle with a shower curtain attached to it. So, in a way, *Mintie* was Andrew's first sailing boat. He has sailed a lot of boats all over the globe since, and has even helped build a few yachts here by the water.

'My life has been an evolution of build it, sail it, and travel around the world with it,' he says. 'But this place has been my grounding. I've always come back to here.'

Little wonder, when you see the view out of the doors. He has observed the harbour changing through those doors, for worse and for better.

'When I first got here, there were no oysters on the rocks,' he explains, 'but now you have to wear shoes when you walk along the shore to the east, and that has to be due to the cleaning up; that's changed the environment.'

Suddenly there's turbulence in the water and the surface looks as though it is boiling.

'There's another sign that the harbour's healthy', Andrew says. It's a school of kingfish – juveniles, but still up to half a metre long – herding baitfish towards the shore.

Andrew has seen a lot of creatures in and out of the water; a seal on the pontoon out the front, little penguins, and in winter 2015, a whale swam within a couple of metres of the shed – and breached. Andrew reckons probably every day of the three decades he has been here, he has pinched himself at how special the location is. 'It is a pretty unique place.'

Plonked in the midst of some scarily imposing architecture, there's something about this little boatshed that invites people to stop and yarn.

'It's like if they see an antique shop, or a vintage car,' muses Andrew. 'And that reaction says something about what we really value, and what we're on the verge of losing.

'People feel attracted to this place, because it makes them feel better about themselves, and they worry what it says about them if these little old buildings disappear.'

Around the harbour, shipwrights' workplaces have been bought and knocked down for residential development, but Andrew is confident this shed will survive. Its heritage significance has been recognised, he explains, and the leasing arrangement attached to the building helps protect it. He looks around the shed, squints out at the light and view washing through the doors, and smiles at Halvo scampering along the deck, tracking a fish.

'This is a lifestyle. I've got to keep my head above water and pay the bills, but my expectation out of this is enjoyment and life experience. If I was seeking money, I'd sell up and look for something else.'

I tell him his attitude is refreshingly non-Sydneyised. He laughs. 'You've got to be non-Sydneyised to do this. We're boat-builders, and that's what we love to do.'

ON THE northern shore of Sailors Bay, the land rears up dramatically, as though nature had built itself a fortress. Little wonder the suburb sprinkled through the bush across the top of it is called Castlecrag. The name was devised by the American architect couple, Walter Burley Griffin and Marion Mahony Griffin. He may be best known for his work in designing Canberra, but Walter Burley Griffin and his wife were smitten with Middle Harbour. He compared the grandeur of the terrain with the Norwegian fiords and the Riviera. He saw the possibility of creating something world-class, yet unlike anything else around the globe. Griffin set up a company, the Greater Sydney Development Association. He plotted his battle plans against the ugliness of suburbia. He wanted people who bought into his vision to escape the streets full of red roofs and paling fences that had infected other arms of the harbour and to be part of nature at Castlecrag, along with Covecrag, which was the estate he planned for the next peninsula to the north, and Castle Cove. Griffin essentially saw the bush as the biggest design feature. The design of the houses, the absence of fences, and the controls protecting the native flora and fauna meant the homes were to blend into the environment and, as Griffin said, each resident could feel as though the whole landscape was theirs. What's more, the houses were like bush fortresses, hunkered along roads that followed the contours of the landscape and were equipped with battle-ready names, such as The Rampart and The Barricade. These bush fortresses were poised to fight off the brick and tile armies inexorably marching over the headlands. Griffin also wanted to stop the alienation of the waterfront, offering reserves and walking tracks.

The Griffins made Castlecrag their home for about a decade, before leaving for India in 1935. While other eminent architects have worked on the peninsula, and the Griffins' ideals have drifted away on some blocks, their mark is still firmly embedded in Castlecrag. Their vision may not have been fully realised, but their legacy is one of the most beautiful and intriguing suburbs by the harbour, and beyond.

The precedent of building bush fortresses, or, at least, of crafting homes from the sandstone, along Middle Harbour had been well and truly set before the Griffins arrived at Castlecrag. For thousands of years, the Cammeraygal people had sheltered in caves scraped out of the escarpments by the elements. In colonial times, the caves had been home to escaped convicts, and in more recent times, they offered refuge to those seeking shelter from the demands of modern life, or the terror of a previous one. A Lithuanian couple, who had arrived in Sydney in the early 1950s, lived in a cave on Middle Harbour for twenty-eight years. Apparently haunted by life under Soviet rule, they were self-sufficient and relied on the bush to keep them out of officialdom's sight and mind. Paddling past the great swathes of bush, and seeing caves and shelters gouged out of the faces of sandstone, I have often wondered how many people still live along here, trying to find what they're looking for, or losing themselves. For this terrain is not only rugged, it also emits in places a forbidding character. It looks like hidey-hole territory.

Whenever I paddle past the peninsula named Castle Cove, I look up at its ridge – at a castle. With its parapets and turrets and a tower, the building looks as though a relic of medieval England has grown among the gums. The home's original owner was a businessman and politician, Henry Willis. After being elected to the new Federal Parliament, Willis had his home built using sandstone quarried on site. Just about everything else had to be brought in by water. When it was completed in 1905, Willis named his home Innisfallen Castle. For many years, the home would have looked spookily Gothic at night from the water; it had no electricity connection until the 1960s.

The water that often carried Willis to and from his castle had also played a part in creating his job in the Federal Parliament. On Easter Sunday in 1891, the Queensland Government's vessel *Lucinda* cruised Middle Harbour, while in its elegant wood-panelled saloons and smoking room, politicians and lawyers worked on the draft Constitution for what would be a new nation. The federation of the colonies of Australia was still a decade away, but it is delicious to think how the debates over the wording of the Constitution may have been smoothed by the harbour waters – and by the contents of the extensive wine racks on board the 52-metre-long paddlewheeler.

Near the entrance to Sugarloaf Bay, a middle-aged couple in their shiny kayaks weave towards me, stitching a messy pattern in the water. They are wearing lifejackets that gleam like tropical fish. Everything looks new – and it is.

'It's our first time out in these,' the man says, before asking, 'Where is the marina?'

He means the marina towards Roseville Bridge. 'Not far away, just around this headland and up a bit,' I reply. 'Maybe half an hour's paddle.'

Figuring they're not locals, I ask where they're from. He replies they have paddled from where they live, along Sugarloaf Bay. The encounter makes me realise how if we remain tethered to the land, we know so little, and see even less, of what's around the next cove. The sum of bays and coves can seem so inhibiting to explore, when viewed from the land. Yet from the water, it just adds to the possibility of accessible adventure.

Around the next point is a spectacular view. Gazing up the water-filled valley, with its high steep walls covered in bush and some tenacious houses, I reckon Middle Harbour has become Middle Earth. Take away the houses, and it could be a scene out of *The Lord of the Rings*. There is not even a breath of wind, and the water is so still, the valley turns upside down in the reflection. Looking at the jagged ridgeline in the water, it looks like a caldera. I gaze at the reflections of the homes along the lip of the ridge. I look behind my kayak to watch the reflected real estate wobble in the wake. Suddenly the houses are invaded by a cloud of psychedelic ghosts. I have paddled into an enormous swarm of jellyfish, which pulsate and seem to radiate an ethereal pinkish light. For a few moments, staring into the water is a simultaneously beautiful and weird experience.

I approach Roseville Bridge, yet another of the structures built across the harbour in the 1960s. The bridge arches over the tightening arm of water. Before the bridge and heading upstream is the last chance to grasp one of the staples of Sydney existence – a good coffee – from a café at the marina tucked in behind Echo Point. In the 1800s, there was a farm on Echo Point, with orchards and mulberries for silk production. By the end of the century, the farm had been converted by the Sydney Temperance Organisation into a centre for recovering alcoholic men. One of its clients was Henry Lawson. He turned his experience into a short story, 'The Boozer's Home', which is a raw observation of the effect of alcoholism on loved ones.

Just before I reach the bridge, I paddle under a pipeline. Along the pipe is a row of black waterbirds, intermittently pooing into the water. I'm running the gauntlet of bomber command. I escape a splattering.

In all the times I had driven over Roseville Bridge, I had never noticed the deck is not straight. But paddling under it, I can see there is a slight curve. Beyond the bridge, the mangroves are crowding the left shore, while a park has been grafted onto the right. A lone trumpeter is sitting there, close to the shore, practising his scales. He waves at me with one hand while still holding and playing the trumpet with the other.

The trumpet notes gradually mute and fall into the water, the traffic on the bridge lowers to a hum, then nothing. Where a few moments ago there were city noises suddenly there is only the music of the bush, with birdsong and water guzzling at the blades' touch. It sounds like I'm a long way from anywhere. That is just how the bloke in the kayak, sitting in the middle of the waterway and waiting for me, likes it. His name is Adrian Tosolini, and I had met him a few months earlier when he was fishing from his kayak further down Middle Harbour in Long Bay.

Adrian is in his mid-30s and is a chef. Every chance he gets, he heads out onto the water to fish. Not to catch fish to cook, as you'd expect, but to relax. No matter what he catches, he releases it.

Adrian is keen, sort of, to show me where he fishes on the upper stretches of Middle Harbour. Unlike most fishermen, Adrian tells me, he doesn't keep secrets. But he'd hate for these spots to be fished out. This area is so important for the future of local fish stocks, he asserts.

'If we keep taking fish from up here, how can we expect there to be any fish up here – or down there,' Adrian says, pointing in the direction of the main part of the harbour.

As we begin paddling upstream, Adrian tells me he caught a bream 40 centimetres long, and he'll show me where, before he quickly adds, 'But you can't write in your book exactly where I caught it.' Now he sounds like a fisherman. Adrian has been coming up this part of Middle Harbour in a kayak since 2010. His craft is a plastic sit-on kayak, which he's equipped with an electronic fish finder and holders for his fishing rod. Yet he's been fishing around here since he was a kid. He and his father would follow bush tracks down to the water's edge.

A stream, Gordon Creek, pushes in from the left, joining the main arm, which continues to shrink as the bush squeezes tighter.

'There's no sound of Sydney up here,' Adrian says. 'I like no noise.' I ask him did he hear the trumpeter before. Yes, Adrian replies. It annoyed him. 'But I figured you arranged that to announce your arrival.'

Beyond Gordon Creek somewhere (I hope that's vague enough, Adrian), he casts his line in about 5 metres of water. This is where he caught that large bream. He points to the muddy shore and indicates the crabs scuttling about. Meantime, his artificial crab lure rests undisturbed in the clean olive-green water.

'Oh, there's a tap now,' he says. 'Sometimes the fish just takes the lure and runs.' But not this time. After casting a few times and drifting, the line goes lank in the water, and he reels it in. He suggests we head upstream.

The main arm splinters into Middle Harbour Creek and Carroll Creek. We follow Middle Harbour Creek, and a little way upstream, between a sandstone escarpment and a sandbank, Adrian casts his line again. He floats and waits. And waits. And casts again. But still nothing. I tell him I must be putting the fish off. But we can see them. He points out a school of whiting swimming by, and luderick. But none is hungry for a plastic crab, it would seem. He also points out clouds of baby fish darting through the water. The sight of fish, just eluding him, impels him to paddle further up the creek, deeper into the landscape. As the banks close in, constricting the water, compressing any sounds and restricting our perspective, the feeling of remoteness grows.

'It's the most secluded part of the harbour, straight out,' Adrian says. 'You go up Lane Cove River and you might get 100 metres of quiet, if that. Not like this; here the quiet goes on for kilometres.'

The water becomes ever more shallow, the sandy bottom tickling the kayak's hull. The water becomes more brackish. I taste it; it's still salty but not as tangy as downstream. We're approaching the harbour's end.

'You know, I've seen baby prawns around here. A cloud of white in the water,' says Adrian.

We paddle cautiously up the last part of the creek, as we hear the sound of running water picking its way through rocks. We round a bend and 100 metres further on, a low wall of rocks, a natural weir, marks the tidal limit, the end of the harbour – and the end of our paddling.

Adrian explains the rocks are known as Governor Phillip's steps. He's also fished in the fresh water up there and has caught Australian bass. For now, he's seeking fish in the salt water. He paddles back down the creek, keen to get in some solitary fishing.

I leave the kayak and hop along the rocks to the natural weir. I taste the water rushing through. It is fresh. Well, as fresh as water running out of a great suburban clump is likely to taste. I imagine Arthur Phillip and his party also tasting the water in this creek on the night of 16 April 1788, when they camped around here during their trek for land to farm. In his journal, one of the exploration party members, John White, described how in this steep valley, they experienced 'the most desert, wild, and solitary seclusion that the imagination can form any idea of'. Almost 230 years on, it still feels secluded here, beautifully so. It is hard to believe this spindly little course picking its way through the landscape broadens and deepens into the drowned river valley that is Middle Harbour.

Paddling downstream, near the junction of the two creeks, I come across Adrian fishing. Still nothing. I leave him to it, so he – and I – can enjoy the solitariness. I've been paddling for only about ten minutes when I receive a text. It's from Adrian. He's sent a photo of himself holding a little bream. A couple of hours later, my phone beeps again. It's a photo of Adrian with a bream that must be 30 centimetres long.

The banks puff out, shedding any reminder that it was a creek. I pass under Roseville Bridge, with the helter skelter of traffic on its deck. Sometimes, when paddling out of the bush, I find there's a reassurance in being greeted by the sounds of time-poor contemporary life. Yet here, I find it an annoyance. I feel like a character out of Conrad's *Heart of Darkness*, wanting to turn around and paddle up the creek, away from civilisation. But I figure my return would only curse Adrian's fishing. I keep paddling back down the main arm, towards the turn into Bantry Bay.

IF THE upper reaches of Middle Harbour Creek reminded me of *Heart of Darkness*, Bantry Bay is the antidote. For years, this gangly strip of harbour wriggling its way into Garigal National

Park has been my escape from a heart of darkness, or a spleen of bile. It is where I have paddled to for years. For me, Bantry Bay is filled not with salt water but a magic potion that clears the head and refreshes the soul. Every time I paddle into it, I find it hard to reconcile that the bay is less than 10 kilometres from the CBD. This bay has allowed me to forget I am in a city. And it has reminded me to be grateful that I am in this city.

For one of the most serenity-inducing places on Sydney Harbour, it has a volatile past. From the 1890s, the New South Wales Department of Explosives used the shores of the bay as a storage base. For more than half a century, barges packed with the dangerous cargo would be towed out of Bantry Bay and down the harbour. Small ships would also head up to the bay to load explosives, with the last vessel making that voyage in the early 1960s. The storage facility shut in 1970, as housing crept closer.

The magazines remain along the western shore. They are stolid brick structures with thick iron doors and an unwelcoming presence. But just to make sure, one of the buildings wears a painted sign that is fading, but it still barks its message clearly: NO ADMITTANCE ON LAND. However, I have seen navy personnel bivouacking in the buildings, throwing open the iron doors at sunrise to let in the light and air, and the occasional fisherman standing on the prohibited shore, ignoring all rules and threats of fines in the hope of a tight line.

Strung along the middle of the bay is a series of public moorings. On weekdays, especially in winter, the buoys bob unused, but on weekends and in summer the bay hosts an archipelago of more than a dozen yachts and cruisers. The poet John Donne may have declared that no man is an island, but when in a boat, a man can pretend he is on an island, floating free of everyone and everything. I find it intriguing when I paddle through the Bantry Bay archipelago that people on their islands pretend I'm not there, that no other boats are there, that nothing and no one is there, except them. That is, until the aroma of coffee wafts across the bay from what looks like a floating can of Vittoria. Then no man is an island; rather, they are all caffeine lovers.

The gilded vision of the big coffee can gliding towards them is skippered by Garry White. Or, as he is better known among boaties in Middle Harbour, Garry the Coffee Boat Man. Each weekend, on public holidays, and throughout January when the harbour is heaving with pleasure craft, Garry putters across the water in his boat, waiting to be waved over by a mariner in coffee distress. Which is frequent.

I wait at the entrance to Bantry Bay, waiting for the flash of gold on the water. I hear the phlegmatic engine first, pushing along the coffee boat at a gentle pace. I give a wave, and over Garry chugs. I grip one of the boat's fenders, and Garry greets me with a smile framed by a beard. Not a hipster barista beard, but one that is salted and nautical.

I order a flat white. In his cabin/café, Garry swivels from the wheel around to his coffee machine. While he makes the coffee, Garry tells me the story of his business.

His boat, a former US Army craft, didn't always look this way. It was once painted blue. The golden livery of his boat and the coffee equipment he uses on board are courtesy of one of those boaties who beckoned to him. For more than two years Garry had been trying without success to speak with Vittoria about the coffee company working with him. After all, that was the brand he was serving. One morning in Sugarloaf Bay, Garry saw someone waving from a large cruiser. The gentleman on board the boat asked for a couple of espressos.

'I didn't know who he was, but I had my suspicions,' recalls Garry.

After the gentleman tasted the coffee, he told Garry he was the boss of Vittoria. Within two weeks, Garry's boat was spray-painted, the cabin was fitted, and inside it was a new coffee machine and grinder.

Just as his boat underwent change, so did Garry to become the Coffee Boat Man. For many years, he was an agricultural economist, and he worked in banking and stockbroking. Then, in 2000, he stepped off the career ladder and onto the water.

'How many people in corporate life dream of the corner office with harbour views?' he says, as he looks around.

Garry loves the freedom of his floating café. With a boat, he says, he has 'no worries about landlords', although café owners usually don't have to worry about physically going under. Garry has had to deal with his boat sinking, but he was quickly back on the water and in business.

In reply to being asked how many cups of coffee he makes each day on the harbour, Garry says he doesn't measure that way, but by how much coffee he goes through. On a very good day, he uses up to 3 kilograms. He estimates that can be up to 200 cups of coffee.

For all the coffee he has served, for all the nautical miles he has covered, Garry White still gets a buzz far better than that provided by caffeine each time he enters Bantry Bay.

'It's just unreal. It has its own feeling. It's a special place.'

And with that, I drain my cup, let go of the fender, and watch Garry chug towards the archipelago to rescue those desperate souls drowning in their desire for a morning coffee.

TO EXPERIENCE the magic of Bantry Bay, you have to go beyond the moored boats and the magazines, past the last vestiges of civilisation, over the shallow sandy bottom, and paddle into the mangroves. Then just sit there.

After visiting the colony in 1885, English historian James Froude wrote rhapsodically about Sydney Harbour, noting, 'There is little tide, and therefore no unsightly mud-banks are uncovered at low water.' He must not have reached the northern end of Middle Harbour. Mud banks suck on the water, helping create a primordial atmosphere. If you paddle onto them, the banks are a bit clingy, but they are hardly 'unsightly'. Yet it is the forest of mangroves rising out of the water that embraces your perspective. Their branches twist and bend like the arms of a Balinese dancer, especially when a breeze nudges the mangroves. The branches are reflected in the water, and the postulating, patterned muddy bottom, garlanded with fallen leaves, reaches up to hold the reflected branches, creating the most beautiful abstract pictures of nature. I have often sat amid those mangroves, just peering into the water.

Since the shoreline is part of Garigal National Park, it is possible to look through the stands of mangroves and, from certain angles, see no evidence of human interference. Of course, if you really want to look for it, there is always the presence of the city and the detritus of ignorance lolling in the shallows, with bits of rubbish that have been washed down the creeks or thrown into the harbour. But when I'm among the mangroves, I want to pretend our rubbish can't reach this bay.

LEAVING BANTRY Bay is always hard, but that feeling is often softened by a white-bellied sea eagle perched in a tree on the eastern shore. The mere sight of the bird is the warmest farewell I can wish for.

Sydney suddenly creeps up through the bush on the eastern slopes. From the water, the houses look as though they are co-existing with the trees for a bit, but the further south I paddle, the more the houses take over, occupying every crag and cranny.

Just before I paddle around a point into Powder Hulk Bay, I pass a harbour pool, armoured with metal mesh to keep out the sharks that apparently cruise into Middle Harbour. I've been told many times that bull sharks head to Bantry Bay to feed and breed. Yet in the hundreds of times I've paddled to the bay, I've never seen a shark. Still, when it comes to sharks, people have long memories. The last fatal shark attack in Middle Harbour, or in any part of the harbour, was in 1963, when a well-known actor, Marcia Hathaway, was mauled in shallow water in Sugarloaf Bay.

Her fiancé, who wrestled the shark in a bid to save Hathaway, later told the media how he straddled its thick body: 'My legs were wide apart and its body touched both of them . . . The water was stained with blood and I never thought I would get her away from it.' The 32-year-old died from her wounds.

The tragic story of the actress is still often the reference point for well-meaning people when they are warning me to be careful on Middle Harbour. And it is why so many will only enter the harbour behind the netting and mesh, for they take their long memories swimming with them.

Powder Hulk Bay remains branded by what it once was. Before the magazines were built at Bantry Bay, the explosives needed to blast and build a colony were stored in old sailing ships moored in the bay. Colonising the slopes around the bay are some big houses and intriguing architecture. One property, a wooden boathouse with a shingle roof and shooji-like doors, looks like a Japanese shrine, as though it has slipped out of a Hokusai print. For a few weeks in spring, the boathouse and its pavilion are dressed in the riotous purple blooms of jacarandas. I almost expect to see samurai sitting in the pavilion, composing haiku in praise of the jacarandas and the harbour. Then again, the words on a stone plaque set into the rock below a historic harbourside mansion, Cabeethon, a few doors – or jetties – further along says it more succinctly than even haiku can: 'Fun by the Water'.

As I paddle around Seaforth bluff back towards The Spit Bridge, mansions loom over me. The grand assemblages of concrete and glass lean out from the bluff, craning for a view. Downstream from the bridge is an inlet called, according to Ken Done's mud map, Stingray Bay. 'Well, that's what I call it,' he told me, 'because you see a lot of stingrays in there.'

Further on is the Clontarf shoreline. It has a languid beach that slowly slides into the harbour, allowing pet owners to walk their dogs in the shallows, a marina, and baths that wear an apron of old iron bars. In the baths, a crowd of children is watched over by their parents. The pine trees along the shore enhance the restful atmosphere. Yet this was not always seen as a gentle family place. *The Bulletin* wagged its finger at the young people disgorged by the steamer load at the privately owned Clontarf picnic grounds on Boxing Day, 1880. Wherever he looked, the reporter saw 'satyrs and bacchantes' drinking and dancing. He fulminated, 'At Clontarf it was not an excursion – it was an orgy'. The picnic grounds owner saw the scene differently. He successfully sued the journal.

Just a few years earlier, Clontarf gained infamy when it was the scene of an attempted assassination of a royal. Prince Alfred, Queen Victoria's son, was on a goodwill tour of the Empire, when he attended a picnic on Clontarf's shores in March, 1868. As the Duke of Edinburgh walked across the lawns, he was shot in the back by a man with a revolver. The would-be assassin, an Irishman named Henry James O'Farrell, was seized. The crowd, according to the newspapers, was yelling for the assailant to be lynched, people fainted, and others were hysterical. The wounded Duke was carried to a steamer and brought back to Government House. He recovered quickly and sailed out of the Heads in early April, leaving behind a colony mortified by the event and deeply divided along sectarian fault lines. It was a dangerous time to be Irish and Catholic in Sydney. As for the Duke's attacker, the crowd calling for O'Farrell to be strung up received delayed gratification. He was found guilty of attempted murder and hanged within weeks of the crime. To recognise the Duke's recovery, people began a public subscription, raising money for the building of the Prince Alfred Hospital in Camperdown.

From Clontarf, I follow Ken Done's map of Middle Harbour. The map is also a guide to his and Judy's past, for they would spend most Sundays at the secluded beaches on the Clontarf side, barbecuing lunch on an old piece of tin, playing cricket on the sand, and swimming out into the clear green water. I reach what Ken has marked as Buddha Beach, 'because you can find a carved Buddha there, and just near it is a Christian symbol of a boat and a cross carved into the rock'.

As I paddle towards Grotto Point, a survey vessel is drawing invisible grids on the surface. It is towing a device emitting a drumming sound. According to a crewman who kindly answers my shouted question, they are surveying for rocks on the bottom. The rock I'm heading for is plainly marked, with a small lighthouse on the tip of Grotto Point. Below the lighthouse, the water swirls from turquoise to creamy froth as it smashes into the rocks. The lighthouse is unmoved by the commotion at its feet. I look up as I paddle just out of reach of the turbulence. Beyond the lighthouse, I'm out of Middle Harbour.

9

NORTH HARBOUR AND MANLY TO NORTH HEAD

ONCE I leave behind the assurance of the little lighthouse on Grotto Point, I feel vulnerable. As I paddle north-east, I'm but one small kayak threading between the surging force of the sea pushing in through the Heads on my right, and the great wall of sandstone, resisting the power of the water, on my left. It is a ceaseless tussle of wills, as Mother Nature stages an awesome arm-wrestle with herself. I don't want to get caught in the middle.

If a harbour is about offering protection, this is the stretch where I feel that the least. The gentle hold of the harbour on my sense of security is loosened by the more assertive power of the sea, especially as it takes its last desperate gasps of life before crashing onto the land. I can feel the sea tugging at the kayak, as if it doesn't want to die alone on the rocks. I paddle a little further away, out of its seductive and destructive grip.

Softening the blows between the water and the rugged cliffs is a wedge of sand called Washaway Beach. The beauty of the scene is at odds with the warning embedded in the name. I'm wondering how often this beach has been washed away by angry seas, as I ride a wave onto the shore.

It is only after I hop out of *Pulbah Raider* and stand on the beach that I notice a man on the sand looking at me. He has a consistent all-over tan. I notice this because he is naked. As I look more carefully along the burnished sandstone escarpment, more figures materialise out of the rocks. They are all nude. And just like the rocks, they look weathered. I seem to have landed on a nudist beach, or perhaps at a clothes-free older men's leisure ground. And I'm the odd one out, in my shorts and shirt. I quickly turn and stare out to sea. The water looks so inviting. I feel as though I should make an effort to fit in with the dress code, rip my clothes off and go for a swim. And then my boldness dissolves. A tourist vessel sneaks around Grotto Point, its decks bejewelled with eyes and lenses. I don't need to spoil all those holiday snaps. I dive in with my pants on.

It is time to get away from Washaway. I track the shoreline and constantly glance up at the bush-crowned escarpment, until it turns and heads to sea. In the crook huddles Crater Cove, and just above it, barely discernible, is the most extraordinary settlement in Sydney.

Fluttering above the cove is an Australian flag. Then I notice a shack on the edge of the bush. I see another shack, then another. Above the cliff straight ahead, indeed, looking like an extension of the rock face, a stone hut balances right on the edge. The hut looks like it has been carried from another sea and washed up here; it reminds me of fishermen's huts from around the Aegean, something you would see on the island of Santorini, perhaps; not on the lip of Sydney Harbour.

The swell puts me and my kayak down gently on the rocks, and I clamber out and carry *Pulbah Raider* onto the shelf, just out of reach of the water. Then I see the first evidence that these rough structures of stone and wood contain flesh and blood. An older woman is peering down from further up the escarpment. I call out, 'Good morning.' She doesn't reply and ambles back towards the huts. I climb the rocks. There is a hand-written note telling passers-by that this is not the way over the hill. I wonder just how many people actually arrive by water to climb the rocks, then traipse through the bush to the top of the hill. At the top of the rocks, standing steadfastly near the hut with the flag, is the woman. Her pose, the body language, is about as welcoming as that of a bouncer outside an exclusive nightclub. I smile but receive a look that could have been carved from the sandstone we're standing on.

I ask her if she lives here. It's a national park, she replies.

I wonder if anyone lives here. It's a national park, she repeats.

I ask how many huts are here. That's for me to work out, I'm told.

She stands there looking at me unflinchingly. Her silver hair is like sea spray, as it whirls in the breeze. I tell her I'm writing a book. The welcome grows cooler. She complains that whenever Crater Cove pops up in public, curious people tramp down from suburbia's fringe on top of the hill at Balgowlah Heights, and they ruin the track.

This place has to be protected, she says.

That statement of protection has become a mantra for Crater Cove over the years. The settlement has been here for the best part of a century. Although the huts look as though they have been tossed together from flotsam and jetsam, this is a community built to survive. For it has withstood more than just what Mother Nature has thrown at it.

When the settlement took shape, it was known to only a few. It existed out of sight and way beyond the bounds of imagination of most Sydneysiders. The huts were mostly used as weekenders and fishing shacks, but during the Great Depression, they were probably lived in. Counter-culture later found its way into the cove. In the 1970s and 1980s, a commune sprung up, with people living simply and cheaply in the huts – but not altogether abandoning life in Sydney. The poet Mark O'Connor stayed in the settlement for a couple of weeks in the early 1980s, hut-sitting for a friend who had been assigned a place in the commune. Mark recalls being amused watching residents scramble up the hill, and at the top, when emerging from the bush, pulling a suit out of their backpack and changing into it, then catching a bus to work in the city.

While he is renowned for creating beautiful environmental poetry, Mark didn't write in his couple of weeks living in a shack by the harbour. For him, it wasn't 'a search for poetry', rather, it was time out, away from the more frenetic rhythms and demands of the city.

'It was a gentle, rather hippy place,' says Mark.

Through the years, however, the city crept closer to Crater Cove. The huts could not escape the ever-tightening net of rules and regulations. The settlement became part of Sydney Harbour National Park, and by the 1980s, the authority administering it decided the huts – and the people using them – had to go. Those using the huts fought to keep them, and the battle ended up in court. They lost. They were evicted and the huts were boarded up. In time, a deal was reached, the hoardings were removed from the huts, and a caretaker group, comprising people who had an association with Crater Cove, was formed. They could protect the huts, and all that they represented.

The woman standing before me tells me she is a caretaker. My repeated attempts to ask if that means people still live here are dispensed with effortlessly. The woman responds by staring out to sea. The long silence gives me plenty of time to follow her gaze. I tell her how beautiful the view is.

Mmmm, is her reply, stretching the consonant almost as far as we can see. She explains arrivals always notice how beautiful it looks, but they don't notice the rubbish. It all washes into the cove, she says, jammed into the crevices, right near where I put my kayak. The biggest problem, she says, is all the plastic. She cleans it out and recently had pulled out enough plastic from the cracks to cover an area six metres long and one metre wide.

And the rubbish is getting worse, she adds.

I tell her it was lovely paddling in. She comments it's a rare day when you can do that. Boats come into the cove, but few can disembark here. She tells me people walk in supplies, because it's usually too rough to bring a boat in.

The woman wonders out loud if that's tailor she can see jumping in the cove. I see nothing but water out there. I turn and look at the huts, trying to count them, as they disguise themselves in the bush and rock. The caretaker volunteers that huts have been here since 1923. She has had a connection to Crater Cove since 1948. I reply it is terrific the huts are still here, because they have become part of our tradition.

That comment seems to annoy her, for she tells me it's not my tradition but hers. And the harbour's.

I want to tell her that if it's the harbour's tradition, then it is *our* tradition. Because that harbour we're looking at is *our* harbour. But I don't.

Then, as if she's been reading my thoughts, she gently says if someone is part of the harbour, they know this place and they want to protect it. Subtly, I guess she's saying to me, you're either with us or against us.

The caretaker mentions some of those who have helped protect the Crater Cove huts; the water police, the passing vessels from the Middle Harbour Yacht Club and local schoolkids, all keeping an eye on the place. Once it's seen, she says, you want to protect it. She says she's spoken with politicians, right up to former Prime Minister Tony Abbott, to do more to protect the settlement. But for a politician to protect it, they would presumably need to talk about it. Which means they can't protect it. For, going by the caretaker's argument, if this place is stuck in the newspapers or on TV – or in a book – it's hard to protect it, and it will be gone.

I thank her for her time. I would love to wander around the huts, have a look at how the salvaged and fossicked bits and pieces have been nailed together with ingenuity and a sense of adventure. I'd love to peer through the salt-mottled windows at the interiors, and get a sense of who stays here on the edge of the world. Indeed, if anyone does.

Instead, I look at her and say I should head off. She nods and walks away.

I negotiate the kayak back into the water and paddle away, figuring the caretaker would be watching from somewhere to ensure I'm gone. Not that I can see her; just a handful of huts. I'm glad to have seen them, and I hope they're always protected, for they are part of our harbour.

The water wobbles like unset jelly, as the waves roll in and hit Dobroyd Head, splintering into spume and silvered specks. Just off the head is a bombora, ruffling the harbour's surface. It doesn't look like much, but that submerged reef can be deadly. In 1874, a wave kicked up by the bombora consumed a boat containing a high-ranking British naval officer, John Thomas Gowlland. He and another man were drowned. They were killed by the very thing Gowlland was in the colony to identify. An eminent hydrographer, Commander Gowlland was surveying Port Jackson, updating charts to keep those on the water safe. The reef is his monument; in 1984, it was named Gowlland Bombora. Yet just because it is known and marked, that doesn't make a bombora benign. At least twenty-five people have died on Gowlland Bombora.

The land around here imposes itself on the skyline. The head is a great untamed slab of earth, wrestled and whittled into the beautiful bluff that it is. From the kayak, it looks untameable, as though it would throw any attempt at development off its cliffs and into the water, to be smashed by the bombora.

As I round the headland, I've paddled into North Harbour. On a map, North Harbour's outline is reminiscent of a water bird, with its beak pecking along the western shores at Balgowlah Heights, its bulbous body forming Manly Cove, and, to the east, its tail feathers are a plume of inlets creating Spring Cove. However, on the water, the bird analogy dissolves, replaced by the quintessential Sydney view of the built and natural environments tussling for the harbour's attention. I gaze north-east to Manly Cove, just over a kilometre away, but as the harbour blossoms and broadens, it looks much further. A ferry is pushing towards the cove, leaving a foamy wake. I don't follow that trail, instead tracing the cartographical bird's beak into Jilling Cove.

The bush gradually gives up the harbour's edge. The shore becomes more manicured, as streets and houses and 21st century suburbia reappear. I pass the wonderfully named Forty Baskets harbour pool, but no one is swimming in it. I'm not surprised, since there is the more enticing option of a string of small beaches occupying indents around Dobroyd Head and in Jilling Cove. The cove is filled with recreational boats, a marina and commercial boatshed, and a weatherboard building occupied by the North Harbour Sailing Club. Moorings exploit the bay until the water becomes so shallow, there is enough depth for only pelicans to land.

Along the cove's eastern shore, the houses are more packed in. But sitting just off the water, there is one handsome green boatshed that has space, and, even rarer, a relaxed air about it. That atmosphere is bolstered by the sight of two men cooking in an open-air 'oven' – a fireplace, really – fashioned out of a crevice in the sandstone face beside the shed. I sidle in and ask the men if I can land here.

'Sure,' replies a big bloke with greying hair and friendly face. 'Fish land on here. Dead bodies . . .' That comment strikes me as curious, but not enough to dissuade me from landing on the sand next to a rowboat.

The big fellow washes his hands in a natural basin scooped out of the rock shelf, and he shakes mine as he introduces himself as Jeff. He goes on to explain the 'dead bodies' comment. Some years ago, a human hand washed into the cove, probably through the nearby stormwater outlet. The fingers had been cut off. 'He mustn't have paid a parking fine,' Jeff adds.

Jeff's mate, an older American fellow, introduces himself. His name is Steve and he is originally from Minnesota but has been living in Sydney for many years. 'Once I got my taste of the harbour, I knew I'd never leave', Steve says.

Jeff and Steve have returned from fishing and are preparing to cook a few flathead for lunch. Jeff tosses a few potatoes in the oven, then sits down on the rocks to yarn. He tells me he bought the boatshed in 1989. The shed had been by the water since the early 20th century, but it seemed it wouldn't have been for much longer, as it was a 'crumbling wreck'. Jeff's line of work is demolition, but with his shed, he was determined to do some serious restoration and rescuing. However, the first thing he did was craft his hole-in-the-wall oven, because 'a man's got to eat'.

The boathouse's renovation is a work in progress, Jeff says. 'You've got to take your time. You've got to think about things for 20-odd years before you launch into it.' Before launching into the boatshed, Jeff restored a timber boat that came with the building. That allowed him to go fishing. Still, he has done more than think about his shed. He raised the roof and gave it a steeper pitch to discourage kids from walking on it. And he installed solar panels.

The barbecue plate is cleaned with beer, and the flathead fillets are laid on it. I ask Steve and Jeff where they caught the fish. 'That's the last thing you'd tell a writer,' Jeff says. Steve then volunteers that if I look, I can see the spot where they caught the fish. From the rock I'm sitting on, I can see down the harbour, through the Heads and out to sea.

'So you caught them somewhere between here and New Zealand?'

'That's correct.'

When the southerlies and south-easterlies roar in through the Heads, the winds charge up North Harbour to Jeff's little shed, so 'it feels like the whole of hell is blowing in'. Still, in fair winds and foul, it's a great spot, the mates agree, being just a few steps from the harbour, sometimes not even that.

'The water comes up over all of this at high tide,' Steve says, gesturing to the rock shelf where we're sitting.

'So it's self-cleaning,' adds Jeff. 'It's on-going. The sea comes in, the sea giveth, the sea taketh away.'

But as he points out, we take away from the sea by what we dump and pour into it.

'I've counted thirty-six stormwater drains just in North Harbour,' he mutters. 'It looks clean, but I reckon there's a piece of plastic for every square foot of water.'

The flathead is ready, and, as he plonks it onto a couple of plates, Jeff asks rhetorically, 'What are these fish ingesting?' He then talks about the shards of broken-down plastic in the water, and the pharmaceuticals ingested by us that then end up in the sea, and in the harbour, when the sewerage system overflows.

'So the fish are on the Pill,' he exclaims.

As Jeff is talking, I think back to what the University of Sydney's Gavin Birch told me about his research into the contamination of the harbour. Gavin and his team took samples near thirty stormwater outlets, and the results revealed surprising levels of drugs, from anti-depressants to painkillers.

Just as I'm wondering whether Jeff is talking about the fish being full of drugs and plastic as a ploy to ensure I don't ask for any, he proffers a forkful.

'Here, try the flathead,' he says. 'It tastes terrific, like the sea.'

Once I'm munching away and nodding in agreement, he provides the punchline.

'Now you can say you've tasted microplastics and medicines.'

The tide is coming in, the rock shelf will soon be under water, and the boys' lunch will be over.

I set off, grateful the harbour still has room along its shores for the likes of Jeff, restoring a boatshed, retaining a sense of what the harbour used to be, and, above all, maintaining a sense of humour, come hell or high water.

JEFF'S RUEFULLY funny comments about eating microplastics soon become dispiritingly real for me in North Harbour.

Fairlight is the name of the suburb along the shoreline, and that could also be a description of the quality of the sunshine. The bathers gleefully splashing around in the harbour pool look as though they are tossing coins in the air, as the light ignites the water drops.

At Delwood Beach, a few hundred metres further on, I slip into the harbour. The water is a lustrous gem, as colours are coaxed to the surface by the sun. I go snorkelling, to see where the colours come from. Yet not long after being in the water, I'm reminded surface beauty can cover something more disturbing.

No more than 30 metres from shore, I glide over a garden of kelp, with the leaves on the long stalks swaying to the rhythm of the water. A few fish float through the garden, before darting off. The garden comprises mostly tones of brown, with a few strokes of purple and mauve. Yet, duck-diving into the kelp garden, I see the intrusion of other colours. The blues and whites of shopping bags splotch the environment. As if that pollution isn't sufficiently confronting, snorkelling back to shore, I have a cloud of plastic in my face. Initially, I presume it is turbulence, that something has stirred up the bottom, but then I realise there are thousands of tiny pieces of plastic floating before my eyes. The plastic blizzard distorts my vision but clarifies my view of what we're doing to the harbour, usually sight unseen. What's uncomfortable for a snorkeller is deadly for marine life. This stuff can end up in their systems, eventually killing them.

Feeling clammy and dirty, I crab my way out of the water onto a rock shelf on the edge of Delwood Beach. Two young women are crouching and peering into the rock pools. They are marine science students, and I talk to one of them about their work.

Nina Schaefer is studying the diversity of life in rock pools, and what is needed to sustain it. For her research, she has been using thermal imaging, shots from above with drones and 360-degree cameras, along with more traditional methods, which is what I observe the pair doing, such as inserting probes into the water to measure salinity and temperature. Nina has been working at four sites around the harbour – Balmain, Berrys Bay, Bradleys Head, and here – but this one is her favourite.

'I think it's pretty diverse from my observations,' Nina says, 'looking at the different species of sea snails, also a lot of algae.'

In the future, Nina's research could be used to help with the design of artificial 'intertidal areas' in foreshore development projects, to try and put back, or, at least, replicate, some of what has already been lost from rocky shores.

Delwood Beach gives me the first inkling of the substance behind the famous marketing slogan devised by a ferry company for Manly, 'Seven Miles from Sydney, a Thousand Miles from

Care'. Standing on the shore, I can see across the harbour to South Head and out to sea, but the city is out of sight, somewhere off to the right, a thousand miles away. The notion of Manly providing an escape is regularly reinforced, every time a ferry pulls into the cove, loaded with another cargo of care-worn commuters from the city. It is only a half-hour's journey on a ferry from Circular Quay. From the 1960s to the early 1990s, there was a hydrofoil service that sliced the travel time in half. But in cutting time on the water, you're also hacking into the pleasure of the journey. For time mixed with water somehow stretches the perception of distance. And not only does distance make the heart grow fonder, it apparently makes it healthier. Maritime historian Graeme Andrews shared a wonderful anecdote from the 1920s about a man whose doctor ordered him to take a three-month sea trip. The man made arrangements with the ferry operators for him to ride their service all day, every day, for three months, going to and from Manly. After the three months, the man's doctor pronounced him healthy.

Yet the appeal of Manly is not only in what is being left behind, or in the journey; it is also in what you see, and feel, as you arrive at the destination. From the harbour, Manly's appearance still has elements of how its earliest developers imagined it; as a holiday village by the water.

Paddling around the point from Delwood Beach, the cove is designed for relaxation. The commercial area and apartment blocks are curtained off by a row of Norfolk Island pines, a species of tree whose very appearance is botanical shorthand for 'beachside holiday' in Australia. In front of the trees is a promenade, where crowds stroll and jog, and below it is a band of sand leading to the harbour. A large netted pool stands guard in the water about halfway along the beach, which is flanked by two iconic structures in Manly: the wharf and the pavilion.

Perched over the water off the western shore, the Art Deco pavilion was built in the 1930s as elaborate change sheds for an earlier, larger harbour pool in the cove. Neighbouring the pavilion is the Sea Life Sanctuary aquarium, which offers visitors the opportunity to dive with grey nurse sharks. These creatures look fierce, with a dental arcade like a sawmill, which gave them an undeserved reputation for eating humans. Their diet is fish. The grey nurse sharks were killed in such numbers that they are a critically endangered species. So chances are the closest anyone would get to a grey nurse shark in Sydney Harbour is in Manly Cove – in a tank.

At the eastern end of the beach, stretching out like a helping hand to ferry passengers, is the wharf. The first ferry wharf was built here in 1855, but Manly Cove had been receiving boats long before then.

On the promenade is a monument, erected in 1928, marking this as the landing place for Governor Arthur Phillip on 21 January 1788, when he and his crew had journeyed up from Botany Bay to explore Port Jackson. A later plaque on another face of the monument says he probably didn't land on that first expedition. Still, the sight of men from the Guringai people wading out to his boats left an impression on Phillip. He later noted that the local men's confidence and 'manly behaviour' prompted him to call the place Manly Cove.

After that first contact here, Manly Cove became a crucible for race relations between the Aboriginal people and the settlers. When Phillip became frustrated that his efforts to follow London's orders to 'open an intercourse with the natives, and to conciliate their affections' were stalling, he decided to try and improve the potential to 'live in amity and kindness with them' by kidnapping one. The man was Arabanoo, although until his abductors learnt his name, they called him 'Manly'. Arabanoo had been snatched from Manly Cove in December 1788, and he was taken to Sydney Cove. Phillip hoped Arabanoo would become a conduit for spreading the word on the good intentions of the British. The Governor also wanted to learn about Aboriginal culture and some of the local language. Yet those plans were dealt a blow. Arabanoo died about six months after his capture, during a severe outbreak of smallpox. His death was mourned by the British, who admired his character and saw in him hope for improved relations. Arabanoo was one of many Aboriginal people killed by the 1789 epidemic. The First Fleet marine and diarist Watkin Tench described it as an 'extraordinary calamity' and painted the awful description of boat crews 'finding bodies of the Indians in all the coves and inlets of the harbour'.

Phillip himself almost died at Manly Cove. The Governor had continued with his practice of kidnapping locals to learn more about them, including the abduction of Bennelong from Manly. After about six months, Bennelong escaped. In September 1790, he apparently sent word, along with a lump of whale blubber, that he was back at Manly Cove. Phillip was rowed to the cove, where a beached whale was the focus of a feast. The Governor talked with Bennelong on the beach, and all was friendly until another man speared Phillip through the right shoulder. Over two excruciating hours, Phillip was rowed back to Sydney Cove with the spear still protruding from him. When he recovered, Phillip said the spearing was a case of misunderstanding and ordered that there be no reprisals.

Manly's distance from the main settlement and its relative inaccessibility meant it was slow to develop. But its superb position, with one side facing the harbour and the other the sea, and just a thin throat of land in between, meant that the dreamers and speculators were bound to find Manly. An English businessman, Henry Smith, both dreamed and speculated when he saw the place. He imagined Manly becoming to Sydney what Brighton was to London, a seaside escape. In the 1850s, he began buying land and built the wharf for the ferries, which were regularly running to Manly by 1856. Smith bought a large double-ended steamer ferry, *Phantom*, to transport more passengers to his wharf. He also planted the first Norfolk Island pines along the esplanade.

As Manly's popularity grew into the 20th century, so did the size of the ferries, carrying up to 1500 passengers, and the wharf kept lengthening. Around it and along the waterfront, the fun industry took hold. Restaurants and hotels sprouted, a cargo wharf beside the main ferry terminal was packed with amusement rides, and there was an aquarium, where visitors could feed their primal fear of being eaten alive by walking through the jaws of a giant fake shark at the entrance. Ferry advertisements proclaimed Manly was Australia's premier seaside resort. The waterfront also found its way into fiction; in D.H. Lawrence's *Kangaroo*, Manly is described as the 'the bathing suburb of Sydney – one of them'.

The fun pier has gone, but the ferries filled with pleasure-seekers keep arriving. About 7,000,000 people pass through the ferry terminal each year. At the eastern end of the beach, I cease paddling and keep my distance from the wharf as the ferry *Freshwater* approaches. The vessel froths the water into a maelstrom as it comes to a halt just before the large buffers, and hundreds of passengers pour out. Some, with surfboards tucked under their arm, head towards the east and the sea, others turn left and stroll along the promenade, a few stop at the cafés on the wharf, but all seem to be sloughing off the city, in one way or another.

The wharf that marks the point of successful escape for many is a shelter for other creatures. Manly, and some of the surrounding coves, is a home for the Little Penguin, or Fairy Penguin. Its scientific name is *Eudyptula minor*, which means, 'good little diver', its Aboriginal name is carangarang binyang, but, when first seen, the Little Penguin is most commonly called 'oh, how cute!'

The Manly area used to have hundreds of breeding pairs, but the encroachment of housing, with its predator residents such as dogs, the increase in the number of powerboats, pollution, and acts of unfathomable cruelty decimated the penguin population through the years. By 1990, there were only about thirty-five left. Governments, the National Parks and Wildlife Service, and the Manly Environment Centre worked to halt the death dive of penguin numbers. They were listed as an Endangered Population, and, in 2002, sites around Manly were declared a critical habitat. Manly is the only breeding colony of Little Penguins on the New South Wales mainland. It is estimated there are about 150 penguins around Manly.

What has also helped the Little Penguins survive is the engagement of the community. One of the first locals to become a penguin protector was Angelika Treichler.

Her first encounter with a penguin was a couple of coves to the east, on Collins Beach, in 2003. National Parks had asked her to help count penguin numbers. So one night she was on the beach, peering into the darkness, looking for penguins, when one waddled up and stood on her foot. It was love at first touch.

Angelika learnt it wasn't just in the more remote coves that the penguins made their nests; they mated and incubated their eggs right under the noses of humans, beneath Manly Wharf. Yet she became more than a penguin observer and counter, when she found out that one of the young females from the Manly Wharf colony had been killed by a dog.

'That was it!' she recalls. 'I was off!' Angelika talked to local dog owners about keeping their pets away from the penguins. Word spread, and so did the desire to help. The National Parks and Wildlife Service set up a penguin warden scheme, training volunteers to help protect the birds. Many more locals just kept an eye out. These days, she says, 'half of Manly is looking out for the penguins'.

As for official wardens, there are about sixty volunteers, aged between eight and eighty-five. They stand on lonely beaches around Spring Cove, and amid the hubbub of Manly Wharf, keeping a protective eye from about May, when the nest-building and mating begins, and remaining on duty every night until about February, when the chicks have hatched and the penguins head out to sea for a few months.

I arrange to meet a group of wardens at the wharf. It is just before 5pm, and the sun is setting on a clear but cold winter's day. A wind sneaking off the water rifles through my clothes, looking for a way to pinch my skin. A few hardy backpackers are walking on the beach, while the flow of ferry passengers thickens.

At a gate on the western side of the ferry terminal, just near a beer café, are three wildlife wardens, identifiable by their jackets. The co-ordinator is Tony Garman. He and his wife Sally have been penguin wardens since 2012. He had been looking for something that combined his interest in the environment with a desire to volunteer. He found what he was looking for on the harbour's edge.

Tony is scanning the shoreline and the sand, which hardens as the light creeps off the beach.

'Around sunset is when the penguins come back out of the water,' he explains, saying the birds spend the day fishing in the harbour and out to sea.

Tonight Tony is joined by two other wardens, Kimberley, a local high school student who has been volunteering for a couple of seasons, and Brad Klose, a hospital scientist. Brad is holding an iPad linked to a remote camera mounted under the boardwalk.

As he looks at his colleagues, Tony mentions how the volunteer numbers are heartening. The penguin numbers aren't. 'We've had more volunteers, and less penguins,' murmurs Tony. He thinks there is one mating pair under the wharf. A penguin has been spotted in recent days.

'I'm guessing it's Lucky we've seen,' says Tony.

Somewhat of a legend among the volunteers, Lucky was born here about five years earlier. He earned his name as a chick, after being photographed.

'When the photo was blown up, we saw all this fishing line around his leg,' Tony says. 'If we hadn't caught him and taken the line off, he wouldn't have survived.' Lucky left the nest under the wharf and 'went travelling for two to three years, as all good Australians do', then, like most male penguins do, returned to where he was born. He paired up with a female penguin the volunteers named Bella. The wardens have helped Bella as well. About two years earlier, they noticed she was limping. She had a gash on her foot, probably from glass, and was treated.

Brad, who has been intently watching his iPad screen, calls Tony over. He has seen a dark shape seemingly making its way out of the water. They watch for a few moments before concluding, 'No, that's a bottle, a plastic bottle'.

Suddenly we hear something, a trill in the cold sharp air. It's a penguin calling. 'Family-planning noises,' explains Tony. 'He's in the nest-building phase, sort of like "Come up and see my etchings".'

The previous year, there were two pairs, including Lucky and Bella, under the wharf. But there have been up to five pairs, Tony says, 'so if we get more than two pairs [this season], we'll be really happy'.

In the summer months, as more people head to the beach in the early evening, more wardens are on duty to ensure the penguins can land freely and are not disturbed. Almost everyone is receptive to a warden's request.

'There's a magic word starting with "p", and it's not "please" but "penguins",' Tony says.

All the while we're talking, more commuters scurry off the ferries. A few stop and ask questions about the penguins. Some seem to know little and are curious, others have a great deal of knowledge and have clearly been tracking the penguins' progress. They hush when the penguin calls, but still there's nothing to be seen on the screen or from under the boardwalk.

'It's a very strange place to do this,' Tony says, of the nesting place, adding that the penguins were first detected under the boardwalk in the 1990s.

A British tourist has his camera trained on the darkness, but warden Kimberley reckons penguins don't like the lens.

'They seem very aware when a camera is pointed at them,' the 17-year-old says. Still, not all penguins are shy. In what sounds like the start of a joke – 'A penguin walks into a bar . . .' – Lucky's father, Stickybeak, waddled into a nightclub across the road, before he was brought back to the beach.

Kimberley remains hopeful of seeing Lucky tonight.

'Lucky was the first penguin I saw here a couple of years ago,' she says. 'And he was so cute.'

To this teenager, volunteering on a Friday night is 'definitely worth it, especially when you see a penguin'.

For Brad, this is his second year of volunteering. In some ways, becoming a warden was a calling for him. He and his wife lived in Kilburn Towers, the distinctive rounded block of apartments on Manly Point, overlooking the harbour. His wife would wake him in the pre-dawn hours, saying she heard penguins calling out. Subsequently, they both volunteered. All the while we're talking, Brad keeps glancing at the iPad, which attracts interest.

'What are you looking at?' asks a passer-by.

'Waiting to look at penguins,' Brad replies.

'What's the best time to see them?' she asks.

'Ah, the number one question,' Brad says.

'November,' Tony replies. It's early July. The passer-by smiles and walks on.

No sooner has she left than Brad excitedly whispers, 'There he is!'

A penguin, small but nuggety, pokes his head out from under the wharf and looks around. He takes a couple of tentative steps, grabs a piece of debris, then disappears back under the wharf.

'That's crazy!' a young tourist utters excitedly.

The penguin pops out again. Tony is fairly sure it's Lucky. The penguin has a white strip along his belly. And he is tiny, maybe 30 centimetres tall, if that. He waddles a little further this time, picking at debris with his beak and being selective about what he grabs. He picks up a feather then discards it in favour of another piece of debris.

'He's collecting for his nest, looking for materials to make it,' says Tony.

A commuter striding purposefully along the promenade stops to watch Lucky at work. She looks enthralled. 'I'll be late home every day, I think.'

In all, Lucky pops in and out from under the wharf seven times, collecting materials for a nest, probably hoping to mate. The wardens share Lucky's hope, so the local penguin population increases. And while they can do little more than watch and wait, the wardens believe they're doing their bit to help nature take its course.

'We have to do the best we can to protect them,' shrugs Tony.

The wardens' hopes were realised later in the season. Lucky and Bella had a chick, which was first seen in October. That little one was named Shadow. Then, on Christmas Day, there was a joy-filled present, with the arrival of a second chick, which the volunteers named Summer.

DODGING A ferry powering away from the wharf, I begin the paddle towards Quarantine Beach. I track along Manly Cove's north-eastern shore. In the bend of the cove, a bunch of older buildings is clustered, as though each of them has been carried in by a southerly. They are the homes of the Manly Cove Launch Club and the Manly Rowing and Sailing Club.

If the buildings haven't been carried in by the winds, just about everything else has been, according to a fellow named Phil, who is climbing into his rowboat at the Launch Club slip.

'When it blows a southerly, it all ends up in Manly,' says Phil. 'Rubbish from everywhere.'

As Phil settles his rowboat out of its metronomic sway, I keep paddling south, passing apartment blocks and swimming pools built right on the harbour's edge, before rounding Manly Point. The tip is marked by Kilburn Towers, which looks like a multi-lensed lighthouse as the windows of its apartments reflect the afternoon sun. Around the point is Little Manly Cove. Along the top of the point is the desired habitat of humans, with a row of big homes, and along the shore is a designated critical habitat of the Little Penguins.

On the other side of the cove is a part of Sydney reimagined. Little Manly Point was the site of a gasworks for more than eighty years, until it closed in 1964. The buildings were demolished in the early 1970s. It remained a contaminated wasteland, fenced off and unloved, for a couple of decades, until it was transformed into a park. The industrial scars have become beauty spots. The concrete wharves where sixty-miler ships laden with coal would berth are now recreational fishing platforms. But the stain of the past can still be seen on rocks close to the water. They are blue. The council has attached a sign to the rocks explaining the discolouration is a substance known as Prussian Blue and is due to a by-product of the coal gasification process. It has gone into the ground then leached out of the sandstone. The notice assures that the substance is 'not known to be toxic' to human health or the environment. Still, those blue rocks are a surreal reminder of what was once here, and an indication of just how difficult it can be to fully remediate a site.

In the next cove is the sight of more blue, but not in a way that disturbs me. It is the water in the long indent of Spring Cove, fringed by bush, and at its head is the delightfully secluded Collins Beach. Never mind Manly being a thousand miles from care; Collins Beach feels a million miles away. Long before a kayak slid into this cove, there were the original inhabitants' canoes. A few days after the First Fleet sailed into Port Jackson, William Bradley was surveying around here when he noted in his journal that 'we were joined by 3 Canoes with one Man in each, they hauled their Canoes up and met us on the beach leaving their Spears in the Canoes'. As I paddle out of the cove, I catch a bare glimpse of the city, as the top of Sydney Tower pokes over the headlands.

Collins Beach is but one strip of sand nuzzling into the bush along this stretch, before the harbour opens to the sea. The harbourscape is wonderful to look at, and to listen to. Just near Shore Beach, an amazing rock formation is guzzling the harbour water through a series of holes. It sounds like the earth is gulching and belching, as the water swills about in the sandstone guts, while above, the twisted branches of an angophora look like the scan of intestinal tracts.

In a line off Shore Beach are bright yellow buoys warning that this is a penguin breeding area and no dogs are allowed on the beach, and threatening a $5500 fine if that is breached. As I paddle through the shallows, the water suddenly shivers as thousands of small fish skitter like a silver cloud in the afternoon light.

It is only a short paddle around to Quarantine Beach, which is marked by another string of buoys to protect the penguin breeding area. Just near one of the buoys is a large cruiser with a dog standing at the stern. The dog jumps into the water and begins swimming towards the shore, its owner frantically calling it back. The dog finally listens and returns.

Quarantine Beach offers protection to penguins these days, but for a century and a half, this site was designed to protect Sydney from the unseen invaders coming through the Heads, the diseases carried by passengers on arriving ships. This was the North Head Quarantine Station. More than 13,000 people passed through here. Many stayed for a while, in the barracks and huts dotting the hill. And hundreds remained here, in the earth on North Head. The site was chosen for the station because it was just inside the Heads, it was far enough removed from the centre of Sydney, and there was a spring nearby to provide fresh water for the internees.

From the water, I can see held in the cleft of the hill an old brick building with a tall chimney, a couple of smaller corrugated iron structures and a sawtooth-roofed warehouse. On a ridge, sitting aloof and peering down into the cove, is a mustard-coloured two-storey building, and, jutting into the water, the wharf, a single finger counting all the ships that berthed and moored here. Between 1828 and 1984, about 580 ships were quarantined at the station. It looks like an old industrial site, which, in a way it is; the station was a fear-reduction industry. It produced a reassurance for a city whose isolation bred concerns about what the rest of the world might bring. Sitting in my kayak, I'm looking at a somnolent place, far removed in atmosphere from the bubbling mix of excitement, anticipation and frustration felt by the ceaseless tides of humanity washing up here for more than 150 years. All I can hear today is the water kissing the kayak's hull.

Once on the beach, I wander into a few of the buildings, which have been preserved and are open to the public. A pale green corrugated iron building looks like a beach shack but it was an inhalation chamber, set up in 1919 in response to the Spanish flu outbreak. Inside, the walls are timber and white. Up to sixty people were packed in here to breathe steam and zinc sulphate. The practice was soon stopped because it didn't work. Standing in the chambers, I can still hear the call of the whipbirds and the waves outside, but in my imagination I'm listening to the heavy, anxious breathing of those placed in here.

The next building, the large brick structure clearly visible from the water because of its chimney, is where passengers' luggage was steamed in large autoclaves to rid them of bugs and disease. These days, the building is a restaurant. Nearby is an old shower block, built in 1913. It held twenty-four showers in corrugated iron cubicles, where new arrivals would wash with water and a solution of carbolic acid to be disinfected. The building feels eerie. Perhaps the fear and uncertainty of all those who showered in here have soaked into the floor.

From here, the quarantined passengers and their steamed luggage would head up the hill, where like on the ship – and in life – they were divided into different precincts: First Class, Second Class and Third Class, along with the 'Asiatics'. The First Class occupants had silver service in their dining hall, a smoking room for the men, and a sewing lounge for the ladies. Irrespective of your 'class', in each precinct you could find tormentingly fine views over North Harbour and down towards the city you were hoping to reach, so near, yet so far. Ironically, these buildings are now used by people who willingly pay to experience the sensation of getting away from it all while still being close to Sydney; they are tourist accommodation.

The name of a road snaking around the border of the Third Class precinct captures how many would have felt, killing time on this headland: Isolation Road. In their daily existence, this was a road the occupants would not have wanted to travel. For it meant your status had changed; you were journeying from 'healthy' to 'sick'. The road led to the isolation precinct and, a little further down the hill, the hospital area, which includes the mustard-coloured building I saw from the water. Here, people were quarantined within Quarantine, when they were diagnosed with contagious diseases. In the hospital precinct, I walk around the verandas that wrap the weatherboard building, taking in the view down the harbour to the city. From the hospital's northern veranda, I can see snippets of Quarantine Beach through the trees. Up the hill, some of the residential buildings can be seen behind the foliage. It is a desperately beautiful place. But from here, the patients could not look back; there are no views of the sea. For that, you have to go much further up the steep headland. But no one wanted to end up there.

The Quarantine Station's Third Cemetery is one of three burial sites that were used by the facility. In all, about 570 people who died while in quarantine are buried on North Head. About 240 are buried in the Third Quarantine Cemetery. The site is overgrown with hardy native bushes that can withstand the buffeting of the winds. The cemetery has fantastic views. The headstones face towards the Heads and along the harbour. It is as though the orientation of the headstones is reminding all who stand before them of where their occupants were hoping to reach, and never did.

While many of the inscriptions have been eaten away by the years and the elements, the headstones still tell stories of the lives and deaths of those they honour. One is etched with anchors and a cross. It is to the memory of William Hay, 'For 20 Years Quarantine Officer'. He died 19 November 1902. There are the graves of children, of a former Customs worker, and a nurse, who died just after the First World War, with the epitaph, 'Her Life Was Sacrificed to Duty'.

One grave is a reminder that not everyone who was sent to the Quarantine Station travelled from the sea; some came from the city. It is the resting place of a woman from a farm in Condobolin, in western New South Wales. Her gravestone says the 40-year-old died while in quarantine in 1900 of bubonic plague, which she contracted in Sydney.

Standing here among the dead, looking at the water, I think of a few lines from an epitaph I had just read, dedicated by a wife to her young husband. It read, 'By the sad and mournful sea/ The dearest one that was to me/Lies sleeping here.' I continue looking at the view, looking at the distant city, where so many are clamouring to own an outlook that is not a patch on this. But as the souls of all those beneath me could attest, a multi-million dollar view is worth nothing if you can't see it.

Yet the most intriguing monument is inscribed in a sandstone escarpment back down near the wharf at Quarantine Beach. The great lump of Sydney sandstone has been etched and crafted into something global. As time dripped and dribbled away for the internees, they would leave their mark on the rock. It is at once an art gallery, diary, memento mori, headstone, and, above all, an extraordinary piece of history. It is cold stone fashioned by the scratches of humanity into something moving to behold. The stone wears roughly hewn names of people and ships, and the dates they arrived. The inscriptions are mostly in English, but I also see Chinese and Japanese characters. The rock also has beautifully composed and delicately etched memorials to those who landed here, and those who never left. A Scottish stonemason, John Howie, who arrived on *Samuel Plimsoll*, carefully carved into the stone that '462 emigrants arrived June 11th 1879'. One who didn't arrive was Howie's one-year-old son, who died at sea. So the tablet is a headstone of sorts to his little boy. RMS *Niagara* appears in a few places on the wall. The reason for this ship having to moor in the cove is summed up in one carving. It is of a fluttering pennant, which reads, 'RMS *Niagara*. Influenza. Oct 1918'.

The names of troopships and servicemen returning home from distant battles are also noted in carved panels. Reading those names reminds me of a story my friend Guy Warren told me about his brief stay off Quarantine Beach. He was among a shipload of soldiers returning from the islands off New Guinea after the Second World War. After a few years away on active service, Guy had been waiting for months in the torpor of the jungle at war's end to be finally given a berth on a ship. He was so excited as they sailed through the Heads and then was thrown into bitter disappointment when the ship veered into Spring Cove. The ship was to moor off the Quarantine Station for its passengers to be checked. The anchor had not even dropped before an arsenal of souvenired Japanese guns and ammunition was being tossed overboard. As he watched this shower of contraband, Guy noticed a couple of blokes sitting in a rowboat, fishing. He gave them a wave. They waved back, and one called out, 'What did you come back for, mate? There's a bloody beer strike on!'

'And in that moment, I knew I was back in Australia,' Guy recalls, chuckling at the memory. 'I *knew* I was home.'

*

IN THE grounds where the authorities tried to shield the harbour city from contagious diseases, Little Penguins seek protection. They have built nests just up from Quarantine Beach. The nests are monitored by cameras and are guarded by volunteers and National Parks and Wildlife Service staff. The penguins are also microchipped, so they can be monitored.

I meet up with Mel Tyas, a long-time NPWS ranger. If I were an endangered species, I'd want Mel looking out for me. She is passionate about protecting the penguins. She is constantly scanning for even the faintest signs of trouble.

As we walk along the beach, she points out a penguin track heading down to the water from a shallow gully filled with a scrabble of lantana. Mel says the penguins have been nesting in the lantana, probably for protection. Before sunrise, she explains, they form up like a train and head down to the water, because there's 'safety in numbers'.

Mel also notices tracks that she thinks could be those of a dog. She looks at the marks in the sand more closely and mutters, 'Or it could be a fox.'

In 2015, in just four days, not far from here, a fox killed twenty-seven penguins. It was devastating to the population; there were just forty-two breeding pairs left.

Among NPWS staff who stayed out until dawn through the winter to protect the remaining penguins were snipers to shoot the fox. None was shot down near the shoreline, but a fox was later killed further up on the headland. It's not known if it was *the* fox, but in any case it was a threat to the penguin colony.

To deal with foxes, there is now baiting all year, and lures are set, using the intoxicating aroma of seal poo. It's enough to make a human retch, but apparently seal poo is like perfume to a fox.

Just off the beach, Mel leads me through a locked gate and wire fence. There is a wooden nesting box, and inside is a penguin with two eggs. It looks beautiful, with its slightly bluish feathers. Mel says it could be either the male or female, because they take turns in minding the eggs.

'Equal opportunity,' she whispers. 'We've got a lot to learn from these penguins.'

I ask Mel why the penguins have come to this part of the harbour and, in particular, Manly Wharf, with so many people around.

'Maybe they've always been here,' she replies, 'but dogs and foxes have wiped so many out. Prior to that, they didn't have as many predators.'

We head over to Store Beach. Mel leads me down a track through the bush. The path dips towards the bay, the gaps between the angophoras scooping up the water. I thought Store Beach was dazzling from the water; it is equally so from the land. We slide down a rock onto the sand, choreographing our steps between the rush of water. Mel peers into a gap in the rock but there are no penguins, just moulted feathers.

We walk along the beach, passing a rock with a small emblem carved into it. Underneath the emblem one word has been chiselled and wrapped in a carved ribbon: 'Smallpox'. Mel says the carving would almost certainly have been done by someone from the Quarantine Station. At the northern end of the beach, we clamber up rocks and into the bush. About 50 metres from the water's edge and perched on the slope are about a dozen nesting boxes. Most of them are plastic. Mel says the penguins don't use those. There are also a few wooden boxes. There is a sign on each box warning the lids are not to be opened; the risk is a $5500 fine. Good thing I'm with a ranger. Mel gently opens the lid, shuts it and whispers for me to come over. I hear the squawking noise within. I figure it's a protest or Penguinese for 'Get lost'. But it transpires it may have been amorous squawking. For when Mel opens the lid again, we see two penguins, looking at us with a 'Do you mind?' expression. I ask why there are two in this box. 'They're getting to know each other.'

The wooden boxes have been made by students at a nearby public school.

'We try to invite kids and the community as much as we can,' explains Mel. 'The more people who know about this the better, as they will try to conserve it.'

We walk amid the little boxes, with Mel gently and discreetly checking if they hold occupants. In one other wooden box, there is a solitary penguin, who shuns the light and our presence.

'It's cool that they're here; it's a shanty town,' she says.

Mel is hopeful that the sum of efforts of the volunteers and her colleagues will mean there will be forty-two breeding pairs again this season. But it is a constant battle for the penguins to survive all the threats that await them in the sea, and on the land.

FROM THE Quarantine Station, I head up the time-welted and weather-beaten headland to another fort designed to repel invaders. Whereas the station faces inward, the North Fort is perched on top of the headland and stares out to sea.

To help mariners into the harbour, an obelisk was erected on North Head as early as 1809, and the strategic importance of the headland was recognised early in the colony. But facilities to deter any enemy coming towards the Heads were built much later, in the mid-1930s. In a newsreel produced in 1940, the defences were called Sydney's own Maginot Line, an assertion probably tinged with wartime hyperbole. But the two guns installed on the headland were powerful, firing 9.2-inch shells up to 30,000 yards, or 27 kilometres, towards the horizon. Under the guns were tunnels and storerooms burrowing into the sandstone. The big guns were tested for the first time in 1938, as war loomed, and, according to a newspaper report at the time, Manly residents were warned to keep their doors and windows open to avoid damage from the concussion. In the same year, the handsome barracks for the 1st Australian Coast Artillery Brigade were grafted onto the headland, and in the years ahead, as the Second World War flared, radar buildings and observation posts were installed amid the scrub and rock on the continent's edge.

With the war's end in 1945, the gradual transition of the site from a strictly military zone to a public sanctuary began. But that would take many years, and the army dug in. Coastal artillery was considered obsolete after the war, so the big guns were removed from the fort and cut up for scrap, and, in time, the fort would become an artillery museum. But from 1953, the School of Artillery took up residence in the barracks complex, and it remained until 1998. One of those soldiers who attended the School of Artillery was Ron Ray.

I had met Ron over at Georges Heights, where he was a volunteer guide around the historic defences. He is performing the same role here, leading tours of North Fort and giving a voice to the nation's military past.

Ron was here in the 1960s, before he went to Vietnam. He lived in the barracks, and he marched in his crisply pressed uniform each morning on the parade ground. It may be decades since he had to march, but to this day, Ron walks around the parade ground, not across it, because 'I regard it as a sacred spot'. Live-fire drills were held in the scrub, and the old tunnels were used for interrogation training. The strict discipline of the place meant Ron gave little thought to his surroundings most of the time.

'Until you were out on your own, you couldn't appreciate what was here,' he recalls.

Half a century on, Ron shares his appreciation. We leave the visitor centre and stroll to an open-air monument to the defence of Sydney. There are constructed tributes around the grounds, including walls of wood salvaged from old wharves. But the greatest monument to the defence of Sydney is the view of the harbour itself, laid out like an exquisite quilt before us, from the Heads all the way down to the CBD.

From vantage points such as this one, Ron used to watch Australian and US Navy ships coming and going during the Vietnam War.

'You could see the city skyline even in those days,' he says, explaining that the trees would be bulldozed and kept at knee-height for clear sight lines. 'So you knew you were in Sydney, but not in the metropolis.'

At night, he could see the Macquarie Lighthouse over on South Head winking at the dark sea. But there was also some-thing creepy about being on guard duty at night, because 'this is the most haunted place in Sydney'. On the track near the Quarantine Station's Third Cemetery, the soldiers reported hearing the clip-clop of a horse and the light of a candle swinging in the dark. They were convinced it was the ghost of a draught horse used to pull the cart carrying corpses to the cemetery.

Ron prepares to take us into the darkness, where ghosts may still hover. Heavy rain is bombarding us, as we head down a camouflage-painted ramp to the skeleton of one gun emplacement. The dish of cancer-eaten concrete and rusting bolts looks naked without a gun. Nearby, there is one disembodied barrel on display, but it was brought here from Middle Head to give people a sense of just how big the guns were.

We venture almost 10 metres underground, out of the rain and into the tunnels. I can still hear water flowing. Rivulets are running in small channels flanking the tunnels. We head into a shell store room, where the powder and shells were kept separately so that if there was an explosion, the hope was everything wouldn't blow up. But Ron says, matter-of-factly, in that stentorian sergeant's voice of his, it would have all blown. We continue to descend into the earth along a straight tunnel, which, in the artificial light, looks interminable. We're accompanied by the incessant sound of running water. Up to eight thousand litres of water seep through the sandstone into the tunnels every day. Ron says the water has been filtered by the rock so is perfect to drink. It was used for domestic purposes in the fortress complex, and, he adds with a smile of satisfaction, it goes very well in whisky. Such was the quality, and reputation, of this water that it was scooped into containers and taken to Vietnam, so that soldiers could have a drop or two of North Head water in their whisky.

'It's just one of those traditions,' he shrugs.

At the end of the passage is an alcove that was a casualty station. As we look back up the tunnel until the yellow light sours and darkens, Ron tells a story about a young electrician who died while working down here. His ghost is said to wander the tunnels. Ron says once the keys were ripped from his hands and tossed. He's convinced the ghost was playing tricks on him. As if to punctuate his story, Ron turns off the lights when we arrive in the cathedral-like space that was the engine room. The blackness is so complete, I can't see my hand in front of my nose. But I can almost see a ghost.

We pass a couple of blast doors and climb the steps back to the surface and into the rain. I ask Ron if he wishes this was still a military base, not a museum. He shakes his head.

'Time moves on, nothing stays the same,' he says. 'What's more, the facilities had had their day.'

But what is timeless is the view. Ron stands with his hands on his hips, peers at the harbour, and, with an air of satisfaction – as though he has just sipped a whisky with a dash of North Head water in it – he murmurs, 'It's still the gem of Sydney'.

NORTH HEAD is referred to as a tied island. When you look at a map, you can see that it is flimsily tethered to the rest of the world by that expensive strip of real estate known as Manly. Yet when you walk to the edges of the headland, it still feels very much like an island, as though it is teetering on the edge of limitlessness.

The headland is stitched with old stone walls that were built under work schemes during the Great Depression. They divided public areas from those that had been scythed off for defence purposes, or for the Catholic Church. The walls cut through the scrub before they stop abruptly at the great cliffs along the eastern face that tumble to the sea. Any pretensions to order that the walls were meant to impose are stripped by the cliffs and the extraordinary sight of the sea, unconstrained and uncontrollable.

I walk a little further south through the wind-bashed and stunted bushland, until I reach Fairfax Lookout, right above where the harbour surrenders to the sea. Two kilometres or so across the water is South Head, looking like a knot of strength and resistance against the sea's ceaseless surge. I watch a group in dragon boats round South Head and paddle at the footing of the great wall of the Australian continent. Whale-watching cruises are heading out to sea. The voices of the tour guides bounce across the water and have splintered into syllables by the time they ricochet off the cliff and reach me. Those pieces of words are quickly washed away by the shushing of the sea. I look over the edge, and below the world is foamy, brittle and breathtakingly beautiful. I look up just in time to see a white-bellied sea eagle drift past at my eye level before it swoops.

I look once more at the band of water binding the headlands, pulling them close. And yet somehow that stretch of water makes the southern shore seem like another country, an ocean apart. Perhaps it only seems that way when you're about to paddle it.

10

BETWEEN THE HEADS

BUMP!

That's all it takes to get me jumping out of my skin, if not out of the kayak. After all, that would not be a wise move, as I'm halfway across the harbour's entrance, paddling towards South Head, about a kilometre ahead. Below me, the water plunges about 30 metres to the floor, and, off to my left, it grows into the sea, chasing the earth's curve to South America.

One bump, and I'm looking nervously at the water all around me, while my thoughts scurry back to shore. I remember Jeff, who I met back in North Harbour, looking at me quizzically when I told him where I planned to paddle.

'Why would you want to go across there in a little kayak?' he asked, before helpfully adding that sharks the size of small buses cruised in and out of the harbour's entrance. 'I wouldn't do it.' I shrugged and laughed. I'm not laughing now.

And it had all been going so beautifully. I had set off at dawn, passing Quarantine Beach, its sand cool blue as it waited to be gilded by the sun. I thought of the Little Penguins waddling down the beach, beating the light to the water. I nudged around the western edge of Quarantine Head, riding the gentle rise and fall of the swell. The great weathered face of North Head revealed more and more of itself. Initially, backlit by the rising sun, the inner and outer headlands were silhouettes, as if they had been lifted from a Chinese ink painting. What the land lacked in colour, the sea more than compensated for. It was as if I were kayaking on burnished metal. But then the colours of the world found their balance, as the sun climbed. While I could see one of the long stone walls cutting down North Head like a scar, and I knew the remains of hundreds of souls lay in the earth up there in the Quarantine Station's Third Cemetery, from out here, the landmark looked unpeopled and remote. It looked as wondrously unconquerable and as wilfully inscrutable as the sea it was rebuffing.

In the harbour's entrance, no other vessel was about. In the distance, pushing along the harbour and preparing to turn left towards Manly, was a ferry. Sometimes in storms, the passengers are taken on a thrill, or terror, ride on the passage across the Heads, as the sea brutally punches and throws the ferries about. In one savage blow in 1972, the ferries were contending with waves about 12 metres high. Yet on this morning, the sea was in a placid mood. I could hear it gurgling as *Pulbah Raider* rubbed across its surface. The only other sound was the faintest thrum of the ferry's engines, creating their own bass notes to bounce across the water.

As benign as the sea appeared, I would not be seduced into paddling any further to the east. The last time I had headed out there in a small vessel, I was breaking a promise I had made to myself. That was back in 2003, to farewell the sailor and adventurer David Lewis on his final voyage.

I had known of David since I was a kid, when I had read his accounts of sailing to Antarctica. David had been the first person to sail solo to Antarctica in his sloop *Ice Bird* in 1972 and 1973. By then, David had already notched up many adventures in his life, sailing all over the globe, particularly around his beloved Pacific Ocean, learning traditional methods of navigation from elders on the islands. Yet he wanted to go further, to the bottom of the world and way beyond the accepted limits of human endurance. So David had sailed through Sydney Heads and into history. More than once, he was almost history, as the yacht was capsized in monstrous seas and screaming gales. David reached Antarctica, his little boat limping into the US base of Palmer. Having read about his escapades, I wanted to be like David Lewis and find adventure. I never really did. But then adventure found me. In 2001, I was told David was moored a few bays around from our Lake Macquarie home, restoring his 28-foot sailboat, *Leander*.

I tracked David down and introduced myself. From the moment I shook his hand, I was in the grip of adventure. David Lewis understood the sea like the back of his hand. Literally. For on his left hand was a tattoo he had received in the Caroline Islands. The design was of dolphins, a shark bite, symbolising danger, and birds, representing guides to land. That tattoo was a constant reminder for David of not only where he had been, but also what he was. For the design meant 'initiated navigator'. In one sense, David had allowed the winds and his imagination to carry him through life, but he always knew where he was headed.

When I met him, the then 84-year-old was preparing *Leander* to sail one last time up Australia's east coast, through a string of islands, and back to his homeland, New Zealand. He invited me to sail with him and two other blokes on the first leg of the voyage, to the Gold Coast. I had never sailed offshore before, and here I was being invited to join the crew for a legend of the seas. I would be as good as an adventurer! I couldn't have wished for more. But as we learn, you should be careful what you wish for.

No sooner had we sailed out of Lake Macquarie than a bunch of dark clouds gathered in the south, just waiting to beat us up. The storm was ferocious, with 6-metre waves pummelling little *Leander*, along with any romantic notions I had of a pleasant sail north. I couldn't stop vomiting, partly from seasickness, mostly from fear. I recall lifting my head from the bucket only to see a mountainous wave looming over us, the wind scream-ing like a banshee, and there was David, with his hand on the tiller, squinting at the blades of rain cutting into his eyes, and all the while smiling. In my mind, that image will always be the portrait of an adventurer.

'That was a terrible first night of sailing for you,' David said to me the next day. 'It was exhilarating sailing, but one can take only so much exhilaration.'

The greatest joy for me on that six-day run along the coast was sitting with David, listening to him talk in that soft, almost timid, voice of his about some of his voyages and what he had learnt about himself. One key lesson he had absorbed was that, like the sea, there was no end to knowledge. He was determined to keep sailing over the horizon in order to keep learning until his final breath. I also learnt a lot on that voyage. What I learnt most of all is what it took to be an adventurer, and that I would never be one. But that didn't mean I couldn't look for adventure and keep stretching myself. After all, the world is not flat but curved; the line on the horizon is only an illusion, so there really is no limit.

As David said to me, 'I know some people think adventure doesn't hold much practical value. But it has an intrinsic value, a spiritual value, a value in personal terms of toning a person up, keeping them fully alive and getting the cobwebs out. Otherwise you risk becoming lethargic.'

However, after that interminably terrifying night in the storm, I vowed I would never go to sea in a small boat again. No one would ever drag me out there again. But David did.

He died in late 2002, and, in early 2003, there was to be a ceremony off Sydney Heads to scatter his ashes on the sea. I accepted a place on a yacht that was heading out for the ceremony.

I remember looking at the horizon, taking in the sea and the sky, and, as thanks for all he had taught me and was still teaching me, I smiled and said, 'You bugger. You got me out here again.'

Desperation, not adventure, impelled some to venture beyond the Heads. The First Fleet marine Watkin Tench was so hungry for news of home after a few years in the colony that he once rowed about 10 kilometres out to sea to meet an approaching ship. Convicts also took to boats, trying to escape. The first recorded attempt was in 1790 when five men set sail in a small, frail craft for Tahiti. They were never heard of again. The following year, there was a celebrated escape, when Mary and William Bryant, along with her daughter and their baby son, stole away with a crew of convicts on a perilous voyage out of the Heads and north to Timor. They had stolen Governor Phillip's cutter for the 5000-kilometre voyage, which took sixty-nine days. In Timor, they were held by the Dutch authorities and handed over to the British. While they had survived the most extraordinary open-boat journey, Mary Bryant lost her husband and children on the voyage to England.

With the daring of the Bryants, and possibly with even less equipment, a lone sailor named Fred Rebell set off on a similarly crazy/brave voyage more than a century later. He wanted to emigrate to the United States of America, but when he was denied a visa, Rebell decided to go anyway, in an 18-foot sailing boat. He sailed out of the Heads in December 1931 relying on a homemade sextant, an old navigation manual, some hand-drawn maps, a couple of watches for chronometers, six months' supply of dried food, and a whole lot of faith. When his watches gave up, Rebell relied on prayers and dreams to find his way to America. They must have been powerful dreams and prayers, because he reached California in January 1933. Rebell was the first person to sail alone across the Pacific from west to east, a feat that still has mariners, especially those who sail in 18-footers on the harbour, talking about him in wide-eyed wonderment.

Yet, through the years, many have felt a sense of escape by coming through the Heads. Journals and diaries, memoirs and reminiscences crackle with the excitement of the first time they set eyes upon Sydney Harbour.

Among the more sober entries are those by the first Europeans to thread between the Heads. Officers on the ships of the First Fleet were aware that with their words they were drawing a path into the harbour for others to follow. Second Lieutenant Philip

Gidley King duly noted 'the entrance is soon discoverd lying between two steep bluff heads, there is no danger in entering the harbour'. Still, others couldn't help but be overwhelmed by the moment, especially after an eight-month voyage from the other side of the globe. Arthur Bowes Smyth, a surgeon aboard the female convict transport *Lady Penrhyn* noted that the descriptions of his fellow mariners painted a picture of a paradise discovered. Then in his diary he too attempted to paint a word picture of the harbour, although he conceded, 'To describe the beautiful & novel appearance of the different Coves and islands as we sail'd up is a task I shall not undertake as I am conscious I cannot do justice to the subject.'

Long after the first European arrivals had noted their impressions, others would excitedly record their thoughts about their introduction to the harbour.

'The entrance to Port Jackson is grand in the extreme,' enthused the writer and illustrator Louisa Anne Meredith, recalling her arrival from England in 1839. Meredith was so enchanted by the harbour and the shoreline that when she saw a rainbow, it seemed 'like a smile of welcome to my new country'.

Four decades on, a visiting American preacher and writer by the name of Dr Talmage rhapsodically recorded his entry into Sydney Harbour. Perhaps he was writing a sermon. 'Safely we rode in between the two great brown pillars of Hawkesbury sand-stone,' he wrote, 'and then began the revelation of a harbour such as nowhere else in the wide world is to be found. The whole scene is an Odyssey, a "Divina Comedia" [sic], an Old Testament and a New Testament of loveliness. You cannot for a moment relax your energy of watching without missing something which you cannot see again.'

Aside from the original inhabitants, Australia has been largely shaped and populated by those coming through the Heads, seeking a new life. In the process, they have brought constant renewal and regeneration. We are a country of migrants, with waves of new arrivals having come in from the sea, shaping the land, as surely as the great rollers from across the Pacific that come to rest on Sydney's sandstone shoreline.

In turn, the harbour immediately set about shaping the arrivals. When the artist Lloyd Rees passed through the Heads, glimpsing North Head and the Manly shoreline through a porthole from SS *Canberra* in 1916, it was love at first sight. The porthole framed the perfect picture.

'Opal-blue water, a band of golden sand, another of olive-green trees; above them a skyline of coral pink shimmering against the limpid air ... In that first long look Sydney cast her spell and it has remained with me ever since, in spite of her brashness and disorder, the crimes she has committed against herself, and, above all, the opportunities she has allowed to pass – opportunities that could have made her more worthy of her setting.'

Rees had travelled only down the coast from Brisbane; for those arriving through the Heads from across the seas, they were seeing more than just the colour of the land change. After the Second World War, ocean liners filled with migrants and refugees cruised into the harbour. Believing the country had to populate or perish, Australia's Immigration Minister Arthur Calwell signed an agreement with the International Refugee Organisation in 1947 to accept displaced persons from camps across Europe. Immigration deals had also been signed with individual countries. And so Australia's post-war mass migration policy was enacted, and the ships began arriving from the war-shattered lands of Europe.

While Arthur Calwell saw on those ships the security of the nation, many standing on the decks as they cruised into the harbour saw their future. In the comedic novel about post-war Australia, *They're a Weird Mob*, by Nino Culotta (who was actually an author with the Anglo-Irish name of John O'Grady), the main character is an Italian journalist who emigrates in order to write about the experience. Nino observes, 'I saw Sydney for the first time the very best way – from the deck of the ship. And at the very best time – early in the morning, with the sun behind us.'

Yet often the sun only illuminated the mixed emotions of those on board. The photojournalist David Moore captured the faces of a group of passengers on a liner's deck in his image, *Migrants arriving in Sydney*, taken in 1966. In that one shot, perhaps the most famous of his celebrated career, Moore managed to compress all the apprehension, excitement, hopes and doubt, the thoughts and worries emanating from the faces of those pressed against the rail. It is the portrait of not just the migrant experience; it is a powerful study of humanity facing change. As was later revealed, the photo was about more than the migrant experience; four of those in the photo were Sydneysiders returning home. Which somehow only reinforces the idea that, in Sydney, nearly all of us can trace our origins to somewhere else, and you can't tell the difference between us.

Some were initially made to feel different. When Teruko Blair sailed into Sydney Harbour in 1953, she was reaffirming life. On more than one occasion, she had all but tasted death. Teruko Morimoto survived the atomic bomb that was dropped on Hiroshima at the end of the Second World War in 1945, then witnessed the extraordinary upheaval of her country, as the Occupation forces imposed new orders and ideas on life in Japan. Teruko was employed as a waitress at the British and Commonwealth Occupation Force's base at Kure, where she met and fell in love with an Australian soldier, William Blair. The soldiers were under strict orders to not fraternise with the locals. Even if a soldier went against the rules and married a Japanese woman, she was effectively banned from entering Australia. With the sweetest, cherubic smile, Teruko told me how she found the thought of her sweetheart sailing back to Australia without her unbearable.

'I thought I couldn't survive,' she said in a soft voice. 'So I decide[d] to kill myself. If he is sent back, that is the day I end my life.'

Teruko prepared a bottle of poison and wrote a letter to the Australian Government condemning it for being so heartless, and another to her parents, apologising. Then she waited for the day William Blair sailed away. But in 1952, Australia lifted the ban on servicemen bringing Japanese wives to Australia, and Bill dashed to tell Teruko the news. They would marry and sail to Australia as husband and wife.

'I took that bottle of poison and threw it into the fire,' Teruko told me. 'And then I started to cry.'

Teruko was one of about 650 Japanese war brides who came to Australia after the war. She was among the first non-Europeans permitted to enter the country when it was still under the restrictive White Australia policy. Teruko recalled her reaction as she stood on the ship's deck coming into Sydney Harbour.

'I felt I could be happy in Australia, that was my first impression,' she said. 'Some of the girls were worried, crying, but I felt I could be happy. I could see nice green trees, beautiful.

'Such a beautiful sight, waiting for me.'

I have been on the decks of cruise ships coming into the harbour, returning from holidays in the Pacific and Papua New Guinea. The only thing at stake for me was the prospect of slipping back into the rhythm of working life. Even so, there was a sense of returning home, which I felt more deeply than when looking out of a plane window at the vast blanket of suburbia rumpled around the harbour. That view diminishes the harbour. From the deck of the ship, everything begins on the water; the harbour takes its rightful place in leaving an indelible impression.

My last cruise ship voyage was on *Pacific Eden* in late 2016. We sailed into the harbour as dawn was breaking. The Hornby Lighthouse on South Head was winking at us across the water. As the sun peeked over the horizon, it set alight the windows of the skyscrapers in the distant CBD. *Pacific Eden* was on a course closer to North Head. Its inner and outer headlands turned from liquid shadows to solid rock as we cruised towards the coastline, until the great bluff was beside us. The ship is 219 metres long and its width is just over 30 metres, big enough to create the sense of filling the space between the Heads as we glided in. But there was still more than a kilometre of water between us and South Head. Off our port side, a couple of fishing trawlers were heading out to sea, and a bunch of kayakers looked like mere marks on the water as they curled around South Head. As we turned south-west, cruising towards Bradleys Head, I looked astern. Perspective was gradually pulling North and South heads together until the gap closed. It appeared as though the sea was shut out and we were encased in the continent. By then, nearly everyone else's eyes were looking forward, up the harbour, particularly those of Captain Chris Norman.

Captain Norman had sailed into Sydney Harbour for the first time just a year earlier, but in the twelve months since, he had been in and out past the Heads about twenty times. A tall Englishman with a young, inquisitive face, Chris had first left the security of land as a teenager, working on fishing trawlers, revelling in 'the challenge of taking an empty piece of equipment to sea and bringing it back with salary'. He had been on cruise ships since 1999, sailing all over the globe, except to Australia. As we sat in the captain's suite on *Pacific Eden* while still out at sea, Chris had told me one of the reasons he accepted a secondment to P&O Cruises was to sail a ship into Sydney Harbour.

When he had that opportunity in November 2015, he was captaining one of five P&O cruise ships entering the harbour at the same time, an event that filled the waterway and the shoreline. Sydneysiders had grown used to seeing cruise ships come and go on virtually a daily basis, but this was the first time five vessels from the one fleet were in the harbour simultaneously. Chris Norman was notching up another milestone in his own life by entering Sydney Harbour. But as he cruised past the Heads for the first time, Chris thought of history.

'I thought of all those sailors who came from X, Y and Z in little wooden boats,' he reflected. 'And looking around, while on the land side there have been a lot of changes, on the sea side little has changed since they sailed in.

'Coming into Sydney as a harbour, I'd venture to say, it must be one of the most famous runs in, it's quite a spectacular run-in,' he said. 'Up until Sydney, the most spectacular place I'd come into was New York on a cold January morning as the sun came up, with a perfect view of the skyline, but coming into Sydney rivalled that. I've been into a lot of ports, but not many have something like the Opera House so close.'

As we sailed through the Heads, I had an inkling how busy Chris Norman was on the bridge. About two hours earlier, he and his team would have communicated with the Port Authority of New South Wales' Vessel Traffic Service, the body helping control ships' movements in and out of the harbour, via email and VHF radio. As *Pacific Eden* neared the Heads, a pilot was brought out on a launch and transferred to the ship to help guide it in. From that point, any communication with shore is on the radio because 'it's in real time'.

'Sydney is, all in all, not a super challenging harbour, but there are challenges, with its usage and the wind,' Chris had told me. 'Wind is something you don't like, because we are effectively one big sail. I don't mind rain, fog doesn't bother me, but wind . . .'

He would be pleased this was a still morning. And there were few other vessels on the water, unlike on the weekends, when all manner of recreational boats are scurrying across the harbour. Not that Chris minds, because he has plenty of watchful eyes on the deck, a Port Authority boat is out front ensuring no vessel gets too close, and, what's more, he likes to see a city engaging with its harbour.

'It is such a busy harbour,' he mused, 'whereas many [harbours] around the world are now empty hulks.'

On the run from the Heads to Bradleys Head, *Pacific Eden* cruised at 10 to 12 knots, then from 6 to 8 knots as she headed to the terminal at White Bay, near Balmain, in the inner harbour. We passed under the Harbour Bridge, cruising at 6 knots. For the passengers on the top deck, it was an exhilarating and breath-holding experience as the ship slid under the steel belly of the bridge deck. The gap between the ship and the bridge seemed to narrow, until it appeared as though the funnel could have touched the steel. Chris had assured there was still up to 3.5 metres clearance. That is sufficient space, according to the Harbour Master's Directions, which stipulates a minimum of 2 metres clearance under the structure, or a metre under the Bridge workers' maintenance gantries. Still, looking up from the ship's deck to the Bridge's underbelly was an awesome sight, as so much of this hour-long run in from the Heads to the wharf was.

For Captain Chris Norman, while the Bridge and the Opera House are exciting to see and provide great photo opportunities, they are not what resonate with him in Sydney Harbour. It is the sense that we are but passing through something much larger and older. He may be at the helm of a massive assemblage of steel as it pierces the harbour, with up to 1500 guests and a crew of 600 relying on him, but Chris Norman feels ephemeral in the face of what time and water have created.

'Yes, the Opera House, yes, the Bridge, but take all that away, and the sea, channels, and the base fabric of the continent remain as they would have been long before we put our own mark onto things.'

SINCE IT is early morning, which is when cruise ships slide in between the Heads, I look to my left. Nothing.

Clear seas, perfect morning. Nothing can spoil this moment. Bump!

That's when I think of Jeff's comment about big sharks. I stop paddling. That bump definitely felt and sounded like it was coming from under the hull. I breathe deeply, as if I might be able to inflate my lungs sufficiently to float away like a balloon, before I figure sitting here caught between two headlands and a whole lot of sea isn't going to help. There's no point turning back, since it's as far either way, so I keep heading south. I place the blade tentatively into the water and drag it slowly. Nothing has bitten the paddle, so the next stroke is a little more confident as I ride over the relaxed arc of the swell. Then . . . Bump!

There can be no doubt about it this time.

It's my water bottle. It has dislodged and is rolling around in the cavity behind the seat. I deflate my lungs and sit for a while as the rhythm of the swell lulls my heart rate.

Peering into the aquamarine, I think of how the harbour's gates are open for all things natural and manufactured to glide through. That rhapsodic 19th century correspondent, Dr Talmage, declared as he sailed into the harbour, 'Room here for all the navies of the earth to ride in and secrete themselves so that they could not be found without much search'. Which is precisely what concerned the defence authorities. The headlands may have been progressively packed with batteries and observation posts to resist an attack from the sea, but as military technology advanced, it was the unseen lurking under the surface that increasingly caused worry. In 1925, a Committee of Imperial Defence report on the requirements for defending Australia stressed the importance of Sydney as a naval and commercial port, and it outlined 'the major form of attack under consideration was by submarines laying mines or firing torpedoes, at shipping both in the harbour and in the approaches to the harbour'. That report prophesied what happened seventeen years later.

On the eve of winter in 1942, three Japanese midget submarines brought into Sydney the fears that had stalked the city virtually since it was born in 1788. For the first time in its history, Sydney came under direct fire. The midget subs had been launched from mother submarines about 12 kilometres off the coast, sneaked between the Heads and created havoc. To find their way to the harbour entrance, one submarine crew used a chart that had been originally surveyed by Captain James Cook. The submarines slipped through the defences by audaciously following Manly ferries.

It was not as though the attack was a complete surprise. Japan was at war with Australia, submarines had been lurking off the coast, harassing merchant shipping, and a few times since February 1942, the Japanese had sent a reconnaissance plane over Sydney without challenge. The last reconnaissance flight had been just a day before the submarines slipped into the harbour. Many years later, the pilot, Susumo Ito, recalled how in the pre-dawn he had flown up the harbour, sometimes as low as 30 metres, over the Harbour Bridge, around the Cockatoo Island dockyard and back out above the headlands along the North Shore.

Even so, the attack was a shock. The harbour that was the heart of the city, and that was cradling dozens of naval ships on the night of 31 May, was the conduit for the enemy to bring destruction and death into Sydney.

Two of the midget submarines did next to no physical damage. One, M27, became entangled in the anti-boom net laid across the harbour from Georges Head to Green Point on

the southern shore. The two men inside blew up the submarine, and themselves. Another, M22, was chased around the harbour before it was finally destroyed by depth charges near Taylors Bay on the northern shore. These days, there is a plaque above the bay, acknowledging the fate of the submarine. You can sit there and contemplate a beautiful scene where two young men died entombed in a small metal tube. Relatives of those men have visited the site, paying tribute by pouring sake into the water and by simply standing on the harbour's edge. As Kazuko Matsuo, the niece of one of the crewmen, told me in 2007 when she visited Taylors Bay for the first time, there were no words, just deep feelings.

The third midget submarine, M24, managed to reach beyond Bradleys Head and fired two torpedoes towards USS *Chicago*, which was moored off Garden Island. They missed the US cruiser, but one torpedo slammed into the seawall near HMAS *Kuttabul*, which was berthed along the south-eastern edge of Garden Island. *Kuttabul* had been a ferry, carrying passengers across the harbour before the Bridge was built. When the war came, the vessel was made useful once more, as a floating barracks. On that Sunday night, *Kuttabul* was filled with sleeping servicemen. When the torpedo struck the wall, the force of the explosion shattered the ship and she sank. Twenty-one died on *Kuttabul*. While the nation was at war, and the city was meant to be on guard, few could believe the Japanese had attacked and killed people in the harbour. Not even survivors from *Kuttabul* could believe it. One later recounted how he laughed dismissively when told there were Japanese submarines in the harbour and had gone back to sleep. He woke up two days later in hospital.

Hearing the explosions and gunfire and seeing the flares and searchlights as the Allied forces hunted the submarines, thousands of Sydneysiders were roused from their sleep and came down to the waterfront to watch. By the time the sun rose, the attack was effectively over. Most people were left in the dark as to what had just happened. Newspaper reports were initially heavily censored but the event inevitably became front-page news. A few days after the attack, Norman Makin, the Minister for the Navy, stood up in the House of Representatives and declared the Japanese attack had been unsuccessful and the harbour defence measures had worked, instantly detecting the midget submarines. The preliminary report of Rear Admiral Gerard Muirhead-Gould, the Naval Officer-in-Charge of Sydney Harbour's defences, gives a different impression of how the defences handled the attack. In his report, Muirhead-Gould liberally used the word 'fail' when appraising those under his charge. Yet in other quarters, Muirhead-Gould's own actions were criticised, including the decision to allow passenger ferries to keep operating in the midst of an attack. His justification was that 'the more boats that were moving about at high speed the better chances of keeping the submarines down until daylight'.

The wreckage of two Japanese midget submarines was salvaged and taken to Clark Island, a loaf of land rising from the harbour just off the southern shore and close to where M24, which was the one sub that had not been found, had fired its torpedoes. On the island, the bodies of the two submariners in each of the craft were removed. A week later, they were cremated with full naval honours and returned to the Japanese. In the face of public criticism for showing too much respect to an enemy that had attacked the harbour, Muirhead-Gould went on radio, praising the 'brave men' for going to their deaths in 'that steel coffin', and he rhetorically asked, 'How many of us are really prepared to make one-thousandth of the sacrifice that these men made?' The wrecks of the submarines were examined then joined into one Frankenstein sub, which was taken on a fundraising tour before being placed on display at the Australian War Memorial in Canberra.

The fear that the submarine attack was the precursor to a full-scale invasion was stoked just over a week later. On 8 June one of the mother submarines, I-24, surfaced off the coast and fired ten shells in the direction of Sydney Harbour Bridge. The shells fell short, landing in the Eastern Suburbs, damaging homes and shops, but no one was killed. Still, it terrified Sydneysiders. Some left the city, wanting to be away from the harbour. For the first time in a long time, Eastern Suburbs real estate could be had for a bargain. Yet there would be no more attacks from the sea.

Fears lingered, as did questions, including, 'What happened to the third midget submarine?' In the confusion that ricocheted around the harbour on 31 May into the early hours of 1 June 1942, M24 slunk back out between the Heads and into deep water. But not nearly as deep as the mystery as to where it had gone. The mystery was finally solved in 2006, when divers found the wreckage off the coast of Sydney's Northern Beaches in about 57 metres of water. The sea had finally given up its secret.

The years reshaped and softened that historic attack on Sydney into an event that could symbolise the journey of two nations; how enemies had reconciled and become firm friends. In 2007, a year after M24 was discovered, Japanese and Australian military and political leaders, along with members of the dead submariners' families, were on board HMAS *Melbourne* for a memorial service above the wreck site. The Japanese families were presented with sand collected from the seabed on which M24 lay, and Rear Admiral Nigel Coates, Commander of the Australian Fleet, read 'Ode to the Fallen (The Sailor's Ode)':

> *They have no grave but the cruel sea,*
> *No flowers lay at their head,*
> *A rusting hulk is their tombstone,*
> *Afast on the ocean bed.*

GRADUALLY THE sense that I could be so easily a plaything of the sea, tossed into the wide blue yonder, subsides as I paddle closer to South Head. Experiencing the harbour's entrance from the water, I more than understand why early travel writers and diarists, grasping for a metaphor, compared the two headlands to arms. I feel as though those arms are embracing me, like a mother's, reassuring me they won't let me out of their grasp. They won't allow the sea to take me.

Where I feel something warmly maternal, Dr Talmage, that late 19th century American preacher and Sydney admirer, saw something more omnipotent when he steamed through the Heads. 'God works by no model, and this harbour was of divine origination,' Dr Talmage sermonised. 'He works with rocks and waters and skies as easily as architects work with pencil and rule and compass; and he intended this harbour not to be a repetition of anything that had ever been done, but to make it impossible for any human engineering or landscape gardening or hydraulics to imitate. It is a winding splendour, an unfolding glory, a transcendent illustration of what Omnipotence can do in the architecture of an ocean.'

Still, that didn't stop at least one designer from imagining he could improve on nature at the Heads. Or perhaps, having vaulted the air and expectations once, he was feeling a little God-like. At the opening ceremony of the Harbour Bridge in 1932, John Bradfield, the man who had nursed it from an idea to an icon in steel, said the structure was 'a stepping stone for greater engineering feats, a bridge across the Heads, maybe . . .'

Looking up, I'm grateful that above me is not a bridge's deck but only sky, which is thickening into a rich blue. More ferries are ploughing across the Heads, to and from Manly, as the day advances.

From half a kilometre or so out, South Head looks like a great ship, with its bow facing resolutely east. The impression is even more pronounced as waves finish their long journey across the sea by disintegrating on the rocks packed along the bottom of the head's sandstone hull. It looks as though South Head is pushing through the seas. But, of course, the headland is going nowhere. It absorbs the sea's energy, compelling it to behave more placidly before it can proceed into the harbour. I can see Hornby Lighthouse on the tip of South Head, painted in candy stripes, and in the distance, poking over the sandstone cliff, is the Macquarie Lighthouse, a stolid white column of dependability. In one form of another, it has been warning mariners that land loomed since 1817. The convict architect Francis Greenway designed the first lighthouse and set the stamp for its replacement in 1880. What I'm looking at is essentially what Greenway envisaged 200 years earlier.

Soon after sailing between the Heads for the first time in January 1788, William Bradley retraced his journey into the harbour, helping survey the vast body of water. Bradley noted, 'As you sail into the opening between the Outer Heads which is near two miles across, steep too on both sides, you will see on the south shore a point off which is a small reef made by the fallen rocks and breaks as far out as any danger can be . . .' I'm mindful of Bradley's advice as I approach the feet of South Head. I make sure to keep my distance, so that the waves don't push me onto the rocks. Having already jumped at the bump of a water bottle, I don't need to feel the bash of Kevlar and fibreglass on sandstone.

A fishing trawler steams in from the sea behind me, its phlegmatic engine hawking in the morning air. I imagine how tired the fishermen on board are, and what a sweet moment it must be each and every time they pass between the Heads, returning to shore. I too head for land. I could paddle a little to the left, and, just before reaching the heft of the sea, land on Lady Bay Beach, discreetly tucked into a cove near the tip of South Head. Instead, I paddle to the right, bound for the beach where British bodies reputedly first lay on the shores of Sydney Harbour.

11

SOUTH HEAD TO DARLING POINT

EVEN ON the shortest of voyages, making landfall is a welcome prospect. Especially when the land waiting to greet you is as beautiful as the harbour shores inside South Head. I paddle away from the sea's influence, out of its swell, and into Camp Cove. Its fringe of sand looks as though it has been peeled off the sandstone headland and meticulously laid like an offering to the water, or to the line of mansions fronting it. On the beach is a sign indicating all vessels are prohibited from landing. But the compulsion of history tells me to ignore the sign and follow Arthur Phillip onto the sand.

The Royal Australian Historical Society and the local council marked this spot as the place where Phillip first stepped ashore in the harbour. On Laings Point, overlooking Camp Cove, the authorities built a small monument in 1927, with a plaque that reads: 'On this beach/Camp Cove/Governor Phillip/first landed in/Port Jackson/Jan 21st 1788.' Despite that plaque's proclamation, there has been a lot of debate about whether this was where Phillip and his party first landed in the harbour on their open-boat journey from Botany Bay. Yet it seems this is where a British person first slept, if not stepped, along the harbour's shoreline. One of Phillip's boat crew, Jacob Nagle, had noted how, after surveying the lower parts of Middle Harbour and Manly, 'we landed on a beach on the south side and there pitched our tents for the night'. As a result, of all the names they could have come up with for the cove, one that perhaps responded to the beauty of the place or the magnitude of the moment, the party instead settled on something perfunctory: 'This place was call'd Camp Cove.' If the first British arrivals underplayed the significance of the site with the name, later generations have soiled it. Right behind the monument, on the knoll with the stunning views, squats a public toilet block.

A small wave gently lifts the kayak and places it on the sand. The beach is gleaming in the early morning light, reminding me of the British writer Louisa Anne Meredith's first impressions of the 'pure white silvery sand' in the coves as she sailed into the harbour in 1839. She wrote that the sand was used as ballast in ships and transported to England, where 'it is much valued, I believe, by glass-makers'.

I have the beach to myself for a few moments, before an older couple arrive to exercise, he to walk along the sand, while she wades into the water and begins swimming slowly the few hundred metres along the cove. A four-wheel-drive crawls slowly along the beach towards me. I immediately think of that 'all vessels prohibited' sign. But it contains two council workers, who are here to clean the beach. I get talking to one of them, Dave. The beach looks clean to me, but Dave knows there will be rubbish, because there have been westerly winds. Winter, when the westerlies mostly blow, is the worst for Camp Cove, he says, because it carries the rubbish of the city onto the beach. In summer, when the crowds descend, it is mainly dropped litter he has to contend with.

Dave cleans eleven harbour beaches between here and Rose Bay. The most littered, he says, is Watsons Bay, which is just around the point to the south.

I ask Dave what's the weirdest thing he's picked up, and he replies diplomatically, 'You name it, I've picked it up.' And with that, he heads off, prodding at the sand, returning the beach to almost-perfection, ready for the crowds to trample and sully it once more.

WATCHING OVER the cove from its perfect position on South Head is the naval base, HMAS *Watson*. The base straddles some of the finest real estate in Australia, as it faces the harbour to the west, and the sea to the east. Approaching the entrance, HMAS *Watson* has the feel of a resort in a fantastic location, but once through the gates, it quickly asserts itself as a military base with a rich history. Near the entrance is an arrangement of shells from the navy's first flagship, HMAS *Australia*, along with a rusted anchor from a 19th century sailing ship. The anchor is leaning against an old fortified wall. This site has held military installations since 1871, when artillery emplacements were built to protect the port.

The navy has been on South Head since the Second World War. The first radar used in Australia was installed on the headland during the war. These days, *Watson* is primarily a training base for maritime warfare. Sprinkled around the site are barracks, and on the crest of the hill is the wardroom, the mess for senior sailors, with views all the way down the harbour to the city and the Bridge. My friend Commodore Peter Leavy recalls the first time he entered that wardroom. It was 1984, and the Western Australian teenager had joined the navy only ten days prior.

'As my group of midshipmen entered for lunch on that first day, we all stopped in unison as soon as we walked in the door, struck by the amazing vista before us,' Pete recalls. 'In subsequent years, I have seen countless other people do exactly the same thing on their first visit to the wardroom.'

Perhaps the most gracious building on the base is Cliff House, the Fleet Commander's residence. When he was the navy's Commodore Warfare, Pete stayed in Cliff House for a while, and his family invited ours to visit in December 2015.

The house was furnished with naval heritage and a few reminders of Pete's career. The dining table was from HMAS *Westralia*. Pete had bought that table for *Westralia* in 1989. Running through the centre of Cliff House was a wide corridor. I stood at the back of the house and looked along it, as though through a telescope, to the harbour. The view widened when I stepped onto the house's flagstone veranda facing south-west. I could see up the harbour to the city skyline, about 11 kilometres away. On the veranda was a cannon cast in 1871, the same year the artillery dug in on South Head. Its barrel was facing towards the sumptuous curve of Camp Cove, just below, perhaps ready to blast any prohibited vessels, such as kayaks, landing on the beach.

From Cliff House, fleet commanders through the years could have watched ships coming and going. This position always held great strategic value. For Pete, the veranda played another role while he was living here.

'One thing I used to wonder about – in fact, I still do – while staring down the harbour was what it must have been like for the First Fleet as they sailed into what was, for them, an unknown harbour,' he recounts later, from his next posting, at the Australian Embassy in Washington DC. 'And, more importantly what the Cadigal (or Gadigal) people of the day thought.

'I think an often undervalued part of Sydney Harbour is the link it provides to the history and traditions of the original inhabitants. Australian Aboriginal culture is the longest continuously surviving culture on the planet – something we should all be proud of and do our utmost to protect – and Sydney Harbour symbolises the links between the Cadigal people and the harmony they enjoyed with their natural environment.'

While the ships go wherever the sea does, cruising around the globe, Sydney Harbour is, in Pete's eyes, 'the spiritual home of the Royal Australian Navy'.

'There is nothing quite like returning to Sydney after six or seven months away on deployment,' Pete explained to me. 'The sight of Centrepoint [Sydney] Tower, while still miles off the coast, serves as the first tangible evidence of Sydney. As you enter the harbour, you immediately pass HMAS *Watson* down the left side. But the best sight of all is rounding Bradleys Head to see the Bridge, Opera House and city itself all open up before you. Nobody ever tires of that sight unfolding.

'I think Sydney Harbour holds something special for all naval officers, and that's saying something from one who hails from Western Australia!'

Pete took us for a walk over to the eastern side of the base, where the continent tumbled off the edge. He had done some of his celestial navigation training standing here on the cliff top. You could look straight out to where the sky touched the sea.

Around where we stood, homesick members of the First Fleet once did the same thing, staring hopefully, expectantly out to sea. In early 1790, Governor Phillip ordered a flagstaff and huts be erected on South Head, so that watch-keepers stationed there could send a signal to Observatory Hill, above Sydney Cove, when a ship was approaching. On 3 June that year, the cry of 'The flag's up!' bounced excitedly around the settlement. One of those who heard the clamour was the marine Watkin Tench. He looked outside his cottage, saw people celebrating and kissing their children, and he guessed what was happening. Tench ran to the top of the hill and, with the help of a telescope, he could see a flag fluttering on South Head. 'My next door neighbour, a brother-officer, was with me; but we could not speak; we wrung each other by the hand, with eyes and hearts overflowing,' Tench noted in his journal. The colony at the bottom of the globe had not been forgotten. The vessel was *Lady Juliana*, packed with a cargo of female convicts.

The convict artist Joseph Lycett used the perspective from South Head to depict the distant settlement of Sydney, and he sketched the view the other way, perhaps wistfully, towards the Heads and out to sea. Lycett tellingly placed in the foreground of his pictures those who were being pushed away by the colonists, portraying the Gadigal walking through their land or watching ships sailing into their harbour. Once the colony took root, and homesickness was quelled by a growing sense of 'home', Sydneysiders would still come to the cliff's top along

South Head to look out and around. One of the colony's most influential figures, William Charles Wentworth, observed how, 'In boisterous weather the surges that break in mountains on the shore beneath you, form a sublime contrast to the still, placid waters of the harbour, which in this spot is only separated from the sea by a low sandy neck of land not more than half a mile in breadth; yet is so completely sheltered, that no tempests can ruffle its tranquil surface.'

A century on, Kenneth Slessor wrote an entire newspaper report about travelling to the best-known stretch of South Head, The Gap, and getting cheap thrills by standing there in a storm. As he told his readers, 'For a five-penny tram-fare yesterday the Sydney citizen had heaven and earth performing beneath his insignificant feet.' That's the beauty of The Gap; it's where nature is so compelling, it puts you in your place. The tragedy is that so many have come here feeling insignificant. The Gap has become renowned as a suicide spot.

The sea has also washed away many lives along the foot of South Head. On a foul night in August 1857, the clipper *Dunbar* was attempting to enter the harbour when it was driven onto the rocks. One hundred and twenty-one passengers and crew perished. It remains one of Australia's worst maritime disasters. There was but one survivor, a crewman who clung to a ledge for more than a day before being rescued. The *Dunbar* disaster horrified and traumatised the harbour city. Corpses and wreckage were washed through the Heads and onto the foreshores. While there are other memorials to those lost from *Dunbar*, the most practical and enduring monument shines out from South Head. The Hornby Light was built in response to the disaster, to more clearly mark the harbour's entrance. This disaster, along with the loss of twenty-one lives when the clipper *Catherine Adamson* foundered off North Head just two months later, highlighted the need for a lifeboat to be stationed close to the Heads. Through the later years of the 19th century and well into the 20th, a lifeboat service was based at Watsons Bay. In vile weather, men would row around the point and through the Heads into monstrous seas to helps crews and passengers on stricken ships. By 1946, the service was finally decommissioned, and the lifeboat that had been based at Watsons Bay since 1907, *Alice Rawson*, was retired. The sea had grown no less tempestuous, but improvements in ship designs and safety methods helped nudge the lifeboat service into history.

WATSONS BAY may be part of Sydney Harbour, but in its look and feel, the village on the shoreline is a community unto itself. The water that connects it to the rest of the world is what also disconnects it. That is a key attraction for those living in the collection of historic and contemporary homes – most of them tasteful, all very expensive – occupying the bay's edge. To its residents, Watsons Bay is like living in a remote fishing village. Which is what it once was.

'There is no place in the estuary . . . so suited for an old tale as this fish-smelling bay, first in the port,' wrote Christina Stead in her beautiful novel of place, *Seven Poor Men of Sydney*. The village where her tale is set, Fisherman's Bay, is Watsons Bay, where she lived for the best part of two decades. 'Life is poor and unpretentious, life can be quiet. The sun rises just over the cliff, and sailing vessels roll in and out as they have done for a hundred years, and a quarter of a mile away unfurl their full sails to catch the Pacific winds.'

Some things have changed from fact to fiction, and from the past to the present. Life is no longer poor in the bay, and the decayed weatherboard cottages and fishermen's shanties that Stead described have been either knocked down or renovated. But the spire of Our Lady Star of the Sea Catholic church is still there, thrusting above the landscape, and boats are still moored in the bay, yet few are working vessels.

In Stead's novel, set in the 1920s, the bay's shoreline is a provider for those who search it: 'The beach provided not only fuel, but also dead fish, swollen fruit, pumpkins, shoes and socks, broken straw-boaters – all varieties of food and clothing cast up from ships and sewers.' The beach is no longer strewn with this sort of flotsam, but people still wander along the shore, fossicking for something far more elusive: peace and quiet. That can be even harder to find. Crowds of people escape to Watsons Bay, many arriving by ferry.

The curve of the bay is interrupted by the wharf, which is like a finger pointing and warning, 'Here comes another load'. People do actually leave Watsons Bay. I've sat in my kayak on a weekday morning, watching commuters amble, not rush, along the jetty to get to the ferry. Their pace seems to fit the feel of the place, and their relaxed attitude is reflected in a sign at the end of the jetty: 'No Waves'. The wharf leads straight to a couple of local institutions by the water, Doyle's seafood restaurant and Watsons Bay Hotel. There's been a pub on this site for about a century and a half.

The restaurant has perhaps the most unpretentious vessel moored in the bay, a rowboat. The sight of the little boat, with 'Doyles' painted in blue on its hull, bobbing on the mooring, holds reminders of the fishing village, and its residents, who – at least in Stead's novel – 'were absolutely fearless, despite the frequency of squalls and sharks, paddling all over the harbour in unseaworthy tubs'.

On the other side of the wharf, I paddle past the swimming baths. I take particular interest in the baths' protective net. It looks intact. If only Robert Hughes were still here, to plunge in and inspect it. When the acclaimed writer and critic was a boy, he learnt to swim in the Watsons Bay baths. Hughes recalled in his memoir, *Things I Didn't Know*, how parents favoured this pool because it was shielded by shark-proof netting. However, young Robert knew better. He had done as he did later in his life as a critic; he put on a mask, dived beneath the surface and saw what others couldn't. There were large holes in the netting. Not that he ever encountered a shark in Sydney Harbour. But he saw plenty of dead ones, caught by game fishermen, hanging on the wharf at Watsons Bay. The Sydney Game Fishing Club still has a home on the wharf, and there are often large cruisers wearing spiky crowns of fishing rods berthed out front.

Just beyond the baths is a two-storey building with the words 'Pilot Station' on its wall. These days, it is a boating safety education centre, but for many years until 2008, this was the base for those who helped guide ships into the harbour. Yet Watsons Bay has been linked to the safe passage of ships for much longer than the existence of this building. Once through the Heads, this was where ships often first dropped anchor, to have their documents inspected or while waiting for a berth further along the harbour. Soon after ships began arriving, pilots were stationed in the bay, rowing out in open boats to meet vessels. The bay is named after one of the earliest pilots. Robert Watson, who served on HMS *Sirius* in the First Fleet, had been granted land on the peninsula.

In 1811, Governor Lachlan Macquarie appointed him senior pilot and then harbourmaster. Watson moved on from those positions, but he remained in maritime safety. When the original Macquarie Lighthouse was completed just up the hill in 1818, he was appointed its first superintendent.

For many years, the pilot service out of Watsons Bay was a haphazard affair and largely unregulated, as crews scrambled out to sea to be first to an arriving ship. With the formation of the Marine Board in 1871, more order was introduced, bringing regularity to pilots' wages and the fees they charged, largely removing the conditions for a frenzied dash for cash on the waves.

While Watsons Bay was remote from Sydney, it was cosmopolitan. The rest of the world not only anchored in its bay but worked on its shores. Among those crewing the pilot boats were Maori and Portuguese mariners. A Russian explorer and biologist, Nikolai Miklouho-Maclay, lived and worked in Watsons Bay. Miklouho-Maclay was accustomed to genuinely remote locations. He had lived and studied cultures in New Guinea. After arriving in Sydney, he believed there was a need for a laboratory to study marine life in the harbour, so he spearheaded the establishment of a biological field station at Watsons Bay. He had the backing of influential figures and organisations in the colony, who were beguiled by the good-looking, bearded Russian. The laboratory didn't last long, and Miklouho-Maclay returned to Russia. But his name remains by the water, further along the harbour at Birchgrove, at the Miklouho-Maclay Park.

The fringe of the harbour city continued to attract those with inquiring minds. John Olsen was already grabbing eyes and interest with his paintings by the time he moved to Watsons Bay in 1963.

As a young man, he had viewed the harbour through the windows of places he lived and painted in. In 1956, he sailed out of the harbour, bound for Europe. John learnt, painted and absorbed new ideas in the Old World, particularly in Spain, before returning in 1960. He vividly remembers the ship carrying him back home through the Heads.

'It was a Saturday evening,' John says. 'We were coming in, there was music playing, there was such jollity, and I thought, "How different this is to what I've experienced in Spain", which was still recovering from a civil war. And here's Sydney Harbour, and it was all bouncing and vibrant. It was just an incredible image.'

For Olsen, the sensation was one of utter seduction, even consummation. To him, there is something sexual about the land opening and a ship penetrating the harbour. As he cheekily tells me, 'Well, you've got to be imaginative too!' Little wonder that one of his paintings is a phantasmagorical burst of colour and sinuous lines titled *Entrance to the Seaport of Desire*.

Yet it wasn't just the harbour's arms and legs that were wrapped around John. He wanted to know every part of it. With paint, he explored its ragged margins and dived under its surface. After a few years, it wasn't enough for John Olsen to be immersed in the harbour only through his art. He and his family moved into a fisherman's cottage at Watsons Bay.

The harbour quickly insinuated itself into his daily routine. He would swim in the morning with his children at Camp Cove, yarn with the fishermen as they returned to the bay after a night out on the harbour or at sea, and he would buy some of their catch. John himself would head out in a rowboat to fish, or to dive over and collect mussels and oysters off rocks. He could easily fill a sugar sack. Once, he recalls through infectious giggles, the *eminence grise* of Australian letters, Patrick White, accompanied him. Not that the writer had any intention of joining John in the water; he would stay in the boat, characteristically observing. But those plans were turned upside down when John returned to the surface with a full sack, handed it up to Patrick, who lost his balance and fell into the water. Patrick wasn't amused, John chuckles.

Each day, when he left the harbour physically, John would dive straight back in creatively. In his studio, the harbour and its profusion of life would splash and squiggle, dart and dance, across his canvases.

'Watsons Bay just served as a wonderful viewing place of the harbour, the activities of ships coming in, of ferries, the different kinds of lights on the harbour – sunshine, as well as night time,' he explains.

'I lived physically in the harbour, and I enjoyed that sense of poetry, that kind of simple village life.'

John constantly saw, heard and felt poetry in the harbourscape and transferred it to his art. He thought Watsons Bay and its resident characters were a Sydney equivalent of the Welsh village in Dylan Thomas' famous radio play-poem, *Under Milk Wood*. John has plunged into the cadences and images of Kenneth Slessor's poetry time and again, particularly that beautiful elegy, 'Five Bells'. And he has been inspired to shape his own words into a tribute to the harbour. For a series of etchings, *Seaport of Desire*, published in 2002, John wrote a poem at Watsons Bay and called it 'The Harbour'. In his verse, he swims through images of ships sliding into the harbour, of tidal pools, spotted fish and 'cranky crabs', before musing in the final lines:

In a turning world, am I the
Bay that called itself
    John Olsen?
or
John Olsen that became
    the bay?

It's a good question. For in the poetry of his painting, John and the harbour have often become so intertwined, they are inseparable. He has lived away from its shores for many years, and yet that body of water that seduced him all those years ago keeps calling him back. Actually, there is no need for that siren song, for the harbour has never left him, or his art. They're good for each other, John and the harbour. They give each other colour, vitality and, above all, love. They're meant for each other.

John refers to the harbour as a 'blue bitch goddess'. I ask him what he means by that.

'She is irresistible, she's beautiful, but she will betray you. She can betray you as quickly as she can draw you in.'

Yet, as he acknowledges in a later conversation, it is we who usually betray the harbour, by being neglectful or even wilfully cruel.

'Love is a fickle thing, and you've got to look after the blue bitch goddess, otherwise she can turn against you,' John says.

'But we often don't look after her,' I reply.

John sighs and utters, 'We're careless, very careless.'

FROM WATSONS Bay, I can see markers warning of peril in the water. Near the main shipping channels is a reef that has caused concern ever since the First Fleet sailed in. The 150-metre-long hazard is known as the Sow and Pigs Reef, which indicates some early colonist had a good imagination. At low tide, the rocks are exposed; at other times, they lurk just below the water. Despite the danger, it wasn't until 1824 that a beacon was erected on the reef. An old ship, festooned with hanging lanterns, was moored near the rocks. Some had other ideas for rendering the reef benign, proposing to build a fort on the reef, so that the Heads could be guarded as well. In the 1830s, enthusiastic harbour reshaper George Barney recommended building a Martello tower on the rocks. He would have his way further along the harbour at Pinchgut. So the reef has defied generations of plans and proposals, steadfastly gripping the harbour floor and, occasionally, vessels.

The worst shipping disaster on the harbour happened not on a reef or near a hazard but out of the blue on a beautiful afternoon in November 1927. The ferry *Greycliffe* was making its way from Circular Quay to Watsons Bay, flitting into wharves along the harbour's southern shore, collecting a mix of workers and commuters, holiday-makers and school students. South of Bradleys Head, the ferry suddenly wheeled to the left. Bearing down on the ferry at 17 knots was the steamship *Tahiti*, about three times the size of *Greycliffe*. Some of the passengers on the ferry could see the inevitable looming, but there was nowhere to escape the collision. *Tahiti* carved into the wooden ferry's port side. Many passengers were trapped in the quickly sinking ferry. Others were tossed into the water.

'I was drawn down by suction and whirled in all directions by the current,' a schoolboy, Leslie Brooke, told the media. 'When I came up I grasped the largest piece of wood that I could find.

There was wreckage everywhere, and it seems as though the boat must have been knocked to splinters, because few pieces of wood were large enough to support anybody. It was terrible to see the scrambling and commotion in the water, which was whirled as though it were boiling.'

Forty died in the collision. Many were residents of Watsons Bay and nearby Vaucluse. Around Sydney there was disbelief at the loss of life; in those two harbourside communities, there was paralysing grief. So many had died in the water that was so much a part of their lives. Outside St Peter's Church in Watsons Bay, the Greycliffe Memorial Gates were built in 1929. Time dismantled the timber gates, but stone memorial plaques survived the years.

PADDLING INTO Parsley Bay, I pass a couple of fishermen on the rocks below a line of mansions. They hold limp lines and wear bored expressions. One says, with a rueful shake of the head, 'No bites, no fish'.

The bay is an elongated finger of water scratching deep into the land between two sandstone hills. The waterway used to be much longer; in the 1930s, a seawall was built and its head was filled in, creating a park. Not that I can paddle far into the bay anyway, because a shark net has been strung across its mouth. Just to ramp up the warning a little more, a sign with a shark icon has been placed on a wharf, trying to ensure that, in the Parsley Bay swimming area, there are no big fish, no bites.

Yet it is not the water that immediately grabs the eye in this bay, but the bridge suspended above it. The pedestrian bridge was built in 1910, and it is still well used. I climb out of my kayak next to the shark sign and walk up onto the bridge, feeling its deck's graceful sponginess. I look through the cables out to the harbour, watching a ferry slide by. The surrounding landscape is studded with large homes, but there are enough trees to create the impression the bay remains flanked by bush.

In the yards of mansions around here, I see a couple of markers of history. On a property boundary between two homes on Parsley Bay's western shore is a sandstone obelisk that served as a navigational mark dating back to the mid-1800s. Just around the point, rising from among a string of houses, is a magical looking white tower, wearing a Moorish crown. I half expect Rapunzel to be letting down her hair at the window, or perhaps to see Juliet. It is, indeed, light that through yonder window breaks. The cylindrical tower, which has been on this site for well over a century, is an operating lighthouse, known as the Vaucluse Bay Range Front Light. I can only look at the tower from the water, for it is on private land. In that respect, when they are locked away on private property, these landmarks of our maritime heritage seem to be Rapunzels of the harbour.

I'm hardly the first to observe how the harbour and elements of its history are cloistered and cut off. Parsley and Vaucluse bays were among the beachheads for a determined battle in the early years of the 20th century for the harbour foreshores.

'Why should, say, a dozen or so owners monopolise the only available beaches, to the exclusion of hundreds of thousands of citizens of the present and future generations?' asked William Albert Notting, the prime mover pushing for the resumption of foreshore land.

'We have only one Sydney harbour in New South Wales, and only one bay like Parsley Bay in Port Jackson, but it will soon be too late to save it, unless the Crown quickly wakes up from its lethargic sleep of indifference or delay . . . Will our citizens awake, or stand idly by and see these priceless gifts of nature locked away from their reach for ever?'

In 1905, the Harbour Foreshores Vigilance Committee was formed 'to keep a watchful eye on all matters of public concern with the harbour and other foreshores'. Notting was elected secretary. He had been agitating for the resumption of land along the harbour for years before that. Notting was motivated in part by what haunted him. On Boxing Day, 1892, a party of picnickers in a yacht *Iolanthe* was thrown into the harbour when the boat capsized. Earlier the group had been ordered off the foreshore near Camp Cove by the landowner, forcing the picnickers to head back onto the harbour as a storm was intensifying. Seven people, including two children, were drowned when *Iolanthe* capsized. Notting had once owned *Iolanthe*. He often referred to the tragedy when citing the need for safe shelter around the harbour and the risk of allowing individuals to own land right down to the high-water mark.

The committee stirred up a swell of interest, attracting dozens of boating and fishing clubs to support them, as well as some newspapers.

'It was bound to come,' thundered a report in the *Sydney Mail and New South Wales Advertiser*. 'For a hundred years we have been throwing away our harbour foreshores recklessly with both hands, as it were, until to-day there is hardly a stretch of beach where a picnic party can land without being ordered off. For scores of years it has been pointed out that this foolish policy should be stopped, if not in the interest of the generation of the day, then in that of posterity. But the process went on. The

Government was warned that the water frontages so recklessly alienated would have to be bought back someday at enormous cost, and now the inevitable has come.'

The committee wanted undeveloped foreshore land to a depth of at least 200 feet, or 61 metres. Like a military leader, Notting would pin a map to the wall at public meetings, and he would point out all the tracts he believed should be in public hands. Notting argued the government had to act quickly, as he rattled off examples of how much the price of waterfront land had jumped in a matter of months.

Notting and the committee grabbed a toehold in Parsley Bay. Land was resumed in 1906 and dedicated for public recreation the following year. The committee was unimpressed with the amount secured, arguing it was insufficient. Notting warned the Government had to be more committed, predicting 'unless we bestir ourselves posterity will wake up to the fact that our much boasted of and beautiful harbour is practically, as it were, a pond in a privately-owned or military-guarded paddock'.

The campaign moved on from Parsley Bay to the next cove, securing land at the head of Vaucluse Bay. The government responded to the committee's pressure by forming the Foreshores Resumption Scheme to buy back more land – the western shores of Vaucluse Bay, the tip of the headland to create Nielsen Park, the Hermitage Foreshore Reserve. More than a century on, those reserves remain, offering respite to an increasingly clogged city. Yet William Notting's vision of returning vast stretches of the foreshores to the people was never realised, while his fears that more and more land would be sliced up, sold off and buried under homes have been. If he were out here on the water, Notting would be perhaps disappointed, but not surprised, by what he would see on the land. After all, he predicted 'the whole of the southern shore and heights above from Point Piper to South Head will be densely populated in years to come'. Yet when I'm on the water, I see the bands of green on sections of the southern shoreline, and I view them as victory flags for William Notting. That tenacious man and ferocious campaigner saved more than some harbour foreshores. He helped Sydney retain some of its very soul.

AT THE head of Vaucluse Bay, I land *Pulbah Raider* on one of Notting's victories. The approach is across shallow water infused with the colours of the bush. The shoreline carries reminders that this belongs to the people, with dinghies stored in racks and dog walkers letting their charges off the leash. Yet just before levering myself out of the kayak, I can see through the trees, about 200 metres away, one of those big, old statements of private wealth by the harbour: Vaucluse House.

This was the home and fortress of William Charles Wentworth and his family. Wentworth stood out in the colony not only because he was tall but because he was an exhausting over-achiever. He was an explorer, being in the trio of the first Europeans to cross the Blue Mountains. He was an author and the publisher of the first independent newspaper in the colony, the *Australian*. He was a barrister and a politician, a reformer and a builder of what this nation would become. Wentworth covered all his bases, if not his past. He was the son of a convict woman, which his detractors were only too ready to remind him of. His father was a surgeon, Dr D'Arcy Wentworth.

Vaucluse House existed before it became part of the Wentworth legend. The core of it, a stone cottage, had been built in 1805 by an Irish aristocrat, Sir Henry Browne Hayes, who had arrived in New South Wales as a convict, having been transported for abducting an heiress. Sir Henry's house was in the bush, so he shared it with snakes. He devised a logical response. 'Being a firm believer in the legendary virtues of St Patrick in expelling serpents from the Emerald Isle, the owner of Vaucluse sent home to Ireland instructions to have several hundred barrels of Irish earth shipped to him from Cork,' according to a report in the *Illustrated Sydney News*. The report recounted how Sir Henry employed a team of convicts to dig a trench around his property, had the barrels of dirt barged from Sydney town, and, on St Patrick's Day, 'the ceremony of filling in the trench was performed, with the result that never a snake thereafter was found in the house or its immediate surroundings'. That wasn't quite the case. Many years after the magic dirt was laid, Wentworth wrote about snakes on the property.

Wentworth bought Vaucluse House in June 1827 for £1500. He loved the harbour's southern shores. 'Looking towards the coast you behold at one glance the greater part of the numerous bays and islands which lie between the town and the heads, with the succession of barren, but bold and commanding hills, that bound the harbour, and are abruptly terminated by the water,' he had written some years earlier in his book, *Description of The Colony of New South Wales*.

The water enticed Wentworth. He and his family would go sailing in their schooner, *Alice*, which was moored at the front of the property in Vaucluse Bay. *Alice* was once hijacked by some of Wentworth's staff, with his butler being the ringleader, who wanted to sail it to New Zealand but only got as far as Port Stephens, north of Newcastle. The proximity to the water also allowed Wentworth to observe his enemies passing. When his nemesis, Governor Ralph Darling, sailed out of the harbour for England in October 1831, Wentworth invited the public to a huge party on his Vaucluse property. According to a report in the newspaper Wentworth had founded, and headlined 'Rejoicings for General Darling's Departure from New South Wales', more than 4000 attended to have an uninterrupted view of the unpopular Governor departing – and to drink the free grog.

After Wentworth bought Vaucluse estate, he kept extending and renovating the home, making it ever grander. Wentworth biographer Andrew Tink noted how the house increasingly looked like a Gothic Revival mansion, not unlike the new Government House that was built half a dozen bays or so further west in the Domain. Perhaps his house helped shape Wentworth's desire for the formation of a local aristocracy, and for him to be a member of it. As a result, Wentworth was disparagingly called the Duke of Vaucluse.

Wentworth's private domain became part of the people's estate when the government bought part of the land and the house more than a century ago. So I can land near the public dinghy racks and stride towards the castle-like building without fear of trespassing. The property makes an overwhelming impression. On the western side there was once a grazing paddock and a vineyard and orchard. To the left is a 'Pleasure Garden', an English ornament beautifully tended, which I skirt around. The native vegetation can't be wholly denied by the imported vision, as sub-tropical rainforest plants are clustered along a creek that provided water for the household. I pass the stables, with their grand façade, and head into the house, which is maintained by the Historic Houses Trust.

In Wentworth's day, this was a largely self-sufficient house-hold, as Sydney town was about a three-hour ride away. The property still has that sense of self-sufficiency, with its kitchen gardens, goat pens, and chicken coops. There is something evocatively disorienting about having the smells of the earth and farmyard animals wafting about in a modern harbour city. Curiously, the stolid containment of the house makes the harbour feel distant. Standing on the veranda wrapped around the ground floor, I can look down the valley to the bay, and from a window on the upper floor, I can see slivers of water. But from the inside, Vaucluse House doesn't feel like what it looks like from the outside – one of the great harbour homes.

Above everything else attached to his name, William Charles Wentworth was a proud Sydneysider. He considered himself a son of this land. He died in England, but his body was brought home, and his remains were placed in a vault cut into the rock on his estate. The family mausoleum is no longer on the property, as parts of the land were sold off. Most likely, that would not have surprised Wentworth. Even as a young man, he knew what Sydney real estate was like. 'The value of land in this town is in many places half as great as in the best situations in London, and is daily increasing,' he wrote. Which only reinforces the idea that some things don't change. But the mausoleum is still in Vaucluse, and so is William Charles Wentworth. He is here, and he is everywhere in Australia. For what he did in his life would help give life to a nation.

ON VAUCLUSE Bay's north-western tip is a clump of rocks that constantly tease the water. Even in the calmest conditions the harbour froths and seethes when it hits the rocks. Or perhaps the harbour is imbibing on them, for they are called the Bottle and Glass Rocks. The formation doesn't look like a bottle and glass any more. Various reasons have been offered for that; depth charges were dropped nearby during the Second World War, a ship fired its cannon at the rocks during the 19th century, vandalism, the effects of water and time. They may be shattered, but the Bottle and Glass Rocks and the shoreline still hold the promise of something delectable, for they are studded with oysters. That is, if you'd be prepared to eat them.

The oyster has its own, not particularly imaginative, name. The Sydney Rock Oyster. Although in Latin its scientific name sounds more impressive, more complex, more in keeping with how they taste: *Saccostrea glomerata*. The oysters are kind of like many Sydneysiders, sweet and generous inside, but with a tough and sharp shell that can cut you deeply.

Despite their formidable exterior, the way oysters feed means they can be hurt by what they live in. They are little pumps, constantly drawing in water and filtering it to obtain food. They take in sediment particles, and, if there are contaminants attached to the sediment, the oyster ingests them as well. Those contaminants accumulate in their bodies. Which is why scientists study oysters as a key indicator of the harbour's health. What some people call delicious, scientists refer to as a biomarker or a biomonitor. One of those who studies oysters is Dr Katherine Dafforn, from the School of Biological, Earth and Environmental Sciences at the University of New South Wales.

'One of the reasons oysters make such good biomonitors is they do tend to accumulate contaminants more than some others species,' Katherine says. 'So people use oysters a lot to see the exposure, to see what the animals in the water column are actually being exposed to, as opposed to just directly measuring what's in the water.'

Katherine has been involved in research that has shown high levels of copper, lead and zinc concentrated in the tissue of oysters from various sites around Sydney Harbour. Some of what the oysters have ingested, she says, is the legacy of the harbour's industrial past. Each time the harbour's bottom is stirred up by a storm or boating activity, the past floats back into the present. But it's not just history being filtered by oysters; we are adding to their toxic intake each and every day.

'Even though we don't have a lot of industrial practice, we are still getting heavy metals introduced to the harbour with storm-water run-off,' Katherine explains. 'Things that are coming off our roads, our roofs and houses and getting into the water column, that's an on-going issue.

'We have a lot of marina moorings all around Sydney Harbour. Anywhere you get a dense accumulation of boats, you get anti-fouling paint, and it produces emissions of copper and other heavy metals.'

Katherine is hopeful for the harbour's future health. But it needs help.

'There's been lots of research into environmentally friendly anti-fouling coating that doesn't have heavy metals, so it would be nice to see some of that get taken up and actually become part of policy.'

'Would you eat an oyster from Sydney Harbour?' I ask her.

'I don't actually like oysters,' replies Katherine. 'But, no, I probably wouldn't eat an oyster from Sydney Harbour. Mainly because they're the kind of animal that's filtering whatever nasties are in the water column. It's the same as fish that live on the bottom in the sediment and feed on things there. They're probably going to accumulate more contaminants than a fish swimming up high in the water column or swimming off the coast. It's thinking about what you're eating, and what it might possibly have eaten. I think that's something to consider.'

GEOGRAPHICALLY, I'VE leaped a couple of kilometres ahead around the shoreline to the south-east, into Rose Bay, and I'm going to paddle my way back to Nielsen Park. Actually, I'm going backwards not just physically. I'm returning to my past, to paddle with someone I met when we were both high school students. He was cool and I wasn't. Then we were at university. He became a rock star. I don't know what became of me. Anyway, apart from running into each other mostly at airports, flying to somewhere for our respective jobs, I haven't seen him in years.

And there he is on the Rose Bay shore. Tim Freedman. He still looks as youthful as he sounds in his songs. He is lithe, still with that cheeky but curious boy's face of his. His skin is still perfect. The only thing old about him is the towelling hat he's wearing.

Tim loves this city. I know, because he recorded a best-selling album of catchy, cleverly lyrical songs titled *Love This City*. Even if in the song, 'You Gotta Love This City', the character screams, 'My city is a whore'. Surely he means the city's like a *Pretty Woman* whore. I forget to ask. Tim frequently references Sydney in his songs, but I don't recall him singing about kayaking on the harbour. Perhaps on the next album.

Tim is to paddle my wife's kayak, which is coloured an incredibly bright candy pink. She chose that colour so that if she was ever lost on the water, a rescue boat could have seen her. I'm fairly confident the occupants of the International Space Station could have seen her. I'm a little concerned Tim might not want to paddle something that looks like it was salvaged from a K-pop clip. Tim doesn't bat an eyelid.

As we push off across the sandy shoals near the Woollahra Sailing Club, Tim looks at the heavy clouds clustering to the east but is unperturbed.

'A symphony of grey,' he mutters. Bloody hell, I think. Freedman sounds lyrical even when he's talking about the weather.

We set off following the languorous curve of Rose Bay, the largest in the harbour. Its unblemished sand is effectively the front yard for a string of mansions and apartments. They are just the first line of eye-watering wealth splayed along the eastern shore and up the hill to the Gothic sandstone edifice of the Kincoppal-Rose Bay School of the Sacred Heart, which has been peering down at sin city and its harbour since the late 19th Century. Tim takes a performer's view of the real estate, a performer who knows what a full house looks like. 'The stalls,' he says looking along the water line, then points up the hill, 'and the dress circle. All the seats are taken.'

We paddle into Milk Beach, which is as delightful as it sounds. It sits below a historic mansion, Strickland House. You would think this beach would be a secret, it seems so secluded. But like the best secrets in Sydney, backpackers know about it. A few girls have found a patch of sand that is glowing in the morning sun.

We walk up the track to Strickland House. The mansion was built in the 1850s by John Hosking, the first Mayor of Sydney, when it became a city in 1842. He called his house Carrara, and it contained plenty of marble imported from Italy. So show-pony behaviour is not a recently developed trait in Sydney property ownership. The house became a convalescent home during the First World War and was named after the Governor, Sir Gerald Strickland, then it was an aged care facility. More recently, Strickland House has been a movie and television star. The Victorian Italianate beauty featured in Baz Luhrmann's *Australia*, but not as a Sydney landmark. It had to pretend it couldn't see the 180-degree views of the harbour and posed as Government House in Darwin. When Tim and I reach the mansion's semi-circular veranda, with its white colonnades gleaming like a perfect grin, we notice it has been turned into a television production set. Windows have been blacked out and crew members scurry about. I wonder if it's a period drama, but no, a technician tells us, it's a contemporary comedy.

We walk back to the beach and set off, following the gnarled shoreline, bejewelled with large sandstone chunks, including one shelf that serves as a popular diving platform, especially on summer weekends. We paddle around Steel Point, and Tim notices a large boulder on the shore that he reckons looks like a skull with one eye, 'like something out of the Batcave'. The cove that the one-eyed skull is guarding is Shark Beach, which may explain the long net defining a large pool. So it is Shark-Free Beach. The harbour beach is better known as Nielsen Park. A boardrider friend tells me when the sea is really angry and spits a large swell through the Heads, it can ricochet off the northern shore and form into surfable waves off Nielsen Park.

Thankfully this day the sea is placid, and we ride a gentle swell onto the sand.

Tim decides to do a couple of laps of the pool, while I feel the need to explore history. In other words, I head to the fancy old stone toilet block. But they are not nearly as fancy as Greycliffe House, further up the hill, with woodwork fretting its gables. Greycliffe House was on part of the Vaucluse estate and built for William Charles Wentworth's daughter, Fanny, when she married. The couple hardly lived here, and it was leased, including to a Lady Isabella Martin, who rented the house in the 1870s so that she and her children could escape the 'lethal air' and 'floating germs' in Sydney.

People still go to Nielsen Park to escape the 'lethal air' in Sydney. On another paddling journey to the harbour pool, I talk with Barbara, who is sitting in the shade, reading the newspaper. She has been coming here regularly from Sydney's inner west for about twenty years. She points to the sand and turquoise water.

'I mean, look at this. How many harbours in the world this close to the city have something like this?' she asks rhetorically. And it's free, she adds. Although she recalls when she came here as a child, you had to pay to enter. But free entry into a slice of paradise comes with other prices.

'On weekends and summer, you have to get up very early, because it's so crowded,' Barbara grumbles.

When I tell Barbara that I'm writing a book about the harbour, she implores me to write how horrible Nielsen Park is, that the water is polluted and shark-infested, there's nothing here, and no one should visit. Tim's assessment is perhaps more apposite, as he emerges from the water off Shark Beach.

'It's fantastic! I can see why this place is famous.'

At his urging, I go for a swim. The floor is sand, but it drops away quickly, leaving only the creamy harbour water below my feet. Floating, I look at the skull rock in the foreground, and the pins and needles of the city skyline in the distance. It is not so much a view as a vision.

We paddle away from Shark Beach and across the harbour to a teardrop of land in Rose Bay's mouth. It is called Shark Island. Yes, there was once a highly publicised shark attack around here. In 1877, in an incident that could have further besmirched Sydney's name in Victorian minds, George Coulthard, a champion footballer and future Test cricketer visiting from Melbourne, was sitting on a boat's gunwale, when a shark apparently bit into the back of his coat and dragged him into the water. Coulthard escaped – minus his coat. As a Victorian news-paper breathlessly reported, the attack showed 'how numerous, ferocious, and daring are the Sharks in Port Jackson'. However, the island apparently received its name because some inventive soul thought it was shaped like a shark. A finless shark perhaps. The Aboriginal name is more evocative: Boam-billy.

With its curtain of trees and an old rotunda sitting like a tiara on its peak, Shark Island has the look of an English park grafted onto the Sydney sandstone. During the 1830s, the island was a quarantine station, to prevent cholera reaching the colony. Even so, intrepid picnickers still came to the island. Later it was used as a quarantine centre for imported cattle and dogs. But there was a growing chorus for the island to be opened to the public for recreation. In 1900, the New South Wales Government responded, and Shark Island became a public reserve. In the early years of the 20th century, the authorities crafted it into a 'truly Edwardian English park'. Grottoes and shelters were carved from the sandstone. In 1975, Shark Island was included in the Sydney Harbour National Park.

Tim and I land beside the jetty protruding from the island's southern end. The plan is to circumnavigate the island on foot – which should take about ten minutes, since it is only 250 metres long and 100 metres wide. We explore a couple of old shelters, built from stone encrusted with shells, so they look as though they have been formed from a piece of petrified harbour. On the eastern side of the island is a modern toilet block, which Tim is rhapsodic about, because of the view. 'It's one of the best dunnies I've ever been in,' he shouts out. I have to see this. Sure enough, it is a fantastic view, over to Milk Beach, along the shoreline, across the harbour to the northern shores, and east towards the Heads. We stand in the toilet gazing out, when it occurs to me it's a little weird to be sightseeing in a toilet.

The rotunda is a more respectable place to take in the view, which is intoxicating wherever you look. Little wonder the island was chosen as the starting point for the inaugural Sydney to Hobart yacht race in 1945. Even though the race's start line has shifted, this little island still attracts a crowd of spectators each Boxing Day.

The symphony of grey has ended. The sky has lightened, and the water is having more blue pulled out of it, as we kayak back into Rose Bay. While paddling, we talk of our various twinges and pains, two middle-aged men who have been on quite a journey. It's been good to catch up on the water. There's no aphrodisiac like loneliness, as a gifted songwriter once noted, but for wiping away the years, there's no medicine like the company of old friends.

*

WHEN YOU paddle on Rose Bay, you're venturing onto an undefined runway. Single-engine seaplanes carrying passengers on scenic flights take off and land on the bay. You can hear a plane chortling as it taxis from the shore. When it is beyond moored boats, the seaplane opens its throat and roars. It is a wonderful sight to be on the water and relatively close as a plane skitters and skips across the bay, before it finally shakes off gravity, and the harbour drops from its floats. Fifteen or so minutes later, the plane will return, gliding in and ploughing across the surface like a pelican.

The invisible runways have been on this bay for many years. There used to be a base for flying boats here. In the early 1930s, Qantas shrank the world a little more by launching a flying boat service to carry mail to England, and later in the decade the planes began carrying passengers. As Trevor Dean, a private pilot and aviation historian who has researched the flying boat era, tells me, 'Sydney's international airport was, you could say, Rose Bay'.

Large four-engine Empire flying boats would heave themselves off the harbour, carrying fifteen passengers and a crew of five. To reach England took nine days, but the destination was only part of the reason for being in a flying boat; it was also about the journey. The passengers were not so much flown but lavished, and they paid handsomely for it. Trevor marvels that a ticket cost roughly the same as an average Sydney suburban house.

Ground – or water – crews would have to sweep the bay before a take-off or landing, to ensure there was no floating rubbish. At night, flares would be laid to create a runway across the harbour.

The Second World War brought an end to leisurely flying boat journeys. The aircraft and its pilots were called to serve. By the time the war was over, advances in aviation had made flying boats all but redundant. But they hadn't been quite pushed out of the air and off Rose Bay. Flying boats carried passengers from the harbour into the Pacific, to destinations without a large airport but plenty of water. From 1947, there were regular flights to Lord Howe Island, the 600-kilometre journey taking three hours.

Back in about 1948, the photojournalist David Moore took a haunting shot of the flying boat base in winter fog. It was as though he had photographed ghosts. In the background, the planes sit like phantom cormorants on the water, their shapes softened by the fog, while in the foreground a crew boat motors away from the planes, leaving an era in its wake. The mood of that photo forecast the fate of the flying boats. By the early 1970s, they had just about disappeared from the bay. The last flying boat journey from Rose Bay to Lord Howe Island was in 1974.

While the flying boats have long gone, the thrill of taking off and landing on Rose Bay remains. Especially for a pilot. Trevor Dean has landed a seaplane on the bay.

'I think there's still a place for the seaplanes,' he reckons, 'even though they are very expensive with the maintenance, because of the salt water.

'I love seeing them fly from Rose Bay.'

The bay is also used for actual boats – or small ships really. Berthed in the marina of the Royal Motor Yacht Club on the western shore, and tethered to private moorings outside the waterfront homes, are some vessels so large you could land a helicopter on their aft deck. A few probably do. As I cut around Woollahra Point, a couple more mini-cruise ships of the super-rich are motoring into the bay. I ride their wake, cast at me like pearls at swine. On a weekend, you can often see these floating palaces moored in Rose Bay, allowing their owners and friends to get away from it all, while still being in sight of their harbourfront mansions.

After paddling around the point, I'm in Felix Bay. This feels like a scooped out serve of the cream of society, with beautiful homes – some historic, some gleaming new – down to its shores, and the Royal Prince Edward Yacht Club resting on the fringe of Lady Martins Beach. The club is in a historic white building with a flagstaff and deep veranda on the first floor. Even without the name, the club looks so proper and upper-class British. Lady Martins Beach may be public, but it seems the only access to the sand is down a narrow path over a stormwater drain.

Beyond the beach and following the western shore of Point Piper is perhaps the most exclusive street in Australia, Wolseley Road. From a kayak, you can see the houses in a way that you could only dream of from the road. Paddling past, I feel like a voyeur spying on obscene wealth. The estates claim everything down to the waterline. Many of the homes have multiple levels. They are escarpments of money. Residing along this stretch is the man who has led the nation, Malcolm Turnbull. When he became the Prime Minister of Australia in 2015, Mr Turnbull had access to Kirribilli House as his Sydney residence. But he chose to stay put in his Point Piper mansion. From one of his verandas or even the jetty, Mr Turnbull can probably see Kirribilli House across the harbour. When I paddle past, however, there's no sign of Mr Turnbull. Perhaps he is also out kayaking, which he is fond of doing. He has even practised kayak diplomacy. Mr Turnbull took John Key, when he was New Zealand's Prime Minister, for a paddle on the harbour.

The pattern of big homes on Point Piper was set by the man after whom the headland is named. Captain John Piper piled the money he earned on the harbour onto the point. For more than a decade from 1814, he was the Naval Officer of the Port of Sydney, which, among his many duties, allowed him to be the collector of customs and harbour dues. As he earned a commission from collecting that money, and shipping into the harbour was growing, Captain Piper became a very rich man. He helped implant the Sydney obsession of a home with a harbour view by spending a fortune building a neo-classical mansion, Henrietta Villa, on his land grant on the point.

When artists wanted to depict a romantic view of the budding colony, as though Utopia were rising among the eucalypts, Henrietta Villa would often feature in their dreamy landscape. As the historian Marjorie Barnard noted of the mansion, 'It marked the spot in the whole Colony that was furthest from reality; its foundations were mirage.' It all turned into a mirage for Piper. He was removed from his post, lost his fortune, and he tried to drown himself before being hauled back into the boat by his crew.

A little further south, the terrain settles into Blackburn Cove, whose shoreline has perhaps the most outrageously inaccurate name in Sydney: Seven Shillings Beach. I land on the sand that hisses at the imposition of my kayak, and I admire the beach-front property before me. I can see a grand old building with a steep pitched roof. A man is tending to the grounds, which lead down to a security wall with a gate and a Woollahra Council sign on it. I presume it is a public park and a council building, the chambers perhaps, which makes sense, since the property is so large. But an older lady resting against the wall puts me straight when I rattle the gate to enter the grounds.

'That's private,' she softly tells me.

'Oh, it's not the council chambers?'

'No, it's Lady Fairfax's house.'

I trudge back to safe territory at the water's edge. The public is granted a little more space just beyond Seven Million Dollars Beach, with the Redleaf Pool, or the Murray Rose Pool, named after the Olympic swimming legend.

In this part of the world, even the kayaks are envy-arousing. A group of older paddlers have arrived on Seven Billion Dollars Beach. They have paddled from Clontarf in Middle Harbour. In the flotilla is a sheeny, sleek kayak created from timber. Its owner, Hans Schmidt, built the kayak from a beam of old cedar, slicing off strips to craft his vessel. It took him 500 hours. Hans points out a few nail holes remaining from the timber's former life. It was once a supporting beam for a pergola. Quite fittingly, he has named his kayak *Reborn*. The kayak has the weight of a log, about 22 kilograms, but it looks as light as a dream. I wait on the beach to watch the paddlers set off, simply to see *Reborn* in the water. To watch that varnished streak of cedar gleaming under the noonday sun while cutting across the turquoise is a beautiful experience.

While paddling across Double Bay, I notice the place name seems true to the appearance. It looks like two bays in one. About halfway along the shoreline, where a wharf juts into the water, there is a change from beach to seawall. And to the west there are more flats along the water's edge. Yet behind them, on Darling Point, are some historic mansions. On the north-east tip of the promontory is a Gothic revival creation in sandstone, Carthona. It seems fitting that the home teetering at the land's limit was built by an explorer and surveyor,

Major Thomas Livingstone Mitchell. The home looks like an aged sandcastle, with cathedral-like windows and the stolid demeanour of a fortress. For more than seven decades, the home has been owned by members of the Bushell family, who are synonymous with tea. A few years ago, I was invited to a dinner in Carthona. While inside the home, I wouldn't have known the harbour was only metres away. I couldn't hear even the slap of a wave against the seawall. But stepping out onto the lawn, looking at the lights of ferries drizzled across the water, and the twinkling from distant lives on the northern shore, I felt I was on Sydney Harbour. Not *by* the harbour, but *on* it. The water was so close that, in the darkness, Carthona could well have been a ship cruising towards the Heads, and I was standing on her deck, breathing salt air and great fortune.

A few hundred metres off Darling Point is Clark Island. This nuggety little piece of land was named after Lieutenant Ralph Clark, who was a marine in the First Fleet. He attempted to grow vegetables and grains on the island with little success, but not due to Mother Nature. As he bemoaned, it was impossible to grow anything before it was stolen. Through the years, the island has been a picnic spot, a spectators' area for skiff races, a storage depot during the Second World War, and an open-air theatre. And it apparently has toilets with an extraordinary outlook. National Parks and Wildlife Service ranger Mel Tyas has told me the toilets are one of the island's highlights, having been carved into the rock. They're like a grotto, which makes for a refreshing change from most public toilets, which are just grotty. The *Sydney Morning Herald* went so far as to say the island had the urinal with the best view in the world. I think that is debatable, having stared out from Shark Island's toilet, but I can't step on shore to refute the newspaper's assertion. The island wears a corset of rocks, and there is no beach for me to land *Pulbah Raider*. And so, having circumnavigated the island, I turn the prow south and paddle away, knowing I may have missed out on using the world's finest toilet. Life is about learning to cope with disappointment – and with holding your bladder.

12

RUSHCUTTERS BAY TO THE OPERA HOUSE

ENTERING RUSHCUTTERS Bay, I'm expecting to be overwhelmed by fabulous maxis and the scent of the 'Blue Water Classic'. After all, this is the home of the Cruising Yacht Club of Australia, which hosts the Sydney to Hobart race.

Instead my introduction in the bay to maritime splendours is a little more modest. An older couple on a yacht call at me to retrieve a dinghy, water-logged and half-submerged in the lane where boats come and go.

'There are also two oars. Grab them too!' the bloke commands.

I know yacht skippers are used to barking orders, but I wonder if he has noticed I'm sitting in a kayak, not on a barge. Still, I get behind the dinghy and push it towards the yacht.

'There's a line at the bow – pull it!' the skipper roars.

'I can't! The dinghy's full of water!' I reply, with lash and mutiny in my tone.

As much as I want to paddle off in protest, I nudge the dinghy towards their yacht, retrieve the oars, and tell them they owe me a beer. The skipper says it's not their dinghy. They presume it has either come loose or been 'borrowed' from the club on the shore, the Royal Australian Navy Sailing Association. But they assure me I'd be welcome to come to the club for a drink.

'Just say you're the man who helped retrieve the dinghy,' the skipper says, a lightness entering his voice.

I have drunk at the RANSA clubhouse before, and I didn't even have to retrieve a dinghy to gain entry. A friend, David Pettett, invited me. David is a club member. We had just competed in a Friday twilight race in his 28-footer, *Pandora*. At least, David had competed; I mostly marvelled. If you want to experience the beauty of not just Sydney but life itself, go twilight sailing on the harbour.

As we sailed away from the clubhouse and out of Rushcutters Bay, a north-easterly puffed far more gently than I was, working the winch and pulling on the sheet. The late afternoon sun turned the water to pewter and the shells of the Opera House into the set of a shadow play. Yachts cut like lasers across the pewter, incising the harbour. At 1800 precisely, the starter's gun popped, and we were off.

I didn't know what the course was. I didn't need to know. I just enjoyed the tilted view, in between working the winch. We avoided a Manly ferry barging through the fleets, and we watched a large cruise ship heading in, which at one point blew its horn quickly five times to warn the pleasure craft to get out of its way. I was amazed by how many boats were on the harbour. If productivity slumps on a Friday afternoon in the city, don't blame the pubs; look to the water. Crowds wash away the cares of the week, some on boats, others along the foreshores. The harbour provides the demarcation between the end of the week and the start of the weekend.

As we wove our way across the harbour, the sun had slunk below the cityscape. The shapes of the CBD buildings and the sails of the yachts ahead of us merged in the wash of the last light. Firm architectural statements shimmered and then darkened, so they looked as though they could be sails; and the sails developed a solidity, their creases ironed out by the twilight. When night arrives, Sydney becomes truly a harbour town, as the delineation between the land and the water fades. It all becomes one.

I had no idea when we finished the race. Except that we did, in a time of one hour, sixteen minutes – apparently. We returned to the RANSA wharf as the water bruised into something dark and mysterious. It was a still evening in the bay. There was no rigging singing and clanging, just the sounds of crews packing up for the night and heading to the clubhouse.

The navy has had a presence on this shore since the 1880s, before the words 'Royal Australian' were attached to it. In colonial days, the New South Wales Navy had a maintenance depot in the bay. During the Second World War, HMAS *Rushcutter*, as it became known, was a recruitment and training centre, and home to some of the RAN's smaller vessels. While the site was handed over to the public in the 1970s, the former drill hall, which looks like a homestead with its second-storey wraparound veranda, remains by the water. And so does RANSA.

The clubhouse is an unpretentious building, with a ramp that leads into a storage area. The bar is housed in a small room, and there are a few tables and chairs in an adjoining area. But on the night I was at the club, everyone headed outside, sitting on plastic chairs, having a drink, and looking at the view to the Bridge, as the lights of North Sydney spattered colour onto the water. A few rowboats and dinghies brought in the last of the sailors from their moorings.

For a facility with the military attached to its name, the club felt very relaxed, almost Rabelaisian, as though it had just turned up and parked itself by the harbour, like some devil-may-care backpacker in a campervan, at the feet of multi-million-dollar apartments and houses on Darling Point. And that feeling only enriched the experience of having a drink at RANSA.

IN RENAMING the coves and bays of Sydney Harbour, the British rarely paid respect to those who were here before them by retaining the Aboriginal words. Instead, many were plastered with the names of those who had 'discovered' or colonised the particular bay in some way. Others were named after some distant personage who had to be honoured. And some bays received something more utilitarian, being named after what they were used for. Rushcutters Bay is one of them. In the swamp at its head, convicts cut reeds for thatching. The bay was also the scene of one of the earliest conflicts between two cultures, as one increasingly encroached on the other. Just a few months after the First Fleet had arrived, two 'rush cutters' were killed by Aboriginal people. Governor Phillip called it 'a very unfortunate circumstance' and noted his doubts that the locals were the aggressors, as the convicts had been seen in one of their canoes. As a result, Phillip later recorded, 'I did not mean to punish any of the natives for killing these people, which it is more than probable they did in their own defence, or in defending their canoes.'

Where there were once rushes and killing in the marshes there is now parkland buttressed by a seawall. But out on the water, just beyond the RANSA club, is a thicket of masts at the marina outside the Cruising Yacht Club of Australia. Money may not grow on trees, but this forest has been grown on money – huge piles of it. Many millions of dollars are berthed in the marina. These are vessels built not just to be stunning in a harbour but to be thrown to the elements. Many of them have competed in the Sydney to Hobart race, considered one of the most demanding yachting events on the globe.

The race was born straight after the Second World War. As the story goes, sailor and maritime artist Jack Earl mentioned he was sailing his yacht to Hobart around Christmas. A couple of others said they would sail down as well, before one of them suggested they make a race of it. When the race began on Boxing Day, 1945, there were nine starters. The man who apparently suggested the race, Royal Navy officer Captain John Illingworth, was the first to Hobart. He completed the 628-nautical-mile voyage in six days, fourteen hours and twenty-two minutes. In 2016, there were eighty-eight starters, and the line honours winner, *Perpetual Loyal*, finished the course in one day, thirteen hours, and thirty-one minutes.

Hobart may hold the promise of glory for a few, but the race's start in Sydney always delivers something spectacular for everyone. More than a million people pack the shores and onto the water each 26 December to witness the fleet setting off. If you're in a kayak, the experience can be both spectacular and scary. Never mind the cricket; my Boxing Day test has been to paddle on the fringes of the race's start lines just to the north-east of Shark Island, without being capsized or run over. What looks like a ballet from the shoreline feels like a chaotic tango when you're part of the water traffic. The water is whipped and whirled as hundreds of vessels jockey for position – and that is just the spectator boats. Historic ferries, sleek cruisers, speedboats, sail boats, gin palace pleasure domes, tall ships, and a few foolhardy kayakers, they're all out on the water. The government department administering water traffic, Roads and Maritime Services, set an area where there is to be no anchoring or 'passive craft'. I presume I'm one of those, but there is nothing passive about paddling near all those boats. We're all kept at bay by the buoys marking the exclusion zone, or perhaps it should be the exclusive zone, given the money and courage required to enter a yacht in this race. Yet I'm still close enough to the competitors to hear the crack of the sails as they scoop up the wind, and to see on the decks the brew of human ambition and toil, as crews will Mother Nature to help take them first out of the harbour, and to not slam them into another yacht.

As the fleet pushes towards the Heads, the choreographed madness recedes into a patchwork of triangular pieces sewn into the sky. The gods of the yachts, the super maxis, seem to almost glide to the sea, while a few of the stragglers are still in the harbour, cross-stitching each other's wakes. Finally, the last couple of sails head out of sight, turning right and heading south. I have sat in my kayak, watching those sails disappear, thinking about the crews, wondering what impels them to do it.

One of those I have watched sail out of the Heads is Wendy Tuck. On Boxing Day 2015, 'Wendo', as she's known, was simultaneously at the start of one race and about halfway through a much bigger one. Wendo was the skipper of a 70-foot yacht, *Da Nang-Viet Nam*. She and her crew of seventeen amateur sailors/adventurers were competing in the Clipper round-the-world race, and the Sydney to Hobart was but one leg, a puddle jump, in their global voyage. Since leaving England in August, *Da Nang-Viet Nam* had already travelled thousands of nautical miles, and her crew had been through so much. But Sydney was the port Wendo had been really looking forward to. She is a Sydney girl, so sailing through the Heads was to be an emotional homecoming.

'We came in at like one o'clock in the morning,' Wendo recalled. Two friends had travelled in their boats to accompany her, then, once inside the Heads she noticed more lights, more boats, more friends, welcoming her.

'Eight boats out there,' she tells me. 'It was really, really cool. I couldn't see my friends' faces, otherwise I would have been really crying!'

As a kid, Wendy Tuck fell in love with the water. She revelled in every opportunity to be on the harbour, as well as heading to the coast to surf. Yet it was only after she returned from years in Europe, backpacking in her 20s, and then working in a travel office, that Wendo realised she could shape her love into a living. In the new century, she changed careers, earning her tickets to be a professional skipper.

'It seemed like a natural progression. I always struggled in offices. This [work on the harbour] is what I was meant to do.'

Wendo has been a sailing instructor, and she has been at the wheel of fast ferries and charter boats, guiding guests, including famous ones, such as Oprah Winfrey.

'The harbour is just a special place,' she says. 'The more you're on it, the more you see.'

Yet Wendo has always wanted to go further out. Before 2015, she had competed in the Sydney to Hobart race eight times. Then came the opportunity to be the first Australian female to skipper a yacht in the Clipper round-the-world race. Knowing that the fourth leg of the race involved competing in the Sydney to Hobart, she told her crew what lay ahead.

'The whole way into Sydney, I was explaining to my crew you've never seen anything like this, the fanfare,' she says.

'Were they surprised by the start of the race, the fanfare?' I ask.

'Yes, but you've got to constantly look around everywhere, to watch out. Your crew want to perform well, but they're distracted.'

Wendo had also made her intentions clear to the other Clipper skippers. *Da Nang-Viet Nam* was going to be first out of the harbour.

'Boys, this is my home town, you're following me for once,' she told them. 'I couldn't believe it, leading them out of the Heads.'

'I guess you don't turn south [out the Heads] that often; it's always a thrill. You don't know what lies ahead.'

For Wendo, what lay ahead was victory. Her yacht was the first of the Clipper fleet across the line in Hobart. Then, while most crews celebrated reaching the finish and began planning for next year's race, *Da Nang-Viet Nam* sailed on through enormous seas and wild storms, surviving a knockdown in the Pacific and thriving in the challenge of the long voyage. Almost a year after leaving England, Wendo returned the yacht and her crew to where they had begun.

Wendy Tuck is one of those extraordinary souls who appreciates the security of a harbour but has the courage to leave all that behind to embrace the life-threatening, life-affirming uncertainty of the sea.

'I love that there is always something going on in the harbour, but I really love the ocean, just its many forms, the vastness of it all,' Wendo muses.

While there are more oceans to sail, more challenges to stare in the face, Wendo's dream lies much closer to home.

'When people ask, "What would you do if you won Lotto?", I answer that I'd buy a house on the water's edge and a tinny, and each day, I'd go out on the harbour and clean rubbish,' she says. 'The cleaning guys do a great job, but I'd do my little piece. It would be like my morning walk.

'Because I've made a living out of the harbour, I'd like to give back to the harbour.'

THE SONGLINES of the points and promontories around this part of the harbour have guided creative types for generations. Perhaps it is because Kings Cross, the city's traditional centre of pleasure in all its incarnations, is just up the hill. So you can place yourself between the devil and the deep blue sea, or at least the harbour. Or perhaps it is because the Art Deco apartments packed along the western edges of Rushcutters Bay and over the headland into Elizabeth Bay offer the best of both worlds; a hint of the northern hemisphere architecturally, but with views that offer the best of Sydney.

For about a decade, David Bowie had an apartment in Elizabeth Bay. The musician lived there sporadically. He particularly loved the harbour outlook. Bowie sold the unit, which he later regretted, as he watched its value climb. During his last tour in Australia in 2004, Bowie mentioned he couldn't believe how much his former property was worth. When a rich rock star is stunned by harbourside real estate prices, you know they must be stratospheric.

Paddling into Elizabeth Bay, I see the apartment block in which Bowie's former neighbour and fellow singer Jeff Duff lives. As well as playing his own songs, Jeff has become well known for his shows paying tribute to Bowie.

Jeff had met Bowie in London in the late 1970s. When he returned to Australia in the late 1980s, Jeff was surprised to find the rock legend living in Elizabeth Bay and sipping coffee in the same café he frequented. Jeff says Bowie once referred to Elizabeth Bay as one of his favourite suburbs on the planet, a sentiment he shares with his musical hero.

For Jeff, Elizabeth Bay is not just his home but an inspiration. He loves to wander down to the jetty outside his home. The jetty is piled with kayaks, and a café has sprouted on its deck. While you can see to the other side of the harbour, Jeff enjoys looking into the water. Even when it is turbid from boats or stormwater, he finds clarity and ideas.

'For my album, *Fragile Spaceman*, I wrote nearly every song while sitting on that jetty,' he mentions. One of the songs is titled, 'Dancing with the Jellyfish'. Jeff called his 2015 album *Elizabeth Bay*. For the cover, Jeff was photographed on the jetty, wearing a sailor's suit, perhaps a reference to his neighbours at the navy's Garden Island base. Not that they disturb him.

'The ship horns become subliminal; you don't notice them,' he says. 'I hear mostly harbour noises, but there are personal trainers [in the park] below my balcony!'

Just near Jeff's little apartment is another connection to Australian music. Boomerang is a Spanish mission-style mansion on expansive grounds behind high walls. On the water's edge there is a mini-Boomerang, a boathouse built in the same style as the mansion, with a long jetty reaching into the bay. Boomerang was built in the 1920s from rhythm and melody. It was the home of Frank Albert, whose family business had imported Boomerang mouth organs before moving into music publishing. The company grew into a powerhouse in media and music production, releasing records by iconic rock bands such as The Easybeats and AC/DC.

I land *Pulbah Raider* at the feet of Boomerang, on a strip of sand below its seawall. A couple of workers are building what looks like a wooden awning along the property's harbour frontage. Apparently it's a splashboard to stop the water curling over the seawall and landing on the lawn, because it kills the grass. It probably also prevents the likes of me peeking at one of Sydney Harbour's best-known homes. Boomerang's perimeter walls serve a purpose other than providing security. Jeff, a keen cricketer, practises his bowling against one of them. That he can play cricket in a little park against a wall that music built is just one reason Jeff Duff can't imagine being anywhere but Elizabeth Bay.

'To me, this place is like my Nirvana,' he says. 'Every time I come back into this area, I just feel at ease and at peace with the world, it's so serene.

'I've lived all around the world, but there's nowhere like this.'

BOOMERANG IS almost modest compared with the property that is perched up the hill, surveying the harbour and all the land that once belonged to it. Elizabeth Bay House was considered the finest house in the colony, taking four years to build from 1835. This two-storey temple to fine living was the home of Alexander Macleay, the Colonial Secretary. The home was built on about 22 hectares of prime bayside land Macleay was granted when he and his family arrived in the colony in 1826. Even back then, when there was not the crush of people along the water's edge, there was controversy that Macleay was given such a lucrative grant, on land that was rapidly increasing in value. The *Sydney Gazette* came to his defence, arguing 'that Gentleman is converting a very small fragment of the most sterile part of the creation into an epitome of the far-famed Eden'.

Almost a decade before building his house, Macleay set about using the land to indulge his passion for gardening. When the Scotsman arrived in the colony, he brought with him plant specimens, including dozens of rose varieties. He also continued to import plants for his garden. He is credited with introducing the jacaranda to Australia, and it's believed one of his daughters may have brought a curse to the landscape when she sailed into Sydney with cuttings of lantana. In all, about 4 hectares of Elizabeth Bay were crafted into a garden.

Macleay's love of the natural world helped shape the house he built. The largest room in Elizabeth Bay House was a library, where he kept natural history specimens in wooden cabinets. He envisaged one day many of these exhibits would be housed in a museum, which would provide 'an essential Service to Science as well as to this Colony'. Macleay's oldest son and nephew inherited the love of natural sciences and history, adding marine specimens to the ever-growing collection. The sum of collecting over two generations ended up forming the core of a museum at the University of Sydney. It is still there, tucked away off the main quadrangle's colonnades, and it is called the Macleay Museum.

Elizabeth Bay House and its grounds attracted many well-known visitors. The Scottish horticulturalist and the man behind Australia's first nursery, Thomas Shepherd, wrote in 1836 how, 'In walking among these lovely trees, you view on the one side an amphitheatre of lofty woods; and on the other you view a large expanse of water with ships, small vessels, and boats, passing up and down the harbour.' The recently arrived artist Conrad Martens painted a watercolour in 1838 of the house shimmering through the foliage.

Macleay's vision splendid didn't last long for him. With the economic downturn in the early 1840s, the grounds shrunk, as allotments were sliced off for sale, and Macleay himself had to move out. But at least the house was saved. What was the private fiefdom of the Macleays is now a public museum, displaying how the fortunate few lived in colonial Sydney.

For a time, Elizabeth Bay House was cut up into flats and was a cauldron of creativity. The author C.J. Koch was a resident. He noted in his novel *The Doubleman* that many of the local apartment blocks had been built in the Jazz Age, 'one of the last periods to allow whimsy and story-book fancy into the design of large buildings'. Not only were many of the apartments built in another time, the suburb had the style of another place. Elizabeth Bay, the narrator observed in *The Doubleman*, was as 'inviting as a dream of pre-war Hollywood, from which it took its style'.

To the poet and journalist Kenneth Slessor, the suburb's attraction lay much closer to home. Slessor was the bard of Elizabeth Bay. Having spent his younger years observing the harbour from a room in Kings Cross, Slessor had gravitated towards what besotted him. He lived in a flat close to the water's edge in the bay. He could throw a line of thought out his window and reel in ideas and images.

Slessor was not a sailor, but he could imagine being one. And then, through his words, he invites all of us to imagine being one. He sails us back in time, to the days of Captain Cook and the other great masters and commanders, who, even to their crew, seemed like magicians under sheets of canvas:

> *Daemons in periwigs, doling magic out,*
> *Who read fair alphabets in stars*
> *Where humbler men found but a mess of sparks.*

And Slessor often sails us to the edges, where time is running out and life is ebbing away, or has gone. That journey is perhaps most moving in 'Five Bells'. The poem is an elegy for a friend who was drowned in Sydney Harbour, after falling overboard from a ferry. In 'Five Bells', Slessor asks:

> *Where have you gone? The tide is over you,*
> *The turn of midnight water's over you,*
> *As Time is over you, and mystery,*
> *And memory, the flood that does not flow.*

Yet as the poem goes on, time and tide, mystery and memory, flow over all of us, as a ship's bell chimes the hours and half-hours passing. It could be such a depressing read, leaving us asking of our own life, 'Where have you gone?', but for the beauty in the final stanza. The poet places himself by the window, looking out into the dark at 'waves with diamond quills and combs of light' and 'Harbour-buoys/Tossing their fireballs wearily each to each'. And he tries to hear his friend's voice but there are only the sounds of the harbour. And those five bells.

I imagine Kenneth Slessor sitting at his Elizabeth Bay window, listening, watching, fishing for ideas. Then, after a lot of preparation, he feeds us what he has caught. Of all the things that have been hooked in Sydney Harbour, none is more satisfying than a Kenneth Slessor poem. And no matter how much of it you consume, you have no concerns of contaminants.

ON THE western side of Elizabeth Bay, I pass a harbour buoy that isn't so much tossing fireballs wearily, in a Slessor sense, but is swaying languidly as the north-easterly takes its first few breaths for the afternoon. The buoy is a warning that I'm approaching 'Naval Waters' – as if the two warships moored ahead of me aren't indication enough.

The 'naval waters' snap to attention against the eastern seawall of Garden Island. The 'island' reference is out of deference to history rather than reality; it is now tethered to the mainland and re-formed into one long peninsula. And from the water, there's no sign of a garden. Instead, with its clock tower, office buildings, historic storehouses and barracks, and huge workshops, it looks like a self-contained harbour town. Which is what it is, really, being the navy's main Sydney base, or Fleet Base East, as those in uniform call it.

In the early colonial years, the island looked unimpressive to some new arrivals, especially those who had been sent here as punishment. In the 19th century novel *Ralph Rashleigh*, purportedly written by convict James Tucker, the main

the twenty-one killed on the barracks ship berthed off the island when it was sunk by a Japanese midget submarine's torpedo the year before. The navy migrated beyond the disappearing island. With a land bridge now established, *Kuttabul* crept up the hill to consume a few historic mansions on Potts Point. Grand gardens that once swept down to the waterfront were reduced to a few walls and stone stairways. The naval past is sprinkled around the base, and it is preserved and on display in a heritage centre on the northern tip of Garden Island.

Sitting forlornly off the north-eastern shore of Garden Island is the decommissioned HMAS *Sydney* IV. This was her home base for more than thirty years. And now it's her retirement home, until her graveyard is determined. I feel for her, languishing in the section of water where *Kuttabul* was sunk, as she waits for the same fate, even if the means is less violent. I also feel for her, because she and I have a past. A brief but enjoyable one. For me, at least.

Just a few years earlier, on 4 October 2013, *Sydney* was the pride of the fleet, as she led seven RAN ships into the harbour, as part of an International Fleet Review. The seven RAN ships were sailing in history's wake.

On 4 October 1913, the young RAN's fleet of warships entered Sydney Harbour for the first time. The flagship then was HMAS *Australia*, but the first *Sydney* was in the line. Hundreds of thousands of Sydneysiders packed along the shores, and the Minister for Defence, Senator Edward Millen, was excited enough to declare, 'Since Captain Cook's arrival, no more memorable event has happened than the advent of the Australian fleet. As the former marked the birth of Australia, so the latter announces its coming of age.' One hundred years on, the navy commemorated that 'coming of age' with the International Fleet Review, involving ships from seventeen nations. The re-enactment of the fleet entering the harbour for the first time was a highlight. I had the great fortune to be on HMAS *Sydney* as a reporter.

A fleet of more than twenty warships, both RAN and foreign vessels, had sailed up from the navy's base at Jervis Bay, bouncing through wind-churned waves under a platinum sky. Then, as the sun sneaked above the horizon on 4 October, *Sydney* led the RAN ships towards the Heads. I was standing on *Sydney*'s port side. I spent a good deal of time looking behind, staring at the ships strung across the sea to the north. It was a formidable sight. But as we slid between the Heads, I looked all around, trying to pull every direction and every sight into the one moment. For, in this moment, the ship was scratching its own signature, making history, on the harbour's surface. Of course, the water would soon forget *Sydney* had ever been here. But I would never forget. I recall saying to myself, just out of sheer wonderment, 'Well, I'm on *Sydney* entering Sydney.'

A flotilla of pleasure craft darted around the ships like excited kids. As the ship rounded Bradleys Head, the air burst with a gun salute. Everyone on board was beaming, from the sailors lining the decks to the invited guests, including the then Premier Barry O'Farrell. I was so caught in the moment, I offered to take the Premier kayaking on the harbour some time. He never did take up that offer.

Sydney was a platform for celebration the following night at the International Fleet Review Spectacular. In other words, a party with fireworks. Sydneysiders have long been brilliant at welcoming fleets by throwing a light-filled party. When the

United States' Great White Fleet arrived in 1908, illuminations were installed on Fort Denison, and, according to the *Sydney Morning Herald*'s report, the water was a fairyland. When the RAN fleet was first in the harbour in 1913, the ships were lit up at night, while the city celebrated. For the 2013 event, the spectacular organisers promised a show the likes of which had not been seen on the harbour before. That promise ensured huge crowds around the harbour's edges. I was on *Sydney*, which was moored just east of the Harbour Bridge and off the Opera House. So it was perhaps the best position on the harbour to experience the spectacular. Above and around me were the choreographed vision, sound and fury of fireworks, light shows and projections onto the Opera House's shells and the Harbour Bridge's pylons, telling the story of the RAN and how it helped build a nation. Not that I was following the story; I was just immersed in the shock-and-awe party. Actually, I'm not sure if many would have been enriched with a greater knowledge of the RAN's history because of the spectacular, but I reckon everyone would have left, saying, 'That navy knows how to throw a great party'.

So as I paddle past her at Garden Island, I not only feel for *Sydney*, I thank her for providing me with an extraordinary harbour experience in 2013.

IF THE term 'working harbour' has drifted away from most promontories and coves in Sydney, it sticks on Garden Island. Its most prominent symbol of heavy work, the enormous hammerhead crane that was on the northern tip, has been dismantled, removing yet another piece of the harbour's industrial heritage. But there is still incessant activity along the edges, and on the water. As I round the peninsula into Woolloomooloo Bay, the frigate HMAS *Perth* is being shunted and pulled by tugs into the main channel. Other warships are berthed along the wharves. When the ships leave for long deployments from here, loved ones, along with politicians and the media, crowd onto the wharves, and passers-by stop and stare through the fence. When a naval base is this close to the heart of the city, 'bon voyage' becomes a public statement. It is part of the vocabulary of Sydney life.

The navy is busy not just on the surface around Garden Island; its divers could be somewhere below my kayak, for all I know.

Able Seaman Paul de Gelder was under the water just around here on 11 February 2009.

As a member of the RAN's Clearance Diving Team 1, Paul's workplace was where very few are allowed to go, beneath the warships. Which means Paul was familiar with an aspect of the harbour that is rarely seen. Not that we would want to, or even could, see through the plumes of silt.

'It was horrible!' Paul says. 'We didn't work in the beautiful parts of the harbour. The harbour floor under the warships is mud, and I don't know how deep the mud is.' When he was working under the decommissioned destroyer HMAS *Vampire*, on display at the Australian National Maritime Museum in Darling Harbour, he estimated the mud would have been at least up to his neck. For all the different characteristics of the harbour on the surface, Paul says, under the water, it is 'mud, silt, and sand'.

What he rarely saw through the gloom were sharks. He was wary of them, 'but I still had a job to do'.

On that February morning in 2009, Paul and his fellow divers were testing new equipment and involved in counter-terrorism training off Garden Island. Paul was on the surface when he felt a whack on his leg, but it didn't hurt. He looked under the water to see the cold eyes of a bull shark, its mouth open and grabbing his leg. Once it occurred to Paul the near-impossible was happening to him, he began fighting for his life. Only he couldn't use his right arm. He realised the shark had bitten into his hand as well. So he fought as much as he could with his left hand, trying to poke the shark in the eye and punch its snout.

The shark shook Paul and dragged him under. Paul kept fighting but he recalls thinking, 'I'm not going to get out of this.'

'Calm came over me, I had no regrets.'

Suddenly the shark was gone. Paul was released. 'It all happens in the blink of an eye,' he says of the attack.

Then came the rush to save Paul de Gelder. He had sustained dreadful injuries. Surgeons amputated his right hand and right leg. Paul spent about two months in hospital. After confronting how his body had been changed, Paul set about changing his life. But first he did as he had done before the attack. He entered the water.

'After the attack, I spent a lot of time snorkelling,' Paul says. 'I had no PTSD, no flashbacks, none of that.'

The experience gave him new perspective, including a desire to learn more about sharks, and about himself.

'It made me appreciate sharks more, because I was forced into learning more about them,' he says. 'Before then, I thought they should all be killed. But then I learnt more about their place in the ecosystem.

'It's all about knowledge.'

I ask Paul what knowledge he has acquired since, which, had he known, he would have applied in that moment of being attacked. Nothing, he replies. He would do nothing different.

'There's nothing I could do. You can't imagine, you can't understand what it's like, to be stuck in the jaws of a 300-plus-kilogram animal. You are totally at its whim.'

Paul has remained in the Naval Reserve as a diver. He has also been determined to share his knowledge and experience, writing a book, speaking at events, and making documentaries about sharks. On one filming expedition in Tahiti, he learnt to hand-feed the very species of shark that had bitten him.

'If I can turn a terrible situation into something beautiful, that's good,' he explains.

It had been almost half a century since the last fatal shark attack in Sydney Harbour, and Paul's experience was the first time a navy diver had been mauled. The city reacted with horror. The attack brought to the surface the fears that lie barely under the water whenever any of us leaves behind the certainty of land and sinks into the beautiful, eerie domain that is the harbour. It has reminded us that when we are in the water, we are in another world, one that is both wondrous and home to dangerous creatures. Yet Paul counters that shark attacks have been very rare in Sydney Harbour.

'Isn't that an indication of how little interest we are to them?' he says. 'You've got to expect an attack, but we humans think we own everything.'

WOOLLOOMOOLOO BAY is wide and deep enough to embrace warships, including the navy's new massive amphibious assault vessels, HMAS *Canberra* and HMAS *Adelaide*, which are berthed, bow to stern, along Garden Island's western shore. Yet the bay is narrow enough to provide me with one of those head-shaking harbour juxtapositions as I paddle along it. On the left are the grey metal cliffs that are the hulls of the amphibious assault ships, and beyond them, plotting the peninsula, is the rigidity and order of military life. On the right shore is the Andrew (Boy) Charlton Pool, with people sunbathing on its deck, a little platform of relaxation. So the inhabitants of these two worlds, the hedonists and the sailors, can wave at each other across the water.

People have been bathing along the shore here for thousands of years. But defined baths, with the dubious enticement of 'hot and cold seawater', were built in the 1830s. There were separate areas for 'gentlemen' and 'ladies'. The first competitive swimming races in the colony were apparently held in the gentlemen's baths in 1846, so it seems fitting that the pool now on the site is named after the 1920s Olympic swimmer Andrew (Boy) Charlton. He used to plough up and down one of the earlier incarnations of the baths in the bay.

With its cascade of vowels and consonants, the very name 'Woolloomooloo' sounds like water flowing. A number of Aboriginal words have been cited as the possible inspiration for the name of the bay and suburb behind it, but one meaning could be 'place of plenty'. By the late 19th century, Woolloomooloo was a place of plenty, and its bay held more than water. It was the site of a major sewage outlet, as Sydney put the loo into Woolloomooloo. The fish markets were also on the shore for about thirty years.

Local fish also helped in the shaping of yachts. In 1858, Dan Sheehy, a boatbuilder working on the harbour's edge in

Woolloomooloo built a yacht, *Australia*, based on his studies of a mackerel he had caught in the bay. Sheehy's transposition of the lines of the dissected fish into the design of his boat must have worked, for *Australia* was a champion racer and influenced yacht designs around the world.

The bay's deep water attracted ships for mooring. But it needed facilities for berthing. So its edges were progressively girdled in wharves, and its head was dredged and buttressed with a semi-circular wharf. Then the bay's head was effectively split in two by a long finger wharf. From the 19th century well into the next, the bay helped push Australian produce, particularly wool, out into the world on commercial ships. From here, an infant nation's youth sailed away, to fight in distant conflicts. And they returned to here, those who survived. After the Second World War, the bay accepted many more arrivals escaping from conflict-scarred lands. The finger wharf became a major passenger terminal.

These days, there are still large vessels berthed outside the wharf, but many of them are pleasure cruisers. For the wharf is no longer a place for people to depart from or arrive at; it is for those who have arrived. What was slowly rotting into the bay in the later years of the 20th century was reimagined into a polished enclave of the well-off. Along the wharf there are a boutique hotel, restaurants and luxury apartments. At the time of the wharf's conversion, the journalist and author David Marr noted that developments such as this marked a new kind of real estate, subdividing the sea. Still, some seriously rich and famous people have put down their roots, along with great wads of cash, on top of the water. The Oscar-winning actor Russell Crowe has an apartment at the end of the wharf. In early 2017, it was reported that Crowe said 'no' to an offer of $25 million for his apartment, which includes a 35-metre marina berth. This place is not exactly a get-away-from-it-all abode for a movie star. Presumably Crowe has uninterrupted views of the hive that is the naval base and, if he were to look down, he could see a kayaker gawking up at his place.

Wedged between two massive berthed cruisers, I realise I could probably paddle right under the wharf. I can even see the other side. But that seems like a short journey into deep trouble, and it's gloomy under there. Instead, I paddle out of the bay, sticking close to the hedonists' shoreline, until I'm back in the main harbour, heading for Fort Denison.

WITH ITS sandstone walls and Martello tower, Fort Denison gives the impression that it owns the middle of the harbour, and it belongs here. Yet that isn't how John Dunmore Lang, the impassioned Scottish-born clergyman, writer and politician, saw it. For he remembered what was there before a fort.

'There was a remarkable rock or islet,' he wrote in 1875. 'A vast mass of grey weather-beaten rock, rising perpendicularly in a slender column to an elevation of seventy-five feet from the deep water.'

When that rock was replaced by a mass of stones, John Dunmore Lang believed the work of God was destroyed by the folly of man.

'I can never pass the island even yet without feeling indignant at the heartless deed which . . . can never be remedied,' he thundered.

The British had defaced the 'remarkable rock' with heartless deeds soon after they arrived. Convicts who had committed some minor misdemeanour were banished to 'Rock Island', as it was called, with nothing but bread and water, which, according to First Fleeter Jacob Nagle, was why it came to be known as Pinchgut. To give a gruesome warning to all sailing into the harbour, in 1796, the body of a murderer, Francis Morgan, was hanged from a gibbet until it was nothing but bones swinging in the breeze. According to the colony's Deputy Judge-Advocate David Collins, the skeleton was far more terrifying to the Aboriginal people, who stayed away from the island they called Mat-te-wan-ye.

It is not skeletons or ghosts that repel me from Fort Denison, but its sea-level armour of oysters on the rocks. That, and the wash of the passing ferries. I have nowhere to land. So Lieutenant Colonel George Barney's creation has succeeded in warding off at least one vessel. For that is why the fort was built. It is the most conspicuous symbol in the harbour of a city's fear that it was open to attack.

On a map he drew within months of arriving in the colony at the end of 1835, Barney had identified Pinchgut as a place waiting to be fortified. But he, and everyone else, would have to wait for years. The fort would be built on not just rock but deception. To overcome budgetary constraints in the early stages of the project, Governor Gipps advised Barney to do some creative accounting to step around London, and, by the early 1840s, the Royal Engineer had launched into the work before funding had been approved. If Barney took a bulldozing approach to the bean-counters back in England, it was gentle compared with what he did to the island. He blew its head off, flattening the rock until it was close to the waterline.

Work stalled when the focus of protecting Sydney shifted from the inner harbour to closer to the Heads. When a new

Governor, Sir William Denison, arrived in 1855, he soon reversed that approach. With England embroiled in the Crimean War, concerns that a Russian fleet could sail into the harbour also helped resuscitate the project. Denison declared the anchorage in front of the town needed protecting, so Barney was back on the island. Perhaps in gratitude, as his fort took shape on the pancake rock, the engineer reckoned it deserved a better name than Pinchgut. And so 'Fort Denison' came to be. The project was finally completed in 1862, almost a quarter of a century after it began.

The fort was built for action. Behind its 4-metre thick walls, the Martello tower housed three large guns, and below in the barracks were up to twenty-five Royal Artillerymen and their families. But the fort didn't really see any action, and from 1881, its role changed, offering protection to shipping and a place to mark time and tides.

The island had a navigation light, which was initially fuelled with whale oil. But when the fog whorled around the fort and erased any hope of clear lines of sight, the light keeper would rhythmically strike a brass gong.

There is no need for a gong's bass rumble the day that I, along with a bunch of tourists, step off a ferry onto the island. It is a flawless Sydney afternoon. Yet in the former barracks are reminders of the most indefatigable of enemies for the fort's occupants: the weather. The remains of old fireplaces are in several rooms, but attempts to drive out the chill must have been futile on winter nights. And yet caretakers and their families loved living here, describing an idyllic island life, of prising oysters the size of saucers off the rocks and watching penguins snoozing in the sun.

Fort Denison remains a wonderful place to view the vignettes of harbour life. Through the embrasures cut into the parapets, I watch sailing boats lean against the wind. I can hear the rhythmic thump of ferry engines mixed with the slap of waves against the rocks. On the island's south-western tip is the cast bronze cannon that used to be fired each afternoon at one o'clock so ships could check their chronometers for accuracy. The gun was silenced during the Second World War, so as not to terrify the locals, but then the daily bang returned to the harbour. On this day, there is no blast; a guide tells me the gun needs to be restored. For now, the cannon at least looks as though it is guarding the island, with its barrel pointing roughly towards the Opera House, as if the greatest threat now comes not from the Heads, but from high culture.

Perhaps the island's greatest threat is gleaned from the tidal measurements taken at the fort. According to a panel displayed near a gauge, studies indicate that sea levels are increasingly rising, and, going by higher predictions, by the year 2100 the forecourt of Fort Denison may be under water by as much as 45 centimetres up to fifty times a year. Looking at the glass as half full, at least that would allow me to arrive on the island by kayak.

PRODDING THE water between Fort Denison and the southern shore is a scaly-backed promontory with a slab of rocks on its headland known as Mrs Macquarie's Chair. When Lachlan Macquarie was Governor, his wife Elizabeth would journey the few kilometres from the clatter and hard scrabble of Sydney town, through the area set aside as a public domain and along the promontory to sit at its tip and watch the harbour. Elizabeth Macquarie has been credited with planning paths and carriage roads through the bush in the Domain. Macquarie had convicts gouge a seat out of the sandstone for her. Yet, as Louisa Anne Meredith observed in her memoir of life in Sydney in the 1840s, the chair was more like a throne, from which one could observe the 'noble estuary with countless bays and inlets, pretty villas and cottages, and dainty little islands, all bright and clear and sunny'. The 'chair' and the attraction to sit at the headland remain. As I can see while paddling the 400 metres across the water from Fort Denison, the memory of Mrs Macquarie has a lot of company these days, with hordes of tourists milling about, gazing out and photographing the harbour. Most eyes and lenses are fixed to the west, towards the view that frames 'Sydney' in one shot – the Bridge and the Opera House.

In recent years, opera has drifted out of the House and across the bay. Each summer, production crews return like migratory birds to a stretch known as Fleet Steps and assemble a massive open-air stage over the waters of Farm Cove and erect seating for 3000 on the shore in preparation for a short season of opera on the harbour.

From the water, the pop-up venue is an extraordinary construction, tucked into the slope yet conspicuous by its scale – and the props. When I paddle into the cove, the stage has been set for a production of *Turandot*. There's a tower that looks like a spaceship, and on each side of the stage is a massive dragon's head, scowling at the seating. A sign facing the water warns, 'Danger. Fireworks. Keep Away.' I heed the sign's advice and enter the venue the conventional way, on foot. I pass under the canopy of Port Jackson figs and the arch of a red pagoda into the fabricated wonderland to meet Louisa Robertson. She is the Executive Producer of Handa Opera on Sydney Harbour.

Louisa has been involved in outdoor events since 2000, but for her, this is 'number one, in terms of scale, complexity and excitement'. She was on board for the first season of opera on the harbour in 2013 and has been helping realise these annual productions since.

Long before a note is sung, a stack of work is done on the shore, on the surface, and below it. Sixteen pylons, including nine to support the stage, have been drilled into the harbour bed. The rear pylons are in 12 metres of water. Mooring lines are also used to hold the floating stage in place. A lot of the major components have been barged in, because, Louisa says, it's simpler than having a procession of trucks. Still, the sight of a dragon's head gliding down the harbour amid the ferries and yachts must have been something.

From the trees' canopy have come more challenges. Cockatoos. The birds behaved like philistines, even eating the giant prop of Nefertiti's head during the production of *Aida* in 2015. To ward off the birds that ate opera, everything from chilli oil to fake snakes have been tried, but Louisa says the most effective line of defence has been 'a rather large water gun'.

Louisa guides me from the foreshore onto a gangway, as though we are boarding a ship. Which in a sense we are. We walk past a couple of rescue boards. Lifesavers are on duty during the production. No audience member has ever had to be plucked from the harbour, but a construction worker had to be fished out. The walkway bobs ever so slightly as we walk towards the stage looming over us.

'Sometimes you feel like you've got sea legs when you're coming off the stage,' Louisa smiles. She explains this production took twenty-two days to set up, and for any given performance, there may be up to 300 workers. Seventy of those are performers, but so many more are never seen. For the stage is like an iceberg; a lot is going on under the stage, just above the waterline.

We enter the 'stage underworld'. A village of shipping containers has been assembled for use as dressing rooms and technical areas. The underworld is also constructed from scaffolding and netting, to ensure no one or nothing tumbles into the harbour. You can hear the water below sloshing and bouncing off the seawall, and above is the music. However, that is largely created down here by fifty-five musicians in their own area. The conductor's image is projected onto a screen near the stage, so the singers can see their cues.

I feel like Orpheus – only without the legendary musician's ability – ascending from the underworld when we step onto the raked stage. It is an awesome sight, looking out across the stage dipping away to the rows of seats on the slope. Technicians are scurrying about, preparing for the night's performance, following leads, checking bits and pieces of technology in the sound and lighting towers, all to celebrate the power and beauty of the human voice.

'I often sit out here and look around. It's a great place to work,' smiles Louisa, a point of calm in the storm of activity. Although 'storm' is a word perhaps best not used at an outdoor venue. Never mind children and animals, Mother Nature must be a horror to work with, especially when you are next to, or on, the water.

'People say to me, "You must stress about the weather", but I don't,' Louisa shrugs. 'It is what it is. I have five [weather] apps on my phone, and I look at them in the morning, but I don't look at them again until three or four o'clock.'

She says only a handful of performances have been cancelled due to wet weather. Costumes have been modified to be rain-resistant, and there are a couple of pop-up drying rooms under the stage. The performers are also rain-resistant.

'I don't recall any principals being divas about the rain,' Louisa says.

But it could happen the night I attend the opera. The setting is dramatic, and not only because of what is on the stage. At twilight, clouds cluster like an evil chorus, the water turns wine dark and, as though ordered by the stage director, the rain falls just as the performance begins. A few flying foxes screech and glide back to the Port Jackson figs behind us.

On stage, a character sings about the moon kissing your face, but it's the rain kissing ours. Actually, it's slapping our faces. Along with the rain comes the wind. Louisa had mentioned there is a wind threshold of 60 kilometres an hour for performances. While it is nowhere near that, the gusts are adding to the theatricality. The stage flags are flapping like a mob of angry seagulls, and the costumes are fluttering wildly. Later in the performance, as the rain intensifies, the female dancers look as though they are performing synchronised mopping, as their long cuffs swish across the stage. It is most certainly a rain dance.

As audience members toss on plastic ponchos and squint determinedly, I wonder how the performers are coping up there, particularly the principal singers.

'If they [the audience] can sit there in the rain, then I can stand there and sing,' Arnold Rawls tells me a few days later.

'But being on a raked stage, and if it's pouring with rain, I have to try and not fall. It's treacherous!'

Arnold is from Louisiana. He has an easy-going lilt in his voice when he talks. The tenor has sung in the great opera houses around the world, including the one just across the water from here. For this production of *Turandot*, Arnold has been cast as Calaf, which means he sings *Nessun dorma*, the aria that has soared out of concert halls and into the universal soundtrack of, 'Oh, I know that!' Audiences just wait for the high notes, so they can release their voices in appreciation. In this production, the appreciation erupts into a roar, when fireworks bloom over the harbour as Arnold holds that final note. He jokes the fireworks take some of the pressure off him when he performs *Nessun dorma*, because, 'I get applause – no matter what!'

The other great distraction, or performer, is the harbour itself. The audience faces not just the stage but the view, which includes the Opera House. Yet that backdrop can accentuate the magic of the experience. During *Nessun dorma*, as the rain falls, the strings swell and Calaf cries out his desire for Turandot, I watch a ferry glide by, its lights glowing like a dream. The arch of the Bridge looks like a tie connecting two notes, two shores, notating the melody that is Sydney Harbour. It is a beautiful counterpoint for what is being sung on stage.

Arnold Rawls doesn't feel as though he is competing with the harbour for the audience's attention.

'Many of them are first-time opera goers, and they're going to see a spectacular stage, with the Opera House, the Bridge, the harbour in the background. Many aren't saying, "I'm going to hear the music of Puccini", they don't care less about that, but this is a great introduction to opera, to the art form.'

Occasionally, when he's on the side of the stage, Arnold himself turns around to see what the audience can. He tells me that the night before, he glanced behind, then whispered to two of his co-performers who were also waiting to go on, 'Look at this'.

'A big cruise ship was going past, and there's the Opera House,' he recounts. 'It made me almost teary eyed. You can't dream of a better view.'

Yet *Turandot* turns into Cinderella. When the season ends, the venue is dismantled, at least for another year. Louisa says the dismantling and bumping out takes about thirteen days. Where there was a stage, there is once more water. That transformation holds echoes of another cultural venue that was built up the hill in the Botanic Garden, only for it to disappear, but far more dramatically and with a sense of finality.

The Garden Palace was a grand vision, designed as a centrepiece of the Sydney International Exhibition in 1879 and 1880. Considered the greatest show on earth, this was the first time an international exhibition had been hosted by a British colony. The Garden Palace was intended to show how far Sydney had come in a century, and yet for anyone who had travelled from the other side of the globe and sailed into the harbour, the building on the hill would have looked reassuringly familiar, like something out of the Renaissance, only eucalypt-scented. The *Sydney Morning Herald* was more prosaic, believing it was reminiscent of the 'fabled palace of Aladdin in the *Arabian Nights*'. The building had a massive central dome, which was the sixth largest in the world. In a pattern that would become familiar to Sydneysiders, before it was built, the Garden Palace stoked controversy, with objections to the design ranging from it blocking people's views to concerns about it leading to traffic congestion. But once it was built, and the world cooed in admiration, Sydneysiders felt a flush of pride in the Garden Palace, including the harbour views it offered. Those views, according to the exhibition catalogue, were 'fairy-like and bewildering . . . for picturesqueness and diversity there are probably few landscapes like it in the world'.

About a million visitors attended the exhibition in its seven-month season, an extraordinary number in a city of 200,000. The newspapers were filled with laudatory prose, and, for a couple of years afterwards, the building became a centre of cultural life in the colony, housing museums and galleries and hosting concerts. It also held government offices filled with plans and blueprints for developing the colony.

But it would all come crashing down. In September 1882, the Garden Palace was consumed by fire.

'An immense flame leapt into the sky, volumes of black smoke rolled up, and with a crash like a peal of thunder the mighty dome fell in,' the *Sydney Morning Herald* reported. The building and its irreplaceable contents were destroyed.

The newspaper noted the blaze was a 'splendid spectacle' from the harbour, with crowds on boats watching from Farm Cove. Yet there was a typically Sydney silver lining to this disaster: 'By 9 o'clock all was over, the residences in Macquarie-street had their view of the harbour restored to them . . .' When the domed vision burnt to the ground, the ruins were cleared and it was landscaped to become part of the Botanic Garden.

PLANTS FROM around the world have flourished for the best part of two centuries in the Royal Botanic Garden. But it was here at the head of the cove that the first British arrivals tried to tease some food out of the thin soil. The livestock loaded off the ships grazed on the slope, and Arthur Phillip had about 4 hectares planted with corn. The indent in the harbour became known as Farm Cove. While the name remained, Phillip quickly transferred his hopes for cultivating food for the infant colony up Parramatta River.

Phillip, or at least his image, remains above Farm Cove. A large statue of him stands on a pedestal in the south-west corner of the Botanic Garden, with his cast eyes gazing over the failed farming land to the harbour that made his reputation. After less than five years in the colony, Phillip returned to England, where he died in 1814. His remains are in a small church in the village of Bathampton. But Australian lawyer and author Geoffrey Robertson believes Phillip should be buried here in the Botanic Garden. Geoffrey has enormous respect for Phillip, calling him 'the first and the finest white Australian' and, because of the founding Governor's insistence that there could be no slaves in the colony, considers him as 'truly our Thomas Jefferson'. What's more, Geoffrey told me, Phillip, more than anyone else, had made the First Fleet's voyage work, which at the time was like going to the moon. One spring afternoon in 2014, while filming a documentary on Arthur Phillip, I was walking with Geoffrey across the garden's lawns, as he explained why it was far more appropriate that Phillip's remains be brought 'home'. Geoffrey argued that Sydney was where Phillip had made his mark and had given his greatest service, and this was where he would be appropriately remembered. So Geoffrey Robertson held a dream of 'repatriation' for Phillip. Yet that very word, let alone the notion of digging up Phillip's remains in Bathampton and reburying them in Sydney, incensed other Phillipophiles. Sir Roger Carrick, the former British High Commissioner to Australia, told me the term 'repatriation' was utterly inappropriate, that Phillip was never an Australian, and, as a Brit, he was buried where he wanted to be. Geoffrey Robertson's dream remains unfulfilled, Arthur Phillip remains where he is, and in the Royal Botanic Garden he has a classical-meets-surreal statue as his memorial – that, and the views of the harbour he sailed into and changed forever more.

This ground was acknowledged as more suited to feeding the soul than stomachs in 1816, when Governor Lachlan Macquarie set aside about 27 hectares for a botanic garden. Two hundred years later, following the curve of its long seawall, I can see that the garden, more than ever, remains an oasis, no longer on the fringe of town, but in the heart of the city. Office workers have unshackled themselves from laptops for an hour to jog around the foreshore, eat their lunch in the shade of trees, or to hide from routine amid the profusion of plants.

Behind the trees, standing upright in its rarefied position above Bennelong Point, is Government House. Its exterior may be Sydney sandstone, but its look is of another place and time. It looks fit for royalty. The architect was Edward Blore, who had worked on Buckingham Palace and whose resume would go on to include Windsor Castle. So he was well qualified to create a building that took off the rough colonial edges, smoothed the ancient Sydney stone, and spoke to all who gazed upon it in modulated tones. This Gothic revivalist building was to replace the more modest Government House that had been constructed in Phillip's day, a little further west down the hill near Sydney Cove. A new Government House, the *Sydney Illustrated* declared in 1843, meant those who expected to see in Sydney a prison instead were greeted with a palace, and, what's more, it helped create a city where any Englishman would have felt at home. And it was home for a string of Englishmen. The first governor to move into the new residence was Sir George Gipps in 1845. The vice-regal role remains, and Government House is the home and office of the New South Wales Governor. In most cities, a castellated and turreted home by the harbour, owning the high point above the Botanic Garden, would be a focal point. Yet in Sydney, this house is overshadowed by its neighbour.

THE SYDNEY Opera House is one of those handful of structures around the world that is so recognisable, and so iconic, it defines an entire city in people's minds. Yet it is a building that defies definition. When people look at it, they see sails, waves, shells on a beach, a flock of birds, nuns scurrying to church. It is at once a building that evokes many things but is incomparable. It all depends on whose eyes you are viewing the Sydney Opera House through. Which is why I want to see the Opera House through the eyes of Mika Utzon Popov. When he looks at the Sydney Opera House, he sees family.

Mika is a grandson of Jørn Utzon, the man who conceived the Opera House. He is the son of renowned architect Alex Popov and internationally recognised artist and Jørn's daughter, Lin Utzon. Mika himself is an artist, designer and sculptor. Mika was born in his mother's native Denmark, he attended art school in Sydney and now lives and creates on the Northern Beaches. He is a beautiful, gentle soul, kind of like the mood the harbour projects on the day we paddle from the North Shore to Farm Cove.

Mika's gentleness comes out in his face, which is enviously youthful, even though it is dressed with a greying beard. His face is made younger by the large glasses he is wearing, accentuating his big eyes that observe and absorb. And Mika is always looking to create. Mika is to paddle my wife's lolly pink kayak, but, before we set off, he swaps over the hatch covers. My turquoise kayak looks as though it has been kissed. His looks as though it has developed an infection.

'That's more artistic,' he declares.

As we paddle out of Careening Cove, he notes how green Sydney looks from the water.

'Even in a big city, I feel like we're here on nature's premises, not the other way around, like in Europe,' Mika muses. 'I reckon if we let it, within a decade, nature would take back the city.'

When he was at art school, Mika loved commuting on the ferries, especially at night. The city from the harbour at night, he says, 'is not so solid, it's more ephemeral'. Halfway across the harbour, just near Fort Denison, we stop and take in the long view of what his grandfather created.

'It's a great angle to see it from,' says Mika. 'You can appreciate the three dimensionality of it, the way shapes seem to shift as we do.' He also points out the Opera House's red granite-faced platform, which Jørn Utzon envisioned as an anchor for the soaring roofs. Mika says because of that base, even without the shells, it would be a substantial and impressive building.

We kayak into Farm Cove and watch the play of the sun on the ceramic-tiled shells. The effect is just as the building's creator intended – dazzling. Mika points out how a couple of the roofs are glowing in the light, while others are in shadow, and how they speak to each other. The smaller shells reflect light onto the two larger shells, illuminating them. The sum of the parts is spectacular. In our view from the middle of the bay, the Bridge sits behind the Opera House. But Mika sees them as soulmates. He can't imagine one without the other now.

'The Bridge provides a beautiful perspective,' he murmurs.

We paddle closer and further to the north, until the Opera House's great petrified waves are cresting over us.

'I've never been this close to it before,' Mika mutters, with his head tilted back.

'I've seen it from the ferry in the past, of course, but the scale of it is very different from the base of the platform. It's like looking up at a giant ship.'

Mika points to the Opera House's base just above us and says of his grandfather, 'He would have stood at that level.'

When he drew the initial concept for the Opera House in 1956, Jørn Utzon had never seen Sydney. But he understood, and loved, water. Utzon lived by it in Denmark and enjoyed sailing. Yet a feeling for water was not enough; Utzon studied naval charts of Sydney Harbour, and he looked at films and photos of the sandstone-stubbled topography, to determine how to create something that would stand out yet belong in the environment. Utzon submitted his ideas, along with more than 230 other entries from around the world, in a design competition staged by the New South Wales Government. The Dane's proposal didn't get far until one of the overseas judges, who viewed the entries with fresh eyes, pointed to Utzon's drawings and declared, 'Gentlemen, here is your Opera House'.

Utzon's design was announced as the winner in 1957. Through the late 1950s and into the next decade, Utzon kept refining his ideas, working out where the lines of geometry and engineering and inspiration intersected, plotting how to fill his fantastic sails and turn his shape-shifting dream into concrete. In 1963, just as his creation was about to seemingly rise out of the harbour, Utzon and his family moved to Sydney. Mika tells me how much his grandfather and grandmother loved living here, that they had made a commitment to stay.

Yet commitments can crumble when politicians get involved. While art at its finest is uncompromising, politics is about the art of the possible; in other words, learning to live with compromise. Utzon designed something that seemed to have few corners, but politicians and bureaucrats managed to find corners to cut anyway, as they hacked at his vision. A change of government and a budgetary squeeze imposed untenable pressures on Jørn Utzon and his creation. In 1966, he and his family left Australia. Utzon never returned, so he never saw the building, which was officially opened in 1973. Yet it was never completed as he imagined it. Like politics itself, the Opera House's gleaming shell distracts you from a stack of compromises, particularly inside it.

So what Mika and I are looking up at is not just his grandfather's imagination and courage set in concrete and glass and tiled in ceramics but also a symbol of the myopia of politics. It was the French writer Gustave Flaubert who said you can't have fine thoughts without beautiful forms. I'm looking at the most beautiful form, but my thoughts about those who squandered what this could have been, and the hurt that brought its creator, are less than fine.

Yet Mika says within the family, around the table, talk is rarely about the 'daily politics' that affected the building. Instead, it is about how architecture can have a dialogue with nature, with society, and with everything else around it. He tells me how he walked across the Bridge, stopping every ten or so metres to take a photo of the Opera House, to appreciate the movement of the building, so that it is like rotating your hand before your eyes, observing your fingers and thumb from different angles.

'Because of what it is, you always notice it, you see that movement, and you don't see that with most buildings,' Mika explains. 'The building is in dialogue with itself, not just with the environment.'

Although he died in 2008, Jørn Utzon, through his creation, is also in a dialogue with the future. He's conversing with a city, indeed, the entire globe, through his Opera House, and perhaps we're listening more attentively now than we did when it was built.

The building is also in conversation with a grandson. Mika has a beautiful way to describe what the Opera House means to him, to his own ambitions, and how it shapes his own dialogue with what he makes. He squints up at what his grandfather created and says, 'It's no longer a goal post', meaning it is not something he has to live up to. Mika pauses and smiles.

'It's a starting line.'

13

BENNELONG POINT TO BARANGAROO

WHEN THE Opera House project was crawling through controversy in the 1960s, many wondered when – and how – it would be completed. The building's skeleton hung on Bennelong Point, as if it were some allusion to the bones of Francis Morgan that swung for years from a gibbet on Pinchgut just across the water. While the Opera House's bones were waiting to be fleshed out, some feared it was already a corpse, a dream that was as good as dead on the water. Just as Morgan's skeleton was meant to warn all who sailed into the harbour in the early colonial days to behave, the Opera House was shaping as a cautionary tale in concrete that the state shouldn't have taken such a risk and spent so much on art. As some Sydneysiders protested at the time, they didn't need the Opera House. Who needs culture when you have that harbour?

Now Sydney, and the world, can't imagine the harbour without the Opera House. Former Prime Minister Paul Keating has said the impact of Utzon's building, like all great art, never weakens, no matter how often you see it, from what angle, or in what light. He reckons it is the greatest building of the 20th century and one of the greatest in history.

This extraordinary piece of art has itself spawned and gifted us so much more art. Comparatively few may attend what is created and performed within the building, but people turn out in droves to see the art projected onto it. Each year for the Vivid festival, when city buildings are used as canvases for eye-popping light installations, the Opera House's shells become giant screens. In 2016, Aboriginal images were a feature of the exhibition. Desert art bloomed on the Opera House's skin, lizards crawled over it, magpies perched on it, and a spirit of place radiated from it.

Less ephemeral visual art has been displayed within the Opera House. Abstract tapestries of John Coburn were commissioned as mesmerising proscenium curtains for the main halls. And through the years, the House has been an inspiration for Australia's best-known artists, from William Dobell depicting the uncompleted building in the late 1960s as a phantom floating in a Turneresque atmosphere to the dazzling, colour-infused iconography of Ken Done's paintings and drawings. Ken has told me of his sustained love of portraying the Opera House, saying, 'It's a game for me, finding new ways to paint it'.

John Olsen's enormous mural *Salute to Five Bells* was born because of the Opera House. John was commissioned in 1972, before the building was finished, to paint the mural for the main foyer of the concert hall. It was to be about 21 metres long and about 3 metres high. What's more, it was to face the harbour. So in scale and positioning, this was an enormous assignment. John had already been depicting the harbour for years, transposing its squiggling foreshores and the cross-current rhythms of its life on and below the surface onto canvas, creating rambunctious, free-form poems in paint. So it seemed appropriate that when John received the commission, he looked not just to the water but into the depths of Kenneth Slessor's poem 'Five Bells' for guidance.

From Slessor's words for a drowned friend, John created something quiet and contemplative. You can get lost in John's harbour, with its wash of blue-purple, and creatures and shapes floating across it. You become another being underwater. When I look at the work, I get a similar feeling to when I'm scuba diving. On the surface, your breath quickens as you flap about. Then, as you descend, you feel the water press in, sounds are dulled and compressed until all you hear is your slowing breath and bubbles, and your view through the mask is simplified and uncluttered. Life underwater becomes elemental, restful yet mysterious. Just as it feels when I look at *Salute to Five Bells*.

But for John, the mural was the result of a lot of restlessness and wrestling with ideas and logistical challenges. He drew on his own relationship with the harbour and his life beside it at Watsons Bay. He remembers while doing some preparatory sketches, 'one of the fishermen at Watsons Bay picked up a squid and held it in his fingers and said, "Put that in the mural, John!"'

'Did you?' I ask him.

'Yes! If you look at the mural, there are several squid actually.'

John also wrote to Jørn Utzon in Denmark. 'I told him what I was doing and what would his suggestions be. "Oh," he wrote, "just swing it left and right to the harbour." So that blue colour that the mural is, it joins up, particularly in moonlight, to the harbour.'

Musing on Slessor's poem of loss as a reference for the mural, John also read in the verse ties to the Opera House.

'Wonderfully enough, the opening lines of "Five Bells" is almost a predictive story of the building of the Opera House itself, with the complaints about how long it would take,' John says, before he recites, from memory, the poem.

Time that is moved by little fidget wheels
Is not my Time . . .

As he recorded in his journal, John finished the mural on 21 April 1973. 'Strange how small it looked,' he noted. 'It really comes into its own at night, when it picks up the lights and movements on the harbour. There is the harbour, there is the mural. It questions "Which is reality?"'

John also wrote that he thought the mural was his finest work and 'Sydney Harbour will never be looked at the same way again'. More than four decades on, John deflects my question about that statement. He's not about to say what others might see. But *Salute to Five Bells* does give you a perspective of the harbour that is different to the one through the Opera House's windows. And if you can't go diving or snorkelling in the harbour, John Olsen's mural offers a creative alternative.

AS WELL as inside and on it, art is created outside the Opera House. Rock concerts have been staged on its forecourt, and so has *Sydney Opera House – The Opera,* or *The Eighth Wonder.*

The drama of how this place came to be, and the impact that had on the lives of those involved, was shaped into an opera by composer Alan John and librettist Dennis Watkins. I have seen the opera performed both inside and outside the building that inspired it; the outdoor experience was particularly moving, as words, music, architecture and place harmonised to create a profound sense of connection.

The 'stage' was set on the monumental steps that lead up to the Opera House, while we, the audience, sat under a perfect sky in late spring, looking at what was being sung about: the building's lit concrete ribs inside; the pointed yet fluid lines of the shells; its skin of tiles that chilled in tone as the sun set. Once the night arrived, the ribs glowed, as though we were peering into a magical, beautiful monster that cradled music in its belly.

As we listened to words about sails swirling, billowing, we gazed up. The breath of the singers seemed to fill those sails with even more meaning, while the architecture, in turn, accentuated the beauty of the voices.

We watched 'the architect' sit on the steps, talking to his daughter about sailing to the other side of the world, to the port of dreams. We listened to the architect outlining what he wanted to create – 'A place of meaning, a palace of music, a wonder of the world.'

And we heard our own harsh voices. This must be the first opera to ever have in its libretto lines such as, 'It's crook, I tell you, bloody crook', 'the lamingtons are melting', and 'it's a bloody white elephant'. But just as surely as that sounds Australian, this building is now part of the vernacular of our nation. The Sydney Opera House is a part of us. It has achieved what the architect sang on that warm November night by the harbour: 'I want the people to feel the power of a special place that belongs to them.'

THE PLACE of belonging was in the early days of the colony a point of cultural dislocation. After the livestock was unloaded from the First Fleet onto the promontory, it was called Cattle Point. From 1790, it came to be known as Bennelong's Point. In a bid to improve relations with the original harbour people, and to keep his intermediary close, Arthur Phillip had a small house built for Bennelong and his wife Barangaroo.

The hut and its pretensions to diplomacy were shoved aside in the name of defence. Governor Lachlan Macquarie ordered a fort be built to defend Sydney Cove and prevent what he called clandestine departures, or convicts escaping. But within a couple of decades, Fort Macquarie was being derided as perfectly useless. Still, it remained, serving for a time as the headquarters of the New South Wales Naval Brigade, until it was replaced in 1902 by a tram depot, which was constructed to look like a fort. When the Opera House was taking shape, some wished the tram shed had remained, arguing that was a much more useful public building.

The debate about what was best for the people on Bennelong Point predated the Opera House. In 1910, that passionate defender of public access to the harbour foreshores, W.A. Notting, wrote a letter to the editor of the *Sydney Morning Herald*, opposing plans for a large wharf. 'The closing of Bennelong Point to the public would be an irreparable loss to the public, who have little enough accessible harbour water frontages left at their disposal,' thundered Mr Notting. The battle of public access versus development along the waterfront echoed through the years around Sydney Cove. In 1998, in his National Trust Heritage lecture, expatriate writer Robert Hughes roasted the new development just along from Bennelong Point at East Circular Quay. In particular, he lashed the luxurious apartment block nicknamed the Toaster. In that mellifluous voice of his, Hughes demanded that the Toaster be torn down, so that what he called the country's greatest building, the Opera House, could be fully appreciated without being obscured, and for East Circular Quay to be restored to the people of Sydney. The Toaster remains, with people paying millions of dollars to live there and assure themselves of uninterrupted harbour views.

LONG BEFORE Jørn Utzon, this cove beguiled another dreamer.

'The different coves were examined with all possible expedition,' wrote Arthur Phillip of his first excursion into Sydney Harbour. 'I fixed on the one that had the best spring of water, and in which the ships can anchor so close to the shore, that at a very small expense, quays may be made at which the largest ships may unload.

'This cove, which I honoured with the name of Sydney, is about a quarter of a mile across at the entrance, and half a mile in length.'

Lord Sydney, or Tommy Townshend as he was known to his friends, was Home Secretary and a chief architect of the idea of a penal colony in New South Wales. He was also a great supporter of Phillip.

Once Phillip had returned to Botany Bay on 23 January 1788, after his exploratory excursion into Port Jackson, he ordered the fleet to head north. *Supply* was first into Sydney Cove on 25 January, and the other ships dribbled in the following day. By the end of 26 January, the fleet was moored in the cove. Those on board the ships shared their leader's enthusiasm for the harbour. Newton Fowell, who was on board *Sirius*, recorded on 26 January that 'here you are intirely Land Locked and it is impossible for any Wind to do you the least damage'. Fowell noted a couple of weeks later when the master of his ship, John Hunter, had completed a survey of the harbour that 'he says it is the finest harbour in the known world'.

Within a couple of months, the settlement formed from another society's cast-offs and criminals was actually taking root on the shores of Sydney Cove. You can see the rough indications of that in a map drawn in March 1788, by Lieutenant William Bradley, marking the placement of tents and buildings, the vegetable gardens, the mooring positions of the ships, and the depth of water in the cove. The marks on the map are made clearer by a watercolour Bradley painted. *Sydney Cove, Port Jackson, 1788* depicts a band of cleared bush, making way for a few buildings around the shores. In the bay sits a moored ship, while another is being careened on the eastern shore. And in the middle of the image, fluttering on the harbour's edge, is the Union Jack.

Louise Anemaat, from the State Library of New South Wales, showed me that watercolour in Bradley's journal. Wearing gloves, Louise also extracted from the archives some sheaves wrapped in wonder and anticipation. They were letters of those first arrivals, including Phillip's correspondence with the Marquis of Lansdowne, praising the harbour. In that one famous phrase from the letter, 'Here a Thousand Sail of the Line may ride in the most perfect Security', lies proof, Louise reckons, that the

Governor always saw this place as much more than a dumping ground for Britain's unwanted. There was a strong strategic and geopolitical reason for the settlement's existence. This land and its resources, including the harbour, had to be protected from rival powers. Anyway, as she added, this experiment had cost so much money, sending almost 1500 souls to the other side of the globe, Sydney had to succeed.

Arthur Phillip may have believed in what Sydney could become, but plenty didn't. Along with the dreamers on those first ships were the doubters. Major Robert Ross, the officer in charge of the marines, was one of the biggest. Ross often argued with Phillip, and he hated New South Wales. Where Phillip saw the buds of an exciting future in a new land, Ross viewed a place where nature was nearly worn out. What's more, he thought this scheme of shipping people to what was a 'vile country' was a ludicrous folly. 'I think it will be cheaper to feed the convicts on turtle and venison at the London Tavern than be at the expense of sending them here,' Major Ross wrote to Secretary of State Nepean in July 1788.

The doubters sailed away; the dreamers prevailed. Their memories shape how Louise Anemaat sees Sydney Cove, especially its crowded and paved head, Circular Quay.

'I find it really hard to walk around Circular Quay and not spend the whole time imagining the beach that was there,' Louise says. 'It was a sandy beach, and you can imagine back then dogs swimming out around the boats, the waves on the sand, the boats clinking away in Sydney Cove, and I imagine all of that because of the letters.'

Bobbing in *Pulbah Raider* on the agitated water just off Bennelong Point, I too can imagine the boats clinking. I can hear other sounds from the water as well, particularly the rumbling beat of ferries pushing in and out of the cove. And as a few of them pass, I see the memory of the First Fleet, in the names of the ferries – *Supply*, *Sirius* and *Charlotte* – and in the unhappy looks among their cargo, only they belong to commuters not convicts. I can't paddle into the cove. It is out of bounds to all but authorised vessels. Yet long before there was a forbidding invisible line stretching between beacons on Bennelong and Dawes points, long before the names *Supply* or *Sirius* were seen in the cove, paddlers would have presided over these waters. Soon after the First Fleet arrived, in an effort to put a figure on those who were here before them, Watkin Tench noted how a survey was undertaken around the harbour, and sixty-seven canoes were counted. Although Tench himself conceded there were doubts about the accuracy of that figure.

Still, the canoes of the first Australians outlasted *Sirius* on Sydney Cove. The ship had survived so many close shaves and scrapes. She had not only journeyed all the way from Portsmouth to Sydney Cove with her convict cargo, but she had helped the young colony survive by sailing to Cape Town and back for supplies. Then in 1790, while on a voyage to the infant satellite settlement on Norfolk Island, *Sirius* came to grief on rocks in, of all places, Sydney Bay. The anchor and a gun from *Sirius* were recovered from the waters off Norfolk Island and brought back to Sydney. These artefacts of the First Fleet's flagship are now only a stone's throw from where *Sirius* first moored. Her anchor and gun are barely noticed memorials, marooned in the deep shadows of the park at Macquarie Place. In early colonial days, this place was near the waterfront, before the cove was beaten back several hundred metres by land reclamation works in the 1800s. More prominent in the park is an obelisk that Governor Macquarie had erected in 1818, 'TO RECORD THAT ALL THE PUBLIC ROADS LEADING TO THE INTERIOR OF THE COLONY ARE MEASURED FROM IT'. Unlike his predecessors, Macquarie was not a navy man; he had risen through army ranks. So it is no surprise he wanted to build roads, to turn away from the sea and look inwards to open up the country. But salt water remained the lifeblood – and the lifeline – of the colony at the time. Overlooking Macquarie Place from a niche in the Victorian-era Lands Department building across the road is a statue of the colony's first Governor. I can almost imagine a tear being shed from Phillip's stone eyes at the sight of those all-but-forgotten relics of his flagship, or perhaps he stares in wonder at how much the cove he chose as the colony's birthplace has shrunk and been reshaped since his time.

Phillip's belief that the cove was capable of accommodating quays at which the largest ships could unload was slowly realised. Perhaps the tardiness to build quays was set by others' belief that nature had already provided what was required. The harbour 'possesses the best anchorage the whole way', declared William Charles Wentworth. 'It is said, and I believe with truth, to have a hundred coves, and is capable of containing all the shipping in the world.' For many years in Sydney Cove, cargo was unloaded from moored ships onto lighters and brought ashore at a public facility on the western shore, the Hospital Wharf. There was also the Governor's Wharf on the southern shore. A merchant, Robert Campbell, who was reshaping the northern stretch of the western shore with his storehouses, had built a wharf by 1802. It was the first private wharf in the colony. The practice of loading and unloading goods out on the water also reduced the opportunity for convicts to escape on ships, or to steal from them.

The first governors had also put in place measures to prevent the harbour being transformed from a form of imprisonment into a means of escape. They banned the building of boats. Yet Phillip had quickly realised boats were needed to transport supplies from the new farming area at Parramatta. So *Rose Hill Packet*, or 'The Lump', was built in a yard at the head of Sydney Cove in 1789. A naval shipyard was built on the cove's western shores in the late 1790s under the orders of Governor Hunter. Gradually merchants and tradesmen crafted their own vessels. Official bans were no match for the imperatives of living by the water.

The small shipyards, including the government's own facility, were pushed out of the cove by development along the shore. The water itself was becoming more clogged with shipping, but the cove was also silting up. The Tank Stream, the creek that Phillip had identified as a reason for settling here and that had sustained life in the early colony, was itself dying. The stream's fate was sealed as soon as the settlers stepped ashore, and its death was foretold by one of those first arrivals, David Collins.

'The spot chosen for this purpose [of clearing ground] was at the head of the cove,' Collins wrote, 'near the run of fresh water, which stole silently along through a very thick wood, the stillness of which had then, for the first time since the creation, been interrupted by the rude sound of the labourer's axe, and the downfall of its ancient inhabitants . . .'

The clearing of land upstream and the sum of unreasonable demands heaped upon the waterway, and dumped into it, by residents and businesses along its course ruined it. The stream that entered the cove in its south-western corner became a storm-water drain. The creek was buried under a growing city and effectively killed. But not quite. As writer Delia Falconer points out in her wonderful love letter to Sydney, the Tank Stream is a ghost creek, haunting the foundations of buildings built over it.

Through the 19th century, the trading and maritime industries clustered ever more tightly around the cove's edges. And the edges themselves were changed to meet the industries' needs. A seawall kept creeping around the waterfront, reaching the Tank Stream. George Barney, the engineer reshaping and rearranging a number of landmarks on and around the harbour, had arranged for sandstone he was blasting off Pinchgut to be transported across the water for the Sydney Cove project. The marshy land behind the seawall was reclaimed. The Tank Stream's muddy mouth was cleaned up and scraped out, and the wall and wharves extended along the cove's western shore. By the early 1850s, Semi-Circular Quay was created.

In time, the quay lost the 'semi' from its name but gained ever greater importance. On the reclaimed land rose fine stone buildings dedicated to collecting and making money: Customs House, staring directly, expectantly, at the docked ships; along the eastern shore were bond stores perfumed with bush paddocks and lanolin, as they were packed with wool to be exported; on the western shore multi-storey warehouses waited to receive what the world brought through the Heads; and, just near Customs House, stood the waterfront edifice that was the Mort & Co storehouse. Thomas Mort was involved in many aspects of shipping. He repaired the ships in his dry dock at Balmain, he stored and sold what was brought in their hulls, and he filled those hulls with Australian produce, particularly wool. He is credited with developing refrigeration for the export of perishable goods. So in his business career, Mort rode both on the sheep's back and the ship's deck.

His Circular Quay building was not just filled with wealth; it was dressed to look rich, with grand colonnades and arches. The store had such an imposing presence on the waterfront that it seemed it would be there for all time. It wasn't. On that site is the AMP building, which was the first to reach for the sky in the city in the early 1960s, after the 150-foot height limit was lifted. Perhaps Mort would not have minded his showpiece being toppled for an insurance giant, for he had been a founder of the Australian Mutual Provident Society. The memory of Mort still holds a small piece of real estate nearby. A statue of him, erected in 1883, five years after his death, stands in Macquarie Place. He is faced away from the harbour, and where his beautiful storehouse used to be.

By the 1870s, Circular Quay had been refashioned sufficiently for a newspaper columnist to declare that if Trafalgar Square were the finest site in Europe, then this was the best in Australia. But it wasn't good enough. It needed 'commercial palaces', paved frontage and better landing stairs to replace the 'slippery and dangerous wooden structure up which our visitors have to scramble when arriving from the ships lying in the harbour'.

'Perhaps the next generation may suggest that at least a portion of our steam-ferry system is capable of improvement, especially as regards the pier arrangements,' the columnist 'Uralla' huffed.

Uralla would have been pleased with the developments over the coming years. The ferries that had sidled in between the larger trade ships to pick up and drop off passengers gradually insinuated themselves deeper into the heart of the quay. Actually, they had already lodged themselves in the heart of a city. The ferries connected one shore of the harbour to the other, and millions of Sydneysiders to their routines. Sydney functioned, in no small part, because of the ferries. They were the city's bridge before there was the Bridge. The ferry wharves at Circular Quay were upgraded and, in the 1890s, they were reordered, so that the sequence corresponded with the destinations. The Parramatta and Lane Cove rivers ferries were at the far western end, the Watsons Bay and southern shore craft berthed at the far eastern wharf. In that way, ferries didn't cross each other dangerously in the quay. On Bennelong and Dawes points were docks for horse ferries.

The numbers using the ferries were enormous. By 1890, about five million passengers and 378,500 carts and buggies, along with 43,800 horse riders crossed the harbour annually. Within twenty years, those passenger numbers had more than doubled, stoking the argument for a harbour bridge. The visiting British author D.H. Lawrence observed through his main character in *Kangaroo* how the city's inhabitants 'seem to slip like fishes from one side of the harbour to the other'. More than eight decades after the Bridge opened, the ferries remain a defining element of harbour life, carrying commuters and tourists on about fifteen million journeys annually. The joy of the ferry journey has remained constant, but the view of the destination has dramatically changed.

Approaching Circular Quay on a ferry deck, there are the 'commercial palaces' the 19th century columnist Uralla had wanted. The buildings must offer wonderful harbour views for their inhabitants. But for those of us on the harbour, they forbid us to see far

up the hill into the CBD, or to get a sense of the rills of a city running down to the water. It wasn't like this a century earlier, when
the towers were but stubs and the view was embracing.

'From the harbour, city towers dominated the skyline –
St Mary's Cathedral, the Queen Victoria Building dome, the
Town Hall, Post Office, and near the Quay, the Lands Office
tower,' recalled the artist and poetic observer Lloyd Rees. 'At
times the Quay could be very beautiful – especially in the evening
peak hours of winter, when in the dusk the ferries would fan out
from Sydney Cove like slow-moving clusters of golden rockets
and spangle their lights across the velvet waters.'

Scything across the towers' feet is the Cahill Expressway. When
it opened in 1958, the roadway was considered a mark of progress
in the city, making life easier for those in cars. A stunning harbour
view even swishes across your side window as you drive east on the
expressway. Yet from the water, the Cahill Expressway, with its
rumbling underbelly of the City Circle railway line, is a perennial
scar. It diminishes the sense of arrival that should course through
us every time we disembark in what is, after all, the birthplace
of Australia. That streak of concrete cuts the CBD off from the
harbour, and it slices through our connection to the past. It is a
miserable greeting to Circular Quay.

What remains around the quay, as it has ever since the beach
and mudflats began being transformed into the entrance to a
harbour town, is the bustle. The musty odours of livestock and
mud have been replaced by the aromas of coffee and cooking from
the cafés and restaurants. The clatter of buggies and carts has
been long drowned out by the guttural noises of motor vehicles
and trains. Where the ferries berth, and along the eastern shore,
you would have once seen bowsprits, hanging like abundant

branches over the wharves, and the sleek lines of clippers with legendary names such as *Cutty Sark* and *Thermopylae*, accepting cargoes of wool and the challenge of setting record sailing times to England. Their sails would eventually wrinkle and fall limp, becalmed by the age of steam.

And there are the people, transiting from home to work, from water to land, from one world to another, and back again. It is always a slightly disorienting, labyrinthine walk around the quay, being jostled by rushing commuters, parrying around tourist groups. Faces, in all their wonderful diversity, form and drift away as you move through the crowd. The quay has always been about the faces, as sailors from around the globe poured off their ships and sauntered and swayed on sea-legs up into Sydney town. Faces tattooed or weather-creased, skin of all pigments, hair from black to snow white, they all melded, sometimes clashed, around the quay. As an English old salt, Stan Hugill, wrote, 'the Circular Quay Sailortown was infested with all sorts of bums and stiffs, as well as sailormen, ex-convicts, remittance men, gold-robbers, bushrangers on a town jaunt, deserters, Larrikins'. Yet not all were welcomed ashore. In 1849, thousands gathered in mizzling rain to protest the harbour being 'polluted with the presence of that floating hell – a convict ship'. The protestors wanted no more transportation of convicts, and it called for a ship in the cove, *Hashemy*, to leave without offloading its human cargo. Water cleanses everything, even memory, for in that crowd there would have been some who chose to forget how they had arrived in Sydney Cove. Four decades later, another convict ship, *Success*, was moored in the cove. Only it was a tourist attraction, filled not with wretched souls in rotting clothes but wax figures and convict artefacts.

The ageing former bushranger Harry Power was apparently a living exhibit on the floating museum, although he denied having ever been transported as a convict.

But mostly Circular Quay was, and is, a place of welcome, and of farewell. From the quay, the young have embarked to serve and fight, even before Australia was a nation. In 1885, when New South Wales sent a contingent to support the Empire in the Sudan War, it was estimated that two in every three Sydneysiders gathered along the procession route and at the wharves to see off the soldiers.

When there was peace in the world but still restlessness in youthful hearts, the young would board liners in the cove, travelling great distances to find themselves. Around the quay, set into the promenade, is a string of plaques dedicated to writers with a connection to Australia, particularly the harbour, in one way or another. The Writers' Walk begins with Dorothea Mackellar's 'I love a Sunburnt Country', and it features a couple of plaques to visiting authors, including Joseph Conrad, who, as a seaman, stepped ashore here a number of times and in later years dipped into his memories of the harbour. Conrad's plaque features a quote from his memoir, *The Mirror of the Sea*: 'Sydney Harbour . . . one of the finest, most beautiful, vast, and safe bays the sun had ever shone upon.' Yet the plaque that most poignantly shows how the harbour is both a place of transition and an anchor for the soul is that of Clive James. The plaque for the expatriate writer, poet and broadcaster is between wharves 3 and 4, offering a view over to the overseas passenger terminal on the western shore, which most days has a massive cruise ship presiding over it, engorging or offloading a couple of thousand passengers on brief holidays. Clive James set off from here on

New Year's Eve, 1961, bound for England and glory. He has never returned to live in Sydney, but, then again, as the inscription on his plaque shows, he has never left either. It is a quote from the final page of his *Unreliable Memoirs*: 'In Sydney Harbour . . . the yachts will be racing on the crushed diamond water under a sky the texture of powdered sapphires. It would be churlish not to concede that the same abundance of natural blessings which gave us the energy to leave has every right to call us back.' The harbour continues to call Clive James home. He wrote in his will that he wanted his ashes to be scattered off Dawes Point. He could end his voyage just near where it had begun.

My fellow Gentleman Kayaker and great mate of Clive James, Bruce Beresford, made the same voyage, sailing for England just a year after his friend, in an Italian passenger ship, *Castel Felice*. Bruce remembers the feeling of the final ties to his homeland and loved ones literally falling away and breaking.

'My parents were on the wharf,' he recalls. 'The whole ship was full of young people, I guess all headed for England, and we'd throw streamers to the dock. After a little while, as you were pulling away, the streamers couldn't reach the wharf. It was a very strange feeling.'

Clustered around the cruise terminal are markers of different eras but all are married to the water in front of them. As you face the cove, to the left of the terminal is a row of sandstone warehouses, known as Campbell's Stores. This was where Robert Campbell's mercantile empire blossomed, as he helped gradually prise open the strict controls imposed on trade in the colony, after he arrived in 1798. More than reshape commerce in Sydney, he changed the scalloped bite out of the shoreline that became known as Campbell's Cove. He built his wharf and warehouses and a large home nearby. Its name acknowledged where his money came from: Wharf House. Onto his wharf, Campbell unloaded products ranging from cattle to spirits, and he became involved in other ventures, including sealing. The existing Campbell's Stores were built later in his career, in the late 1830s. These days, they house restaurants.

Just up from the stores and behind the passenger terminal is the former Australasian Steam Navigation Company building, a Flemish red-brick confection, built in the 1880s. If the architecture looks far removed from its location, the building's ground floor now looks very much a part of the harbour. Its windows radiate colour, as it is a gallery and studio of Ken Done.

Further south along the shore, past stoic stone buildings that once housed the Mariners' Church and the Sailors' Home, is the former Maritime Services Board building. The MSB was a state agency that oversaw most of the public facilities and functions on and around the harbour. The MSB's headquarters at the quay were built on the crushed bones of the convict-built Commissariat store. It was completed just after the Second World War. Harry Seidler, who was developing his name as a modernist architect, hated the building, calling it 'an utter disgrace, regressive, copying old Greece and Rome'. That 'regressive' building is now the repository of the cutting edge; it has been recycled as the Museum of Contemporary Art.

Just back from the water is one of the oldest remnants of the colony's connection with the harbour. Cadman's Cottage was built in 1816. The stone cottage was the home for many years of John Cadman. He came by ship as a convict and ended up as Superintendent of Government Boats. So that little building is more than a rare reminder of the convict past; it symbolises that in Sydney town, you could leave behind your convict past.

Yet if I'm looking for how the past can flow into the present around Circular Quay, I find it just near Wharf 1. Aboriginal musicians, daubed with ceremonial paint, are playing the didgeridoo and rhythm sticks, while a young man dances. The performers are silhouetted against the sun-lit water, which is shimmying and shaking. I know it is just the churn of the ferries, but I'd like to think that it is the culture of the Gadigal people enticing the harbour to dance.

IN SYDNEY, the fortunes of where you live seem to be set on an east–west axis. Generally speaking, the Eastern Suburbs, close to the sea and southern shores of the harbour, have been for the well-connected and well-off. The Western Suburbs, out on the sun-baked plains, have been home to the 'battlers'. The East–West real estate and social divide has been there since Sydney's foundation. The division was roughly marked by the creek that gave them all, regardless of class, drinking water, the Tank Stream. The Governor and his staff took the ground to the east of the stream, and the convicts, along with the marines, were mostly on the western side. As the settlement developed beyond tents, many of the convicts picked their way along the craggy spine of the western shore, over the rocks. And so their home became The Rocks. To the east, Phillip imposed a sense of order, creating something that looked planned. To the west, the terrain shook off regularity. And the terrain suited the character of many of those who lived there. They built rough homes from the rocks and stones on the rocks and stones, paying little heed to roads or tracks, rules or order. Most didn't wait for land grants, they just put ground beneath their feet and a roof of sorts over their heads. When he was Governor, Lachlan Macquarie tried to push order between the cracks and boulders, with street names and numbers. But the locals largely ignored that. They knew who lived where, and they had their own paths to follow. It may not have been orderly, as the government would have liked, but for the residents it worked. And that's how The Rocks grew; organically, wildly and insistently.

If early colonial visitors were searching for a part of Sydney that matched their preconceptions or prejudices of what a penal settlement would look like, The Rocks provided it. After his examination of the colony near the end of Macquarie's gover-norship, John Thomas Bigge reported back to London that The Rocks area was mainly inhabited by the most profligate and depraved part of the population. When a merchant, Richard Jones, was asked in 1819, as part of a House of Commons inquiry, whether a stranger arriving in Sydney would view it as a settlement principally populated with convicts, he answered, 'No; I should think if he kept from the Rock part of the town, he would rather regard himself as in some country town in England'.

Yet the inhabitants of The Rocks knew which way to look. They faced not towards authority, but down the harbour. Historian Grace Karskens, in her study of The Rocks, noted how the area's townscape was unified by the houses' orienta-tion towards the sea. This, she said, defined the character of early Sydney as a maritime town. After serving their time, many who lived in the area worked as labourers, or in transporting goods and people. But through the years, The Rocks attracted plenty of money that washed in from the harbour. Many a sailor walked past the moral gatekeepers of the Mariners' Church on the waterfront and lurched into the maze between the rocks, seeking out inns, licensed and unlicensed, and the pleasures licentious to be found on the peninsula. The Rocks had a reputation among sailors for being a dangerous place, and they were sometimes assaulted and robbed. But more likely, they would lose their money in establishments with wonderful nautical names such as The Three Jolly Sailors and The Sheer Hulk. In his memoir of Sydney around the 1830s, Alexander Harris recalled how he would visit The Rocks and find it hard to keep a straight line because of the 'crags, quarries, and rows of houses'. But it was even harder to stay on the straight and narrow. He mentioned The Sheer Hulk, which was 'full to suffocation of the lowest women, sailors and ruffians'. As Harris noted, because of its terrain, you didn't so much walk but tumble or climb in The Rocks – especially after visiting one of its inns.

As the city grew, the public gaze receded from The Rocks, and the convict generation died away. Yet it remained a ramshackle home to many on the fringes of the city. Those who lived there often described themselves as residents on The Rocks. Not in The Rocks, but *on*, as if they were squatting. Just as a eucalypt works its way through the toughest of terrains to embed its roots, perhaps the very landscape of The Rocks has taught its inhabitants how to adapt, and to tenaciously hold on. In their history, the people of The Rocks have had to face forces trying to uproot them.

Bubonic plague broke out on the peninsula in January 1900. The unwelcome import was brought ashore by ships' rats and spread through the crowded quarters on The Rocks and neighbouring Millers Point. The area was effectively quarantined, and authorities set about cleansing the peninsula, lime-washing homes, sweeping and collecting huge amounts of rubbish, which was dumped out to sea, and catching more than 100,000 rats. Within eight months, there were 303 plague cases, and 103 people died in the city. Politicians responded by introducing legislation that was like a bureaucratic broom sweeping around the harbour's edge. The Sydney Harbour Trust was formed in 1901. The Trust's main thrust was to administer the port, taking control of much of the commercial areas of the waterfront. But its power extended beyond the shoreline, with the Trust resuming more than 600 properties. The Trust pushed into The Rocks, and it seemed that as part of the 'cleansing', the area regarded by many as a slum and a moral sewer would be flattened. Fearing 'Old Sydney' was about to disappear, a group of artists, led by Julian Ashton, traipsed through The Rocks, preserving the straggly streets and stone buildings on canvas. Homes were demolished, but the community survived. Yet The Rocks continued to be gnawed away at through the 20th century. The building of the Harbour Bridge in the 1920s and the Cahill Expressway's construction three decades later led to many homes and businesses being toppled.

In the 1960s, as the eastern pillar of Sydney Cove was being transformed with the Opera House's construction, the State Government decided to smarten up the western side as well. It held a design competition for the redevelopment of The Rocks. In 1970, it established the Sydney Cove Redevelopment Authority, and, once again, it seemed as though Australia's oldest suburb was under threat. The historic terraces were to tumble in favour of high-rise development. But the people of The Rocks clung on. A residents' action group was formed and enlisted the help of the Builders' Labourers Federation, which applied a green ban to the area. The fight intensified, and a clash between protesters and police in 1973 became known as the Battle of The Rocks. The protesters may have lost that battle, with seventy-seven of them arrested, but they eventually won huge concessions to save the area. The retention of many of the buildings allowed tourism to flourish. What was once considered old and ugly came to be seen as historic and beautiful – and profitable. Yet those qualities have pushed The Rocks once again into the sights of government planners and developers, who have had bigger plans for the peninsula. But first, they had to move residents. A new battle had begun.

In 2014, the State Government began selling off almost 300 properties in The Rocks and Millers Point. Politicians argued that it would have cost $100 million to restore and maintain the historic properties, and with the money raised from the sell-off, it could build many more public housing homes.

Those buying the historic homes have to be wealthy. One property alone, Darling House, was sold in February 2016 for $7.7 million. The smaller terraces are selling for seven-figure sums. Those moving out of the homes are public housing residents. But they have not been leaving without a fight. Walking around the peninsula, I see the protest signs stuck outside houses, and hanging from wrought-iron-adorned verandas.

A focal point of this battle is a building that arose after the last fight to save The Rocks. The Sirius building is just to the east of the Sydney Harbour Bridge approach. It was built in 1979, in response to the plans to redevelop the area. Sirius looks like a neatly stacked pile of cubes in concrete and glass. It is a prominent example of what is called brutalist architecture, but many feel it has been the residents' lives that have been brutalised by government policy in recent years.

Sirius has seventy-nine units and, when I visit, just a handful of occupants. The New South Wales Government has been moving out the social housing residents, because it wants to sell the building. Walking across the Harbour Bridge, I have noticed how much the soul of the building has been stripped. In the window of one unit almost at eye level with the Bridge's deck, there used to be a 'One Way. Jesus' sign always on display, much to the bemusement of many passers-by. The sign has gone, and I can now see to the other side of the unit, as though I'm peering through a ghost. To better understand how much the soul of Sirius, and the lives of those who have called it home, has been changed, I meet up with one of the few still living there.

Cherie Johnson has lived in the Sirius building since 1980. She moved in with her 'Mumma', Betty. Cherie still recalls that first day, when they opened the door and looked straight through the apartment to the main window. As Mumma said, 'Gosh, Cherie, it's like winning the lottery.'

The view is like something that would feature in a lottery ad. Sydney pours into the unit through the window that reaches from just above the floor to the ceiling. We walk to the window. Cherie, with her mass of hair backlit, looks down at the roofs of old terraces and smiles wistfully – 'there were families in there, but only a couple remain' – then points at a former clothing factory that is now a luxury hotel with a rooftop pool. Further on, over the stepped gables of the former Australasian Steam Navigation Company building, is a massive cruise ship. If the ship weren't there, we would be able to see the Opera House. To the left of us, we can see ferries pushing across to the North Shore, and if I really turned my head, I would be able to see the Bridge. To the right is Circular Quay, and the CBD buildings behind, and off in the distance over the ship are the Eastern Suburbs, from where Cherie and Mumma moved.

'It's like an enormous TV screen, always has been,' Cherie says. Through that window, she has seen so much life, so much of Sydney. She has seen the spectacular, with each New Year's Eve and Australia Day, the sublime, with whales just near the Bridge, the historic, such as the Bicentennial celebrations, and the everyday.

Cherie's life has been entwined with that world out there. It has been since they moved into the area, and on that first morning, when Cherie went for a walk to buy a newspaper, she realised, 'My gosh, it's like I'm in a little country town'. She worked for many years at the historic Fortune of War Hotel, a popular watering hole down near the Quay, and she made friends in her area, and in her building. Never mind that many thought it was a monstrosity.

'When we first moved in here, people used to say, "Gosh, you live in the butter boxes, or the beehive. It's an ugly building",' she recalls. 'I think anyone who doesn't like the look of it is uncultured and ignorant. That's how I feel. They say it doesn't fit in with the area, but I think it does. It was state of the art when it was built.'

Cherie says the most beautiful thing about the building is what people can't see, the community that formed inside it. She recalls the diversity of residents – young, old, families – and many who had long and deep links to work and life on the waterfront. One neighbour's family had lived on the peninsula for five generations.

But that community has largely gone, leaving little more than a concrete shell. Cherie finds it bitterly ironic that Sirius was built for those who were being displaced by a previous government's vision, and now they are being moved on to accommodate a new regime's grand plan. A prime reason for them being moved on, she says, is that view out her window. When it was built, many felt Sirius had no place being in The Rocks. Now that this is a highly sought after area, Cherie feels the attitude is that Sirius is no place for social housing residents. Her life and those of her neighbours, she believes, are being sold out for a view.

'It was an area where many moons ago no one wanted to live,' she murmurs. 'It was only full of workers. It was okay before for us to move into the area, whereas now, all I can see are the dollar signs in their [the government's] eyes. Suddenly we're not worthy of living here.'

Cherie catches her breath and looks out the window. The source of pain brings her pleasure once more.

'You never felt alone, even if you were alone,' she says, using the past tense, as though she has already left. Housing NSW has offered other accommodation. But she's holding on, not for the view, but mostly for what this place means to her, for the memories it holds and the community it once had.

For now, Cherie is alone. Her Mumma has died. And she is the last one to be living on this floor. The last of her neighbours moved out about eighteen months earlier. There is a resident upstairs, but she is the only one on that floor as well.

'It's like a ghost town,' she says. 'It's social classing, it's getting the working class out [of the area].'

Just as her future remains unclear, so does that of Sirius. Despite expert advice, the government said it would not heritage list the building. Now that it has lost its soul, Cherie worries Sirius will have its body crushed.

'I'd hate to see this torn down, it shouldn't be,' Cherie says with a determination that can't be softened by even her smile. 'That would be sacrilege. It's not a holy place, but it's my holy place!'

BACK IN the water, having timed my paddle between the flurry of ferries and their angry wakes, I reach the western point of Sydney Cove. Or, in the language of the first Australians, War-ran, or Warrang. We know this is what Sydney Cove was traditionally called because of the man after whom the cove's western point is named, Lieutenant William Dawes. In the earliest days of the colony, he must have stood out as an extraordinary man. Dawes was practical. No sooner had the First Fleet arrived than he had built a simple earthen redoubt on the eastern point, cradling two guns from *Sirius*. It was the first fortification built in the colony. He then built a redoubt on the western point. Yet Dawes also gazed at infinity. On the western point, he established an observatory. Dawes studied this strange night sky through equipment given to him back in England by the Astronomer Royal, Nevil Maskelyne. As payment of sorts, the promontory was named Point Maskelyne for a time. But it quickly became known by the name of the man living there, looking outwards and up. The observatory itself was accorded permanence on the point's high ground. That was initially known as Flagstaff Hill, as it held the signal station that communicated with South Head to alert the town of any ships approaching. But with the construction of a stone observatory, it became Observatory Hill. From the 1850s, a time ball on the observatory's tower would plummet at one o'clock each day, a simple action keenly observed by mariners in the harbour, so they could set their ship's chronometers. Sydney's night sky may be smeared and scrawled on by the city's lights, making it harder to see the stars, but there on the hill, rising above, and remaining aloof from the commotion all around it, is an observatory still. And people still seek the infinite here; Observatory Hill is a favourite place for wedding photos.

William Dawes was more than an observer. He was a listener. He established a relationship with a young Gadigal woman, Patyegarang, and they taught each other their languages. Dawes scratched down what he learnt in his notebooks. What is apparent, in any language, is the intimacy the Englishman and the Gadigal woman shared. It is beautiful to read the local phrase for 'You winked at me', or how the action of warming your hand by a fire and then gently squeezing the fingers of another is summed up in one word, Putuwá. And while Dawes recorded how to say it, we are – as a nation – still learning how to enact this phrase: Gatu piryala, or 'we two are talking to each other'.

On Dawes Point, the earthen redoubts were pounded and reinforced into something more substantial, as the defence complex was upgraded. It offered greater protection than the remnants of the incomplete Fort Phillip, further up the hill. When the fort was begun in the early 1800s, it was as much about offering protection from rebellious convicts as it was from enemies coming through the Heads. Yet within a couple of years, the project was abandoned, and it surrendered the hill to windmills. While Dawes Point was the command post for fortifications along the harbour, its guns never fired in anger.

They were muzzled once and for all in the 1920s, when the area was cleared for the construction of Sydney Harbour Bridge.

The remnants of the fort, etched in the sandstone slabs and with a few mute guns pointing eastwards, now shelter under the great iron geometry of the Bridge's southern approach. The Harbour View Hotel, which is crouching under the approach, is not where it has always been. The original pub had to be moved in 1925 for the Bridge. The silver lining was the hotel had a new, thirsty clientele – the workers. And the new location still had a harbour view.

Tracing Dawes Point in my kayak, I crane my neck and watch the sky turn into iron. No matter how many times I paddle under the Bridge, I'm in awe, as though I'm seeing it for the first time. The arch is majestic, but it is when you're underneath that you feel the power of the Bridge, the sum of all those straining muscles, all that sweat, all the risk, it took to build it. Not that I can ever look up for too long, as I also feel the power, and the potential sinking sensation, of the harbour ricocheting off the sandstone seawall.

Many have paddled here before me. One of the colony's earliest watermen, the legendary Billy Blue, rowed his passengers from the North Shore to Dawes Point. The watermen were among the original taxis of Sydney, transporting people across the harbour, or from ship to shore and back. The colonial surgeon and author Peter Cunningham noted that many of Sydney Harbour's watermen had formerly plied their trade on the Thames. In the early years of the 20th century, a watermen's shelter was built on Dawes Point, but it was already on its way to becoming a memorial. The trade was dying, its fate all but sealed by the Bridge shadowing the watermen's shelter. Yet watermen – and women – still take passengers around the harbour. The waves of the passing ferries and water taxis bouncing off the seawall jostle me to not forget that.

I paddle into the bay that for many years had no name. It was simply the bay between Dawes Point and Millers Point. That it was close to Sydney town, particularly the earthy delights scattered in the lanes up the hill and over into The Rocks, yet it was a little removed, would have been a reason it was a popular mooring area with whaling ships in the middle of the 19th century. The ships' cashed-up sailors may have been welcome but the stench of the cargo was not.

In this bay with no name, Captain Robert Towns, a trader and whaler who founded Townsville, built the first wharf around this area in 1845, and soon the bay had more and more private wharves spiking into it. In this part of the harbour, out of sight of the authorities, there was a lot of smuggling, including of crew members. Convicts could pose as seamen or stow away, but, as both the town and maritime trade grew, increasingly the problem for captains was their sailors deserting in Sydney, losing themselves in the sandstone warren beyond the wharves. Those crew members had to be replaced, by hook or by crook. There were quite a few crooks involved in procuring sailors. They were known as crimps, working out of, or milling about, sailors' boarding houses and inns. The *Sydney Morning Herald* reported in 1906 of a parliamentary debate about how some boarding-house keepers and publicans in Sydney and Newcastle were involved in the trade. The sailors' welfare group, the Mission to Seamen, wrote in response that more could and should be done to help mariners while they were on shore, and to stop 'the plundering of sailors'. Usually the crimps' method was persuasion with money, but occasionally there were reports of some poor sailor – and even landlubbers – waking up on a ship, having been knocked out with grog, or with a blow to the head, and carried to the harbour.

I walk, and climb, from the waterfront, along dog's-leg lanes that are like dried-up creek beds and on streets flanked with tightly packed terraces to a pub that has been around since the days of sail and whalers. The Hero of Waterloo hotel is a wedge of history. The pub was built in 1842 by a Scot, George Paton, and it opened a year later. Paton was a master stone-mason. He had convicts cleave out blocks of sandstone from the nearby Argyle Cut, a chasm being hacked out of the rock to ease passage from one side of the peninsula to the other. At the pub, the convict stonemasons' efforts can be still seen etched into the blocks. Paton left his own mark around town; he was involved in the building of the Garrison Church just up the road in 1840, the Sydney Post Office, and the Australian Museum.

Inside the Hero of Waterloo, there is a distinct air of the colonial. The floors are wooden, the walls are sandstone, and great timber beams, like cross-trees on a sailing ship, buttress the ceiling. There is a fireplace that has blackened the blocks above it. I sit near a large sash window, sipping my beer (a James Squire, in deference to the convict brewer) and look at the Georgian and Victorian houses across the road. Yet it is the raw but warm lumps of stone and wood cocooning me that conjures up the past. I imagine this place filled with unleashed sailors going mad over grog and women. And all being well, they stumbled out of here, back to their own ship. Or they may have ended up on another ship. I had heard rumours of a tunnel from the pub to the then-unnamed bay. The story goes it was used for smuggling grog but also for 'shanghaiing' sailors. I ask the bartender if the story is true, and he points to a trapdoor in the floor, just near the bar. He tells me the tunnel was blocked off many years ago, so no one knows its exact route. I tell him I'm relieved, but he jokes I would've been safe, because I haven't drunk enough. I order another beer.

For as long as there were those leading sailors into temptation, others tried to save them. Among the protectors were the clergymen and volunteers of the Mission to Seamen. In their memoirs, sailors write appreciatively of the Mission workers' hospitality, and how they would take ships' apprentices, or brassbounders, on picnics with local young women to the Blue Mountains. One old English-born captain, William H.S. Jones, recalled how meaningful a Mission picnic was for him, and other 'lads so far from home', during his first visit to Australia in 1906, especially 'after our months of drudgery, monotony and anxieties afloat'.

The organisation is now the Mission to Seafarers, and it is still on the peninsula, huddled near the water at the bay that once had no name, still helping mariners. One of the Mission's workers, Gary King, says the shipping industry has dramatically changed. For one thing, the commercial vessels now mostly dock not in Sydney Harbour but in the waterway rejected by Arthur Phillip as less suitable for ships, Botany Bay. And once in port, sailors are stripped of one luxury they used to have: time.

'It's a totally different world,' Gary says. 'The seafarers used to have longer R&R [rest and recreation], and we had accommodation for them. They might have been in port for days or weeks. Now sometimes they have only four hours. They're in and out. So all they want is to have a quick look at the city, to be tourists for a few hours, buy souvenirs, and phone or email their families.'

So Gary and his colleagues drive a small bus to Port Botany, pick up ships' crews, give them a quick tour and bring them to the Mission headquarters. There, amid ships' models, artefacts and mementos of a more gently paced but perilous time in seafaring, the crew members can contact home, before they are driven back to their ship and push out to sea once more.

While the seafarers would have a little more time ashore in Sydney if their ships docked in the harbour rather than Port Botany, Gary says that would not be practical. In 1788, Arthur Phillip may have considered the harbour big enough for a thousand ships to moor securely, but in the 21st century, the vessels are much larger, and Gary says it would be one congested waterway if they were all squeezing in and out of the port.

'It's all romantic when you see ships coming in, but you can't contemplate that now,' Gary muses. 'It's a different city to what it was, and the harbour was getting just too crowded.'

Still, with commercial shipping having largely headed south to Port Botany, I question how much Sydney has been diminished as a harbour town, now that it doesn't have sailors from around the world wandering, and having a good time, along its waterfront. But Gary puts that notion in perspective.

'Even if the ships were coming into here, that culture has gone, that kind of seafaring has gone,' he counters. 'The turnover is so quick.'

Gary says as the industry continues to change, and time is compressed ever tighter, the Mission's role is more important than ever for seafarers.

'We're giving them a little break from the monotony of the ship,' Gary concludes, his words echoing what Captain Jones had said in praising the Mission's work more than a century earlier.

THE BAY between Dawes Point and Millers Point finally received its official name years after the Sydney Harbour Trust resumed the waterfront and much of the peninsula in 1901. It came to be known as Walsh Bay, named after the Trust's first chief engineer and later commissioner, H.D. Walsh. Yet the change to the bay was more than in name. The clutter of private wharves in the bay was resumed by the port authority. The design of many of the old wharves provided high-density living for rats. After the plague outbreak, those old wharves were demolished. Walsh devised new wharves, as he did for other bays and inlets around the port, and a rat-proof sea wall was installed. Thousands of tonnes of silt had to be dredged and barged out to sea to accommodate larger ships. Just over a decade after the Trust took control of the port, Walsh Bay began to resemble a giant hand, with finger wharves stretching out into the bay. The wharves were bejewelled with handsome stores crowned with gabled roofs, and the past was pushed aside along the waterfront to make way for new buildings and a series of roads to transport cargo. From the early years of the 20th century, the world's ships slipped in between those fingers. Yet as the years pushed on, the wharves became arthritic and increasingly neglected, as shipping embraced containers and unloaded their cargo elsewhere. Walsh Bay became a backwater on the doorstep of the city.

As the century drew to an end, the bay was rediscovered and

revitalised. At Wharf Number 1, a hotel was built, luxury apartments sprouted on Wharf 6/7, as well as along the shoreline, offices and restaurants colonised the area, and at Wharf 4/5, members of the Sydney Theatre Company and Sydney Dance Company began treading the boards.

Along Pier 2/3, there is a stretch called Theatre Walk, and plaques wearing names such as Nevin and Cracknell, Livermore and Blanchett are spaced along the deck. It is also a thoroughfare of anglers. Having barely glanced at the gilded names at their feet, the fishing folk form a curious democracy at the end of the wharf, each finding their own space to cast a line and keep to themselves. That is, until a line tightens. Individuals suddenly become a team.

'Quick, someone grab that net and bring it over,' I hear someone yell. A net is brought over, just as a young man lands a fish, which looks as though it has swum through a rainbow and absorbed its colours.

'It's an amberjack,' a middle-aged fellow explains. The young man receives high-fives and handshakes. A few take photos on their phones.

'Don't see many amberjack around here,' mutters another man. He says that amberjack are more of a tropical fish. The middle-aged bloke grabs a measuring mat to check the legal size limits on an amberjack.

'It's legal!' he declares. The amberjack measures in at about 45 centimetres.

Then, just as quickly as it had formed, the team drifts apart like bubbles and returns to the satisfied insularity of fishing – until the next big one is hooked and help is needed to land it.

ON THE peninsula, no section has been more dramatically transformed than the area now called Barangaroo. For decades, a massive block of concrete imposed its mass on the water along the peninsula's western shore, providing somewhere for shipping containers to be stacked. The concrete apron was ripped up in the early years of the 21st century, and the waterfront is being redeveloped. In twenty-two hectares of waterfront land, there is a marked contrast in what 'redevelopment' means. To the south, towards Darling Harbour, a cluster of towers has risen. The developers have explained how the buildings' designs were inspired by the shapes to be found on and by the harbour, from yachts' sails to cockle shells. Yet from the water, it is hard for me not to see the buildings as being the shape of big piles of money.

To the north, however, there is an alternate future. The headland has been reshaped into something verging on the incredible in this city: a return to an approximation of how this foreshore once was, before there were wharves and ships, before there were towers and people living and working on top of each other. It has been turned into parkland, but not flat green expanses, like what you find at the head of most bays around the harbour; it is an undulating, rocky, straggly landscape. The 6-hectare reserve has been meticulously sculpted, including the placement of about 10,000 sandstone blocks and the planting of more than 75,000 native plants, to create the impression that it is very natural and attractively unkempt. It is the Sydney Harbour equivalent of a hipster.

Over the years, while paddling around the headland, I have been watching the area's transformation. The unremitting wintry grey of the concrete was replaced by the formation of a hill that progressively turned green and shaggy with foliage. The shoreline was unshackled from the boring certainty of a straight line, instead squiggling along the water's edge and sprinkled with large crumbs of sandstone. I have nuzzled into the small cove that has been scooped out along the reserve's southern shores. While the cove itself is a recent creation, or recreation, its name is a reminder of the many generations of paddlers on Sydney Harbour. It is called Nawi Cove, named after the bark canoes of the original harbour people. Sitting in my own version of a nawi in the cove, I have looked up and around at the new-old terrain.

For a time, the emerging landscape was loomed over by the Sydney Harbour control tower. The building was erected in the early 1970s and was almost 90 metres high. It was nicknamed The Pill, because it controlled berths in the harbour. The tower had the shape of a World War Two German stick grenade, and its critics believed it had about the same effect on the surrounding area's aesthetic appeal. The tower was no longer used for controlling vessel movements after 2011, so when the reserve was taking shape, it was decided to bring the tower down. Some, including the National Trust, fought to save the tower, arguing it symbolised Sydney's shipping tradition, and that there was so little left of the harbour's industrial heritage. The National Trust posed alternative uses, such as it being a viewing tower or part of a Museum of Sydney Harbour. However, in 2016, the tower's concrete column was encased in scaffolding and dismantled.

From Nawi Cove, I can also see the crowded western face of Millers Point. I see Hickson Road, which was cut and pushed along the shoreline a hundred years earlier, and it passes a colonial sandstone warehouse converted to offices. I look up at the tiers of heritage, including the workers' cottages built by the Sydney Harbour Trust to replace those it had knocked down as part of the peninsula's redevelopment. Crowning the hill is the observatory. Yet I experience a greater sense of history by stepping onto the sandstone shoreline and walking up to the headland at Barangaroo Reserve. From here, you can see all the way to the past. As former Prime Minister and champion of the headland reserve Paul Keating told the crowd at its official opening in 2015, this was where many Aboriginal people had lived. They could travel the short distances in their canoes to Ballast Point to the west, and over to Balls Head on the North Shore, and, in between, Goat Island. So Mr Keating saw this park as helping reconnect these key points of geography, and of history. He also thought the redevelopment would change how we looked at the harbour.

'We always looked north through Circular Quay,' Paul Keating said. 'Now I think we'll look west.'

The area's very name is a link to the past. Barangaroo was a Cammeraygal woman with an indomitable presence, much to the consternation of the British arrivals. She was disdainful of many of their ways and commands, and she apparently ignored their appeals for her to wear clothes. Yet her husband, Bennelong, tried to straddle both cultures, which she didn't like.

Barangaroo was also a fisherwoman. She and all the fishing women from the harbour groups have been honoured by Peta Strachan, the artistic director of the Jannawi Dance Clan. Peta conceived a performance piece called *Net Fishing Dance*, which she and her troupe performed on the Barangaroo headland on Australia Day in 2016. Like the harbour itself, the dance had a compelling energy. The women performers, wearing flowing dresses the colour of ochre, danced with a fishing net.

The choreography gave the net fluency, creating the impression the performers were dancing with a wave.

Peta has told me she conceived the dance to acknowledge and celebrate the skills and athleticism of the women, as they fished from their nawi, sometimes with their babies on their backs, and cooking what they caught, feeding their families.

'Their skills were amazing,' says Peta, who is a Dharug woman. 'They were pretty impressive. Imagine doing all of that now.'

Peta herself doesn't fish. Instead, she developed her ideas for the dance from research, reading about Barangaroo and other harbour fisherwomen. The women would make their own fishing equipment, including lines from the fibre of trees and plants, and hooks from shells. Just as the harbour nourished the women and their families, those women, their stories, and their relationship with the harbour have fed the soul of Peta Strachan and led to her *Net Fishing Dance*. It also reiterated what Peta has always known and felt: the harbour is a special place.

'It is the connection to all the different clans,' she says.

And through her dance, Peta helps all of us connect to each other, and to the harbour. While watching *Net Fishing Dance* being performed by the Jannawi performers on the Barangaroo headland, I thought that this was the realisation of what Paul Keating had said at the reserve's opening: 'This is going to be an absolutely magic area.'

14

DARLING HARBOUR TO GOAT ISLAND

THE NOTION of Sydney Harbour as a major commercial port has been largely carried away on the king tides of history and progress. But from my kayak, I find traces of it in the water and in snippets along the shore around Darling Harbour. Which is where I'd least expected to find any sense of what this place used to be. This stretch of the harbour has undergone not just some serious cosmetic surgery through the years; it has had a character transplant.

The shores of this long bay gouging into the south-west edges of the CBD were once a source of food for the original inhabitants. They collected cockles along the tidal flats. Before it was known as Darling Harbour, the British called this Cockle Bay. The name has been retained for one section of the waterway, which is still a source of food. It's lined with restaurants and bars.

Food was a motivation for the development of Cockle Bay in early colonial days. The first major wharf beyond Sydney Cove was built on the eastern shore in 1811. Produce was unloaded and taken up the hill to the marketplace. Through the 19th century, a ragged string of wharves and piers spread along the shores. They were the conduit between the water and the businesses that sprouted on the harbour's edge. As well as accepting farm produce from up Parramatta and Lane Cove rivers, the wharves held timber unloaded for boatyards, coal for industries, including the Australian Gas Light Company's works on the shore, and grains for flour mills. Multi-storey warehouses impressed themselves on the waterfront, and steam ships that had traced the coast and traversed the seas docked in Darling Harbour. This waterway became clogged with commerce. Lighters and cranes loaded and unloaded cargo, and the waterfront factories belched a Dickensian smoke into the sky.

When the Sydney Harbour Trust redeveloped the wharves in the first years of the 20th century, it only intensified activity in and around Darling Harbour.

'The ordinary observer of the new wharves of Darling Harbour ... cannot fail to see what a metamorphosis the foreshores will present when a continuous system of similar structures, flanked by a wide thoroughfare, is completed, and what a convenience that will be for the maritime commerce of Sydney,' declared a report in Sydney's *Evening News*.

While there had been reclamation work around this bay since the mid-1800s, Darling Harbour's head was filled in during the 1920s, using spoil from the city's underground railway construction project. That made room for more wharves and stores, and an extensive rail freight system.

If Sydney Cove was the gateway to the city, Darling Harbour was the tradesmen's entrance. As Circular Quay and its arms were increasingly beautified or at least made monumental, the hard graft of the maritime trade was pushed around the peninsula into Darling Harbour and the tendrils of water attached to it. Yet in the course of the 20th century, as the city grew and ships bulked up with containerised cargoes, pressure increased on the port. That was relieved by diverting ships to Port Botany. Darling Harbour began to stagnate, an industrial has-been of rusting rail lines, rotting wharves and warehouses filled with little more than cobwebs and dust.

Where water is involved in Sydney, nothing stays neglected for long. Through the late 1970s and into the 1980s, the southern end of Darling Harbour was brought back to life to handle a form of commercial cargo that had been rarely seen in this part of the harbour: tourists. The New South Wales Government, along with private money, set about redeveloping more than 50 hectares of waterfront land, forming an administrative authority and drafting legislation for the construction of tourist, entertainment, cultural and commercial facilities. Some people hated it, believing the waterfront development was far removed from the soul of the harbour's heritage; indeed, removed from any sort of soul. But the government viewed this as a Bicentennial gift to the nation, and it was opened to the public just ten days before Australia Day, 1988. As a tourist attraction, it is the gift that keeps on giving, bringing in millions of visitors annually. As a development, it continues to divide opinion.

From the water, at least, Darling Harbour is pumping. The lifeblood, however, has changed. It is a working harbour, dedicated to recreation. I paddle past finger wharves populated with showboats, whale-watching boats, sightseeing boats, charter boats, water taxis, and ferries.

Ahead of me, spanning the harbour like a portcullis, is the historic Pyrmont Bridge. A bridge has been here since the mid-1800s, carrying traffic across the water from the city to the west. The original wooden structure was replaced by this iron bridge in 1902. It had a swing-span mechanism to allow larger ships through to the head of Darling Harbour. The bridge now carries only pedestrians but it still opens, basically to allow through yachts and large cruisers. Which provides another tourist attraction, as crowds stand at the barriers of the split bridge, watching a mast glide past just in front of them.

Standing sentinel on each side of the harbour are buildings with roofs that crest and roll like waves. The one on the city shore is an aquarium. Having somewhere to be within comfortable viewing distance of the mysteries of the deep right beside the harbour makes sense. That's what the president of the local Linnaean Society thought back in 1879, when he declared in a speech, 'there are few places in the world in which the requisite buildings could be placed with such advantage for the supply of all conceivable forms of marine life for exhibition to a large city population, such as in Sydney'.

The building on the Pyrmont shore is the Australian National Maritime Museum. Inside are thousands of exhibits, tracing the country's relationship with water. Outside is a flotilla of historic boats, from yachts to a boat used by South Vietnamese asylum seekers to reach Australia, from the replica of James Cook's *Endeavour* to two decommissioned navy ships, the destroyer HMAS *Vampire* and the submarine HMAS *Onslow*. I have paddled to *Onslow*'s stern. It is like creeping up on a sea monster, its black flanks forbidding. I have also kayaked around the *Endeavour* replica, looking up through the geometry of its rigging, and peering at the windows along the lavishly decorated stern to the captain's cabin, imagining Cook sitting in there, making marks on a chart, tracing a line towards the future and into history.

The museum's wharves are at their most beguiling when it is hosting the Classic and Wooden Boat Festival. I have paddled in among the boats on display, placing my Kevlar and fibreglass craft almost within touching distance of some legends crafted from timber. Among the vessels are Halvorsen cruisers, preened and polished like nautical show dogs, and small yachts with gigantic reputations. I fawn over *Kathleen Gillett*, a double-ended, wooden cruising ketch, which was born on the banks of Parramatta River and sailed around the world by maritime artist Jack Earl. I see *Anitra V*, a timber yacht also built on Parramatta River at the Halvorsen family's boatyard and raced by the brothers Trygve and Magnus Halvorsen in a string of Sydney to Hobart races. And there is an intriguing motor boat, *Mount Pleasant*. She has an intriguing aura, and an extraordinary history, as I learn from her owner, Simon Mitchell, who is standing at her stern.

Simon has made his money in finance and now spends much of his time messing about on boats, particularly this century-old one.

'You know what BOAT stands for?' he asks, before answering. 'Bust Out Another Thousand!'

Simon should know. He has spent the past few years and a stack of money restoring *Mount Pleasant* on the state's South Coast. Like a proud parent, he shows me photos of her restoration, from a worn-out shell to the royal-blue-hulled beauty she is today. While he was restoring *Mount Pleasant*, Simon tried to balance respecting her past and incorporating modern comforts.

'One of the dilemmas was what to conserve, where to compromise, because we're not a museum,' he says, as he points behind. 'Look! Period detail. USB chargers!'

Simon is a generous soul, constantly inviting festival visitors on board his 12-metre boat for a look below deck and encouraging them to open the door with the fine glass panels to admire the fancy shower. He says he installed it principally to win his partner over to the idea of cruising.

I must have been sufficiently impressed by the handiwork, because Simon invites me to cruise on *Mount Pleasant* the following day on a special tour. This is a homecoming and 100th birthday present for her. Simon had researched the life – or lives – of *Mount Pleasant*, and now he is going to take her back to some key places of her early years.

We cruise the harbour not chronologically through the boat's life, but geographically. First we circumnavigate Cockatoo Island, where, Simon explains, she used to ferry workers after the Second World War. We then putter a little south to Goat Island, where she had worked for the Maritime Services Board in the 1950s. She had been a 'G' boat, as the MSB's Goat Island workboats were called.

We carve the few hundred metres across the harbour towards the northern shore, heading for an old slipway incised into the shore near McMahons Point.

'And this is where she was born,' Simon says.

Mount Pleasant was built in 1916 in the boatyard of William Holmes for a ferry operator on the New South Wales Central Coast. She could carry seventy passengers and was the star of the delightfully named Saratoga and Mount Pleasant Original Ferry Service. By the 1920s, she was back on Sydney Harbour, with her whistle, connected to the exhaust, turning heads whenever it hollered.

The whistle still chimes, and it still turns heads. As we pass *Alexander*, Simon blows the whistle, as if one old ferry is talking to a younger thing. The other ferry's passengers look up, surprised to hear the sound of the past, full of energy, bounding across the water to them.

We chug east to Garden Island, skirting around the naval base. The skipper explains *Mount Pleasant* was put to work for the navy during the Second World War and was alongside HMAS *Kuttabul* the night of the Japanese midget submarine attack. When the *Kuttabul* was sunk, it's believed *Mount Pleasant* helped carry the dead and others caught up in the attack to shore.

We turn to head back out into the main channel, but *Mount Pleasant* takes her time. A dignified old lady is not about to be rushed.

'Be a good girl,' Simon coaxes, as he manoeuvres the boat.

The skipper wants fish and chips from Doyles in Watsons Bay. As we cruise further east, Simon talks about the ferry's life until he bought her. After her time in the Maritime Services Board, she was sold as a pleasure craft and was in Botany Bay. She was taken to the South Coast in the early 1990s. And there she stayed, slowly dying, until Simon came along, looking for a new challenge.

'She's a bit of a mongrel,' he says of her new look, 'with elements of the workboat, but her style is closer to when she was a ferry.' I look around at the plush royal blue and white interior, and the gleaming wheel. She doesn't look like an old workboat.

'Honestly, I think it's the best she's ever been,' Simon says.

As we saunter along the harbour, *Mount Pleasant* receives plenty of admiring waves and hoots. We can see the Heads, and I ask him what it was like to bring her between those great bluffs, back home, for the first time in decades. Simon looks ahead and grins.

'You know you're an Australian when you're coming into Sydney Harbour, especially coming into the harbour in a boat you've restored yourself, and on her centenary.'

WITH ONE slab of forlorn and neglected waterfront land having been transformed into something eye-catching and money-spinning, the redevelopment fever spread a little further west along the harbour, around the Pyrmont peninsula.

On the north-eastern side of the peninsula, the redevelopment has crept to the water's edge, and then kept going. I kayak past finger wharves, built for commercial shipping in the post-World War Two years. Now those wharves prop up apartment blocks and offices that have the look of warehouses but are cocoons of luxury.

Along the north-western stretch of Darling Harbour is *James Craig*, a fully restored tall ship. She was built in 1874 and for many years carried cargoes around the globe, until the age of steam reduced her to menial tasks, such as being a coal hulk. *James Craig* was eventually left abandoned on a beach in Tasmania, before she was rescued by volunteers from the Sydney Heritage Fleet, who spent years restoring her body and dignity. Now *James Craig* carries tourists around the harbour and often out through the Heads. Yet she, and other tall ships on the harbour such as *Soren Larsen* and *Southern Swan*, also carries the romance of sail.

Once you have experienced that romance, you remain smitten. *Soren Larsen* doesn't have the age of *James Craig*, having been built in Denmark in 1949, but she has a wonderful history. The square rigger was a star in the BBC television series *The Onedin Line*, and she was part of the First Fleet re-enactment voyage for Australia's bicentenary, sailing from Portsmouth and arriving in Sydney Harbour on 26 January 1988. Twenty-seven years later, I was on *Soren Larsen* for an Australia Day tall ships race along the harbour. What a joy it was watching the crew members work with each other, and with the ship, their efforts bringing her to life; that, and the breeze. People often use sailing as a metaphor for relaxing, taking it easy, accepting wherever the wind blows. It all sounds so passive. But standing on *Soren Larsen* that day, it occurred to me that sailing was about working hard and making the most of the moment to get somewhere. As the saying goes, a pessimist whinges about the wind, the optimist expects it to change, while the realist adjusts the sails. So sailing is a lesson in reality.

Yet the very vessel that teaches you to be a realist also seduces you to be a dreamer. The mere sight of a sailing ship is a dream. While kayaking, I've often seen *James Craig* out on the harbour. When her sails are filled with the winds, she looks as though she is off to the ball. But even as I paddle past *James Craig* docked in Darling Harbour, her sails furled, and her sleek black hull snuggling into the wharf, she is still a dream. Hers is a timeless beauty.

Off the peninsula defining Darling Harbour's western shoreline, there was once a small island. But as the point was industrialised, development extended to the island. Darling Island, as it was called, was the site of a slipway. The Australasian Steam Navigation Company built its maintenance yard here for its ships. By the 1870s, the march of industry had trampled any distinction between the peninsula and the island, as land was reclaimed.

On the former island, the Royal Edward Victualling Yard was built for the Royal Navy, to supply its ships as they cruised around the eastern edges of the British Empire. The complex was handed over to the Commonwealth after the Royal Australian Navy was born. A towering remnant of those times stands above the seawall on the western shore. It is an eight-storey building of brick and stone with gabled parapets. As I sit in the kayak and look up, the tower is more than a landmark; it exudes authority. The building commands you to notice it. Its face is tattooed with the letters of another age, another reign: 'GR', or 'George Rex', for King George V. The structure also wears what was a rarity when it was constructed. Each of its eight floors has external fire escape stairs, because in early 20th century Sydney, this was a tall building, and pumped water, if needed, could reach only so high. At the building's feet on the quay is an old crane, reminding me I'm floating on the invisible prints of ships. For much of the past century, in wartime and peace, vessels were loaded and unloaded here. In the future, the building will accommodate only the loaded. It is being converted into apartments.

I paddle out of the lonely quay and follow the peninsula's shore, which is pinned with a promenade that looks like a wooden wharf, as though ships could still dock here. But it is built for recreation, not industry. A group is practising yoga on the deck, looking down at the water where there were tidal baths until the 1940s. I can't imagine swimming in this part of the harbour now, let alone then.

In the 19th century, Pyrmont was progressively dug up and carried across the water to make the CBD look more impressive. Pyrmont stone was used in the construction of major public buildings, including the General Post Office and the Art Gallery of New South Wales. All the while, the beauty of the peninsula, which early colonial picnickers called Pyrmont because it reminded them of a German spa resort, was disappearing into holes.

Yet as I can see from the water, in recent years the peninsula has been refilled with building materials. Medium-density housing has been packed along the ridges and at the base of the shaved sandstone faces. If the celebrated photographer Max Dupain were still here, I wonder what his eye would make of the change. He used to have a studio on the other side of Darling Harbour, and through his window, he would photograph the ships and wharves, the industries and jammed-in working class housing, catching with his cameras and light the texture and grit of those lives. If he could look across at the shinier, cleaner Pyrmont, with its proclamations and promises of wealth in the apartments and offices and the Star Casino, would Dupain see the makings of a compelling image, or a place that is now having its soul quarried?

At the end of the peninsula, along Johnstons Bay, the Colonial Sugar Refining Company presided over a large area for more than a century. Raw materials from as far away as Fiji were unloaded at the wharves then distilled and refined into sugar, golden syrup, molasses and alcohol, as well as building materials. In the early 1990s, when CSR moved off the 11-hectare site, the developers moved in to create a new community. A few of the old industrial buildings were retained and recycled, but shadowing them are high-rise residential blocks. Moping around the walking areas near the waterfront are a few artefacts of the site's industrial and shipping past, including two large iron balls. I don't know what their purpose once was, but when I paddle past them, I cannot help but think they may be symbols of a castrated maritime industry around the harbour.

Straight ahead is the David and Goliath, or the past and present, of bridges.

Any modern bridge that sets out to be noticed, rather than merely be driven over, is up against it in Sydney. What has been built across the harbour before and Mother Nature ensure that. But Anzac Bridge projects a monumental presence. The then-Premier Bob Carr must have been confident of the bridge's profile as he officially opened it in 1995, because he cut the ceremonial ribbon using the same pair of scissors as his political forebear Jack Lang did in 1932 for the opening of Sydney Harbour Bridge. Anzac Bridge has the architecture to substantiate the ceremony. It has twin 120-metre-high concrete towers, each fanning stay cables ever so delicately towards the deck. As I paddle towards the bridge, I marvel at those cables knitting the sky.

Sitting below the Anzac Bridge like Banquo's ghost is the structure it replaced, Glebe Island Bridge. The original bridge was built from wood in 1857. To allow ships to pass, the operator – and toll collector – would turn a winch, and a section would rise like a drawbridge. The wooden structure was replaced in 1901 with a steel bridge, which had a swing-span in the middle. What was impressive technology at the start of the century was a source of frustration for motorists near the end of it, before Anzac Bridge was opened. My friend and fellow Gentleman Kayaker George Ellis grimaces when we paddle this section of the harbour, because he remembers sitting in his car and waiting in a long queue of traffic, while the bridge swung open, cutting a main artery to the west.

Time and lack of use have rendered the structure sclerotic. In an insult to any bridge, it is no longer fixed in the position that made it useful – crossing the bay. Instead, the swing span is left open to allow through the array of vessels that berth in the bays on the southern side. Some locals want the bridge rejuvenated as a pedestrian and bicycle crossing. Gliding past its time-worn sandstone pylons, then looking up at its replacement, I reckon the old bridge remains a beautiful gateway to Blackwattle and Rozelle bays.

Having passed through the narrow throat of water into these two bays, I've been swallowed into a bizarrely diverse part of the harbour. It is working hard to offer something for everyone. A glass half-full view would say it looks eclectic; half empty, it's a bit of a mess. Along these two bays that peel off in opposite directions like a feuding couple, there are elements of what the harbour once was, markers of how it has changed, and predictors of what it will increasingly be. There is a concrete plant but also extensive parklands and a waterfront walking track. There are tasteful apartments and townhouses yet derelict patches and ramshackle wharves that are an eyesore, unless you're a planner or developer. There is a marina swaddling large pleasure cruisers, yet also mooching about on the shores, waiting to work, are barges, ferries and showboats. Sculls cut across the water from the Glebe Rowing Club, and paddling teams in dragon boats and outriggers huff and puff in unison towards Anzac Bridge.

These two bays combined have the feel of a working harbour but in places look like a backwater, as though the same levels of development and beautification that have washed over other parts of the harbour haven't yet been carried into here. All of which makes it an intriguing place to paddle.

I turn left into Blackwattle Bay. I'm paddling in the wake of convict labourers, who rowed across the bay then waded into the swamps to cut wattle trees and reeds for building materials. As the area was cleared, factories and timber yards rose out of the mud. The bay that was named for its black wattle is now synonymous with fish.

The Sydney Fish Market is on the bay's south-eastern shores. It turns away from the hubbub of the city and ignores the scuttling and shuffling of traffic on the spider web of arterial roads and ramps above its head to create its own energy. The market is reminiscent of a shopping mall, as visitors cruise through the retail areas, looking for a feed. Just before Good Friday and in the lead-up to Christmas, the complex is filled with not just the scent of the sea but desperation, as hordes spiral into a buying frenzy, snapping up a couple of hundred tonnes of prawns and about 900,000 oysters. Each morning, beginning before dawn, the market holds a wholesale auction, selling what is bound for plates in restaurants and cafés. About fifty tonnes of seafood are traded each day. With seafood, Sydneysiders are insatiable. It seems to be part of our identity as harbour people, literally nourishing who we are. It has been that way for many thousands of years.

For the original inhabitants living around its shores, the harbour helped sustain them. But no sooner had the British arrived than there was competition for fish. Jacob Nagle was part of Arthur Phillip's crew exploring Sydney Harbour. Nagle noted how on the night before they headed back to Botany Bay to tell the others they had found a place to settle, he tossed out a line from his boat.

'I ketched a large Black Brim,' Nagle recorded, adding that Phillip had asked who caught the fish. 'I inform'd him that I had. Recollect he Said that you are the first white man that ever caught a fish in Sidney Cove.'

According to the First Fleeters, when they first threw out their nets and hauled in large catches, the Aboriginal people responded positively. Surgeon John White wrote how in one encounter the day after the fleet had arrived in Sydney Cove, the 'natives' helped drag the catch ashore and 'were liberally rewarded with fish, which seemed to please them and give general satisfaction'.

But satisfaction dimmed as fish stocks were reduced during winter, while the demand from the newcomers increased, and the original inhabitants' precious fishing equipment and canoes were sometimes stolen. In a letter to his father on 12 July 1788, Newton Fowell wrote the Aboriginal people passed his ship, *Sirius*, daily but never came close. 'We could often see them strike fish,' he wrote. 'I have often gone to them & given them things which they readily accept but will never part with anything, particular their fish which is their only Subsistance [sic] & I believe they have little enough for themselves.'

As the colony developed, it was not just competition for food that put pressure on fish stocks in the harbour. The development around the shores, and treating the harbour as somewhere to dump a city's waste, sullied the waters to the extent that governments had inquiries, and Sydneysiders asked what was happening to their jewel. 'Our harbour has partaken largely of the character of a "dead sea",' declared a newspaper, after a die-off of oysters and mussels in 1891.

Yet for decades, the harbour remained a sink trap and dumping ground for the city, and the results of that can be seen – or, more to the point, can't be seen – in the fish market. You can't buy Sydney Harbour fish at Sydney Fish Market. The seafood comes from beyond the Heads. Commercial fishing in Sydney Harbour ended in 2006 due to concerns about contaminants, particularly dioxins, in the water. The State Government bought back commercial licences and warned recreational anglers where not to fish. That move meant the livelihoods of commercial fishermen were poisoned by the past actions of other industries.

In Iron Cove, just a few bays to the west of the fish market, I come across a man named Frank. He is gently pulling up onto the shore a much-patched and repainted dinghy. With a beanie pulled towards his weathered face, and his lithe body covered in a thick-cabled jumper, jeans and gumboots, Frank looks like a fisherman. The way his face ignites as we get speaking about water, and the mysteries and bounties it contains, tells me Frank is a fisherman. And that's before I hear Frank's story.

Frank was born into fishing. His father had been a fisherman in Sicily, before he emigrated in 1948. In new waters in a new land, he practised his old ways, fishing on the harbour. Four years later, the teenage Frank, his siblings and mother also arrived in Sydney, stepping off a ship at Walsh Bay.

In 1954, Frank's father launched a boat that had been built in Berrys Bay, over on the North Shore. It was a 25-foot craft constructed from kauri pine. A priest blessed the boat, and it was named *San Giuseppe*, to remember the family's home back in Sicily. Frank joined his father on *San Giuseppe*, working the harbour, creating a life. They fished for bream, whiting and John Dory, and they trawled for prawns in the bays, including this one, Leichhardt Bay, where I've met Frank.

'Leichhardt Bay prawns, they were beautiful – this big,' Frank enthuses, opening his thumb and forefinger as wide as he can.

The father and son headed out in the afternoon and fished late into the night, before delivering their catch in the early hours to the market. It was a hard way to make a living – 'I was a fisherman during the summer, and a painter during the winter' – but he loved the life. Then it ended.

Frank shakes his head. He reckons shutting down commercial fishing in the harbour was a big mistake. It caused economic pain in so many quarters, from those who sold nets to those supplying fuel for the boats. But, he says emphatically, it also hurt the community. It changed people's way of life, the social activities and culture, associated with fishing. Frank squints at the water, seeing what is no longer there, as he mutters there used to be up to forty fishing boats in this bay.

I ask Frank what happened to *San Giuseppe*. He smiles and points to her, a blue and white vessel with her name lovingly hand-painted on her bow. He can no longer make a living from her, but she remains part of his life. Frank has just spent a few hours on her, replacing a plank and painting. His loved ones tell him he should sell the boat, but, he shrugs, 'I can't. I won't.' For Frank, *San Giuseppe* maintains a connection to his father, to his past, to what he did, and to who he was – and still is.

'I like the water. I'm happy when I see the water,' says Frank, as he gives his battered little dinghy one last heave onto the shore.

You can still see trawlers travelling across the harbour. Their engines reliably grumble as they go out of the Heads and come back in again, wearing a halo of gulls flapping and screeching for a free feed. You can usually find a small fleet docked outside the fish market in Blackwattle Bay, in between their voyages out to sea.

Early one morning, I paddle up to a man standing in a rocking tinny beside a trawler. He is painting the hull with a hand-held roller. It looks an enormous job, like painting the Harbour Bridge, and I tell him so. As he keeps working, he tells me he has sanded, undercoated and painted most of the hull in one night. I ask him if he's the skipper.

He stops rolling, turns cautiously, and looks at me quizzically. 'Do you think a skipper would be doing this job?'

WHILE THE cause of the damage to the fishing industry lies in the sediments under the water, just a few hundred metres from the market is a team dedicated to keeping the harbour's surface and shorelines looking clean and free of rubbish.

The Roads and Maritime Services' environmental teams are based on the northern side of Rozelle Bay. They're responsible for inspecting 200 locations around the harbour. Every day, the teams head out in barges, removing rubbish from the shores and anything on the water that could be a hazard to boating.

I'm invited out with Troy Polidano, who is skipper today, and deckhand Jarrod Bernhardt on *ES5*, a catamaran barge with a bow ramp. The 12-metre barge can be loaded with almost 5 tonnes of garbage. We set off from the wharf and glide under Anzac Bridge.

The team's first job is to check the pump-out stations at White Bay and the King Street commercial wharves, where many of the tourist boats dock. Troy and Jarrod say the commercial sector is highly aware of avoiding pumping out waste in the harbour, but they know a few recreational boats still do it; they've seen the evidence on the water.

We trundle around into Walsh Bay, where Jarrod scoops up a soccer ball. Usually they collect tennis balls.

'I could keep twenty tennis balls every day,' says Troy, as he manoeuvres the wheel and levers to steady the barge for his colleague. The teams also retrieve stacks of headwear, which they hang on a 'hat tree' back at the base.

We edge into Sydney Cove, after Troy contacts the Port Authority's Vessel Traffic Service for permission to enter what is a restricted area. As we bob at the base of a white mountain that is a berthed cruise ship, Troy explains a lot of plastic rubbish can be trapped in the cove and has to be removed, to keep paths clear for ferries, and it is not a good look in tourists' photos.

We turn west and head under the Bridge. 'I think I've been under the Harbour Bridge more than I've been over it,' says Troy, who joined the team in April 2015, after years working as an aircraft mechanic. Jarrod, who had been working in the commercial maritime industry, joined the service a few months later.

Jarrod and Troy are on the 'river run' today. They are inspecting Parramatta River as far as the weir, a course of just over 20 kilometres, to ensure it is clear for the RiverCats.

'Our primary function is to make sure there's safe navigation in the harbour,' Jarrod explains.

'We try to get things before they're a hazard, so if we see potential hazards on the shore, we grab them,' Troy adds. As if on cue, he notices a palm frond splayed on the surface. The barge crawls up on the frond, and Jarrod fossicks it out. The worst time for debris on the harbour, they say, is after a king tide has flushed out all the rubbish along the shores.

'After king tides, there are just lines of debris, and they're really thick,' mutters Jarrod. He says they can collect more than 3 cubic metres of rubbish from just one little cove.

Sometimes, amid the thick refuse of the city, are things they would prefer not to have to deal with, such as animals' corpses and 'Sydney Harbour squids' (used condoms).

On the journey up and down the river, Troy nudges the barge onto the slips of beaches in small coves and lowers the ramp, so Jarrod can collect rubbish off the shore. Jarrod tells me the weirdest item he's fished out of the harbour is a quad bike. He had to use a small crane on the barge to lift it out of Powder Keg Bay in Middle Harbour. For Troy, the most disconcerting item he's retrieved is a complete artificial breast.

I'm transferred to another Environmental Services vessel at 'Naval Beach', a secluded cove beside HMAS *Waterhen*, tucked in around Balls Head. As I bid Troy and Jarrod farewell, they are frowning at the line of plastic on the shore. They had cleaned here only yesterday.

'It's never ending, really,' says Jarrod.

The 'never-ending' clean-up voyage continues with Ken Wark and deckhand Louise Nelson on their skimming boat. It has a cage that drops through the deck to scoop rubbish. Ken and Louise are cleaning the 'City Circle', the stretch of heavily used water just east of the Harbour Bridge.

Ken has been working on, or beside, the harbour for more than thirty years and has been on the Environmental Services barges since 1994. He reckons that, while there's less rubbish on the water, a lot of problems continue to flow from the catchment areas.

'This is the lowest point,' Ken mutters. 'So it all ends up in here.'

'One thing I've seen less of are cigarette butts, they're not in the concentrated levels of the late 1990s.'

Near Bradleys Head, Louise spots a bottle of household cleaner in the water. It's still full and can be put to use sprucing up the cabin.

'You see,' smiles Ken. 'The harbour provides.'

Louise explains how each officer seems to focus in on certain things when inspecting the harbour.

'I've been on a straw tangent, and also styro, or polystyrene,' she says. Louise also has a skill for spotting floating money – 'I found a $50 note off Luna Park' – although it's becoming less common with the advent of ways to pay without cash. Ken's forte, she says, is navigational hazards, such as logs.

Sadly, both have spotted bodies in the water. In her eight years on the boats, Louise has found four. Ken has seen one in his time.

Ken lowers the cage into the bay just beyond Milsons Point. The water bubbles furiously, as lines of rubbish are scooped from along the seawall. There's not a lot today, but they know that will soon change. Rain is forecast.

After the wet weather, Louise says, 'you play the goalkeeper almost, and stop the debris coming down [the river] and washing on shore'.

'We're on top of it much quicker now,' says Ken. 'And so the harbour gets back to its state much quicker.'

In a disposable society, what Ken and Louise, Jarrod and

Troy, and the others do for the harbour is indispensable. It is, as Jarrod says, the never-ending job on Sydney Harbour.

THE AUTHOR and Sydney lover Ruth Park once observed that Blackwattle Bay and Rozelle Bay were places where old boats came to die. But these days, just along from the RMS depot, is where old boats are resuscitated and reborn.

Sydney Heritage Fleet has its docks and workshop on the shore. It was here that a team of volunteers restored the tall ship *James Craig* to be the majestic vessel she is once more. The shipyard reverberates with the soundtrack of vitality; clanging and banging and busy voices. It is the sound of a harbour working. The centre of attention is the coastal steamer *John Oxley*, which was built in 1927 and served as a pilot boat and lighthouse tender off Queensland for many years. She was one of many coastal steamships that traced the east coast. Near the end of her working life, *John Oxley* was considered a rust bucket, but as I stand under her bow, looking up at the immensity of her in the slave dock, I can see the years are being scraped off her steel skin. From this angle, she looks awesome, as though she can't wait to slide back into the water. Yet she has been on the dock for the best part of twenty years. As the 450 volunteers know all too well, to do time-honoured work takes time. But the rewards of patience are berthed in front of the yard, including the fleet's flagship, the graceful 1902 steam launch, *Lady Hopetoun*. The fleet has nine historic vessels, from tugs to a gentlemen's schooner – and *James Craig*.

While looking at the century-old harbour ferry *Kanangra*, which still has salt water rubbing her belly while she is being restored, I meet up with Tim Drinkwater, Sydney Heritage Fleet's Operations Manager.

While Tim is talking, I keep gazing at the steam tug *Waratah*, which is beside *Kanangra*. 'Come on,' says Tim, following my stare. 'Let's go see her.'

Waratah was born on Sydney Harbour, at Cockatoo Island in 1902. At the end of her working life in the late 1960s, she was to be scrapped, until Sydney Heritage Fleet saved her. She is the oldest tug in working order in Australia. What's more, *Waratah* is a living, steam-breathing reminder of what the harbour has lost. As Sydney's role as a working harbour drifts away, so too have the tugs. In old photos of the harbour, tugs are a constant presence, exhaling coal-black breaths as they stoically push and pull ships in and out of wharves.

'Without them, a port would be a chaotic place to berth a ship,' Tim says.

Tugboats have been crucial in developing Sydney Harbour as a port. In 1831, the first steam-powered vessels appeared on the harbour, and, among their various roles, they were tugs. Before then, ships were moved at the variable mercy of Mother Nature, or slowly pulled by oarsmen, as Randi Svensen points out in her book on tugs, *Heroic, Forceful and Fearless*. Once there were tugboats, Randi explains, ships no longer had to wait for fair winds and currents to go in and out of port.

With fewer ships berthing in the harbour, you don't see many tugs. It is only when I'm at Sydney Heritage Fleet's yard that I realise how rarely I see them on the harbour. Not that they've ever demanded attention. Tugs are not very Sydney. They are not flashy, and they are not something you notice; they just get on with the job, usually while in the service of something much bigger and more eye-catching, such as a cruise ship.

What we once barely noticed we now keenly feel. It is as though there is a hole in the soul of Sydney Harbour with so few of these little workboats going about their business. Yet here in Rozelle Bay, that soul is restored and the hole at least partially filled. You can see a small fleet of tugs nuzzled in together, with *Waratah* and two former navy vessels, *Bronzewing* and *Currawong*.

Bronzewing is used to manoeuvre *James Craig*. On an earlier visit to Sydney Heritage Fleet, I accompanied Tim and a retired tugboat worker, Terry, on an excursion down the harbour to tow the tall ship. While Tim was at the wheel, Terry worked the lines at the bow. It was labour-intensive and vocally driven, as instructions were hollered from ship to ship, and from the tug's bow to the wheelhouse and back again. But Tim and Terry made it look seamless, as *Bronzewing* persuaded *James Craig* to move out from its Darling Harbour berth.

'It's just a quiet gentle movement,' Tim told me. 'And every now and then, you just give it a little more pull.'

To see *Bronzewing* once more resting beside *Waratah* provides a good feeling, which I mention to Tim. He's not surprised, for that is one role of Sydney Heritage Fleet, 'to reassure people that this was a working harbour, and this place is living evidence of that'.

We take a ladder down into the heart of *Waratah*, to her meticulously kept engine. Tim explains how it works, but I see only a jigsaw of wheels and shafts. He also shows me where the coal is shovelled to fuel *Waratah*, and the tray of soot that has to be emptied. I ask who does all this.

'Volunteers,' he replies.

As we inspect *Waratah*'s inner workings, Tim talks about the flesh and blood that keeps this steel and wood alive. Among the fleet's 450 volunteers are former maritime tradesmen and waterfront workers, but there are also retired professionals, such as surgeons and lawyers. And it's not a boys' club; there are women among the workers. Tim observes that, for many, the volunteers are giving new life not just to the vessels they work on but also to themselves, as they develop new skills and new friends. What's more, he says, the Heritage Fleet is saving skills.

'Without a place like this, we'd have lost so many of the skills that have been here on the harbour for a long, long time,' he says. 'These skills keep vessels afloat.'

And as he watches his neighbours, such as those who build and maintain wharves, being pushed out by the dollars and desire for waterfront living, Tim knows those skills will become even rarer.

'It's the Catch-22 here; the harbour becomes the carrot to bring people here, but then that population gets so big and the price of real estate goes up so much, it just gets too expensive to operate near the water, and it's just for the very, very wealthy,' Tim muses.

'I think the saddest part is that the commercial operators are being squeezed out. People forget that what they do is maintain the harbour, maintain those waterfront properties. I'd like to see the commercial operators along here stay, to keep Sydney Harbour in the beautiful state it is today, because without them, it would go to wrack and ruin very quickly.

'Aesthetically, some of the harbour looks absolutely beautiful, but we can't live on beauty alone. We still have some shipping, and those wharves need to be maintained. So I'm hoping common sense might prevail, that a compromise be made, and we remember what the harbour is about. So lock in the infrastructure, keep the harbour operational, and ensure it's not only interesting to look at but viable.'

WHAT IS collected and cherished at Sydney Heritage Fleet still holds some relevance back out under Anzac Bridge and along the western shore of what is called Glebe Island and around into White Bay. Tugs still chaperone ships into deeper water here. This section still looks kind of like a working harbour. The wharves wrapping around Glebe Island into White Bay handle bulk goods. For many years, Glebe Island – which is actually not an island – was part of the change to containerisation in shipping. Containers were also handled along the opposite shore at White Bay. But then that all moved to Botany Bay, leaving a huge expanse of concrete and a whole lot of head scratching as to what it could become. Still, the area has been through change before.

In the 1850s, an abattoir was developed on Glebe Island, with refined sandstone buildings constructed for the slaughter of animals. The waste was pumped into the harbour in such quantities that Blackwattle and Rozelle bays would sometimes look as though they were flowing with blood. Sharks would also feast on the waste. Residents complained about not just the pollution in the water but in the air. The odours were rank. Despite the complaints and a government inquiry, the abattoir didn't close until 1916, moving upriver to Homebush.

Along the north-western side of Glebe Island is a row of grain silos. They've been here since the 1920s, and in a city that was not yet reaching for the sky, the silos were considered landmarks. In the lead-up to the Olympics, they must have been seen as ugly. From the Anzac Bridge side, the complex was tarted up with a bizarre *trompe l'oeil*, so that the silos looked like ancient temple columns, with indents depicting muscular athletes who have vaulted from the decorations on a Grecian urn. From the silos' other side, however, on the water, there's no hiding what they are, and they're painted in dun colours of grey, brown and cream.

Near the silos, at the end of the bay, is the disused and derelict White Bay Power Station, with its twin chimneys. When I turn and look back down White Bay, I barely notice the industries and businesses flanking it as I'm fixed by the view to the Harbour Bridge. That view tends to block out everything else from the vision – or, at least, it can shape how everything else around it is seen.

When he was the New South Wales Premier, Mike Baird called this area an urban wasteland. The New South Wales Government's development arm has had a grand plan for this stretch, which is part of what it calls the Bays Precinct. As Mike Baird outlined, the power station and Glebe Island could become an 'innovation hub'. He forecast how this could become a vibrant waterfront destination, where, instead of importing sand, it could be used for exporting silicon. The term 'wasteland' came as a surprise, and as a bit of an insult, to the maritime businesses operating on Glebe Island and around White Bay. Where the Premier and his planners saw potential, those who relied on access to the harbour could see their livelihoods ebbing away, and more of the waterfront's traditions being wiped out.

Further along White Bay on its northern shore, where containers used to be stacked, the shipping industry is flourishing. It is a cruise ship terminal. The gentle waves of the terminal's steel roof sit under industrial girders, so that the past and present co-exist. Not that some of the neighbours are happy about the terminal. In his 'A Portrait of Sydney', Kenneth Slessor wrote evocatively about being able to look down streets into ship's funnels at the bottom of the garden. The present-day residents are concerned about what comes out of the ships' funnels. They have argued emissions from the fuel burnt by the docked cruise ships have been damaging their health. A little further past the terminal, I see outside a waterfront home a placard facing the harbour that reads, 'Cruise Emissions Poison Us'.

I've sailed on cruise ships out of and into the White Bay terminal. From the ship's top deck, I could look over the terminal to the row of terrace houses that marked the edge of a thick clump of homes on the Balmain peninsula. The division between the suburb and harbour life is the width of a narrow street, which is what makes Balmain so attractive to so many. Wandering over to the ship's starboard side, I could see to Pyrmont, where the cruise liners used to berth in the post-war years. That wharf area has been colonised by apartments and offices, so cruise ships would not fit there anymore.

But the cruise ships are coming in and out of the harbour with ever increasing regularity. In the 2015/2016 financial year, there were about 325 cruise ship visits in New South Wales, most of them to Sydney. Demand exceeds wharf availability, and the biggest cruise companies have reportedly pulled some of their ships out of Sydney, because there are not enough berths. Yet again, the harbour is over-loved, and there's simply not enough of it to go around to satisfy all those who want a slice of it.

As I paddle on around Peacock Point, which is marked by an old anchor, I can't help but wonder what the early occupants of the small cottages scrambling up the steep hill would have made of the change to their suburb. If they could return from the 19th century, they would recognise some of the structures, built from local stone, but they would notice their workplaces at the bottom of the hill had gone, and then they would faint when they heard the prices their humble cottage or terrace house now sold for. This area, then as now, has willed many to fall in love with water. The bookseller James R. Tyrrell, who grew up overlooking Johnstons Bay, reminisced about his Tom Sawyer existence by the harbour in the 1880s, even being allowed to play pirates on a visiting sailing ship. All around him lived seamen and captains, with tales and mementos of a life on ships, and down at the waterfront were timberyards and slipways.

Along the shore, there are scant reminders of those little industries. Just near the Balmain East ferry terminal at the end of Darling Street is a two-storey sandstone building. It was a boat store, believed to have been built in the late 1800s. But vessels have taken shape on this site since the 1830s. A boat-builder, John Bell, established a yard here in the 1830s. Bell's shipyard was bought by brothers John and Thomas Fenwick in 1883. The Fenwicks had a tugboat company, which would grow into one of the biggest around the harbour. Well into the 20th century, Fenwick tugs could be seen tied up at a private wharf outside the boat store. The tugs and the wharf have gone, but the stone building has been restored, clinging onto the shore and the waterfront traditions that created it.

The maritime character of Balmain East remains not just in a physical way. Its spirit wanders up the streets and lanes, past the rows of cottages and somnolent veranda-hooded shops. It whorls around the corner buildings that were once pubs crammed with seamen unsteady on their legs, searching for something like home, or perhaps trying to forget where they came from, or maybe they were just beyond remembering. Balmain East still looks and feels like a maritime town even from the water, as I sit in my kayak, riding the ferries' wakes. This place was essentially made by the water. It is a community built on stone and scented with salt. Water has defined many of those who have lived here.

In rugby league terms, Neil Bevan (no relation) is a Balmain boy. He was at the 1939 grand final, which was won by the Balmain Tigers. Actually, his mother was there. And, therefore, so was he. Neil was in his mother's womb.

In territorial terms, Neil Bevan is a Balmain East boy. He grew up in a sandstone house with a slate roof, built in 1880, down a pathway overlooking Jubilee Bay on the southern side of the peninsula. The bay received its name from a floating dock opened in 1880s, known as the Victoria Jubilee Floating Dock, in honour of Queen Victoria. By the time Neil was a boy, the dock was gone, and so was Queen Victoria, but the shoreline remained pebbled with boatyards and ship repair businesses.

The harbour provided for Neil and his family. Around the rocks, they would catch crabs, and they would string out a fishing net in the bay. More than nourish him and his neighbours, the harbour filled the community's work and leisure hours.

'Down the east end, just about everyone worked around the waterfront,' he says.

Neil trained at Cockatoo Island as a shipwright and followed his trade around the harbour and out to sea. There was work always to be found.

'The harbour was full of ships at every berth, all the way around Pyrmont, Darling Harbour and into Walsh Bay, and a few around in Woolloomooloo Bay,' he remembers.

Neil has studied the traditions of his trade, particularly an organisation that was formed to protect workers, the Shipwrights' Provident Union of New South Wales. It seems to make sense that Neil's interested in union history. After all, the Australian Labor Party is considered to have been born in Balmain, at a meeting in a local pub, the Unity Hall Hotel, in 1891, just a year after a massive maritime workers' strike across the colonies. Neil despairs at seeing those traditions and the touchstones of his childhood disappear from around the peninsula. Even his own boyhood home was demolished for a block of units. And although he now lives away from the harbour, he still visits the peninsula and identifies himself as belonging there.

'People say, "You come from Balmain",' Neil says, 'and I say, "No. I come from Balmain East".'

Tracing the Balmain East shoreline, I pass a few slipways on the properties of mansions, and anaemic-brick apartment blocks from the later 20th century. On a few of the balconies are residents – a young woman sipping coffee, a middle-aged man tending to plants, a father playing with a small child – each doing their own thing, unaware of each other's presence, sharing a harbour view, but not with each other. It is as though an Edward Hopper painting has sprouted by the harbour.

Leaving behind the shore and the seeming disconnect of those living on it, I paddle the couple of hundred metres north to Goat Island.

*

TO MY eyes, Goat Island looks like a large sandstone lump that managed to keep its head above water when the valleys were drowned and the harbour was shaped. To Aboriginal people, it was known as Mel-Mel, or 'eye'. On a map, the island looks a little like an eye, but perhaps it was Mel-Mel because from its high ground, about 40 metres above the water, you could see in all directions around the harbour. The British gave it the less poetic name of Goat Island. It's uncertain why, but it may have been that the goats brought on the First Fleet were landed on the island to graze.

For a small island of little more than 5 hectares, a lot of history and roles have been stacked upon, and gouged from, it since 1788. It has been a quarry, a military installation, a prison, a water police station, a fire brigade base, a biological laboratory, a harbourmaster's quarters, a depot for the Maritime Services Board, a shipyard, a television production set – and a home.

Approaching the island along its south-western side, I see the different eras packed in together, as colonial sandstone buildings jostle with a row of boatsheds, a wharf and a couple of slipways, one with a large cruiser on it. Looming over the shipyard is a large 1920s hammerhead crane. I don't land on the western side, as the shipyard is being run as a commercial operation. I paddle around to the northern face of the island, where there is an old marina, with a small weatherboard shed on the wharf at its entrance. Hundreds of workers used to hop on and off ferries around here when the Maritime Services Board depot and shipyard were in full swing half a century ago. Today the marina is empty but for one National Parks and Wildlife Service launch and the forlorn slap of waves. But the launch tells me the island's resident ranger is home.

I see Ben Cottier, a field officer for NPWS, outside a rust-mottled and sawtooth-roofed workshop at the end of the marina. Ben, a gentle, lean man with an easy smile, indicates for me to land on a small indent of a beach near the workshop. He later explains the indent is part of a deeper incision cut into the island. It was a moat to separate the convicts from water police officers, when they were based on the eastern end of the island from 1837.

Ben guides me through the island's past. We walk up the hill to a beautiful Federation home perched on the high point. Popping out of the roof is a stubby tower with windows on all sides. This was the Harbourmaster's home and office in the early 20th century. No one lives here now, and inside the house is fading and peeling into disrepair. But as a real estate agent might say, never mind the interior, look out the windows. From the second storey, we climb very steep stairs – virtually a ladder – into the little tower. For the Harbourmaster, this would have been an empowering view, with its aspects to the west, along the North Shore and to the east. The chimneys outside the windows are studded with small stones and shells, so the harbour is embedded in the home. The house may be empty and the Harbourmaster no longer needs a small tower on a roof to monitor ships, but out the front, there are still large navigational markers and lights to guide vessels.

Beside the Harbourmaster's house is a row of historic cottages. Ben and his family live in one. They're the only people living on the island. They have been here for thirteen years. He and his partner take their boys across to Balmain by boat to attend school, and they have to plan their housekeeping; they can't just run down to the shops. At one point in the 1930s, when it was the base for so many harbour activities, about 120 people lived on Goat Island. Ben shows me where there used to be a tennis court and a hall where dances were held.

'There was quite a community here.'

We stand on the high ground, looking west over the convict-era buildings and powder magazine and the shipyard, which I had seen from the water. It is a grand view across history. We follow a sandstone wall down the hill and head through an arched entrance. On one side are the convict-cut walls, on the other a 1960s amenities block, only a metre or so between them, but architecturally worlds apart. In the stone walls, visitors to the island made their mark through the years. Ben shows me etched messages, including one left by a soldier in 1914.

Beyond the wall is a cluster of sandstone buildings, including a large gunpowder magazine. Ben opens the magazine's thick doors to reveal the vaulted ceiling. It has the beauty and stillness of a cathedral yet was crafted from convicts' suffering. A century later, during the Maritime Services Board's time, it was used for stores. Now it is eerily empty.

Across a courtyard is a former cooperage. A stone on the building indicates, in a lavish font, it was built in 1836. Between the magazine and cooperage is a strange-looking wooden box on wheels, with a barred door. It is a replica of the boxes that convicts slept in, while they were based on the island to construct the buildings. Inside the box are a couple of platforms and a dunny. Twenty men used to sleep in here, Ben says. Stooping in the confined space, I feel claustrophobic.

We look over into the shipyard, just as the cruiser glides down the slipway into the water. Through the 20th century, vessels frequently splashed into the water here. This island was like a port within the harbour. The port authority's tugs and dredges were stationed here, as were fire-fighting vessels. On the three slipways, vessels were built and maintained by up to 500 workers, including thirty-five shipwrights. Then, in the 1970s, the Maritime Services Board began winding back its operations on the island, and, by the early 1990s, it had all but left.

The National Parks and Wildlife Service has been administering the island since 1994. But Ben constantly sees the reminders of who and what was here before. On the southern shore, he points out two stone lines running through the shallows, the remains of an early slipway. A little further around, he shows me a hollowed-out section in a boulder. This was Bony Anderson's 'chair'. Charles 'Bony' Anderson was a convict but also a former sailor who had sustained a brain injury during his service in the Royal Navy. He was considered hard to manage and was chained to this rock on the island. Depending on the story, he lived in this cavity for anywhere between several weeks to a couple of years. Looking at that cold, hard stone and imagining a damaged soul being chained to it, any time seems too long. Bony was sent to Norfolk Island where, Ben says, he had the good fortune to 'get a kind commandant', and eventually he was a free man.

From Bony's chair, we can look across the water to the Barangaroo development. The significance of that name washes back to the island. Barangaroo and her husband Bennelong apparently liked to visit Mel-Mel during the colony's early days. Bennelong claimed deep connection to the island through his father. Ben has watched the emergence of the Barangaroo development over the past few years.

'When I came here, it was still being used for containers, and you could watch the container ships come in,' murmurs Ben.

The eastern shore is sprinkled with great shards of concrete. Ben says they are the remains of wharves that skirted the island. He points to the forest of old pylons, where Maritime Services Board boats used to moor. The only vessels that come close to shore now are pleasure boats.

We cross a footbridge above the 'moat' to the island's eastern tip, and the partly restored 19th century water police station. There have been water police on Sydney Harbour since Governor Phillip's day, when he appointed watchmen to row along the shores. They became known as the Rowboat Guard. These days, the water police are based in Balmain East. While this location on Goat Island would offer an unhindered view east, the officers would feel the chilling effects of the harbour and the winds.

Ben has to leave in the launch to pick up his boys from school. I ask him what he loves about living on Goat Island. He smiles and says, 'We're surrounded by the city, but we're not part of it'.

'It's a lot noisier than you'd think; you can hear the trains on the Bridge, party boats on the water, and the tugboats, when they pass. They get the windows shaking.

'You can hear the fog horns early in the morning, and you get up and see the harbour is fog-bound. That's a couple of mornings a year. The boys can't get to school on those mornings.'

Having seen the historic water police headquarters, I check out the pretend water police headquarters. The popular television series *Water Rats* was filmed here from 1996 to 2001. The former Port Emergency Services building was the main base in the show.

The building is now a faded and forgotten star. Police logos remain on salt-smudged glass doors, and stairs lead to an empty first floor, with a sign giving the hollow warning, 'NO ENTRY. POLICE ONLY'. In the yard nearby is a rusted anchor attached to nothing. The dilapidated building seems like a potent symbol of the ephemeral nature of television. One minute, everyone is watching you; the next, you're washed up and weather-beaten. Yet I turn around, and I see *Water Rats*' biggest star is as ravishing and as undimmed as ever. That view.

15

FROM MORT BAY BACK TO HENRY

AROUND EVERY bay in Sydney Harbour there is a water view. But it is the bay scraping out the northern edge of the Balmain peninsula that was accorded the honour, or lumbered with the bleeding obvious, of the name Waterview.

Paddling into the bay, it is evident many have taken up residence here for the water view. But they occupy sites where the work that used to be done was water-based. The motivation to make money was water-driven. In the 19th century, the bay was packed with ships, and its shores were made higgledy-piggledy by a rambunctious brew of maritime businesses, from boatyards to docks.

The maritime industry still hugs the shore in places.

The Sydney Ferries' workshop is straight ahead. A few ferries are docked in front of the workshop. Yet as I paddle towards the complex, I'm caught in a pincer movement of the wakes of *Scarborough* and *Golden Grove*, as one ferry heads into the bay and the other pushes out to work. With the water momentarily hissing and seething, it sounds like I'm paddling through a nest of snakes.

Further east around the shore is a commercial marina, and a barge carrying a large wooden pole chugs purposefully across the water. So, for a moment, it looks like a working harbour. And then I turn and see the Waterview Wharf Workshops, a clump of buildings painted in breezy colours of apricot, orange, green and blue. The buildings have been here for a long time, but they haven't always been dressed to look like a rainbow landing in the bay. They were once the workshops of the Adelaide Steamship Company. The shipping company had bought the site, which had been a timber yard, in 1900 to use as a depot to maintain and repair its fleet. Along the pathway zig-zagging down the steep hill to the workshops, casual workers would gather each morning. They would stand at a zig or a zag, according to their trade, hoping it would provide a straight path to employment by the water.

For more than sixty years, ships berthed out the front of the workshops. When the maritime workers moved out, artists moved in. My friend Guy Warren had a studio in the workshops for a few years from the late 1970s.

'Fifty dollars a week, and it was huge!' he enthuses.

Guy worked on the ground floor, with wide-planked decking and the lap of the water beneath his feet, while he was cocooned in the workshop's corrugated iron skin. In his rented space, Guy would stand amid a grove of ancient hardwood beams and columns as he explored the Australian landscape with his paints and imagination.

'A lot of watercolours came from there,' Guy remembers.

He still has sketchbooks filled with visual notes, especially of changing weather and shapes on the water, from ships to swimmers. For ideas, Guy only had to open the large double doors that looked straight onto the water. The view was still overwhelmingly industrial sometimes.

'I'd look out and suddenly everything was black. It was a huge black tanker gliding past or turning around in the bay,' he recalls.

'At high tide, I had been known to swim out there, but I think I stopped when I found a dead dog floating in the water.'

The harbour increasingly flowed into his work. Lines of soft colour, light-infused, wash across the paper in his *Balmain* series. More than make marks on the paper, Guy began ripping and perforating the surface. He had observed small workboats chugging past, ruffling the water, with the froth and foam sopping up the sunlight. So to replicate how the water could be punctured or torn, he did the same to the paper he was creating on.

'I stayed overnight sometimes,' Guy says. 'I would open the doors, and there was the harbour sparkling in the morning sunshine, it was just unbelievable. We knew it wouldn't last.'

It didn't last. Guy had to move out. The workshops were redeveloped into offices.

'In the end, in a way, I was almost happy to leave,' Guy reflects. 'It was almost too powerful, because I found that everything I was doing was related to the harbour.'

'But . . .' And he smiles and his eyes crinkle, giving the 90-something-year-old the look of a mischievous boy. 'I never got another studio as good as that!'

AS COMPELLING as the water view is, the bay's name was changed. It came to be known as Mort Bay. It is named after

Thomas Sutcliffe Mort, who has left his stamp on the harbour's character, and on the shores of this bay.

I paddle west along the bay, past the ferry maintenance depot and the former Colgate-Palmolive buildings on the shore. The air around the bay used to be scented by the manufacturing of body- and household-cleaning products in the factory. The sweet smells were enough to quell the grittier odours of industry. Guy Warren can sniff the air in his memory, saying 'it wasn't unpleasant!' In the late 1990s, the buildings were converted into apartments.

Tucked into the bay's western corner are remains of Thomas Mort's maritime vision. As shipping boomed in the early 1850s, particularly with the gold rushes luring people from across the seas, Mort saw opportunity. He had seen a lot of potential business sailing and chugging out of the Heads, as there were not suitable maintenance facilities for many visiting ships. So it was here in the bay that Mort built the colony's first large-scale dry dock, which was completed in 1855.

The dock helped build Mort's wealth and influence in the colony, and his vision kept expanding. His company serviced not just vessels but built machines for the country's develop- ment, from bridges to railway locomotives. In the early 1870s, Mort's Dock and Engineering Company was formed, and the complex spread over ten hectares at the head of the bay, and into the harbour. Mort's Dock was a major provider of jobs in Balmain, with up to 1000 workers. It continued to construct and repair ships well into the 20th century. During the Second World War, corvettes and frigates were built here. In the late 1950s, eighty years after Thomas Mort's death, the company went into liquidation. For a time during the 1960s and 1970s, a container terminal was on the site. Now it is a park.

The reminders of Mort's dock and the container days meld along the shore, with the rusted iron of the old caisson sharing the water with sandstone seawalls, concrete aprons, and bollards that remain defiantly red. The caisson that held back the harbour now feels the surge of time. The dock has been filled in, and where vessels once squatted, dogs and kids now run. In the lawn is a ghostly line in the shape of a ship.

For a few moments, I sit in *Pulbah Raider* near the caisson. What a stirring sight it must have been as a ship settled into the water here and cruised away. Now all that is in this part of the bay are fish flittering about. The noises of industry have reverberated into history. I hear nothing but the murmur of water as it nuzzles around the kayak, and the laughter of children in the park. To Thomas Mort, it would have been the sound of ruination.

The shoreline bends around to what is called Ballast Point. This was where the oil tankers that Guy Warren used to see from his studio were headed. On this headland, there were about thirty storage tanks at the Caltex terminal. The skeletons and footprints of those tanks have now been incorporated into a park that acknowledges what the Sydney Harbour Federation Trust has called the industrial ecology. When it came into being, the Trust said harbour-side industrial structures no longer needed for the port's infrastructure could form the basis of inspiring public spaces. That call has been heeded on Ballast Point. It is marvellous to wander among the exposed bones of industry here.

The largest storage facility, called Tank 101, is remembered in a structure built from recycled curved sheet steel retrieved on the site. Tank 101 once contained crude oil; now it holds words. Punched into the steel are the first two lines from Les Murray's poem, 'The Death of Isaac Nathan, 1864':

Stone statues of ancient waves/tongue like dingoes on shore

The poet has said the inspiration for those lines came from looking at the hollowed-out sandstone along the foreshores, and the way the light reflected by the harbour quivered in the hollow of the rocks. Men made things here, but nature made the headland they worked upon. Those layers of history to prehistory to the waterline can be viewed all around the headland, as the remains of concrete walls and caged constructions of stones and boulders press into the ancient sandstone.

From Ballast Point, I can look over into Snails Bay, with its eclectic and eccentric collection of harbour life tethered to concrete dolphins strung along its mouth. That eccentricity is best experienced from the water.

I paddle past the diverse fleet of tugs, barges, and lighters, and a disembodied pontoon from the Cremorne Point ferry terminal. It makes the bay look like a waiting room for the discarded and forgotten. It is a marked change from what used to float here: timber.

Logs would be unloaded from ships into the water, then tugs would nudge and push them into rafts, and they would be towed to timber yards around the harbour and up Parramatta River. Occasionally, the chains corralling the logs would break, and timber would drift around the bay like lost cattle until it could be rounded up. Timber would also be loaded directly onto barges that chugged in and out of the bay.

When I was in the Environmental Services boat with Ken Wark, we talked about the timber trade as we passed Snails Bay.

'Imagine how much valuable timber must be on the harbour

bottom,' Ken remarked. He explained that timber also used to be floated in Rozelle Bay, where this workboat was kept. When the bay was being cleared for new marinas, the sonar revealed large lumps on the bottom. Divers were sent down, and it was discovered those lumps were massive logs. Ken said about thirty logs were retrieved and were auctioned off for very high prices.

The floating logs represented a healthy business to Nicholson Bros, which kept its fleet and base in Snails Bay. The company had grown from operating a launch carrying picnickers up Lane Cove River to the biggest private ferry service in the port, especially on the harbour's western side. After the Second World War, Nicholson Bros had tugs, which helped move the imported timber to where it needed to go around the harbour. The company's fleet featured dozens of craft with the prefix 'Pro-' in their name, from *Providore* to *Proclaim*.

Snails Bay is named in honour of the pace that the Gentleman Kayakers' Club sets on the harbour. That's not true. Otherwise, it would be called Leopards Bay. However, many an adventure has begun and ended in Snails Bay, as Gentleman Kayakers Bruce Beresford and George Ellis live in nearby suburbs.

'Growing up in the western parts of Sydney, I knew nothing about the harbour,' Bruce mentions during one of our adventures. 'We had the occasional trip to the beach, but the harbour was somewhere I knew nothing about. So the idea of living near it is a revelation.'

The heads of most bays around the harbour, with their parks and reserves on reclaimed land, are symbols of the natural environment lost. But for rugby league followers, the head of Snails

Bay is hallowed ground. It holds Birchgrove Oval. Two of the first rugby league matches were played here on 20 April 1908. So it is regarded as a birthplace of the sport. The oval was the home ground of the Balmain Tigers from that foundation year until 1932. On weekends, the sounds of crowds lining the oval, cheering on sports teams, still filter down to the water.

Along the bay's western shore is a thin strip of land, with large homes teetering on either side of its spine. This protuberance from the suburb of Birchgrove is called Long Nose Point. Those on the point's eastern side have colonised just about every skerrick of land, for they have box seat views to the Bridge. The maritime industry used to be concentrated along here, with small yards and boatsheds. Historian Graeme Andrews referred to the Sydney Harbour Trust's 1922 handbook to indicate the sheer number of little businesses and workboats that once existed, particularly west of the Bridge. Among the vessels listed were 559 lighters and sixty-eight tugs, along with cranes and dredges – and thirty-six watermen's boats, the prototype for the water taxi. Jammed in between the yards along this shoreline was the Snails Bay Sabot Sailing Club. It began in the early 1960s, and these little sailboats would scurry around Snails Bay and between the tugs and lighters each weekend for about a decade. As the repair yards and boatsheds began to disappear off the point, so did the sailing club. A crumbling reminder of those days used to hide between the houses on Long Nose Point, with an old boatyard on the water's edge. But in recent years, I watched the yard being demolished, its industrial footprint wiped over and replaced with multi-million-dollar townhouses. The removal of any trace of the working harbour from Long Nose Point is almost complete. Almost.

At the tip of the point is a sandstone seawall and ramp to the water. It is all that remains of the Morrison and Sinclair shipyard, which had taken up residence soon after the end of the First World War. The company built ferries and luxury cruisers, even a patrol ship for the colonial administration in New Guinea. The state bought the site in the early 1970s for $185,000. It is now a park and popular fishing spot. The point's tip is always finely webbed with fishing lines, setting the subtlest of traps for an unsuspecting kayaker. Pushing into the harbour, the point is also frequently harassed by passing boating traffic, particularly with ferries stopping at its tip. Water smacks into the seawall then eddies and whirls angrily. It is as though the harbour is protesting at 'Long Nose Point' and is demanding a return to the Aboriginal name, Yurulbin. It would be more appropriate; Yurulbin means 'swift running water'.

Once I have paddled around Long Nose Point's tip, I'm back in Parramatta River. The sandstone face and industrial remnants of Cockatoo Island are ahead of me, a kilometre or so upstream. I turn left and trace Long Nose Point, its shore and ridgeline pebbled with houses, historic and sparkling new. Some are designed to stand out; others try to blend into the harbour environment. One home looks like a scaled amphibian, armoured in tiles the colour of stormy water.

One of those living along here is artist Ken Unsworth. He has lived in a semi-detached house in the Louisa Quays development since the early 1990s. The waterfront development is built on the site of old boatyards. Ken kind of wishes the maritime industries were still on the shore.

'My house is okay,' he jokes, 'but all these other houses should still be boatbuilders' yards!'

Ken loves his place, viewing the water through the trees he has planted, but he worries, 'Sydney Harbour is rapidly becoming an ornamental lake.'

As I paddle south-west along Birchgrove's shores I'm thinking about Ken's lament for the harbour, when I see a couple of old wooden boatsheds. One of them is shedding its skin of shingles, but their appearance, and their defiance, is heartening. May they continue to defy the years and the developers.

The shoreline grows steeper, yet there are buildings above and below the escarpment, and clinging onto it. Along here, there used to be a coal mine. The Sydney Harbour Colliery first broke through the earth in 1897 and kept digging for about twenty years, under the Balmain peninsula and beneath the harbour bed, chasing the dark vein. The two shafts were named the Birthday and the Jubilee, in honour of Queen Victoria. The colliery closed in 1915 but reopened in 1924. The Balmain Colliery, as it became known, tunnelled almost a kilometre underground, burrowing below the harbour towards Goat Island and the North Shore. The colliery was a tolerated neighbour in Birchgrove as it provided about 300 jobs, but for those in the shafts, it was hot, humid and dangerous work. Ten were killed in the life of the colliery. Coal ceased being mined in the early 1930s, and gas was extracted from the operation for another twenty years. The shafts were filled in, and part of the site was eventually transformed into a housing development.

At the bottom of the escarpment, just near where the coal mine used to be, is Balmain Sailing Club. A steep set of stairs lead down to the clubhouse, so it is easier, and less demanding on the legs, to approach it from the water.

The club provides a link back to 1849, when the first Balmain Regatta was staged, bringing watermen and sailors from around the harbour to test their skills and have some fun. The club continues to stage the Balmain Regatta on the last Sunday of October.

One of the great custodians of the harbour's maritime traditions, Ian Smith, regularly participates in the regatta in *Britannia*, his homage in wood to Balmain hero 'Wee Georgie' Robinson. In 2016 he entered *Britannia* in the Vintage Skiffs division, and he invited me to join the crew. We were towed from the Sydney Flying Squadron clubhouse at Careening Cove, under the Bridge and up the river to Balmain Sailing Club. Long before we reached the club's jetty, we slalomed through a crowd on the water, and Ian recognised many of those in the boats.

'There's "Dog-boat Dave!"' Ian said animatedly, pointing to David Glasson, who chugs around the harbour in a century-old boat, which in its former life was used to retrieve dogs' corpses from the harbour. David is renowned for respecting and reviving old workboats, when others have given them up for dead. He has recently restored a wooden launch that had been used to transfer personnel to and from HMAS *Parramatta*. During the week, David works on the maintenance of bridges around the harbour. And very early each day, long before the sun is up, he is out on the water in his old boat. It's how he gets around. 'My boat is my car,' David says. 'I still can't walk on water. I'm still trying to perfect that!'

For the regatta, the sleek 1903 'gentleman's' schooner, *Boomerang*, was moored proudly in the cove, wearing a colourful shawl of flags. There was also a tiny dinghy darting about.

'There's our little sister, our baby sister!' exclaimed one of our crew. Her name was *The Balmain Bug*, and she was built by Ian and launched in 1994. The 6-foot dinghy looked so cute, her cedar hull gleaming, but Ian said she was a volatile little thing to sail and easily turned over.

Striking a pose among the boats were yellow female mannequins, with bikinis painted onto them and mounted on floats. They were the 'goils', as opposed to buoys, that would be marking the course we were to sail: past Cockatoo Island, down to Goat Island, then back up to Drummoyne Bay and across to the clubhouse.

Soon after we had begun racing, Ian ordered for the 'Tigers' spinnaker to be unfurled. It seemed appropriate, since we were deep in Balmain Tigers territory and in 'Wee' Georgie's heartland. The north-easterly had the Balmain Tigers' logo puffing its chest out as we carved across the harbour. *The Balmain Bug* scurried in front of us, and a photographer snapped the scene, presumably catching two of Ian's 'Balmain' creations in the one frame.

We won our division. As we waited for the trophy presentation, we stood on the deck outside the clubhouse and watched kids jumping and diving into the harbour. I took that as a vote of confidence in the health of the water. Ian looked doubtful, before telling me how he once had to dive in here to retrieve a keel, and he could not see for the mud. He figured all that mud would have been contaminated with the legacy of the industries that had been along these shores.

The final race was run. It was a rowing competition, the watermen's race. As though symbolising the dwindling of that tradition, there were only two competitors in the watermen's race.

At the presentation ceremony on the deck, Ian accepted the division winner's trophy, which was a carved lump of hardwood. It was called the 'Commonwealth Bowsprit Trophy'. But true to Ian's boatbuilding knowledge, he pointed out the wood was not from a bowsprit but a tiller. No sooner had the ceremony ended than rain started sprinkling the harbour. Hardly a sailor sought shelter. They reached for their drinks and stood resolute, watching Cockatoo Island being wrapped in a skein of rain.

JUST A few hundred metres further along the shore is a monument to one of Balmain's favourite people, the Olympic swimming legend Dawn Fraser. Fittingly, the monument is a harbour pool. It is called the Dawn Fraser Baths.

The pool predates Dawn. It is reputed to be the oldest operating pool in Australia, having been built in the 1880s. But it's Dawn's pool. Always was, long before it was named after her. Dawn was the youngest of eight children in a local family, and she would come to the baths to swim. Swimming helped her breathe. She had asthma. Harry Gallagher, her future coach, met the teenage Dawn here. Actually, he was confronted by her. She was bombing the kids he was trying to train in 'her' pool. Harry thought Dawn was just a local tough, until he saw her swim. Harry invited Dawn to the other side of the river, to train with his squad in Drummoyne. She was dismissive. But Dawn did go to the other side of the river, trained with Harry, and swam to glory. She won the gold medal for 100-metres freestyle at three consecutive Olympic Games.

Dawn Fraser is still revered in Balmain. She remains the true north in many locals' compass. While paddling around the harbour, I've met quite a few people who grew up in Balmain, and each of them found their way home in their story-telling with a reference to Dawn. They swam with her or her older brothers in the baths, they worked with her father at Cockatoo Island, they had a drink with her.

I want my own moment associating with Dawn Fraser on the Balmain peninsula. Or at least with the Dawn Fraser Baths. On a late April afternoon, I decide to go for a swim. Approaching from the water, the Dawn Fraser Baths could not look more Australian. Its perimeter walls are made of corrugated iron. It could well be one huge outdoor dunny. At a time when the harbour's water quality was dodgy, that was perhaps what swimmers felt they were in. But the harbour's water on this day looks clear, so I'm confident the pool's will be beautiful, if a little chilly.

I head to the entrance, crowned in stolid concrete. But the roller doors are down. Then I see the sign: 'Closed for Winter'. I reckon Dawn would be disappointed by that. How soft, closing the pool during the cold months. And it's not even winter. Balmain boys don't cry, according to former resident and ex-New South Wales Premier Neville Wran, but maybe they shiver and tremble.

Denied the opportunity to swim, I climb to the neighbouring headland which holds Elkington Park and a long, wide view to the north and west. On the headland, which is called White Horse Point, there are signs warning people to keep away from the cliff. But I bet the sandstone ledge over the water has been used as a jumping platform by local kids for generations. At the foot of the headland is a small beach tucked into the cove. Gentleman Kayaker Bruce and I have landed on that beach for a mug of tea. Sipping on a drink, and shielded by the sandstone from the rest of Sydney, it is one of those magical places on the harbour. It offers a solitude that is harder to find the further you go along the shoreline. Unless you can pay for it.

On the next headland, at Sommerville Point, there is a new housing development, which has boasted in its marketing that it is Sydney's hidden exclusive sanctuary. I wonder how the neighbours feel about that. The new development is across the road from a cluster of public housing blocks that have been on the point for more than sixty years. The residents look out upon one of the few remaining commercial maritime operators along here. At the Balmain Marine Centre, a couple of yachts are on the slips, and the jetty is flanked with boats. As I paddle past, I cannot help thinking the public housing complex and the marine industry will be probably pushed off its valuable land in time to create more hidden exclusive sanctuaries.

Residential developments have been popping up right along this stretch in recent years. The site of a former pharmaceutical and chemical factory that dated back to the 1860s was turned into medium-density housing. Neighbouring that reinvention, the Balmain Shores housing development is built on the site of the former power station complex. For more than six decades, coal was shipped to the station to be burnt and generate electricity for the surrounding homes and industries. The complex was a rubbish dump of sorts as well, because Balmain Power Station 'A' burnt garbage. The complex was decommissioned in the 1970s and was demolished in 1998. There is little evidence a massive Balmain power station was ever here, other than a few plaques and the shell of a 1930s pump house, which drew water from the river for use in the cooling process.

Whenever I come to a bridge, I'm like the troll in *Three Billy Goats Gruff*. I love to sit under there. However, unlike the nasty troll in the fairytale, the only thing I want to devour is the atmosphere. I also love the sense that time is only nibbling at me, whereas I can hear it almost gnawing at those rushing across the bridge above me. And so I stop paddling and sit under the Iron Cove bridges, connecting Rozelle to Drummoyne. The older steel truss bridge was opened in 1955, and it maintains a fairly straight line across the cove. Right beside it, on its southern side, is the concrete bridge, opened in 2011, and it slightly curves around the older structure. So I can look up at the semi-circle framing the sky between the bridges. Around a pylon near the Rozelle shore is a nice fishing spot. At least, that's according to the graffiti painted on the pylon. A cleaner from the local Leichhardt Council is reaching across with a paint brush on a long pole, erasing the graffiti. The 'Nice fishing spot!' declaration, however, is out of reach. I ask the cleaner if the graffiti is correct. No idea, she tells me. But it's been there for about eight years. Still, it's a nice spot for trolls and kayakers to sit for a while.

I track the joggers and walkers on the path along the meandering shoreline. The water's edge is kept in order by a seawall, before a weathered rocky outcrop reasserts the power and beauty of unshaped stone. Beyond the shore, on the rise, a few sandstone towers and turrets poke above the trees. They mark the site of the former Callan Park Mental Hospital. The Inspector of the Insane, Frederick Norton Manning, whom I had learnt about back at the former Gladesville Hospital, further up Parramatta River, worked with the Colonial Architect James Barnet to create a group of beautiful neo-classical buildings for patients. It was hoped a new facility would alleviate the problem of overcrowding in the colony's asylums.

The buildings were constructed in the 1880s from sandstone mainly quarried on the 40-hectare site. Just as he had done at Gladesville, Dr Manning shaped the institution according to his belief in the therapeutic benefits of calm surroundings, with gardens and views, and well-designed buildings. While it underwent changes through the years, eventually becoming known as Rozelle Hospital, the complex remained a centre for the treatment and study of mental illness for more than a century. Since the hospital closed in 2008, some of the historic buildings have been a nursery for creativity, with tenants including the Sydney College of the Arts and the New South Wales Writers' Centre. After all, the philosophies that Dr Manning espoused about the connection between well-being and beautiful surroundings also have a place in feeding the muse.

For rowers in search of calm waters, Iron Cove offers some hope, as it peels off the main harbour, yet it is a huge expanse of water. The run from the bridges to the south-western edges of the cove is more than a kilometre. As a result, there are a couple of large buildings, the Leichhardt Rowing Club and the UTS Rowing Club – on the eastern shore, and Drummoyne Rowing Club on the opposite side. Although there are obstacles and potential distractions. In the bay in front of Leichhardt Park, I see a slalom course for rowers, with a couple of dozen boats moored.

I circle around the bottom part of the cove, which is fed by a couple of creeks that are now really canals, disgorging into the harbour the run-off from the suburbs to the south and south-west of here. Heading back up the western shore, I land at Rodd Point, which sticks into Iron Cove like swollen tonsils. I'm intrigued by an austere stone cross standing on raised ground.

It gives the impression that someone wanted to be left alone in death. Traipsing up the hill to the cross, I find it was the resting place for the Rodd family.

Brent Clement Rodd was a lawyer and extensive landowner around these shores for more than half a century through to his death in 1898. He may have left this world, but Rodd wasn't about to leave his harbourside land. A family vault had been carved into the rock on the point, with the sandstone cross marking it. In 1903, Rodd's body and those of other family members, along with the cross, were transferred to Rookwood Cemetery. But as a plaque indicates, the Rotary Club of Five Dock moved the cross, if not the bodies, back in 1975, 'to complete the restoration of Rodd Point'.

Arguably, the restoration is not quite complete. There's still the 'landmark' at the tip of Rodd Point. As further proof this city has so many beautiful locations that authorities are left with few choices for ugly conveniences, there is a public toilet built into the knoll. The block has all the appeal of an air-raid shelter. And the roof of the toilets is a lookout. It is while standing here, looking all the way to the harbour's northern shore, that I reflect on how many toilets with a view I've visited on this journey. I may have found my next book subject . . .

From this point, Rodd could have gazed over at the small island that he coveted but could never own, despite a lot of effort to buy it from the government. While he didn't acquire the title deeds, the island acquired his name. It is called Rodd Island. The paddle from Rodd Point to the island is only a few hundred metres, but the destination feels wonderfully remote. I trace the northern shore, which is leaning against a thick stone seawall, and admire the palm trees, picnic pavilions and main building, painted a burnished tangerine and russet, as though a bushfire were in full flame above the water.

Pulbah Raider slides onto the sand in a tiny cove indented on the island's north-eastern side. I climb some rough stone stairs through a glade and onto an emerald lawn. The main building I could see from the water is even more beautiful up-close. It is an old dance hall, sheathed in corrugated iron, and with a long veranda pressing the slanting sun off its decking. But the magic appears when I peer through the window into the hall. Its wooden floor is so polished and gleaming, it is like a mirror reflecting the view through the hall's windows. So I can see the reflections of Port Jackson figs and palms, a snippet of the older Iron Cove Bridge, and the harbour, pooled and shimmering. It is as though everything beautiful about Sydney Harbour is contained in that hall.

Before it held dancing feet and magical reflections, the hall was part of a research centre, set up to try and find a biological method to combat the rabbit plague that was ravaging the landscape and rural industries. The New South Wales Government had offered the massive reward of £25,000 for the development of a method. In 1888, the renowned French microbiologist Louis Pasteur sent his nephew, Adrien Loir, to Sydney to conduct experiments, and the island became his base.

Loir and his team's research were deemed ineligible for the reward, but they stayed on the island to develop a vaccine for livestock. The island also became a de facto quarantine station. Sarah Bernhardt, who was one of the biggest stars in the world at the time, arrived in Sydney in 1891. The actress was travelling with her dogs, and when the pets had to go into quarantine, Loir suggested they be held on the island. In that way, the French actress could see her pets, and quite possibly Loir could see Bernhardt.

By 1894, the laboratory was closed and the island had returned to being what the Rodd family loved about the place – a picnic spot. Apart from being used as a training depot for the United States Army during the Second World War, the island has remained a public reserve, and a place to escape from Sydney in the middle of Iron Cove.

HEADING NORTH, I arrive in Half Moon Bay. I'm attracted not by the prospect of paddling into something lunar but a rare sight on the harbour: a fibro shack on piers, with a deck and jetty, and a ramp. It wears on its side a slipway and a shaggy fringe of mangroves. A well-dressed man is leaning over the railing on the club's deck and smiles as I approach.

'This is the Half Moon Bay Yacht Club,' he answers, when I ask about the building. His name is Craig Kann, and he's one of twenty-eight club members.

Membership is closely guarded, he explains. Basically, you have to wait until 'someone goes to the big boatshed in the sky'. Craig had to wait fourteen years and has been a member for four years. He is now the Vice Commodore.

I ask Craig how's the water quality around here, and he tells me it's healthy.

'It's not uncommon to stand here and look down and see stingrays, kingfish,' Craig says. 'Look around you. It's awash with bait fish. Something big will come in and eat that.'

Perhaps it's that comment that encourages me to ask Craig if I can land and have a quick look at the club. He invites me up.

I paddle under the piers and pull the kayak onto the sand and crawl out from under the building. The entry takes you through a long shed, lined with dinghies. The number of dinghy places basically determines how many members the club can have, Craig explains, as we walk through the no-nonsense shed. A peek into the club room tells me the members don't spend their dues on interior decoration. But this club was never meant to be fancy, right from the time it was formed just after the Second World War.

Craig tells me I should meet life member Harry Downie to talk about the club's early days. And later I do. Harry lives just up the road from the yacht club in the same house he's been in for donkey's years.

Harry's a welcoming bloke. And he's the working harbour personified. Harry tells me he was born in Balmain in 1927. He began work at Cockatoo Island in 1944 and was apprenticed to Ken Fraser, Dawn's dad. He talks about going to sea in 1950, working on ships, and sailing from New Guinea into Sydney Harbour with a cargo of animals, Noah's Ark-like, for Taronga Park Zoo. Harry still has his 'Seaman's Document of Identity', even though it is many years since he has worked on a ship. Actually, he still does – in a miniature way. He meticulously creates ships in bottles.

Harry mourns the loss of the working harbour, and shakes his head at what his workplace and favourite pubs have become.

'There was history then, there's nothing now!' he says. 'You know, the Ship Inn was full of wharfies. Now it's full of la-de-das drinking cocktails!'

Harry is a wonderful talker, until the conversation turns to the Half Moon Bay Yacht Club. He'd prefer not to talk about that, in the hope I don't write about it. Basically, he doesn't want people to know about the club. Sorry, Harry.

Although he does tell me that, when the club started, there was no building. The members sat on a large rock on the shore. If it was raining, they met in a nearby house.

Perhaps to divert me from asking him any more questions about the club, Harry directs me to another long-time member, Frank Matthews, who lives just around the corner. Frank lives in the same house he grew up in. His grandfather, a shipwright, bought the home a century ago. Its big windows offer a view straight down to Half Moon Bay and the yacht club. Through those windows, young Frank watched the Half Moon Bay Yacht Club take shape around the rock.

Most of the men, Frank recalls, were wearing white singlets and shorts, so when his mother saw them gathering around the rock, she nicknamed them 'the seagulls'. Those blokes mostly worked in the maritime industries. They were tradesmen and labourers at Cockatoo Island or worked at Mort's Dock at Balmain. And that was handy when it came to building the club's facilities.

'Those industries made their contribution to the club's slipway and cradle,' Frank smiles.

Frank joined the club at sixteen, when he started work. The club's rule was you had to be employed to be a member, so that it didn't cost the family. Frank has been a member for about sixty years. As for the club's profile, Frank says, 'we don't advertise and we decided to remain a mystery'.

Frank turned water into a livelihood. He worked on the waterfront and on the harbour, from woolstores to tugs, from lighters to the Maritime Services Board at Goat Island, before buying Rosman ferries. For about twenty years, he operated the company's historic ferries, transporting people around the harbour, from Cockatoo Island workers to school kids.

'Ferries had a fascination,' he says. 'The movement of people outweighed the movement of cargo. It was more complex but more satisfying.'

However, Frank vividly remembers the moment he realised change was creeping along the shores and leaching into the water. It was the mid-1990s, a Monday morning at 7.30, and Frank was out on the harbour in one of his ferries. What Frank saw – or didn't see – disturbed him.

'We were the only moving thing I could see on the water,' Frank recalled. 'Years ago, there would have been boats heading in all directions; barges being towed, ferries running, a hive of activity at that time of the day. That's when I understood the change. It was no longer a working port.'

Frank sold the company in 2008 and retired from operating ferries, but he remains in love with boats and the harbour. That is reaffirmed every time he looks out his window.

Back down at the clubhouse, Craig Kann says one of the shining qualities of this spot is that it remains a gathering place for ordinary folks who love being on boats.

'I think it adds to the diversity of the boating public,' Craig says. 'It's not just for rich people. It says you don't have to be a "multi-"[millionaire].'

PADDLING OUT of Iron Cove, past the Drummoyne Pool on the western shore and under the bridges, I'm struck by the lack of boating traffic in this part of the harbour. For more than half a day I've been kayaking in Iron Cove, and *Pulbah Raider* has been barely nudged by another vessel's wake. Little wonder there are still a few rowing clubs in this part of the harbour.

At Birkenhead Point, which marks the western side of Iron Cove's mouth, I pass the former Dunlop rubber factory. It has been turned into a massive shopping and retail hub. This is consumerism on an industrial scale. Even the nearby Birkenhead Point marina advertises 'Shopping Berths Available'.

While I'm heading back out into the main part of Parramatta River, the waterway looks like something more expansive. Before me I can see three islands; Cockatoo to the north-east, Spectacle and, a couple of hundred metres ahead, Snapper Island.

When the British first sailed into Port Jackson, there were fourteen harbour islands. The sight of those islands enriched the first arrivals' wonder. In his description of the 'truly luxuriant' port, naval surgeon George Worgan, noted 'a Number of small Islands, which are covered with Trees and a variety of Herbage, all which appears to be Evergreens'. Yet natural beauty was never going to save the islands from being put to work, scarred, or obliterated, as they were joined to the mainland or each other. Of those fourteen islands, eight remain. The three I can see in front of me used to be four; Spectacle was once two islands connected by a sandy isthmus, but that was filled in. Even the colonial government knew something had to be done to save the islands and ensure they were still accessible to the public. In 1879, the government set aside Snapper, Rodd and Clark islands as public recreation reserves.

Approaching Snapper Island, however, it is glaringly clear this place is off limits to the public. 'DO NOT ENTER. UNSTABLE STRUCTURES. TRIP AND FALL HAZARDS', reads one sign.

'HAZARDOUS MATERIALS AREA' and 'ASBESTOS' read others. The island looks run-down and abandoned to moulder in the middle of the river. Yet someone had hopes for it at some stage. There are two palm trees, one denuded and the other looking as though it will soon give up on island living, along with rusting buildings and sheds. On one shed is a sign fading into the corrugated iron but still able to provide a clue to what this island had been used for: 'SYDNEY TRAINING DEPOT'.

For many years, the smallest island in Sydney Harbour was barely visited, and for a time was used as a storage base for the navy. But then in 1930, Leonard E. Forsythe, the founder of the Navy League Sea Cadets at nearby Drummoyne, saw Snapper Island as like a ship on which he could train his charges. He leased the island from the Commonwealth Government and set about making it ship-shape. He blasted about 1000 tonnes of rock from the crown to flatten it, he reclaimed land to make the island larger, and he built a seawall to sculpt the island's outline into that of a vessel. He referred to the buildings and sheds as decks and cabins. Forsythe named his creation the Sydney Training Depot, in honour of the Australian warship that had sunk the German raider *Emden* during the First World War. When *Sydney* was stripped at nearby Cockatoo Island in 1932, he even retrieved items to display as memorabilia on his island/ship. And it was Leonard E. Forsythe who planted those cabbage palm trees.

During the Second World War, Forsythe had to share the island with Allied troops who used it for training and recreation, but it was returned to him in 1946. After the war, the cadet unit flourished, and the public could visit the island and see *Sydney* relics in a small museum. But when Forsythe died, his vision foundered. The island is now in the care of the Sydney Harbour Federation Trust, which has written there is a plan for rehabilitating and maintaining the island. But from where I sit in the kayak, the warning signs suggest there is still a vast gap between plans and reality, and, with each passing year, Forsythe's 'ship' sinks deeper into ruin.

I HAD intended to paddle to Spectacle Island. When I stood on the foreshore at Drummoyne Sailing Club, I could clearly see the island, a few hundred metres away, hunkered in the harbour and covered in historic buildings. I could even see on the southwestern shore a little beach on which to land *Pulbah Raider*. But the navy put that intention in its place. There would be no landing of a kayak on the beach. Surrounding the island are 'naval waters'. Even from the shore, I could see the sign warning vessels to stay 100 metres away from the island, otherwise risk imprisonment or a big fine.

The navy runs Spectacle Island. Naval officers have had a connection with the island for a long time really. They were the first British people onto the island, when John Hunter and his crew camped here while surveying the harbour in February 1788. Hunter named it 'Dawes Island', after his colleague Lieutenant William Dawes, but by the 1820s it was called Spectacle Island, possibly because the two lumps of land joined by the sandy isthmus resembled a pair of spectacles.

So to visit Spectacle Island, I play by the navy's rules. No kayak. I'm delivered by a navy workboat. The skipper steers the boat past a couple of old concrete lighters standing sentinel in front of the island like those lion statues you find at the front stairs of many homes, and we nestle into the east wharf.

Waiting on the wharf to guide me around is Lindsey Shaw. Lindsey is a former senior curator at the Australian National Maritime Museum. She now helps out on Spectacle Island as a curator.

'This was a dangerous island,' Lindsey says. 'Now it's the main repository for naval heritage.'

We begin with the 'dangerous' era. From the 1860s, the island was one big storage depot for gunpowder. It was also an armaments depot for the Royal Navy.

'Every time a new [navy] ship came in or went out of the harbour, this is where the gunpowder came from,' Lindsey explains.

She shows me some of the original buildings. One of the powder magazines has the date '1865' cut into the stone above the front door. On the island's north-eastern point is a two-storey building with a veranda. It looks both elegant and immovable, as though neither gunpowder nor a blast of the fiercest wind across the harbour could affect the building. This was the residence of the island's superintendent and family. While the town was close by, the occupants were expected to be largely self-sufficient. Below the seawall outside the superintendent's house, a rock platform is exposed at low tide, and Lindsey says it is a happy hunting ground for archaeologists and historians. All manner of artefacts, from tiles to bottles, have been uncovered. The archaeologists' treasure was trash then, and the island garbage disposal system was simple: 'Just toss it into the water.'

We walk around the island, past sandstone walls and over long shadows. The island doubled in size over time to 2 hectares, with the rock dug out of nearby Cockatoo Island for the creation of its Sutherland Dock transported here for land reclamation.

As we pass one building, Lindsey says, 'somewhere around here we would have been walking into water'. This was where the isthmus was, before it was filled in. On the western end of the island, the land rises. Aside from a Second World War gun emplacement on top, Lindsey reckons the hillock is perhaps the best indication of how the island looked before it was reshaped by the military, 'a bit lumpy and scrubby'.

Fifty-eight buildings were constructed on the island to hold gunpowder or accommodate those guarding it. During the world wars, this was a major munitions factory. In the Second World War, hundreds worked around the clock, preparing ammunition for the Allied nations' navies. So for the best part of a century, this was an island dedicated to destruction. It was built for it. Lindsey shows the thickness of the buildings' walls, and their design, so that any blast or shock pushed inwards, not out, over the island and across the water. But I imagine that wasn't assurance enough for those living nearby, particularly along Drummoyne's shores. The potentially volatile island must have looked too close for comfort to those residents. What's more, there was more danger on the water. Ringing the island were moored ammunition storage lighters. By the 1980s, the armaments had been moved up the river to Newington.

Today, this defused island is beautiful, not just because of the view when you look out but also for what you see inside the buildings. For many of them hold the artefacts and stories of a naval power, a harbour city, and an island nation.

In a former workshop, memorabilia are on the walls, floor, and they hang from the ceiling. They are part of a submarine history collection, transferred from HMAS *Platypus*, when the base in Neutral Bay shut. Some exhibits you expect to find, such as models and an old periscope, its metal sheath still gleaming, as though it were still polished by sailors. Others are arcane and tell much about life on the subs, and for submariners on shore: a cricket trophy mounted on a beer can, and a board marked, 'Drinking Records'. On the workshop's mezzanine floor are stacks of maritime art, and the walls are lined with commemorative plaques, most from visiting ships, and they are but a small sample on the island. 'We have 50,000 commemorative plaques,' says Lindsey. She reckons you can tell how much a ship has cared about its visit by the quality of the plaque or trophy its company has given. If the visitors didn't really care, the trophy often suggests some sailor rummaged through the cupboards, found something they wanted to get rid of, and presented that. It sounds like the naval equivalent of re-gifting.

Lindsey takes me through the doors of a cavernous old store, which now holds the bulk of the navy's heritage collection. In here, basically, is an example of everything ever used in the navy, no matter how menial, from the tiniest buttons to old canvas shoes. Lindsey estimates there about 150,000 items in the collection. We walk under a banner that reads ADVANCE AUSTRALIA and into an Aladdin's Cave. The treasures and touchstones of history are packed in and seemingly go on and overwhelmingly on. I see barrels and casks that would have been on some of the earliest naval ships in these waters. There are captured German guns and uniforms, meticulously kept. There's part of the bow of HMAS *Warrego* – 'the first one' – mounted like a trophy, and the captain's cabin from HMAS *Parramatta*. Lindsey opens drawers to reveal ceremonial swords, and an original letter, which may not tell a story about this harbour but is intriguing. The contents are night orders for the Battle of Cadiz. It is signed by Horatio Nelson.

At least one kayak has made it onto this island. There's a black canvas model, one that could be folded up, just like the one used in Operation Jaywick, the secret raid by commandos on Japanese ships in Singapore Harbour in September 1943.

Bells are stacked on shelves, and on the walls are name plates and life-rings from decommissioned ships, which have slid off the sea, or below it, and out of our memory.

'Every time a ship is decommissioned, the P, R & T (presentations, relics and trophies) come here,' Lindsey says, before pointing to HMAS *Betano* name plates. 'So if we get another *Betano*, for example, they [the ship's company] can come here and get this.'

Lindsey opens a cupboard to reveal a small wooden box. She opens the hinged lid, and I'm confronted with a face. It is the face of someone I have never seen, but he is part of the reason I have been spending so much time on the harbour. It is the death mask of Commodore James Goodenough. The mask is cradled under a folded Union Jack. I'm surprised not so much by seeing a death mask in the cupboard (although that's a fair shock), but by a sense of familiarity. I've lived near where Goodenough lies. He is buried at St Thomas' Rest Park, which I used to walk through each day and night. Having stood in front of his grave and read the explanation about his death from arrow wounds in 1875, I always imagined the Commodore would look older, gruffer, more worn by a life at sea and in action. He was forty-four when he died. But I'm face to face with someone who looks younger. The absence of hair, and of blemishes, perhaps restores youth to the face. In any case, I'm glad to be able to put a face to the man whose connection to the harbour and the sea had indirectly encouraged me to improve mine.

The collection on Spectacle Island continues to grow. On the way back to the wharf, we pass a building with its doors open, and I see the honour boards from the recently decommissioned HMAS *Sydney*. Sprinkled around the grounds are old armaments, including a mortar system that is roughly facing the Drummoyne shoreline.

'It's an anti-submarine system,' Lindsey explains.

'Or anti-Drummoyne,' I add.

'Yes, but they tend to behave themselves.'

As I'm taken back to the Drummoyne shore in the launch, I'm trying to process the experience I've just had. To be in the midst of so much of this country's naval history for a couple of hours has been extraordinary and overwhelming. Which is perhaps why I keep thinking of a hydrangea. I saw the plant blooming below a rock overhang and near an old 'whaler' on the island's south-western side. I was wondering who planted it, bringing a soft blush of colour to a place of machines and warfare. The hydrangea reminded me of a naval man and artist I had spoken with a few times. Ray Parkin was serving on HMAS *Perth* when it was sunk in a ferocious battle against Japanese warships off Java in 1942. He survived the sinking but was captured by the Japanese. Mr Parkin (for I never called him Ray and was never invited to) ended up on the Burma–Thailand Railway as a prisoner of war. Despite the cruelty of his captors and the ravages of Mother Nature, Mr Parkin secretly continued drawing and watercolour painting. To Mr Parkin, this was the most effective medicine for what he considered the biggest threat to a man in his situation: self-pity. Miraculously, a lot of his artwork survived, smuggled out of the jungle by another POW, Lieutenant Colonel Edward 'Weary' Dunlop, who returned them to Mr Parkin after the war. When Mr Parkin showed me the drawings, I remember being stunned by not just the attention to detail in each image but the subject matter; they were mostly of little plants and insects. He particularly loved depicting butterflies. These were meticulous studies of natural beauty. I asked him why he drew these things, rather than capturing the adversity he was stuck in, and he replied beauty made you feel better. What's more, he advised, no matter where you were, you could always find beauty – if you looked. As a POW, Mr Parkin was once enchanted by the sight of toadstools growing out of elephant dung. Most of us would see the dung; Ray Parkin saw the toadstools. An eye for beauty helped Ray Parkin survive the war and shaped how he viewed life.

On and around Sydney Harbour, even the laziest observer can't miss its beauty. However, it is on such a grand and intoxicating scale, you can be blind to the small and subtle moments of beauty – unless you look for them. And so when I saw that hydrangea on Spectacle Island, I thought of Mr Parkin, and his lessons in beauty. He has helped me see this harbour for what it is.

IN THE years since the removal of the potential powder keg on the water, the only thing exploding along the Drummoyne shores are property prices. The paddle west takes me past a mix of apartment blocks and restored older homes, along with a few new creations, including one with a glass-fronted pool right on the harbour's edge. So a swimmer could be underwater and still enjoy harbour views, even if they're wobbling and warping.

At the western end of Drummoyne Bay, on Wright's Point, is an old landing stage. The steps themselves are armoured in oysters, and the stone balustrade ripples as it drunkenly stumbles along the edge of the point. From the water, it is obvious the steps are all that is left of something grand. A plaque set into one of the sandstone posts by the local council and historical society explains this was once the landing stage for Drummoyne House, built by William Wright in 1853. Wright had made his fortune trading across the Tasman, importing New Zealand kauri pine. When his mansion was being built, Wright was apparently obsessive about its quality, inspecting every block of stone and smashing any that he considered defective. In 1971, Wright's carefully constructed home was demolished. These days, just beyond the remains of the stone landing stage, is a sleek creation in steel and glass. The modern mansion is both beautiful and severe, like the look a supermodel gives whenever a camera lens is pointed in her direction.

As I paddle around the point, that imposing piece of architecture and almighty pile of concrete, Gladesville Bridge, vaults into view. Yet it is something more modest moored just in front of me that politely asks for my attention. It is a 28-foot yacht called *Pandora*. The boat is owned by a friend, David Pettett. *Pandora* is moored at the marina which huddles under the bridge. The Gladesville Bridge Marina's catchphrases on its promotional material are 'The answer to all your prayers' and 'Have faith in us', which makes it all the more appropriate that David moors his *Pandora* here. David is a man of God. He has worked as a chaplain for the navy, in prisons, and as a missionary in Japan.

My meeting him was almost providential. It was certainly very 21st century. While kayaking on Middle Harbour, I photographed a little yacht that passed me. The sailor said, 'Good morning' and ploughed on. A day later, I received a message on social media from this bloke, David Pettett, asking for a copy of the photo. Which told me two things: David was internet savvy, and that he was an observant gentleman. The good news for me was a picture was worth not only a thousand words but an invitation to go sailing.

Seeing *Pandora* at her mooring reminds of the first time I sailed with David, along with his friend Jacqui. It was a sulky day, with the sky on the verge of tears and the water a succulent olive colour, but I was feeling a lightness that resembled liberation. I had just resigned from my job and had decided to spend some time kayaking around the harbour.

The little yacht quickly gobbled up the breeze and we ripped across the water, as *Pandora* zig-zagged east.

'The winds get fluky in this river and around the headlands,' David explained, looking every bit a skipper, with his neatly trimmed beard, and his eyes constantly scanning around, looking for trouble.

We sailed under the Bridge and into a busier harbour, with the Saturday sailing traffic. David took us to the southern side of Fort Denison, explaining there was a current that carried you more quickly. Like that current, David had a deep knowledge of the harbour that lay just under the surface, and it bobbed up in anecdotes and snippets as we sailed. David is a Sydney Harbour boy. He grew up at Balgowlah on North Harbour and sailed on those waters through his teenage years. He swam in Manly Cove and caught the ferry to the city for work. The harbour shaped him then, and it continues to do so. David later told me the harbour both energised him and provided calmness. Above all, the harbour was 'home'.

The south-easterly pushed us to 6 knots, which was as fast as *Pandora* wanted to go. David looked for somewhere to moor along the northern shore. But the wind was ruffling those coves, so we moored near Watsons Bay. I could see Our Lady Star of the Sea's spire trying to burst the clouds. Further up the headland, the Macquarie Lighthouse's white paint was licking up the sun to look pristine.

As we sailed back to Drummoyne, darting and pirouetting around the thick Saturday afternoon boating traffic, I remember feeling a sense of excitement that I would soon be paddling into all these places we were passing. And I felt a little overawed at the enormity of what I wanted to do, in trying to learn about the individual characters of the dozens of bays and coves, and, in the process, better understand why the harbour meant so much to so many. I wondered how long it would take, and where it would take me. Then I remembered something Jacqui had said to me earlier in the day, when I asked where we would head for lunch.

'Sailors don't tend to ask where they're going,' she smiled. 'They just sail.'

I would do the same. I would just paddle.

DESPITE MY resolution on that day, I always had in mind my destination. I knew where this journey would end. Back at the monument to champion sculler Henry Searle.

The end is almost in sight.

First, by way of thanks to the original inhabitants, I paddle into Wallumatta Bay on the northern bank of Parramatta River. I walk over the rock shelf at the water's edge. The rock is striated, holding the scars and marks of millennia in its skin, and the surface is pocked with dozens of little pools. I peer into one, admiring the reflected bush and sky cupped in the water. On the foreshore is a rack of dinghies clumsily hugging, and set into a rock is a plaque honouring and acknowledging the Wallumedegal people. We could honour them, and respect what we have, more meaningfully yet simply by keeping the shore cleaner. The rubbish I see on the tideline is besmirching the traditions and beauty of this part of the harbour.

Heading upriver, I see the broken column protruding from the water. The monument marking the tragic end to a young life, erected on the finish line for competing rowers on the river, is also my finish line for this book.

When Mark Twain sailed into Sydney in 1895, he was beguiled by what he saw, charmed by what he heard, and inspired to write about the experience, embellishing it with a tale entwining two obsessions of the harbour city: sharks and making oodles of money quickly. Twain observed the harbour was beautiful, but made all the more so by the city. With respect to one of my favourite novelists, Mark Twain viewed Sydney the wrong way. The city is beautiful because of the harbour. For all the ugly structures we have built around it, the harbour remains undiminished. Without the harbour, everything we have built in Sydney would be sorely diminished. Even the Opera House, even the Harbour Bridge. Newcastle upon Tyne has a similar bridge, and I doubt many people would travel around the world to see it. It is an impressive bridge, but it doesn't span Sydney Harbour.

Yet everything has its limits, even the seemingly bottomless beauty of Sydney Harbour. We can't keep ignoring it, encroaching upon it, imposing our expectations and demands on it, pouring our polluted water and tossing our rubbish into it, and abusing it. And it is not enough to occasionally look at the harbour, or to skite about it to visitors. We have to engage with it, nurture it, protect it, and cherish it. We have to do that, otherwise, one day we'll look at the harbour and realise it isn't as beautiful as it once was. And in that moment, we'll realise how ugly we are, and how stupid we've been. If John F. Kennedy was right about us being drawn to the sea because, in a sense, that is what flows through us, then by abusing the harbour, we are hurting ourselves.

Storm clouds gathering in the west are backlit by the lowering sun, and a gum tree on the bank is aflame in the dying light. Henry's monument is almost glowing, like a navigational beacon. Perched on top of the broken column is a pelican. Watching the majestic bird, I wonder if the pelican is somehow a sign from Henry, telling me to keep paddling and cross the finish line. With the day ebbing away, I forget about symbols and immerse myself in the beautiful sight of a pelican-crowned column hardening into a silhouette as the silken water wraps around its base.

Even so, while looking at Henry's column, I can't help but think of what's ahead. I don't know what I'll do next. Maybe I'll apply for a job on a Sydney ferry. I had read how applicants used to be advised to row or sail the shores of the harbour to commit to memory the names of all the inlets, bays, hazards, reefs, buoys and currents, for they would be questioned about it. Even after all my paddling, I'm not sure I would pass that test, but through the journey, I have come to know the harbour, and myself, better. Anyway, sometimes you don't need to know all the names and details of somewhere before setting off; you just have to trust instinct and go there.

THE JOURNEY is finished, but my relationship with the harbour will never end. One September Friday evening, while walking through St Thomas' Rest Park, past the headstones of sailors and boatbuilders, I hear the distant moan of a cruise ship blowing its horn. I had seen the ship preparing to depart White Bay about an hour earlier. That mournful but warming moan wraps itself around the headstones, around the memories of the departed mariners, and around me, calling us all down to the harbour, back to the water.

THE HARBOUR

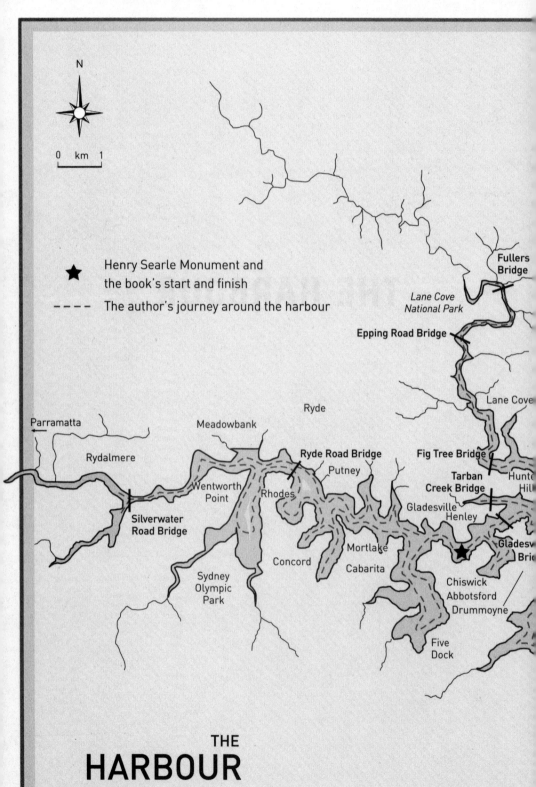

N

0   km   1

★ Henry Searle Monument and
    the book's start and finish

- - - - The author's journey around the harbour

Fullers
Bridge

*Lane Cove
National Park*

Epping Road Bridge

Lane Cove

Ryde

Meadowbank

Ryde Road Bridge

Putney

Fig Tree Bridge

Tarban
Creek Bridge

Hunte
Hill

Parramatta

Rydalmere

Wentworth
Point

Rhodes

Silverwater
Road Bridge

Gladesville

Henley

Gladesv
Brid

Mortlake

Concord

Cabarita

Sydney
Olympic
Park

Chiswick

Abbotsford

Drummoyne

Five
Dock

THE

HARBOUR

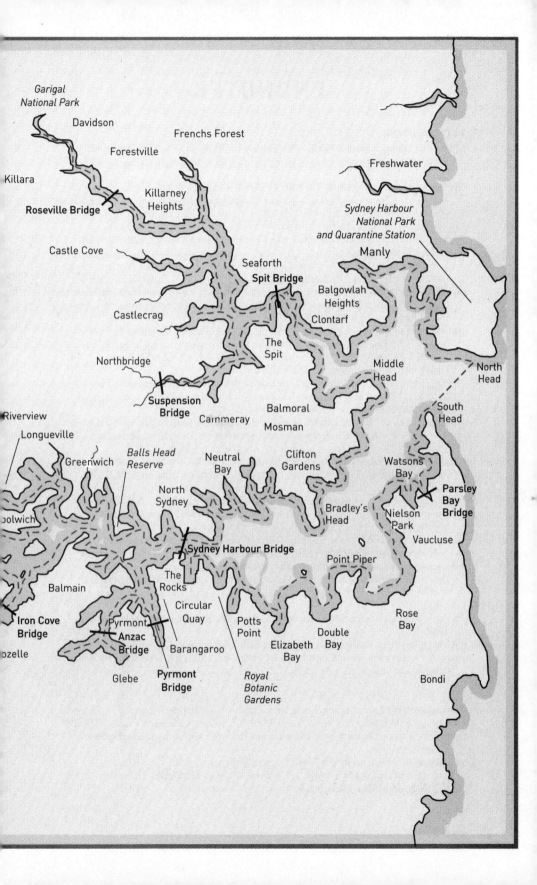

ENDNOTES

INTRODUCTION

'abreast of a Bay ... which I call'd *Port Jackson*': Cook, James, *The Journals of Captain Cook*, selected and edited by Philip Edwards, Penguin Books, 1999, p130.

'the finest and most extensive harbour in the universe ...': White, John, *Journal of a Voyage to New South Wales*, a Project Gutenberg of Australia ebook, accessed at www.gutenberg.net.au/ebooks03/0301531h.html on 13 January, 2017.

unequalled in its 'Spaciousness and Safety': Worgan, George, 'Journal Kept on a Voyage to New South Wales with the First Fleet', http://www2.sl.nsw.gov.au/archive/discover_collections/history_nation/terra_australis/journals/worgan/, accessed 13 January, 2017, from Collection 10: George Bouchier Worgan – letter written to his brother Richard Worgan, 12–18 June 1788. Includes journal fragment kept by George on a voyage to New South Wales with the First Fleet on board HMS Sirius, 20 January 1788–11 July 1788: Courtesy of Mitchell Library, State Library of New South Wales [Safe 1/114].

'satisfaction of finding the finest harbour in the world': Phillip, Arthur to Lord Sydney, 15 May, 1788, quoted in Barton, G.B., *History of New South Wales from the Records. Vol 1 – Governor Phillip, 1783-1789*, Charles Potter, Government Printer, Sydney, 1889, p268.

'Here a Thousand Sail of the Line may ride in the most perfect Security': The letter can be read at http://www2.sl.nsw.gov.au/archive/discover_collections/history_nation/terra_australis/letters/phillip/

'compares it to the Bay of Naples or the entrance to Rio Janiero [sic]': Dr Talmage, 'Cosmos', *The Kiama Independent and Shoalhaven Advertiser*, Thursday, 4 October, 1894, p4, accessed on trove.nla.gov.au on 21 July, 2016.

'You gotta love this city for its body and not its brain': Words from 'You Gotta Love this City' by Tim Freedman, used with permission of Sony/ATV Music Publishing.

'No one in Sydney ever wastes time debating the meaning of life ...': Williamson, David, *Emerald City*, Currency Press, Paddington, 1987, p2, reproduced with permission of Currency Press.

Kenneth Slessor verse: from 'Captain Dobbin', *Selected Poems*, HarperCollins Publishers Australia, Sydney, 2014, reproduced with permission.

I decided to take my time exploring the 316 kilometres or so of the harbour's shoreline: Dimensions of Sydney Harbour taken from 'Operational Brief and Profile, Maritime Environmental Services', Roads and Maritime Services, 2017.

'many lobed': Lawrence, D.H., *Kangaroo*, Angus & Robertson (reprint), Sydney, 1991, p5.

'So much has been said and written about Sydney Harbour ...': 'Sydney Harbour', *Sydney Morning Herald*, Saturday, 7 November, 1903, p4, accessed on www.trove.nla.gov.au on 21 July, 2016.

1

Australians ruled the sculling world title: Figures from Bennett, Scott, *The Clarence Comet: The Career of Henry Searle 1886-89*, Sydney University Press, 1973. I'm indebted to this book for the information I've used about the life and career of Henry Searle.

gripped with 'fear travelling by sea': Quoted in Bennett, p51.

'expressions of unfeigned sorrow ...': *Sydney Morning Herald*, 11 December, 1889, p7, accessed Mitchell Library archives.

'he did us honour, for he was of us ...': *Sydney Morning Herald*, 11 December, 1889, p6.

'the best samples of wool ever exported': *Sydney Morning Herald*, 11 December, 1889, p7.

'a monument be erected on the Brothers rocks ...':'A Memorial to the Late Champion', *Sydney Morning Herald*, 12 December, 1889, p5.

'one of the most imposing and remarkable events': *Sydney Morning Herald*, 16 December, 1889, p7, accessed via trove.nla.gov.au

'covered by wreaths from every one of the Australian colonies': *Sydney Morning Herald*, 16 December, 1889, p8.

'the development of biceps, not brains, is most desirable ... ': in Bennett, Scott, *The Clarence Comet*, p89.

verse, written by 'O.S.W: 'Henry E. Searle', *The Sydney Mail*, 14 December, 1889, p1337.

would 'derive eternal benefit' from the views: 'Minutes of Evidence Taken Before the Select Committee on Lunatic Asylums', 1863, reproduced in Johnson, Beverley & Rosen, Sue, 'History of Gladesville Hospital' report, Sue Rosen Pty Ltd, 1994 (Collection of Peter Colthorpe, Friends of Gladesville Hospital).

'a splendid piece of perfect drainage in itself': Dr Francis Campbell, 1863, quoted on National Parks and Wildlife Service information board, Bedlam Point.

'We stoped [sic] at a Neck of land to Breakfast': Bradley, William. 'A Voyage to New South Wales', December 1786–May 1792; journal, compiled 1802, Friday, 15 February, 1788, p82, Mitchell Library, State Library of New South Wales, accessed at http://acms.sl.nsw.gov.au/_transcript/2015/D02131/a138.html, 14 February, 2017.

'The Governor gave this Man a hatchet & a looking glass ...': Bradley, William, 'A Voyage to New South Wales ...' journal, p83.

'causing great delays and much strong language and worry ...': Campbell, W.S. 'Parramatta River and its vicinity, 1848-1861', Royal Australian Historical Society Journal, Vol. v, Part vi, 1919, p254.

'the man who's born a bushman, he gets mighty sick of town': Paterson, A.B., line from 'An Answer to Various Bards' (1892), reproduced in *The Penguin Banjo Paterson Collected Verse*, selected and introduced by Clement Semmler, Penguin Books Australia, 1993, p45.

The song of the river/That sings as it passes/For ever and ever: Paterson, A.B., 'The Daylight is Dying', reproduced in *The Penguin Banjo Paterson Collected Verse*, p58.

Information about Harold Meggitt Limited and the campaign to save Rockend: from 'Rockend Cottage, 38-40 Punt Road, Gladesville Conservation Management Plan', prepared for NSW Department of Urban Affairs & Planning, Land Management Branch, by Clive Lucas, Stapleton and Partners Pty Ltd, Kings Cross, 2001.

Rockend had become ... a burnt and ragged wreck: 'Rockend Cottage ... in 1984' information pamphlet, Banjo Paterson Park Committee (Collection of Ross Pitts).

The organisation warned it would make rowing more dangerous: 'We're on a collision course': NSW Rowing takes on state government', Melanie Kembrey, smh.com.au, 12 February, 2016, retrieved 13 February, 2016.

'there were few mangroves ... and the rocky outcrops encrusted with oysters': This information is from a plaque on the Wulaba Track.

the pressure on river ferries increased: Details on the history of ferries on Parramatta River from the first chapter of Graeme Andrews' book, *The Ferries of Sydney*, A.H. & A.W. Reed, Sydney, 1975.

a sailor was 'easing himself' ... when he fell overboard and drowned: The story recounted in a footnote in Karskens, Grace, *The Rocks: Life in Early Sydney*, Melbourne University Press, 1997, Footnote 27 in 'Many Laybouring People', p155.

Buried in the bed ... is the keel of HMAS *Stuart*: www.navyhistory.org.au/3-april-1947, accessed 29 April, 2016.

Errol Flynn had another *Sirocco* built: Svensen, Randi, *Wooden Boats, Iron Men: The Halvorsen Story*, Halstead Press, in association with the Australian National Maritime Museum, Sydney, 2007, p47. I'm indebted to Randi and her book for many of the details on this section about the Halvorsens.

pioneered the concept of mass production: Svensen, *Wooden Boats, Iron Men*, p83.

became known as 'the Hollywood Fleet': Svensen, *Wooden Boats, Iron Men*, p82.

The Ryde yard 'was ahead of its time ...': Email interview with Randi Svensen by the author, 3 May, 2016, reproduced with permission.

'I will make it felony to drink small beer': The character of Jack Cade in Shakespeare, William, *Henry VI, Part 2*, Act IV, Scene 2, 75-76.

one of the wealthiest men in the colony: Some of the details here from Glenda Miskelly, www.fellowshipfirstfleeters.org.au/james_squire, www.jamessquire.com.au/about, G. P. Walsh, 'Squire, James (1755–1822)', *Australian Dictionary of Biography*, National Centre of Biography, Australian National University, http://adb.anu.edu.au/biography/squire-james-2688/text3759, published first in hardcopy 1967, accessed online April 27, 2016.

'Not me go to England no more. I am at home now': Bennelong to 'Mr Phillips', 29 August, 1796, reproduced in Flannery, Tim (edited and introduced by), *The Birth of Sydney*, Text, Melbourne, 1999, pp146-147.

The ... oranges became so popular they would be transported by water: Stephensen, P.R., *The History and Description of Sydney Harbour*, Rigby Ltd, Adelaide, 1966, p316.

Some common fruits are grown out here/Where once were fields of waving beer!: McKee Wright, David, 'Night Thoughts at Ryde', reproduced in Langford, Martin (editor), Harbour City Poems, Puncher and Wattmann, Glebe, 2009, p42.

'he would bring it ashore at Meadowbank': Blaxell, Gregory, *The River*, p169, Halstead Press, Ultimo, 2009.

'What greatness had not floated on the ebb of that river ...': Conrad, Joseph, *Heart of Darkness*, Penguin, 1983 (reprint), p7.

'the tide ceased to flow; and all further progress ... was stopped ...': White, John, *Journal of a Voyage to New South Wales*, first published 1790, reproduced as an e-book by Project Gutenburg of Australia. gutenberg.net.au/ebooks03/0301531.txt, accessed 9 May, 2016.

Phillip sent Henry Dodd upriver: Pembroke, Michael, *Arthur Phillip: Sailor, Mercenary, Governor, Spy*, Hardie Grant, Melbourne, 2013, p204.

Marketing for Royal Shores development: www.royalshores.com.au, accessed February, 2016.

Barges carried the crude oil upriver: Stephensen, P.R., *Sydney Harbour*, Rigby, Adelaide, 1966, p307.

One sign prohibits fishing: Sign read at Silverwater boat ramp on 18 February, 2016.

A terminal was built near ... Parramatta and Duck rivers: Stephensen, *Sydney Harbour*, p292.

2

'felled trees for logs ... for building materials': Gregory, *The River*, pp206-207.

'the largest "household" in the district': Coupe, Sheena, *Concord, A Centenary History*, Council of the Municipality of Concord, NSW, 1983, p100.

in 150 years ... there was never an explosion: Andrews, Graeme, *The Watermen of Sydney: Memories of a Working Harbour*, Turton & Armstrong, Wahroonga, 2004, p77.

A regional environmental plan was made: Toon, John & Falk, Jonathan, *Sydney, Planning or Politics*, Planning Research Centre, University of Sydney, 2003, p159.

nine million cubic metres of waste and contaminated earth: www.sopa.nsw.gov.au, accessed 12 February, 2017.

creating a new suburb ... was a developer's dream: Introduction, *Newington: a New Suburb for a New Century*, Mirvac Lend Lease Village Consortium, North Sydney, 2000, p9.

a tangle of scrub in the early days of the colony: Keneally, Tom, *Homebush Bay: A Memoir*, Minerva Books, Melbourne, 1995, p1.

not a native tree, not even a stump, was visible: Meredith, Louisa Anne, *Notes and Sketches of NSW*, 1844. Accessed via gutenberg.net.au

The Australian Jockey Club held its first meetings at the course: Stephensen, P.R., *Sydney Harbour*, pp286-287.

Just ten metres from the shore ... sits the wreck of SS *Ayrfield*: For the sites and some of the history of the shipwrecks in Homebush Bay, I'm indebted to Gregory Blaxell's *The River*, pp197-200, and his article 'The Wrecks of Homebush Bay' in *Afloat* magazine, May 2008, accessed at www.alfoat.com.au on 23 May, 2016.

one of the remarkable aspects ... was its diverse birdlife: 'A Bicentennial Park for Sydney', Macquarie University Centre for Environmental Studies, 1978, in Coupe, Sheena, *Concord*, p290.

more than 200 native bird species have been recorded: Figure from www.sydney olympicpark.com.au, accessed on 18 May, 2016.

dioxins were detected more than 10 kilometres upriver: Davies, Anne, 'The poison that got away', *Sydney Morning Herald*, 30 October, 2010, accessed at www.smh.com.au on 18 May, 2016.

Any fish caught west of Sydney Harbour Bridge should not be eaten ...: www.dpi. nsw.gov.au/fishing/closures/location-closures/sydney-harbour-port-jackson, accessed 18 May, 2016.

Levy repeated the process ... his house collapsed: Coupe, Sheena, *Concord*, p163.

'a veritable Paradise': *Beautiful Sydney*, 1896, in Coupe, Sheena, *Concord*, p76.

'the most magnificent charity ...': *Review of Reviews*, 1894, in Coupe, Sheena, *Concord*, p78.

Among those who sought refuge ...was the poet Henry Lawson: Roderick, Colin, *Henry Lawson: A Life*, Angus & Robertson, Sydney, 1991, p272.

The Walkers ... would often have a band playing on a pontoon: For many of the historical details about Yaralla and the lives of the Walkers, I'm indebted to Sheena Coupe's book, *Concord*.

Yaralla ... was a self-contained estate: Coupe, Sheena, *Concord*, p84.

'free from any humidity injurious to the constitution': *Sydney Morning Herald*, 14 September, 1840, reproduced in Coupe, Sheena, *Concord*, p72.

Tyrrell joined the 'swarms' making 'the pilgrimage': Tyrrell, James R., *Old Books, Old Friends, Old Sydney*, Angus & Robertson, Sydney, 1952 (reprinted 1987), p10.

Cabarita is ... believed to mean 'by the water': Coupe, Sheena, *Concord*, p113.

a large rock was like a hen, and a group of smaller ones like chickens: Variations of the name story appear in Coupe, Blaxell and Stephensen's books. P.R. Stephensen also raises the possibility of the crew seeing the emu and chicks.

wearing skis ... based on a magazine photograph: www.skirace.net/water-skiing-in-australia, accessed 1 June, 2016

'miserable wretches' harnessed to carts: Ducharme, Leon, *Journal of a Political Exile in Australia* (Australian Historical Monographs, vol.2), Review Publications, Dubbo, 1976, p31, reproduced in Coupe, Sheena, *Concord*, p49.

'but he dismissed them with threats ...': King, Philip Gidley, *Remarks & Journal Kept on the Expedition to form a Colony on His Majestys Territory in New South Wales ...* (vol. 1) 27 January-1 February 1788, Manuscript ML Safe 1/16, p88-89, accessed from www.sl.nsw.gov.au/archive/discover_collections/society_art/french/perouse/botanybay.html, on 29 May, 2016.

the shoreline was used in filming ... *For the Term of His Natural Life*: Information from www.canadabayconnections.wordpress.com, accessed 30 May, 2016.

Two of the coves remain: Information from a plaque at the headland, Drummoyne Municipal Council and Drummoyne & Districts Historical Society, 1978.

3

Les Murray verse: from 'The Sydney Highrise Variations. 1. Fuel stoppage on Gladesville Road Bridge in the Year 1980 and 2. View of Sydney, Australia, from Gladesville Road Bridge', from Murray, Les, *Collected Poems*, William Heinemann Australia, Melbourne, 1994, pp171-172, reproduced with permission.

a large arch that spans the creek: Information on the bridge from http://www.rms. nsw.gov.au/projects/sydney-north/tarban-creek-bridge/index.html, accessed 16 June, 2016.

waiting at the wharf with a wheelbarrow: Story reproduced in Brodsky, Isadore, *Hunters Hill, New South Wales, 1861-1961*, John D. Jukes for the Council of the Municipality of Hunters Hill, 1961, p39.

'vines are coming along very well ...': Quoted in Maguire, Roslyn & Drake, Diana, *The Priory at Hunters Hill, N.S.W.*, Hunters Hill Trust, 1992, p3, accessed from www.huntershilltrust.org.au on 15 June, 2016.

'the very worst characters find an undisturbed place of abode': 'Kissing Point Common', *Sydney Morning Herald*, 14 February, 1851, p3, accessed via trove. nla.gov.au.

expect to sell the house ... for about $6 million: According to www.realestate.com. au, the house sold on June 25, 2016, for $6,500,000, accessed 15 February, 2006.

'all other harbours dwindled down to almost insignificance': Joubert, Jules, *Shavings and Scrapes from Many Parts* (1890), quoted in Sherry, Beverley, *Hunter's Hill: Australia's Oldest Garden Suburb*, David Ell Press, Balmain, 1989, p18.

the service provided ... was so haphazard ...': Andrews, Graeme, *The Ferries of Sydney*, p27.

'the face of the district will change considerably': R.D. Stuckey, in Brodsky, Isadore, *Hunters Hill, New South Wales, 1861-1961*, p69.

more than 220 places listed on the Register of the National Estate: www. huntershilltrust.org.au/about, accessed 21 June, 2016.

the slag ... was dumped around the site: Ewald, Connie, *The Industrial Village of Woolwich*, The Hunters Hill Trust, 2000, p60.

'The unborn Australian will ... be handed a piece of concrete': Quoted in Oppenheimer, Melanie, *Volunteering*, UNSW Press, Sydney, 2008, pp130-131. Details about the Kelly's Bush campaign were learnt from Melanie's book.

'the finest views of any known spot in the Colony': *Sydney Gazette*, 23 November, 1841, reproduced in Hall, Richard (editor), *Sydney: An Oxford Anthology*, Oxford University Press, Melbourne, 2000, pp32-33.

'had the appearance ... of the Abomination of Desolation': Stephenson, P.R., *The History and Description of Sydney Harbour*, p344.

188 metres long and about 27 metres wide: dimensions from www.woolwichdock. com/history, accessed 28 June, 2016.

the wives would walk up ... to the households ... and sell their catch: Ewald, Connie, *The Industrial Village of Woolwich*, p45.

the island was apparently snake-infested: Parker, R.G., *Cockatoo Island*, Nelson, Melbourne, 1977, p1.

fluctuations in food supply and prices, and housing convicts : Much of the detail about Cockatoo Island is from Clark, Mary Shelley and Clark, Jack, *The Islands of Sydney Harbour*, Kangaroo Press, Sydney, 2000. Figures also from excerpts of 'Cockatoo Island Dockyard – Conservation Management Plan, Vol.1, June 2007,

Godden Mackay Logan, on www.cockatooisland.gov.au, accessed on 6 July, 2016.

'grain ... may be preserved in them for years': Gipps quoted in Parker, R.G., *Cockatoo Island*, p2.

referred to the cells as a tomb: Brodsky, Isadore, *Hunters Hill, New South Wales, 1861-1961*, p18.

'mast, paddle and sail discovered ... an attempted escape': Excerpt from diary of James Rush, quoted in Parker, *Cockatoo Island*, p7.

'a wretched, exhausted creature clinging ... to the oyster-covered rocks ...': Becke, Louis, *Old Convict Days*, pvii, reproduced in Day, A. Grove, *Louis Becke*, Hill of Content, Melbourne, 1967, p26.

'An island which does not provide itself with ships ...': Quoted in Parker, R.G., *Cockatoo Island*, p73.

images of people talking freely on mobile phones in open fields: The author visited the 20th Biennale of Sydney on Cockatoo Island on 3 June, 2016.

the workers had a choir, which practised on the ferry: Andrews, Graeme, *The Ferries of Sydney*, p106.

4

Hunter explored the lower reaches: 'Plan of Port Jackson, Coast of New South Wales ... as Survey'd by Cap'n. Hunter 1788', reproduced in Groom, Linda, *A Steady Hand: Governor Hunter and his First Fleet Sketchbook*, National Library of Australia, Canberra, 2012, p38.

the house that is synonymous with the river: Brodksy, p29.

'we have plenty of sea fish ...': Sherry, Beverley, *Hunter's Hill. Australia's Oldest Garden Suburb*, p29.

'we could hardly work the long oars to make any headway ...': Harris, Alexander, *The Secrets of Alexander Harris*, Angus and Robertson, Sydney, 1961, p126.

the shark tore a chunk of flesh from his thigh: 'The Lane Cove Shark Again. Youth Fiercely Attacked.' *Evening News*, Sydney, Tuesday, 30 January 1900, p6, accessed on www.nla.gov.au on 15 August, 2016.

He died from a 'frightful' wound: 'Killed by a Shark in Lane Cove', *Sydney Morning Herald*, Saturday, 27 January 1912, p15, accessed on www.trove.nla.gov.au on 15 August, 2016.

operators would ... lead the passengers in 'sing-songs': Andrews, Graeme, *The Ferries of Sydney*, p95.

stirred up by launches 'that were going up and down all the time': 'Killed by a Shark in Lane Cove, *Sydney Morning Herald*, Saturday, 27 January 1912, p15.

'a factory ... would go very far to destroy it': 'Wool-washing', *Sydney Morning Herald*, Wednesday, 8 September 1886, p7, accessed at www.trove.nla.gov.au on 9 August 2016.

'converting ... [a] ... rocky creek into a pretty ... sheet of water': 'Another Beauty Spot. A Lane Cove Improvement', *Sun*, Friday, 11 April 1913, p5, accessed at www.trove.nla.gov.au on 9 August 2016.

'impossible to prevent the factories from emptying their waste': 'Lane Cove River Resident Complains Soapy-Colored Water', *Sun*, Saturday, 29 March 1920, p8, accessed at www.trove.nla.gov.au on 9 August 2016.

using his jacket to try to scoop up more wind: Harris, Alexander ('an Emigrant Mechanic'), *Settlers and Convicts*, (London, 1847), Melbourne University Press, 1954, pp85-87.

he chopped, loaded and unloaded the wood: Harris, Alexander, *The Secrets of Alexander Harris*, Angus and Robertson, Sydney, 1961, p114.

A journalist wrote about a fleet of 'Lane Cove Varnishers': 'The Varnishers', *Evening News*, 12 December, 1912, p6, accessed at www.nla.gov.au on 9 August, 2016.

An old boatman often bedded down under the overhanging rocks: Harris,

Alexander ('an Emigrant Mechanic'), *Settlers and Convicts*, p87.

'other places do seem so cramped up and smothery': Twain, Mark, *The Adventures of Huckleberry Finn*, Penguin (reprint 1987), p176.

the possibility that the pair had died from accidental poisoning: *Who Killed Dr Bogle and Mrs Chandler?* (2006), directed and written by Peter Butt, produced by Film Australia and Blackwattle Films.

considered a weir or lock near Fig Tree Bridge: 'Locking the Lane Cove River', *Cumberland Argus and Fruitgrowers Advocate*, 15 September 1900, p12, accessed on www.trove.nla.gov.au on 9 August, 2016.

The pleas kept coming: 'Locking Lane Cove River', *Sydney Morning Herald*, Friday 30 December 1904, p4, accessed on www.trove.nla.gov.au on 9 August, 2016.

'made tea and ate fish just caught in the river' then '... sang sentimental songs': Stead, Christina, *Seven Poor Men of Sydney* (1934), Sirius reprint 1987, p197.

the five fingers of Lane Cove: Farlow, Margaret, in piece on Lane Cove for www.dictionaryofsydney.org/entry/lane_cove, accessed on 29 August, 2016.

only this part of the main building ... was built: Details from www.riverview.nsw.edu.au/our-school/#history_of_riverview, accessed 29 August, 2016.

So I sit and muse in this wayside harbour and wait ...: 'The Wanderer', reproduced in Heseltine, Harry (edited by), *The Penguin Book of Australian Verse*, Penguin Books Australia, 1982, p109.

'straddled its hill in isolation, a self-contained and monosexual world ...': Hughes, Robert, *Things I Didn't Know*, Knopf, 2006, p146, © Robert Hughes, 2006, reproduced by permission of Penguin Random House Australia.

'the fleet ... gave the river quite an animated appearance': 'Annual Regatta – Saturday, June 8th', in *Our Alma Mater*, 'A School Annual Edited by the Students of St Ignatius' College S.J. Riverview', Sydney, 1890, p71.

received its name because a woman who sang and played a tambourine: Bethel, Walter E., 'Haymaking. Earliest Use of Lane Cove Names and Legends', in *Sun*, 11 October, 1930, p7, accessed on www.trove.nla.gov.au on 9 August, 2016.

half of Sydney's seagrass beds have disappeared: Chettle, Nicole, 'Sydney Harbour boat moorings are impacting sea floor marine life: researchers', www.abc.net.au, 22 March, 2015, accessed 30 August, 2016.

'these baths were rather frightening ...': Phelan, Nancy, *A Kingdom by the Sea*, A&R, Sydney, 1969, reprinted 1980, pp144-145.

the run-off rises, and so do the levels of microbial contamination: I read the table at www.environment.nsw.gov.au/beach/ar0910/sydneyestuarine.htm, accessed on 16 February, 2016.

pollution was likely and to avoid swimming in the baths: www.environment.nsw.gov.au/beach/Reportstar.htm, last accessed 31 August, 2016.

he fell into the water and survived: Ewald, Connie, *The Industrial Village of Woolwich*, The Hunters Hill Trust, 2000, p22.

'confronted by the golden sandstone portals of Sydney Harbour': Rees, Lloyd, *Peaks and Valleys*, Collins Australia, Sydney, 1985 (reprinted 1989), p113.

there was a half-hour service until midnight: Rees, Lloyd, *Peaks and Valleys*, p214.

'I don't want to go to Heaven because it can't be as beautiful as this': Quoted in Free, Renée (in collaboration with Lloyd Rees), *Lloyd Rees. The Last Twenty Years*, Craftsman House, Sydney, 1990, p167.

5

The good mates almost drowned once: The story of the leaky canoe is recounted in Dundy, Elaine, *Finch, Bloody Finch*, Holt, Rinehart and Winston, New York, 1980, p55.

'the immense numbers of tree stumps ...': Harris, Alexander ('an Emigrant Mechanic'), *Settlers and Convicts*, p89.

the sea was about 30 kilometres east of the Heads: For a fine summary of the harbour's formation, read Tim Flannery's introduction in his *The Birth of Sydney*, Text Publishing, Melbourne, 2000, pp8-10, and Proudfoot, Peter, *Seaport Sydney: The Making of the City Landscape*, University of NSW, Sydney, 1996, pp5-7.

'Australasia': Wentworth, William Charles, 1823, accessed at setis.library.usyd. edu.au/ozlit. Transcription based on the facsimile version available in: *W. C. Wentworth Australasia* [With an Introduction by G. A. Wilkes], Sydney: Department of English, University of Sydney, 1982. The original publication appeared in 1823 as 'Australasia — A Poem written for The Chancellor's Medal at the Cambridge Commencement, July 1823, by W. C. Wentworth, An Australasian; Fellow-commoner of Saint Peter's College', London: G. and W.B. Whittaker, 1823, pp.xii, 28.

'A large firm ... [will] establish large petroleum works': 'A New Industry', *Goulburn Evening Penny Post*, 8 February, 1900, p4, accessed www.trove.nla.gov.au on 9 August, 2016.

'the industry is not of a noxious or offensive character ...': 'A New Industry', *Goulburn Evening Penny Post*, 8 February, 1900, p4.

Tingira ... mouldered in nearby Berrys Bay: Information from www.navy.gov.au/hmas-tingira, accessed on 7 September, 2016.

used teak decking from the wreck of the *Tingira*: Svensen, Randi, *Wooden Boats, Iron Men: The Halvorsen Story*, p117.

'on the brow of a ridge overlooking the Harbour ...': Berry, Alexander, 27 January, 1837, quoted in Russell, Eric, *The Opposite Shore*, p59.

'"I have got enough land, now let other people get a little also"': 'The Shoalhaven Incubus', *The Illawarra Mercury*, 23 December 1858, reproduced in Russell, Eric, *The Opposite Shore*, p69.

the owner of the largest freehold estate in the colony: Wonga, 'Alexander Berry of Crows Nest 1781-1873', unpublished manuscript, entry for the Isabella Brierley Prize for History, 1995, p83.

'The Sacrifice of Ball's Head': Lawson, Henry, (1916), reproduced Roderick, Colin (editor), *Henry Lawson Collected Verse, Volume Three: 1910-1922*, Angus & Robertson Australia, 1981 (reprint), p401, reproduced with permission of the publisher, ETT Imprint, Sydney.

the whales ... dived under his boat: 'Whales in Sydney Harbour', by 'Resident in Elizabeth-street', *Sydney Morning Herald*, Monday, 30 September, 1889, p5, accessed www.trove.nla.gov.au on 17 July, 2016.

no formal maritime facility on the beach: 'Berrys Bay Waverton Scoping Study', Arup Pty Ltd for NSW Roads and Maritime Services, Sydney, July 2012, p31.

The Fords built colliers ... and luxury motor yachts: Some of this information from the Boatbuilders' Walk plaque on site, North Sydney Council.

A plan for a marina ... has been opposed by an action group: www.saveberrysbay. org.au

'could be castellated on top to resemble mediaeval castles': 'Harbour Foreshores,' *Sydney Morning Herald*, Thursday, 13 August, 1931, p8, accessed www.nla.gov. au on 8 August, 2016.

'WARNING. Trees in this area have been wilfully destroyed ...': I read the sign while visiting Carradah Park on 9 September, 2016.

no country would allow such a beautiful foreshore to be defiled: Quoted in Spigelman, Alice, *Almost Full Circle: Harry Seidler, A Biography*, Brandl & Schlesinger, Rose Bay, 2001, p204. This book, along with Kenneth Frampton and Phillip Drew's and Helen O'Neill's, provided much of the background information about Seidler's vision for McMahons Point, and the building of Blues Point Tower.

towers [were] built on the waterfront, blocking the view: Frampton, Kenneth and Drew, Phillip, *Harry Seidler*, Thames and Hudson, London, 1992, pp70-71. Information on Blues Point Tower is from p72.

Blues Point Tower was ...larger than anything that was in [Seidler's] plans: O'Neill, Helen, *A Singular Vision: Harry Seidler*, HarperCollins Publishers Australia, Sydney, 2013, p179.

'We pulled him across in his own boat, and paid him our fares': Harris, Alexander, *Settlers and Convicts*, p90.

The poster featured the words, 'True Blue!': The poster, along with biographical information, is in Warne, Catherine, *Pictorial History: Lower North Shore*, Kingsclear Books, Alexandria, 2005, pp5-7.

'No one is interested until it's too late': *Bob Gordon: Lavender Bay Boat Builder*, DVD, North Sydney Council & Life Captured, June 2005.

6

'a big want in the lives of Sydney and North Sydney': Quoted in Warne, Catherine, *Pictorial History: Lower North Shore*, p132.

Luna Park had its critics: Marshall, Sam, *Luna Park: Just for Fun*, Luna Park Reserve Trust, Sydney, 1995, p55.

a ... Dutch submarine was moored next to the park: Marshall, Sam, *Luna Park: Just for Fun*, p82.

The first recorded burials on the North Shore: The headstones' story is told in Lawrence, Joan, *Pictorial History: Lavender Bay to The Spit*, Kingsclear Books, Alexandria, 1999, p7.

'Young men in their dozens line the sides [of the ferry] ...': Rees, Lloyd, *Small Treasures of a Lifetime*, pp47-48.

the Port Authority discovered ... a ship's propeller: 'Lost and found in Sydney Harbour: Port Authority of NSW finds giant propeller using sonar technology', www.abc.net.au, accessed 2 November, 2015.

'The Bridge is 20 miles high ... and feeds on paint': Slessor, Kenneth, 'A Portrait of Sydney', reproduced with permission of the publisher, ETT Imprint, Sydney, and Paul Slessor, originally published in *A Portrait of Sydney*, Ure Smith, 1952, republished in Haskell, Dennis (editor), *Kenneth Slessor*, UQP, St Lucia, 1991, p78.

'Visit of Hope to Sydney Cove, near Botany Bay': Darwin, Erasmus, reproduced in Langford, Martin (editor), *Harbour City Poems*, Puncher & Wattmann, Glebe, 2009, p18.

The young scientist was also impressed by the evolution of Sydney: Pearn, John, 'The Antipodes of Erasmus Darwin: The Place of Erasmus Darwin in the Heritage of Australian Literature and Biology', in Smith, Christopher Upham Murray & Arnott, Robert, *The Genius of Erasmus Darwin*, Aldershot, Hampshire, England, 2005, p106.

a bridge from 'Dawes Battery to the North Shore': Francis Greenway, writing to *The Australian* in April 1825, quoted in Lalor, Peter, *The Bridge*, A&U, Sydney, 2005, p49.

thirteen million passengers a year were being carried across: Lalor, Peter, *The Bridge*, p37.

'I will see my Romance of the Bridge become a Reality': Quoted in Lalor, *The Bridge*, p82.

'Old North Sydney': Lawson, Henry, in Roderick, Colin (editor), *Henry Lawson: Collected Verse, Volume 2*, Angus & Robertson, Sydney, 1968 (reprinted 1981), pp68-69, reproduced with permission of the publisher, ETT Imprint, Sydney.

telling them their lives were to be upturned: From *Shifting Old North Sydney: Sydney Harbour Bridge and the Local Community*, (DVD), North Sydney Council, 2007.

'A telephone call, that a fine wall was coming down ...': Cash, Frank, *Parables of the Sydney Harbour Bridge*, self-published, Sydney, 1930, pix.

'no part of New South Wales has undergone such far reaching change': Cash, Frank, *Parables of the Sydney Harbour Bridge*, p13.

the Reverend Cash was the only one ... to have unlimited access to the work: Ennis, Lawrence, 'Foreword', in Cash, Frank, *Parables of Sydney Harbour Bridge*, pvii.

Reverend Cash often put his faith in beams and platforms: Cash, Frank, *Parables of Sydney Harbour Bridge*, p122.

'the same gift, as the Sacred Word speaks of God conferring upon the whole world': Cash, Frank, *Parables of Sydney Harbour Bridge*, pp459-460.

'a colossal work of modern sculpture against a background of eternity': Rees, Lloyd, *The Small Treasures of a Lifetime*, p50.

Sydneysiders ... jumped out of bed ... and added to the symphony: Lalor, Peter, *The Bridge*, p26.

'The pylon features ... destroyed the visual reality of the steel bridge ...': Boyd, Robyn, *The Australian Ugliness*, published by Text Publishing, Melbourne, reproduced with permission, © Robyn Boyd Foundation 2010, originally published by Australian Pelican, Ringwood, Victoria, 1968 (revised edition), p38.

'safe conduct over the Bay of Despond on the Bridge of Faith ...': 'The Bridge', *The Age*, Friday, 18 March, 1932, p3, www.trove.nla.gov.au, accessed 27 February, 2017.

no fish or crustaceans caught west of the Bridge should be eaten: www.dpi.nsw.gov.au/fishing/recreational/fishing-skills/fishing-in-sydney-harbour.

the toilet bag ... splatted on the deck of a ferry: Story told in Lalor, *The Bridge*, p202.

he doesn't know how anyone can work on the Bridge anymore: Lalor, Peter, *The Bridge*, p345.

'every reason to hope' work would begin that year: *Freeman's Journal*, Saturday 25 June, 1887, p19.

7

the lanolin-soaked floors created ... a furnace: 'Wool Store Burnt', *The Argus*, 14 December, 1921, p19, http://trove.nla.gov.au/newspaper/article/4613650, accessed 27 October, 2016.

Wee Georgie ... won at least thirty championships: For additional information about Robinson and the 18-foot skiffs, I'm indebted to the article by John Cadd, '18 ft skiffs: Sydney's Flying Circus', in *Classic Boat* magazine, August 2007, pp38-42.

he would be ordered overboard and left to swim back: Jackson, Jacqueline, *James R. Jackson: Art was his life* ... Bay Books, Sydney, 1991, pp11-12.

used to listen to the subs' engines rumble to life: Kayaking with Mika Utzon Popov, 23 June, 2016.

More than $40 million have been spent: 'Platypus Management Plan' (Draft Plan Factsheet & Plan Possibilities Consultation Summary – July 2016), The Sydney Harbour Federation Trust. Also the Trust's book, *Shaping The Harbour*, Sydney, 2011, pp62-65.

In the days after the controversial opening: Lalor, Peter, *The Bridge*, p312.

one section ... has been revered locally: Details of Lex and Ruby Graham's garden come from the information plaque on site, as part of the Cremorne Point Foreshore Walk, read 10 November, 2016.

whale exports were valued at £140,220: Ancher, Edward A., *The Romance of an Old Whaling Station*, 1909, republished 1976 by the Mosman Historical Society, p15.

'very favourable to a ship of war ...': F.P. Blackwood, RN, letter published in an advertisement in the Sydney *Shipping Gazette*, 9 May, 1846, quoted in Ancher, *The Romance of an Old Whaling Station*, p13.

'a rough, rural and romantic place worth seeing ...': Quoted in Ancher, *The Romance of an Old Whaling Station*, p37

'the soft, dark breath of the harbour playing through my hair': From a letter from Arthur Streeton to Tom Roberts, December 29, 1891, in Croll, R.H., *Smike to Bulldog: Letters from Sir Arthur Streeton to Tom Roberts*, Ure Smith, Sydney, 1946, p28.

'fascinating, warm, grey sky and yellow rock': Letter from Arthur Streeton to Tom Roberts, 14 July, 1907, in Croll, R.H., *Smike to Bulldog: Letters from Sir Arthur Streeton to Tom Roberts*, p88.

'Sydney-Side': Lawson, Henry, reproduced in Roderick, Colin (editor), *Henry Lawson Collected Verse: Volume One*, Angus & Robertson Australia, 1981 (reprint), p349, reproduced with permission of the publisher, ETT Imprint, Sydney.

intent on turning the city into a South Pacific town: Pringle, John, *Australian Accent*, Chatto & Windus, London, 1958, pp187-189.

the facilities were grossly overdue: 'The New Fortifications', *Illustrated Sydney News*, 18 February 1871, p12, accessed trove.nla.gov.au, 5 July 2017.

the most extensive playground in Australia: From a 1913 ferry guide, quoted in Aplin and Storey, *Waterfront Sydney*, p133.

About 575 fish species have been recorded: Those figures are from the Sydney Institute of Marine Science's website, www.sims.org.au/research/long-term-projects/sydney-harbour-research-program/about-sydney-harbour, accessed January 24, 2017.

the 'military road' was an impressive 66 feet wide: *Illustrated Sydney News*, 18 February, 1871, p12, accessed trove.nla.gov.au, 5 July 2017.

'better entitled to his rank than the English to his land': O'Connell, James, *A Residence of Eleven Years in New Holland and the Caroline Islands*, an excerpt from which is reproduced in Flannery, Tim (editor), *The Birth of Sydney*, Text Publishing, Melbourne, 1999, pp230-231.

the third largest facility in Australia: For more on the Georges Heights hospital, read Fletcher, Patrick (editor), *The Hospital on the Hill*, Sydney Harbour Federation Trust, Sydney, 2012.

writers also stayed, including Robert Louis Stevenson: The reference to Robert Louis Stevenson comes from Gavin Souter's *Time & Tides*, Simon & Schuster Australia, Sydney, 2004, p209.

designed to 'prevent any attack from without': King to Duke of Portland, March 1801, quoted in Oppenheim, p10.

the first time there had been loss of life: '*Edward Lombe*: Wreck Inspection Report.' Prepared by Tim Smith and David Nutley, Underwater Cultural Heritage Program, NSW Heritage Office, Department of Planning, June 2006.

8

'The country ...was rather high and rocky ...': White, John, *Journal of a Voyage to New South Wales*, accessed at www.gutenberg.net.au/ebooks03/0301531 on 17 January 2017.

'fear heightening the night's enchantment': Phelan, Nancy, *Kingdom by the Sea*, Angus & Robertson, Sydney, 1969 (reprint 1980), p118.

If he saw another artist's paint marks on a rock, [he] would get annoyed: Jackson, Jacqueline, *James R. Jackson: Art was his life ...* Bay Books, Sydney, 1991, p94.

She called them 'Treasure Island' beaches: Phelan, Nancy, *Kingdom by the Sea*, p54.

'stretches like a natural bridge nearly across the channel': Tackra, 'Vignettes of Sydney Harbour', in *Sydney Mail and New South Wales Advertiser*, Wednesday, 30 December 1908, p1705, accessed trove.nla.gov.au on 17 July, 2016.

The traffic on the deck above has continued to grow: Information from http://www.rms.nsw.gov.au/maritime/using-waterways/bridge-opening-times, accessed 27 December, 2016.

'Wonder ... that the houseboat idea has not been adopted': 'Sydney Harbour Residential Club', *Sydney Mail and New South Wales Advertiser*, Saturday, 10 June 1899, page 1351, accessed on trove.nla.gov.au on 17 July 2016.

there was even a boarding house boat on the harbour: 'House boats for Sydney Harbour', *Clarence and Richmond Examiner*, 27 February, 1909, page 3, accessed on trove.nla.gov.au on 17 July, 2016.

for 'gentlemen only' to live on board: 'Sydney Harbour Residential Club Company', *Australian Star*, Sydney, Friday, 2 June 1899, p5, accessed on trove.nla.gov.au on 17 July, 2016.

'a world of delight, adventure and privilege': Moore, David. *Sydney Harbour*, p8.

'with a confidence that was discernible by the spectators': 'A Daring Feat', *Illustrated Australian News*, 16 April, 1877, p62.

'walked fearlessly at the rate of eighty steps to a minute': 'L'Estrange's rope-walk over Middle Harbour', *Sydney Morning Herald*, 16 April, 1877, p5.

'The Bridge to Health and Wealth at Northbridge': Raine and Horne advertisement, 1913, quoted in Clifford, Pam, *Northbridge – Building a New Suburb*, self-published, Sydney, 2014, p49.

even the state's road authority officially accepted the name : Clifford, Pam, *Northbridge – Building a New Suburb*, p37.

The owner apparently thought the land ... was suitable for only goats: Clifford, p23.

made Fig Tree House pleasant for the human species: Clifford, p165.

'waves of fire and smoke were rolling out of the vessel with such fury: 'The *Itata* Completely Destroyed', *Sydney Morning Herald*, 13 January, 1906, accessed on trove.nla.gov.au on 29 December, 2016.

one of the smallest tidal rock pools: Information from a plaque at the site, read on 22 August, 2016.

as though the whole landscape was theirs: 'Griffin legacy at Castlecrag' on www.griffinsociety.org, accessed on 2 January, 2017.

The caves had been home to escaped convicts: I'm indebted to Gavin Souter's wonderful book, *Time & Tides*, and for his wealth of information and knowledge of Middle Harbour.

debates ... may have been smoothed by the harbour waters: Details of the yacht from Miles, Patricia, *Lucinda: Little Ship of State*, Australian National Maritime Museum, Sydney, 2001.

converted into a centre for recovering alcoholic men: Information from a plaque at Echo Point Park, read 28 May, 2016.

'the most ... solitary seclusion ...': White, John, *Journal of a Voyage to New South Wales*, accessed at www.gutenberg.net.au/ebooks03/0301531 on 17 January, 2017.

'no unsightly mud-banks are uncovered at low water': Froude, James, *Oceana, or England and her Colonies*, Longmans Green, London, 1886, reproduced in Hall, Richard, *Sydney*, p73.

'The water was stained with blood ...': 'Shark kills actress in shallow cove: fight by fiance', *Sydney Morning Herald*, 29 January, 1963, p1.

'At Clontarf ... it was an orgy': *Bulletin*, 9 January, 1881, reproduced in Hall, Richard (editor), *Sydney*, pp70-71.

9

They were evicted and the huts were boarded up: Details of the residents of Crater Cove and the battle to evict them are from Grayson, Russ, 'Hidden path to a cove's history', on www.pacific-edge/2007/2008/hidden-path-to-a-coves-history, accessed 6 May, 2016.

twenty-five people have died on Gowlland Bombora: Figure from the article 'Gowlland Bombora ended a brilliant career', Morecombe, John, published on 26 February, 2016, at http://www.dailytelegraph.com.au/newslocal/northern-beaches/gowlland-bombora-ended-a-brilliant-career/news-story/e948265ad8f16c1c8ce2f84b041e98e1, accessed on 22 January, 2017.

the man's doctor pronounced him healthy: Andrews, Graeme, *The Ferries of Sydney*, p111.

to try ... to 'live in amity and kindness with them': Reproduced in Eldershaw, M. Barnard, *Phillip of Australia*, Angus & Robertson, Sydney, 1972, p29.

'finding bodies of the Indians in all the coves ...': Tench, Watkin, *A Complete Account of the Settlement at Port Jackson*, G. Nicol and J. Sewell, London, 1793, republished by the University of Sydney library, Sydney, 1998, accessed at www.setis.library.usyd.edu.au/ozlit on 22 January, 2017.

'the bathing suburb of Sydney – one of them': Lawrence, D.H., *Kangaroo*, p21.

there were only about thirty-five left: A lot of the details about the Little Penguin come from Pulman, Felicity, *The Little Penguins of Manly Wharf*, Sydney, 2013.

the substance is 'not known to be toxic': Read by the author on 4 May, 2016.

'joined by 3 Canoes with one Man in each ...': Bradley, 29 January, 1788.

warned to keep their doors ... open to avoid damage: Oppenheim, Peter, *The Fragile Forts*, p232.

10

the first to sail alone across the Pacific from west to east: Details on Fred Rebell from Fulloon, Gillian, 'Rebell, Fred (1886-1968)', *Australian Dictionary of Biography*, National Centre of Biography, Australian National University, accessed at www.adb.anu.edu.au on 5 June, 2016.

'soon discoverd lying between two steep bluff heads ...': www.sl.nsw.gov.au/archive/discover_collections/society_art/french/perouse/botanybay

'To describe ... the different Coves ... I cannot do justice ...': Smyth, Arthur Bowes, *Journal of Arthur Bowes Smyth*, 1787 March 22-1789 August, accessed at http://nla.gov.au/nla.ms-ms4568 on 6 February, 2017.

'like a smile of welcome to my new country': Meredith, Louisa Anne, *Notes and Sketches of New South Wales*, J., Murray, London, 1844, pp34-35, reproduced as a Project Gutenberg of Australia ebook, accessed at http://gutenberg.net.au/ebooks16/1600201h.html on 7 February, 2017.

'two great brown pillars of Hawkesbury sand-stone ...': 'Dr Talmage', in 'Cosmos', *The Kiama Independent, and Shoalhaven Advertiser*, Thursday 4 October 1894, p4, accessed at trove.nla.gov.au on 21 July, 2016.

'Opal-blue water, a band of golden sand ...': Rees, Lloyd, *Small Treasures of a Lifetime*, p45.

'I saw Sydney for the first time the very best way ...': Culotta, Nino, *They're a Weird Mob*, Ure Smith, Sydney, 1958, p14.

'I felt I could be happy in Australia ...': As well as speaking with Teruko Blair on the telephone in February, 2017, I spoke with her in May, 2007, in Canberra, for a story I did for *The 7.30 Report*, titled 'Japanese war brides reflect on their journey', which was broadcast on ABC Television on 14 May, 2007.

2 metres clearance under the structure: 'Harbour Master's Directions', Port Authority of New South Wales, July 2016, p14, accessed www.portauthoritynsw.com.au on 27 February, 2017.

'Room here for all the navies of the earth ...': 'Dr Talmage, in 'Cosmos', *The Kiama Independent, and Shoalhaven Advertiser*, Thursday 4 October 1894, p4, accessed at trove.nla.gov.au on 21 July, 2016.

'the major form of attack under consideration ...': Quoted in Oppenheim, Peter, *The Fragile Forts*, p207.

three Japanese midget submarines brought into Sydney: Carruthers, Steven L., *Japanese Submarine Raiders, 1942: A Maritime Mystery*, Casper Publications, Narrabeen, 2006, p116.

The pilot had ... flown up the harbour: Ito's flight is recounted in Jenkins, David, *Battle Surface! Japan's Submarine War Against Australia, 1942-44*, Random House Australia, Sydney, 1992, pp186-192.

there were no words, just deep feelings: My story, titled 'Remembrance service held for midget sub crews', was broadcast on *The.730 Report*, on ABC TV on 6 August, 2007.

attacked and killed people in the harbour: Carruthers, Steven L., *Japanese Submarine Raiders, 1942*, p145.

'the better chances of keeping the submarines down until daylight': Muirhead-Gould, G.C., 'Japanese Midget Submarine Attack on Sydney Harbour – Preliminary Report'., No B.S. 1518/37, 22 June, 1942, reproduced in Carruthers, Steven L., *Japanese Submarine Raiders, 1942*, p244.

'How many of us are really prepared to make ... the sacrifice ...?': Quoted in Jenkins, David, *Battle Surface! Japan's Submarine War Against Australia, 1942-44*, p230.

Ode to the Fallen (The Sailor's Ode): printed in 'Memorial Service for Japanese Midget Submarine M24, Sea Ceremony, HMAS Melbourne', Monday, 6 August, 2007, program, Department of Veterans' Affairs.

'He works with rocks and waters and skies ...': Dr Talmage, in 'Cosmos', *The Kiama Independent, and Shoalhaven Advertiser*, Thursday 4 October 1894, p4, accessed at trove.nla.gov.au on 21 July, 2016.

'a stepping stone for greater engineering feats ...': Bradfield, quoted in Lalor, Peter, *The Bridge*, p332.

'As you sail into the opening between the Outer Heads ...': Bradley, William, *A Voyage to New South Wales*, 1802, p83, facsimile copy at Mitchell Library, Sydney, ML. Ref.1/981/54A3-4

11

'This place was call'd Camp Cove': Nagle, Jacob, Collection 08: Jacob Nagle – memoir, titled 'Jacob Nagle his Book A.D. One Thousand Eight Hundred and Twenty Nine May 19th. Canton. Stark County Ohio', 1775-1802, compiled 1829, p83, State Library of NSW, MLMSS 5954 (Safe 1 / 156), www.sl.nsw.gov.au.

'it is much valued, I believe, by glass-makers': Meredith, Louisa Anne, *Notes and Sketches of New South Wales*, J. Murray, London, 1844, p35, reproduced as a Project Gutenberg of Australia ebook, accessed at http://gutenberg.net.au/ebooks16/1600201h.html on 7 February, 2017.

'a brother-officer, was with me ...': Tench, Watkin, *A Complete Account of the Settlement at Port Jackson*, originally published by G. Nicol and J. Sewell, London, 1793, reproduced by University of Sydney Library, 1998, accessed at http://setis.library.usyd.edu.au/ozlit/pdf/p00044 on 4 March, 2017.

'In boisterous weather the surges ... break in mountains ...': Wentworth, W.C., *Description of The Colony of New South Wales and Its Dependent Settlements in Van Diemen's Land*, G. and W.B. Whittaker, London, 1819 (Facsimile Edition, Griffin Press, Adelaide, 1978.), p15.

'heaven and earth performing beneath his insignificant feet': Slessor, Kenneth, 'Storm Troops', *The Sun*, 12 December, 1920, reproduced in Haskell, Dennis, *Kenneth Slessor*, pp205-207.

The Gap has become renowned as a suicide spot: Lifeline: 13 11 14.

a lifeboat service was based at Watsons Bay: 'The "Alice Rawson" and the Port Jackson lifeboat service', p4, accessed at www.woollahra.nsw.gov.au on 8 March, 2017.

'Life is poor and unpretentious, life can be quiet ...': Stead, Christina, *Seven Poor*

Men of Sydney, first published Peter Davies, London, 1934, reprinted Sirius
Quality Paperback, Sydney, 1987, p2.

'The beach provided not only fuel, but also dead fish ...': Stead, Christina, *Seven
Poor Men of Sydney*, p3.

residents 'were absolutely fearless ...': Stead, Christina, *Seven Poor Men of Sydney*, p3.

'The Harbour': Olsen, John, *Seaport of Desire*, Port Jackson Press, Melbourne,
2002, seen at *John Olsen: The City's Son*, Newcastle Art Gallery, November 5,
2016-February 19, 2017, reproduced with permission.

'I was drawn down by suction ...': 'Ferry Disaster', *The Argus* (Melbourne),
5 November, 1927, p35, accessed at www.trove.nla.gov.au on 7 March, 2017.

'We have only one Sydney harbour ...': 'Our Harbour Foreshores' (letter to the
editor), *Sydney Morning Herald*, 19 April, 1906, p11, accessed at www.trove.nla.
gov.au on 8 August, 2016.

'to keep a watchful eye on all matters of public concern ...': 'Vigilance Committee
Formed', *Sydney Morning Herald*, Thursday, 2 November 1905, p5, accessed at
www.trove.nla.gov.au on 8 August, 2016.

'It was bound to come ...': 'The Harbour Foreshores', *Sydney Mail and New South
Wales Advertiser*, Wednesday, 23 October 1907, p1049, accessed at www.trove.
nla.gov.au on 8 August, 2016.

'unless we bestir ourselves ...': Letter to the Editor, *Sydney Morning Herald*,
19 December, 1907, p10, accessed at www.trove.nla.gov.au on 8 August, 2016.

'the southern shore ... will be densely populated ...': Letter to the Editor, *Sydney
Morning Herald*, December 19, 1907, p10.

'the ceremony of filling in the trench was performed ...': Wilson, The Rev. Canon,
'Old Sydney', in *Illustrated Sydney News*, 4 April, 1889, p11-13, accessed on
www.trove.nla.gov.au on 8 August, 2016.

'Looking towards the coast ...': Wentworth, W.C., *Description of The Colony of
New South Wales and Its Dependent Settlements in Van Diemen's Land*, G. and
W.B. Whittaker, London, 1819 (Facsimile Edition, Griffin Press, Adelaide, 1978),
p13.

Alice was ... hijacked by some of Wentworth's staff: Tink, Andrew, *William Charles
Wentworth*, Allen & Unwin, Sydney, 2009, pp135-136.

more than 4000 attended to have an uninterrupted view: 'Rejoicings for General
Darling's Departure from New South Wales ...' *Australian*, 21 October, 1831, p2,
accessed www.trove.nla.gov.au on 8 August, 2016.

the house ... looked like a Gothic Revival mansion: Tink, Andrew, *William Charles
Wentworth*, p129.

'The value of land in this town ... is daily increasing': Wentworth, W.C.,
Description of The Colony of New South, p7.

'My city is a whore': Words from 'You Gotta Love this City' by Tim Freedman, used
with permission of Sony/ATV Music Publishing.

could escape the 'lethal air' and 'floating germs': Details from the information
plaque outside Greycliffe House, read on 2 November, 2016.

'how numerous ... are the Sharks ...': 'Local Intelligence', in *Kilmore Free Press*,
Kilmore, Victoria, 20 September, 1877, p2, retrieved from nla.trove.gov.au on
30 June, 2017.

a 'truly Edwardian English park': Term used on information notice on Shark Island,
NPWS.

'It marked the spot ... that was furthest from reality ...': Barnard, Marjorie,
Macquarie's World, originally published 1941, republished by Angus &
Roberstson, Sydney, 1971, p49.

impossible to grow anything before it was stolen: Clark, Mary Shelley and Clark,
Jack, *The Islands of Sydney Harbour*, p179.

the urinal with the best view in the world: *Sydney Morning Herald*, 22 November,
1994, cited in Clark and Clark, p176.

12

'I not mean to punish any of the natives ...': Quoted in Barton, G.B., *History of New South Wales from the Records. Vol 1 – Governor Phillip, 1783-1789*, Charles Potter, Government Printer, Sydney, 1889, p301.

'... an epitome of the far-famed Eden': *Sydney Gazette*, 16 February, 1827, p2, quoted in Cherry, Derelie, *Alexander Macleay: From Scotland to Sydney*, Paradise Publishers, Kulnura, 2012, p105.

she sailed into Sydney with cuttings of lantana: Cherry, Derelie, *Alexander Macleay: From Scotland to Sydney*, pp289-290.

'an amphitheatre of lofty woods ...': Shepherd, Thomas, *Lectures on Landscape Gardening in Australia*, 1836, p89, quoted in Cherry, pp315-316.

'one of the last periods to allow whimsy ...': Koch, C.J., *The Doubleman*, Chatto & Windus, The Hogarth Press, London, 1989, p139.

'inviting as a dream of pre-war Hollywood ...': Koch, C.J., *The Doubleman*, p134.

'*Daemons in periwigs* ...': Slessor, Kenneth, 'Five Visions of Captain Cook', *Selected Poems*, HarperCollins Publishers Australia, 2014, published in Haskell, Dennis (editor), *Kenneth Slessor*, UQP, St Lucia, 1991, p22, reproduced with permission.

'Five Bells': Slessor, Kenneth, Selected Poems, HarperCollins Publishers Australia, 2014, published in Haskell, Dennis (editor), *Kenneth Slessor*, pp46-47, reproduced with permission.

'a doubly sterile mass of rugged grey rocks ...': Tucker, James, *Ralph Rashleigh*, Angus & Robertson, Sydney, 1952, published as an ebook by Project Gutenberg Australia, accessed at www.gutenberg.net.au/ebooks03/03012291.txt on 25 March, 2017.

'Since Captain Cook's arrival, no more memorable event has happened ...': Read at www.awm.gov.au/royal-australian-navy-fleet-entry-1913, accessed on 25 March, 2017.

marked a new kind of real estate: Marr, David, 'The irresistible city', *Sydney Morning Herald*, 2 December, 1997, p3.

'no' to an offer of $25 million: Macken, Lucy, 'Russell Crowe pulls his Finger Wharf apartment off the market, says no to $25m', 5 February, 2017, accessed at www. domain.com.au on 6 February, 2017.

'I can never pass the island ... without feeling indignant ...': Lang, John Dunmore, *An Historical and Statistical Account of New South Wales*, 1875, quoted on information plaque at Fort Denison.

Convicts ... were banished ... with nothing but bread and water: Nagle, Jacob, Collection 08: Jacob Nagle – memoir, titled 'Jacob Nagle his Book A.D. One Thousand Eight Hundred and Twenty Nine May 19th. Canton. Stark County Ohio', 1775-1802, compiled 1829, p84, State Library of NSW, MLMSS 5954 (Safe 1 / 156), www.sl.nsw.gov.au.

advised Barney to do some creative accounting: Semple Kerr, James, *Fort Denison*, The National Trust of Australia, Sydney, 1986, pp9-10.

sea levels are increasingly rising: Read at Fort Denison, 17 February, 2017.

'noble estuary with countless bays and inlets ...': Meredith, Louisa Anne, *Notes and Sketches of New South Wales*, p34.

'fabled palace of Aladdin in the *Arabian Nights*': 'Destruction of the Garden Palace by Fire', *Sydney Morning Herald*, 23 September, 1882, p7.

'fairy-like and bewildering ...': 'Notes of the Sydney International Exhibition of 1879', Government Printing Office, 1880, reproduced in Proudfoot, Peter; Maguire, Roslyn: and Freestone, Robert (editors), *Colonial City, Global City: Sydney's International Exhibition 1879*, Crossing Press, Sydney, 2000, p26.

a 'splendid spectacle': 'Destruction of the Garden Palace by Fire', *Sydney Morning Herald*, 23 September, 1882, p7.

'the first and the finest white Australian': Robertson, Geoffrey, 'Beyond the Bicentennial', in *Dreaming Too Loud*, Vintage, Sydney, 2013, p9, © Geoffrey

Robertson 2013, reproduced by permission of Penguin Random House Australia.

'repatriation' was utterly inappropriate: I spoke with Sir Roger Carrick and Geoffrey Robertson for *Arthur Phillip: Governor, Sailor, Spy*, ABC DVD, 2015.

those who expected … a prison were greeted with a palace: Information from www.governor.nsw.gov.au, accessed on 31 March, 2017.

'Gentlemen, here is your Opera House': Matthiesen, Stig; Bente Jensen; and Molvig, Thomas, *The joy is not in owning – but in creating*, Utzon Center, Aalborg, Denmark, 2011, p53.

13

the greatest building of the 20th Century: Keating, Paul., 'Building a Masterpiece: The Sydney Opera House', in *After Words: The Post-Prime Ministerial Speeches*, Allen & Unwin, Sydney, 2011, p5.

'It questions "Which is reality?"': Olsen, John, excerpt from journal entry, 21 April, 1973, in *Drawn to Life*, Duffy & Snellgrove, Potts Point, 1997, p105.

Lyrics from *The Eighth Wonder*: composer Alan John, librettists Dennis Watkins and Alan John, 1995, revised as *Sydney Opera House: The Opera (The Eighth Wonder)*, 2016, reproduced with permission of Alan John and Dennis Watkins.

Fort Macquarie was being derided: *Sydney Gazette*, 13 September, 1834, quoted in Kerr, 'Fort Denison', p7.

'The closing of Bennelong Point … would be an irreparable loss …': 'Letter to the Editor', *Sydney Morning Herald*, 1 June, 1910, p11, accessed at trove.nla.gov.au on 8 August, 2016.

demanded that the Toaster be torn down: An extract of that speech was published as 'Little but shame to build on', *The Australian*, 29 April, 1998, p13.

'This cove … is about a quarter of a mile across': Phillip, Arthur to Lord Sydney, May 15, 1788, quoted in Barton, G.B., *History of New South Wales from the Records. Vol 1 – Governor Phillip, 1783-1789*, Charles Potter, Government Printer, Sydney, 1889, p269.

a chief architect of the idea of a penal colony: For more on Lord Sydney, see Tink, Andrew, *Lord Sydney: The Life and Times of Tommy Townshend*, Australian Scholarly Publishing, Melbourne, 2011.

'the finest harbour in the known world': Fowell, Newton (Irvine, Nance – editor), *The Sirius letters: the complete letters of Newton Fowell, midshipman & lieutenant aboard the Sirius flagship of the first fleet on its voyage to New South Wales*, Fairfax Library, Sydney, 1988. p73.

'Here a Thousand Sail of the Line may ride in the most perfect Security': The letter can be read at http://www2.sl.nsw.gov.au/archive/discover_collections/history_nation/terra_australis/letters/phillip/

'I think it will be cheaper to feed the convicts on turtle …': Quoted in Barton, G.B. *History of New South Wales from the Records. Vol 1 – Governor Phillip, 1783-1789*, Charles Potter, Government Printer, Sydney, 1889, p500.

sixty-seven canoes were counted: Tench, Watkin, *A Complete Account of the Settlement at Port Jackson*, G. Nicol and J. Sewell, London, 1793, p9, republished by the University of Sydney library, Sydney, 1998, accessed at www.setis.library.usyd.edu.au/ozlit on 22 January, 2017.

'possesses the best anchorage the whole way': Wentworth, W.C., *Description of The Colony of New South Wales*, p12.

'The spot chosen … was at the head of the cove': Collins, David, *An Account of the English Colony in NSW Vol 1*, T. Cadell Jun and W. Davies, London, 1798, reproduced by Project Gutenberg Australia, accessed at www.gutenberg.net.au/ebooks/e00010.html on 4 February, 2017.

the Tank Stream is a ghost creek: Falconer, Delia, *Sydney*, New South, Sydney, 2010, pp33-34.

'our steam-ferry system is capable of improvement': 'Vagrant Musings', by Uralla, *Illustrated Sydney News and New South Wales Agriculturalist and Grazier,* 6 September, 1879, p3, accessed at www.trove.nla.gov.au on 30 October, 2016.

The numbers using the ferries were enormous: Figures from Lalor, Peter. *The Bridge,* p37.

'seem to slip like fishes from one side of the harbour to the other': Lawrence, D.H., *Kangaroo,* p5.

'From the harbour, city towers dominated the skyline ...': Rees, Lloyd, *Small Treasures of a Lifetime,* p46.

'infested with all sorts of bums and stiffs': Hugill, Stan, *Sailortown,* Routledge & Kegan Paul Ltd, London, 1967, p279.

'polluted with the presence of that floating hell ...': 'The Great Protest Meeting', *Sydney Morning Herald* report, 12 June, 1849, p2.

'the yachts will be racing on the crushed diamond water under a sky the texture of powdered sapphires ...': James, Clive, *Unreliable Memoirs,* Picador, London, 1981, p174, reproduced with permission.

his ashes to be scattered off Dawes Point : 'Clive James makes poetic appeal for final trip home', Kaya Burgess, *The Times,* 28 July, 2016, reproduced in www.theaustralian.com.au, accessed 15 April, 2017.

'an utter disgrace ... copying old Greece and Rome': Quoted in Spigelman, Alice, *Almost Full Circle: Harry Seidler,* p191, reproduced with permission.

the most profligate and depraved part of the population: Karskens, Grace, *The Rocks: Life in Early Sydney,* Melbourne University Press, 1997, 167.

'he would rather regard himself as in some country town in England': Reproduced in Neville, Richard, 'Sydney Watercolours: Portrait of a Town', in McPhee, John (editor), *Joseph Lycett: Convict Artist,* Historic Houses Trust of NSW, Sydney, 2006, p123, reproduced with permission of Sydney Living Museums.

This defined ... early Sydney as a maritime town: Karskens, Grace, *The Rocks: Life in Early Sydney,* p18.

'full to suffocation of the lowest women ... and ruffians': Harris, Alexander, *Settlers and Convicts,* p6.

Gatu piryala, or 'we two are talking to each other': Some of the phrases recorded by Dawes were published in Flannery, Tim (editor/introduction), *The Birth of Sydney,* Text, Melbourne, 1999, pp111-115.

Sydney Harbour's watermen had ... plied their trade on the Thames: Karskens, Grace, *The Rocks: Life in Early Sydney,* p185.

more should be done to help mariners: 'Poor Jack', letter to the Editor, *Sydney Morning Herald,* 18 August, 1906, p9.

recalled how meaningful a Mission picnic was for him: Jones, William, H.S., *The Cape Horn Breed,* first published 1956, reprinted 1999, Ibex, Melbourne, p197.

a viewing tower or part of a Museum of Sydney Harbour: www.nationaltrust.org.au, accessed 9 February, 2016.

'We always looked north ... Now I think we'll look west': Paul Keating at the Barangaroo Reserve opening, 22 August, 2015.

14

'The ordinary observer ... cannot fail to see [the] metamorphosis: 'The Wharves of Sydney', *Evening News,* 23 June, 1905, p7, retrieved from trove.nla.gov.au, on 8 August, 2016.

'there are few places in the world ...': 'Linnaean Society', *Sydney Morning Herald,* 8 February, 1879, p8, retrieved from trove.nla.gov.au on 6 March, 2017.

its eight floors has external fire escape stairs: Fire safety information for Royal Edward Victualling Yard from www.environment.nsw.gov.au

the same pair of scissors as Jack Lang in 1932: 'Anzac Bridge', www.environment.nsw.gov.au, accessed 3 May, 2017.

fifty tonnes of seafood are traded each day: Figures from www.sydneyfishmarket.
com.au, accessed 2 May, 2017.
'the first white man that ever caught a fish in Sidney Cove': Nagle, Jacob, Collection
08: Jacob Nagle – memoir. Titled 'Jacob Nagle his Book A.D. One Thousand
Eight Hundred and Twenty Nine May 19th. Canton. Stark County Ohio',
1775-1802, compiled 1829, pp83-84, State Library of NSW, MLMSS 5954
(Safe 1 / 156), www.sl.nsw.gov.au.
The 'natives' ... 'were liberally rewarded with fish': White, John, *Journal of a
Voyage to New South Wales*, from http://gutenberg.net.au/ebooks03/0301531.
txt, accessed 9 May, 2016.
the Aboriginal people passed his ship daily but never came close: Fowell, Newton
(Irvine, Nance – editor), *The Sirius letters: the complete letters of Newton
Fowell, midshipman & lieutenant aboard the Sirius flagship of the first fleet on
its voyage to New South Wales*, Fairfax Library, Sydney, 1988, p79.
'Our harbour has partaken largely of the character of a "dead sea"': 'Discoloration
of Sydney Harbour', *Goulburn Herald*, Monday 27 April, 1891, page 4, accessed
trove.nla.gov.au on 21 July, 2016.
places where old boats came to die: Park, Ruth, *Ruth Park's Sydney*, revised edition,
revised by Ruth Park and Rafe Champion, Duffy & Snellgrove, Sydney, 1999,
p166.
ships were moved at the mercy of Mother Nature: Svensen, Randi, *Heroic, Forceful
and Fearless: Australia's Tugboat Heritage*, Citrus Press, in association with the
Australian National Maritime Museum, Ultimo, 2011, p16-18.
could be used for exporting silicon: Clennell, Andrew, 'The Dawn of a New Bay',
Daily Telegraph, 22 October, 2015, pp4-5.
there are not enough berths: Markson, Sharri, 'Cruising for a Bruising', *Daily
Telegraph*, 27 April, 2017, pp8-9.
reminisced about his Tom Sawyer existence: Tyrrell, James R., *Old Books, Old
Friends, Old Sydney*, pp5-7.
the MSB began winding back its operations: For some of the details of the history of
Goat Island, I'm indebted to Mary Shelley Clark and Jack Clark's *The Islands of
Sydney Harbour*.

15
zig-zagging down the steep hill, casual workers would gather: Information from
www.lakeview.net.au. accessed 10 May, 2017.
the company went into liquidation: For more on Thomas Mort's business career, see
Barnard, Alan, *Visions and Profits*, Melbourne University Press, on behalf of the
Australian National University, 1961.
industrial structures ... could form ... inspiring public spaces: 'Reflections on a
Maritime City: An Appreciation of the Trust Lands on Sydney Harbour', the
Interim Sydney Harbour Federation Trust, Mosman, 2000, p29.
Les Murray verse: Lines from 'The Death of Isaac Newton, 1864', from an
information plaque at Tank 101, read on 30 October, 2016, reproduced with
permission.
The company's fleet featured craft with the prefix 'Pro-': Andrews, Graeme, *The
Watermen of Sydney*, Turton & Armstrong, Wahroonga, 2004, p29-34.
Among the vessels listed were 559 lighters ...: Andrews, Graeme, *The Watermen of
Sydney*, p59.
Yurulbin means 'swift running water': Details from information plaque in the park,
read 18 April, 2016.
The colliery was a tolerated neighbour: Details from information plaque, located on
site, River St, Leichhardt Council, read 18 April, 2016.
little evidence a massive Balmain power station was ever here: Details from
information plaque, located on site, read 18 April, 2016.

the **Rotary Club of Five Dock moved the cross:** Details from plaque on site, read
5 September, 2016.
'a Number of small Islands, which are covered with Trees ...': Worgan, George,
'Journal Kept on a Voyage to New South Wales with the First Fleet', http://
www2.sl.nsw.gov.au/archive/discover_collections/history_nation/terra_australis/
journals/worgan/, accessed 12 January, 2017, from Collection 10: George
Bouchier Worgan – letter written to his brother Richard Worgan, 12–18 June
1788. Includes journal fragment kept by George on a voyage to New South
Wales with the First Fleet on board HMS Sirius, 20 January 1788–11 July 1788:
Courtesy of Mitchell Library, State Library of New South Wales [Safe 1/114].
Of those fourteen islands, eight remain: Clark and Clark, *The Islands of Sydney
Harbour*, p1.
now in the care of the Sydney Harbour Federation Trust: 'Shaping the Harbour', the
Sydney Harbour Federation Trust, 2001-2011, 2011, p95.
once the landing stage for Drummoyne House: Plaque read on 1 June, 2016.
Wright was obsessive about its quality: Blaxell, Gregory, *The River*, p84.
commit to memory the names of all the inlets: Andrews, Graeme, *The Ferries of
Sydney*, p109.

SELECT BIBLIOGRAPHY

BOOKS
Ancher, Edward A., *The Romance of an Old Whaling Station: The Story of the
Pioneers of Mosman and Cremorne*, first published in the Australian Historical
Societies' Journal, Vol.2, parts 10 and 11, 1909, republished in 1976 by the
Mosman Historical Society.
Anderson, Patricia, *Art + Australia*, Pandora Press, Sydney, 2005.
Andrews, Graeme, *The Ferries of Sydney*, A.H. & A.W. Reed, Sydney, 1975.
Andrews, Graeme, *The Watermen of Sydney*, Turton & Armstrong, Wahroonga,
2004.
Aplin, Graeme and Storey, John, *Waterfront Sydney 1860-1920*, Allen & Unwin,
1991.
Barnard, Alan, *Visions and Profits: Studies in the Business Career of T.S. Mort*,
Melbourne University Press on behalf of the Australian National University,
Melbourne, 1961.
Barnard, Marjorie, *Macquarie's World*, Angus & Robertson, Sydney, 1971
(republished).
Barton, G.B. *History of New South Wales from the Records, Vol 1 – Governor
Phillip, 1783-1789*, Charles Potter, Government Printer, Sydney, 1889.
Bennett, Scott, *The Clarence Comet: The Career of Henry Searle 1866-89*, Sydney
University Press, 1973.
Blaxell, Gregory, *The River: Sydney Cove to Parramatta*, Halstead Press, Ultimo,
2009.
Boyd, Robin, *The Australian Ugliness*, Australian Pelican, Ringwood, Victoria, 1968
(revised edition).
Brodsky, Isadore, *Hunters Hill, New South Wale: 1861-1961*, John D. Jukes for the
Council of the Municipality of Hunters Hill, 1961.
Carlton, Mike, *First Victory: 1914*, William Heinemann, Sydney, 2013.
Carruthers, Steven L., *Japanese Submarine Raiders, 1942: A Maritime Mystery*,
Casper Publications, Narrabeen, 2006.
Cash, Frank, *Parables of the Sydney Harbour Bridge*, self-published, Sydney, 1930.

Cherry, Derelie, *Alexander Macleay: From Scotland to Sydney*, Paradise Publishers, Kulnura, 2012.

Clark, Mary Shelley and Clark, Jack, *The Islands of Sydney Harbour*, Kangaroo Press, Sydney, 2000.

Clifford, Pam, *Northbridge – Building a New Suburb*, self-published, Sydney, 2014.

Cook, James, *The Journals of Captain Cook*, selected and edited by Philip Edwards, Penguin Books, 1999.

Croll, R.H., *Smike to Bulldog: Letters from Sir Arthur Streeton to Tom Roberts*, Ure Smith, Sydney, 1946.

Coupe, Sheena, *Concord: A Centenary History*, Council of the Municipality of Concord, NSW, 1983.

Culotta, Nino, *They're a Weird Mob*, Ure Smith, Sydney, 1958.

Day, A. Grove, *Louis Becke*, Hill of Content, Melbourne, 1967.

Doak, Frank, *Australian Defence Heritage*, The Fairfax Library, Sydney, 1988.

Dundon, Gwen, *A History of Ferries on the Central Coast of NSW*, self-published, in association with Deerubbin Press, Berowra Heights, 2010.

Dundy, Elaine, *Finch, Bloody Finch*, Holt, Rinehart and Winston, New York, 1980.

Eldershaw, M. Barnard, *Phillip of Australia*, Angus & Robertson, Sydney, 1972.

Emanuel, Cedric (drawings) & Dutton, Geoffrey (text), *Waterways of Sydney*, J.M. Dent, Melbourne, 1988.

Emmett, Peter, *Sydney: Metropolis. Suburb. Harbour.*, Historic Houses Trust of New South Wales, Sydney, 2000.

Ewald, Connie, *The Industrial Village of Woolwich*, The Hunters Hill Trust, 2000.

Falconer, Delia, *Sydney*, New South, Sydney, 2010.

Flannery, Tim (editor), *The Birth of Sydney*, Text Publishing, Melbourne, 1999.

Fletcher, Patrick, *The Story of Bungaree*, Sydney Harbour Federation Trust, Sydney, 2009.

Fletcher, Patrick (editor), *The Hospital on the Hill*, Sydney Harbour Federation Trust, Sydney, 2012.

Fowell, Newton, *The Sirius Letters: The Complete Letters of Newton Fowell* (edited and with commentary by Nance Irvine), the Fairfax Library, Sydney, 1988 (reprinted 2007).

Frampton, Kenneth and Drew, Phillip, *Harry Seidler*, Thames and Hudson, London, 1992.

Free, Renée (in collaboration with Lloyd Rees), *Lloyd Rees: The Last Twenty Years*, Craftsman House, Sydney, 1990.

Groom, Linda, *First Fleet Artist*, National Library of Australia, Canberra, 2009.

Groom, Linda, *A Steady Hand: Governor Hunter and his First Fleet Sketchbook*, National Library of Australia, Canberra, 2012.

Hall, Richard (editor), *Sydney: An Oxford Anthology*, Oxford University Press, Melbourne, 2000.

Harris, Alexander ('an Emigrant Mechanic'), *Settlers and Convicts* (London, 1847), Melbourne University Press, 1954.

Harris, Alexander, *The Secrets of Alexander Harris*, Angus & Robertson, Sydney, 1961.

Hart, Deborah, *John Olsen*, Craftsman House, Sydney, 1991.

Haskell, Dennis (editor), *Kenneth Slessor*, University of Queensland Press, St Lucia, 1991.

Hawley, Janet, *Wendy Whiteley and the Secret Garden*, Lantern, Sydney, 2015.

Heseltine, Harry (edited by), *The Penguin Book of Australian Verse*, Penguin Books Australia, 1982.

Hoskins, Ian, *Sydney Harbour*, New South, Sydney, 2009.

Hoskins, Ian, *Coast*, New South, Sydney, 2013.

Howard, Robyn, *Picturesque Sydney Harbour*, View Productions, Sydney, 1984.

Hughes, Robert, *The Fatal Shore*, Pan Books, London, 1988.

Hughes, Robert, *Things I Didn't Know*, Knopf, 2006.
Hugill, Stan, *Sailortown*, Routledge & Kegan Paul Ltd, London, 1967.
Jackson, Jacqueline, *James R. Jackson: Art was his life ...* Bay Books, Sydney, 1991.
Jenkins, David, *Battle Surface! Japan's Submarine War Against Australia, 1942-44*, Random House Australia, Sydney, 1992.
Jones, William H.S., *The Cape Horn Breed*, first published 1956, reprinted 1999, Ibex, Melbourne.
Karskens, Grace, *The Rocks: Life in Early Sydney*, Melbourne University Press, 1997.
Keating, Paul, *After Words: The Post-Prime Ministerial Speeches*, Allen & Unwin, Sydney, 2011.
Keneally, Tom, *Homebush Bay: A Memoir*, Minerva Books, Melbourne, 1995.
King, Philip Gidley (edited by Fidlon, Paul G. and Ryan, R.J.), *The Journal of Philip Gidley King: Lieutenant, R.N. 1787-1790*, Australian Documents Library, Sydney, 1980.
King, Robert J., *The Secret History of the Convict Colony*, Allen & Unwin, Sydney, 1990.
Koch, C.J. , *The Doubleman*, Chatto & Windus, The Hogarth Press, London, 1989.
Lalor, Peter, *The Bridge*, Allen & Unwin, Sydney, 2006.
Langford, Martin (editor), *Harbour City Poems*, Puncher & Wattmann, Glebe, 2009.
Lawrence, D.H., *Kangaroo*, Angus & Robertson (reprint), Sydney, 1991.
Lawrence, Joan, *Pictorial History: Lavender Bay to The Spit*, Kingsclear Books, Alexandria. 1999.
Loney, Jack, *Wrecks on the New South Wales Coast*, Oceans Enterprises, Yarram, Victoria, 1993.
Luck, Peter, *The Sydney Harbour Bridge: 75 Fascinating Facts*, New Holland (Australia), Sydney, 2006.
Maguire, Roslyn and Drake, Diana, *The Priory at Hunters Hill, N.S.W.*, Hunters Hill Trust, 1992.
Marshall, Sam, *Luna Park. Just for Fun*, Luna Park Reserve Trust, Sydney, 1995.
Matthiesen, Stig, Bente Jensen and Thomas Molvig, *The joy is not in owning – but in creating*, Utzon Center, Aalborg, Denmark, 2011.
McKillop, Bob, *Pictorial History: Willoughby*, Kingsclear Books, Alexandria, 2015.
McPhee, John (editor), *Joseph Lycett: Convict Artist*, Historic Houses Trust of NSW, Sydney, 2006.
Miles, Patricia, *Lucinda: Little Ship of State*, Australian National Maritime Museum, Sydney, 2001.
Morgan, Chris, *Life & Death on the North Side: A History of St Thomas' Church & Cemetery, North Sydney*, Stanton Library, North Sydney Municipal Council, 1988.
Moore, David (text by Rodney Hall), *Sydney Harbour*, Chapter & Verse, in association with State Library of NSW Press, Sydney, 1993.
Murray, Les, *Collected Poems*, William Heinemann Australia, Melbourne, 1994.
Olsen, John, *Drawn to Life*, Duffy & Snellgrove, Potts Point, 1997.
O'Neill, Helen, *A Singular Vision: Harry Seidler*, HarperCollins Publishers Australia, Sydney, 2013.
Oppenheim, Peter, *The Fragile Forts*, Australian Military History Publications, Loftus, 2005.
Oppenheimer, Melanie, *Volunteering*, UNSW Press, Sydney, 2008.
(Revised by Park, Ruth and Champion, Rafe), *Ruth Park's Sydney*, Duffy & Snellgrove, Sydney, 1999.
Parker, R.G., *Cockatoo Island*, Nelson, Melbourne, 1977.
Paterson, A.B., *The Penguin Banjo Paterson Collected Verse*, selected and introduced by Clement Semmler, Penguin Books Australia, 1993.
Pearce, Barry, *Michael Johnson*, The Beagle Press, Sydney, 2004.

Pembroke, Michael, *Arthur Phillip: Sailor, Mercenary, Governor, Spy*, Hardie Grant, Melbourne, 2013.

Phelan, Nancy, *A Kingdom by the Sea*, Angus & Robertson, Sydney, 1969 (reprinted 1980).

Proudfoot, Peter, *Seaport Sydney: The Making of the City Landscape*, University of NSW, Sydney, 1996.

Proudfoot, Peter; Maguire, Roslyn, and; Freestone, Robert (editors), *Colonial City, Global City: Sydney's International Exhibition 1879*, Crossing Press, Sydney, 2000.

Pulman, Felicity, *The Little Penguins of Manly Wharf*, National Parks and Wildlife Service, Sydney, 2013.

Rees, Lloyd, *Peaks and Valleys*, Collins Australia, Sydney, 1985 (reprinted 1989).

Rees, Lloyd, *The Small Treasures of a Lifetime*, Collins, Sydney, 1984.

Robertson, Geoffrey, *Dreaming Too Loud*, Vintage, Sydney, 2013.

Roderick, Colin, *Henry Lawson: A Life*, Angus & Robertson, Sydney, 1991.

Roderick, Colin, *Banjo Paterson: Poet By Accident*, Allen & Unwin, Sydney, 1993.

Russell, Eric, *The Opposite Shore: North Sydney and its People*, the North Shore Historical Society and the Council of the Municipality of North Sydney, 1990.

Semmler, Clement, *A.B. Paterson*, Oxford University Press, Melbourne, 1972.

Sherry, Beverley, *Hunter's Hill: Australia's Oldest Garden Suburb*, David Ell Press, Balmain, 1989.

Shore, Harvey, *From the Quay*, New South University Press, Sydney, 1981.

Souter, Gavin, *Time & Tides: A Middle Harbour Memoir*, Simon & Schuster Australia, Sydney, 2004.

Spigelman, Alice. *Almost Full Circle: Harry Seidler, a Biography*, Brandl & Schlesinger, Rose Bay, 2001.

Stead, Christina, *Seven Poor Men of Sydney*, first published Peter Davies, London, 1934, reprinted Sirius Quality Paperback, Sydney, 1987.

Stephensen, P.R., *The History and Description of Sydney Harbour*, Rigby, Adelaide, 1966.

Svensen, Randi, *Wooden Boats, Iron Men: The Halvorsen Story*, Halstead Press, in association with the Australian National Maritime Museum, Sydney, 2007.

Svensen, Randi, *Heroic, Forceful and Fearless: Australia's Tugboat Heritage*, Citrus Press, in association with the Australian National Maritime Museum, Ultimo, 2011.

Tink, Andrew, *William Charles Wentworth*, Allen & Unwin, Sydney, 2009.

Tink, Andrew, *Lord Sydney: The Life and Times of Tommy Townshend*, Australian Scholarly Publishing, Melbourne, 2011.

Toon, John and Falk, Jonathan, *Sydney: Planning or Politics*, Planning Research Centre, University of Sydney, 2003.

Tyrrell, James R., *Old Books, Old Friends, Old Sydney*, Angus & Robertson, Sydney, 1952 (reprinted 1987).

Warne, Catherine, *Pictorial History: Lower North Shore*, Kingsclear Books, Alexandria, 2005.

Wentworth, W.C., *Description of The Colony of New South Wales and Its Dependent Settlements in Van Diemen's Land*, G and W.B. Whittaker, London, 1819 (Facsimile Edition, Griffin Press, Adelaide. 1978).

White, Jill, *Dupain's Sydney*, Chapter & Verse, Sydney, 1999.

Williamson, David, *Emerald City*, Currency Press, Paddington, 1987.

Wilson, Gavin, *Harbourlights: The Art and Times of Peter Kingston*, Craftsman House, Victoria, 2004.

JOURNALS, PAPERS AND REPORTS

'Alexander Berry of Crows Nest, 1781-1873', Wonga, unpublished manuscript, entry for the Isabella Brierley Prize for History, 1995.

'Berrys Bay Waverton Scoping Study', Arup Pty Ltd for NSW Roads and Maritime
    Services, Sydney, July 2012.
'Bungaree: The First Australian' exhibition catalogue, Mosman Art Gallery,
    31 January–8 February, 2015.
Edward Lombe: Wreck Inspection Report', prepared by Tim Smith and David
    Nutley, Underwater Cultural Heritage Program, NSW Heritage Office,
    Department of Planning, June 2006.
'Fort Denison: An investigation for the Maritime Services Board of NSW', James
    Semple Kerr, National Trust of Australia, New South Wales, 1986.
'Gladesville Hospital Conservation Plan', Environmental Studies Assignment, School
    of Landscape Architecture, University of New South Wales, November 1994.
'Gladesville Hospital: A Walk in Your Past', Information pamphlet, 1996, from the
    collection of Peter Colthorpe, Friends of Gladesville Hospital.
'Harbour Master's Directions', Port Authority of New South Wales, July 2016.
'Memorial Service for Japanese Midget Submarine M24: Sea Ceremony, HMAS
    Melbourne', Monday, 6 August 2007, program, Department of Veterans' Affairs.
Newington: a New Suburb for a New Century, Mirvac Lend Lease Village
    Consortium, North Sydney, 2000.
Our Alma Mater: 'A School Annual Edited by the Students of St Ignatius' College
    S.J. Riverview', Sydney, 1890.
'Platypus Management Plan' (Draft Plan Factsheet & Plan Possibilities Consultation
    Summary – July 2016), Sydney Harbour Federation Trust.
'Reflections on a Maritime City: An Appreciation of the Trust Lands on Sydney
    Harbour', Interim Sydney Harbour Federation Trust, Mosman. 2000.
'Rockend Cottage, 38-40 Punt Road, Gladesville Conservation Management Plan',
    prepared for NSW Department of Urban Affairs & Planning, Land Management
    Branch, by Clive Lucas, Stapleton and Partners Pty Ltd, Kings Cross, 2001.
'Rockend Cottage ... in 1984', pamphlet, Banjo Paterson Park Committee, April 1984.
'Rockend: Part of our Colonial Heritage', pamphlet, Banjo Paterson Cottage
    Restaurant, undated.
'Shaping the Harbour', Sydney Harbour Federation Trust, Mosman, 2011.

FILMS & DVDS
Arthur Phillip: Governor, Sailor, Spy, ABC DVD, 2015.
Bob Gordon: Lavender Bay Boat Builder, DVD, North Sydney Council and Life
    Captured, June 2005
Fanta, short black and white film, Hobbs Kingston Shead Production, Sydney, 1973,
    on *Films of Peter Kingston* DVD, self-released, 2012.
Shifting Old North Sydney: Sydney Harbour Bridge and the Local Community,
    DVD, North Sydney Council, 2007.

NEWSPAPERS AND ARCHIVES
Mitchell Library/State Library of NSW
North Sydney Heritage Centre, Stanton
    Library
Freeman's Journal
Goulburn Evening Penny Post

Sydney Gazette
Sydney Morning Herald
Daily Telegraph
The Sun

WEBSITES
abc.net.au
adb.anu.edu.au
afloat.com.au
anmm.gov.au (Australian National
    Maritime Museum)

anu.edu.au
aviationwriter.org
awm.gov.au
baragoola.com.au
dictionaryofsydney.org

domain.com.au
dpi.nsw.gov.au
environment.nsw.gov.au
finance.gov.au
friendsoflanecovenationalpark.org.au
gg.gov.au
gnb.nsw.gov.au
governor.nsw.gov.au
griffinsociety.org
gutenberg.net.au
huntershilltrust.org.au
lakeview.net.au
mvcapedonsociety.org
navy.gov.au
navyhistory.org.au
northsydney.nsw.gov.au
openboat.com.au
pacific-edge.info
portauthoritynsw.com.au

rms.nsw.gov.au
ryde.nsw.gov.au
saveberrysbay.org.au
setis.library.usyd.edu.au
shf.org.au (Sydney Heritage Fleet)
sims.org.au
skirace.net
sl.nsw.gov.au
smh.com.au
sopa.nsw.gov.au (Sydney Olympic Park
   Authority)
sydneyfishmarket.com.au
sydneylivingmuseums.com.au
sydneyolympicpark.com.au
theaustralian.com.au
theaustralianafund.org.au
trove.nla.gov.au
visitsydneyaustralia.com.au
woolwichdock.com

AUTHOR INTERVIEWS

Steven Adams, Gladesville, 4 March, 2016; Louise Anemaat, Mitchell Library, February 2015, and phone, 31 March, 2017; Harrison Ashton, Elizabeth Bay, 14 October, 2016; Bruce Beresford, various harbour kayaking adventures over the years; Jarrod Bernhardt, Rozelle, 8 November 2016; Neil Bevan, Drummoyne, 16 September 2016, and phone interview, 7 May, 2017; Gavin Birch, telephone, 20 October, 2016; Teruko Blair, telephone, 13 February, 2017; Colin Campbell, Bedlam Bay, 30 March, 2016; Wayne Cartner, Rozelle, 8 November, 2016; Reg Chard, Brays Bay, 22 May 2016 and phone interview 24 May, 2016; Donald Chivas, Kissing Point, 18 February 2016 and phone interview April 2016; Stephen Coburn, Lower Georges Heights, 10 November, 2016; Peter Colthorpe, Gladesville, 16 April, 2016; Ben Cottier, Goat Island, 9 November, 2016; Joan Croll, Drummoyne, 10 June, 2016; Ossie Cruse, phone interview, 12 June, 2016; Katherine Dafforn, telephone interview, 8 February, 2017; Trevor Dean, phone interview, 7 November, 2016; Paul de Gelder, phone interview, 15 August, 2016; Simon Dobrée, Homebush Bay, 22 May, 2016, and subsequent email correspondence; Ken and Judy Done, Chinamans Beach, 2–3 March, 2016; Harry Downie, Drummoyne, 16 September, 2016; Tim Drinkwater, Rozelle Bay, 4 May, 2017; Jeff Duff, telephone, 18 October, 2016; George Ellis, various kayaking locations over several years; Marshall Flanagan, Careening Cove, 8 October, 2016; Dennis Foley, phone interview, 14 September, 2016; Les Fordham, Lavender Bay, 31 December, 2015–1 January, 2016; Tim Freedman, Rose Bay, 1 March, 2016; Ross Gardner, Onions Point, 25 and 29 February, 2016, and phone interview 23 May, 2016; Tony Garman, Manly, 1 July and 16 September, 2016; Jeff Garrick, North Harbour, 4 May, 2016; Professor William Gladstone, Chowder Bay, 10 November, 2016; David Glasson, phone interview, 18 July, 2017; Lloyd Hammond, Bedlam Bay, 3 February, 2016; Henry Hart, Henley, 3 February, 2016; Andrew Hay, Sailors Bay, 20 May, 2016, and 19 August, 2016; Catherine Hobbs, Riverview, 29 January, 2016, and email correspondence; Charles Jensen and Barry Jensen, Lavender Bay, 31 December, 2015–1 January, 2016; Cherie Johnson, The Rocks, 8 November, 2016; Craig Kann, Half Moon Bay, 5 September, 2016; Gary King, phone interview, 21 April, 2017; Peter Kingston, Lavender Bay, 7 October, 2016; Brad Klose, Manly, 1 July, 2016; Roger Kyle, Abbotsford, 1 June, 2016; Sean Langman, Berrys Bay, 14 September, 2016; Peter Mann, Dawes Point, 24 October and 31 October, 2016; Frank Matthews, Half Moon Bay, 16 September, 2016; Marshall

Michael, Brays Bay, 18 February, 2016; Steve Middendorf, North Harbour, 4 May, 2016; Simon Mitchell, Darling Harbour, 17 April, 2016, and on the harbour, 18 April, 2016; David Mort, Riverview, 29 January, 2016; Louise Nelson, various locations on Sydney Harbour, 8 November, 2016; Paul Nind, Rose Bay, 29 March, 2016; Captain Chris Norman, on board *Pacific Eden*, at sea, 27 November, 2016, and email correspondence; Mark O'Connor, phone interview, 21 January, 2017; John Olsen, Southern Highlands, 27 September, 2016, and phone interview, 2 March, 2017; Graham Percival, Hunters Hill, 24 May, 2016; David Pettett, various locations while sailing, November 2015–February 2016; Ross Pitts, Looking Glass Bay, 24 February, 2016; Troy Polidano, Rozelle, 8 November, 2016; Lyndie Powell, telephone interview, 26 February, 2017; Arnold Rawls, phone interview, 7 April, 2016; Ron Ray, Georges Heights, 1 May, 2016, and North Head, 16 and 25 September, 2016; Margaret Reidy, phone interview, 30 August, 2016; Warwick Richardson, Woolwich, 25 February, 2016; Louisa Robertson, Farm Cove, 8 April, 2016; Paul Roman, Abbotsford Cove, 30 March 2016, and phone interview, 31 May, 2016; Nina Schaefer, Delwood Beach, 5 May, 2016, and subsequent emails; Hans Schmidt, Seven Shillings Beach, 14 October, 2016, and phone interview, 16 March, 2017; Eric and Pam Sellix, Balls Head Bay, 25 February, 2016; Lindsey Shaw, Spectacle Island, 19 January, 2016; Ian Smith, various interviews and conversations, between January and May 2016; Tim Smith, phone interview, 22 December, 2016; Michael Stevens, phone interview, 27 February, 2017; Randi Svensen, Darling Harbour, 14 April, 2016; Angelika Treichler, telephone interview, 7 April, 2016; Adrian Tosolini, Middle Harbour, 18 August, 2016; Wendy Tuck, telephone interview, 13 January, 2016, and email, January 2015, 2016; Mel Tyas, North Head, 21 July, 2016; Ken Unsworth, Birchgrove, 16 July, 2016; Mika Utzon Popov, kayaking, 23 June, 2016; David Ward, Hunters Hill, 8 June, 2016; Ken Wark, various locations on Sydney Harbour, 8 November, 2016; Guy Warren, various interviews, and canoeing in Middle Harbour, 23 March, 2016; Debbie Watson, phone interview, 14 June, 2016; Garry White, Bantry Bay, 9 October, 2016, and telephone interview, 10 October, 2016; Wendy Whiteley, Lavender Bay, 28 September, 2016; John Wood, phone interview, 30 May 2016.

ACKNOWLEDGEMENTS

This journey in a kayak, and in words, required more than water under the hull of *Pulbah Raider* and a paddle in my hands. It was dependent on the generosity and kindness of a lot of people, on the harbour and along the shore.

Firstly, my thanks to everyone who spoke with me for the book. I can only imagine how disconcerting it must have been for many of you, as this middle-aged stranger paddled into your piece of the harbour, and your peace, and started asking questions. So for your patience and good humour, and for sharing your knowledge and opinions of the harbour, I thank you all.

My appreciation and thanks to the following for inviting me onto your vessels, or for organising interviews with those at the helm: David Pettett; Simon Mitchell; Charles Jensen, Barry Jensen and Les Fordham; David Jones, Corporate Communication Manager, Carnival Australia; Whittney Jago and Cassandra O'Connor, Roads and Maritime Services; Wayne Cartner, Team Leader of RMS' Environmental Services; Pam and Eric Sellix; Marina Thomas, Clipper Events; Tim Drinkwater, Operations Manager, Sydney Heritage Fleet.

A huge thanks to Ian Smith, a superb skipper and an erudite and patient man. Thank you for all you've taught me, Ian, on the harbour and through our conversations.

And I raise a glass of red (in preference to that rum) to the wonderful crew of *Britannia* for tolerating the least competent 'bailer boy' to ever sail in an 18-foot skiff on the harbour.

Thank you to the staff of the State Library of New South Wales, particularly Senior Curator Louise Anemaat; the staff of the North Sydney Heritage Centre at Stanton Library; Catherine Hobbs, College Archivist, Saint Ignatius' College, Riverview; Steven Adams and Gareth Dyer, The Scots College; Shirani Aththas, Australian National Maritime Museum; Commodore Peter Cole, Naval Heritage Centre, Garden Island; Graham Percival, Hunters Hill Historical Society, and; Katherine Roberts, Senior Curator, Northern Beaches Council.

I tip my hat to the writers, musicians, artists and poets who have been inspired by the harbour and whose work I reference in the book. To a master of words, Simon Winchester, I'm honoured and humbled by what you've written about this book. Thank you.

For sharing your wealth of information or introducing me to your wonderfully knowledgeable friends and colleagues, my thanks to: Peter Mann; Mel Tyas; Michael Pembroke; Lyndsey Shaw; Randi Svensen; Amy Hetzel; Liz Hinton; Ben Hawke, and; Keiko Tamura.

To Dan Ruffino and all the team at Simon & Schuster Australia, thank you for your support and belief in this project. A special thank you to my publisher Roberta Ivers, for your patience, wonderful humour and gentle encouragement in helping bring this book to life. For all your work and advice, my thanks to Publishing Director Fiona Henderson, Anabel Pandiella, Publicity Director Anna O'Grady, Marketing Director Jo Munroe and Editor Michelle Swainson. Thank you as well to editor Janet Hutchinson, proofreader Mark Evans, and indexer Patricia Holloway for your care with the words. For the beautiful cover design, my thanks to designer Christa Moffitt.

The cover image is by harbour icon, gifted artist and a cherished friend, Ken Done. Ken, you prove that a picture is worth even more than a thousand words. The fact my words are wrapped in your image is an honour and a source of delight. Thank you as well for your words about the book, Ken, and my hugs to you and Judy for your support for the project.

Thank you to Simon & Schuster Australia's terrific sales team for taking *The Harbour* out into the world. Indeed, my thanks to all the booksellers and librarians for what you do in spreading the word – and words.

And thank you to Larissa Edwards for accepting me into the Simon & Schuster Australia fold in the first place.

For your advice and admonishment, therapeutic drinks and healing laughs, my hugs and kisses or firm handshake (take your pick) to my friends who have pushed the kayak out and helped keep its paddler afloat: Craig Hassall, former CEO of Opera Australia; Commodore Peter Leavy, Sharon Wood and Robert Kingdon, and; Guy Warren.

To my fellow Gentleman Kayakers and dear friends, Bruce Beresford and George Ellis: Groucho Marx may have said he didn't want to belong to a club that accepted people like him as a member, but I'm honoured to be part of ours. Thank you, Bruce and George, for your guidance and humour, and for being slower and older than me.

To Tom and William, oceans of love to you both for encouraging me on the water, and off it, and for your patience while I've been writing.

And to Jo, for your research and editing, advice and encouragement, for lending an ear and a shoulder to lean on, for sharing your heart, soul and brilliant mind, and for paddling with me, on the harbour and through life . . . I'm lost for words.

Scott Bevan

INDEX

character, who was also a prisoner, was nonplussed by what he saw as he sailed into the harbour: 'But alas, the so-called Garden Island presented nothing to his view but a doubly sterile mass of rugged grey rocks rising from the bosom of one of the numerous bays, and crowned with the same unvarying livery of russet green.' Perhaps being a convict dimmed his view, for a vegetable garden had been established on the island within a couple of weeks of the British arriving. As my friend and senior navy officer Pete Leavy explained, the garden was established on the island 'presumably to minimise theft when most convicts couldn't swim'.

Even if the vegetables didn't flourish on Garden Island, the navy did. While ships had anchored off Garden Island's shores since the earliest days, and a couple of guns were implanted on its northern end in 1799 to guard the town, the naval presence dug in during the second half of the 19th century. The Royal Navy used the island as a depot for its ships, as part of its Australian Station. A few of the buildings that arose on the island to service Her Majesty's vessels remain along the shore, their warm colours of brick and stone a contrast to the clinical grey of the ships berthed in front of them. In 1913, soon after the Royal Australian Navy came into being, the island was handed over to the Commonwealth to be its major naval base. During the Second World War, it ceased being an island. The barrier of water was filled with concrete and steel for a massive dry dock, nearly 350 metres long, to repair and refit ships. The Captain Cook Graving Dock, as it was named, was finished just before the war did.

The conflict brought changes beyond the physical. The naval base here was named HMAS *Kuttabul* in 1943, in honour of